Statistics for Research and Life

Gary W. Lewandowski, Jr.

Monmouth University

Kevin P. McIntyre

Trinity University

worth publishers

Macmillan Learning

New York

Program Director: Suzanne Jeans
Senior Executive Program Manager: Daniel DeBonis
Associate Director, Digital Content: Anna Garr
Development Editor: Thomas Finn
Senior Media Editor: Shoba Emanuel
Editorial Assistant: Emily Kelly
Executive Marketing Manager: Katherine Nurre
Marketing Assistant: Claudia Cruz
Senior Director, Content Management Enhancement: Tracey Kuehn
Executive Managing Editor: Michael Granger
Manager, Publishing Services: Ryan Sullivan
Senior Lead Content Project Manager: Kerry O'Shaughnessy
Senior Workflow Project Supervisor: Susan Wein
Executive Manager of Workflow and CMS: Jennifer Wetzel
Production Supervisor: Lawrence Guerra
Director of Design, Content Management: Diana Blume
Senior Design Services Manager: Natasha A. S. Wolfe
Senior Cover Design Manager: John Callahan
Art Manager: Matthew McAdams
Executive Permissions Editor: Robin Fadool
Director of Digital Production: Keri deManigold
Advanced Media Project Manager: Hanna Squire
Composition: Lumina Datamatics, Inc.
Printing and Binding: King Printing Co., Inc.

ISBN 978-1-319-24717-1 (Paperback)
ISBN 978-1-319-54074-6 (Loose-leaf Edition)

Library of Congress Control Number: 2023937238

Printed in the United States of America

1 2 3 4 5 6   28 27 26 25 24 23

Acknowledgments

Text acknowledgments and copyrights appear in the References at the back of the book (starting on page R-1), which constitute an extension of the copyright page. Art acknowledgments and copyrights appear on the same page as the art selections they cover.

Worth Publishers
120 Broadway
New York, NY 10271
www.macmillanlearning.com

We dedicate this book to all the students who will become counselors, mental health professionals, behavioral scientists, market researchers, social workers, human resource professionals, parents, spouses, friends, and individuals who will all benefit from applying statistical concepts to their research and lives.

We also dedicate this book to Colleen, Avery, Michele, and Isla for their love and support.

About the Authors

Gary W. Lewandowski, Jr., grew up in a suburb of Philadelphia and went on to receive his B.A. from Millersville University of Pennsylvania and then his Ph.D. in Social/Health Psychology from Stony Brook University. Gary is a husband, father, dog owner, professor and former chair in the Department of Psychology at Monmouth University, author of *Stronger Than You Think: The 10 Blind Spots That Undermine Your Relationship . . . and How to See Past Them,* and co-author of *Discovering the Scientist Within: Research Methods in Psychology.* He has published over 75 academic articles and book chapters and given over 120 conference presentations (most co-authored with undergraduates). Dr. Lewandowski's research, writing, and public speaking focus on the self and relationships. His research also examines ways to improve research methods and statistics instruction. He is a nationally recognized teacher who the *Princeton Review* recognized among its Best 300 Professors from an initial list of 42,000. He has also won Distinguished Teaching Awards at Stony Brook University and at Monmouth, and had his Intimate Relationships course featured in a *USA Today* article. He has given a TEDx talk, *Break-ups Don't Have to Leave You Broken,* which has over 2.4 million views. Currently, Dr. Lewandowski writes the *Psychology of Relationships* blog on PsychologyToday.com. His expertise and articles (200+ of them) have appeared in mass media outlets such as the *New York Times,* the *Wall Street Journal, Business Insider,* the *Washington Post,* CNN, *APA Monitor,* WebMD, and *Scientific American,* and have been enjoyed by over 7 million readers.

Kevin P. McIntyre earned a B.S. degree in Psychology from the University of Illinois at Urbana-Champaign and a Ph.D. in Social Psychology with a graduate minor in Research Methods and Statistics from Saint Louis University. He is currently a Professor and Chair of the Department of Psychology at Trinity University in San Antonio, Texas, where he primarily teaches courses in statistics and research methods, social psychology, and introductory psychology. He is the creator of OpenStatsLab.com, which is a resource for the teaching of statistics. McIntyre's research focuses on how romantic relationships affect individuals' perceptions of self and identity, and his research has been published in the *Journal of Social and Personal Relationships, Self and Identity,* and *Personal Relationships.* He co-edited a book entitled *Interpersonal Relationships and the Self-Concept* and his work has been supported by grants from the Association for Psychological Science and the Society for Personality and Social Psychology. In addition to his teaching and research, McIntyre has worked as a statistical consultant on a variety of medical, educational, and psychological research projects. He has also served as a statistical consultant in legal proceedings involving professional sports teams, international technology firms, and financial investment services. McIntyre was born in Naperville, Illinois, where he developed a lifelong interest in rooting for sports teams that have very little chance of winning. He is an avid golfer who once shot an even par round of 72. He currently lives in San Antonio, Texas, with his wife, Michele, and daughter, Isla, who are the loves of his life.

Brief Contents

Detailed Table of Contents

Preface

To the Student

Welcome!

Of the many courses you take in college, this one may surprise you the most. Know why? Because statistics aren't what you think. First off, you might think that this course involves a lot of scary math, but it's really not the case. For example, you might flip through this book and see the symbol Σ and assume it indicates some complicated mathematical procedure. But, in reality, it simply indicates that we should add numbers together (similar to a plus sign). In fact, this entire textbook relies on simple mathematical operations that you probably learned in grade school. If you can add, subtract, multiply, and divide, as well as use the square and square root buttons on your calculator, you have the math skills needed to succeed.

All of which is to say, don't psych yourself out about this course. Too many students start their statistics course convinced they aren't going to like it and aren't going to be good at it. The fact is, right now, no one in your class is a statistical expert. That's why you're here. You must embrace the power of "yet." If you think this course isn't your thing, maybe it isn't . . . yet. You may not be good at stats . . . yet. You may not be confident about your math skills . . . yet. Give it a chance and take it easy on yourself.

You may not completely understand a concept the first time—and that's ok! Many of the ideas in statistics are counterintuitive and, as a result, seem confusing at first. But don't stress yourself out. Between your class, this textbook, and its associated resources (including video explanations of each of the main analyses), you're going to get a lot of repetition and practice. You'll get there. You might even surprise yourself to find that you like statistics! And if you love math and statistics already, we hope that this book helps you to deepen your understanding and appreciation for how statistics are more than just a means (pun!) to an end.

You're also going to be surprised by how useful this course is. We've all had those courses in high school where you and your classmates wondered, "When am I ever going to use this in real life?" (Sometimes, rightfully so). That's why our primary emphasis is on how statistics can change the way you think about the world. We call this textbook *Statistics for Research and Life* because we think statistics are a great way to answer questions that we encounter in everyday life, as well as in academic research.

Beyond the practical usefulness of the material in this course, learning about statistics will help you develop skills that you can take with you into your career. We can all agree that critical thinking is useful and an important skill to have. In fact, 95% of employers consider critical/analytical thinking a skill that is "very" or "somewhat important" for college graduates to have (Finley, 2021). In other words, the skills you learn in this course may help you get a job.

Finally, it's easy to see how important numbers and data are to top-tier companies like Meta, Apple, Microsoft, Google, and Amazon. We use quantitative information to pick the best products, restaurants, and even dating partners. But numbers can be deceiving, unless you know what questions to ask. This course will also build your critical thinking evaluative skills and help you become a better consumer of data. In short, these skills will help you not only throughout the rest of your college career, but for the rest of your life.

Best wishes for a transformative course that will change the way you look at the world,

—*Dr. L and Dr. M*

To the Instructor

Why this book? Because we've been there. We've seen the look of fear in our students' eyes on the first day of class. That fear makes difficult material even more intimidating and discourages those who are already reluctant to learn statistics from fully engaging. We certainly don't want those fears realized when students open their textbook hoping to find clarity and all they find is overly complex and unapproachable explanations that seem written more to impress other academics than to help students learn.

So our book takes a different approach. We wrote a book that's student-centered—that meets the students where they are and builds on that starting point to get them where we want them to go. To do that, we have structured this book around these key principles:

1. **Meet Students Where They Are.** Being "student-focused" is one of the most frequently espoused values from instructors. But how many textbooks, especially statistics texts, are truly written in a way that places students' interests at the forefront?

   We know that most students are (at best) apprehensive about this material, and at worst enter the course planning to despise it. The antidote is to capture students' interest and curiosity with relatable research questions and topics. We start slowly by introducing the basics of each analysis and then add complexity. We do this by breaking each chapter into two halves: *Statistics for Life* and *Statistics for Research*.

   In the *Statistics for Life* half of the chapter, we introduce the main concepts that students need to analyze data or perform a statistical test. In this section, students will gain practice thinking through problems and applying statistical concepts to their life to help make sense of data. Importantly, we do not inundate them with every concept and nuance of a test in this section. While it's tempting to describe all the assumptions, follow-ups, and caveats to each particular test right away, we find that this fire-hose-of-information approach is too difficult for students to appreciate when they are new to statistics. Instead, we reserve additional complexity and nuance for the second half of each chapter.

In the *Statistics for Research* section, we delve into more detail. Because students have already encountered the basics, they are now ready to broaden their understanding by applying the same concepts, but with an added layer of sophistication. We can now cover the material with additional rigor and detail that is necessary because we have helped students warm up to the new ideas.

Another aspect of being "student-focused" is that every chapter applies the material to two engaging examples. This may not seem like a major advancement in statistics education, but take a look at other textbooks. We bet that many of the examples used to illustrate statistical concepts are boring and/or irrelevant to your students. In our book, we sought to use examples that students will connect with and that will enhance their learning experience.

In the *Statistics for Life* half of each chapter, the examples entail "problems" that students may encounter in their everyday lives, such as picking a movie for date night or evaluating if brain training apps work. In the *Statistics for Research* half of each chapter, the examples build on existing research from across the disciplines of psychology, such as determining the capacity of working memory or understanding the association between screen time and cognitive development among children.

2. **A Critical Thinking Text, Not Just a Statistics Text.** There is a fundamental difference between being able to follow a series of steps that produce the right answer, and actually knowing what you're doing. Too often, statistics courses overemphasize getting the correct answer above all else. Though the final result of any statistical analysis is important, the journey toward the final answer is where the most important learning occurs. Far too many students emerge from statistics courses able to generate answers but having no idea what they're doing and why. That is a missed opportunity. Rather than have students "plug and chug," we emphasize the underlying logic of each statistic and the purpose of each step along the way. For this reason, we forsake computational formulas in favor of definitional ones and explain how to calculate each analysis by hand, in addition to using software.

3. **Improve Thinking and Information Literacy.** Our focus on process has an underlying motive. We want students' understanding of statistics to change the way they think about the world. Deviations from the

mean are so much more than a part of a statistics formula. They provide a lens through which to interpret all types of information. That's important because the vast majority of our students are not going to be career researchers or statisticians. But, if taught well, statistics will mold how students understand their lives, approach problems, or think about issues. Statistics also help students cultivate employable skills and make them more savvy consumers of information. The importance of statistical/information literacy will only grow in our increasingly data-driven world. These outcomes are important for every student.

4. **Breaking Down Silos.** As you likely are well aware, students have a low opinion of statistics and their usefulness. What's worse, however, is that their views only worsen after learning more about statistics (Sizemore & Lewandowski, 2009)!

    By focusing on statistics as tools to solve not only research problems but also real-world problems, we hope to make their usefulness more apparent. *Statistics for Research and Life* poses questions that statistics help answer and then helps students interpret and communicate the findings. By doing so, students see the intersection of research methods and data analysis in context, enabling them to see the practical value of statistics in their personal lives. When students see statistics' role in answering questions they care about, their appreciation for statistics' usefulness will grow.

5. **An Alternative to YouTube University.** When students find that their textbooks are unapproachable or confusing, they often turn to online resources (e.g., videos, websites) to help them learn the material. Some of these resources are excellent and do a nice job of explaining key concepts and the steps to perform various analyses. However, the quality is uneven. Even when they're good, students may encounter problems such as unfamiliar formulas or notations, which might confuse them even more. To help avoid these problems, we've developed a series of video tutorials that guide students through the hand calculations that they encounter in each of the chapters. We also include video tutorials that guide them step-by-step through running the analyses using SPSS. In each case, the videos map precisely to what we cover in the text.

Book and Chapter Organization

The Society for the Teaching of Psychology created a Statistical Literacy Taskforce and charged them with creating guidelines for statistics education in psychology. The resulting report, "Statistical Literacy in the Undergraduate Psychology Curriculum" outlines five key goals. Within our chapters, we have made sure that we have fully incorporated each of the goals and have noted placement below.

The early chapters serve as the building blocks for the later chapters that focus on specific statistical tests. Chapter 1 begins the journey by serving as a primer on why statistics are so important. With that discussion setting the tone, we turn toward ways of describing and simplifying data, including frequency distributions and an introduction to visual displays of data (Chapter 2), and measures of central tendency and variability (Chapter 3). We then pivot toward inferential statistics with discussions of Z-scores (Chapter 4) as well as the normal curve, sampling, and probability (Chapter 5). These concepts pave the way for an introduction to hypothesis testing (Chapter 6), including hypothesis testing with distribution of means (Chapter 7), as well as statistical significance, confidence intervals, effect size, and power (Chapter 8). (This includes a heavy emphasis on the taskforce's *Goal Four: Distinguish between Statistical Significance and Practical Significance.*)

In the remaining chapters we focus on specific statistical tests that provide us with answers to our real-world and research questions. As we begin to cover the most commonly used statistics, chapters share a common approach:

1. **Learning Outcomes:** We introduce each chapter's goals for what students should take away.
2. **Statistics for Life:** We start with an interesting observation or curiosity from everyday life that statistics can help us better understand or solve.
   a. **Where Do the Data Come From?** Here we pinpoint key features of the problem that ultimately influence the statistics we use. In many cases, we provide tasks and questions for students to complete that generate data that are similar to the problems described in each chapter.
   b. **What We're Trying to Accomplish:** This section leads readers through the logic behind the test and maps out the test's goal and what it hopes to accomplish. Here we draw parallels to nonstatistics contexts as we work through definitional formulas to help illustrate what the statistics does to arrive at the answer. (*Goal Two: Apply Appropriate Statistical Strategies to Test Hypotheses.*)
   c. **How Does It Work? Step by Step:** To facilitate creation of tables, figures, or hand calculations, we break down the process into easy-to-follow steps. These steps often conclude with a "Check Yourself" step designed to be part quality control, but also a review of key logical points in the process to further solidify students' understanding.
   d. **Video—Hand Calculation Tutorial:** Sometimes it's just easier to figure something out when you see someone else do it first. In our hand calculation video tutorials, we show students every step of the process in narrated videos that guide students through all key analyses.
   e. **Video—SPSS Calculation Tutorial:** Although we think that learning hand calculations is helpful for students to learn why a test works,

most research uses statistical software to perform analyses. Because it can be difficult to learn how to use technology by reading about it in a text, we created a series of narrated videos that show students how to navigate SPSS.

f. **Communicating the Result:** Here we model how to explain findings and what they mean in an easy-to-understand fashion. The goal is to help students learn how to communicate statistical information so that someone who is not entirely familiar with statistics can understand. We also show how results may appear in an online article, newspaper, or magazine. (*Goal One: Interpret Basic Statistical Results.*)

g. **Forming a Conclusion:** In this section we help students use their critical thinking skills to properly interpret what the numerical findings from the example can (and cannot) actually tell us.

3. **Statistics for Research:** This section follows a similar structure, but instead of a problem from students' everyday experience, the second example features a research question inspired by a published journal article. Once again, we focus on a topic that students find interesting. The one key difference is that the "Communicating the Result" step gives an example of an APA-Style results section, table, and/or figures. (*Goal Three: Apply Appropriate Statistical and Research Strategies to Collect, Analyze and Interpret Data, and Report Research Findings.*)

4. **Focus on Open Science:** Throughout the book we highlight ways to incorporate open science practices and emphasize the ethical considerations that enter into the data analysis process. Why is this so important? Well, psychological science (and science in general) is undergoing major changes with respect to how we conduct research. Nearly all scientific journals require some form of open scientific practice, whether it be open data, open materials, or preregistration of hypotheses. This is for good reason. With several failures to replicate high-profile studies in science, open science practices help restore our confidence and trust in the scientific method. Incorporating these ideas throughout will help students master these principles, avoid mistakes of the past, and fully prepare them as the next generation of researchers.

5. **Become a Better Consumer of Statistics:** This section focuses on helping students become better consumers of statistical information. Through the use of interesting research articles and nonacademic sources, we focus on proper evaluation and interpretation of statistics, tables, and figures so that students have the tools to critically evaluate the scientific and nonscientific information that they encounter in everyday life. (*Goal Five: Evaluate the Public Presentation of Statistics.*)

6. **Statistics on the Job:** To help students appreciate the broad application of statistics, we provide several examples of how the skills they learn in their statistics course can help them in a variety of careers and vocations.

Pedagogical Features

- **Writing Style:** The most essential feature that we hope encourages learning is our writing style. We sought to adopt a conversational writing style that draws students into the ideas and makes the material more approachable.

- **Bridging the Gap Between Life and Research:** To help make information more relatable and concrete, chapters always start with an example that students may commonly experience. Using that as the foundation, the chapter's second example explores concepts within the context of an interesting study inspired by published research.

- **Realistic Problems:** Real data is messy and full of extraneous information. You have to wade through and really know what information you need to get the right answer. Our examples and practice problems avoid the artificial simplicity of the typical "canned" or "cookie-cutter" types that students often encounter in texts.

- **Data Visualization:** As data becomes more prevalent in psychology and also in our everyday lives, being able to work with visualization of data across many formats is critical. We emphasize ways of presenting data in both APA Style and other contexts.

- **Video Tutorials:** It can be hard to follow the sequences of steps in a complex formula or hypothesis test. So, chapters include narrated video tutorials to explain hand calculations and SPSS analyses.

- **Statistically Speaking:** These margin notes provide students with examples of how concepts from the chapter might come up in everyday conversation, helping students gain familiarity with key terms and an understanding of how to apply them both in and out of the classroom.

- **Open Stats Lab:** We highlight opportunities for students to work with data sets from actual research studies, available to them via Open Stats Lab (www .OpenStatsLab.com). This website provides instructors with actual data sets from published research in psychology and activities for students to work through the analyses reported in the research.

- **Bolded Key Terms:** To facilitate note-taking, we bold key terms and provide in-text definitions, as well as definitions in the margin and glossary.

- **Your Turn Practice Questions:** Research in cognitive science suggests that testing does more than assess knowledge; it also helps form memories that can be recalled in the future. At key points in each chapter, we provide students with an opportunity to check their progress and test their understanding by asking thought-provoking questions that emphasize critical thinking and the application of chapter concepts.

- **End of Chapter Review Questions:** The end of each chapter provides an opportunity for students to practice the skills from the chapter. Solutions to both Your Turn and chapter review questions appear at the end of each chapter.

- **Data Sets:** There's no substitute for extra practice working with data. To facilitate that, we make the data sets from the chapter examples available so students can practice the analyses and replicate what we discuss.

The text's table of contents and chapter structure allow instructors to easily incorporate this book into a wide variety of course approaches. Most importantly, the text demonstrates the use and application of statistics in both everyday and research contexts. By modeling a scientist's natural process of becoming intrigued by a thought-provoking question and then using statistics as a tool to help provide useful answers, we hope that *Statistics for Research and Life* develops students' appreciation for statistics and changes the way they think about their world.

Achieve for *Statistics for Research and Life*

Macmillan Learning's Achieve is a comprehensive online learning platform that makes it easy to integrate assessments, activities, and analytics into your teaching. Built from the ground up for today's learners, it includes an interactive e-book, formative and summative assessment tools, and additional resources to boost student learning—in a powerful new platform with a clean, intuitive, mobile-friendly interface.

Achieve was co-designed with instructors and students, on a foundation of years of learning research, and rigorous testing over multiple semesters. The result is superior content, organization, and functionality. Achieve is effective for students at all levels of motivation and preparedness, whether they are high achievers or need extra support.

Achieve was built with accessibility in mind. Macmillan Learning strives to create products that are usable by all learners and meet universally applied accessibility standards. In addition to addressing product compatibility with assistive technologies such as screen reader software, alternative keyboard devices, and voice recognition products, we are working to ensure that the content and platforms we provide are fully accessible.

Macmillan Learning offers deep platform integration with all LMS providers, including Blackboard, Brightspace, Canvas, and Moodle. With integration, students can access course content and their grades through one sign-in. And you can pair Achieve with course tools from your LMS, such as discussion boards and chat and gradebook functionality. LMS integration is also available with Inclusive Access.

Macmillan Learning's Achieve for *Statistics for Research and Life* includes the following resources:

- The **interactive e-book** allows students to highlight, bookmark, and add their own notes, just as they would in a printed textbook. The text resizes to different screen dimensions to provide a convenient and accessible reading experience on a wide range of devices.

- Each chapter comes with two **homework problem sets:** one for formative assessment and one for summative assessment. The questions are written specifically for this text and are organized by the major learning outcomes for the chapter. Instructors can track students' progress on each learning outcome in real time in the Reports area of Achieve. This allows instructors to identify the topics that students are understanding versus those they need additional help to grasp.
- Students can view the authors' own **video tutorials** on calculating the statistics by hand or using SPSS software. These videos are embedded in the e-book for easy access, and they can also be assigned.
- The **Lecture Slides** reimagine the content for in-class presentation with abundant images, concise presentation of the major points and questions for discussion. The **Instructor's Resource Manual** includes tips for teaching and other resources to help build effective and engaging classroom experiences. Additional slide decks are available for the images and figures from the book, as well as a set of questions designed to be used in class with the iClicker polling system.
- The **Test Bank** was written to match the content and learning outcomes of *Statistics for Research and Life*. Assessment authors worked to craft an assessment package as carefully constructed as the book and media. It comprises over 1,500 multiple-choice and essay questions written at several levels of Bloom's taxonomy.
- Instructors have access to a variety of supplementary video resources, including **StatClips**, **StatClips Examples**, and **Statistically Speaking "Snapshots."** StatClips lecture videos, created and presented by Alan Dabney, Ph.D., Texas A&M University, are innovative visual tutorials that illustrate key statistical concepts. In 3 to 5 minutes, each StatClips video combines dynamic animation, data sets, and interesting scenarios to help students understand the concepts in an introductory statistics course. In StatClips Examples, Alan Dabney walks students through step-by-step examples related to the StatClips lecture videos to reinforce the concepts through problem solving. Snapshots videos are abbreviated, student-friendly versions of the Statistically Speaking video series, and they bring the world of statistics into the classroom.
- **EESEE Case Studies**, taken from the *Electronic Encyclopedia of Statistical Exercises and Examples*, offer students additional applied exercises and examples.

Acknowledgments

Writing a textbook takes a tremendous amount of time, resilience, and patience. Even more so when that work occurs in the midst of a pandemic. Everyone involved in this project showed a remarkable degree of tenacity and flexibility to help create a new way of delivering statistics instruction. We have benefited tremendously from the team's talents and know that students will as well.

We are particularly indebted to Dan DeBonis, the executive program manager for psychology, who always believed in this book's vision and the unique value that it brings to students. The early stages of the project benefited from Katie Pachnos' organization and eye for detail. But ultimately, the project would not have come together without the steady guidance of our development editor, Tom Finn, who helped us focus in on what would be most essential to students.

We would also like to thank our content project manager, Kerry O'Shaughnessy, for coordinating the book's copyediting, proofreading, typesetting, and production; copyeditor Matt Van Atta for his careful attention to each line of the text; accuracy checker Melanie Maggard for making sure all of the calculations were accurate; photo editor Robin Fadool for outstanding photo research and permissions work; and design managers Natasha A. S. Wolfe and John Callahan, who helped create a visually appealing and approachable statistics book that students will enjoy. In addition, we would like to thank Macmillan Learning's leadership team for their support throughout this process.

Special thanks go out to Catherine Phillips, who did an excellent job preparing the end-of-chapter questions and chapter learning objectives, as well as helping us resolve various issues that came up along the way.

As with all textbooks of this scope, we benefitted from the expertise of colleagues at a diverse group of institutions who assisted via focus groups and chapter reviews:

Alexa Anderson
University of Wisconsin, Milwaukee

Elizabeth Arnott-Hill
College of Du Page

Marisa Beeble
Russell Sage College

Jennifer Blessing
University of Tampa

Reagan Brown
Western Kentucky University

Robert Butler Eastern
Oregon University

Cecilia Cheung
University of California, Riverside

Baine Craft
Seattle Pacific University

Christina Crosby
San Diego Mesa College

Lydia Eckstein
Allegheny College

Laura Edelman
Muhlenberg College

Amanda El Bassiouny
California Lutheran University

Stacey Farmer
Siena College

Kathy McGuire
Western Illinois University

Timothy Servoss
Canisius College

Catalina Flores
University of Akron

Charisse Nixon
Penn State Behrend

Royce Simpson
Spring Hill College

Antonya Gonzalez
Western Washington University

Jamie O'Bryant
Spring Hill College

Vivian Smith
Cabrini College

Christopher Hayashi
Southwestern College

Allyson Phillips
Ouachita Baptist University

Tara Stoppa
Eastern University

Jessica Hehman
University of Redlands

Bridget Reigstad
Normandale Community College

Chris Ward
University of Houston, Clear Lake

Joe Johnson
Miami University

Aurora Rosales
Los Angeles Mission College

Gary Welton
Grove City College

Julie Lindenbaum
Russell Sage College

David Rudek
Aurora University

Michelle Williams
Holyoke Community College

AJ Marsden
Beacon College

Diane Sasnett-Martichuski
Florida Gulf Coast University

Chrysalis Wright
University of Central Florida

We also want to mention our mentors who helped us nurture our love of psychology, research, and statistics: Susan Luek (Millersville University of Pennsylvania), Art Aron (Stony Brook University), Donna Eisenstadt (Saint Louis University), Michael Leippe (Saint Louis University), and Hisako Matsuo (Saint Louis University). Our mentors challenged and supported us as students, and we are honored to be able to do the same for our own students. This book wouldn't be possible without them. It was only through decades of teaching and continuously focusing on what our students truly needed to get out of a statistics course, and refining our style, that we were able to create our current approach.

Finally, we'd like to acknowledge the love and support our families, who had a front row seat throughout the process, the sacrificed weekends, late nights, and obsession with trying to write a truly innovative textbook. Without their support, this wouldn't have been possible.

CHAPTER 1

Why Statistics Are So Important

Learning Outcomes

After reading this chapter, you should be able to:

- Define statistics and identify the reasons that people and researchers can benefit from statistical knowledge.

- Differentiate between heuristics and algorithms.

- Explain the role of samples and populations.

- Differentiate between variables, values, and scores.

- Define different types of variables.

- Describe levels of measurement.

- Explain the role of ethics in research.

- Explain how statistics can increase your ability to evaluate scientific claims.

statistics the science of identifying, gathering, organizing, summarizing, analyzing, and interpreting numerical information to draw conclusions about the world.

Your eyes flutter open. It's 7:25 A.M. and you have one thought: coffee! And not the weak brown water you make at home, but a serious 16-ounce cup of coffee. You check your phone to look up that new coffee shop your friend told you about. As you start typing, your phone offers suggestions for what you might want. Sure enough, it finds the right place. Before heading out, you hop on Instagram and notice you have three new followers. Must be those new pics you posted. You run out the door, not wanting to be late for your 200-level course at 8:15 A.M. Your 3.60 GPA certainly can't afford for you to be late on the first day. In the car, you fire up Spotify to get you going. As you drive and start singing along, you find yourself amazed by how Spotify always knows *exactly* what you want to hear. Just then you remember to watch your speed as you go through town, mindful that if you're even 2 miles per hour over the speed limit, you'll get a ticket you can't afford. Forty-nine minutes after starting your day, you roll into Room 113 with 60 seconds to spare. That's just enough time to wonder why you need to take this statistics course in the first place—because you're pretty sure that statistics and numbers aren't a big part of your life.

Read that previous paragraph again. Better yet, take a closer look at your day. Your life is full of numbers. Whether it is the time of day, the speed limit, your GPA, a room number, a course level, a search engine's predictions, social media algorithms, or music services' uncanny ability to pick songs you love, the fact is your world is increasingly reliant on data. As data become more important, your ability to understand numbers and think logically about them is essential. In other words, **statistics,** or the science of identifying, gathering, organizing, summarizing, analyzing, and interpreting numerical information in order to draw conclusions about the world, are more important than ever before. Statistics are the backbone of the algorithms that help you search the Internet, purchase the best products online, and get the best movie recommendations. Statistics are also at the heart of the psychological research findings that help

Your day doesn't just start with coffee, it also involves a lot of numbers.

Shutterstock

you understand personality, memory, mental health, and even love. By understanding statistics, you will have a better understanding of the world around you. You will also have the tools to solve the problems that confront you every day.

The Essence of Statistics

Chances are this is the first statistics course you have ever taken. Understandably, you may be wondering what to expect. Rest assured that you are heading along a well-worn path traveled by students all over the globe. Even though statistics is a near universal requirement for most behavioral science students, there are a number of misconceptions about the course.

What Statistics Isn't: Super Complex Math

Let's address the most common misconception about statistics. Most people think that statistics involves a lot of complicated math. We have good news! The math involved in a statistics course is likely more basic than what you encountered in high school. We created our very own Statistics Readiness Quiz to see if you have what it takes to get started in this course. Ready? Here are seven questions, with no calculators allowed. Go!

1. $7 + 6 + 3 =$ _____
2. $5^2 =$ _____
3. $64/4 =$ _____
4. $38 - 30 =$ _____
5. $(7 + 6 + 3)/4 =$ _____
6. $\sqrt{25} =$ _____
7. $2 + (3 \times 6)/2 =$ _____

Here are the answers:

1. 16
2. 25
3. 16
4. 8
5. 4
6. 5
7. 11

How many questions did you answer correctly? Now, imagine how much easier they would have been with a calculator.

The math in this course will not be any more challenging than the operations you used above: add, subtract, multiply, divide, square, and square root. Remembering the order in which you must complete operations (see Question 7) poses the greatest challenge. If you can remember the correct order of operations (PEMDAS: parentheses, exponents, multiplication, division, addition, subtraction), you'll do just fine.

Realizing that statistics is not a hardcore math course is the first step for setting yourself up for success. You also need to have confidence in your abilities. Your school would not have allowed you to enroll in a course if you weren't prepared. Like in any course, there are going to be difficult lessons, but remember that even seemingly simple things can be tough at first. Can you read a book? When you first set out to understand a single sentence, you probably struggled. But look at you now! When you keep working at things, they get easier and easier.

Remember, too, that when it comes to your abilities, you are not a finished product. You can grow and improve, and research shows that when you have this type of growth mindset about your math abilities, you do much better at math (Boaler, 2013). If you have more of a fixed mindset and think that "you're just not a math person," you may be setting yourself up for failure before you even start. Here's the thing: No one expects you to be perfect, and you shouldn't expect that, either. Mistakes are part of the process and important for learning statistics. We, the authors of your textbook, are still learning new things about statistics after 20 years and still sometimes make mistakes. Calculation errors aren't a sign that you can't do math; rather, they're a sign that you're human.

This brings us to another point: As you work on building your skills and solving problems, avoid simply going through the motions to get the right answer. Although finding the correct answer is ideal, much more important is your ability to think through the process. If you truly understand each step, you will make fewer mistakes in the first place and be more likely to catch errors along the way.

What Statistics Is: Training You to Think Differently

Time for your second Statistics Readiness Quiz. Grab a piece of paper, read the directions in **Figure 1.1** carefully, then get started.

DIRECTIONS: Number your paper 1 through 7. Complete this activity to the best of your ability, but as quickly as possible. Please read the instructions for all 7 items carefully before taking the quiz. When you have finished, continue reading the chapter.

1. Write the word "statistics" backwards. Try to pronounce it out loud or in your head. Try to avoid giggling.

2. Give yourself a high-five, because, let's be honest, everyone needs a high-five.

3. Add your year of birth to today's day, subtract 72, and then add your favorite number.

4. Did Question 3 equal 81? Why or why not?

5. With your non-dominant hand, write, "Stats will be my favorite class" in large capitalized letters.

6. Go to page 256 of the text. Describe what you see.

7. There are a lot of "secrets" to success in this course: reading the book, following directions, listening carefully to all instructions, giving yourself enough time to do things well, following examples, and using the resources provided. Now that we know the importance of paying careful attention and being detail-oriented, please only complete Question 1.

Figure 1.1   Statistics Readiness Quiz

Welcome back. How did you do on the quiz? We hope you aced it, because being able to carefully follow directions might just be the most important skill in this course—even more important than math skills. To do statistics, you need numbers, the ability to understand the logic of an analysis, and the ability to ignore nonscientific influences such as assumptions, personal experiences, and beliefs. Here is an equation that sums up the essence of statistics:

$$\text{Statistics} = \text{Math} + \text{Logic} - \text{Intuition}$$

In other words, a statistics course should train you to think differently—specifically, to think more critically and more logically.

What does this mean? If you are like most people when they make decisions and solve problems, you probably rely on taking your best

What is the best way to successfully conquer an escape room: searching for clues systematically, or haphazardly?

guess and using mental shortcuts, what researchers call **heuristics.** These quick solutions are often practical but imperfect. The opposite approach, an **algorithm,** relies on following a clearly planned and logical sequence of rules. To give you a sense of the difference between using heuristics and algorithms, imagine that you and your friends visit an Escape Room where you have to search throughout a room for clues and solve a series of puzzles in order to gain your freedom. If you use heuristics, you might look for keys in typical places (e.g., a desk drawer). The problem is that, in Escape Rooms, the room is designed to be tricky. If you really want to find hidden items, you need to be more like an algorithm and systematically check everywhere. Learning statistics will help you think more like an algorithm—that is, in a more sequential, more logical, and less haphazard way.

heuristic a strategy that relies on mental shortcuts, or quick solutions that are often practical but imperfect.

algorithm a strategy that relies on carefully following a clearly planned and logical sequence of rules.

Why Do You Need to Study Statistics?

Consider why you are taking a statistics class. In our experience, most students take statistics because it is required for their university curriculum or their major. Why do you think your university and/or major requires you to take stats? As implied by the name of this book, we think that understanding statistics can be useful to understanding research—and life!

As you advance in your studies, you will need to be able to read and understand statistics to evaluate research findings, including the research's strengths and weaknesses. Not surprisingly, 77% of undergraduate psychology programs require students to take a statistics course, while 23% require students to take a course that combines research methods and statistics (Messer et al., 1999). Why? The answer may not be what you think. Your professors are not trying to turn you and your classmates into statisticians. In reality, they are helping you prepare for life.

Understanding statistics is also important for developing critical thinking skills. Every day, we encounter "research-based" claims about the world that may or may not be true. For example, you might see a news report suggesting that new research finds support for some health supplement. "Sharks don't get cancer, so take this pill made out of shark cartilage!" Does it work? Is it worth buying? A background in statistics can help you critically evaluate these questions, the answers to which can impact your everyday life. The world is more data-reliant than ever, and being able to understand concepts such as randomness, uncertainty, and probability is critical.

In addition, many career paths benefit from or require statistical knowledge. Maybe you haven't considered a career in statistics or data science—but you should! The ability to conduct, analyze, and evaluate research is a very marketable skill that is in high demand by employers. Throughout this book, we'll highlight several ways that you might use statistics at work in the "Statistics on the Job" sections.

Have we convinced you that your statistics course is more than a degree requirement to endure on your way to graduation? We hope so! This course is a golden opportunity for you to develop problem solving, critical thinking, database management, data analysis, data visualization, and mathematical communication—key skills that are becoming increasingly important in everyday life and that you will be able to feature on your résumé or curriculum vitae. The world has awoken to the power of data and being able to understand, interpret, and utilize statistics will contribute to your success in research and in life. Can you live by the statistics "rules" for life (see **Figure 1.2**)?

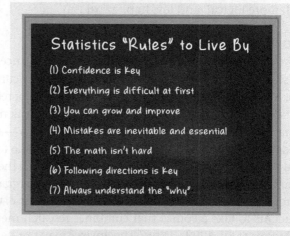

Figure 1.2   Statistics "Rules" to Live By

Your Turn 1.1

1. Think about taking a trip to your favorite destination. Describe how that experience is full of numbers.

2. In your own words, define "statistics."

3. After getting back from class, you realize that you don't have your student ID. (a) How would you search for it using an algorithm? (b) How would you search for it using heuristics?

4. Why do most psychology programs require students to take statistics? What skills will you learn?

Why Do Researchers Need Statistics?

Every research study starts the same way: with a question based on the researchers' observations, experiences, literature searches, or educated guesses. Statistics provide researchers with tools to answer their questions. Although statistics is important in many academic disciplines, including biology, neuroscience, engineering, medicine, accounting, advertising, meteorology, economics, political science, physics, and sociology, it is absolutely essential for psychology and behavioral sciences. Why? When they conduct research on human behavior, psychologists must contend with extraordinary *variability* and *uncertainty*.

Human Behavior Is Variable

Human behavior is incredibly variable or inconsistent. No two people act the same way all of the time (even identical twins!). Heck, you don't even act the same way all of the time. This variability can make it hard to see patterns in behavior and, therefore, to make conclusions about how different factors relate to one another. Take, for example, the case of a clinical psychologist testing the efficacy of a new anxiety treatment. For half of the participants in a study, the treatment may successfully reduce anxiety levels. For the other half of the participants, the treatment may show no effects whatsoever. As the researchers, we need to be able to answer the question "Does the treatment work?" in the face of these inconsistent outcomes.

This is where statistics come in. Statistics allow us to see the signal (i.e., the fixed or meaningful patterns) in the noise (i.e., variability/inconsistency). In other words, what is consistent and clear amid the haphazard or accidental things that occur in the background?

We Can't Measure Everyone All the Time

In an ideal world, any time we had a question, we would answer it by gathering information from every single individual to whom the question applies. This group is called our **population** and represents all of the people, objects, or animals that we are interested in studying. To know

population every single person, animal, or object that has relevant data about a research question.

what college students think about student debt, for example, we could ask every single college student in the world (the entire population of college students).

But you can see the problem: Researchers do not live in an ideal world and often lack the time, money, access, or other resources to collect data from everyone in a population. Instead, researchers are often only able to gather information from a subset of the population, called a **sample.** The hope is that the information from this smaller group can provide insights into the larger population. Statistics make this process possible.

As we will see in the coming chapters, we can use a branch of statistics called **descriptive statistics** to summarize the basic or essential characteristics of a sample. If instead we wanted to draw conclusions about a population based on a sample of data, we could use a branch called **inferential statistics.** For example, if we wanted to know how many cups of coffee students at our college drink per week, we would use descriptive statistics. If we wanted to use that information to draw conclusions about all of the college students in the country, we would use inferential statistics.

We Can't Measure Everything Directly

Another source of uncertainty in our conclusions comes from the fact that many variables in psychology and other behavioral sciences don't exist in a concrete form. Consider a cognitive psychologist who wants to study memory. What *is* memory, really? Memory is not a physical thing that we can measure directly; it is an abstract idea. Nevertheless, we can observe that people are able to retain information over time, whether it be song lyrics, the name of their pet goldfish, or the definition of a statistical term. We can label each of these behaviors "memory" because each involves the common outcome of recalling information over time. We call the labels we give abstract ideas, such as memory, **constructs** because they are mental constructions that we build by observing traits, behaviors, or cognitions that seem to have common features or outcomes.

Because we are interested in measuring constructs, our first step in the research process is to specify **operational definitions** that translate our construct into a set of concrete, observable, and measurable characteristics. Although memory is a construct, we can operationally define it in a way that makes it measurable. For example, if we wanted to measure memory, we could give our participants a list of 30 words to review for 3 minutes, take back the lists and wait 10 minutes, and then ask participants to write down as many of the 30 words as they can remember. Their "memory score" would be the number of words

sample a subset of cases selected from the population.

descriptive statistics a branch of statistics used to summarize the basic characteristics of a sample dataset.

inferential statistics a branch of statistics used to make conclusions about a population based on the data from a sample.

> Want to learn more about making inferences about a population from a sample? SEE CHAPTER 5 ↗

construct a variable that is not directly observable but describes a collection of traits, behaviors, or cognitions related to the same idea or concept.

operational definition a description of a construct in terms of concrete, observable, and measurable characteristics.

that they correctly remembered. Of course, this is not the only way to operationalize memory. We could, instead, give participants a list of 30 words, wait 10 minutes, and then give them a list of 100 words and ask them to identify the 30 words that we gave them initially. Again, their "memory score" could be the number of correctly identified words, minus the number of incorrectly identified words. The key point here is that, whichever approach we take, we must operationally define our constructs in such a way that we can clearly measure them.

Your Turn 1.2

1. Which of the following is an operational definition of the construct "anxiety"?

a. A mental state characterized by feelings of worry and nervousness

b. A feeling of agitation with little or no reason

c. Participants' scores on the State-Trait Anxiety Inventory

d. A persistent feeling of tension

2. (a) Why do we study samples instead of populations? (b) Give your own example of when it would

be useful to use a sample instead of a population in everyday life.

3. A political pollster collects data from 1,200 registered voters to estimate the overall job approval of a state governor. What is the name of the branch of statistics that the pollster is interested in using?

4. A market researcher wants to check the impact of viral videos on brand engagement. In this example, what are (a) the construct and (b) a potential operational definition?

Understanding Variables

Some movies are real tearjerkers. For example, many online lists include the opening scene of the movie *Up* (2009) as one of the saddest scenes of all time. Spoiler alert: If you haven't seen the movie, here's a quick synopsis of the opening scene. Ellie and Carl grow up, fall in love, get married, and plan their futures together. Unfortunately, life does not go according to their plans. Ellie and Carl learn that they are not able to conceive children and are not able to live the adventurous lives they had dreamed about. Eventually, we see Ellie get sick and pass away, leaving Carl a widower.

It's a gut-wrenching scene. But it also makes you wonder: Is the scene gut-wrenching to everyone? Our job as psychologists is to understand why some people cry while watching this scene, while others seem unaffected. What are the sources of these differences, and what might help explain their variability? Are there personality traits that lead some people to cry and others not to cry? Are there situational cues that increase or decrease the likelihood of crying? Are there developmental, cognitive, or perceptual processes that influence the tendency to cry?

Variables vs. Values vs. Scores

To begin to answer these questions, we need to differentiate between variables, values, and scores. If we are interested in measuring how long a person cries while watching *Up*, then time spent crying is our **variable,** because different people have different outcomes (that is, outcomes vary). A variable is anything that can be varied, altered, or changed. Every variable has a set of **values,** or any of the possible outcomes for the measurement of that variable. In the case of our crying example, a person might not cry at all (0 seconds crying) while another might cry a lot (60 seconds crying). Although there are many possible values, each participant will get a **score** that reflects their individual result. For example, Participant 59's score might be 22 seconds, while Participant 176's score is 8 seconds.

variable anything that can change.

values any possible outcomes for a variable.

score a participant's individual result on a variable.

Types of Variables

To understand why people act the way they do, we first need to distinguish between independent and dependent variables. **Independent variables** are the variables in studies that we either manipulate or measure to examine their impact on some outcome. **Dependent variables,** in contrast, are the outcome variables in studies that we measure to see whether they have changed in response to the independent variable(s). Independent variables are the presumed cause, whereas dependent variables are the presumed effect. If you wanted to see how watching cat videos online makes people experience cuteness overload, the videos are the independent variable, and the participants' reactions are the dependent variable. Importantly, other variable types exist as well, but we'll save discussion of those for future chapters.

independent variable the variable in an experiment that is manipulated to determine if it causes a change in the dependent variable; the cause.

dependent variable the variable in a study that changes in response to the independent variable; the outcome or effect.

When it comes to *Up*, we might guess that people are more likely to cry when they care more about connections to other people. To test this, we might have one group of participants do an activity that emphasizes their similarities and connection to others, and another group of participants do an activity that emphasizes how unique and different they are from others. We could then have all of the participants watch the opening scene of *Up*, and we would then record participants' crying behavior. In this experiment, the activity that participants complete (the connection-to-others or different-from-others) is the independent variable because it is the variable we manipulate to determine whether it impacts our dependent variable, which, in this case, is crying behavior.

Levels of Measurement

After we identify our independent and dependent variables, we need to measure them. Because we can operationally define our variables in different ways, there are four ways to map our measurements onto a numbering system. This aspect of our variables is called the **level of measurement** (sometimes called the *scale of measurement*), or the types and characteristics of the information that numbers convey. You can easily remember the four measurement scales with the mnemonic NOIR (the French word for "black"), which you may have seen in the context of films, novels, or pinots.

Nominal Scale Nominal scale variables use numbers to indicate categories (e.g., 0 = Sophomore, 1 = Junior, 2 = Senior; 1 = Left-handed, 2 = Right-handed; etc.). As you can see, the numbers we assign to a category are merely labels that we use instead of the category name. For example, if we were measuring whether or not a person cries in response to the movie *Up*, we could assign the value "1" to any participant who doesn't cry, and the value "2" to any person who does cry. Note that the value "2" does not mean twice as much crying as the value "1." The numbers themselves are arbitrary, which is why assigning them is also called *dummy coding*. So, we could alternatively assign a value of "0" to the group of participants who do not cry and a value of "1" to the group who does cry, or just as easily use numbers like 27 and 83, because the numbers are merely labels not actual scores.

Ordinal Scale Ordinal scale variables are those that we can rank order by magnitude but without knowing exactly how much of the variable is present. That is, we may know one score is greater than another score but be unable to quantify by exactly how much, because the distance between values can differ. For example, we might want to rank order our participants in terms of crying intensity while watching the opening scene of *Up*. We could give a ranking of 1 to the participant who displayed the most intense crying, a rank of 2 to the participant who displayed the second-highest intensity of crying, a rank of 3 to the participant with the third-highest intensity of crying, and so on. Here, it's possible the difference between the second and third ranks is quite small, while the difference between the first- and second-ranked criers is quite large. The numbers we assign to each participant reveal the order in which the participants fall on our variable (crying intensity) but not how intense their crying was.

Interval Scale Interval scale variables allow us not only to order the values from lowest to highest but also to quantify the amount of the variable that is present. For example, we might ask participants a series of questions that allows us to indicate their crying intensity while watching *Up*'s opening scene. One participant may have a score of 1

level of measurement (or **scale of measurement**) the types and characteristics of the information that numbers convey.

nominal scale a level of measurement in which scores reflect not an amount of a variable but, rather, membership within a group or category.

ordinal scale a level of measurement in which scores can be rank ordered.

interval scale a level of measurement in which scores reflect the actual amount of a variable and differences of one unit reflect the same amount across the number line; zero, however, does not reflect an absence of the variable.

(low crying intensity), whereas another participant has a score of 8 (extreme crying intensity). Thus, we are not only able to determine the order of crying intensity but also how much difference there is between the two participants (7 units). An important property of interval scales is that a difference of one unit is the same amount of difference across the entire scale. So, the difference between scores 1 and 2 (1 unit) should be the same amount of the variable as the difference between scores 9 and 10 (1 unit).

Ratio Scale Ratio scale variables have all of the characteristics of interval scale variables, plus two important properties. First, these variables have a meaningful or true zero. A score of zero indicates the complete absence of the variable (which is not necessarily true for interval variables). Second, these variables map onto the underlying construct in such a way that we can calculate meaningful ratios of the variable. When we say "meaningful," it is to say that we can determine whether one participant has twice as much of the variable or one-third less of the variable as another participant. For example, we could measure crying while watching the movie *Up* by collecting all of the tears produced by participants. We could then determine the liquid volume of their tears. This would be a ratio variable because a volume of 0 would indicate the absence of tears. Moreover, if one participant produced 5 ml worth of tears, we could say that this is half as much as a participant who produced 10 ml worth of tears. Similarly, because we are using a ratio scale, we can accurately say that 5 ml is twice as much as 2.5 ml.

Now, you might be wondering why the level of measurement is so important. The answer is that there are different statistical techniques for different levels of measurement. The analysis for two nominal variables will be different from the analysis for two ratio variables. For this reason, understanding these four levels of measurement, shown in **Table 1.1**, is critical.

One thing that you'll notice about the levels of measurement listed above is that some measurements fall into separate distinct categories (e.g., are you a college student or not?), while others fall along a series of possibilities (e.g., how many college credits have you completed?). **Discrete variables** can take on values that are whole numbers, meaning that they do not contain fractions or decimals (e.g., 1, 2, 13). For example, the number of times that a person wipes tears from their eyes while watching the opening scene of the movie *Up* would be discrete (a person can wipe their tears 1 time or 2 times, for example, but not 1.22 times). All nominal and ordinal variables are discrete because we assign whole, positive integers for different categories of a nominal

ratio scale a level of measurement in which scores reflect the amount of a variable present, and a zero score indicates the absence of the variable; ratio variables have the property that one can calculate meaningful ratios.

discrete variable a variable whose value is obtained by counting and, as a result, can only take the form of a whole, positive integer; often nominal and ordinal scale data.

Table 1.1

Summary: Four Types of Measurement Scales

Type of Scale	Key Characteristics	Examples
Nominal	• Numbers represent categories or labels • Numbers have no numeric meaning	• Handedness • Political party • Zip code, phone number
Ordinal	• Ordered or ranked observations • Differences between values are not equal	• "Top 10" list • Socioeconomic class • Class rank
Interval	• Equal differences between each value	• Standardized test scores • Credit score • Stress ratings
Ratio	• Equal differences between each value • True zero point	• Number of song plays on your playlist • Height, weight, time • Frequency of activity (e.g., going to the gym)

variable or different rankings of an ordinal variable. For example, if we coded people's responses to watching *Up* using the scale 1 = yes, they cried, or 2 = no, they did not cry, this would be a discrete, nominal variable. Importantly, for nominal variables, the discrete values that we assign to different categories are arbitrary and often serve as stand-ins for other information; they can be easily replaced with letters or other symbols (e.g., instead of room number 113, you could simply call it the blue room).

In contrast, **continuous variables** can take on any value and can include fractions or decimals (e.g., 1.7, 2.33, 5.72, 10.10012). For example, we could measure the loudness of each sob that a person makes while watching *Up* (e.g., how many decibels was the crying?). This is continuous because a participant could have a sob that measures 23.52 decibels in loudness. With continuous variables, we can create a measure that uses several different factors to gauge crying intensity (e.g., a combination of tear volume, loudness, frequency, duration, and overall distress). As such, continuous variables have the ability to capture much more information. Throughout this book, we will need to consider discrete and continuous variables in order to determine the proper statistic to use.

continuous variable a variable whose value is obtained by measuring and, as a result, can include fractions or decimals; often interval or ratio scale data.

Your Turn 1.3

1. Give your own example of each of the following: variables, values, and scores.

2. For her 12th birthday, Olivia goes to the amusement park with her family. On the way home, she writes in her diary about her favorite rides at the park. For each of the experiences below, identify the level of measurement and whether the variable is discrete or continuous.

a. Olivia ranks 5 of the rides from lamest to scariest. She gives the carousel a rank of 1, the bumper cars a rank of 2, the Ferris wheel a rank of 3, the roller coaster a rank of 4, and the tower drop a rank of 5.

b. Olivia reflects on how some of the rides really got her heart pumping, while others didn't have much of an effect. Based on the activity monitor that she wears on her wrist, she discovers that riding the Deathtrap caused her heart to race at 139 beats per minute, riding the Space Sling caused her heart to beat at 115 beats per minute, and riding the Ghost Coaster caused her heart to beat at 91 beats per minute.

c. Olivia remembers that some of the rides made her feel queasy. Next to each ride description in her diary, she records a 0 if the ride did not make her feel nauseated and a 1 if it did.

d. Olivia decides that the best rides are the ones that have high g-forces. Based on the information on the park's website, she learns that her three favorite roller coasters cause riders to experience 3.4G, 2.2G, and 1.9G.

Open Science and Ethics in Statistics

As a student, a researcher, or a human being in everyday life, ethics should guide your decision-making and behavior. **Ethics** involve a set of moral guidelines that shape behavior and inform decisions. Although we commonly think of ethical dilemmas in research (e.g., is it permissible to administer strong electrical shocks to others?), how you handle, interpret, and communicate data has ethical implications as well.

One potential ethical issue involves how researchers use data. For example, TikTok, Snapchat, and other social media sites and apps have access to a lot of your personal data. In what ways can they use that data? Are some uses of that data unethical? The same principles hold true for researchers. When we ask participants to answer questions about themselves, we are asking people to share information that might be sensitive or embarrassing if that information became public. Because it's hard to tell what information may be sensitive for a person, we should treat all information carefully. We will make sure that we protect the identities of individual participants so that if a data breach does occur, it won't cause harm to participants.

It's also possible that researchers are biased and only seek to confirm their pre-existing ideas. An extreme example of this ethical issue involves data fabrication or making up data, or, more colloquially, "fudging the numbers." Obviously, this is a clear ethical violation.

ethics a set of moral guidelines that shape behavior and inform decisions.

Although it is rare, sadly, data fabrication has occurred within psychology and across the sciences. The psychologist Diederik Stapel, for example, fabricated data showing that messy environments promote stereotyping. Similarly, the physician Andrew Wakefield faked data linking vaccines to autism. Thankfully, these types of cases are the exception, but because people use data to make decisions about their lives, faked data can have a profoundly negative impact.

Because of these egregious ethics violations, as well as the identification of other questionable practices, psychologists have been changing the ways we do research, conduct our statistics, and report our findings. Specifically, there is a growing movement toward **open science.** The mission of open science is to encourage greater transparency in the research process so that researchers use only the highest-quality research practices. For example, researchers are now encouraged (or required) to use **preregistration,** where they declare a study's purpose and hypotheses before data collection. Researchers may also publish all study materials and analyses on the Internet, so that other scientists can corroborate and reproduce their results. Throughout this book, we will emphasize the role of ethics in data analysis and interpretation and discuss more specific issues related to open science, including easy-to-implement practices for conducting the best science possible.

Become a Better Consumer of Statistics

Every person who reads this book will regularly encounter numbers and statistical information in their everyday lives. It is inevitable—just think of poll results, test scores, credit ratings, interest rates, and graduation rates, not to mention the variety of percentages, averages, correlations, and study results that you'll read in books, articles you find online, and published research. That's right—you should continue to read journal articles well after graduation.

Think of it this way: If you go to a medical doctor with a serious ailment, do you expect that they have kept up-to-date in their field and know the latest research findings that relate to your illness? Of course you do! As you think about your future career, it's hard to imagine that your job would not benefit from your being able to understand and interpret cutting-edge research. If you're a therapist, you'll want to read up on the latest research to help you grow and refine your counseling techniques. If you go into human resources, you may want to learn about which new interview techniques are best. If you pursue a marketing career, you might want to pick up the latest and most effective social influence strategies. Even outside of your career, you may want to learn about the latest findings that will help you live a happy and

open science a series of key practices, including preregistration, sharing study methods, and sharing datasets, designed to encourage greater collaboration and transparency in the research process.

preregistration openly and clearly stating a study's purpose and hypotheses before collecting any data.

healthy life—findings that will help you have a satisfying romantic relationship, or findings that will help you be a good parent. Across all of the areas of your life, science helps.

Being able to understand statistical results will make science more meaningful to you. Even if you do not read the original journal publications, you may read other material that uses scientific sources and describes the results. Having a working understanding of statistics will give you a distinct advantage. Having an appreciation for where numbers come from, and for what they are and are not able to tell us, will allow you to spot false and misleading information that unscrupulous authors may promote. Consider this: If you have extensive experience with a particular clothing brand, you're more likely to spot the fake versions you see online or on the streets. The same is true for data: When you have a little experience with data analysis, you'll be able to detect convincing results in the midst of flukes and fake results.

 SPSS VIDEO TUTORIAL: Need an introduction to statistical software? Check out the video tutorial Introduction to SPSS!

What Numbers Do and Don't Tell Us

Knowledge is power—specifically, the power to not let others deceive you. Either intentionally or through carelessness, deception via data and numbers is common. This is why it is important to be an informed consumer who considers where numbers are coming from and what information they really convey. You may think this point is more appropriate when considering complicated statistical analyses in dense reports. The reality is that being an informed statistical consumer starts with a math skill you've been honing since you were in diapers.

Even Counting Has Its Flaws What could be more basic than counting? Surprisingly, even counting is not perfect. If you've ever watched the ball drop on New Year's Eve in Times Square in New York, you've inevitably heard the host proclaim that there are a million people there partying and having a good time. How did they come up with that number? They didn't count every single person; rather, they estimated. Not only that—how could the host possibly know that every single one of those people was having a good time? Often, the cold temperatures, confined space, and lack of bathroom access make the experience anything but pleasant. That is, the operational

Based on this picture, count how many people are having a good time. How confident are you that your answer matches your classmates' answers? After all, counting is easy—right?

Ryan Rahman/Pacific Press Media Production Corp./Alamy Stock Photo

definition of a "good time" matters. As you can see from this example, even something as simple as counting requires you to understand the process in order to interpret the numbers correctly. Being a savvy consumer of statistical information starts with being curious about how data get created.

Where Data Come From Matters There is an old saying in computer programming: "garbage in, garbage out." When you look at statistical output, reports, charts, and other findings, it is very difficult to ascertain whether the numbers are garbage. That's because results from a poorly designed study can look very similar to numbers from carefully conceived and executed research. The more you can learn about the data's origin, the better, and you'll want to pin down a few key pieces of information: (1) Who did they study? Do the researchers have any potential special interest in the results (e.g., cigarette research funded by tobacco companies)? (2) How did they measure or manipulate key variables? Did they use high-quality materials that have been used in other studies? If not, are the questions clear and specific enough? Are the questions leading? (3) What was their sample like? Was it large enough? Was it representative? Who do they claim the results apply to? (4) Did their conclusions stick to the data, or were the findings exaggerated or misstated?

> **Want to learn more about research methods, or just need a refresher? SEE APPENDIX B.**

Statistics on the Job

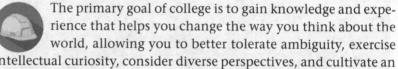

The primary goal of college is to gain knowledge and experience that helps you change the way you think about the world, allowing you to better tolerate ambiguity, exercise intellectual curiosity, consider diverse perspectives, and cultivate an innate desire for further knowledge. The second goal is to help you start a career that will pay the bills.

Well, you're in luck. As we mentioned earlier in this chapter, the statistics course is not one of those courses where you wonder, "When am I ever going to need this again?" Instead, a course in statistics may be one of the most valuable courses you can take to prepare you for future employment. What types of skills do employers want? Here are the top 5 skills and the percentages of employers who consider it very important for college graduates to have these skills: (1) oral communication (85%); (2) working effectively with others (83%); (3) written communication (82%); (4) ethical judgment and decision-making (81%); and (5) critical/analytical thinking (81%) (Hart Research Associates, 2015). Not coincidentally, we have already touched on how you will develop skills #4 and #5 in your statistics course, and we will highlight written communication throughout the text as well. Statistics will also likely give you the chance to work with others and practice presenting your results during class.

As you can see, even if you do not want to be a statistician, whatever career you pursue will benefit from the skills you develop in your statistics course, including your ability to think like a statistician. Of course, if you want to pursue a career in statistics, there is even better news. According to the U.S. Bureau of Labor Statistics' *Occupational Outlook Handbook*, jobs for statisticians will grow by 35% through 2030, with half of them having a starting salary of $95,570 or higher (Bureau of Labor Statistics, 2022). Similarly, data science jobs are expected to grow by 28% through 2026, with average annual salaries of $111,100

(Schroeder, 2021). Clearly, not only are statistical skills in demand on the job market, but the market is also willing to pay very well for those skills.

Statistically Speaking

Learning statistics can feel like you're learning an entirely new language. You may wonder if it's worth it if you don't plan on becoming a statistician in the future. Remember: Taking a statistics course helps you to *think* more statistically. It's not about understanding foreign ideas in isolation; it's about opening your eyes to the statistical concepts that already exist in your life.

Throughout this book, look for the Statistically Speaking margin notes to see just how relevant the course content is to daily life. Here are examples of the types of statistical statements that you might already be hearing:

- *The search algorithm Google uses is so good because it can consider every possible option very quickly.*
- *I know you say that Taylor is "cool," but how would you operationalize "cool"?*
- *When it comes to liking country music, my friends show considerable variability. Some love it while others hate it.*
- *The questions on that health exam were so random. It was like there wasn't any explanation or pattern to how the professor picked the questions.*
- *The school newspaper always wants to know what the student population thinks, but it solicits opinions only from a small sample of students for their stories.*
- *That paint sample I got from the store wasn't representative at all of the paint can I bought. The two looked nothing alike.*

Review Questions

1. You are upset that you are required to take a statistics course. You want to study psychology, not math! Your older brother points out that, last semester, you were complaining that you didn't understand an article you read for your psychopathology course, and that a statistics course might help. Why might your brother be right?

2. You accidentally left your glasses where a toddler could reach them. The glasses have, naturally, been relocated from where you left them.
   a. Give an example of how you might search for your glasses using a heuristic.
   b. Give an example of how you might search for your glasses using an algorithm.
   c. Which approach is more likely to result in your glasses being found? Why?

3. Concussions among hockey players are a serious issue. A researcher wants to evaluate the concussion risk among hockey players in the National Hockey League (NHL).
   a. What is the researcher's population?
   b. What might their sample be?
   c. If the researcher were interested in evaluating concussion risk across all professional sports, not just hockey, would your answer to Part a be a population or a sample? Why?

4. In your own words, describe and differentiate descriptive statistics and inferential statistics.

5. In your own words, why do we need to use operational definitions in psychological research?

6. Extraversion is defined as "the qualities of being confident, lively, and enjoying social situations." Is this an operational definition? Why or why not?

7. Stress is defined as "a worried or nervous feeling that stops you relaxing, caused, for example, by pressure at work or financial or personal problems." How could you modify this definition to operationally define the construct of stress?

8. You notice that you feel better after you interact with your pets. After reading this chapter, you are considering researching the topic rather than making assumptions based on your personal experience. For each item related to your research below, identify whether it is a variable, value, or score.
   a. Anxiety measured with a standardized questionnaire.
   b. How messy do you think house pets are, on a scale from 1 (extremely messy) to 10 (extremely tidy)?
   c. What type of pet do you own? 1 = cat, 2 = dog, 3 = bird, 4 = other
   d. Thiago owns 2 dogs.
   e. Attitudes toward pet ownership measured with the Pet Attitude Scale (Templer et al., 1981).
   f. Cameron spends an average of 56 minutes walking the dog each day.

9. Researchers evaluated whether children's understanding of sarcasm could be improved with training (Lee et al., 2021). Children were read stories that included sarcastic and literal phrases, or stories that only had literal phrases. Afterwards, children watched puppet shows that ended with either sarcastic

or literal phrases. Then they were asked a series of questions that, among other things, allowed the researchers to assess sarcasm detection. In this experiment:

a. What was the independent variable?
b. What was the dependent variable?

10. The math grades of high school students who were taught using a growth mindset curriculum combined with study skills increased more than the math grades of high school students who were taught only study skills (Blackwell et al., 2007). Students in the growth mindset group also showed an increase in classroom motivation. In this experiment:

a. What was the independent variable?
b. What were the dependent variables?
c. What was the population of interest?
d. What was the sample?

11. Ji-min has just started working in a day-care center. She is assigned to a room where some children are being potty trained, others are still in diapers, and still others can use the toilet consistently. After a week of cleaning up accidents, she realizes that some children require more attention than others, at least when it comes to reminding them to use the toilet. She considers how to measure this idea. For each item below, identify the level of measurement and whether the variable is discrete or continuous.

a. The children are at different points in the potty-training experience. Ji-min records a 0 if the child is not potty trained, a 1 if the child is currently being potty trained, and a 2 if the child is fully potty trained.

b. Ji-min remembers from her child psychology class that one aspect of potty training is biological maturity. She looks at the children's profiles to determine how old they are.

c. Some children have more accidents than others. Ji-min records the number of accidents that each child had over the course of a week.

d. Ji-min realizes that, because some children have more accidents than others, they may need more reminders than the children who have fewer accidents. She ranks the children from most to fewest accidents.

12. What is preregistration, and what is its role in research ethics?

13. Why do some researchers publish their study materials and analyses? How does this relate to research ethics?

14. Give an example of how the statistics course can improve the top 5 skills that employers consider important for college graduates to have.

a. Oral communication
b. Working effectively with others
c. Written communication
d. Ethical judgment and decision-making
e. Critical/analytical thinking

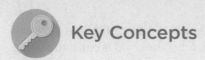

Key Concepts

Answers to Your Turn

Your Turn 1.1

1. Answers will vary but could include type of travel vehicle (e.g., BMW 325, Boeing 737-700), vehicle speed, train or flight numbers, speed limit signs, road or station numbers, addresses, how you would quantify your favorite destination (e.g., 10 out of 10), etc.

2. Answers will vary. Statistics is a field of math that we use to understand numerical information to make conclusions about the world.

3. (a) Systematically retrace every step since the last time you saw your ID. (b) Think of what you consider the most logical places to look for your ID (your bag, your desk, outside your door, etc.), and check there.

4. Psychology programs require statistics to help students evaluate research's strengths and weaknesses (not because programs expect all students to be statisticians/researchers). Students will learn problem

solving, critical thinking, database management, data analysis, data visualization, and mathematical communication.

Your Turn 1.2

1. (c) An operational definition describes the operations or procedures that we use to measure a construct. Here, we will measure anxiety by measuring participants' scores on a questionnaire. Options a, b, and d all define the construct, but not the procedures we will use to measure it.

2. (a) Accessing populations is difficult, time-consuming, and/or expensive. Samples are easier to work with and, if representative, give insights into the population. (b) When selecting a college, you attend one sample class instead of attending all of the potential classes.

3. Inferential statistics because the pollster is using a sample to estimate a characteristic of the population.

4. (a) Brand engagement. (b) Several answers are possible. Potential answers include clicks on an advertisement, app usage, visits to a website, sales, etc.

Your Turn 1.3

1. Answers will vary but would be similar to the following: variable = happiness; value = 1, extremely unhappy, through 7, extremely happy; score = an individual participant's result (e.g., score of 5).

2. (a) ordinal, discrete; (b) ratio, continuous; (c) nominal, discrete; (d) ratio, continuous.

Your Turn 1.4

1. (1) It will help you spot fakes. (2) You will focus more on operational definitions and what "counts." (3) You will know the right questions to ask regarding study design.

2. d

Answers to Review Questions

1. Understanding statistics helps you evaluate and understand research results. A statistics course helps you develop your critical thinking skills, which, in turn, can help you evaluate the strengths and weaknesses of a research study. Finally, depending on your chosen career, understanding and evaluating research—including the statistical results—is important to many careers (including being a therapist).

2.
   a. Answers will vary but could include searching in all the regular places you put your glasses. Answers could also include all the places the toddler has hidden things in the past.
   b. Answers will vary but could include searching the house systematically and room by room, including in strange places like the dishwasher. The answer should involve a systematic process that has a clear plan and a logical sequence of steps.
   c. Although it might take much longer, the algorithm is more likely to result in your glasses being found because the toddler may have put your glasses somewhere that isn't particularly logical to an adult.

3.
   a. All hockey players playing in the NHL.
   b. Answers will vary but could include a subset of 30 players or one team of players (e.g., Vancouver Canucks).
   c. The answer to Part a would be a sample because all hockey players would now be only part of the larger group that the researcher is interested in. The new population would include athletes from all professional sports.

4. Descriptive statistics are used to summarize fundamental or basic characteristics of a sample. In contrast, inferential statistics are used to make conclusions about the population from sample data.

5. We need operational definitions in psychology because many of the things we are interested in studying cannot be directly measured. There may be multiple ways of measuring the construct, and we need to clearly communicate how we are measuring the construct in our study.

6. This is not an operational definition because it does not describe how we would measure extraversion.

7. Answers will vary but must include how stress will be measured. Answers could include a self-report rating on a scale from 1 (low) to 10 (high) measuring how stressed you feel; saliva cortisol measures; heart rate variability; and how long (in minutes) it takes you to fall asleep.

8. a. variable
   b. value
   c. value
   d. score
   e. variable
   f. score

9. a. The type of stories children were read: stories with sarcastic and literal phrases or stories with only literal phrases.
   b. How well the children detected sarcasm after the training.

10. a. What the students were taught: either growth mindset and study skills or just study skills.
    b. Math grades of the students and classroom motivation.
    c. High school students.
    d. The students who participated in the study and who were taught using one of the curricula.

11. a. Nominal, discrete
    b. Ratio, continuous
    c. Ratio, discrete
    d. Ordinal, discrete

12. Preregistration is a form of open science. With preregistration, researchers state and share their purpose and hypotheses before they collect their data. Unfortunately, there have been instances where hypotheses were developed after data collection. It is easy (but unethical) to say that what you "expected" to find matches your data if you already know the results of your study.

13. Sharing materials and data is a form of open science. The purpose is to allow other researchers to evaluate your data and methods, and to potentially reproduce your results. If you engage in unethical behavior—for example, fabricating the results—the ethical violation may be detectable by other researchers if they can thoroughly evaluate your data and methods.

14. a. Answers will vary but could include presenting research findings to the class.
    b. Answers will vary but could include forming study groups to learn the material.
    c. Answers will vary but could include writing up the results for a research publication or presentation.
    d. Answers will vary but could include evaluating whether there is a conflict of interest that could influence the research (did the researchers have a special interest in the outcomes of the research?) and how data should be handled to maintain privacy of the participants.
    e. Answers will vary but could include evaluating whether the scale of measurement is sufficient for the statistical analysis, evaluating whether the sample is representative of the population (and why that matters), and whether the conclusions made by the researchers are supported by the data and the type of analysis that was run.

OPEN STATS LAB

Sharpen your statistics skills with real-life data! Check out OpenStatsLab.com, created by coauthor Kevin McIntyre, to practice running analyses for real published research studies.

2

Frequency Distributions and Visual Displays of Data

Learning Outcomes

After reading this chapter, you should be able to:

- Explain why researchers use tables and figures to summarize data.

- Create a frequency table and histogram.

- Identify key features that are observable in histograms, including modality, skew, and kurtosis.

- Identify potential issues in histograms, including ceiling and floor effects and outliers.

- Use statistical software to generate frequency distributions and histograms.

- Create tables and figures in APA Style.

- Identify the characteristics of misleading charts and graphs.

- Describe the common types of tables and figures that researchers use to summarize data.

Relationships are full of questions: "Will you go out with me?" "What are we?" "Do you love me?" "Will you marry me?" But perhaps the hardest question of all is this: "What do you want to watch tonight?" Finding the right answer to this question is key because there is no better way to ruin an evening than to sit through a bad movie. Because you're in charge of "date night" this week, the choice—and the pressure—is all yours. So what's it going to be? The latest super-hero saga? A romantic comedy? A horror movie? Of those options, a rom-com seems like the safest option for a date night. In particular, you have a vague memory that someone told you *Love Actually* (2003) is a wonderful date movie.

Smartly, before locking that in as your final choice, you decide to double-check if it really is a good choice. First, you ask your room-mate Steve, a man of few words, who gives it two thumbs up and a wink. This type of feedback is difficult to decipher. Next, you send out a text blast to your friends and ask them to rate *Love Actually* on a 1- to 5-star scale. As a handful of text responses roll in, it is clear that most friends didn't take the question seriously, offering zero-star ratings, 100-star ratings, and an assortment of sarcastic remarks like, "I can't believe anyone would actually want to watch a movie with you." The feedback isn't super helpful, and it's part of a poor response rate overall.

You quickly realize you need more data—and not just from people you know. To get that information, you check out the Pungent Potatoes movie rating app to see what the world has to say about *Love Actually*. Here are 50 of the most recent ratings:

8	7	8	2	1	6	10	1	9	1
4	10	2	3	9	10	8	9	10	1
2	1	8	6	7	5	3	10	9	9
9	1	6	5	9	2	7	5	4	8
7	3	4	1	3	1	10	6	5	1

When deciding what to watch, how can you easily make sense of feedback from thousands of people?

FG Trade/E+/Getty Images

As you scroll, you see that all of the scores are like this—seemingly random numbers with no easily discernible pattern. Making sense of the scores in this format is nearly impossible. You need to simplify things in order to find patterns in the data.

Statistics for Life

Data help us make decisions. More data help us make better decisions. The problem is that we have difficulty forming accurate conclusions based on large quantities of numbers. To make numbers more useful, we need to organize them in a user-friendly way.

Where Do the Data Come From?

Whenever we encounter numbers, we need to understand their origin. Without a proper understanding of how the numbers were generated, we cannot have much confidence in their meaning. In the case of Pungent Potatoes, a few pieces of information are important. First, the app and its corresponding web-site have a worldwide user base, though the majority of users are from the United States and Canada. Second, users are casual movie fans, not trained experts or movie critics. Third, users rate movies on a 10-point scale, with 1 = Plain-Boiled/Po-Ta-No and 10 = French-Fried Deliciousness—so, in this case, high scores indicate that users like a movie more.

What We're Trying to Accomplish

Our goal? Bring order to the chaos. We need to identify tools and techniques that allow us to more easily recognize patterns in a large group or set of numbers. Once we can see tendencies within the numbers, we can begin to interpret their meaning and make more informed decisions.

Frequency Tables: How Do They Work?

Let's start with the easiest technique we know: counting up similar responses. How many people gave the movie an 8, and how many gave it a 3? In other words, let's determine how frequently each response occurs. To make our counting easier to understand, we can create a table. The most logical table format is an ordered list of all possible responses or values (i.e., the possible ratings of 1 through 10), along with a tally of how often or how many times each response occurred (i.e., your count of each rating). In statistics, we call this a **frequency table.** By creating a frequency table for a movie, we can see if more people gave it high ratings, if more gave it low ratings, and which ratings users gave most and least often. In other words, we can start to see patterns emerge.

Step by Step: Creating a Frequency Table Remember in Chapter 1, when we said that statistics is less about complicated math and more about following the proper steps? Starting with frequency tables is perfect because all we need to do is count. Here is the first opportunity (of many) to closely follow instructions.

Step 1: Create a List of Possible Values Our first column, all the way on the left, should be a list of every value that a person could potentially provide for a variable. On Pungent Potatoes, users can rate movies from 1 to 10. When listing, organization is key, so we will list from lowest to highest (we could also have listed from highest to lowest). Label this column the variable name—in this case, "Movie Rating."

Step 2: Count Up the Responses The next column to the right (labeled "Frequency") is our count of how often each value from the first column occurred. How many 1-star responses were there? (There were 9.) How many 2s? (There were 4.) And so on. We should also note if a value does not occur by giving that value a 0. With a large data set, this process can be tedious. Good news: Later in this chapter we will discuss how to use statistical software to tally responses automatically.

There may also be an additional column for cumulative frequency, which serves as a running count of the total number of responses. For 1-star scores, the cumulative total is 9 because that is the first category. For the 2s, there are 4 additional responses, so the cumulative total would be 13 (9 + 4).

Step 3: Determine Relative Frequency and Percentages A shortcoming of a basic count of responses is that it does not give you

frequency table an ordered list of each specific possible value, along with a tally of how often or how many times each data point occurred.

a sense of how that number or category compares to all others. That is, we may know there were 9 people who rated the movie a 1, but, compared to other ratings, is that a lot or a little? One way to give a sense of relative size of each response is to calculate **relative frequency,** which captures the proportion of the sample providing the same response. Instead of just knowing how many people responded with a 1, we can determine how many 1-star responses there were relative to the number of responses overall. To find the relative frequency, we need to count up the total number of responses (in this case, there are 50). We calculate the relative frequency of a 1-star rating by dividing the frequency (f) or number of 1-stars (9) by the sample size (N) or the total number of responses (50). Thanks to our calculator, we divide f/N, (9 / 50), and we know that the answer is 0.18.

Once we have the relative frequency, we can calculate the percentage of responses that fall into each category. We multiply our relative frequency by 100 ($0.18 \times 100 = ?$) and add the % symbol. So, 18% of movie reviewers gave *Love Actually* a rating of 1, the lowest possible rating (see **Figure 2.1**). Here is that idea expressed as a formula:

$$percentage = \frac{f}{N} \times 100$$
$$f = \text{frequency}$$
$$N = \text{sample size}$$

Here is the math in everyday terms:

(Your Count for a Category Divided by Overall Number of Responses) Multiplied by 100 = Percentage of Responses in that Category

And in numbers:

$$\frac{9}{50} \times 100 = 18\%$$

Step 4: Check Yourself . . . It is always a good idea to ensure that the numbers we calculate are correct and make sense. Sometimes that involves recalculating to double-check what we did, but there are often other ways to verify your answers. For frequency tables, we can sum or add up the numbers in the frequency column to make sure that the answer matches what we used for "Overall Number of

Movie Rating	Frequency	Cumulative Frequency	Percent
1	9	9	18
2	4	13	8
3	4	17	8
4	3	20	6
5	4	24	8
6	4	28	8
7	4	32	8
8	5	37	10
9	7	44	14
10	6	50	12

Figure 2.1 Frequency Table of Pungent Potatoes Ratings for *Love Actually*

Responses." Similarly, we can sum up the values in the percentage column to be sure they add up to 100% (accounting for minor variations in rounding).

Again, statistics is less about doing hardcore math and more about following directions, including knowing when to do calculations, understanding why we are doing it, thinking about what the numbers mean, and communicating our results (see **Figure 2.2**).

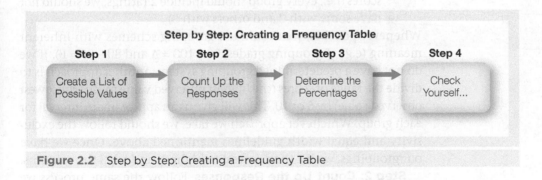

Step by Step: Creating a Frequency Table

Step 1	Step 2	Step 3	Step 4
Create a List of Possible Values	Count Up the Responses	Determine the Percentages	Check Yourself...

Figure 2.2 Step by Step: Creating a Frequency Table

Step by Step: Creating a Grouped Frequency Table In some cases, we are not as interested in individual values (e.g., whether someone gave a 1 vs. a 10), but rather how many people fall into a broader range of scores that we group together, in what statisticians call an **interval.** For example, to get the gist of a movie's quality, we may only want to know how many people gave really high ratings (e.g., an interval of 9 or 10) and how many people gave really low ratings (e.g., an interval of 1 or 2).

interval the range of scores used to create a grouped frequency table or histogram.

grouped frequency table an ordered list of groupings of values, along with a tally of how often values in each interval occurred.

In these cases, we would create a **grouped frequency table,** which displays an ordered list of grouped values along with a tally of how often values in each interval occurred. Grouped frequency tables are especially useful when there are many possible values (e.g., 1–100) because the groupings allow us to see patterns in the data more clearly. Let's follow the steps below to create a grouped frequency table (see **Figure** 2.3).

Movie Rating Interval	Frequency	Cumulative Frequency	Percent
1–2	13	13	26
3–4	7	20	14
5–6	8	28	16
7–8	9	37	18
9–10	13	50	26

Figure 2.3 Grouped Frequency Table for Movie Ratings

Step 1: Create a List of Possible Values First, we need to determine the size of our intervals in the first column. When doing so, we should use the following guidelines:

1. Exclusivity: Each observation (i.e., movie rating) must belong to one and only one group.
2. Equal width: Each group should capture the same range of scores (i.e., every group should include 2 ratings; we should not have some with 2 and others with 3).

Whenever possible, we should use grouping schemes with inherent meaning (e.g., if grouping grades, 90 – 100 = A and 80 – 89 = B). If we do not have a predetermined grouping system, another approach is to divide the range of scores (the highest observed value minus the lowest observed value) by 5 or 10. This will give us an approximate interval for each group. Whichever approach we take, we should follow the exclusivity and equal width guidelines mentioned above. Once we have our groupings, we list them lowest to highest, and label the columns.

Step 2: Count Up the Responses Follow the same process we used with a frequency table.

Step 3: Determine Relative Frequency and Percentages Again, follow the same process we used with a frequency table.

Step 4: Check Yourself . . . When we group scores together, it is possible that we have too wide of an interval per group. If this occurs, we might actually lose information and therefore our ability to see patterns in the data. For example, if we created a frequency distribution of grades on an exam, we could group them 0–50 and 51–100.

But because most exam scores fall between 51 and 100, this group scheme would not allow us to see any differences. For example, someone with a 55 and someone with a 95 would be in the same interval, and nearly everyone else would be in this same group, too. So, whenever we create a grouped frequency table, we should check ourselves to make sure that we choose an appropriate number of groups. We want to reduce the number of groups in our table but not at the expense of seeing the patterns in the data (which is the whole point of creating a frequency distribution in the first place!).

Histograms: How Do They Work?

Why is Instagram more popular than other forms of social media like Twitter? One word: pictures. We like pictures because they convey a lot of information in an easily digestible format. The same is true for numbers. Visual representations of data are often much easier to comprehend. Generally, the goal of data visualization (e.g., charts, graphs, figures, and tables) is to make it simpler to make sense of **raw data,** or numerical information that has not been processed, changed, or analyzed in any way. As much as a frequency table is an improvement over a group of raw movie ratings, converting tables to charts would make patterns even easier to see. We can create a **histogram,** which plots the different values of a variable on the x-axis and the observed frequencies of those values on the y-axis. Although a histogram looks like a **bar graph,** there are important differences. Most importantly, the bars in a histogram touch, which indicates that the variable on the x-axis is continuous. In a bar graph, the bars do not touch, indicating that the variable on the x-axis is nominal. Because the bars are right next to each other in a histogram, the resulting chart looks like a Tetris puzzle piece or the city skyline in the background of the New York Mets baseball team's logo. Let's follow the steps below to create a histogram (see **Figure 2.4**).

raw data numerical information that has not been processed, changed, or analyzed in any way.

histogram a visual representation of data for a single variable that uses bars to chart values on the x-axis and shows frequencies on the y-axis.

bar graph a chart for displaying frequencies of nominal data.

Step by Step: Creating a Histogram

Step 1: Create a Frequency Table We just did this. Let's use the frequency table in Figure 2.1 to construct a histogram.

Step 2: Label the X-Axis On the horizontal line at the bottom of the histogram, provide a label that describes what information the histogram displays. Next, mark off a spot for each possible value (or group interval) using equal spacing between each marking. Label each interval with the appropriate value, starting with the lowest value on the left.

Step 3: Label the Y-Axis On the vertical line, we need to determine what the uppermost value will be. This could be equivalent to

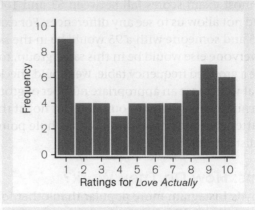

Figure 2.4 Histogram Using Frequency Table of Pungent Potatoes Ratings for *Love Actually*

your uppermost frequency (e.g., if the most frequent value is 12, the top value could be 12), or it could be slightly higher than the uppermost frequency (e.g., if the most frequent value is 21, the top number could be 25). If we choose a slightly higher frequency, it should be a logical number (e.g., often a number ending in 0 or 5). After we determine the top value, start labeling possible values, starting with 0 at the bottom. If we have a limited number of possibilities (e.g., the highest frequency is 10), we can label each possibility. If we have more, we can label key intervals (every 5, every 10, etc.).

Step 4: Add in the Histogram Bars Using the information in the frequency table, add in a bar for each observed value. We should plot values on the x-axis and counts/frequencies on the y-axis. The height of each bar should match the corresponding frequency count from our table (see **Figure 2.5**).

Step 5: Check Yourself . . . If you find that the histogram has blank spaces because some values of the variable did not occur in the data

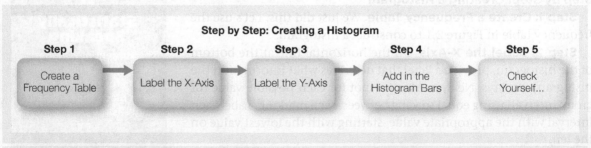

Figure 2.5 Step by Step: Creating a Histogram

set (in other words, there were zero people who responded in a certain way), consider creating a histogram from a grouped frequency table. To create a histogram with grouped frequencies, the process is virtually identical to the one we just used. The big exception is in Step 2. When charting a group of values, we can use the middle value as the label (e.g., we label an interval of 8–10 with a 9) or we can use the left endpoint (e.g., we label an interval of 1–2 as a 1, 8–10 as an 8, and so on; see **Figure 2.6**).

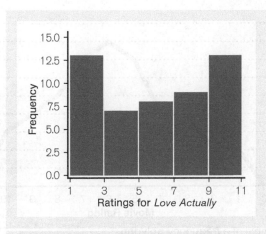

Figure 2.6 Histogram Using Grouped Frequencies of *Love Actually* Movie Ratings

Your Turn 2.1

1. You challenge 14 of your closest friends to a buffalo chicken-wing eating contest. You record the number of wings that each friend eats below. Create a frequency table.

| 6 | 8 | 6 | 7 | 6 | 7 | 1 | 3 | 2 | 4 | 4 | 2 | 6 | 6 |

2. Using the buffalo chicken-wing eating contest data from Question 1 above, create a histogram.

3. Why do researchers create frequency tables and histograms? Select the best response below.

　a. Frequency tables and histograms allow researchers to summarize lots of data in an easily interpreted format.

　b. Frequency tables and histograms allow researchers to observe key patterns within their data.

　c. Frequency tables and histograms help researchers make conclusions about their data.

　d. All of the above.

4. In a grouped frequency table, the _____ principle states that each score must belong to one and only one group, while the _____ principle states that each grouping should capture approximately the same range of values.

Frequency Distributions: How Do They Work?

frequency distribution any graphical representation of data frequencies.

Any graphical representation of data frequencies is called a **frequency distribution.** Histograms are one type of frequency distribution within this broader category. Regardless of what the resulting image is called, our goal is to discern patterns in order to better understand our data. To help identify patterns more easily, we can graph frequencies using a continuous line, sometimes called a **frequency polygon.** Doing so helps us see how the data are spread out or distributed more clearly.

frequency polygon a graph of frequencies that uses a continuous line to visualize the shape of a frequency distribution.

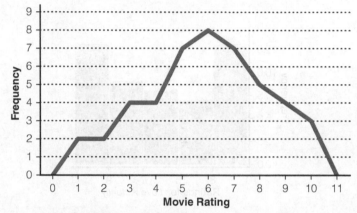

An example of a frequency polygon.

How Many "Bumps"? The first thing you may notice is the number of "bumps" or raised areas in the distribution. The "bumps," also known as "modes," represent the most frequently occurring value(s). When a distribution has only one "bump" or "mode," we call it a **unimodal distribution** because one value obviously occurs more frequently than the others. Take a movie like *Legally Blonde* (2001). You could imagine a distribution in which the most frequent rating is an 8, with all of the other ratings occurring less frequently. That is, most often, viewers consider it a really good, but not exceptional, movie (see **Figure 2.7**).

unimodal distribution a distribution that has one "peak," representing the most frequently occurring value.

Consider a different movie, *Mean Girls* (2004). It is possible that ratings are not as consistent or clear because the movie has a couple of different ratings that occur fairly frequently. Perhaps 5s and 9s are both much more common than other ratings (see **Figure 2.8**). In cases where there are two "bumps" or values that occur most frequently, we have a **bimodal distribution.** Take another look at the histogram of *Love Actually* movie ratings (see Figure 2.6). See how ratings pile up at both ends? This shows that *Love Actually* is a polarizing film that viewers typically love or hate. Note that in a bimodal distribution the two top values do not have to be identical

bimodal distribution a distribution that has two "peaks," indicating the two most frequently occurring scores.

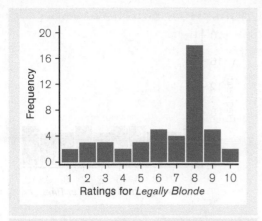

Figure 2.7 Unimodal Distribution of Movie Ratings for *Legally Blonde*

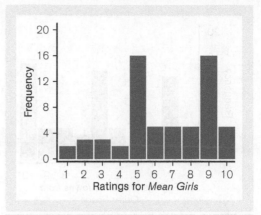

Figure 2.8 Bimodal Distribution of Movie Ratings for *Mean Girls*

to each other; they both just have to be clearly more frequent than the other values (see Figure 2.8).

It is also possible that several values happen most frequently or that you have a **multimodal distribution.** In this case, the graph has multiple "bumps," where people's opinions are far-ranging and vary from love to hate to indifference. Consider a movie like *Killer Klowns from Outer Space* (1988). Some people love it because it is a unique and kitschy horror film that does not take itself seriously. Others hate it because, well, it is about clowns that try to kill you. Some viewers have a distinct love/hate opinion and fall solidly in the middle (see **Figure 2.9**).

Finally, it is possible that all values in a data set occur at approximately the same rate. When this happens, we do not see any distinct "bumps." We call this a **uniform distribution.** For example, the movie *A Wrinkle in Time* (2018) had evenly mixed reviews, with no one reaction to the movie occurring more frequently than any other reaction (see **Figure 2.10**).

What Does the Shape Look Like? We can also take a big-picture view and look at the graph holistically to get a sense of its overall shape. The first thing we might notice is whether we have a **symmetrical distribution,** meaning that, if we drew a line down the middle of the graph, both sides would be the same shape. We may see this with a movie like *Red Sparrow* (2018) with Jennifer Lawrence, where most people consider it solidly mediocre, with fewer people rating it strongly favorable or strongly unfavorable. The key for a symmetrical distribution is that similar numbers of ratings fall on either side of the middle.

multimodal distribution a distribution that has more than two modes.

uniform distribution a distribution in which all of the values occur with approximately the same frequency.

symmetrical distribution a type of distribution where the pattern of scores to the left of the middle is approximately identical to the pattern of scores to the right of the median; the median, mean, and mode occur at the same point.

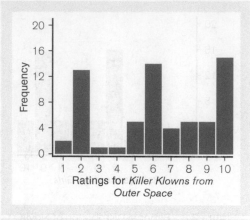

Figure 2.9 Multimodal Distribution of Movie Ratings for *Killer Klowns from Outer Space*

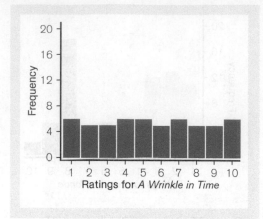

Figure 2.10 Uniform Distribution of Movie Ratings for *A Wrinkle in Time*

Interested in learning more about normal distributions, which are an important symmetrical distribution? SEE CHAPTER 4 ↗

skewness the degree to which a distribution is not symmetrical; distributions can be positively or negatively skewed.

positive skew values on the left side of a distribution are more frequent than values on the right.

negative skew values on the right side of a distribution are more frequent than values on the left.

Other distributions, however, are somewhat asymmetrical, with one half of the graph displaying higher frequencies than the other half. In statistical terms, a distribution's amount of asymmetry is called its **skewness.** Higher frequencies can occur on either the left or the right side.

If we were to graph movie ratings for a nearly universally hated movie like *The Emoji Movie* (2017), we would see a frequency distribution with many scores on the low end of the scale and just a few on the positive end (see **Figure 2.11**). In contrast, if we graphed ratings for uber-popular and critically acclaimed films such as *Pulp Fiction* (1994) or *Inside Out* (2015), we would see that the vast majority of people give those movies top-end ratings, with just a few ratings on the negative end (see **Figure 2.12**).

When determining a graph's skew, we focus on the location of the "tail" or the part of the distribution with less frequent values. If the "tail" is on the right side of the peak, the graph's skew is positive; if it is on the left side of the peak, the graph is negatively skewed. So, because the tail of the distribution of scores for *The Emoji Movie* ratings is on the right, we say that this distribution is **positively skewed.** In contrast, because the tail of the score distribution for the *Pulp Fiction* ratings is on the left, this distribution is **negatively skewed.** Importantly, to get the full picture of the patterns in our data, we need to consider both modality and skewness together. The

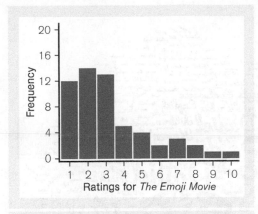

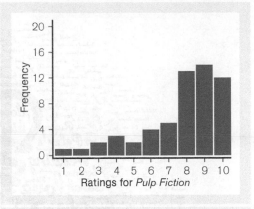

Figure 2.11 Positively Skewed Distribution for *The Emoji Movie*'s Ratings

Figure 2.12 Negatively Skewed Distribution for *Pulp Fiction's* Ratings

combination of these features will give us the most complete idea of what our data look like.

Communicating the Result

  Statistics are fundamentally about finding answers to questions. Before finalizing our decision on whether to spend an evening watching *Love Actually*, we should consider a few other pieces of information. First, what are the main themes in the movie?

To find out, we can read *Love Actually*'s plot description on its Wikipedia page. Here, we have the same problem that we had with the numbers: there is a lot of information, and it would be helpful to simplify it in some way. To do that, we can look at how frequently each word occurs in the description. Although not typically used in research, we can see visualizations of frequencies of nominal data using a *word cloud*, which organizes words into an image, with each word's size indicating how frequently it occurs. In word clouds, all of the possible words are closely packed together (sometimes into a recognizable shape), with larger words representing more frequently occurring words. A word cloud of the *Love Actually* plot reveals that words like "Christmas," "Natalie," and "Juliet" are large. From this cloud, we might conclude that these elements are more prominent in the movie's plot. This is where it is important to be a good consumer of seemingly statistical information. Although word clouds provide information, they are imprecise, as differences in word size are too

Figure 2.13 Word Cloud of *Love Actually*'s Plot

difficult to reliably identify. Hence, word clouds are more of a novelty than a useful tool (see **Figure 2.13**).

To make a final decision, we probably also want an idea of what people have to say about the movie. That is, beyond numerical ratings, what words do viewers use in their reviews? We could gather this information from Pungent Potatoes' review section. But, again, that would produce a lot of data and make it difficult to find patterns. We could instead count the number of times key words appear in the 50 most recent ratings. To do that, we can create a histogram based on nominal data.

Step by Step: Creating a Bar Graph When we have nominal data, we create a bar graph.

Step 1: Create a Frequency Table First, create a frequency table using the categories as the values. Instead of values from the scale (e.g., "1," "2," and "3"), we will use the nominal data categories (e.g., use of the words "Awesome," "Enjoyable," and "Awful"). We should follow the same steps for creating frequency tables that we used previously.

Step 2: Label the X-Axis On the bottom line, mark off a spot for each category using equal spacing between each while leaving space so that the bars for each category do not touch. Label accordingly.

Step 3: Label the Y-Axis This is identical to the procedure we used previously for histograms.

Step 4: Check Yourself . . . Confirm that we have included all categories on the x-axis and frequencies on the y-axis (see **Figure 2.14**). Make sure the height of each bar matches the frequency count from our table and matches the proper value. Finally, be sure that there is space between the bars to make it clear that the x-axis is categorical.

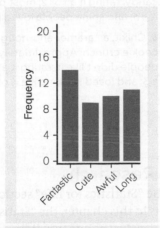

Figure 2.14 Bar Graph Using Nominal Data of Movie Review Key Words

Forming a Conclusion

Throughout this book, we will show how we can use statistics to solve everyday problems. This chapter started with a common conundrum that we all face—namely, should we watch the movie *Love Actually* tonight? By inspecting our frequency distribution and histogram, we can see that people have mixed opinions about *Love Actually*. Some people love it and some people hate it. This is critical information to have because, if we had just looked at the overall rating on Pungent Potatoes, it would have seemed like people were generally neutral about this movie. By digging into the data, we see otherwise. Factoring in the word cloud of the plot and the histogram of the most common words in user ratings, we have a lot to consider. Ultimately, given how polarizing *Love Actually* seems to be, it is worth watching just to see where you and your partner fall in the debate of whether *Love Actually* is actually a good or bad movie.

Now that we have seen how we can use frequency tables and histograms to look for the patterns in everyday data, we want to apply these same skills to research.

Your Turn 2.2

Marcus wants to determine the best candy to hand out on Halloween. He surveys 20 of his neighbors and asks them to rate various types of candy on a 1–5 scale, with 1 indicating that they don't like the candy and 5 indicating that they love it. Based on the information provided, (a) sketch out what the frequency distribution generally looks like for each type of candy, and (b) label the distribution based on its modality and skewness.

1. Cashew Bliss, a chocolate-covered coconut candy bar with cashews: The vast majority of people didn't like it, rating it 1 or 2. A few people, however, loved it, rating it 4 or 5.

2. Cackles, a peanut-and-nougat candy bar covered in chocolate: Some people didn't like this candy, rating it a 1 or 2; most people liked it, rating it a 3; and some people loved it, rating it a 4 or 5.

3. Chixit, a caramel-and-nougat candy bar with a cookie crunch: Approximately the same number of people didn't like it, rating it a 1 or 2; liked it, rating it a 3; and loved it, rating it a 4 or 5.

Statistics for Research

Now that the "Statistics for Life" section has introduced the key concepts in this chapter, the "Statistics for Research" section will review key points to solidify what we have learned. This section uses a different, more research-based example to provide additional depth and nuance, fostering an even better understanding. What topic will we explore today?

Sex. Few topics raise as many questions. The great thing about being fluent in statistics is that we can get answers to our questions. Perhaps one of the most common questions people have about sex is "How much are people having?" Researchers in 2017 investigated whether adults living in the United States today have more or less sex on average than adults did 30 years ago (Twenge et al., 2017). These researchers wanted to examine whether societal changes have impacted people's sex lives.

Without data, the answers to this question are not obvious. Some societal changes might make us think that adults have more sex now than in the past. People generally have more liberal attitudes toward casual sex than they did in the past; people have greater access to birth control; new drugs help people with sexual dysfunction engage in sex; and dating apps make it easy to find sexual partners. At the same time, other societal changes might make us think that adults have less sex now than in the past. People work longer hours now than in the past; smartphones, video games, and streaming platforms provide people with endless entertainment; people have easy access to pornography that might reduce their interest in sex; and people are more likely to take drugs that have side effects that impair sexual functioning and arousal (e.g., antidepressants).

Based on this information, what is the answer? Do people today tend to have more or less sex than people 30 years ago? Why do you expect this outcome? Based on your guess, sketch out what you think the histograms will look like for these groups (now vs. 30 years ago). Hold onto these predictions; we'll come back to them in a moment.

Where Do the Data Come From?

 How could we collect data to answer the researchers' question? Obviously, we can't go 30 years back in time and survey people in the past. Instead, we need to see if any existing data sets include questions about participants' sexual behaviors—which is exactly what the researchers studying sexual frequency did. They turned to the General Social Survey (GSS), a survey of a nationally representative sample of adults living in the United States. Although the GSS has been around since 1972, the survey started measuring sexual frequency in 1989. Over the years, more than 26,000 people have answered the question "About how often did you have sex during the last 12 months?" using this scale: 0 (*Not at all*), 1 (*Once or twice a year*), 2 (*Once a month*), 3 (*2–3 times a month*), 4 (*Weekly*), 5 (*2–3 times per week*), or 6 (*4+ times per week*).

Remember: any time we use or interpret statistics, it is important to know where the data come from and what the numbers mean. Here, we want to be careful when thinking about individual scores because the scores are not exactly equivalent to frequency of sex. That is, a score of "5" does not mean 5 times a month, and a score of "2" indicates having sex once a month or about 12 times a year.

What We're Trying to Accomplish

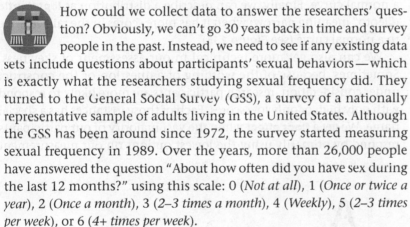 The GSS is great because it provides a ton of data from a large sample across many decades. Digesting over 26,000 scores will be difficult, so we need to organize these data in order

kurtosis a measure of the "tailedness" of a distribution; kurtosis is high when a distribution has many extreme scores, and kurtosis is low when there are few or no extreme scores.

mesokurtic distribution a distribution that is similar in kurtosis to a normal curve.

platykurtic distribution a distribution that has fewer scores in its tails than a normal curve.

leptokurtic distribution a distribution that has more scores in the tails than a normal curve.

floor effect a positively skewed distribution that occurs when most participants respond at the extreme low end of the measurement scale.

to quickly observe and diagnose key patterns. Histograms would help. As we discussed in the first half of this chapter, for any histogram, we should be able to identify whether it is unimodal, bimodal, multimodal, or uniform, and whether it is symmetric or skewed.

Now that we are familiar with the basics, we can consider a few more histogram characteristics in this part of the chapter. One new characteristic to consider is **kurtosis,** which describes the "tailedness" of a distribution (Westfall, 2014). A distribution with many extreme scores (i.e., scores in the tails of a distribution) will have a high kurtosis. In contrast, a distribution with few extreme scores, such as a uniform distribution, will have a low kurtosis. Perhaps the easiest way to consider a distribution's heavy or light "tailedness" is by comparing it to a particular type of distribution called a *normal curve*. We will learn more about normal distributions in Chapter 4, but, for now, we can describe a distribution as **mesokurtic** ("meso" meaning middle, and "kurtosis" meaning bulge) when it has the same level of kurtosis as a normal curve. We can describe a distribution as **platykurtic** ("platy" meaning broad or flat) when it has fewer scores in the tails relative to a normal curve. Finally, we can describe a distribution as **leptokurtic** ("lepto" meaning narrow) when it has more scores in the tails relative to a normal curve (see **Figure 2.15**).

We can also get more technical in our assessment of skewness. Sometimes, because of the wording of a question or the construct under consideration, research participants are more likely to respond with only high or only low scores. Each of those instances has a special name. We get a **floor effect** when the vast majority of our participants respond by primarily using the lowest options on our measurement

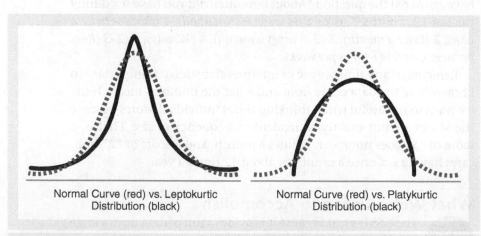

Normal Curve (red) vs. Leptokurtic Distribution (black)

Normal Curve (red) vs. Platykurtic Distribution (black)

Figure 2.15 Comparison of Normal (Mesokurtic), Leptokurtic, and Platykurtic Distributions Outliers

scale (e.g., answering 0 or 1 on the GSS item asking about their sex frequency). If a floor effect occurs, we will almost certainly have a positively skewed distribution, because most people will respond at the extreme low end of the scale and only some participants will respond using the other options.

Alternatively, we get a **ceiling effect** when most participants respond using the highest options on a measurement scale (e.g., answering 5 or 6 on the GSS item asking about their sex frequency). If a ceiling effect occurs, we will almost certainly have a negatively skewed distribution, because most people will respond using the extreme high end of the scale and only some participants will respond using the other options. Regardless of whether a ceiling or floor effect occurs, the consequence is that we will observe lower variability in participants' responses. This makes it harder for us to make broad conclusions about our data because we will not know for sure whether the pattern observed in the data reflects the true pattern or is a byproduct of our scale. So, anytime we interpret a skewed distribution, we want to consider whether a floor or ceiling effect is present and what might have caused this effect.

We can describe all histograms in terms of their modality, skewness, and kurtosis. But some histograms have an additional feature that we should look out for — scores that are atypical from other scores, called **outliers**. As shown in **Figure 2.16**, outliers are scores that occur far away from all the other observations. We will define exactly

ceiling effect a negatively skewed distribution that occurs when most participants respond at the extreme high end of the measurement scale.

outlier an extreme score; more technically, a score that occurs at least three standard deviations away from the mean.

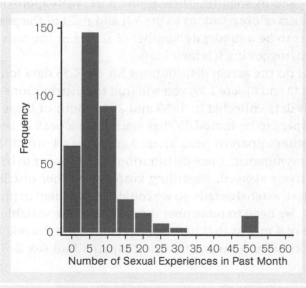

Figure 2.16   Histogram with Outliers

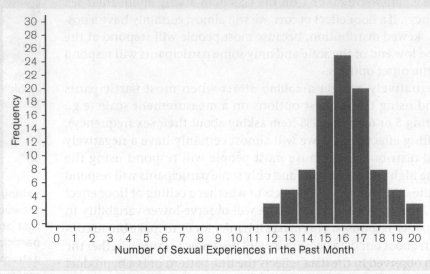

Figure 2.17 Symmetric Histogram

how far away these scores need to be from the other observations in Chapter 4.

Let's put our histogram knowledge to the test. Consider **Figure 2.17** and diagnose the modality, symmetry, and kurtosis. Without any calculations, we can quickly see that this distribution is unimodal, symmetric, and mesokurtic. There is one peak, with approximately equal numbers of observations to the left and right of the peak, and there seems to be a moderate number of scores in the tails of the distribution, suggesting it is mesokurtic.

So, what do the actual distributions for the GSS data look like? In **Figure 2.18** and **Figure 2.19**, you will find the distributions for the participant data collected in 1989 and 2016. Both of these distributions appear to be bimodal! They both have a peak at response 0 and another apparent peak around responses 4 and 5. Rather than being symmetric, these distributions both appear to be somewhat positively skewed. Regarding kurtosis, neither distribution seems to have extensive tails, so we could classify them as platykurtic. Finally, we need to remember the scaling of the variable. Here, a response of 4 means that participants had sex on a weekly basis, and a response of 5 means that participants had sex 2–3 times per week.

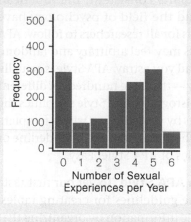

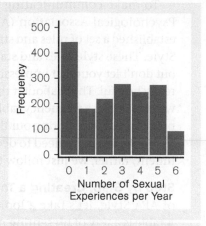

Figure 2.18   GSS Data for 1989

Figure 2.19   GSS Data for 2016

Your Turn 2.3

1. Most zombies eat about the same amount of brains per day (between 2.6 and 4.4 ounces). However, Dave the Zombie eats 11.2 ounces of brain per day. In statistical terms, we would call Dave a(n) _____ because he is an extreme observation.

2. A developmental psychologist asks parents to rate their feelings about their children on a scale from 1 (hate) to 10 (love). What issue is likely present in the resulting data set? Why?

a. Ceiling effect

b. Outlier

c. Floor effect

d. Kurtosis

SPSS VIDEO TUTORIAL: Want to use statistics software to create frequency tables and histograms with measures of skewness and kurtosis? To learn how, check out the video tutorial for Chapter 2: Frequency Distributions, Histograms, Skew, and Kurtosis!

Communicating the Result

Researchers use frequency tables and histograms in their research papers to describe large groups of numbers. Most often, researchers use frequency tables and histograms at the beginning of the study's Results section, or to help describe the sample's demographic characteristics (e.g., age, ethnicity, etc.). When we create our own frequency tables and histograms, we want other researchers to have just as easy a job identifying this relevant information.

To make communicating our results consistent, the American Psychological Association (APA) and the field of psychology have established a set of rules and standards for all researchers to follow: APA Style. These style rules and standards may feel arbitrary and random, but don't let your first impressions lead you astray. APA Style is actually really helpful. Think about it this way—there are hundreds of different ways to depict a frequency table or histogram. APA Style simplifies the process of disseminating our findings by providing us with a template to follow. We don't need to decide whether to italicize or underline or indent; rather, we just follow the rules of APA Style. Easy.

Step by Step: Creating a Table in APA Style To get our first taste of APA Style, let's take a look at the guidelines for creating tables. A table is a way of presenting numeric information by organizing that information into columns and rows. **Figure 2.20** is a frequency table for participants' responses by year from the GSS data set, formatted in APA Style. We can see that the various response options form the columns of the table and the years of response determine the rows. The frequencies observed for each year are the numbers within the body of the table. Follow these steps to create an APA-Style table.

Step 1: Identify the Table At the top of the page, provide a table number. The table number helps readers know which table to look at when. Label the first table mentioned in the paper "Table 1." The second table is "Table 2," and so on.

Table 1

How Often Do People Have Sex? Frequency of Responses by Year

Year	Not at All	Once or Twice	Once a Month	2–3 Times per Month	Weekly	2–3 Times per Week	4+ Times per Week
1989	298	99	114	221	258	307	64
1998	516	175	263	358	425	458	125
2004	445	160	240	364	376	377	147
2010	440	174	194	284	257	304	99
2016	439	178	216	274	244	271	90

Note. This table presents five years' worth of results out of the 16 years in which this question was measured.

Figure 2.20 Sample Table Formatted in APA Style

Step 2: Table Title On the next line, provide a short yet descriptive title for the table that explains what information the table contains.

Step 3: Define Table Area Add a horizontal line at the top and bottom of the table body.

Step 4: Define Rows and Columns Give descriptive labels to each column, including a label for the rows as the left-hand column. To help distinguish the labels from the actual data, add in a horizontal line under the label row. Also, include a line after the data and before any table notes.

Step 5: Data! Add in the numeric information. According to APA Style, we should round most statistical numbers to two decimals. There are two exceptions to this rule. First, if we are reporting means and standard deviations for discrete scores, which are scores that can take on only whole numbers (such as responses to questionnaires), we should report only one decimal place. If we are reporting p-values, we can report three decimal places.

Step 6: Table Note Below the horizontal rule created in Step 3, add in a table note. The table note provides any additional information that the reader should know but otherwise isn't that obvious. For example, if there are any abbreviations or acronyms in the table, explain them in the table note.

Step 7: Check Yourself . . . APA Style never uses vertical lines within tables. However, many word processing programs automatically add in vertical lines between columns. Be sure not to simply copy and paste tables from SPSS or other statistical programs. Those programs rarely format tables in perfect APA Style. Also be sure to consult the most recent edition of the *Publication Manual of the American Psychological Association* (commonly called "the APA Manual") to double-check the formatting. Tables should appear after the references in a full APA-Style paper.

Step by Step: Creating a Figure in APA Style Before continuing, we should distinguish figures from tables, because they are not the same. Basically, a figure is any way of depicting numeric information that is *not* a table. A figure could be a graph, a chart (similar to a graph, but for non-quantitative information), a map, a drawing, or a photo. In other words, as long as it is not a table, it's a figure. All of the histograms that we looked at earlier are examples of figures.

As with tables, APA Style mandates how we should format figures, making our job of creating figures much easier. An example of a figure formatted in APA Style is provided in **Figure 2.21**. Here are the steps for creating a figure in APA Style.

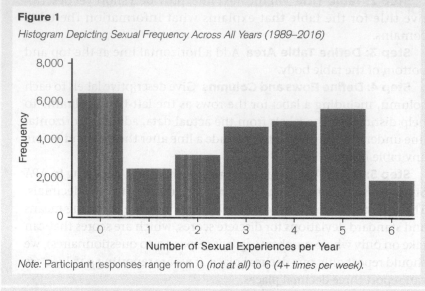

Figure 1

Histogram Depicting Sexual Frequency Across All Years (1989–2016)

Note: Participant responses range from 0 *(not at all)* to 6 *(4+ times per week)*.

Figure 2.21 Sample Figure Formatted in APA Style

Step 1: Number the Figure Each figure gets a figure number, printed in bold font. The first figure mentioned in our paper should be called Figure 1, and subsequent figure numbers should be determined by the order in which they are mentioned in the text.

Step 2: Title the Figure Give the figure a title. The figure title should explain what information is depicted in the figure, in a brief manner. The figure title should be printed in italic font.

Step 3: Create the Content of Your Figure Typically, we will create figures in one computer program (e.g., Microsoft Excel and SPSS) and then paste them into a word processing program (e.g., Microsoft Word and Google Docs). The figure image should be placed between the figure title and figure note.

Step 4: Create a Note The figure note provides the reader with additional information to explain what the figure depicts. For example, if the figure includes any symbols that can take on more than one meaning (e.g., error bars could represent standard error, standard deviation, or confidence intervals), we should explain them in the figure note.

Step 5: Check Yourself . . . Let's make sure we have labeled our axes. If our figure has an x- and a y-axis, we should always have a label for each. All text that occurs in a figure should be in a sans serif font (such as Arial) and sized between 8 and 14 points.

Forming a Conclusion

After inspecting the various frequency tables and histograms for the GSS sex frequency data, we still need to address the key research question of whether people are having more or less sex now than they were 30 years ago. To answer this question, we cannot look at the data for any one year; instead, we need to compare across the years. Take a look at the overall frequencies for each of the responses, presented in Figure 2.20. As you can see, in 1989 the number of participants that reported having no sex in the previous year was lower than it was in 2016. In 1989, 298 participants (21.9% of responders) reported having no sex in the previous year, while in 2016, 439 participants (25.6% of responders) reported having no sex. Not only did fewer people have no sex in 1989 compared to 2016 but more people in 1989 had frequent sex. In 1989, 629 participants (46.2% of responders) reported having sex on at least a weekly basis, while in 2016, only 605 participants (35.3% of responders) reported having sex on at least a weekly basis. Based on this information (and other analyses), the authors' main conclusion from their analysis of this data is that American adults have sex less frequently now than they did 30 years ago! What do you think of these results?

Focus on Open Science: Open Data

If the sexual frequency study's findings were a surprise and you want to dig deeper, there is good news! The author's data set is available online to double-check. The GSS data are available to anyone online at https://gssdataexplorer.norc.org/. Although the GSS data have been available for general use for many years, historically it was uncommon for researchers to share their data with other scholars. On one level, this makes sense. Some researchers may fear that others will "scoop" their ideas by using the researchers' data to publish a paper before the original authors can publish the findings themselves (Gewin, 2016). Other scholars may focus on the costs associated with data collection. For example, a sexual frequency study that tracked the same participants over 10 years would take a long time and a lot of money to complete. As a result, some researchers may be hesitant to give their data and labor away to others for free.

Despite these objections, making study data open and freely available to all is becoming the standard in science. Many federal funding agencies, such as the National Science Foundation and the National Institutes of Health, strongly encourage scholars to post their data in online repositories. Similarly, if the authors of an article post their data online, many journals now reward articles with open data badges. Most importantly, by making their data open, scholars are increasing the

Many journals include graphics such as this Open Data badge to signal that other researchers may access the study's data online.

Center for Open Science

ability for others to reproduce their work. That is, if other researchers question a particular study's findings, they can re-analyze the original data to either challenge or confirm the original authors' conclusions. This is what science is all about: evaluating the evidence to determine which ideas we should keep, and which we should not. These processes increase our confidence in the study results, and, for this reason, the benefits of open data far outweigh the costs (LeBel et al., 2017).

Become a Better Consumer of Statistics

Because graphs and charts help us see information more clearly, they are a standard feature on news programs, in articles, and in textbooks.

Common Mistakes When Creating Graphs and Charts

When making our own charts, it is important to avoid common mistakes such as mislabeling the axes, using colors and fonts that are difficult to read, not having our numbers add up correctly, and omitting information (title, legend, etc.). To avoid these basic issues, we will always be sure to complete the "Check Yourself" step when creating graphs and charts.

Misleading Graphs and Charts

Occasionally, problems with graphs and charts go beyond basic mistakes and are downright deceptive, sometimes purposefully so. We need to be able to critically evaluate these images so that we are not misled into forming wrong conclusions.

Not Starting at 0 The y-axis should start at the lowest possible value, which is often 0 (or 1, depending on your measure; see **Figure 2.22**). Graphs that fail to start at 0 often truncate or shorten the range of possible values on the y-axis. Thus, differences between categories appear much larger. Imagine if the data show that Canadian couples typically have sex 50 times a year, while American couples have sex 55 times a year. If the y-axis started at 0 and ascended up to 60, the differences in size between those two bars would not appear that large, which is accurate. But if the y-axis started at 45 and ascended to 60, that same 5-point difference between the countries would appear much larger than it should (see **Figure 2.23**).

Not Using Equal Intervals In this similar problem with y-axis labeling, the y-axis may start at 0 but then ascends using uneven differences between values. That is, the values may start ascending by 10, only to ascend by 5 or 1 near the top. The end result is that differences between the bars look much larger than they really are (see **Figure 2.24**). This also happens when the y-axis starts at 0, but then the jump to the first interval is large (e.g., "20"), with all subsequent intervals ascending by a lower amount (e.g., "5").

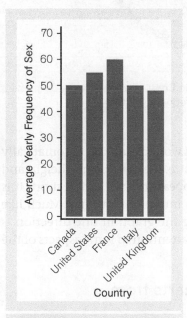

Figure 2.22 Histogram of Sex Frequency by Country with Y-Axis Starting at 0

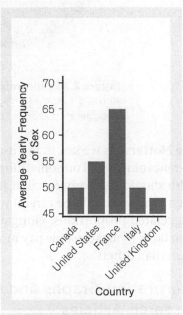

Figure 2.23 Histogram of Sex Frequency by Country with Y-Axis Starting at 45

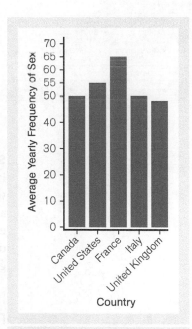

Figure 2.24 Histogram of Sex Frequency by Country with Y-Axis Using Unequal Intervals

pie chart a circle that represents 100% of responses and is divided to represent categories as percentages.

Exaggerating Proportions A misleading chart may use an oversized bar to represent a number that the creator wants viewers to think is bigger. Exaggeration of proportions can also happen in a **pie chart,** a circle that represents 100% of responses and is divided to represent percentages of categories. Each numerical percentage should match up with the area shaded in the chart. For example, while only 26% of movie viewers rated *Love Actually* a 1 or a 2, if someone wanted to make the movie reviews look even worse, they could shade in half of a pie chart and label it as 26%. This chart would be misleading because half of the pie realistically should correspond to 50% of the ratings (see **Figure 2.25**).

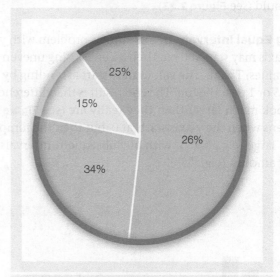

Figure 2.25 Incorrect Pie Chart of *Love Actually*'s Movie Rating Frequency with Exaggerated Proportions

Size Matters As we saw in the use of word clouds, we automatically infer meaning based on something's size. Ideally, a chart's height and width should be nearly equal. If it appears too tall or too short, it is a sign that we should be careful with interpreting things. Much like exaggerated proportions, elongating the graph in one direction is often done to make people pay more attention to some aspects of the graph than others.

Interpreting Graphs and Charts from Research Articles

Scientists are bound by ethical codes of conduct and should never attempt to purposefully mislead readers using graphs and charts (or any statistical information). As part of the peer review process required in journals, experts in the field carefully review each study prior to publication. Nonetheless, we want to carefully interpret visual information in order to draw proper conclusions.

Let's look at **Figure 2.26** from the article on sex frequency (Twenge et al., 2017). By looking at the figure title, we know that the data represent participants' estimates of sexual frequency each year over a 15-year period. The figure legend tells us that one line represents never-married individuals, while the other line represents married participants. The axis labels tell us the nature of the data depicted on the x- and y-axes. Interestingly, the y-axis starts at 50 instead of 0. Although it is best to start at 0, when the lowest value in the data range starts so high (in this case, 55), patterns in the data can be easier to see when starting at a higher number. As we can see from the figure, in previous decades married individuals reported having sex more frequently than never-married individuals. However, more recently that pattern has reversed, with never-married individuals reporting greater sexual frequency than married participants.

Be careful here not to assume that marital status directly causes or leads to sexual frequency (i.e., if someone wants to have more sex, the answer isn't necessarily to avoid marriage). To be a good consumer of statistics, we need to think about other factors. One possibility is that

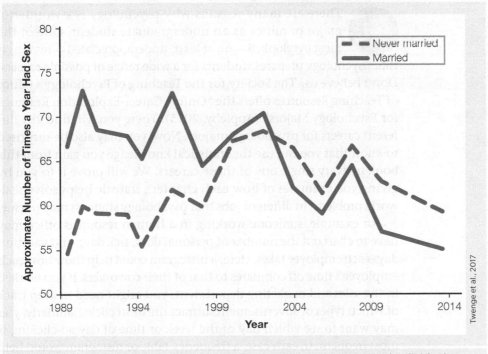

Figure 2.26 Estimated Sexual Frequency for Married and Never-Married Individuals

the age of marriage has increased over time, such that ages at which people are most sexually active (i.e., their 20s) are also the ages when people are not married. That wasn't necessarily true in the 1980s.

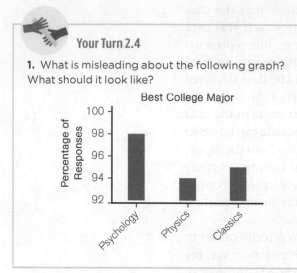

Your Turn 2.4

1. What is misleading about the following graph? What should it look like?

2. The Novice Statistician: Create a graph with at least three major errors. Explain where the errors are.

3. True or false: APA Style requires all figures to have a figure title placed above the figure.

Statistics on the Job

There are many reasons why psychology is a wonderful major or minor as an undergraduate student. One of the most overlooked—or, at least, underappreciated—reasons is that psychology prepares students for a wide range of possible careers. Don't believe us? The Society for the Teaching of Psychology's Office of Teaching Resources offers the "Online Career-Exploration Resource for Psychology Majors" (Appleby, 2015). There you will find 281 different careers for psychology majors. Now, you may also be surprised to know that you can use the statistical knowledge you gain from this book in every single one of those careers. We will prove it to you by giving you examples of how each chapter's statistic helps solve real-world problems in different jobs that psychology students may pursue.

For example, someone working in a human resources office may have to chart out the number of personal days, sick days, and vacation days each employee takes. Here, a histogram could help show how each employee's time off compares to that of their coworkers. If you worked in the sales and marketing department, you might need to keep track of which types of advertisements attract the most clicks. Similarly, you may want to see which day of the week or time of day ad-clicking is most frequent. In each case, a frequency table or histogram would help you summarize the data and see patterns more clearly.

CHAPTER 2 > Review

Review Questions

1. Jody works at a university and needs to present data on the number of college credits completed by the most recent graduates from the college. Her slides have a lot of numbers that may be difficult to interpret. Based on what you learned in this chapter, what would you recommend she add to her presentation, and why?

2. José is determining the average class size in his college's math department. This semester, they offer 20 courses. Create a frequency distribution for his data.

   24, 23, 26, 25, 18, 23, 24, 22, 19, 22, 20, 23, 25, 22, 19, 23, 26, 20, 24, 23

3. The following are the number of sections offered in a fall semester in a state university's psychology department. What is the most appropriate type of figure for these data, and why?

Course Name	Number of Sections
Introduction to Psychology	34
Human Sexuality	4
Adolescent Psychology	1
Child Psychology	2
Lifespan Development	10
Psychology of Personality	2
Statistical Methods in Psychology	3
Social Psychology	3
Abnormal Psychology	7
Biological Psychology	3

4. Latoya works in the customer service department of an Internet service provider. She knows that people get frustrated and are more likely to change providers if they must wait on hold for a long time before speaking to a representative. As a result, her department has set goals for average wait times. She takes a random sample of customer wait times from today and creates a frequency distribution (below). Help her identify and fix the mistakes in the frequency distribution.

   4, 15, 36, 20, 18, 12, 7, 21, 42, 16, 11, 49, 32, 19, 18

Wait Time (minutes)	Frequency	Relative Frequency
45–50	1	0.06
40–45	1	0.06
35–40	1	0.06
30–35	1	0.06
20–25	2	0.13
15–20	5	0.31
10–15	3	0.19
4–10	2	0.13

5. Latoya decides to follow up on her research by reviewing recent survey data. After each call, customers complete a brief survey. Customers rate their satisfaction on a scale from 1 = very unsatisfied to 7 = very satisfied. She randomly selects 25 surveys from each day over the past week. Help Latoya by creating a frequency polygon for the data. Then, describe the modality, skew, and kurtosis. Are there any values that might be outliers?

Satisfaction Rating	Frequency
7	38
6	29
5	37
4	28
3	21
2	14
1	8

6. You are hired to assess a group of kindergarteners' language skills. This task is outside of your area of expertise, and you underestimate the children's skills. As a result, most children score above 90% on your measure even though you know that there are greater differences in their skill levels. What issue is likely present in the resulting data set? If you were to graph the data, what would it look like? What impact might this have on the statistical analyses you had planned?

7. If instead you had made the kindergarten language skills test too difficult, and most children had scored below 30%, what issue might be present in your data, and what would the graph of the data look like? Would it have the same or a different impact on the statistical analyses you had planned?

8. Your local news station presents a graph that doesn't start at 0. You start yelling at the television and your roommate asks why you are so upset. How would you explain to your roommate the effect that not starting at 0 has on the interpretation of the graph?

9. You are working on a presentation about postsecondary education, and you want to include national data about the types of degrees people are earning. Your work is shown in the table below. It's a good thing you're working in a group, because you've made a few mistakes in your APA formatting that your classmate tactfully points out to you. What errors did you make?

Table 1

Degree Earned. Frequency of Responses

Year	No Answer	Less than High School	High School	Associate/ Junior College	Bachelor's	Graduate
1980	3	445	745	45	158	71
2000	16	439	1,501	206	435	218
2021	9	246	1,597	370	1,036	760

Note. Data from the General Social Survey / NORC at the University of Chicago.

10. You are interested in the number of pets students have, so you create a poll and send a link to your classmates. Interpret the following SPSS output.

Statistics		
Number of pets		
N	Valid	70
	Missing	0
Skewness		1.507
Std. Error of Skewness		.287
Kurtosis		1.462
Std. Error of Kurtosis		.566

a. What is your sample size?
b. Is the distribution positively skewed, is it negatively skewed, or is there no skew? How can you tell?
c. Is the distribution mesokurtic, platykurtic, or leptokurtic? How can you tell?

11. You tend to swear a lot when you are frustrated and/or stressed. You've just started studying statistics, so you start collecting data on how many times you swear per day. You started collecting data 30 days ago, have entered the data into SPSS, and are wondering what the distribution looks like. Look at the SPSS output to answer the following questions.

Statistics		
Swears		
N	Valid	29
	Missing	0
Skewness		1.784
Std. Error of Skewness		.434
Kurtosis		6.267
Std. Error of Kurtosis		.845

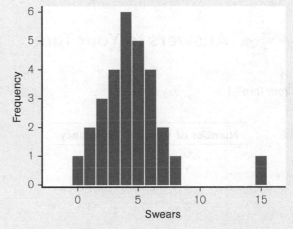

a. Did you collect data for every day? How can you tell?
b. Identify any potential outliers.
c. Describe the skew and kurtosis of the distribution. What influence do(es) the outlier(s) seem to have on the shape of the distribution?

Key Concepts

Answers to Your Turn

Your Turn 2.1

1.

Number of Wings	Frequency
0	0
1	1
2	2
3	1
4	2
5	0
6	5
7	2
8	1

2.

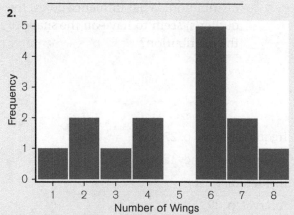

3. d. All of the above.

4. exclusivity; equal width

Your Turn 2.2

1. Cashew Bliss:

(a)

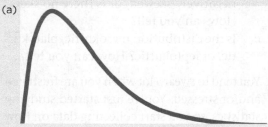

(b) unimodal, asymmetrical, positive skew

2. Cackles: (a)

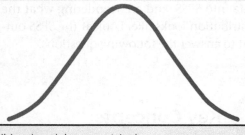

(b) unimodal, symmetrical

3. Chixit: (a)

(b) uniform, symmetrical

Your Turn 2.3

1. outlier

2. a. Ceiling effect. The vast majority of parents are going to respond at the extreme positive end of the scale.

Your Turn 2.4

1. The graph doesn't start at zero. It should look like this:

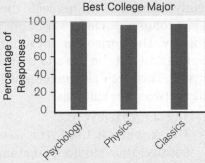

Best College Major

2. Answers will vary but will include errors such as not starting at 0, unequal intervals, mislabeled axes, incorrect data, missing information, and features with varying sizes (bars too big or small relative to their value).

3. True. APA Style requires a figure title below the figure number and above the figure body. The title should be in italics.

Answers to Review Questions

1. Jody should include a visual representation of her data, such as a histogram or a polygon, because visual representations summarize data in an easy-to-interpret format and allow us to see patterns in the data.

2.

Class Size	Frequency	Percent
26	2	10
25	2	10
24	3	15
23	5	25
22	3	15
21	0	0
20	2	10
19	2	10
18	1	5

3. The most appropriate is a bar graph because the variable is nominal.

4. There should be no skipped intervals, the intervals should be of equal width, and each observation should belong to only one group (exclusivity). Adding up the frequencies should sum to 15 (the overall number of responses) but instead sums to 16.

Wait Time (minutes)	Frequency	Relative Frequency
45–49	1	0.07
40–44	1	0.07
35–39	1	0.07
30–34	1	0.07
25–29	0	0
20–24	2	0.13
15–19	5	0.33
10–14	2	0.13
5–9	1	0.07
0–4	1	0.07

5. The distribution is bimodal (peaks at rating = 5 and rating = 7), with negative skew. Kurtosis may be hard to discern, but the distribution is platykurtic.

6. You likely have a ceiling effect. The data would be negatively skewed. Most of the scores will be clustered to the right-hand side of the distribution with the tail pointing to the left-hand side. Your data will have low variability, which can make it difficult to draw conclusions about the general population from our data.

7. In this case, you would have a floor effect. The data would be positively skewed. Most of the scores would be clustered to the left-hand side of the distribution with the tail pointing to the right-hand side. The impact would be similar to having a ceiling effect.

8. When a graph doesn't start at 0, it tends to make differences between groups look larger.

9. See the corrected table at the bottom of the page. The table number was not formatted correctly. The title of the table was not sufficiently descriptive. The header in the second to last column (Bachelor's) was not aligned properly. The horizontal lines that define the table area at the top and bottom were missing. There were also unnecessary vertical lines between the columns.

10. a. The sample size is 70.
    b. The skewness is 1.507. The skewness is positive, which indicates that the distribution is positively skewed.
    c. The distribution has positive kurtosis, which indicates that the distribution is leptokurtic (more scores in the tails relative to a normal distribution).

11. a. Your sample size is 29, but you've been collecting data for 30 days, so you missed one day.
    b. There is one potential outlier: the value of 15 seems to be atypically high.
    c. The distribution is positively skewed and leptokurtic. The outlier is increasing the positive skew and the "tailedness" of the distribution (without it, the data look normally distributed).

Table 1

Highest Degree Earned. Frequency of Responses by Year

Year	No Answer	Less than High School	High School	Associate/Junior College	Bachelor's	Graduate
1980	3	445	745	45	158	71
2000	16	439	1,501	206	435	218
2021	9	246	1,597	370	1,036	760

Note. Data from the General Social Survey/NORC at the University of Chicago.

OPEN STATS LAB

Sharpen your statistics skills with real-life data! Check out OpenStatsLab.com, created by coauthor Kevin McIntyre, to practice running analyses for real published research studies.

Measures of Central Tendency & Variability

Learning Outcomes

After reading this chapter, you should be able to:

● Differentiate between three measures of central tendency: mode, median, and mean.

● Identify which measure of central tendency is best for different types of data.

● Differentiate between three measures of variability: range, variance, and standard deviation.

● Calculate measures of central tendency and variability by hand.

● Calculate measures of central tendency and variability using SPSS.

● Identify common errors that people make when interpreting measures of central tendency.

L ate at night, procrastinating on a paper you would rather not write, you find yourself on Amazon.com and stumble upon the DinoPet. The DinoPet is a micro-aquarium shaped like a dinosaur that you fill with microscopic creatures that absorb light during the day and glow blue at night without any help from electricity or batteries.

Who really needs that? You do. Right now. Before spending money you don't have, though, you need to determine if the DinoPet is as awesome as it seems. So you check out the reviews. There are hundreds of them, which is great; unfortunately, the overall customer review rating is a 3.0. You can't get any more middle of the road than that in their 5-star rating system. You need to figure out if that 3.0 rating is good or bad, and ultimately whether you're about to become a proud owner of a DinoPet.

Statistics for Life

To know whether a 3.0 rating is a good sign, we need to first figure out what a 3.0 even signifies. One thing is for sure: Amazon customers use that one number as an indication of what everyone thinks about a product. But as someone with an increasingly sophisticated understanding of statistics and numbers, you want to dig deeper. For example, the 3.0 stars could simply be the most common rating, it could be the value where half of the ratings are above it and half are below, or it could be the average rating. Depending on what the 3-star rating actually refers to, we might come to a completely different interpretation of what it tells us. That is, if everyone mostly gives it a "3," that indicates one thing, while many people rating it a "5" with others rating it a "1" or "2" tells a different story. We need to know a bit more about these ratings before we can answer the question, "Is buying the DinoPet a good idea?"

Where Do the Data Come From?

Amazon has over 300 million active customers worldwide. A product like the DinoPet very likely has been sold to many thousands of people. Of those, a small percentage of customers

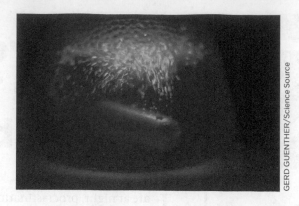

will give a rating, with an even smaller number taking the time to give written feedback. That's important to keep in mind because the ratings are not from a randomly selected sample. Thus, we have to ask ourselves whether people who provide ratings are meaningfully different from those who don't give ratings. Depending on our thoughts here, we might adjust our view on the ratings' accuracy, including whether we think they may be overly enthusiastic and positive, unnecessarily harsh, or both (i.e., only those with extreme views tend to write reviews). In any case, we need to consider these types of issues when deciding how much to allow customer ratings and reviews to influence our purchases.

Measures of Central Tendency: What We're Trying to Accomplish

When a product only has six ratings, it is hard to know what the overall rating really can tell us because the sample size is so small. However, in those cases, the benefit is that we can carefully review each individual rating. The more information we have to make a decision, the better. The only problem is that once we have a dozen or more reviews and ratings, looking through them individually becomes overwhelming. Drawing conclusions is nearly impossible because we have to be careful that we are not allowing some ratings to have greater influence than others (e.g., a particularly glowing 5-star rating is still only one person's experience).

In these cases, what we need is one number that best captures the entire collection of ratings. This number would serve as the representative for the other numbers. This is just like when groups send a single representative to convey their thoughts. Whether it is one student who represents all students' views to the faculty or administration, or the local politician who advocates for her constituents in the House of Representatives, one entity stands in and characterizes everything else.

This one person attempts to convey the group's sentiment as accurately as possible. Does that imply that every single person in the group feels exactly the same? No. But the representative's view should be most similar to most of the members. That is, it should reflect the **central tendency,** or value that summarizes all of the other obtained measurements or values for a particular variable. Central tendency conveys the main idea of all the information in that group. We can do the exact same thing with numbers.

All three types of central tendency have the same goal: describe the larger set of scores. Measures of central tendency are one type within the broader category of descriptive statistics, which, you'll recall from Chapter 1, is a category of statistics including any treatment of data meant to summarize, depict, draw, or show the nature of the data. We have three main ways of expressing the central tendency of a group of numbers: mode, median, and mean. As with all concepts in the book, we will first give a basic introduction in this section, Statistics for Life, to give you a solid foundation. Then in the Statistics for Research section, we'll build on what you know and provide more depth.

central tendency value that summarizes all of the other obtained measurements or values for a particular variable.

Mode: How Does It Work?

The easiest way to answer the question about what is most typical in a group of values is to figure out which value occurs most often. If you were to look at all of the different star ratings on Amazon, you could count how frequently customers gave each rating. The number or category that occurs most often is the **mode.** Thus, if a 5-star rating is most common, that is the modal response. The modal response is at the histogram's peak, which is why we call a distribution "unimodal" if there is one mode and "bimodal" if there are two modes.

mode a measure of central tendency indicating the number that occurs most often.

The nice thing about the mode is that it works with categorical or nominal data (i.e., variables that use numbers to indicate categories). If instead of number of stars, Amazon asked people to give nominal/categorical ratings of Excellent, Good, Average, Poor, or Awful, we would still be able to count up the number of responses, see which response occurs most frequently, and determine central tendency based on the mode. To keep things simple, let's just work with the first 10 ratings we find on the site: 3, 4, 2, 5, 2, 2, 1, 4, 2, 5. Rest assured, everything we are about to do works the same with hundreds or thousands of numbers, but it is easier to see how it all operates with a more manageable number of responses.

> ❝
> ### Statistically Speaking
> I asked everyone I could about the best place to go for Spring Break and the modal response was Cancun.
> ❞

Step by Step: Calculating a Mode

Step 1: Create a Frequency Table We would do this exactly the same way that we did in Chapter 2. No symbols, no formulas, just counting.

Step 2: Compare Values Based on the counts we gave for each value (i.e., how many 4-star ratings, 3-star ratings, etc.), determine which one has the most. We have one "1," four "2's," one "3," two "4's," and two "5's." Because "2" occurs the most, that is the mode.

Step 3: Check Yourself . . . It is wise to double-check our counts for each value. In addition, we want to see if there is a tie for the top spot. It is possible to have multiple modes or a multimodal distribution, in which two values share the highest frequency (e.g., the same number of 5-star and 1-star ratings).

Median: How Does It Work?

The mode, or value that occurs most frequently, can be from any value on the scale. That is, any value can occur most frequently, and it does not necessarily have to be from the middle or central part of the scale. Often, a product's overall rating will fall around the 5-star scale's midpoint (i.e., a "3"), but the most frequently given rating is a "5." After all, people buy products expecting to like them, so 5-star ratings should be common. Thus, it may be best to determine the **median,** or the place in a series of numbers that represents the midpoint location where half of the actual scores are above the midpoint and half of the actual scores are below it. Essentially, we want to identify the 50th percentile or the exact middle ranking. As a result, medians are an ideal measure of central tendency for ranked or ordinal-level data.

Step by Step: Calculating a Median

Step 1: Sort the Scores Arrange all of the scores in order from lowest to highest. If our original scores were: 3, 4, 2, 5, 2, 2, 1, 4, 2, 5, we would line them up as follows: 1, 2, 2, 2, 2, 3, 4, 4, 5, 5.

Step 2: Count the Number of Scores Simply count up the number of scores that we have on a variable (e.g., the number of ratings for the product). The statistical abbreviation for the number of scores is N (see **Figure 3.1**).

median a measure of central tendency that indicates the place in a series of numbers that represents the midpoint location where half of the actual scores are above and half of the actual scores fall below.

N = Number of Scores
X = An Individual Score
Σ = Sum of Scores

Figure 3.1 Statistical Symbols Used in This Chapter

Step 3: Identify the Midpoint Location To do this, we want to take our total number of scores (N), add 1, and then divide by 2.

$$\frac{N+1}{2}$$

That tells us which place in the order is the median. So if we have 10 ratings ($N = 10$), then

$$\frac{10+1}{2} = \frac{11}{2} = 5.5$$

This indicates that, starting from the left, we should count 5 scores. The ".5" tells you that your midpoint won't be an exact value, but rather a space between two numbers. In this case, you count 5 scores from the left and realize, the midpoint is a space between a "2" and a "3." When that happens, add up the two numbers and divide by 2.

$$\frac{2+3}{2} = 2.5$$

Thus, the median is 2.5.

Step 4: Check Yourself . . . To confirm you did things correctly, make sure there are the same number of scores to the right of the median as there are to the left.

Mean: How Does It Work?

Although the median, by definition, falls in the middle of a distribution of scores, it does not tell us that much about the scores themselves. These three scores, 5, 37, 99, have the exact same median as these three scores, 35, 37, 38. But as you can see, the numbers themselves are quite different. Remember, a measure of central tendency should be the one number that best represents the rest of the group. To do that, we really need to account for what each value in our distribution is. We do that by finding the **mean,** sometimes called the arithmetic mean, through calculating the average of the numbers. The mean represents the mathematical balancing point for all of your scores.

mean sometimes called the arithmetic mean, a measure of central tendency that indicates the average of the numbers (sum of all numbers divided by the number of cases).

A teeter-totter is designed to balance out the weight of the individuals. Similarly, a mean should balance the value of the scores on each side. However, if one score is too extreme, it can throw off the balance.

The idea here is that the mean works similarly to the fulcrum or pivot point of a teeter-totter. If the mass on the left side of the teeter-totter is equal to the mass on the right side, the teeter-totter will be balanced. If the mass is unequal, the teeter-totter will fall to the side with greater mass. The mean works the same way for any set of scores. The mean captures the point at which the low and high values in a distribution will balance out.

Step by Step: Calculating a Mean

Step 1: Find the Sum of the Scores Take each score (X) and add them up:

$$3 + 4 + 2 + 5 + 2 + 2 + 1 + 4 + 2 + 5 = 30$$

In statistics, rather than say "add them up" or "find the sum," we simply use a symbol (Σ, the Greek letter sigma) to indicate the same thing. So, we could have also said

$$\Sigma(3, 4, 2, 5, 2, 2, 1, 4, 2, 5) = 30$$

Step 2: Count the Number of Scores Just like we did for the median, we find N by counting the number of scores that we have on a variable. In this case, we have 10 ratings total.

Step 3: Calculate the Mean To calculate the mean (M) (also commonly symbolized as $\overline{X}$ or "X-bar"), we essentially divide the answer from Step 1 by the answer from Step 2.

$$M = \frac{\Sigma X}{N}$$

In everyday terms: The Sum of All Scores divided by The Total Number of Scores = Mean (see **Figure 3.2**).

$$M = \frac{\Sigma X}{N} = \frac{30}{10} = 3$$

Words: (The Sum of All Scores divided by The Total
　　　Number of Scores) = Mean
Symbols: $(\Sigma X / N) = M$
Numbers: $(30 \div 10) = 3$ or $(30 / 10) = 3$

Figure 3.2 Words/Symbols/Numbers: The Mean

Step 4: Check Yourself . . . Once we find the answer, make sure that it is not less than the bottom score and not greater than the top score. In other words, it has to fall between 1 and 5. Take a minute to line up all of the scores (like we did to find the median) and see where the mean falls along that sequence. As the balancing point, the mean should fall somewhere within the middle of the scores such that it balances out the low and high values.

Before you read on, take a look at this video, which demonstrates how to calculate measures of central tendency.

HAND CALCULATION VIDEO TUTORIAL: To learn more, check out the video tutorial Calculating the Mean, Median, and Mode by Hand!

Your Turn 3.1

1. Please match each symbol to the correct description:

____ *X*　　a. Mean

____ *M*　　b. Sum

____ Σ　　c. Individual Score

____ *N*　　d. Number of Scores

2. Summer's here and you need a raft. You learn you can buy a raft shaped like bacon (because of course you can), but you want to check the ratings. Here are the most recent ratings: 5, 5, 5, 4, 5, 1, 5, 2, 1, 5. Calculate the (a) mode, (b) median, and (c) mean.

3. Give 5 scores that have the exact same mode, median, and mean.

4. Below you will see SPSS output for the movie ratings of *Love Actually*, described in Chapter 2. Based on this output, the mean rating of *Love Actually* is _____, the median is _____, the mode is _____, and the sample size is _____.

Statistics		
Rating_for_Love_Actually		
N	Valid	50
	Missing	0
Mean		5.5200
Median		6.0000
Mode		1.00

Measures of Variability: What We're Trying to Accomplish

 A measure of central tendency, especially the mean, tells us a lot about the middle of a frequency distribution. In particular, the mean gives us that one value that best represents all of the other values. However, the mean does not tell us how closely it matches up with the other values. That is, does the mean fall relatively near the other scores, or is it further away?

Consider this: you can have the same mean for groups of very different scores. For example, if you saw that the DinoPet's ratings were 3, 3, 3, the mean is obviously 3 and does a perfect job of representing all of the scores in the group. Now, if the ratings were 2, 3, 4, the mean is still 3. Though it's not a perfect representation of the other scores, it is still very close. However, if the DinoPet's ratings were 1, 3, 5, the mean is still 3, but it is relatively far (2 full stars) away from most of the scores.

These situations highlight the need to have a sense of the scores' **variability,** or how spread out the scores are in a distribution. In cases where the scores are all the same (3, 3, 3), the scores are all piled up in one area and have low variability. When the scores are very different (1, 3, 5), the scores are spread widely and have high variability. We have three main ways of expressing the variability of a group of numbers: range, variance, and standard deviation, each of which are also types of descriptive statistics.

variability how spread out the scores are in a distribution.

range a measure of variability that indicates how far apart the top score is from the bottom score.

Range: How Does It Work?

At the most basic level, if we want to see how much something spreads out, we need to know where it begins and where it ends. If we know our DinoPet has an average rating of 3.00, that may tell us something different depending on what the highest and lowest ratings were. For example, if the lowest score was 2 and the highest was 4, it shows people don't differ all that much in their rating. But if the top score is 5 and the bottom is 1, then it suggests people have a wider range of experiences with their DinoPet. When considering variability, the **range** is a numerical indication of how far apart the top score is from the bottom score.

Step by Step: Calculating the Range

Step 1: Sort the Scores This is just like what we did to calculate a median: 1, 2, 2, 2, 2, 3, 4, 4, 5, 5.

Step 2: Identify the Top and Bottom Scores In other words, what are the lowest and highest scores in our data set?

Step 3: Calculate the Range In everyday terms, find the range by subtracting the lowest score from the highest score, or Range = Highest Score – Lowest Score. In numbers: $5 - 1 = 4$.

Step 4: Check Yourself . . . Since we have all positive numbers, the range cannot be greater than the highest value or lower than the lowest value.

Variance: How Does It Work?

Knowing something about the distribution's endpoints is helpful, but it does not tell the whole story. Imagine if someone wanted to take a road trip and travel the entirety of Interstate 95, the longest stretch of road running North–South in the United States that traces the Eastern Seaboard. If the would-be travelers wanted to get a sense of their experience, knowing the endpoints (Maine and Florida) is useful. However, they do not tell them much of what they'll experience throughout the middle of their journey. It is the same with a distribution. We may know a DinoPet's ratings begin and end (almost always 1-star and 5-star), but the more useful information is how all of the ratings are distributed between those endpoints. For example, there could be a couple of 1-star ratings, and a ton of 5-stars, or a few 1-star and 5-star ratings, but an abundance of ratings near the middle.

We know that variability in general tells us how much numbers are spread out in the distribution. But spread out from what? The most logical reference point in the distribution is the mean. If we want to know what most scores are like, the mean gives us that value. From there, it would be useful to know how much other scores are similar or different (i.e., how far they are) from the mean. **Variance** (SD^2) (also commonly symbolized as S^2) is a statistic that measures the average of the squared differences between each score and the mean—in other words, the average squared deviation from the mean.

Step by Step: Calculating the Variance of the Population

Step 1: Find the Mean (M) We can follow the steps described earlier to calculate the mean of our scores: 3, 4, 2, 5, 2, 2, 1, 4, 2, 5 (see **Figure 3.3**). When we did that, the answer was 3, or $M = 3$.

Step 2: Find the Deviation Score ($X - M$) A **deviation score** is a calculation of how far each score is from the mean by subtracting the mean (M) from each score (X). We can determine a deviation score as follows: ($X - M$) (see **Figure 3.4**).

If we try to add up the deviation scores, they will always sum to 0. That's because, as we mentioned earlier, the mean is the balance point

variance (SD^2) a measure of variability that generally lets us know how far, on average, numbers in the distribution are spread out from the mean, $\Sigma(X - M)^2/N$, or SS/N.

deviation score a calculation of how far each score is from the mean by subtracting the mean (M) from each score (X), or ($X - M$).

Score (X)
3
4
2
5
2
2
1
4
2
5
Sum $\Sigma(X) = 30$
$N = 10$
Mean $\Sigma(X)/N = 3$

Figure 3.3 Computation Sheet: Calculating a Mean

$$(X - M) = \text{Deviation Score}$$
$$(X - M)^2 = \text{Squared Deviation Score}$$
$$\Sigma(X - M)^2 = \text{Sum of Squared Deviation Scores}$$
$$\Sigma(X - M)^2 = SS$$

Figure 3.4 Statistical Symbols: Deviation Scores

of a distribution. As a result, the scores' distance above the mean will always be the same as the scores' distance below the mean (see **Figure 3.5**).

Score (X)	Deviation Score (X – M)
3	0
4	1
2	–1
5	2
2	–1
2	–1
1	–2
4	1
2	–1
5	2
Sum $\Sigma(X) = 30$	$\Sigma(X - M) = 0$
$N = 10$	
Mean $\Sigma(X) / N = 3$	

Figure 3.5 Computation Sheet: Calculating Deviation Scores

Step 3: Find the Squared Deviation Score $(X - M)^2$ If the sum of every distribution's deviation scores is always 0, it becomes impossible to find the total amount of deviation. To counteract this problem, we square the deviation scores (see **Figure 3.6**). This has two immediate benefits. First, it makes all of our deviations positive. Now when we add them up, we won't have positive and negative values cancelling each other out.

There's a second, even bigger benefit. Squaring the deviation amplifies large differences. Think of it this way: If a score deviates from the mean by 1, when we square that, the difference is still 1. But if a

Score (X)	Deviation Score (X − M)	Squared Deviation Score (X − M)²
3	0	0
4	1	1
2	−1	1
5	2	4
2	−1	1
2	−1	1
1	−2	4
4	1	1
2	−1	1
5	2	4
Sum $\Sigma(X) = 30$ $N = 10$ Mean $\Sigma(X) / N = 3$	$\Sigma(X − M) = 0$	$\Sigma(X − M)^2 = 18$ $SS = 18$

Figure 3.6 Computation Sheet: Calculating Sum of Squared Deviation Scores

score is far off the mean and deviates by 3, squaring that becomes 9. Essentially, we are punishing scores for being further from the mean. In Chapter 2 we discussed outliers and the issues they present. If we have an outlier, our scores are going to be more spread out. Here, by squaring deviations, we represent just how different those outliers are from everything else in mathematical terms.

Step 4: Find the Sum of Squared Deviation Scores (*SS*) We do not just want to know about how one score deviates from the mean. We also want to get a sense of how much all of the scores in our distribution differ from the mean. To get a sense of that, we need to add up all of the deviations. In other words, we need to find the sum of the squared deviation scores, also known as **sum of squares.** Or, in symbols, $SS = \Sigma(X − M)^2$.

We might wonder why we need to do any more calculations. Isn't the sum of squares a good measure of the total amount of variation in a distribution? Yes, it is! Because of this, we will use the sum of squares in some analyses later in this textbook. Unfortunately, it has a limitation as a measure of variation. As we add additional observations to a data set, the sum of squares will typically increase, even if the overall amount of variation in the data remains the same. Ideally, we want a measure of variation that only captures the amount of variability in a data set and isn't affected by the sample size.

sum of squares (*SS*) the sum of the squared deviation scores, or $\Sigma(X − M)^2$.

Step 5: Calculate the Population Variance We can get around this issue by finding the average of the squared deviation scores. The sum of squares will tell us how much total squared deviation we have among all of our scores. But it would be more useful if we had a sense of how much, on average, each score deviated from the mean. To determine that, we need to divide the sum of squared deviations (SS) by the number of cases (N), or $\Sigma(X - M)^2/N$, or SS/N. The result is the population variance (SD^2), or the average of the squared differences between each score and the mean.

$$SD^2 = \frac{\Sigma(X - M)^2}{N} \qquad SD^2 = \frac{SS}{N}$$

In everyday terms, (The Sum of All Squared Deviation Scores divided by The Total Number of Scores) = Variance (see **Figure 3.7**).

$$SD^2 = \frac{SS}{N} = \frac{\Sigma(X - M)^2}{N} = \frac{18}{10} = 1.80$$

Words: (The Sum of All Squared Deviation Scores divided by The Total Number of Scores) = Population Variance

Symbols: $(SS/N) = SD^2$

Numbers: $18/10 = 1.8$

Figure 3.7 Words/Symbols/Numbers: Population Variance

Step 6: Check Yourself . . . The first thing to double-check is that the mean is the balance point of our distribution (see **Figure 3.8**). We can do this by making sure the sum of the deviation scores is zero. Next, check the squared deviation scores to verify that they are all positive numbers. Finally, check to see if the variance that you calculate makes sense. Variance can be zero if all of the scores are identical, but otherwise it must be a positive number. There's either variation in our data or there isn't. We can't have negative variance.

Standard Deviation: How Does It Work?

The variance does exactly what we would want. It gives us an indication of how much our scores typically vary or deviate from the mean. The only problem is that because

Score (X)	Deviation Score (X − M)	Squared Deviation Score (X − M)²
3	0	0
4	1	1
2	−1	1
5	2	4
2	−1	1
2	−1	1
1	−2	4
4	1	1
2	−1	1
5	2	4
Sum Σ(X) = 30 N = 10 Mean Σ(X)/N = 3	Σ(X − M) = 0	Σ(X − M)² = 18 SS = 18

Variance (SD²) = Σ(X − M)²/N
Variance (SD²) = SS/N
Variance (SD²) = 18/10
Variance (SD²) = 1.8

Figure 3.8 Computation Sheet: Calculating Population Variance

variance uses squared differences, it can be challenging to interpret. For example, if we calculated a variance of 16 and wanted to interpret what that tells us, we know that 16 is greater than a variance of 12 or of 1.83. But it is hard to wrap our heads around what a variance of 16 might indicate relative to our scores. What exactly does our variance represent for your 5-point rating scale? What if we had a 7-point scale?

Though we had a good reason for doing so, when we squared all of our numbers it created this issue. If only we could undo it! Think back to your middle school math class. What is the opposite of squaring a number? Taking the square root. When we do that, we put the variance back within the context of scale's original values. This **standard deviation (SD)** (also commonly symbolized as S) is a measure of how far scores are dispersed from the mean using the same units as the original scale. That is, if the measure went from 1 to 7, a standard deviation of 1 equates to 1 point on the measure.

In other words, we have standardized the deviation scores relative to the original scale and now know the average amount scores differ from the scale's mean. Because standard deviation uses the same units

standard deviation (SD) a measure of variability that indicates how far scores are dispersed from the mean using the same units as the original scale. It is the square root of the variance, or $\sqrt{SD^2}$. They are the most widely used statistic for describing variability.

as the original scale, it is easier to understand. If your standard deviation is 1, it indicates that scores vary by 1 point on the scale. If the standard deviation is 12, it represents 12 points on the scale. Since it is much more intuitive than variance, standard deviations are the most widely used statistic for describing variability. Once you have the variance, calculating standard deviation is simple.

Step by Step: Calculating Standard Deviation

Step 1: Calculate the Variance (SD^2) Do this using the steps outlined above.

Step 2: Calculate the Standard Deviation (SD) This is as straightforward as taking the square root of the variance.

$$SD = \sqrt{\frac{\Sigma(X - M)^2}{N}} \qquad SD = \sqrt{SS/N}$$

In everyday terms, The Square Root of the Variance = Standard Deviation (see **Figure 3.9**).

$$SD = \sqrt{\text{Variance}} = \sqrt{SD^2}$$
$$SD = \sqrt{1.8} = 1.34$$

Words: (The Square Root of the Variance) = Standard Deviation
Symbols: $\sqrt{\text{Variance}} = \sqrt{SD^2} = SD$
Numbers: $\sqrt{1.8} = 1.34$

Figure 3.9   Words/Symbols/Numbers: Standard Deviation

Step 3: Check Yourself . . . The standard deviation should be less than the range. It should also be lower than the highest possible value in your scale (see **Figure 3.10**). In our case, it should not be higher than 5. Also, take a look at your answer and see if it makes sense relative to your scale. Our mean star rating was a 3, so having our scores differ by an average of 1.34 makes sense, especially since our ratings were not clustered all around 3 (we had some 1's and 5's). If more of the scores are closer to the mean, you should expect a lower standard deviation.

Still unsure how to compute the standard deviation of a population? Take a look at this video, which walks through the steps for

Score (X)	Deviation Score (X − M)	Squared Deviation Score (X − M)²
3	0	0
4	1	1
2	−1	1
5	2	4
2	−1	1
2	−1	1
1	−2	4
4	1	1
2	−1	1
5	2	4
Sum Σ(X) = 30 N = 10 Mean Σ(X)/N = 3	Σ(X − M) = 0	Σ(X − M)² = 18 SS = 18

Variance (SD²) = Σ(X − M)²/N
Variance (SD²) = SS/N
Variance (SD²) = 18/10
Variance (SD²) = 1.8

Standard Deviation (SD) = $\sqrt{SD^2}$
Standard Deviation (SD) = $\sqrt{1.8}$
Standard Deviation (SD) = 1.34

Figure 3.10 Computation Sheet: Calculating Standard Deviation

calculating the deviation scores, the sum of squares, the variance, and the standard deviation.

 HAND CALCULATION VIDEO TUTORIAL: To learn more, check out the video tutorial Calculating the Standard Deviation of a Population by Hand!

Communicating the Result

The DinoPet's three measures of central tendency were different. The mode was 2.00, the median was 2.50, and the mean was 3.00. The variability measures for the DinoPet were a range of 4.00, a variance of 1.80, and a standard deviation of 1.34. Of the variability measures, standard deviation is the easiest to interpret and shows that rating scores typically differed from the mean by over a point. Because the mean and standard deviation are the most useful numbers, you will see them used most frequently to describe a group of scores. You could simply say that the DinoPet's mean rating was a 3.00 with a standard deviation of 1.34. You may also want to draw some conclusion and support it with data. To report that in APA Style, you could write something like "The DinoPet's ratings are near the middle of Amazon's star rating scale (*M* = 3.00; *SD* = 1.34)." When communicating with statistical symbols, remember to always put them in italics when writing in APA Style.

Forming a Conclusion

As you can see, an overall rating of "3" on Amazon tells you part of the story, but not the whole story. When you start digging into the numbers a bit, you might form different conclusions based on which measure of central tendency you use. With the mode and median both at or below 3 stars, it should not give us much confidence in the product. The standard deviation of 1.34 gives some hope, because it indicates that there were several scores above 3 stars. But it cuts both ways. It also means there were several scores 1.34 points below 3 stars that fell close to 1 star.

In conclusion, the measures of central tendency and variability should make you hesitant to buy a DinoPet. Though a few people gave a 5-star rating, the most common rating was a 2, and 50% of raters rated it below at 2.50. To have more confidence in a purchase you should probably look for a product with lots of ratings that have a mean above a 4.0 with low variability.

Your Turn 3.2

1. Give five numbers with (a) low variability; (b) high variability; (c) repeat (a) and (b), but make sure each set of numbers has the same mean.

2. Please match each symbol to the correct description (Note: One will be used twice):

____ *SD*   a. Standard Deviation

____ $\Sigma(X - M)^2$ b. Variance

____ *SD*²   c. Squared Deviation Score

____ (*X* – *M*)   d. Deviation Score

____ (*X* – *M*)²   e. Sum of Squares

____ *SS*

3. Earlier you figured out that the mean rating for the bacon raft was 3.80. Now, you want to get a sense of the ratings' variability. Here are the most recent ratings again: 5, 5, 5, 4, 5, 1, 5, 2, 1, 5. Calculate the (a) range, (b) variance, and (c) standard deviation.

4. What is a deviation score? If we sum the deviation scores for any distribution, what is always the result?

5. How might you pay someone a compliment using the concepts of mean and standard deviation?

6. Below you will see SPSS output for the movie ratings of both *Love Actually* and *Black Panther* (2018). Based on this information, for which movie is there greater agreement among the raters? Explain your answer.

Statistics		Rating_for_Love_Actually	Rating_for_Black_Panther
N	Valid	50	50
	Missing	0	0
Std. Deviation		3.23400	1.58101
Variance		10.459	2.500
Range		9.00	7.00

Statistics for Research

Now that you have the basic idea behind measures of central tendency and variability using a fun example, we're going to use these concepts in a more formal research-based example. This will not only give you a bit of helpful repetition and review, but will also allow us to deepen your understanding.

Scrolling through social media sites, you've probably wondered about why people post the things they post. Sometimes people post about truly remarkable experiences: a vacation, the birth of a child, the death of a pet. But more often than not, they post about their everyday lives: their time in the 5k race, the clothes they bought at the mall, the fancy meal they made. Do these posts give us deeper insights into our friends' psychology?

Research has sought to answer questions such as this one to determine whether people's use of social media reveals something about their psychological well-being. For example, research reveals that viewing the posts of Instagram influencers tends to result in more negative emotions among people who are socially anxious (Parsons et al., 2021).

In another study, researchers wanted to study people's use of negative emotion words on Facebook (Settanni & Marengo, 2015). These researchers found that people who reported higher levels of depression, anxiety, and stress reported more negative emotion words in their Facebook posts. But is this true for other social media platforms? Some people argue that Twitter is a more toxic social media platform than Facebook (Gordon, 2020). Let's imagine that we wanted to measure the use of negative emotion words on Twitter. How might we determine the central tendency and variability of negative emotions on Twitter?

Where Do the Data Come From?

To answer this research question, we could recruit a random sample of participants who regularly post to Twitter. For each of our participants, we could collect their 50 most recent tweets. We could then analyze our participants' frequency of emotion words using a computer program called the Linguistic Inquiry and Word Count, or LIWC for short (pronounced "Luke"). LIWC has a built-in dictionary that scans text passages for over 6,400 psychologically relevant words, including the use of positive and negative emotion words. (Note: If you want to analyze your own writing, find a passage that you have written about a personal experience and visit https://www .liwc.app/demo. Paste your writing passage into the text analyzer and click on "Analyze Text.")

Let's imagine that **Figure 3.11** presents the results of one of our participants' 10 most recent tweets. As we can see, the participant wrote 836 words, of which the first 500 were analyzed. Of those 500 words, 1.1% (or about 6 words overall) referred to negative emotions.

Your text sample is 836 words. The LIWC2015 analysis of the text sample you entered is below. If you entered more than 500 words, only the first 500 words were analyzed. Note that LIWC2015 actually produces about 90 different output dimensions. Always remember that the more text you have, the more trustworthy the results.

TRADITIONAL LIWC DIMENSION	YOUR DATA	AVERAGE FOR SOCIAL MEDIA: TWITTER, FACEBOOK, BLOG
I-WORDS (I, ME, MY)	1.9	5.51
SOCIAL WORDS	12.1	9.71
POSITIVE EMOTIONS	3.6	4.57
NEGATIVE EMOTIONS	1.1	2.10

Figure 3.11   Sample LIWC Analysis Results

We could then combine the results for all of our participants and measure the central tendency and variability to calculate the descriptive statistics for our participants' display of negative emotions on Twitter (see **Figure 3.12**).

1	2	3	4	5	6	7	8	9	**10**	**11**	12	13	14	15	16	17	18	19	20
0.7	1.1	1.1	1.4	1.6	1.8	1.9	1.9	1.9	**1.9**	**2.0**	2.0	2.1	2.1	2.3	2.4	2.5	2.6	2.9	3.4

Figure 3.12   Negative Emotions Words Sample Data Sorted From Lowest to Highest Values for 20 Participants

Measures of Central Tendency: What We're Trying to Accomplish

As we discussed earlier, our goal when calculating measures of central tendency is to summarize a distribution numerically by finding its most representative score, and we

determine the most representative value in a distribution by figuring out the mode, the median, and the mean.

We might, at this point, ask why we need three measures of central tendency. Why can't we just have one? Well, we need three measures because there are different scenarios that we encounter in research that make one a better representative for a distribution than the others.

Want to review skewed vs. symmetrical distributions? SEE CHAPTER 2. ↗

Mode: When Do We Use It?

We use the mode when we want to calculate central tendency for nominal-level data. Indeed, it is meaningless to compute the median or mean for nominal data. For example, let's say that we measured participants' favorite social media platform (1 = Facebook, 2 = Twitter, 3 = Reddit, 4 = TikTok). If we calculated the mean of our distribution to be 1.70, what would this tell us? Nothing. It would be impossible to interpret. So, when it comes to nominal data, the mode is our only and best available option for measuring central tendency (see **Figure 3.13**).

Measure of Central Tendency	When Do We Use It?
Mode	Nominal data
Median	Ordinal data Interval or ratio data, distribution is skewed
Mean	Interval or ratio data, distribution is symmetric

Figure 3.13 Summary Table of When We Use the Mean, Median, and Mode

Aside from measuring central tendency for nominal data, we won't generally use the mode. The mode is simply too limited in what it reveals about a distribution. Knowing the most frequent score in a distribution doesn't actually tell us that much about the distribution as a whole. To understand why this is the case, take a look at **Figure 3.14**.

Here, we see a positively skewed distribution on the left and a negatively skewed distribution on the right. These two distributions are almost completely different in every way. Yet, they have the exact

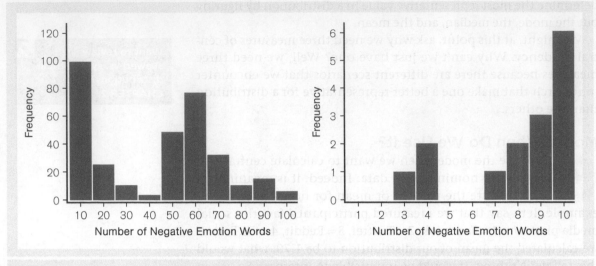

Figure 3.14 Two Histograms Showing Skewed Distributions That Have the Same Mode

same mode. So, the big problem with the mode is that it reflects only the most frequently occurring score in a distribution. It doesn't reflect *all* of the scores in the distribution. Ideally, we want our measure of central tendency to capture the most representative score for the entire distribution.

Median: When Do We Use It?

Want to review levels of measurement? SEE CHAPTER 1.

We use the median as our measure of central tendency in two situations. First, we use it when we have ordinal-level data. Recall that with ordinal data, the median tells us the rank at the middle of a distribution. For example, if we ranked 11 participants from lowest to highest based on their use of negative emotion words, the median would be 6. This would be the middle rank in the distribution.

Second, we use the median when there are outliers or extreme scores in a distribution. For example, let's imagine that we record negative emotions word use on Twitter for a sample of participants. The first four of the participants use 2.30, 1.79, 1.99, and 1.84 negative emotion words per 100 words. Overall, when we sum the scores and divide by 4, this group of four participants has a mean of 1.98 negative emotion words and a median of 1.92 (the median is 1.92 because we must add the two middle scores, 1.84 and 1.99, and divide by 2). Now imagine that we measure a fifth participant, who happens to be a melancholy poet who uses 17.22 negative emotion words in their tweets. Importantly, the inclusion of this one extreme score has a huge effect on the mean, but not on the median. With our melan-choly poet included in our sample of five participants, the group has a mean of 5.03 negative emotion words and a median of 1.99. As you can see, the mean went up a lot when we included the one outlier, while the median increased only slightly. The fact that the median doesn't change much in response to outliers is helpful because our goal in calculating central tendency is to generate a number that best represents the entire distribution and does not give too much weight to extreme scores. So, when outliers are present, use the median.

Mean: When Do We Use It?

When it comes to measuring central tendency, we use the mean most of the time. There are a couple of key reasons for this. First, unlike the mode and median, the mean is sensitive to the exact value of all of the data set's scores, making it a better reflection of the entire data set. If any score in a distribution changes, we will see a corresponding change in the mean. Second, because the mean accounts for every score in a distribution, it is a key component in our measures of variability. As we saw earlier, deviation scores $(X - M)$ determine how far each score is from the mean, and we use deviation scores to calculate the sum of squares $\Sigma(X - M)^2$, the variance $\Sigma(X - M)^2/N$, and the standard deviation $\sqrt{SD^2}$.

Why do we use the mean when calculating measures of variation? Well, recall that in the first part of this chapter, we said that the mean represents the mathematical balancing point for a distribution of scores. As a result, the sum of the deviation scores is always zero. That is, the mean is the point in a distribution where the deviation scores to the left side of the mean equal the deviation scores to the right side. Because the deviation scores to the left of the mean will have a nega-tive sign (because those scores are smaller than the mean), they will cancel out the deviation scores to the right of the mean, which have a positive sign (because those scores are larger than the mean). As a consequence, when we add them up, they will sum to zero, reflecting that the deviation scores have balanced out.

Weighted Means

Amazon is a multibillion-dollar company, so their overall customer ratings use something more complicated than a basic arithmetic mean. According to Amazon, they calculate "a product's star rat-ing using machine-learned models instead of a simple average" (Amazon.com). In other words, all ratings are not considered equally. The machine learning part sounds fancy, but at its core, the process uses a **weighted average** in which some ratings are adjusted to give

> ""
> ## Statistically Speaking
> Sure, the mean salary at that company is $75,000, but the CEO makes $250 million a year. Because the CEO is such an outlier, I'd rather know the median salary.
> ""

weighted average a way of calculating the mean in which some ratings are multiplied in order to give them more importance.

them more importance. As for which ratings are more important, consider these questions:

- Who do you think will provide better information, someone who has made a lot of ratings, or someone who has made only a few?
- Someone who has previously left helpful reviews, or someone who leaves less helpful reviews?
- Is a review better if it is more recent, or older?
- Should it matter if Amazon verified the reviewer actually purchased the item?

Logically, ratings from customers who leave more frequent and helpful reviews, made verified purchases, and reviewed an item more recently should all influence your judgment of the product more and hence are allowed by Amazon to have a greater influence on the overall rating.

There are also times when you might want to give some information more credit—for example, if you are averaging data across several different samples, some of which are larger than others. In these cases, you may want to give more weight to data from larger samples than to data from smaller samples.

Researchers commonly use weighted averages to combine sample means together. Let's say, for example, that we measured the negative emotion words on Twitter across two sets of people: one comprised of 100 university students, with a mean of 2.17, and another comprised of 900 adults living in the United States, with a mean of 1.66. We might be (mistakenly) tempted to simply find the average of the two means

$$\frac{2.17 + 1.66}{2} = ?$$

Why is this wrong?

It's incorrect to combine the means in this way because it's weighting both samples equally. That's a problem here because one of the samples is much larger than the other. In general, larger samples are more likely to match the population. Therefore, we want to combine group means so that their impact on the overall mean is proportional to their individual sample sizes. To give the larger sample more credit in our calculation of the weighted mean, we will use a modified formula for the mean.

$$M_1 \times \frac{N_1}{N_1 + N_2} + M_2 \times \frac{N_2}{N_1 + N_2}$$

As you can see in **Figure 3.15,** when we combine the means of two (or more) groups, we multiply each group mean by its contribution to the overall sample size. Using our example from a moment ago, the mean for the first sample of 100 university students was 2.17, and this sample contributed 100 out of 1,000 total participants, so when calculating the overall mean, we need to weight this mean based on its contribution to the total sample (100 out of 1,000). The second sample of 900 adults had a mean of 1.66, and this sample contributed 900 out of 1,000 total participants, so again, when calculating the overall mean, we need to weight this mean by its relative contribution to the total sample (900 out of 1,000).

Sample 1 University Students (x_1)	Sample 2 U.S. Adults (x_2)
$$M_1 \times \frac{N_1}{N_1 + N_2}$$ $$2.17 \times \frac{100}{100 + 900}$$ $$2.17 \times 0.10 = 0.217$$	$$M_2 \times \frac{N_2}{N_1 + N_2}$$ $$1.66 \times \frac{900}{100 + 900}$$ $$1.66 \times 0.90 = 1.494$$
Weighted Mean $$M_1 \times \frac{N_1}{N_1 + N_2} + M_2 \times \frac{N_2}{N_1 + N_2}$$ $$0.217 + 1.494 = M$$ $$1.71 = M$$	

Figure 3.15 Weighted Mean When Combining Two Samples

Thus, the combined mean of the two samples is 1.71. Importantly, this value is closer to the mean for the sample of U.S. adults ($M = 1.66$), relative to the sample of university students ($M = 2.17$), reflecting the fact that the sample of U.S. adults was much larger than the sample of university students.

Measures of Central Tendency and the Shape of a Distribution

 When describing a distribution, we typically focus on the measure of central tendency that is most appropriate for the level of measurement of our variable and the shape of the distribution. However, we can also learn something about a distribution by considering all three measures of central tendency at the same time. Taken together, the mean, median, and mode reveal if a distribution is symmetrical or skewed. Take a look at **Figure 3.16.**

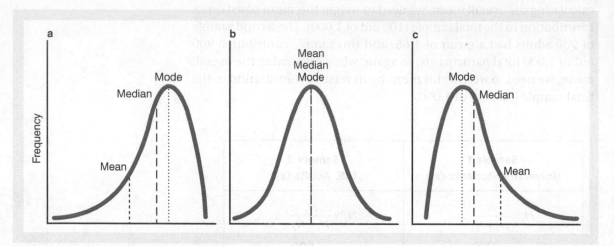

Figure 3.16 Negatively Skewed Distribution, Symmetric Distribution, and Positively Skewed Distribution, With Mean, Median, and Mode Labeled

Notice that for the symmetric distribution in the middle of the figure, the most frequent score (the mode) is equal to the middle score (the median) and is also equal to the average score (the mean). As it turns out, the three measures of central tendency will always be equal for a symmetric distribution.

What about for skewed distributions? Look at the left panel of Figure 3.16. Here we can see that the mode is greater than the median and the median is greater than the mean. This makes sense because the mode is sensitive only to the most frequent score, so it will always be at the peak of the distribution. The median is sensitive only to the middle score, so it wouldn't matter if one tail of the distribution was longer than the other. However, the mean is sensitive to these scores, so it will be pulled in the direction of the tail of the distribution. So, for a negatively skewed distribution, the mode is greater than the median and the median is greater than the mean.

This pattern is reversed for positively skewed distributions, as depicted in the right panel of Figure 3.16. The mode will always be at the peak of the distribution. The median will be in the middle. The mean is affected by the scores in the tail of the distribution, so it will be greater than the median. So, for a positively skewed distribution, the mode will be less than the median and the median will be less than the mean.

Measures of Variability: What We're Trying to Accomplish

 In the Statistics for Life portion of this chapter, we learned that there are different ways of calculating variability. As we delve deeper into this topic now in Statistics for Research, we'll learn when we use each measure of variability.

To get us started, consider the three distributions in **Figure 3.17.**

Participants	Distribution A	Distribution B	Distribution C
1	0.61	−1.59	30.20
2	1.26	−13.81	16.15
3	2.19	11.71	−69.07
4	1.74	21.80	8.52
5	1.87	8.66	−54.30
6	2.41	6.19	20.20
7	0.46	−7.69	26.50
8	2.01	−9.60	−61.70
9	2.33	−8.89	27.85
10	1.62	9.72	72.15
M	**1.65**	**1.65**	**1.65**

Figure 3.17 Figure With One Low Variation Distribution, One Medium Variation Distribution, and One High Variation Distribution, All With a Mean of 1.65

Each of these distributions has the same mean, 1.65, yet these distributions are very different from one another. In particular, these distributions differ in terms of their dispersion or variability. The scores in Distribution A are very similar to each other, with almost all the scores hovering around the mean. The scores in Distribution B are more varied than those in Distribution A, with some of the scores positive and some negative. Finally, the scores in Distribution C are even more varied than Distribution B, with huge differences between the scores. Yet again, each of these distributions has the same exact mean.

The key here is that just knowing the central tendency of a distribution isn't enough to understand what's going on within a distribution of scores. We also need to know something about variation. Are the scores in a distribution really similar to one another, or are they very different? So, let's take another look at our measures of variation, this time focusing on when we should use each of them.

Range: When Do We Use It?

The range is easy to calculate and easy to interpret. Unfortunately, it's also terribly limited as a measure of variation. The main limitation with the range is that it takes into account only the highest and lowest scores in a distribution. To give you a sense of why this is a problem, take a look at the two sets of scores in **Figure 3.18.**

Which of the two sets of scores seems more variable to you? In Set A, all of the scores differ from each other. In Set B, the three middle scores are the same, and only the first and last scores differ. Based on this information, we would say that there is greater variation among the scores in Set A compared to Set B. Yet, if we calculate the range for these sets of scores, we will find that the ranges are the same (both data sets have a range of 4)! This example reveals the main problem with the range. It is sensitive only to the two most extreme scores. Whatever happens in a data set between those two scores doesn't matter when it comes to the range, so ultimately we won't use it very often when measuring variability.

That said, there are a few situations in which we might use the range. First is if we are making very "quick and dirty" or rough estimates of variability. We can easily calculate the range when looking at a frequency table or histogram, whereas it's more time consuming to calculate the variance or standard deviation. Second, we might use the range as a measure of dispersion when explaining our results to people who have little or no background in statistics (such as nonscientists). People without training in statistics may not understand what the variance or standard deviation reveal but will likely understand the range (see **Figure 3.19**). Finally, in research papers, we're most likely to see ranges given when describing measures (e.g., the scale ranged from 1 to 7) or describing samples (e.g., the participants ranged in age from 18 to 77).

Variance: When Do We Use It?

The fact that the range only measures the two most extreme scores limits our ability to describe the entire distribution. Variance, on the other hand, is sensitive to all the scores in a distribution. As we learned in the first half of this chapter, variance (when measured for a population) is the mean of the squared deviation

Set A	Set B
1	1
2	3
3	3
4	3
5	5

Figure 3.18 Two Sets of Scores With the Same Range, but Differing Amounts of Variation

Measure of Central Tendency	When Do We Use It?
Range	Ordinal data; limited use
Variance	Interval or ratio data; primarily used while calculating other statistics
Standard Deviation	Interval or ratio data; used to report descriptive statistics; used while computing other statistics

Figure 3.19 When We Use the Range, Variance, and Standard Deviation

scores. For each score in the distribution, we calculate its deviation score by subtracting the mean, squaring it, summing up the squared deviation scores, and then dividing by N.

As with the range, however, there is a practical problem with the variance that makes it less commonly reported in research articles. The problem relates to our having to square the deviation scores. When we square the deviation scores, we also square the units of the variable that we are measuring. For example, if we wanted to measure the variation in the number of negative emotion words people use on Twitter, the variance would reflect the number of emotion words squared. This is a problem because our measure of variation isn't in the same units as the variable itself. This mismatch between the units of our variable and the squared unit of variance is an extra layer of complexity that makes variance more difficult to conceptualize. As a result, researchers tend to prefer using standard deviation when reporting variability. We should note that there is nothing inherently wrong mathematically about variance. It's just a bit harder to interpret than the standard deviation.

So, when will we use the variance? Well, not often. Given that standard deviation is easier to interpret, we tend to report that instead of the variance. Nevertheless, we will use variance (or formulas that are conceptually related to variance) while performing other statistical analyses (e.g., analysis of variance).

Step by Step: Calculating the Variance of a Sample Earlier in this chapter, we learned how to calculate the variance of a population. We did this because we had the entire set of ratings for DinoPet, which was our population. For our study of emotion use on Twitter, we don't have data for the entire population. We only have the scores for a random sample of people whom we recruited into our study. Because we are calculating the variance of a sample, we will introduce a new wrinkle to our formula. Let's use our Twitter data set (see **Figure 3.20**) to see how much variance there is for negative emotion words in our sample.

Score (X)	Deviation Score (X − M)	Squared Deviation Score (X − M)²
0.7	−1.28	1.64
1.1	−0.88	0.77
1.1	−0.88	0.77
1.4	−0.58	0.34
1.6	−0.38	0.14
1.8	−0.18	0.03
1.9	−0.08	0.01
1.9	−0.08	0.01
1.9	−0.08	0.01
1.9	−0.08	0.01
2.0	0.02	0.00
2.0	0.02	0.00
2.1	0.12	0.01
2.1	0.12	0.01
2.3	0.32	0.10
2.4	0.42	0.18
2.5	0.52	0.27
2.6	0.62	0.38
2.9	0.92	0.85
3.4	1.42	2.02
Sum $\Sigma(X)$ = 39.6 N = 20 Mean $\Sigma(X)/N$ = 1.98	$\Sigma(X − M)$ = 0	$\Sigma(X − M)^2$ = 7.55 SS = 7.55

Variance $(SD^2) = \Sigma(X − M)^2 / N − 1$
Variance $(SD^2) = SS / N − 1$
Variance $(SD^2) = 7.55/19$
Variance $(SD^2) = 0.40$

Standard Deviation $(SD) = \sqrt{SD^2}$
Standard Deviation $(SD) = \sqrt{0.40}$
Standard Deviation $(SD) = 0.63$

Figure 3.20 Computation Sheet: Calculating Deviation Scores

Step 1: Find the Mean (M) To calculate the mean, we need to add up all of the raw scores in Column 1 of Figure 3.20 and divide by the number of scores. As we see in the figure, the mean of our sample is 1.98.

Step 2: Find the Deviation Scores ($X - M$) We need to calculate deviation scores for each of the scores in the distribution by taking the score and subtracting the mean. Here's the first one:

$$(X - M) = (0.7 - 1.98) = -1.28$$

Try the rest on your own, and then compare your answers to the second column of Figure 3.20.

Step 3: Find the Squared Deviation Score ($X - M)^2$ Because the mean is the balance point of the distribution, the deviation scores to the left of the mean will always balance out the deviation scores to the right of the mean. As a consequence, the sum of the deviation scores is always 0. So, before we can calculate to sum of the deviation scores, we need to square them. For the first deviation score:

$$(X - M)^2 = (0.7 - 1.98)^2 = -1.28^2 = 1.64$$

We repeat the same process for the rest of the scores, which are reported in the third column of Figure 3.20.

Step 4: Find the Sum of Squared Deviation Scores (SS or $\Sigma (X - M)^2$) Now that we have the squared deviations for each score, we need to add them all up. Although typically we call this the "sum of squares," it might be more helpful to think of this as the "sum of squared deviations scores." After adding up the squared deviations on your own, compare your result with the bottom row of Figure 3.20. Hopefully, your result is 7.55 or close to it. As before, be aware that you might have slight differences in your calculation due to rounding differences.

Step 5: Calculate the Variance of a Sample To determine the variance of our sample, we need to make an important modification to the way that we calculated the variance of a population earlier in the chapter. If you look back at Figure 3.10, you'll see that to calculate the variance of a population, we divided the sum of squared deviations (SS) by the number of cases (N). This makes sense because variance represents the average of the squared deviation scores.

Here's the new wrinkle when calculating the variance of a sample: Divide the sum of squared deviations (SS) by the sample size minus 1 ($N - 1$), as indicated below:

$$SD^2 = \frac{\Sigma(X - M)^2}{N - 1}$$

Why do we divide by $N - 1$ rather than N? Well, there are two explanations to consider (both of which might seem confusing at first).

First, when we calculate the variance of a population, we know about each of the scores in the population *and* we know the mean of the population. However, when we calculate the variance of a sample, we know the scores in our sample and the mean of the sample, but the mean of our sample is itself based on the scores in the sample. As a result, the mean of our sample is not an additional, independent piece of information. If we were to use it in our formula to calculate the variance of our sample, we would be "double dipping"; that is, we would be treating the scores and the mean as if they were each independent pieces of information. Because they're not, we need to modify the denominator of our formula for the variance of a sample to be $N - 1$, so that our estimate of the variance is based on the number of independent observations. Another name for this general idea is that we use the **degrees of freedom,** that is the number of independent pieces of information, in the denominator of the formula for variance of a sample.

A second explanation is that when we calculate the variance of a sample, the scores in our distribution are going to be closer, on average, to the mean of our sample than they would be to the mean of the population. This is because the mean of our sample is always based on the scores within our sample, whereas the mean of the population is based on scores that are not included in our sample. As a result, when we calculate the variance of a sample, we typically underestimate the actual amount of variation in the population. Dividing by $N - 1$ typically reduces this bias.

To show how this works, let's work through an example. Say we calculate the sum of squared deviations to be 100 based on a sample size of 25. If we divide 100 by 25 (i.e., 100/25), the result is 4.00. If we instead divide 100 by 24 (one less than 25), we have 100/24, which is 4.17. So, dividing by a slightly smaller number (24 vs. 25) results in a slightly larger estimate of variance (4.17 vs. 4.00). This higher estimate is on average closer to the actual variance of the population, and so we will use it whenever calculating the variance of a sample.

degrees of freedom the number of independent observations in a sample that are free to vary.

SPSS and other statistics software also use this unbiased version of the formula.

Returning to our problem, because we are calculating the variance of a sample, we need to divide the sum of squared deviation scores by the sample size minus 1:

$$SD^2 = \frac{\Sigma(X - M)^2}{N - 1} = \frac{7.55}{20 - 1} = \frac{7.55}{19} = 0.40$$

Step 6: Check Yourself . . . The variance of a sample can never be a negative number. The lowest possible variance is zero. Think of it this way: If a distribution's scores are all the same (e.g., they are all "5"), there's no variation in the data, and the variance will be zero. However, as soon as you have different scores (e.g., 5, 4, 6, 2, etc.), the deviation of those scores from the mean will be greater than 0. When we square these deviation scores, the sum of squares and variance will become positive numbers.

Standard Deviation: When Do We Use It?

When reading research articles or conducting our own research, standard deviation is the most used measure of variability. Not only does it have all of the good properties of the variance (in that it's sensitive to all of the scores in a distribution), but it is also more intuitive than variance because it avoids squared units. That is, it uses the same units as our measured variable. For example, when we measure negative emotion words on Twitter, our measure of dispersion is in words, not words[2].

Step by Step: Calculating Standard Deviation of a Sample Most of the time, when performing research, we collect a sample of scores, as opposed to measuring everyone in the population. Because of this, we won't use the formula that we used in the Statistics for Life portion of this chapter. That formula is used to calculate the standard deviation of a population.

Instead, we use $N - 1$ in the denominator of our formula for the standard deviation of a sample, just as we did a moment ago when calculating the variance of a sample. The reasons for this are the same. We use $N - 1$ because it reflects the degrees of freedom, or the number of independent pieces of information gathered in our study. Also, using the $N - 1$ correction typically results in a more accurate estimate of the population standard deviation. Let's see how this works.

Step 1: Calculate the Variance of a Sample (SD^2) Do this using the steps outlined above to calculate the variance of a sample.

Step 2: Calculate the Standard Deviation (SD) This is as straightforward as taking the square root of the variance. Go ahead and make the calculation, and then compare your response to the bottom row of the following equation:

$$SD = \sqrt{\frac{\Sigma(X - M)^2}{N - 1}}$$

In everyday terms, The Square Root of the Variance = Standard Deviation. In symbols:

$$\sqrt{Variance} = \sqrt{SD^2} = SD$$

$$\sqrt{0.40} = 0.63$$

Step 3: Check Yourself . . . Whenever we calculate the standard deviation, we need to think about our data set. Is it data for a population or sample? If we have measured every entity of interest, we use the formula for standard deviation of a population. If we have measure a sample, then we use the formula for standard deviation of a sample. So, we should always confirm that we are using the correct formula based on our research scenario.

Before reading on, watch this video. It demonstrates the computations needed to find the deviation scores, the sum of squares, the variance, and the standard deviation for a sample.

 HAND CALCULATION VIDEO TUTORIAL: To learn more, check out the video tutorial Calculating the Standard Deviation for a Sample by Hand!

SPSS Video Tutorial: Measures of Central Tendency and Variability

 Now that we know how to calculate different measures of central tendency and variability, we are ready to learn how to compute those statistics using SPSS. Take a look at this video, which presents click-by-click instructions to generate the mean, median, and mode as well as the range, variance, and standard deviation.

 SPSS VIDEO TUTORIAL: To learn more, check out the video tutorial Descriptive Statistics!

Communicating the Result

An APA-Style paper has six main components: A title page, abstract, introduction, method section, results section, and a discussion. In this textbook, we are going to focus primarily on the results section because this is where we write about most of our statistical analyses.

We should write the results section of a paper in a straightforward and simple manner. We want to express to the reader what analysis we performed and what the results of the analysis revealed in an efficient and straightforward way. Where possible, we want to keep the focus on our variables, hypotheses, and research questions, and not on the statistical information.

First, a bad example, "The mean percentage of negative emotion words in Twitter posts was 1.98 and the standard deviation was 0.63. This indicates that, on average, participants use slightly less than 2 negative emotion words per 100 words when writing on Twitter." Notice how this puts all the focus on the statistical information. It's wordy and requires the reader to wade through some numbers to get to the result. Here is a better way that uses APA Style:

Results

Overall, the participants' use of negative emotion words on Twitter is rare ($M = 1.98$, $SD = 0.63$), with slightly less than 2 percent of all words characterizing negative emotions.

Notice how the focus is on the conclusion, and the statistical information serves only as evidence to support the conclusion. This approach is compact and helps the reader keep their attention on the important information.

Forming a Conclusion

Our original research question asked how often people use negative emotion words on Twitter. We answered this question by calculating the central tendency and variability. By doing so, we found the average number of negative emotions that individuals express (per 100 words) and the amount of variability between people. Is this a lot of negative emotions? Well, it's hard to say. We would need to conduct a similar analysis for other social media platforms, and compare their means, to get a sense of whether Twitter posts differ from other social media posts.

Your Turn 3.3

1. Cabral played nine holes of golf, with a mean number of strokes per hole of 4.00. Unfortunately, his golf pencil smudged and his score for his final hole was lost. The scores for the first eight holes are listed below. Figure out what his score on the ninth hole must have been *using your knowledge that the sum of the deviation scores must equal zero* to guide your calculations.

Hole	1	2	3	4	5	6	7	8	9
Raw Score	5	5	4	3	4	4	5	3	?
Deviation Score	+1	+1	0	−1	0	0	+1	−1	?

2. For each of the following variables, identify the appropriate measure of central tendency. Explain your response.

    a. Heart rate

    b. Responses to a questionnaire measuring anxiety symptoms

    c. Gender

    d. Rank runners finish in a race

3. Without looking back through the chapter, or at your notes, write down the formula for the standard deviation. Hint: Think about the steps needed and build the formula step by step.

4. What is the correction we need to make to the formulas for the variance and standard deviation of a sample? Why do we need to make this correction?

5. A clinical psychologist wants to determine the average number of days it takes for an anti-depressant drug to become effective. She collects a sample of 12 participants and finds a mean latency of 32 days. Her colleague collects a sample of 25 participants and finds a mean latency of 26 days. What is the weighted average for the two samples combined?

6. Here is the SPSS output for the mean and standard deviation of our frequency of sex data for 2016 described in Chapter 2.

a. 1989:

Descriptive Statistics					
	N	Minimum	Maximum	Mean	Std. Deviation
Frequency of sex during last year	1361	0	6	2.90	1.963
Valid N (listwise)	1361				

b. 2016:

Descriptive Statistics					
	N	Minimum	Maximum	Mean	Std. Deviation
Frequency of sex during last year	1712	0	6	2.51	1.966
Valid N (listwise)	1712				

Using the guidelines for communicating the results described above, write a sentence describing the results.

7. What is the best measure of central tendency for (a) ratio data; (b) nominal data; (c) ordinal data?

Become a Better Consumer of Statistics

Media outlets know that consumers are short on time and are not interested in wading through large quantities of data to form a conclusion. Producers of media content are not wrong. Who has time to really dig into all of the data and make sense of thousands of numbers? Consequently, the media delivers neatly packaged soundbites and graphics that capture vast amounts of information in a few numbers. Better to just get the TL;DR (or super short) version and move on. Not so fast. We cannot change what type of information the media provides, but we can change how carefully we interpret that data. If we make just the slightest of efforts, we can avoid making common errors when interpreting statistical information.

Median ≠ Mean

When covering news stories about politics, the media often doesn't pay attention to the differences between the mean and the median, but we should, because it can make a big difference in our interpretation of the news. In 2017, Congress passed a large tax cut, and the media reported that the average tax cut would be around $1,000. Should we conclude from this that most people will pay $1,000 less in taxes? No. The key here is that the $1,000 tax cut is the mean tax cut, not the median. Remember that outliers can have a huge impact on the mean, but they do not impact the median.

Let's say, for example, that we have 11 taxpayers, and we want to determine their mean tax cut. We might have one taxpayer get a tax cut of $10,000 while the remaining 10 people get a tax cut of $100. What would the mean tax cut be? $1,000. In contrast, what would the median tax cut be? $100. Which do you think is the better indicator of how much people can expect to save in taxes in this situation, the mean or the median? We'd argue that the median is a better measure of central tendency in this situation in that it represents most of the people in the scenario.

When Bill Gates enters a room, the average income of everyone in it increases by millions of dollars.

The Flaw of Averages

We also want to be wary of media reports that include a description of the central tendency, but not the variability. To illustrate this point, imagine that Guillermo is running late for work. To get a sense of whether there is traffic that will make him even more late, he turns on the news for the traffic report, which says that traffic on the highway is moving at 45 mph on average. Does this mean that there won't be any traffic jams that will delay Guillermo further? No! It could be the case that all of the cars are moving at 45 mph. But, it could also be the case that some cars might be moving at 90 mph, while other cars are going zero mph. Without knowing the variability, we don't have enough information to make an accurate conclusion.

Averages Are Theoretical

Although the mean is very useful for giving us a sense of a distribution, it doesn't always perfectly reflect reality. For example, you might read a news report that the average birth rate has declined to 1.84 births per woman (Miller, 2018). While this is the average of the population, it

Does it look like these two people are having the same experience of the weather? Even though the average temperature is the same for both of them, there is a lot of variability based on whether they are in the shade or not. We need to remember that measures of central tendency tell us a lot about a distribution, but they don't tell us about variability.

Ollyy/Shutterstock

does not describe any particular observation within the data set. Obviously, no one has 1.84 kids. Children come only in whole numbers. As consumers, we need to be careful to avoid overinterpreting means and taking them literally.

What Variability Does and Does Not Tell You

To be a good consumer of statistics, we not only have to know what a number can tell us, we also have to be aware of what it does *not* tell us. That is, we have to be careful to not go beyond our data. We'll return to this theme throughout the text. When it comes to variability, standard deviations and variance indicate how much scores vary. Importantly, they do not tell us why those scores vary. That's important because there are a ton of potential explanations for variability. It can be easy to assume you know why. For example, high variability in the DinoPet ratings may result from people not following the directions and giving a low rating. That is certainly a plausible guess, but our current data does not provide the type of information we would need to make that conclusion. Ultimately, we have to remember that descriptive statistics merely tell us *what* is happening; they can't tell us *why* those things happen. If that feels limiting, don't worry. The statistics we will learn about in later chapters help us to test more interesting ideas.

Interpreting Graphs and Charts From Research Articles

We've all been there. We have a deadline approaching, and we need to find sources for a paper we are writing. One option, which is often the strategy taken by students, is to read the abstract of the paper and to look for a quick summary of the findings. Taking this approach is like seeing

	Age > 25 (n = 111)		Age 18 – 25 (n = 90)			Total	
	M	SD	M	SD	t	M	SD
LIWC codings							
Positive emotions	1.16	0.49	1.32	0.60	–2.08*	1.23	0.54
Optimism	0.55	0.36	0.56	0.26	–0.23	0.55	0.32
Negative emotions	1.53	0.83	1.79	0.86	–2.17*	1.65	0.85
Anxiety	0.26	0.74	0.24	0.20	0.25	0.25	0.56
Anger	0.43	0.31	0.53	0.45	–1.86	0.47	0.38
Sadness	0.56	0.34	0.71	0.35	–3.07**	0.63	0.35
Positive emotions	0.92	1.20	1.56	1.38	–3.51**	1.21	1.35
Negative emotions	0.07	0.14	0.17	0.25	–3.60**	0.11	0.20

Figure 3.21 Descriptive Statistics for Different Types of Words on Facebook

a movie preview instead of the full movie. It tells you something, but it leaves a lot out. Abstracts, by their nature, are very short and, consequently, don't contain enough information to be helpful. In contrast, we can learn a lot about a paper's findings by looking at tables and figures.

Figure 3.21 presents the results from a study on word usage on Facebook (Settanni & Marengo, 2015). As you can see, there is a lot of additional information in the table that might help us better understand the study and write our own paper. First, in the left-hand column, we can see that in addition to analyzing negative emotions, the authors also looked at other types of words: positive emotions, optimism, anxiety, anger, and so on. Next, we see that the authors also analyzed the means and standard deviations separately for older participants (ages greater than 25) and younger participants (ages between 18 and 25). Finally, we have the means and standard deviations for the total sample. You'll notice in the middle set of columns that there is an additional statistic called *t*. We will discuss what this statistic tells us in Chapter 10.

Focus on Open Science: Open Materials

Imagine that you wanted to conduct your own study examining people's use of words on social media. Perhaps you want to examine whether the emotions people express on Instagram are different from the emotions they express on Reddit. Performing this study would be incredibly difficult without access to the LIWC software that automatically counts up the number of

Authors of research articles that post their study materials publicly can earn this open materials badge, created by the Center for Open Science.

emotion words in written text. If you had to create your own software program, this would take years of work. For this reason, psychology and other disciplines are beginning to emphasize an important aspect of open science called **open materials,** which is the idea that researchers should post all of their study materials (e.g., software, questionnaires, instructions to participants) online for other researchers to use. Having access to these materials makes it easier for researchers to replicate a study's findings or conduct new research that extends a study's findings.

Statistics on the Job

We're only in Chapter 3, but already the concepts and tools that we are learning can help you on the job. Understanding how measures of central tendency and variability work can impact tons of decisions made by companies and professionals. Tech companies, for example, spend large amounts of money trying to understand the User Experience (called UX for short). By asking users questions about how they interact with a website, their emotions and attitudes about particular products, or their intention to use a product in the future, UX analysts gather mountains of data that they need to analyze.

One of the first things that these analysts look at is the descriptive statistics, comprised mainly of means and standard deviations. By knowing these values (e.g., what was the average overall rating of the new home screen?), the analysts can get a broad understanding of whether the UX was positive, neutral, or negative, and how much people differed in their experience.

Means and standard deviations can also impact billion-dollar lawsuits. Back in 2010, one of the authors of this textbook worked as a statistician for a group of lawyers. The lawyers were trying to identify the 10 best arguments that they could use to help support their case. The issue was that the lawyers had 40 possible arguments that they might use in court, but the judge ruled that they would only have a certain number of hours to present their argument. Hence the need for the list of top 10 best arguments. With the help of a team of litigation consultants, the lawyers conducted a mock trial with around 50 mock jurors. During the mock trial, the lawyers presented all 40 arguments and then asked the mock jurors to rate each argument in terms of how persuasive it was. By examining the means and standard deviations of the items, it was possible to identify the most persuasive arguments.

We hope that you walk away from this chapter realizing that measures of central tendency and variability are useful to solve real-world problems. As we move forward in this textbook, we will learn about the many different ways that businesses and professionals use statistics to solve problems in the workplace.

Review Questions

1. For each of the following variables, identify the appropriate measure of central tendency. Explain your decision.
   a. Favorite rollercoaster at a theme park near you
   b. Height required to ride on the rollercoaster (inches)
   c. Wait time to ride (minutes)
   d. Quality of service at a restaurant (1 = great, 5 = horrible)

2. Average household income is positively skewed and unimodal. What does this indicate, and what would the relative positions be for the mean, median, and mode?

3. It is wintertime, and you're taking a ski vacation in Canada next week. You check the weather report and see that the average daily temperature (in Celsius) for the next week is as follows:

   −10, −14, −10, −8, −9, −5, 2

   a. Calculate the mean, median, and mode temperature for the week.
   b. Is the distribution positively or negatively skewed? How do you know?

4. It is the end of the term, and you want to get a sense of your grade before you write the final exam. The course website is glitching, so you need to compute your mean homework grade by hand. Thankfully, you have the grades written down in a notebook.

   84, 86, 91, 95, 83, 88, 87,

   85, 90, 92, 93, 87, 100, 85

   a. What is your mean homework grade?
   b. Let's say you got off to a rough start this term and earned a 0 on the first homework assignment instead of an 84. If this were the case, do you expect your mean homework grade would increase or decrease? Why?
   c. What would your mean score be if the situation in part b occurred?

5. You are interested in the amount of added sugar in some of your favorite juices and sports drinks. You calculate the mean to be 10.5 grams of sugar across a sample of 9 different products. Then you find one more beverage that you want to include. It has 5 grams of sugar per serving.
   a. When you calculate the revised mean, with 10 beverages included, do you expect your mean will increase or decrease? Why?
   b. Calculate the new mean, including the 10 different products you are evaluating.

6. Over the past two summers you have collected data on the factors that influence employee retention. You collected a sample of 49 employees last summer and found a mean age of 24.7 years. This summer your sample was 201 employees, and you found a mean age of 28.1 years.

    a. When you compute the weighted average, do you expect the answer to be closer to 24.7 or 28.1? Why?

    b. In your write-up of the study, you will report the average age of your overall sample. What is the weighted average for the two samples combined?

7. You forgot to empty your pockets before putting your clothes in the wash, and one of the numbers is now illegible. You remember that you had 15 data points, and the mean was 66. The data you can read is as follows:

    86, 50, 102, 78, 65, 45, 38,
    78, 40, 95, 58, 62, 81, 39

    If you originally had 15 data points, and the mean was 66, what is the value of the missing number?

8. The Beck Depression Inventory II (BDI-II) contains 21 items that are scored from 0 to 3. Total scores can therefore range from 0 to 63, with higher scores indicating more severe symptoms. Suppose you have the following sample of 5 scores:

    15, 20, 12, 26, 22

    a. What is the greatest possible range of scores that could be obtained on the BDI-II?

    b. What is the range of scores that you obtained in your sample?

    c. What is the variance and standard deviation that you obtained in your sample?

    d. What measure of variability would most likely be reported in an academic research article? Why?

9. Hope is related to better psychological health. Considering this, you decide to include the State Hope Scale (Snyder et al., 1996) when assessing your client's psychological health. Total hope scores can range from 6 to 48, with higher scores corresponding to higher levels of hope. Consider the following data set and then complete the following two problems:

    42, 40, 26, 31, 27, 39, 33

    a. If these scores represent a population, calculate the range, variance, and standard deviation.

    b. If these scores represent a sample, calculate the range, variance, and standard deviation.

10. Phantom limb syndrome, which is the perceiving of sensory stimulation in a limb that no longer exists, occurs in many patients with amputations. A recent meta-analysis estimated that over 60% of people with limb amputations experience phantom limb pain (Limakatso et al., 2020). Mirror therapy is a promising intervention for phantom limb pain. Following 4 weeks of mirror therapy, patients experienced decreases in pain ratings when measured on a 100-mm visual analogue scale (Chan et al., 2007). Larger negative values indicate greater decreases in pain. You decide to replicate their study and find the following in your sample of 9 patients:

−16, −99, −25, −20, −39, −19, −27, −30, −22

   a. Calculate the range, variance, and standard deviation.
   b. You visually inspect your data and notice that one score, −99, is unusually high. You go back to your original files and discover a data entry error. The score was actually −9 (not −99). Recalculate the range, variance, and standard deviation.
   c. Explain the influence of an outlier on the three measures of variability.

11. Why should you be cautious when interpreting the following statements?
   a. If you were hurt in a motorcycle accident, call us today! The average settlement made by our lawyers is over $500,000!
   b. The average class size in our school is 15.3 students.

12. You just returned from a vacation, and you feel jet lagged. You're wondering how long it will take for your circadian rhythms to return to normal. You do some searching and discover a data set that someone has shared from participants who had crossed one time zone. Using the SPSS output, answer the following questions:
   a. What is the sample size of the data set?
   b. What are the mean, median, and mode?
   c. Is the data normally distributed or skewed? (Hint: Use the relative locations of the mean, median, and mode.)
   d. What is the range, standard deviation, and variance?
   e. Using the APA guidelines for communicating results, write a sentence describing the results.

Statistics		
jet_lag_hours		
N	Valid	92
	Missing	0
Mean		3.060
Median		3.000
Mode		2.5
Std. Deviation		1.4710
Variance		2.164
Range		9.0

Key Concepts

central tendency, p. 63

degrees of freedom, p. 90

deviation score, p. 69

mean, p. 65

median, p. 64

mode, p. 63

open materials, p. 98

range, p. 68

standard deviation (*SD*), p. 73

sum of squares (*SS*), p. 71

variability, p. 68

variance (SD^2), p. 69

weighted average, p. 81

Answers to Your Turn

Your Turn 3.1

1. From top to bottom, the answers are: C A B D

2. (a) 5; (b) 5; (c) 3.8

3. Any 5 numbers that are exactly the same or represent a symmetric distribution, such as 1, 2, 3, 4, 5

4. 5.52; 6.00; 1.00; 50

Your Turn 3.2

1. (a) 4, 4, 4, 4, 4; (b) 2, 8, 55, 62, 999; (c) 5, 5, 5, 5, 5 and 1, 3, 5, 7, 9

2. a, e, b, d, c, e

3. (a) 4.00; (b) 2.76; (c) 1.66

4. A deviation score is a raw score minus the mean. The sum of the deviation scores is always zero.

5. This will vary, but should be similar to "You're not just smart, but your intelligence is easily 2 or 3 standard deviations about the mean."

6. There is more agreement in the ratings for *Black Panther* than there is for *Love Actually*. The standard deviation for *Black Panther* (1.58) is smaller than the standard deviation for *Love Actually* (3.23), indicating that there is less spread in the distribution.

Your Turn 3.3

1. Because the mean is the balance point of the distribution, we know that the sum of the deviation scores equals zero. To solve, we can sum the deviations scores: $1 + 1 + 0 + (-1) + 0 + 0 + 1 + (-1) = +1$. These deviation scores sum to +1, so the missing deviation score must be a –1 (because we know that when we add all nine scores together, they must sum to zero). Thus, if the missing value has a deviation score of –1, we know that it must be one less than the mean, which would be a score of 3.

2. (a) Mean; this is a ratio variable, so the mean is the best measure of central tendency. (b) Mean; this is likely an interval variable, so the mean is the best option. (c) Mode; gender is a nominal variable, so the mode is the best option. (d) Median; rank variables are ordinal, so the median is the appropriate option.

3. $SD = \sqrt{\dfrac{\Sigma(X - M)^2}{N - 1}}$

4. We divide the squared deviation scores by $N - 1$ instead of N. We make this correction because otherwise, we would underestimate the variance and standard deviation of the population.

5. 27.94 days

6. Participants in 1989 reported having more frequent sex, on average, (*M* = 2.90, *SD* = 1.96) compared to participants in 2016 (*M* = 2.51, *SD* = 1.97).

7. (a) Mean; (b) mode; (c) median

 ## Answers to Review Questions

1. **a.** Mode; the data is nominal level.
b. Mean; the data is ratio level.
c. Mean; this is a ratio variable.
d. Median; this is an ordinal variable.

2. The positive skew means that most values are on the left side of the distribution and there is a longer tail extending to the right side of the distribution. The unimodal means that there is only one mode. The mean will be higher than the median, and the median will be higher than the mode.

3. **a.** Mean is –7.71, median is –9, mode is –10.
b. Positively skewed—the mean is pulled to the right relative to the other measures of central tendency.

4. **a.** 89
b. Expect a decrease, because the extreme score is lower than the mean calculated in part a and an outlier will pull the mean towards it.
c. 83

5. **a.** The mean will decrease because the score being added is lower than the original mean (the one that includes 9 beverages).
b. 9.95 grams

6. **a.** The weighted mean will be closer to 28.1 because it is associated with the larger sample size.
b. 27.43 years

7. **a.** 73 (The sum of X must be 990 if there were 15 data points with a mean of 66. The legible data sums to 917; therefore, 990 – 917 = 73.)

8. **a.** The greatest possible range is 63.
b. The actual obtained range is 14.
c. Variance = 31, standard deviation = 5.57.
d. The standard deviation is the most commonly reported because it is sensitive to all scores in the distribution, and it is in the same units as the variable itself. The range is sensitive only to the two most extreme scores, and the variance is not measured in the same units as the variable.

9. **a.** The range = 16, the variance = 35.43, and the standard deviation = 5.95.
b. The range = 16, the variance = 41.33, and the standard deviation = 6.43.

10. **a.** The range = 83, the variance = 659.5, and the standard deviation = 25.68.
b. The range = 30, the variance = 74.5, and the standard deviation = 8.63.
c. An outlier increases all three measures of variability.

11. a. In this case, the median would be a better measure because the mean is likely being affected by some extremely high settlements. The median would be a better measure of how much a person should expect in a settlement (though even then it would be quite flawed).

b. By itself, this isn't enough information. It is possible that some classes are very tiny and other classes are quite large. A measure of variability is needed. In addition, you cannot have 0.3 of a student. Be careful about taking a value literally.

12. a. The sample size is 92.

b. The mean is 3.060, the median is 3.0, and the mode is 2.5.

c. The distribution is positively skewed—the mean is larger than the median, and the median is larger than the mode.

d. The range is 9, the standard deviation is 1.471, and the variance is 2.164.

e. Participants reported slightly more than 3 days of jet lag symptoms ($M = 3.06$, $SD = 1.47$).

OPEN STATS LAB

Sharpen your statistics skills with real-life data! Check out OpenStatsLab.com, created by coauthor Kevin McIntyre, to practice running analyses for real published research studies.

Z-Scores and the Normal Curve

Imagine that you've been selected to be the guest judge on *America's Got Talent.* Your job is to decide which of the performers deserves to move into the next round. Sounds easy, except of course that each act is a completely different performance. There is a singer, a dancer, a gymnast, a magician, a trapeze artist, a knife thrower, a comedian, and even a little kid who raps. How are you supposed to identify which act is the best when they are all different? What if, for example, you simply like singers more than you like comedians?

Scenarios where you attempt to make comparisons across different areas isn't all that different from a common conversation that you've probably had sitting around with your friends. You know, the "who's best?" discussion in which you argue about which singer is best, which team is best, who the best player is, or even which pizza place serves the best slice. To really get things heated, try to figure out who's the best of the best, regardless of genre or domain. If you take a group of clear superstars in their field like Ellen DeGeneres, LeBron James, and Ariana Grande, who shines the brightest? This question is sure to spark a difficult debate because it is nearly impossible to make direct comparisons in a fair way that is free of subjectivity or individual biases. That is, unless you use statistics. If you want to answer these endless debates about "who's best," you can use statistics to help resolve the issue!

Statistics for Life

The question we want to answer is: Who's the most successful star, Ellen DeGeneres, LeBron James, or Ariana Grande? If you and your friends attempt to subjectively parse these superstars' greatness, several issues are likely to creep in. First, each person will have favorites. A person they already like, or a genre they enjoy more (e.g., a friend may not care for basketball at all) may affect their overall judgment. Next, each friend will have different degrees of knowledge about each area, with some friends knowing a ton about an area and others knowing virtually nothing. For example, most of you will know that Ellen DeGeneres is a TV personality with several shows,

Which of these stars is most successful?

Matt Winkelmeyer/Getty Images

Albert L. Ortega/Getty Images

Steve Granitz/WireImage/Getty Images

but everyone is unlikely to know exactly how big her audience is, how many championships LeBron James has won, or how many sold-out concerts Ariana Grande has had. If one of your friends knows a lot more about a particular field, they inevitably win the debate. Clearly, you need some ground rules.

First, you need to decide on what you mean by success. Granted, that will mean different things to each superstar. You could pick a different measure of success for each one: album sales for Ariana, audience size for Ellen, and games won for LeBron. The problem with each of them is that their success transcends any one genre or category. Take LeBron, for example. Sure we can measure games or even championships won or gold medals earned, but he's also had success as an author, a celebrity endorser of products (e.g., Sprite), an actor, a TV show writer, a producer of documentary and mainstream films, and a musician. The same is true for Ariana Grande and Ellen DeGeneres; both have numerous successful ventures in many areas.

But there is one aspect that unites them all: how much money they have earned. Though it is debatable whether money equates to success, for our purposes, earnings are a decent indicator of success because they capture success in multiple dimensions. Thus, the specific way that we will describe and assess our variable (success), called our **operational definition** (see Chapter 1 to review operational definitions), will be earnings in 2020. Keep in mind that the researcher gets to decide which definition works best for their study (e.g., a different researcher may decide that a better measure of success is media mentions). Using earnings does level the playing field in terms of determining success, but you'll see that it still isn't a perfectly even comparison.

operational definition the specific way a researcher describes and assesses a variable.

Where Do the Data Come From?

It just so happens that Forbes.com (2020) published a list of "The World's Highest-Paid Celebrities" where they rank the top 100 earners. Clearly, data such as this are much more objective than relying on our friends' opinions, or even those of other "experts." In reviewing the overall list, it is important to note that the list heavily favors stars from the United States. Also, the earnings figures are only from one year. Though that does provide fairly recent information, it does not consider previous earnings over the star's lifetime, which is fine. As the ones asking the question, we get to decide how we want to measure things, and looking at recent earnings feels like a good way to determine who the most successful star is right now.

What We're Trying to Accomplish

Looking over the list (see **Figure 4.1**), that year Ellen DeGeneres earned $84 million, LeBron James earned $88.2 million, and Ariana Grande earned $72 million. Problem solved, question answered. LeBron James is the most successful because he earns the most. Right? Not so fast.

Remember, each of our stars falls into different categories. We have a TV personality, an athlete, and a musician. Those professions are distinct in important ways. For example, it may simply be easier to earn more money as an athlete or a TV personality than as a musician.

Rank	Name	Age	Earnings	Category
1	Kylie Jenner	24	$590 M	Fashion & Retail
2	Kanye West	44	$170 M	Fashion & Retail
3	Roger Federer	40	$106.3 M	Athletes
4	Cristiano Ronaldo	37	$105 M	Athletes
5	Lionel Messi	34	$104 M	Athletes
6	Tyler Perry	52	$97 M	Media & Entertainment
7	Neymar	30	$95.5 M	Athletes
8	Howard Stern	68	$90 M	Media & Entertainment
9	**LeBron James**	**37**	**$88.2 M**	**Athletes**
10	Dwayne Johnson	49	$87.5 M	Actor/Actress
11	Rush Limbaugh	71	$85 M	TV Personality
12	**Ellen DeGeneres**	**64**	**$84 M**	**TV Personality**
13	Bill Simmons	-	$82.5 M	Media & Entertainment
14	Elton John	74	$81 M	Musician
15	James Patterson	74	$80 M	Author
16	Stephen Curry	33	$74.4 M	Athletes
17	**Ariana Grande**	**28**	**$72 M**	**Musician**
18	Ryan Reynolds	-	$71.5 M	Actor/Actress
19	Gordon Ramsay	55	$70 M	TV Personality
20	Jonas Brothers	32	$68.5 M	Musician

Forbes.com

Figure 4.1 Forbes List of 2020 Celebrity Earnings

If you look at the top 100, there is support for this idea. Out of the top 100 celebrities, only nine TV personalities made the list. However, 34 athletes and 33 musicians appeared in the top 100. All of a sudden, Ellen DeGeneres's earnings seem a bit more impressive. She's one of nine, while LeBron James and Ariana Grande are both one of many. In addition, the top athlete on the Forbes list earned over nearly $20 million more than LeBron, and the top musician earned nearly $100 million more than Ariana. As you can see, overall earnings miss the entire story.

Comparing Individual Scores to Means and Standard Deviations To truly understand each star's success, we need to consider earnings in the context of the other stars from their category. How does Ellen DeGeneres compare to other TV personalities, LeBron James to other athletes, or Ariana Grande to other musicians? The only way to answer that is to know what the group's average is and generally how much everyone is spread out. In other words, we need to know what the mean and standard deviation is of everyone in that group. By taking the mean and standard deviation (see Chapter 3 for review on how to calculate these) into account, we will be able to get a better sense of just how extraordinary each celebrity is within their group, and as a result, we will have a better ability to compare the celebrities to each other.

Based on our calculations, for TV personalities ($M = 59.44$; $SD = 17.15$), athletes ($M = 55.27$; $SD = 20.74$), and musicians ($M = 50.06$; $SD = 11.50$), if you compare each star's earnings to their group's mean, you see that they are all above their group's mean. But, some are more above the mean than others (LeBron is about $33 million above the athlete's mean, while Ellen is about $24 million above the TV personality mean, and Ariana is only $20 million above the musician's mean).

Although we know where individual stars fall relative to their category mean, it is less clear how far they are away and how that compares to how much scores typically vary from the mean. In other words, we need to account for the group's standard deviation.

Step by Step: Plotting Individual Scores on a Number Line You can compare the numbers, but it is much easier to visualize the differences between them by setting up each group's mean and standard deviation on a number line, and then plotting out where an individual score falls. The further the individual score is to the right of the mean, the better that individual is doing compared to their own group. We should do this for each celebrity category to see where Ellen, LeBron, and Ariana each fall relative to their peers.

For now, let's focus on doing this for the musician category by following these steps:

Step 1: Create a Line Draw a single horizontal line. At the midpoint, place a medium-sized vertical line. In between each end and the midpoint, place two small vertical lines evenly spaced apart, leaving a bit of room at the endpoints.

Step 2: Plot the Mean Place the mean of the data underneath the middle line.

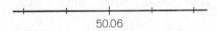

50.06

Step 3: Plot the Standard Deviations First, we want to identify the values that correspond to one and two standard deviations above the mean. To find one standard deviation above the mean, we will take the mean and add one standard deviation

$$(M + SD)$$

$$(50.06 + 11.50 = 61.56).$$

We would then place the result under the first vertical line to the right of the mean. For two standard deviations above the mean, it would be

$$(M + SD + SD)$$

$$(50.06 + 11.50 + 11.50 = 73.05).$$

We would then place the result under the second vertical line to the right of the mean.

To find the values for one and two standard deviations below the mean, we will follow the same procedure but will now *subtract* the standard deviation from the mean. To find one standard deviation below the mean, we will take the mean and subtract one standard deviation

$$(M - SD)$$

$$(50.06 - 11.50 = 38.57)$$

We would then place the result under the first vertical line to the right of the mean. For two standard deviations below the mean, it would be

$$(M - SD - SD)$$

$$(50.06 - 11.50 - 11.50 = 27.07)$$

We would then place the result under the second vertical line to the right of the mean.

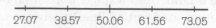

Step 4: Plot the Score Identify the score you want to use. In this case, for musicians, we want to see where Ariana Grande's earnings of $72 million fall. Find the corresponding spot on the number line, mark it with an X, and label it.

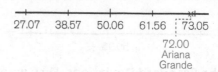

72.00
Ariana
Grande

Step 5: Check Yourself . . . Make certain that your vertical lines are equidistant from each other. The values to the right of the mean should be greater than the mean and should always be the same interval apart (which should be equivalent to the standard deviation). Similarly, the values to the left of the mean should be less than the mean, with each interval equal to one standard deviation.

Once we have created a number line and plotted out the scores for one category, in this case musicians, we next need to do the same for the other categories. Plotting out these scores is the first step toward comparing them. The next step is a bit more complicated and requires us to have an understanding of the normal curve.

Your Turn 4.1

1. You get your psychopathology test back and learn you earned a 65 out of 100. Yikes! Now you want to know the classes' mean (**M**) and standard deviation (**SD**). What combination of **M** and **SD** would make you feel much better about your grade?

2. Ryan Seacrest earned $60 million in 2020. The average earnings and standard deviation for TV personalities was **M** = 59.44; **SD** = 17.15. Using this information, please plot Seacrest's individual score on a number line.

---

normal curve the theoretical symmetrical distribution shape when there is a large number of observations that are continuous scores. The curve depicts the probability or likelihood of observations occurring. Also known as the normal distribution, Gaussian distribution, or bell curve.

Normal Curve: How Does It Work?

As we learned in Chapter 3, the mean and standard deviation from a set of scores establishes the shape of the scores' distribution. The mean establishes the center, while the standard deviation determines how spread out the distribution is. A larger standard deviation indicates a flatter distribution, while a smaller standard deviation indicates a distribution with more of a bump in the middle.

One of the most common distributions that we will observe is the **normal curve**, which depicts the probability or likelihood of observations occurring. Also known as a normal distribution, or Gaussian distribution (named after Carl Friedrich Gauss, who developed the mathematical formula describing the normal curve), the normal curve relies on the premise that often when we make a lot of observations, the measurements tend to bunch up around the mean, with fewer occurrences at the extremes. In other words, most things in nature tend to fall close to the average. That said, the normal curve is theoretical, and we may never know for certain whether a variable in nature falls into a perfectly normal distribution.

Characteristics of a Normal Curve Every normal curve shares the same qualities. First, the curve is always symmetrical such that if you drew a line down the middle, the left and right sides would be mirror images of each other. Because the normal curve is symmetrical, the mean, median, and mode are always equal to each other. Recall that we saw this in Chapter 3. Any time a distribution is symmetrical, we know that the mean, median, and mode must all be equal. Normal curves are unimodal with a majority of the scores clustered around the mean, with fewer scores at the tails or extremes. These qualities give the normal curve a bell-shaped appearance, which is why scientists also refer to normal curves as a "bell curve."

Why Are Normal Curves Common? The normal curve is nature's default. Let's consider an example straight from nature: the height of a blade of grass (see **Figure 4.2**). If in early spring, you went out to an un-mowed lawn, randomly selected 1,000 blades of grass, and then

ROBYN BECK/AFP/Getty Images

The normal curve is typically described as "bell-shaped," which is similar to the shape of Pharrell's hat.

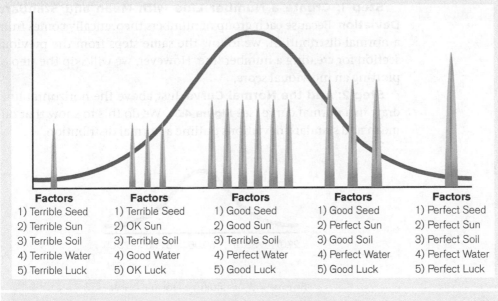

Factors	Factors	Factors	Factors	Factors
1) Terrible Seed	1) Terrible Seed	1) Good Seed	1) Good Seed	1) Perfect Seed
2) Terrible Sun	2) OK Sun	2) Good Sun	2) Perfect Sun	2) Perfect Sun
3) Terrible Soil	3) Terrible Soil	3) Terrible Soil	3) Good Soil	3) Perfect Soil
4) Terrible Water	4) Good Water	4) Perfect Water	4) Perfect Water	4) Perfect Water
5) Terrible Luck	5) OK Luck	5) Good Luck	5) Good Luck	5) Perfect Luck

Figure 4.2 Blades of Grass and the Origins of the Normal Curve

created a histogram of each blade's height, you would see that most blades of grass are average. Few will be exceptionally short or exceptionally tall.

Why? Because a multitude of factors influence everything we measure. For grass height, that includes the seed quality, amount of sun, soil quality, water quality, proximity to other seeds, presence of pesticides, amount of fertilizer, weather, climate, air quality, and so on. The list is nearly endless. Not to mention random luck. Some blades of grass get eaten by insects, while others get trampled on and stuck to the ground. You get the idea. A lot of factors influence grass (and even more that influence any psychological variable).

Now think about what it would take for a blade of grass to be the tallest in your sample. That blade would need nearly every possible factor to be in its favor: perfect seed, sun, soil, water, and luck. The opposite is true of the shortest blade. For blades in the middle, they would have a mixture of factors for and against them. With so many factors influencing any outcome, it is most likely for some factors to help and some to hurt. The result is that most outcomes end up in the middle. Extremes or extraordinary outcomes are rare, which is why the tails of a normal distribution are so low.

Step by Step: Building a Normal Curve Normal curves featuring blades of grass help make the concept clear. However, you will want to be able to create normal curves based on numbers. Earlier, we went through the steps for plotting individual scores on a number line. To build a distribution, you do essentially the same thing, with one very small wrinkle. Here are the steps:

Step 1: Create a Number Line with Mean and Standard Deviation Because each group of numbers theoretically comes from a normal distribution, we follow the same steps from the previous section for creating a number line. However, we will skip the step of plotting an individual score.

Step 2: Add the Normal Curve Just above the horizontal line, draw in a normal curve (see **Figure 4.3**). We do this to show that our mean and standard deviations outline a normal distribution.

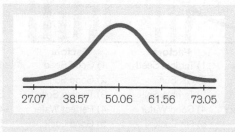

Figure 4.3 Building a Normal Curve

Step 3: Check Yourself . . . Be sure that the middle of your curve lines up with the midpoint of the number line (i.e., the mean).

For the purposes of our question about which star is most successful, we must remember that each star comes from a different category (TV personality, athlete, musician). As a result, each group has its own mean and standard deviation. Each group also has its own unique normal distribution. We could see where each individual falls within their group's normal distribution (i.e., where does LeBron fall on the normal distribution of athletes?). But because all three are on different distributions, we still can't make direct comparisons between Ellen, LeBron, and Ariana. We need one more conceptual tool to help us solve our problem: Z-scores.

Your Turn 4.2

1. All of the following are true of normal curves, EXCEPT:

   a. unimodal.

   b. asymmetrical.

   c. identical mean, median, and mode.

   d. most scores fall near the center.

2. How happy are you? Plot your answer on a normal curve. What factors influence your happiness?

3. Give your own example of something that is normally distributed. Explain what caused it to be a normal distribution.

4. A school psychologist has a population of 7-year-olds who take an aptitude test with the following results: *M* = 29, *SD* = 4. Build a normal curve based on this information.

5. In Chapter 3, we saw that participants' use of negative emotion words on Twitter was unimodal and symmetrical. Here, we see that the distribution resembles a normal curve. Describe the likely factors that caused this variable to be normally distributed.

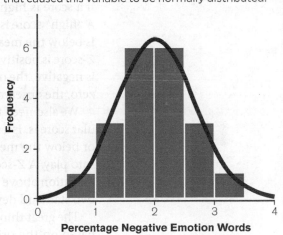

Z-Scores: How Do They Work?

Imagine we met three people, each with money from their country. One person from France has 100 euros, another person from the Philippines has 500 pesos, and another from Norway has 65 kroner. If we had to figure out who has the most money, how would we do it? First we need to establish common ground. We

Z-score a transformation that takes an individual raw score and coverts it into a standardized format where the mean is 0 and standard deviation is 1.

could do that by putting them all on the same scale by converting everyone's money to U.S. dollars. With everyone's money utilizing the same basis for measurement, we can now make a direct comparison.

It's the same basic idea with our three different superstars. To measure success most accurately, we need to value each star's earnings differently based on their profession. Statistics help us solve problems. Like a toolbox, we use different statistics to solve different challenges. In this case, we can use a **Z-score**, which is a transformation that takes an individual raw score and converts it into a uniform format where the mean is 0 and standard deviation is 1. Thus, a Z-score indicates how many standard deviations a score is above or below the mean. In other words, the scores are standardized to a theoretical normal distribution with a *M* of 0 and a *SD* of 1.

Think of it this way: Z-scores are just like social comparison. Knowing a single score is useful, but we don't fully know what it indicates. To figure that out, we need to see how the score compares to everyone else in a group. Maybe you take one of those online credit score tests and get a score of 400. Great! Or is it? If you find out that, according to CreditKarma, the average credit score is 630, suddenly your score doesn't look so good. As this example illustrates, we can determine if a score is high or low only by comparing it to the mean response. A "high" score is one that is above the mean. A "low" score is one that is below the mean. This is what the sign of a Z-score tells us. When a Z-score is positive, the observation is above the mean. When a Z-score is negative, the observation is below the mean. When a Z-score equals zero, the observation equals the mean.

We also need to consider how far above or below the mean a particular score is. Is a score just above or below the mean? Or is it far above or below the mean? This is where the magnitude of a Z-score comes into play. A Z-score of 1.00 indicates that a raw score is one standard deviation above the mean. A Z-score of −2.00 indicates that a score is two standard deviations below the mean.

The great thing about Z-scores is that because they are standardized based on the original scale's mean and standard deviation, we can compare scores across variables or groups. Essentially, by converting raw scores to Z-scores, we put our variables on a level playing field. What's a better score on a standardized test—a 528 on the SAT Math, or a 20.4 on the ACT Math? On the surface, it would seem like a 528 is 507.6 points higher than a 20.4. But because the SAT and ACT are measured on different scales, we can't compare these scores directly. However, if we convert them both to Z-scores, we see that both fall exactly on their respective means, so they both have a Z-score of zero, reflecting the average performance. In other words, these scores equate to performances that are exactly equal.

We can take the same approach to making other comparisons across variables or groups. Who's the better athlete, Simone Biles or Serena Williams? We can't compare their "scores" directly (gymnastics uses a different scoring system from tennis, after all), but we can evaluate how far above the mean each athlete is by quantifying their performance and comparing it to the average performance in their category. For example, we might calculate Simone Biles's Z-score for number of gold medals (versus the average Olympian) versus Serena Williams's Z-score for number of major championships (versus the average professional tennis player). We could then compare the Z-scores and determine which athlete had the more extraordinary performance, because the Z-score would tell us just how many standard deviations above average each athlete is.

Returning to our example, we need to compare a TV personality to an athlete to a musician. First, we compare each star to their own group by calculating each star's Z-score. This will tell us how many standard deviations they are above or below the mean. Next, we will be able to directly compare the stars to each other.

Step by Step: Calculating a Z-Score To convert an individual score into a Z-score, you don't need to do much that is different from what you already practiced in Chapter 3. The math is the same; it's just a matter of what you do with the numbers. Here, we'll lead you through the steps for calculating Ellen DeGeneres's Z-score.

Step 1: Calculate Scores' Mean We would do this exactly the same way that we learned to do in Chapter 3, using the data for all of the TV personalities.

Using the raw data provided in **Figure 4.4**

$$M = \frac{\Sigma X}{N} = \frac{85 + 84 + 70 + 65.50 + 60 + 51 + 43 + 39.50 + 37}{9}$$

$$= \frac{535}{9} = 59.44$$

Step 2: Calculate Scores' Standard Deviation We would do this exactly the same way that we did in Chapter 3. That is, standard deviation $(SD) = \sqrt{\Sigma(X - M)^2 / N}$ (see Figure 4.4). (Note that we are dividing by N, instead of $N - 1$, because we are focusing solely on Forbes's celebrity earnings list and considering that data as the full population.)

Name	Scores (X)	Mean (M)	$X - M$	$(X - M)^2$
Rush Limbaugh	85.00	59.44	25.56	653.09
Ellen DeGeneres	84.00	59.44	24.56	602.98
Gordon Ramsay	70.00	59.44	10.56	111.42
Dr. Phil McGraw	65.50	59.44	6.06	36.67
Ryan Seacrest	60.00	59.44	0.56	0.31
Simon Cowell	51.00	59.44	−8.44	71.31
Sean Hannity	43.00	59.44	−16.44	270.42
Heidi Klum	39.50	59.44	−19.94	397.78
Oprah Winfrey	37.00	59.44	−22.44	503.75
$\Sigma =$	**535**		$SS =$	**2647.72**
$N =$	**9**		$SD =$	**17.15**
$M =$	**59.44**			

Figure 4.4 Ingredients for Calculating a Z-Score

Step 3: Calculate Z-Score At the heart of a Z-score, we want to see how much an individual score differs from all of the scores' mean $(X - M)$, then compare that to how much scores in the data typically differ (SD). That is, we can see that Ellen DeGeneres's \$84 million falls above Forbes's list group mean for TV personalities of \$59.44 million by about \$24 million, but is that a lot? This is the essence of the Z-score calculation $Z = (X - M) / SD$, which will tell us how many standard deviations away a score is from the mean (see **Figure 4.5**).

$$Z = \frac{(X - M)}{SD}$$

Figure 4.5 Statistical Formula: Z score

In everyday terms: (The Score's Deviation from the Mean divided by The Average Difference from the Mean) = Z-Score (see **Figure 4.6**).

$$Z = \frac{X - M}{SD} = \frac{84 - 59.44}{17.15} = \frac{24.56}{17.15} = 1.43$$

So, Ellen DeGeneres has a Z-score of 1.43, which indicates she is close to one and a half standard deviations above the mean. Essentially, Ellen's individual earning score of 84 equates to a Z-score of 1.43.

> **Words:** (The Score's Deviation from the Mean divided
> by The Typical or Standard Difference from the
> Mean) = Z-Score
> **Symbols:** $(X - M) / SD = Z$
> **Numbers:** $(84 - 59.44) / 17.15 = 24.56 / 17.15 = 1.43$

Figure 4.6   Words/Symbols/Numbers: Z-Scores

Step 4: Check Yourself . . . One thing to be mindful of is that Z-scores can be positive or negative. If it is negative, make sure the individual score is less than the mean. Similarly, if the individual score is above the mean, the Z-score should be positive. Theoretically, Z-scores have no set range. That said, Z-scores almost always fall between –3 and +3, and most typically fall between –2 and +2. If the calculated Z-score falls outside of that range, be sure to double-check the math or confirm that the individual score is actually widely different from the mean.

Step by Step: Plotting Z-Scores on a Standard Distribution To see how each celebrity's earnings compare, we can plot each star's Z-score on a **standard normal distribution,** which is a normal curve with a mean of 0 and a standard deviation of 1.

Step 1: Draw a Number Line with a Normal Curve Follow the steps we used previously when we plotted individual scores.

Step 2: Label the Mean and Standard Deviations We base a standard distribution on Z-scores, so the mean is 0. We should label the vertical lines to the right +1 and +2, the lines to the left, –1 and –2.

> **standard normal distribution** a normal curve with a mean of 0 and a standard deviation of 1.

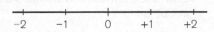

Step 3: Calculate the Z-Scores We know that Ellen DeGeneres's Z-score was a 1.43. We can calculate LeBron James's Z-score using the Forbes list data as follows:

$$Z = \frac{X - M}{SD} = \frac{88.20 - 55.27}{20.74} = \frac{32.93}{20.74} = 1.59$$

Similarly, we can calculate Ariana Grande's Z-score as follows:

$$Z = \frac{X - M}{SD} = \frac{72 - 50.06}{11.50} = \frac{21.94}{11.50} = 1.91$$

Step 4: Plot the *Z*-Scores Just as we did with an individual score, for each star's *Z*-score, find the corresponding spot on the number line, mark it with an X, and label it (see **Figure 4.7**).

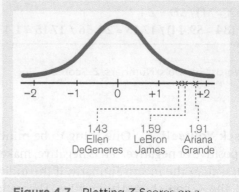

1.43
Ellen
DeGeneres

1.59
LeBron
James

1.91
Ariana
Grande

Figure 4.7 Plotting *Z*-Scores on a Standard Normal Distribution

Step 5: Check Yourself . . . Because we can convert any normal curve to a standard normal curve that displays *Z*-scores, those *Z*-scores will correspond to the original scale's means and standard deviations, and the placement on the number line should be the same. For example, the "X" on the number line signifying Ariana Grande's *Z*-score should be the same distance to the left of the +2 as her individual score of 72 was from 50.06, which was the value that was one standard deviation greater than the musician group's mean. The same will be true for Ellen's and LeBron's individual and *Z*-scores.

Your Turn 4.3

1. Match each formula to the correct description (Note: One answer is used twice):

_____ $(X - M)/SD$ a. Mean

_____ $\sqrt{\Sigma(X - M)^2/N}$ b. Variance

_____ SS/N c. Standard Deviation

_____ $\Sigma X/N$ d. *Z*-Score

_____ $\sqrt{SS/N}$

2. Curious about where other stars earnings' fall relative to the mean and standard deviation of their group?

a. Lionel Messi made $104 million. Athletes: $M = 55.27$; $SD = 20.74$

b. Lady Gaga made $38 million. Musicians: $M = 50.06$; $SD = 11.50$.

HAND CALCULATION VIDEO TUTORIAL: To learn more, check out the video tutorial Calculating a *Z*-Score by Hand!

Communicating the Result

Figure 4.7 essentially conveys our key results. Looking at the standard distribution, we can see that Ariana Grande has the highest Z-score of our three celebrities. Though it has the information we need, it isn't the most aesthetically appealing way to convey this information. Though not something you would see in an APA-Style paper, a common data visualization you will see is an **infographic,** which is a visual technique for conveying data that relies on images, figures, and tables presented in an appealing way.

infographic a visual technique for conveying data that relies on images, figures, and tables presented in an appealing way.

For example, we could create an infographic for our data by vertically arranging stacks of money representing increasing earning levels (see **Figure 4.8**). We would have to indicate on the infographic that we are using "adjusted earnings" and include a footnote generally describing the Z-score calculations we did in this chapter (i.e., Ariana's Z-score was highest, LeBron's was next highest, followed by Ellen's).

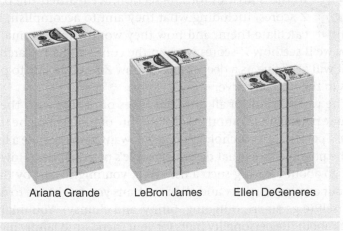

Ariana Grande   LeBron James   Ellen DeGeneres

Figure 4.8 Infographic of Celebrities' Adjusted Earnings From 2020

Forming a Conclusion

Our original question was, "Who's the most successful star, Ellen DeGeneres, LeBron James, or Ariana Grande?" The answer, despite LeBron actually earning more money, is Ariana. In essence, though Ariana made less money than LeBron ($72 million vs. $88.2 million) her earnings were more impressive. Among her own celebrity type (musicians), she was further above the mean. That's important because, for a variety of reasons, it could be harder to make money as a musician and easier to make money as an athlete. Think of it this way: When you learn that someone at your school has a 3.75 GPA, does your interpretation of that GPA depend on what their major is? Without naming names, chances are you find that GPA much more impressive for some majors than others.

While Ellen DeGeneres had the lowest Z-score, you want to keep that in perspective. Statistics can't provide an absolute and definitive answer to a question. Instead, they help us to have a more informed discussion that hopefully includes a critical evaluation of the numbers. For example, one consideration is that she is a woman in a category dominated by men. As a result, Ellen's earnings relative to the entire world of TV personalities are in some ways even more impressive. Remember, statistics can tell you a lot, but it is always up to you to look beyond the numbers and think critically about what the results are really telling you.

Statistics for Research

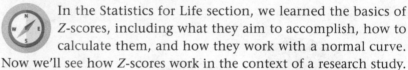 In the Statistics for Life section, we learned the basics of Z-scores, including what they aim to accomplish, how to calculate them, and how they work with a normal curve. Now we'll see how Z-scores work in the context of a research study. That will also give us a deeper look at how Z-scores relate to percentages in the normal curve.

The world is full of all different types of people with their own unique personality comprised of a mixture of traits. Imagine that you were a personality psychologist and you wanted to compile a list of all of the possible traits that describe people's personalities. How would you go about creating such a list? Well, you might start by thinking of your own personality and all of the traits you might use to describe yourself (e.g., smart, outgoing, funny, and clumsy). You might then think about the personality traits for your friends and family members. How many traits do you think you could come up with?

Back in the 1930s, a social psychologist named Gordon Allport had this same idea: create a list of all possible personality traits. Rather than think about himself or his friends, he went to the dictionary and wrote down every single word that could describe a person. In the end, he developed a list of 17,953 traits. That's a lot of traits.

Too many, in fact, to be useful. Imagine having to complete a personality questionnaire with 17,953 questions! Since the time that Allport developed his list of traits, other psychologists have worked to reduce the number of traits to those that are the most descriptive of personality. In the end, personality psychologists have settled on a list of five traits that are the most important characteristics of personality.

Collectively, these are called the Big Five personality traits, and they include: Openness to new experience, Conscientiousness, Extraversion, Agreeableness, and Neuroticism (or OCEAN, if you want a helpful mnemonic to remember them all). If you want to learn more about these traits, check out **Figure 4.9**.

Big Five Trait	Description
Openness to New Experience	Willingness to try new things
Conscientiousness	Tendency to be organized and self-disciplined
Extraversion	Tendency to be outgoing and sociable
Agreeableness	Degree to which a person is trusting and helpful
Neuroticism	Tendency to be emotionally unstable and prone to negative emotions

Figure 4.9 Descriptions of Big Five (OCEAN) Personality Traits

When we have several variables, as we do when measuring the Big Five traits, we often want to answer several questions: Is a particular score high, moderate, or low on a trait? How does a score for one variable compare to scores on different variables? How does a score for a variable compare across different people? To answer these questions, we'll need to further develop our understanding of the normal curve and Z-scores.

Where Do the Data Come From?

One of the most commonly used questionnaires to assess the Big Five personality traits is the Big Five Inventory (John et al., 1991). This inventory consists of 44 total items, some of which measure each of the Big Five traits. For example, an item measuring Extraversion asks participants to respond by indicating their agreement with the statement, "I am someone who is outgoing, sociable." To complete the Big Five Inventory yourself, visit the website www.outofservice.com and select the Big Five Personality Test option.

If you complete the test at this website, you won't be the first person to do so. Over 15 million people have completed the personality tests that the site hosts, and several research papers have been published using data from the site. One such paper examined whether personality traits become fixed when individuals enter adulthood, or whether personality changes with age (Srivastava et al., 2003). To test this, the researchers measured 132,515 respondents. Using this large sample, the researchers found the means and standard deviations for each of the Big Five traits for age cohorts ranging from 21 to 60 years old.

What We're Trying to Accomplish

We saw earlier in this chapter that the normal curve and Z-scores help us to compare different people on a single variable (e.g., comparing celebrities in terms of success). We can also use the normal curve and Z-scores to evaluate where a particular score falls on a variable. That is, we might want to determine whether a person is high, moderate, or low on a personality trait.

For example, let's imagine that we are conducting a case study of a client at a counseling center. We want to examine the Big Five personality traits of our client as part of a general client assessment. Note that we will refer to our client by their initials, CR, as is commonly done in case studies. We want to evaluate where CR's scores on the Big Five traits fall, relative to the population. **Figure 4.10** presents the raw scores for each of the Big Five traits for CR, as measured by the Big Five Inventory.

Trait	CR's Score
Openness	3.91
Conscientiousness	4.07
Extraversion	3.77
Agreeableness	4.88
Neuroticism	2.22

Figure 4.10 CR's Raw Scores on the Big Five Inventory

In order to evaluate whether a person like CR is high or low in a trait, or compare across traits (e.g., Extraversion score vs. Agreeableness score), we need to understand more about how the normal curve works. The normal curve, in addition to being common in nature, has specific mathematical properties that allow us to identify where any particular score falls relative to the other scores in a distribution. As we will learn in the next section, by knowing the mathematical characteristics of the normal curve, we will be able to identify the particular percentile to which a score belongs.

We will also need to know more about how Z-scores work. To solve our problem, and evaluate where CR falls on the Big Five, we will need to convert each trait to a Z-score, because each of the Big Five traits has its own normal curve, and so we will need to standardize our variables. Only by converting each trait to a Z-score will we be able to compare CR's traits to each other.

Normal Curve: Understanding the Ratio of Scores in the Peak Versus the Tails

Earlier in this chapter, we saw that normal curves are symmetric and unimodal, have scores that tend to cluster around the mean, and appear bell-shaped. As it turns out, though, not all bell-shaped curves are normal curves. What makes a normal curve unique is that it has a specific ratio of scores that occur in the peak of the distribution in the middle relative to the tails on the far left and right sides.

In particular, a normal curve is any bell-shaped curve where approximately 68% of all observations occur within plus or minus one standard deviation of the mean. In other words, 68% of all personality trait scores fall in this range, with 32% of scores falling outside of this range. Similarly, approximately 95% of all observations occur within plus or minus two standard deviations of the mean, and approximately 99% of all observations occur within plus or minus three standard deviations of the mean. This 68–95–99 ratio is sometimes called the **68-95-99 approximation** and is found in all normal curves and allows us to make general conclusions about how typical any specific score is relative to the overall distribution. That is, we shouldn't be surprised to observe scores that are within one standard deviation above or below the mean, because we know that 68% of all scores occur in this range. But scores that are more than two standard deviations above or below the mean should be surprising since only 5% of scores will occur in this range. Scores that occur more than three standard deviations above or below the mean should be rare as about 1% of scores will fall in this range. Now, it's important to note that these percentages are approximations and not the exact percentages of scores that fall within these regions (e.g., the number of scores that fall within plus or minus three standard deviations is actually closer to 99.7% of scores). But, the 68–95–99 approximation is a useful summary to help us get a rough estimate of where scores should fall in a normal distribution. **Figure 4.11** shows us where this 68–95–99 ratio comes from.

68-95-99 approximation in any normal distribution, there are similar percentages of cases between standard deviations (roughly 68% within 1 *SD* of the mean, 95% within 2 *SD* of the mean, and 99% within 3 *SD*).

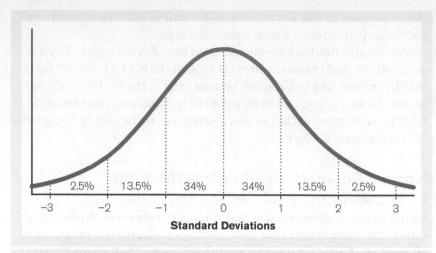

Figure 4.11 A Standard Normal Curve With the Approximate Percentage of Scores

As you can see, a normal curve has a specific percentage of scores that fall within plus or minus 1, 2, and 3 standard deviations of the mean. In a normal distribution, 50% of all scores will fall above the mean and 50% of all scores will fall below the mean, and 100% of all scores will fall somewhere under the curve. Moreover, approximately 34% of the scores fall between the mean and +1 standard deviations above the mean, and another 34% fall between the mean and −1 standard deviations. If we sum these two values, it tells us that 68% of all scores for a normally distributed variable fall between −1 and +1 standard deviations.

An additional 13.5% of scores fall between +1 and +2 standard deviations above the mean, and similarly between −1 and −2 standard deviations below the mean. If we sum these two values, it tells us that an additional 27% of all observations will fall between −2 and +2 standard deviations from the mean, or 95% overall (68% + 27% = 95%). If we go a bit farther away from the mean, we will find that approximately 2.5% of scores fall between +2 and +3 standard deviations above the mean, and similarly 2.5% fall between −2 and −3 standard deviations below the mean. If we sum these two values and add the sum to what we had previously, we will find that nearly 100% of all scores in a normal distribution (99.73%, to be more precise) will fall between −3 and +3 standard deviations from the mean.

As you will see, because these percentages are predictable in every normal curve, each standard deviation value is consistently associated with a specific percentage. This will allow us to use Z-scores to determine what percentile corresponds to a specific score.

Finding the Percentile Rank for Any Score in a Normal Distribution

While the 68–95–99 ratio is useful for identifying the percentage of scores that occur in various regions of the normal curve (e.g., the region between +1 and –1 standard deviation), we can, in fact, find the percentage likelihood for any value of a variable.

Namely, we are able to determine the **percentile rank** of a score, which tells us the percentage of scores that fall below a specific value. For example, we might find that a person who is extremely diligent, hard-working, studious, careful, and dedicated scores in the 90th percentile for the trait Conscientiousness. This would tell us that this person is more conscientious than 90% of other people on this trait. To find the percentile rank of a score, we first need to convert our normal distribution to a standard normal distribution (i.e., a normal distribution with a mean of 0 and a standard deviation of 1).

Why do we need to convert to a standard normal distribution? Because normal curves, while they have the same shape, and while 68–95–99 percent of scores fall within +/ – 1, 2, and 3 standard deviations, respectively, have different means and standard deviations. For example, according to Srivastava et al. (2003), the normal curve for the personality trait Extraversion has a mean of 3.25 and a standard deviation of 0.90. In contrast, the normal curve for the personality trait Agreeableness has a mean of 3.64 and a standard deviation of 0.72. Notice that these two traits are both normally distributed but have different means and standard deviations. So, to find the percentile rank for these variables, we need to first standardize them so that they have the exact same mean and standard deviation. This way differences in various personality traits' means or standard deviations do not affect our ability to compare them to each other.

percentile rank reflects the percentage of scores that occur below a particular value on the normal curve.

> **"**
> ### Statistically Speaking
> How crazy is it that my roommate and I both had high school GPA's of 3.45, but I was in the 90th percentile, while my roommate was in the 60th. Clearly, my roommate's school had a lot of high grades.
> **"**

We standardize our variables by using Z-scores. Remember, a Z-score is a standardized score that tells us the number of standard deviations that a raw score is above or below the mean. To calculate a Z-score, we use the same formula as we did earlier, as shown previously in Figure 4.5. To get some additional practice calculating Z-scores, let's convert our client CR's raw scores on the Big Five Inventory into Z-scores using what we learned earlier in this chapter.

Step by Step: Calculating a Z-Score To calculate the Z-scores for these traits, **Steps 1** and **2** from Calculating a Z-score described earlier in this chapter state that we need to calculate the mean and standard deviation for each trait.

In this case, because we only have data for our client, we need to rely on previous research. Srivastava and colleagues (2003) established the means and standard deviations for 21-year-olds for all five of the Big Five traits (shown in **Figure 4.12**).

Trait	M	SD
Openness	3.92	0.66
Conscientiousness	3.45	0.73
Extraversion	3.25	0.90
Agreeableness	3.64	0.72
Neuroticism	3.32	0.82

Figure 4.12 Means and Standard Deviations for the Big Five Inventory

Step 3: Calculate Z-Score As we did in the *Statistics for Life* section, to convert each raw score into a Z-score, we need to subtract the mean from the raw score $(X - M)$, and then divide by the appropriate standard deviation (SD). Try to convert each of CR's raw scores from Figure 4.10 into a Z-score, and then compare your results to those in **Figure 4.13**.

Step 4: Check Yourself . . . We've already stated that nearly all scores (approximately 99%) in a normal distribution will fall between −3 and +3 standard deviations from the mean. Thus, if we calculate a Z-score that is smaller than −3 or larger than +3 standard deviations from the mean, we should double-check our math. It is certainly possible that we will observe these values of Z, but it should be uncommon.

Step by Step: Using the Z-Table to Find the Percentile Rank of a Z-Score Looking at Figure 4.13, you can see how CR's scores on each trait compare to the mean (e.g., the Conscientiousness score

Trait	M	SD	CR's Score	Calculation	Z-Score
Openness	3.92	0.66	3.91	$\dfrac{3.91 - 3.92}{0.66}$	−0.02
Conscientiousness	3.45	0.73	4.07	$\dfrac{4.07 - 3.45}{0.73}$	0.85
Extraversion	3.25	0.90	3.77	$\dfrac{3.77 - 3.25}{0.90}$	0.58
Agreeableness	3.64	0.72	4.88	$\dfrac{4.88 - 3.64}{0.72}$	1.72
Neuroticism	3.32	0.82	2.22	$\dfrac{2.22 - 3.32}{0.82}$	−1.34

Figure 4.13   Client CR's Z-Scores for the Big Five Inventory

was 0.85 standard deviations above the mean). Which one of these scores is the most typical for the population, and which is the most unusual? Well, we know that in a normal distribution, values that are near the mean occur most frequently in the population. We also know that values at the mean will have a Z-score of 0. Client CR's Z-score for Openness was −0.02, which is very close to 0, meaning that CR is very close to the population mean on the trait Openness. For the trait that is the most unusual for the population, we know that as we move away from the mean for a normal curve, either above or below, the likelihood of making an observation decreases. So, we can determine that CR's score for Agreeableness was the most unusual, in that it has the most extreme or largest Z-score from the mean at 1.72.

Just how uncommon was CR's score for the trait Agreeableness? To figure out a score's exact percentile rank, we next need to refer to the Z-table (see **Figure 4.14**). The Z-table presents the probabilities of observing any Z-score rounded to two decimals. We will discuss probabilities in greater detail in Chapter 5. But for now, we just need to know that if we multiply each value in the body of the table by 100, it tells us the percentile rank for the Z-score. For example, if the number in the table is a probability of 0.6217, we can multiply this by 100 and convert it to a percentile rank of 62.17%. To use the Z-table, follow the steps below.

Step 1: Locate the Value of Z to the First Decimal The table's first column presents Z values to the first decimal. If the Z-score is negative, make sure to use the Z-table with negative values of Z. To find CR's probability for the trait Agreeableness, with a Z-score of 1.72,

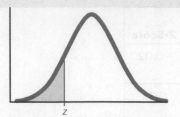

Standard Normal Probabilities

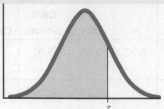

Table entry for z is the area under the standard normal curve to the left of z

Standard Normal Probabilities

z	.00	.01	.02	.03	.04	.05	.06	.07	.08	.09
−3.4	.0003	.0003	.0003	.0003	.0003	.0003	.0003	.0003	.0003	.0002
−3.3	.0005	.0005	.0005	.0004	.0004	.0004	.0004	.0004	.0004	.0003
−3.2	.0007	.0007	.0006	.0006	.0006	.0006	.0006	.0005	.0005	.0005
−3.1	.0010	.0009	.0009	.0009	.0008	.0008	.0008	.0008	.0007	.0007
−3.0	.0013	.0013	.0013	.0012	.0012	.0011	.0011	.0011	.0010	.0010
−2.9	.0019	.0018	.0018	.0017	.0016	.0016	.0015	.0015	.0014	.0014
−2.8	.0026	.0025	.0024	.0023	.0023	.0022	.0021	.0021	.0020	.0019
2.7	.0035	.0034	.0033	.0032	.0031	.0030	.0029	.0028	.0027	.0026
−2.6	.0047	.0045	.0044	.0043	.0041	.0040	.0039	.0038	.0037	.0036
−2.5	.0062	.0060	.0059	.0057	.0055	.0054	.0052	.0051	.0049	.0048
−2.4	.0082	.0080	.0078	.0075	.0073	.0071	.0069	.0068	.0066	.0064
−2.3	.0107	.0104	.0102	.0099	.0096	.0094	.0091	.0089	.0087	.0084
−2.2	.0139	.0136	.0132	.0129	.0125	.0122	.0119	.0116	.0113	.0110
−2.1	.0179	.0174	.0170	.0166	.0162	.0158	.0154	.0150	.0146	.0143
−2.0	.0228	.0222	.0217	.0212	.0207	.0202	.0197	.0192	.0188	.0183
−1.9	.0287	.0281	.0274	.0268	.0262	.0256	.0250	.0244	.0239	.0233
−1.8	.0359	.0351	.0344	.0336	.0329	.0322	.0314	.0307	.0301	.0294
−1.7	.0446	.0436	.0427	.0418	.0409	.0401	.0392	.0384	.0375	.0367
−1.6	.0548	.0537	.0526	.0516	.0505	.0495	.0485	.0475	.0465	.0455
−1.5	.0668	.0655	.0643	.0630	.0618	0606	.0594	.0582	.0571	.0559
−1.4	.0808	.0793	.0778	.0764	.0749	.0735	.0721	.0708	.0694	.0681
−1.3	.0968	.0951	.0934	.0918	.0901	.0885	.0869	.0853	.0838	.0823
−1.2	.1151	.1131	.1112	.1093	.1075	.1056	.1038	.1020	.1003	.0985
−1.1	.1357	.1335	.1314	.1292	.1271	.1251	.1230	.1210	.1190	.1170
−1.0	.1587	.1562	.1539	.1515	.1492	.1469	.1446	.1423	.1401	.1379
−0.9	.1841	.1814	.1788	.1762	.1736	.1711	.1685	.1660	.1635	.1611
−0.8	.2119	.2090	.2061	.2033	.2005	.1977	.1949	.1922	.1894	.1867
−0.7	.2420	.2389	.2358	.2327	.2296	.2266	.2236	.2206	.2177	.2148
−0.6	.2743	.2709	.2676	.2643	.2611	.2578	.2546	.2514	.2483	.2451
−0.5	.3085	.3050	.3015	.2981	.2946	.2912	.2877	.2843	.2810	.2776
−0.4	.3446	.3409	.3372	.3336	.3300	.3264	.3228	.3192	.3156	.3121
−0.3	.3821	.3783	.3745	.3707	.3669	.3632	.3594	.3557	.3520	.3483
−0.2	.4207	.4168	.4129	.4090	.4052	.4013	.3974	.3936	.3897	.3859
−0.1	.4602	.4562	.4522	.4483	.4443	.4404	.4364	.4325	.4286	.4247
−0.0	.5000	.4960	.4920	.4880	.4840	.4801	.4761	.4721	.4681	.4641

z	.00	.01	.02	.03	.04	.05	.06	.07	.08	.09
0.0	.5000	.5040	.5080	.5120	.5160	.5199	.5239	.5279	.5319	.5359
0.1	.5398	.5438	.5478	.5517	.5557	.5596	.5636	.5675	.5714	.5753
0.2	.5793	.5832	.5871	.5910	.5948	.5987	.6026	.6064	.6103	.6141
0.3	.6179	.6217	.6255	.6293	.6331	.6368	.6406	.6443	.6480	.6517
0.4	.6554	.6591	.6628	.6664	.6700	.6736	.6772	.6808	.6844	.6879
0.5	.6915	.6950	.6985	.7019	.7054	.7088	.7123	.7157	.7190	.7224
0.6	.7257	.7291	.7324	.7357	.7389	.7422	.7454	.7486	.7517	.7549
0.7	.7580	.7611	.7642	.7673	.7704	.7734	.7764	.7794	.7823	.7852
0.8	.7881	.7910	.7939	.7967	.7995	.8023	.8051	.8078	.8106	.8133
0.9	.8159	.8186	.8212	.8238	.8264	.8289	.8315	.8340	.8365	.8389
1.0	.8413	.8438	.8461	.8485	.8508	.8531	.8554	.8577	.8599	.8621
1.1	.8643	.8665	.8686	.8708	.8729	.8749	.8770	.8790	.8810	.8830
1.2	.8849	.8869	.8888	.8907	.8925	.8944	.8962	.8980	.8997	.9015
1.3	.9032	.9049	.9066	.9082	.9099	.9115	.9131	.9147	.9162	.9177
1.4	.9192	.9207	.9222	.9236	.9251	.9265	.9279	.9292	.9306	.9319
1.5	.9332	.9345	.9357	.9370	.9382	.9394	.9406	.9418	.9429	.9441
1.6	.9452	.9463	.9474	.9484	.9495	.9505	.9515	.9525	.9535	.9545
1.7	.9554	.9564	.9573	.9582	.9591	.9599	.9608	.9616	.9625	.9633
1.8	.9641	.9649	.9656	.9664	.9671	.9678	.9686	.9693	.9699	.9706
1.9	.9713	.9719	.9726	.9732	.9738	.9744	.9750	.9756	.9761	.9767
2.0	.9772	.9778	.9783	.9788	.9793	.9798	.9803	.9808	.9812	.9817
2.1	.9821	.9826	.9830	.9834	.9838	.9842	.9846	.9850	.9854	.9857
2.2	.9861	.9864	.9868	.9871	.9875	.9878	.9881	.9884	.9887	.9890
2.3	.9893	.9896	.9898	.9901	.9904	.9906	.9909	.9911	.9913	.9916
2.4	.9918	.9920	.9922	.9925	.9927	.9929	.9931	.9932	.9934	.9936
2.5	.9938	.9940	.9941	.9943	.9945	.9946	.9948	.9949	.9951	.9952
2.6	.9953	.9955	.9956	.9957	.9959	.9960	.9961	.9962	.9963	.9964
2.7	.9965	.9966	.9967	.9968	.9969	.9970	.9971	.9972	.9973	.9974
2.8	.9974	.9975	.9976	.9977	.9977	.9978	.9979	.9979	.9980	.9981
2.9	.9981	.9982	.9982	.9983	.9984	.9984	.9985	.9985	.9986	.9986
3.0	.9987	.9987	.9987	.9988	.9988	.9989	.9989	.9989	.9990	.9990
3.1	.9990	.9991	.9991	.9991	.9992	.9992	.9992	.9992	.9993	.9993
3.2	.9993	.9993	.9994	.9994	.9994	.9994	.9994	.9995	.9995	.9995
3.3	.9995	.9995	.9995	.9996	.9996	.9996	.9996	.9996	.9996	.9997
3.4	.9997	.9997	.9997	.9997	.9997	.9997	.9997	.9997	.9997	.9998

Figure 4.14   Standard Normal Cumulative Probability Table

we would go about halfway down the first column of the table on the right, which corresponds to a Z of 1.7 because this is the value of Z to the first decimal.

Step 2: Locate the Value of Z to the Second Decimal   After you've identified the appropriate row, we need to find the appropriate column. At the top of the table, each column gives the second decimal of our Z-score.

For the Agreeableness of CR, with a Z-score of 1.72, our second decimal is 0.02 so we would scroll to the third column of the table.

Step 3: Find the Probability of the Z-Score Line up the row for the value of Z to the first decimal with column for the value of Z to the second decimal. The value in the table's body is the probability associated with the Z-score (see **Figure 4.15**). CR's personality trait Agreeableness, with a Z-score of 1.72, has a probability of .9573.

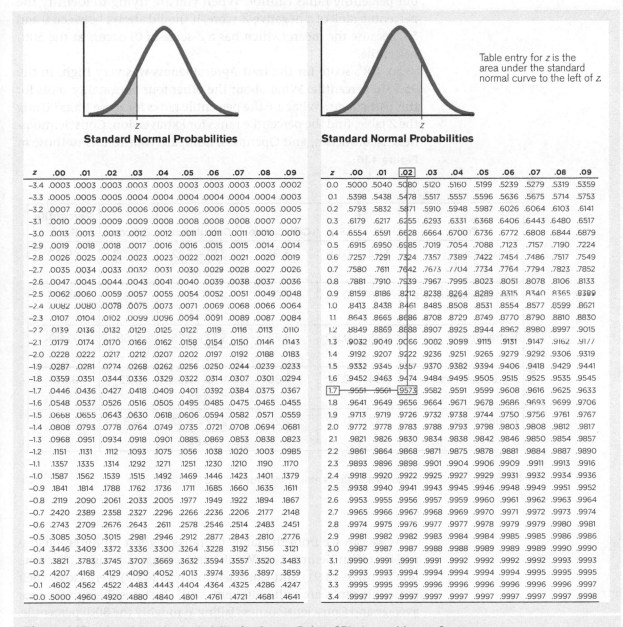

Table entry for z is the area under the standard normal curve to the left of z

Standard Normal Probabilities

z	.00	.01	.02	.03	.04	.05	.06	.07	.08	.09
-3.4	.0003	.0003	.0003	.0003	.0003	.0003	.0003	.0003	.0003	.0002
-3.3	.0005	.0005	.0005	.0004	.0004	.0004	.0004	.0004	.0004	.0003
-3.2	.0007	.0007	.0006	.0006	.0006	.0006	.0006	.0005	.0005	.0005
-3.1	.0010	.0009	.0009	.0009	.0008	.0008	.0008	.0008	.0007	.0007
-3.0	.0013	.0013	.0013	.0012	.0012	.0011	.0011	.0011	.0010	.0010
-2.9	.0019	.0018	.0018	.0017	.0016	.0016	.0015	.0015	.0014	.0014
-2.8	.0026	.0025	.0024	.0023	.0023	.0022	.0021	.0021	.0020	.0019
-2.7	.0035	.0034	.0033	.0032	.0031	.0030	.0029	.0028	.0027	.0026
-2.6	.0047	.0045	.0044	.0043	.0041	.0040	.0039	.0038	.0037	.0036
-2.5	.0062	.0060	.0059	.0057	.0055	.0054	.0052	.0051	.0049	.0048
-2.4	.0082	.0080	.0078	.0075	.0073	.0071	.0069	.0068	.0066	.0064
-2.3	.0107	.0104	.0102	.0099	.0096	.0094	.0091	.0089	.0087	.0084
-2.2	.0139	.0136	.0132	.0129	.0125	.0122	.0119	.0116	.0113	.0110
-2.1	.0179	.0174	.0170	.0166	.0162	.0158	.0154	.0150	.0146	.0143
-2.0	.0228	.0222	.0217	.0212	.0207	.0202	.0197	.0192	.0188	.0183
-1.9	.0287	.0281	.0274	.0268	.0262	.0256	.0250	.0244	.0239	.0233
-1.8	.0359	.0351	.0344	.0336	.0329	.0322	.0314	.0307	.0301	.0294
-1.7	.0446	.0436	.0427	.0418	.0409	.0401	.0392	.0384	.0375	.0367
-1.6	.0548	.0537	.0526	.0516	.0505	.0495	.0485	.0475	.0465	.0455
-1.5	.0668	.0655	.0643	.0630	.0618	.0606	.0594	.0582	.0571	.0559
-1.4	.0808	.0793	.0778	.0764	.0749	.0735	.0721	.0708	.0694	.0681
-1.3	.0968	.0951	.0934	.0918	.0901	.0885	.0869	.0853	.0838	.0823
-1.2	.1151	.1131	.1112	.1093	.1075	.1056	.1038	.1020	.1003	.0985
-1.1	.1357	.1335	.1314	.1292	.1271	.1251	.1230	.1210	.1190	.1170
-1.0	.1587	.1562	.1539	.1515	.1492	.1469	.1446	.1423	.1401	.1379
-0.9	.1841	.1814	.1788	.1762	.1736	.1711	.1685	.1660	.1635	.1611
-0.8	.2119	.2090	.2061	.2033	.2005	.1977	.1949	.1922	.1894	.1867
-0.7	.2420	.2389	.2358	.2327	.2296	.2266	.2236	.2206	.2177	.2148
-0.6	.2743	.2709	.2676	.2643	.2611	.2578	.2546	.2514	.2483	.2451
-0.5	.3085	.3050	.3015	.2981	.2946	.2912	.2877	.2843	.2810	.2776
-0.4	.3446	.3409	.3372	.3336	.3300	.3264	.3228	.3192	.3156	.3121
-0.3	.3821	.3783	.3745	.3707	.3669	.3632	.3594	.3557	.3520	.3483
-0.2	.4207	.4168	.4129	.4090	.4052	.4013	.3974	.3936	.3897	.3859
-0.1	.4602	.4562	.4522	.4483	.4443	.4404	.4364	.4325	.4286	.4247
-0.0	.5000	.4960	.4920	.4880	.4840	.4801	.4761	.4721	.4681	.4641

Standard Normal Probabilities

z	.00	.01	.02	.03	.04	.05	.06	.07	.08	.09
0.0	.5000	.5040	.5080	.5120	.5160	.5199	.5239	.5279	.5319	.5359
0.1	.5398	.5438	.5478	.5517	.5557	.5596	.5636	.5675	.5714	.5753
0.2	.5793	.5832	.5871	.5910	.5948	.5987	.6026	.6064	.6103	.6141
0.3	.6179	.6217	.6255	.6293	.6331	.6368	.6406	.6443	.6480	.6517
0.4	.6554	.6591	.6628	.6664	.6700	.6736	.6772	.6808	.6844	.6879
0.5	.6915	.6950	.6985	.7019	.7054	.7088	.7123	.7157	.7190	.7224
0.6	.7257	.7291	.7324	.7357	.7389	.7422	.7454	.7486	.7517	.7549
0.7	.7580	.7611	.7642	.7673	.7704	.7734	.7764	.7794	.7823	.7852
0.8	.7881	.7910	.7939	.7967	.7995	.8023	.8051	.8078	.8106	.8133
0.9	.8159	.8186	.8212	.8238	.8264	.8289	.8315	.8340	.8365	.8389
1.0	.8413	.8438	.8461	.8485	.8508	.8531	.8554	.8577	.8599	.8621
1.1	.8643	.8665	.8686	.8708	.8729	.8749	.8770	.8790	.8810	.8830
1.2	.8849	.8869	.8888	.8907	.8925	.8944	.8962	.8980	.8997	.9015
1.3	.9032	.9049	.9066	.9082	.9099	.9115	.9131	.9147	.9162	.9177
1.4	.9192	.9207	.9222	.9236	.9251	.9265	.9279	.9292	.9306	.9319
1.5	.9332	.9345	.9357	.9370	.9382	.9394	.9406	.9418	.9429	.9441
1.6	.9452	.9463	.9474	.9484	.9495	.9505	.9515	.9525	.9535	.9545
1.7	.9551	.9561	.9573	.9582	.9591	.9599	.9608	.9616	.9625	.9633
1.8	.9641	.9649	.9656	.9664	.9671	.9678	.9686	.9693	.9699	.9706
1.9	.9713	.9719	.9726	.9732	.9738	.9744	.9750	.9756	.9761	.9767
2.0	.9772	.9778	.9783	.9788	.9793	.9798	.9803	.9808	.9812	.9817
2.1	.9821	.9826	.9830	.9834	.9838	.9842	.9846	.9850	.9854	.9857
2.2	.9861	.9864	.9868	.9871	.9875	.9878	.9881	.9884	.9887	.9890
2.3	.9893	.9896	.9898	.9901	.9904	.9906	.9909	.9911	.9913	.9916
2.4	.9918	.9920	.9922	.9925	.9927	.9929	.9931	.9932	.9934	.9936
2.5	.9938	.9940	.9941	.9943	.9945	.9946	.9948	.9949	.9951	.9952
2.6	.9953	.9955	.9956	.9957	.9959	.9960	.9961	.9962	.9963	.9964
2.7	.9965	.9966	.9967	.9968	.9969	.9970	.9971	.9972	.9973	.9974
2.8	.9974	.9975	.9976	.9977	.9977	.9978	.9979	.9979	.9980	.9981
2.9	.9981	.9982	.9982	.9983	.9984	.9984	.9985	.9985	.9986	.9986
3.0	.9987	.9987	.9987	.9988	.9988	.9989	.9989	.9989	.9990	.9990
3.1	.9990	.9991	.9991	.9991	.9992	.9992	.9992	.9992	.9993	.9993
3.2	.9993	.9993	.9994	.9994	.9994	.9994	.9994	.9995	.9995	.9995
3.3	.9995	.9995	.9995	.9996	.9996	.9996	.9996	.9996	.9996	.9997
3.4	.9997	.9997	.9997	.9997	.9997	.9997	.9997	.9997	.9997	.9998

Figure 4.15 Identifying the Probability for Scores Below CR's Agreeableness Score

Step 4: Multiply by 100 To convert the probability to a percentile rank, we need to multiply the probability from the table by 100: $0.9573 \times 100 = 95.73\%$. Thus, a participant with an Agreeableness raw score of 4.88, which corresponds to a Z-score of 1.72, would be in the 95.73rd percentile. This indicates that CR's score is higher than 95.73% of all scores on the trait Agreeableness.

Step 5: Check Yourself . . . Z scores can be positive or negative, but percentile ranks cannot. When you are trying to identify the percentile rank of a negative Z-score, it should always between 0 and 50, because the mean (which has a Z-score of 0) occurs at the 50th percentile.

So, CR's score for the trait Agreeableness was very high, in the 95.73rd percentile. What about the other four personality traits for this participant? What are the percentile ranks for these traits? Using the Z table, find the percentile ranks for Extraversion, Conscientiousness, Neuroticism, and Openness. Compare your results to those in **Figure 4.16**.

Trait	*M*	*SD*	CR's Score	Calculation	*Z*-Score	Percentile Rank
Openness	3.92	0.66	3.91	$\dfrac{3.91 - 3.92}{0.66}$	−0.02	49.20
Conscientiousness	3.45	0.73	4.07	$\dfrac{4.07 - 3.45}{0.73}$	0.85	80.23
Extraversion	3.25	0.90	3.77	$\dfrac{3.77 - 3.25}{0.90}$	0.58	71.90
Agreeableness	3.64	0.72	4.88	$\dfrac{4.98 - 3.64}{0.72}$	1.72	95.73
Neuroticism	3.32	0.82	2.22	$\dfrac{2.22 - 3.32}{0.82}$	−1.34	9.01

Figure 4.16 CR's *Z*-Scores and Percentile Ranks for the Big Five Inventory

As we can see from the table, CR ranks highest on Agreeableness and lowest on Neuroticism. We also can see that although CR's scores on Openness (3.91) and Conscientiousness (4.07) were close, their percentile ranks are quite different, with Openness being very near average and Conscientiousness falling at roughly the 80th percentile.

Your Turn 4.5

1. David takes the GRRR, a frustrating standardized test, because he wants to attend a veterinary medicine graduate program. His test results reveal that he scored a 158 on the verbal portion of the test and a 155 on the math portion of the test. According to the information provided with his results, the GRRR Verbal has a mean of 150 with a standard deviation of 6 (*M* = 150 and *SD* = 6), while the GRRR Math has a mean of 148 with a standard deviation of 6 (*M* = 148 and *SD* = 6). Complete the following tasks:

  a. Convert David's raw scores for the GRRR Verbal and GRRR Math into *Z*-scores.

  b. Find the percentile ranks for David's test scores.

Finding the Raw Score That Corresponds to a Percentile Rank in a Normal Distribution

As we just saw, we can use the *Z*-table to find the percentile rank for any value of *Z*. We can also do the opposite. If we have a percentile rank, we can find the *Z*-score that corresponds to it. Let's say, for example, that we are conducting a study where we want to recruit participants who are high in Neuroticism (a trait that captures a person's proneness for experiencing negative emotions). Perhaps we decide to recruit only participants who are above the 75th percentile for the trait Neuroticism. To do this, we need a way to determine the raw score that corresponds to a percentile rank of 75.

Step by Step: Using the *Z*-Table to Find Raw Scores Based on Percentile Rank To find the raw score that corresponds to a particular percentile rank, we work backwards from what we did to find the percentile rank based on a raw score. Essentially, we start by looking in the body of the *Z*-table for the probability for our target percentile rank (75%). This will help us find the relevant *Z*-score. Once we know the value of *Z*, we can convert the *Z*-score to a raw score, using the *Z*-score formula.

  Step 1: Divide the Percentile Rank by 100 We need to start by converting our percentile rank to a probability by dividing by 100. So, if our percentile rank is 75, our probability is 75/100 = 0.75.

  Step 2: Find the *Z*-Score That Most Closely Corresponds to the Probability We now look up 0.75 in the *Z*-table's body and identify the *Z* value to the first and second decimal place (see **Figure 4.17**). In this case, the probability of 0.75 does not occur precisely on our *Z*-table. Instead, the probabilities of 0.7486 and 0.7517 are listed. These two probabilities correspond to *Z*-scores of 0.67 and 0.68, respectively. Because the probability of interest falls between these two values, we

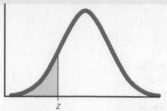

Standard Normal Probabilities

Table entry for z is the area under the standard normal curve to the left of z

Standard Normal Probabilities

z	.00	.01	.02	.03	.04	05	.06	.07	.08	.09
-3.4	.0003	.0003	.0003	.0003	.0003	.0003	.0003	.0003	.0003	.0002
-3.3	.0005	.0005	.0005	.0004	.0004	.0004	.0004	.0004	.0004	.0003
-3.2	.0007	.0007	.0006	.0006	.0006	.0006	.0006	.0005	.0005	.0005
-3.1	.0010	.0009	.0009	.0009	.0008	.0008	.0008	.0008	.0007	.0007
-3.0	.0013	.0013	.0013	.0012	.0012	.0011	.0011	.0011	.0010	.0010
-2.9	.0019	.0018	.0018	.0017	.0016	.0016	.0015	.0015	.0014	.0014
-2.8	.0026	.0025	.0024	.0023	.0023	.0022	.0021	.0021	.0020	.0019
-2.7	.0035	.0034	.0033	.0032	.0031	.0030	.0029	.0028	.0027	.0026
-2.6	.0047	.0045	.0044	.0043	.0041	0040	.0039	.0038	.0037	.0036
-2.5	.0062	.0060	.0059	.0057	.0058	.0054	.0052	.0051	.0049	.0048
-2.4	.0082	.0080	.0078	.0075	.0073	.0071	.0069	.0069	.0066	.0064
-2.3	.0107	.0104	.0102	.0099	.0096	.0094	.0091	.0089	.0087	.0084
-2.2	.0139	.0136	.0132	.0129	.0125	.0122	.0119	.0116	.0113	.0110
-2.1	.0179	.0174	.0170	.0166	.0162	.0158	.0154	.0150	.0146	.0143
-2.0	.0228	.0222	.0217	.0212	.0207	.0202	.0197	.0192	.0188	.0183
-1.9	.0287	.0261	.0274	.0268	.0262	.0256	.0250	.0244	.0239	.0233
-1.8	.0359	.0351	.0344	.0336	.0329	.0322	.0314	.0307	.0301	.0294
-1.7	.0446	.0436	.0427	.0418	.0409	.0401	.0392	.0384	.0375	.0367
-1.6	.0548	.0537	.0526	.0516	.0505	.0495	.0485	.0475	.0465	.0455
-1.5	.0668	.0655	.0643	.0630	.0618	.0606	.0594	.0582	.0571	.0559
-1.4	.0808	.0793	.0778	.0764	.0749	.0735	.0721	.0708	.0694	.0681
-1.3	.0968	.0951	.0934	.0918	.0901	.0885	.0B69	.0853	.0838	.0823
-1.2	.1151	1131	.1112	.1093	.1075	.1056	.1038	.1020	.1003	.0985
-1.1	.1357	.1335	.1314	.1292	.1271	.1251	.1230	.1210	.1190	.1170
-1.0	.1587	.1562	.1539	.1515	.1492	.1469	.1446	.1423	.1401	.1379
-0.9	.1841	.1814	.1788	.1762	.1736	.1711	.1685	.1660	.1635	.1611
-0.8	.2119	.2090	.2061	.2033	.2005	.1977	.1949	.1922	.1894	.1867
-0.7	.2420	.2389	.2358	.2327	.2296	.2266	.2236	.2206	.2177	.2148
-0.6	.2743	.2709	.2676	.2643	.2611	.2578	.2546	.2514	.2483	.2451
-0.5	.3085	.3050	.3015	.2981	.2946	.2912	.2877	.2843	.2810	.2776
-0.4	.3446	.3409	.3372	.3336	.3300	.3264	.3228	.3192	.3186	.3121
-0.3	.3821	.3783	.3745	.3707	.3669	.3632	.3594	.3557	.3520	.3483
-0.2	.4207	.4168	.4129	.4090	.4052	.4013	.3974	.3936	.3897	.3859
-0.1	.4602	.4562	.4522	.4483	.4443	.4404	.4364	.4325	.4286	.4247
-0.0	.5000	.4960	.4920	.4880	.4840	.4801	.4761	.4721	.4681	.4641

z	.00	.01	.02	.03	.04	.05	.06	.07	.08	.09
0.0	.5000	.5040	.5080	.5120	.5160	.5199	.5239	.5279	.5319	.5359
0.1	.5398	.5438	.5478	.5517	.5557	.5596	.5636	.5675	.5714	.5753
0.2	.5793	.5832	.5871	.5910	.5948	.5987	.6026	.6064	.6103	.6141
0.3	.6179	.6217	.6255	.6293	.6331	.6368	.6406	.6443	.6480	.6517
0.4	.6554	.6591	.6628	.6664	.6700	.6736	.6772	.6808	.6844	.6879
0.5	.6915	.6950	.6985	.7019	.7054	.7088	.7123	.7157	.7190	.7224
0.6	.7257	.7291	.7324	.7357	.7380	.7422	.7454	.7486	.7517	.7549
0.7	.7580	.7611	.7642	.7673	.7704	.7734	.7764	.7794	.7823	.7852
0.8	.7881	.7910	.7939	.7967	.7995	.8023	.8051	.8078	.8106	.8133
0.9	.8159	.8186	.8212	.8238	.8264	.8289	.8315	.8340	.8365	.8389
1.0	.8413	.8438	.8461	.8485	.8508	.8531	.8554	.8577	.8599	.8621
1.1	.8643	.8665	.8686	.8708	.8729	.8749	.8770	.8790	.8810	.8830
1.2	.8849	.8869	.8888	.8907	.8925	.8944	.8962	.8980	.8997	.9015
1.3	.9032	.9049	.9066	.9082	.9099	.9115	.9131	.9147	.9162	.9177
1.4	.9192	.9207	.9222	.9236	.9251	.9265	.9279	.9292	.9306	.9319
1.5	.9332	.9345	.9357	.9370	.9382	.9394	.9406	.9418	.9429	.9441
1.6	.9452	.9463	.9474	.9484	.9495	.9505	.9515	.9525	.9535	.9545
1.7	.9554	.9564	.9573	.9582	.9591	.9599	.9608	.9616	.9625	.9633
1.8	.9641	.9649	.9656	.9664	.9671	.9678	.9686	.9693	.9699	.9706
1.9	.9713	.9719	.9726	.9732	.9738	.9744	.9750	.9756	.9761	.9767
2.0	.9772	.9778	.9783	.9788	.9793	.9798	.9803	.9808	.9812	.9817
2.1	.9821	.9826	.9830	.9834	.9838	.9842	.9846	.9850	.9854	.9857
2.2	.9861	.9864	.9868	.9871	.9875	.9878	.9881	.9884	.9887	.9890
2.3	.9893	.9896	.9898	.9901	.9904	.9906	.9909	.9911	.9913	.9916
2.4	.9918	.9920	.9922	.9925	.9927	.9929	.9931	.9932	.9934	.9936
2.5	.9938	.9940	.9941	.9943	.9945	.9946	.9948	.9949	.9951	.9952
2.6	.9953	.9955	.9956	.9957	.9959	.9960	.9961	.9962	.9963	.9964
2.7	.9965	.9966	.9967	.9968	.9969	.9970	.9971	.9972	.9973	.9974
2.8	.9974	.9975	.9976	.9977	.9977	.9978	.9979	.9979	.9980	.9981
2.9	.9981	.9982	.9982	.9983	.9984	.9984	.9985	.9985	.9986	.9986
3.0	.9987	.9987	.9987	.9988	.9988	.9989	.9989	.9989	.9990	.9990
3.1	.9990	.9991	.9991	.9991	.9992	.9992	.9992	.9992	.9993	.9993
3.2	.9993	.9993	.9994	.9994	.9994	.9994	.9994	.9995	.9995	.9995
3.3	.9995	.9995	.9995	.9996	.9996	.9996	.9996	.9996	.9996	.9997
3.4	.9997	.9997	.9997	.9997	.9997	.9997	.9997	.9997	.9997	.9998

Figure 4.17 Finding Z-Scores for Probability of 0.75 (Percentile Rank of 75)

can split the difference $(0.67 + 0.68/2)$ and conclude that a probability of 0.75 corresponds roughly to a Z-score of 0.675.

Step 3: Convert the Z-Score to a Raw Score Using the formula for the Z-score in Figure 4.5, we enter the Z-score that we just found (0.675) and the mean and standard deviation for Neuroticism ($M = 3.32$, $SD = 0.82$). Solving for the raw score, X, we enter in the numbers as follows: $(X - 3.32)/0.82 = 0.675$. Next, we need to solve for X using some basic math: $X = (0.675 \times 0.82) + 3.32$. Therefore, $X = 3.87$. Thus, to recruit participants above the 75th percentile for the trait Neuroticism, we would want to recruit participants with scores of 3.87 or higher on the Neuroticism subscale of the Big Five Inventory. Or, you can use a formula to directly convert your Z-score to a raw score:

$$X = (Z)(SD) + M$$
$$X = (0.675)(0.82) + 3.32$$
$$X = 0.554 + 3.32 = 3.87$$

$$\boxed{X = (Z)(SD) + M}$$

Step 4: Check Yourself . . . Remember that the percentile ranks that we get using the Z-table always reflect the percentage of scores that fall below a specific value. This means that 75% of all scores will be less than a raw score of 3.87 for the trait Neuroticism. It also means that 25% will be higher than 3.87. We know this because all scores fall under the normal curve, and so the percentage of scores that fall to the left of a percentile rank added to the percentage of scores that fall to the right of a percentile rank must sum to 100%.

Your Turn 4.6

1. Isla is also taking the GRRR. She knows that in order to have a good shot at getting into the graduate program at Prestigious University (PU), she needs to score in the 75th percentile or higher on the GRRR Verbal and in the 65th percentile of the GRRR Math. Again, she knows that the GRRR Verbal has a mean of 150 with a standard deviation of 6 ($M = 150$ and $SD = 6$), while the GRRR Math has a mean of 148 with a standard deviation of 6 ($M = 148$ and $SD = 6$). What raw scores does Isla need to get on the GRRR Verbal and Math in order to meet the admission standards at PU?

2. Stevie wants to be in the top 5% of students applying to Prestigious University for the GRRR Verbal, because she intends to be an English major. What score does Stevie need to achieve her goal?

Comparing Normal Distributions Using Z-Scores

Figure 4.18 presents the raw scores for Extraversion and Agreeableness for two different clients at the counseling center, MT and JH. Imagine that client MT completed the Big Five Inventory and scored a 3.50 on the trait Extraversion and a 3.50 on the trait Agreeableness. Would these scores indicate that this person has the same level of Extraversion and Agreeableness? No. The distributions for Extraversion and Agreeableness have different means and standard deviations. As a

	Extraversion		Agreeableness	
	Raw Score	Z-Score	Raw Score	Z-Score
Client MT	3.50	0.28	3.50	−0.19
Client JH	4.15	1.00	4.36	1.00

Figure 4.18 Raw Scores and Z-Scores for MT and JH on Extraversion and Agreeableness

consequence, we cannot directly compare raw scores on the two traits to one another. In order to compare across normally distributed variables that have different means and standard deviations, we need to standardize our scores using Z-scores.

As we can see in Figure 4.18, the Extraversion score for client MT of 3.50 corresponds to a Z-score of 0.28, indicating that MT is 0.28 standard deviations above the mean. In contrast, MT's raw score of 3.50 for Agreeableness corresponds to a Z-score of −0.19, indicating that this client is 0.19 standard deviations below the mean (a negative Z-score). So, we can conclude that this client is relatively higher in Extraversion than Agreeableness.

If we look at client JH, we can see that although this client's raw scores for Extraversion and Agreeableness are different (4.15 vs. 4.36), the Z-scores that correspond to these raw scores are both 1.00. This tells us that JH is one standard deviation above the mean for both traits, suggesting that this client is equally high in Extraversion and Agreeableness. So, in order to compare across variables, whether it be personality traits or any two variables, we need to standardize the raw scores into Z-scores before we can compare them directly.

 Your Turn 4.7

1. Isla and Jalen are comparing their performances on the GRRR. Jalen reveals that he got a score of 158 on the GRRR Verbal, while Isla reveals her score of 156 on the GRRR Math. Using the means and standard deviations provided in Your Turn 4.6, identify which person had the better performance.

Using Z-Scores to Identify Outliers

In Chapter 2, we noted that some scores occur at the extreme tails of our distributions. We called these scores "outliers." When outliers are present in our samples, they can have large influences on our overall sample's descriptive statistics (i.e., the calculation of the mean and standard deviation). Thus, as researchers, we need to decide whether we should leave these scores in our data set or exclude them. We might choose to retain these scores if we think that they accurately reflect the variability that exists in the population. However, we might choose to exclude these scores if we think they reflect sloppy measurements or carelessness on the part of study participants.

Because outliers are so influential on our calculations of our sample's mean and standard deviation, we need to easily identify outliers in our data set. One way that we can do this is by establishing a benchmark for what constitutes an outlier. Although there are different standards across different areas of science, one common standard is to define an outlier as any score that is more than three standard deviations away from the mean. In other words, an outlier would be any score that has a Z-score of greater than 3 (or less than -3). So, if we are analyzing a data set, we should start by converting all of the raw scores to Z-scores and remove any values greater than plus or minus 3. This is reasonable because we know that approximately 99% of scores fall within three standard deviations from the mean, so any score outside that range is highly atypical.

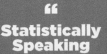

"
Statistically Speaking
Did you hear that Sabela is making $200K a year in her first job out of college? That is easily more than what 99% of other college graduates make. That salary is clearly an outlier.
"

Your Turn 4.8

1. The GRRR Verbal has a mean of 150 with a standard deviation of 6. What raw scores, above *and* below the mean, would we need to observe in order to designate those scores as outliers?

SPSS Video Tutorial: The Normal Curve, Z-Scores, and Outliers

When performing analyses, we can use SPSS to provide us with information regarding the normal curve and Z-scores that helps us understand aspects of our data. To see how this works, watch this video, which demonstrates how to overlay a normal curve onto a histogram, how to compute Z-scores, and how to inspect Z-scores for outliers.

SPSS VIDEO TUTORIAL: To learn more, check out the video tutorial Normal Curve and Z-Scores!

Communicating the Result

When writing about Z-scores and other statistical information in APA Style, there are a few rules that we should follow. First, APA Style designates that all non-Greek statistical symbols should be italicized, while statistical symbols that are Greek letters should not be italicized. So, because Z is not a Greek letter, it should always be italicized. Similarly, other statistical symbols that we have learned so far that should also be italicized include N, M, and SD. In contrast, we would not italicize Σ, μ, or σ because these are all Greek letters.

Second, all numbers should be rounded to two decimals (except for p-values, which we will talk about in Chapter 6). Third, if a number you are reporting can take a value greater than 1, use a zero before the decimal point. For example, you would write 0.88, not .88. Fourth, you should never begin a sentence with a numeral. If beginning a sentence with a number, use words rather than numerals. For example: "Fifty-nine participants completed the experimental session." Finally, use words to express numbers less than 10, but use numerals to express numbers greater than 10. For example, "Nine participants were outliers, and an additional 13 failed an attention check." Putting all of these rules together, here's an example of how this would look in an APA-Style paper:

Results

Based on our preregistered analysis plan, we defined outliers as observations with a Z-score greater than 3. Nine participants were outliers, and an additional 13 failed an attention check. We tested all hypotheses at the $\alpha = .05$ level. Results based on our remaining sample ($N = 1,231$) revealed that participants were high in conscientious ($M = 4.21$, $SD = 1.11$).

Forming a Conclusion

Our goal for this section was to evaluate whether a particular score is high, moderate, or low on a variable, compare scores across different variables, and compare scores across different people. In particular, we were examining the scores of a specific case study, client CR, on the Big Five Inventory. Because each trait has its own normal curve, each with different means and standard deviations, we needed to standardize the raw scores so that we could compare them to each other. In doing so, we learned that CR is close to the mean for the trait Openness, landing in the 49.20th percentile; is relatively high in Conscientiousness and Extraversion, landing in the 80.23rd and 71.90th percentiles, respectively; is very high in Agreeableness, landing in the 95.75th percentile; and is low in Neuroticism, landing in the 9.01st percentile.

Become a Better Consumer of Statistics

As we discovered in this chapter, the "who's best" or "what's best" disputes we engage in often occur because we are evaluating performance across different scales. We can't directly compare variables when they each have different means and standard deviations. One way statistics can help settle such disputes is by standardizing our scores so that they are on the same scale using Z-scores. By measuring our variables in standard deviation units, we can better judge just how extraordinary a particular performance is compared to others.

So one way that we can become better consumers of statistics is by considering whether we are comparing apples to apples, or apples to oranges. That is, are the variables measured on the same metrics or on different metrics? If we are buying cold medicine and one product claims to be long-lasting and another claims to be fast-acting, we need to recognize that these are different scales. The only way that we can compare their effects to each other is to standardize our variables. If that isn't done, we should approach those claims with additional skepticism.

Focus on Open Science: Outliers and Questionable Research Practices

We learned in this chapter how to identify outliers. Any raw score that corresponds to a Z-score greater than plus or minus 3 can be considered an outlier. This is straightforward. However, what we do with outliers is not. Should we leave them in the data set? Exclude them? These are often difficult questions to answer because the reason why certain observations are outliers is unknown to us as researchers.

We might be tempted to analyze our data both ways, to see how the results change when the outliers are retained or excluded. It then becomes tempting to use whichever analysis worked better. However, this is a **questionable research practice,** or **QRP,** that can create serious problems (John et al., 2012). QRPs are gray areas in science because they are techniques that are appropriate to use under certain circumstances but inappropriate under others. For example, it is appropriate to exclude outliers when the researchers base their decision on predetermined criteria, such as whether a score is a certain number of standard deviations above or below the mean. It is not appropriate to exclude outliers solely on the basis of whether doing so helps the result confirm a researcher's hypotheses.

The real issue is how and when researchers make that decision. For example, if a researcher bases their decision about how to handle outliers on what yields the best results, the published research may not be entirely accurate. In particular, making analytical decisions to increase good results increases the overall rate of **false-positive findings.** In other

questionable research practice (QRP) analytical techniques that are acceptable under certain conditions but that can be exploited to produce a specific result or confirm a particular hypothesis.

false-positive findings results that support a hypothesis, even though the hypothesis is incorrect.

words, a study looks like it worked, when in reality it didn't because the researchers wrongly concluded that a hypothesis was correct when in fact it was incorrect.

As you could imagine, being able to make decisions that help make your study successful is tempting. So tempting that open science advocates suggest that researchers should determine the criteria for when they should include or exclude data BEFORE they run the study. This way, the rules the researchers will follow are established before they have any data or results to tempt them. As an extra layer of transparency, open science practices also suggest that researchers publicly post their plan for their analysis on the Internet where anyone can see it. These strategies should help reduce the likelihood that researchers commit questionable research practices, including those related to handling outliers.

Statistics on the Job

Many professions rely on the ability to evaluate excellent, average, or poor performances of their employees. Take, for example, people who work in human resources departments and industrial-organizational psychologists. They often need to evaluate workers throughout the entire business or company, which often includes a wide variety of departments and job responsibilities.

Would it make sense to evaluate all employees on the same scales? No! Salespeople, marketers, engineers, product fabricators, and CEOs all have different duties, and they should be evaluated accordingly. However, it might make sense to compare performances across departments. If a product fails to meet its sales target, was it because the marketing department didn't reach enough potential consumers? Was it because the engineers developed a defective product? To evaluate across different departments with different criteria for success, we need to standardize our variables and use the normal curve to interpret what constitutes exemplary performance from average performance. To do that, we would need to establish the best measure of success in each department, then compare employees in that department to that standard. This would tell us who is above or below average and allow us to compare across departments.

School psychologists use similar skills. School psychologists often administer standardized tests to diagnose students with learning disabilities, perform assessments to identify behavioral problems, and evaluate cognitive abilities (APA, 2018). In order to make these assessments, school psychologists must understand how characteristics and disorders are distributed in the population, and thus need an understanding of how the normal curve and Z-scores work. By doing so, they can more accurately identify the students with scores that fall in the upper or lower ends of the distribution and help provide those students with more personalized forms of instruction that better match their abilities.

Review Questions

1. You're having an argument with your friends about which sport is the best. You maintain that it is hockey. Your friends disagree, and name other sports (e.g., football, soccer, tennis, etc.). There are many ways of defining "best," but as a group you decide that you will measure popularity. How might you operationally define your variable?

2. You just got your child psychology test back, and you earned 83 out of 100. The professor tells you that the mean was 75 and the standard deviation was 7. Plot your individual score on a number line.

3. What is the mean, median, and mode of the standard normal distribution?

4. IQ scores are normally distributed with a mean of 100 points and a standard deviation of 15 points. Build a normal curve based on this information.

5. You recently discovered that watermelons that are heavy for their size tend to be more flavorful and juicier. You're at the supermarket, and you see two types of watermelons. You see standard watermelons that have a mean of 22.5 lbs and a standard deviation of 1.25 lbs. You also see personal size watermelons that have a mean of 5.0 lbs and a standard deviation of 0.85 lbs. You buy a standard watermelon that weighs 23.44 lbs and a personal-size watermelon that weighs 5.84 lbs. Complete the following:
   a. Convert the watermelon weights into Z-scores.
   b. Find the percentile ranks for the watermelons.
   c. Based on weight, which one is likely to be sweeter?

6. It is well known that CEOs are typically paid substantially more than their employees. One way to evaluate companies is to compare the ratio between what the chief executive officer (CEO) is paid and what the median employee is paid. This is known as the company's pay ratio. In 2018–2019 the average pay ratio for publicly traded companies was 275, with a standard deviation of 355.
   a. The pay ratio for Netflix was 178. What percentile rank does this correspond to?
   b. The pay ratio for Apple was 283. What percentile rank does this correspond to?
   c. If the scores are normally distributed, what percentage of scores would fall between –80 and 630?

7. The Centers for Disease Control in the United States has pediatricians and other health care providers monitor the growth of children. One metric that is measured is head circumference. For those assigned female at birth, at 12 months the mean head circumference is 45.1 cm with a standard deviation of 1.3 cm.

   a. Your child's head circumference is 45.7 cm. What is their percentile rank?

   b. What score is associated with the top 15%?

   c. A child whose head circumference is below the 5th percentile or above the 95th percentile should be flagged for follow-up. What raw scores would we need to observe to designate them for follow-up?

8. Your roommate has been complaining about the number of shoes you own and is adamant that you have way more than the average person in the United States. That is, they say your shoe collection is an outlier. You both agree to use statistics to settle your argument. You own 32 pairs of shoes, and a quick search on the Internet reveals a recent survey report that Americans own an average of 20 pairs of shoes with a standard deviation of 5.

   a. Is your shoe collection an outlier? How do you know?

   b. A close friend has more than one pair of shoes for each day of the year. Is their shoe collection an outlier? How can you tell? (Hint: What raw score above the mean would we need to observe in order to designate the shoe collection as an outlier?)

9. In Chapter 2, you visually inspected data that were collected on swearing behavior. You identified one value, 15, as a potential outlier. The raw data have been converted into Z-scores.
   Using the following SPSS output, determine whether that value was an outlier.

Z-score (swears)				
		Frequency	Percent	Valid Percent	Cumulative Percent
Valid	−1.60200	1	3.4	3.4	3.4
	−1.24463	2	6.9	6.9	10.3
	−.88726	3	10.3	10.3	20.7
	−.52989	4	13.8	13.8	34.5
	−.17252	6	20.7	20.7	55.2
	.18485	5	17.2	17.2	72.4
	.54222	4	13.8	13.8	86.2
	.89959	2	6.9	6.9	93.1
	1.25696	1	3.4	3.4	96.6
	3.75854	1	3.4	3.4	100.0
	Total	29	100.0	100.0	

10. The onboarding process for new employees is expensive in terms of both time and money, so employee retention is important. You have been hired by a company to measure job satisfaction amongst the company management personnel. You use a variety of standardized measures and create a composite score that ranges from 0 to 75, with higher scores indicating higher levels of satisfaction.

a. If the standard deviation of this variable is 9.127, use your knowledge of the formula for Z to find the value of the mean for this variable.

b. If a person had a score of 52, what would their Z-score be?

c. If a person had a Z-score of 1.28, what would their job satisfaction score be?

d. Are there any outliers in the data set?

If there are, what are they?

Case Summaries[a]		
	job_satisfaction	Z-score (job_satisfaction)
1	21	−3.74264
2	48	−.78446
3	48	−.78446
4	49	−.67490
5	50	−.56534
6	51	−.45578
7	53	−.23665
8	53	−.23665
9	53	−.23665
10	54	−.12709
11	55	−.01753
12	55	−.01753
13	55	−.01753
14	57	.20159
15	57	.20159
16	57	.20159
17	58	.31116
18	59	.42072
19	60	.53028
20	61	.63984
21	61	.63984
22	63	.85897
23	64	.96853
24	66	1.18765
25	71	1.73546
Total N	25	25
a. Limited to first 100 cases.		

Z-score (job_satisfaction)					
		Frequency	Percent	Valid Percent	Cumulative Percent
Valid	−3.74264	1	4.0	4.0	4.0
	−.78446	2	8.0	8.0	12.0
	−.67490	1	4.0	4.0	16.0
	−.56534	1	4.0	4.0	20.0
	−.45578	1	4.0	4.0	24.0
	−.23665	3	12.0	12.0	36.0
	−.12709	1	4.0	4.0	40.0
	−.01753	3	12.0	12.0	52.0
	.20159	3	12.0	12.0	64.0
	.31116	1	4.0	4.0	68.0
	.42072	1	4.0	4.0	72.0
	.53028	1	4.0	4.0	76.0
	.63984	2	8.0	8.0	84.0
	.85897	1	4.0	4.0	88.0
	.96853	1	4.0	4.0	92.0
	1.18765	1	4.0	4.0	96.0
	1.73546	1	4.0	4.0	100.0
	Total	25	100.0	100.0	

Key Concepts

68–95–99 approximation, p. 123

false-positive findings, p. 137

infographic, p. 119

normal curve, p. 110

operational definition, p. 106

percentile rank, p. 125

questionable research practice (QRP), p. 137

standard normal distribution, p. 117

Z-score, p. 114

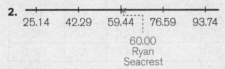 ## Answers to Your Turn

Your Turn 4.1

1. Lots of possibilities, but generally you should pick a mean that is lower than your score, and a small standard deviation. For example, a mean of 50 with a standard deviation of 1 would mean most people got around a 50, making your 65 look really good by comparison.

2.

| 25.14 | 42.29 | 59.44 | 76.59 | 93.74 |

60.00
Ryan
Seacrest

Your Turn 4.2

1. b (normal curves are symmetrical)

2. The most typical answer is that your happiness is near the middle of the normal curve because most people are average. That's because there are a large number of factors that influence your happiness. These factors include genetics, upbringing, schooling, life experiences, where you grew up, socioeconomic status, your intelligence, your attractiveness, and your personality, to name a few (clearly there are many more).

3. These will vary, but the explanation should focus on how a large variety of factors combine in such a way that they largely offset each other. The result is that most people or cases are average. It should also explain how it takes most factors working for you to have an exceptionally high score (which is rare) or most factors working against you to have an exceptionally low score (which is also rare).

4.

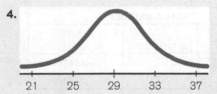

| 21 | 25 | 29 | 33 | 37 |

5. We could imagine many reasons for why the distribution of negative emotion words was normally distributed. For example, the bell-shaped curve could be due to differences among Facebook users, such that the vast majority of participants write posts containing a few negative emotion words, and a smaller number write posts contain almost no or very many emotion words. Alternatively, it could be due to the types of posts that people typically make on Facebook. Perhaps most Facebook posts describe emotionally neutral experiences with relatively fewer extremely happy or extremely sad posts.

Your Turn 4.3

1. d, c, b, a, c

2. (a) $(104 - 55.27) / 20.74 = (48.73) / 20.74 = 2.35$. Lionel Messi earns 2.35 standard deviations above the mean for top athletes. (b) $38 - 50.06 / 11.50 = (-12.06) / 11.50 = -1.05$ Lady Gaga earns −1.05 standard deviations below the mean for top musicians.

Your Turn 4.4

1. False. Only bell-shaped curves that have the 68–95–99 ratio of scores in the peak versus the tails are normally distributed.

2. a

Your Turn 4.5

1. (a) (158 − 150 / 6) = 1.33 (Verbal), 155 − 148 / 6 = 1.17 (Math). (b) .9082 × 100 = 90.82% (Verbal), .8790 × 100 = 87.90% (Math)

Your Turn 4.6

1. 0.675 = (X − 150) / 6, X = 154.05 (GRRR Verbal), 0.385 = (X − 148) / 6, X = 150.31 (GRRR Math)

2. We need to first divide our percentile rank by 100, 5 / 100 = .05. Next, we need to consider that our area of interest is the scores that fall to the right of the Z-score that we are looking for, but our Z-table gives us only the area to the left. Because of this, subtract our probability from one, 1 − .05 = .95. In other words, if a score that is in the "top 5%" is in the 95th percentile, which corresponds to a probability of .95. Next, we use our Z-table to look up the Z-score that corresponds to a probability of .95. The probability of .95 falls between the Z-scores of 1.64 and 1.65, so we can state that Stevie's score needs to correspond to a Z-score of 1.645. Finally, we can convert this Z-score to a raw score using the formula X = (Z)(SD) + M. X = 1.645(6) + 150, X = 159.87.

Your Turn 4.7

1. Both Jalen and Isla were 1.33 standard deviations above the mean on their respective tests, so they performed equally well.

Your Turn 4.8

1. We can define outliers as scores that are more than three standard deviations above or below the mean. Thus, for the GRRR Verbal, outliers would be scores that are less than 132 or greater than 168.

Answers to Review Questions

1. Answers will vary, but could include revenue, number of people who watch matches, number of countries where the sport is played, and risk of injury.

2. The line will have the following markings on it: 61, 68, 75, 82, 89. A line with the score of 83 will be on the line—much closer to the 82 than the 89.

   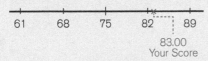

3. The mean is 0, because the distribution is unimodal and symmetrical; the median and mode are also 0.

4. Normal curve, centered on 100, with markings on the x-axis at 70, 85, 100, 115, and 130.

   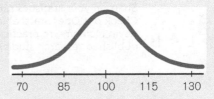

5. a. Standard-size watermelon, Z = 0.75; personal-size watermelon, Z = 0.99.
   b. Standard-size watermelon, 77.34%; personal-size watermelon, 83.89%.
   c. The personal-size watermelon is likely sweeter because it is a higher percentile rank.

6. a. Z-score = −0.27, percentile rank = 39.36%
    b. Z-score = 0.02, percentile rank = 50.80%
    c. −80 corresponds to a Z-score of −1, and 630 corresponds to a Z-score of +1; therefore, if the data are normally distributed, then 68% of the scores should fall between −80 and 630.

7. a. Z-score is 0.46, percentile rank is 67.72%.
    b. Find the 85th percentile; closest on the table is 85.08. Z-score = 1.04, score = 46.45.
    c. The 5th percentile has a Z-score = −1.645, and a score of 42.96 cm; 95th percentile has a Z-score = 1.645, and a score of 47.24 cm.

8. a. Z = 2.40; your collection is less than 3 standard deviations above the mean and therefore is not an outlier.
    b. Their shoe collection is an outlier. Having 35 or more pairs of shoes would result in a Z-score greater than or equal to 3. Your friend has at least 366 pairs of shoes, which is clearly an outlier.

9. The output indicates that one score was abnormally high, with a computed Z-score of 3.76. This Z-score is linked with the raw score of 15, since that was the largest value in the data set. The value was an actual outlier because the Z-score was above +3.

10. a. Mean = 55.16
    b. Z-score = −0.346
    c. Score = 66.84
    d. There is one outlier in the dataset—a Z-score of −3.74264, which corresponds to a raw score of 21.

Sharpen your statistics skills with real-life data! Check out OpenStatsLab.com, created by coauthor Kevin McIntyre, to practice running analyses for real published research studies.

Probability and the Distribution of Sample Means

Learning Outcomes

After reading this chapter, you should be able to:

● Describe the features that increase or decrease the likelihood that a sample is representative of the population.

● Describe the features of a distribution of sample means.

● Calculate the probability of an event.

● Calculate joint and additive probability.

● Distinguish between frequency distributions and a distribution of means.

● Calculate the mean and standard error of a distribution of means.

● Describe the Central Limit Theorem and explain its implications for the shape of a distribution of means.

sample subset of people selected from the population using some defined procedure.

population every single person that has relevant data about the research question.

We each get one lifetime. What do you want to accomplish in yours? As you ponder your life goals, you probably have certain "can't miss" or "must do" experiences that you want to check off your lifetime to-do list, or your "bucket list." How much progress have you made on your "bucket list"? Are you doing better than most people? You only live once, #YOLO; better get busy!

Statistics for Life

Let's take this opportunity to figure out where you are with your bucket list. For example, how common are your bucket list items to most people? If you asked your friends about their bucket lists, how likely would your friends' lists resemble that of the general population? Perhaps more importantly, how likely are you to complete the items on your bucket list? To answer these questions, we're going to explore what makes a **sample,** or a subset of people more or less likely to represent the **population,** or every single person that has relevant data about the research question. We'll also learn how to calculate probability so we can determine just how likely you are to complete bucket list items.

Where Do the Data Come From?

If you search on the Internet, you can find popular bucket list items. LiveStrong.com, for example, published "The World's 20 Most Popular Bucket List Activities" (Manning-Schaffel, 2018), which included the following:

1. See the Northern Lights
2. Run a Marathon
3. Take an African Safari
4. Write a Story
5. Walk Along the Great Wall of China
6. Learn to Play an Instrument
7. Snorkel at the Great Barrier Reef (or just go snorkeling)
8. Skydiving
9. Own a Dog

Joe McBride/The Image Bank/Getty Images

10. See the Pyramids of Giza
11. Learn Another Language
12. Ride a Venetian Gondola
13. Drive Across the Country
14. View Paris From Atop the Eiffel Tower
15. Hike the Pacific Crest Trail
16. Take an Alaskan Cruise
17. See Your Favorite Band
18. Go Glamping
19. Visit Stonehenge
20. Climb Mt. Kilimanjaro (or another big mountain of your choosing)

As usual, before we use this (or any) information, we need to consider the source, especially when searching the Internet. In this case, we should be curious about the site's authors giving few details about their methodology, other than to say, "We spent some time researching 20 of the world's most popular bucket list activities and present them here for your consideration." Umm, that's pretty vague! We could certainly devise a research strategy that would effectively produce a list such as this, but we have no way of knowing whether the article's authors did anything like that.

face validity extent to which, on the surface, something appears to effectively accomplish its goal.

Even so, the list has what researchers call **face validity,** which means that on the surface, something appears to effectively accomplish its goal. In other words, this looks like a perfectly reasonable list of experiences most people would want to do in a lifetime and doesn't include anything that seems out of place. Though this would not be sufficient for published research, for our purposes in this chapter, a face-valid list works just fine.

Samples and Populations: What You're Trying to Accomplish

Our original question focused on how much progress we've made on the bucket list and how that compares to most people. This leads immediately to the question, who are "most people"? In other words, who is our population? The answer is really up to us as researchers based on who we want to study.

For example, we could ask older adults 65 and over about their bucket lists. That would certainly provide interesting information, but it seems unfair to compare a college student's bucket list progress to someone in such a different stage of life. Instead, it would be more informative to compare college students to other college students. Now, we could certainly be even more specific and focus just on other psychology students, or only on those who are taking statistics this semester. But realistically, learning about the population of current college students will provide a good gauge of how your bucket list progress measures up to others.

Of course, the absolute best way to learn about college students' progress on their bucket list is to ask them. All of them. If we collected each and every college student's information in the entire world, we could be extremely confident that our conclusions would be accurate. If you're thinking that sounds like an impossible amount of work, you're right! Entire populations are nearly impossible to study unless the population is really small (e.g., you only want to compare yourself to everyone in your class). Luckily, it's possible to gather information from a subset or sample of the population, as we talked about in Chapter 1, and use that smaller group to tell us about the rest of the population.

Sample Representativeness: How Does It Work?

When generating a sample, we want that smaller group to be a **representative sample,** which means the smaller sample shares the same characteristics of the broader group or overall population. For example, if we asked a sample of four students how many bucket list items they've completed, we hope that their response represents what we would learn if we asked the entire population (i.e., all of the other students whom we were not able to ask).

Of course, whenever we rely on samples to make inferences about the broader population, we will always have some degree of uncertainty when making conclusions. There will always be a chance that our

representative sample a smaller subset that shares the same characteristics of the larger overall population.

"
Statistically Speaking

Before I buy an entire block of cheese, I need to sample a representative piece as a taste test.

"

generalizability the ability to make accurate conclusions about those who were not in the study.

sampling technique how participants were recruited into the study.

random sampling (also called *random selection*) a sampling strategy by which every single person in the entire population has the same chance of being included in the sample.

volunteer bias a problem encountered when recruiting participants for a study where the people who volunteer to participate in a study are systematically different than the people do not volunteer. As a result, a sample may not be representative of the population.

convenience sample a sampling strategy in which a researcher selects participants based on the ease at which they are recruited into the study.

conclusion is wrong, and that the results have poor **generalizability,** or ability to make accurate conclusions about the population. The good news is that our statistics knowledge will allow us to quantify our level of uncertainty. In short, smaller, less representative samples will lead to greater uncertainty. Obtaining a truly representative sample is challenging, but several factors affect whether our sample is representative.

Sampling Technique The first factor is how we recruited participants into the study, called the **sampling technique.** A sample is more likely to represent the population if we select people from the population based on chance. For a sample to truly have **random sampling,** also called *random selection,* every single person in the entire population needs to have the same chance of being part of the sample and therefore all possible samples have the same chance of being selected. For example, every college student in the population should have an equal chance of responding about their bucket list, not just your friends or those nearby.

Now, although random selection is the best sampling method for generating a representative sample, researchers in psychology are not able to use it that often. The main reason is that random sampling is actually quite difficult to implement. It's hard to identify every person in the population. Not all people have a phone number, e-mail, or mailing address that we can use to contact them. Even if we were able to get an exhaustive list of every person within a population, we can't compel them to participate in our study. They might lack the time, interest, or motivation to participate. As a result, even if we start out using random sampling, our sample will always include only those people willing to participate, which can introduce problems. That's because the people who volunteer to participate may differ from the rest of the population on key variables, reducing the likelihood that our sample is representative of the population. We call this particular issue **volunteer bias.**

Consequently, many psychology studies don't use random sampling at all and instead rely on convenience sampling. A **convenience sample** is one in which a researcher selects individuals to participate based on how easy it is to recruit them into the study. For example, we might obtain participants from an introductory psychology participant pool or use students in a particular residence hall. The main consequence of using a convenience sample such as this is that it may not be representative of the population.

Variability A second factor that can affect our sample's representativeness is how much those in the population differ on the trait we're measuring. Although (as we noted in Chapter 1) most characteristics are highly variable (e.g., mood), some are less variable than others (e.g., intelligence). Imagine for a moment that you ask 10 friends to rate their interest in completing two bucket list items, seeing your favorite band in concert and skydiving, and you record in the data in **Figure 5.1**.

Friends	Seeing Favorite Band in Concert (1 = Not at All; 5 = A Lot)	Skydiving (1 = Not at All; 5 = A Lot)
Monica	5	5
Rachel	5	1
Ross	5	3
Joey	4	2
Phoebe	5	4
Chandler	5	5
Janice	4	3
Barry	5	2
Emma	5	1
Gunther	5	3

Figure 5.1 High Variability Versus Low Variability in Bucket Item Ratings

As you can see, your friends' interests in seeing their favorite band are relatively consistent from person to person. If you selected a sample of three of these friends, the sample's average would be similar to the population's average (i.e., the overall average of all of your friends). So, when the variable of interest is relatively consistent across the population, it is much more likely that our sample will be representative, or similar to, the broader population.

However, consider what happens when you're interested in learning about something more variable, like how much people want to go skydiving. Looking again at Figure 5.1, the numbers vary a lot from person to person because some of your friends are really interested in going skydiving and others are not. Now if you were to draw a sample of three friends, the sample may not closely resemble the population because there is a chance that your sample could only include people who really love the idea of skydiving or only those people who despise it. So, when there is a lot of variation from person to person, there is a greater chance that our sample will not be representative and not match the characteristics of the population.

Of course, true differences are not the only reasons that people may have different scores on a variable. The scores we observe may also differ due to **error,** or the fluctuations in scores caused by how we measure

error fluctuations in scores caused by how we measure a variable (i.e., measurement error), experimenter expectations and biases (i.e., experimenter error), or participants' expectations and biases (i.e., participant error).

a variable (i.e., measurement error), experimenter expectations and biases (i.e., experimenter error), or participants' expectations and biases (i.e., participant error). Anytime we seek answers to a question, our job should be to minimize the amount of error that occurs in that process. Similarly, our job as statisticians is to think about how error creates noise or distractions from the signal, or what we want to learn, from our data.

Sample Size A third factor that can affect a sample's representativeness is the sample size. As our sample size increases, the tendency for our sample to be representative of the population goes up. This makes sense. If we were able to measure everyone in a population, our sample would always be perfect. But as our sample size includes fewer and fewer people, we miss more of the population, and the chances that our sample is representative goes down. For example, if you want to know how people in the country feel about a given topic (e.g., "What is the best TV show?"), are you better off asking a lot of people or a few? If you ask only a few, you may get some weird or at least less common answers. But if you ask more people, the results will more accurately reflect what most people consider the best shows. This is why you should be really skeptical of those "person on the street" interviews or personal testimonials that you might see. Any time you ask one person about their experience, you can't be sure to know all of their eccentricities and idiosyncrasies (e.g., perhaps the one person interviewed doesn't watch TV at all and only watches Internet cat videos). But if we can collect data from lots of people, we can identify that group's central tendency, which should give us the one value that best represents the entire group.

Regardless of the cause, any time our sample does not reflect the population, we are adding uncertainty to our conclusions (see **Figure 5.2** for a summary of factors). Later in this chapter, we will see how we will take both the amount of variability and the sample size into account in order to quantify our level of uncertainty.

Increases a Sample's Representativeness	Decreases a Sample's Representativeness
Random Sampling	Convenience Sampling (and other non-random sampling methods)
Low Variability in Population	High Variability in Population
Larger Sample	Smaller Sample

Figure 5.2 Factors That Impact a Sample's Representativeness

Creating a Distribution of Sample Means As we can see, whether a sample matches the population depends on a number of factors. As a result, we'll never know for sure whether a particular sample is representative. That's a definite bummer. But what happens if we combine information from many samples? With more data, we should be able to get a better estimate of the population. We will explore this idea next.

Rather than considering the individual scores that make up a population, a **distribution of sample means,** or distribution of means for short, is a theoretical distribution created by taking an infinite number of samples of a certain size (e.g., it could be a sample of 2 people, 10, or 20; see **Figure 5.3**) from a population. We determine the "set size" based

distribution of sample means a distribution that depicts the means of all possible samples drawn from a population.

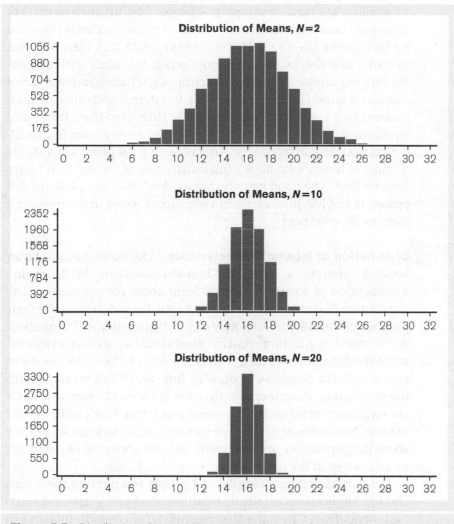

Figure 5.3 Distribution of Means' Shape Depends on the Sample Size

on the size of our sample. If we have a sample of 4 students' bucket list progress, we would create a distribution of means that portrays an infinite number of samples with 4 people each. If our sample had 30 people, our distribution of means would be from samples of 30 people each. Where does the distribution of means come from?

Distribution of Means: Where Does It Come From? Imagine that we have everyone in the world available to us, and we are able to know the number of items on their bucket lists that they completed. If we were interested in individuals, we'd simply plot everyone on a distribution. However, we are working with a mean from a particular sample of 4 people, so we need to stay consistent with that. To do so, we would take a random sample of 4 people, identify their number of completed bucket list items (e.g., 7, 8, 6, 14 items), calculate the mean for this sample $(7 + 8 + 6 + 14)/4 = (35/4) = 8.75$, and then plot that to start a new distribution. We could repeat this again with a different random sample of 4 people, identify their individual number of completed bucket list items (e.g., 12, 3, 9, 9 items), and calculate their mean $(12 + 3 + 9 + 9)/4 = (33/4) = 8.25$, then plot that. Rinse and repeat, over and over and over. By doing so, a more complete distribution would begin to emerge. After repeating the process an infinite number of times, we'd have a full distribution of means. Don't have time for that? The good news is that we don't ever complete the full process in real life. Instead, we can rely on the power of mathematical logic we describe next.

Distribution of Means: Characteristics Why do we need to know about distributions of means and how to create them? Well, creating a distribution of means helps us to learn about the population. The distribution of means and the overall population contain all the same people. The only difference is how they're being grouped. Think about it. The overall population consists of individual scores from everyone, while the distribution of means takes samples of those same people in groups of 4. The people we're drawing from are still all the same, with the same scores. *Because of this, the mean of the distribution of means is always the same as the mean of the overall population.* That's really helpful to know, because most of the time we take samples to learn something about the population, and being able to learn about the population's mean is a step in the right direction.

The process of taking samples of 4 people and plotting the means also has implications for the distribution of means' shape and variation. Recall from Chapter 4 that plotting scores from individuals in a large population results in a normal distribution, with most people scoring near the mean and fewer people scoring at the extremes. In terms of how many bucket list items most people have completed, we might find that most people have completed 12 items, with very few having completed only 3 items or 18 items. In other words, completing very few or very many items from a person's bucket list is rare. If we're plotting individual's scores, extremes like 3 or 18 are highly uncommon, but they do happen.

When we're working with means from samples, those extremes will be even rarer. Let's think through why that's the case. If we have a sample of 4 people, to get an extremely low sample mean, all 4 people would need to have extremely low individual scores (e.g., 2, 4, 1, 5). Remember, each of those scores is extremely rare by itself. If getting one low score is unlikely, how likely is it that a random sample of 4 people would get four low scores? Highly unlikely. It is difficult enough to have one rare thing happen, but to have it happen four times is a lot less likely.

The end result is that that when we use means of samples to create a distribution, extreme scores are rare. This impacts the distribution's shape because it shortens the tails and results in more scores being closer to the mean (see **Figure 5.4**).

Why does this happen? We know from our discussion of the normal curve in Chapter 4 that scores are more likely to be near the mean simply because in any sample, scores similar to the mean are more common. That is, we're much more likely to get samples of 4 people that look like (12, 9, 13, 14) or (11, 12, 11, 14), where all four scores are near the mean. That's not to say extreme scores aren't possible, but in a sample with several scores, any extreme score will be balanced out by scores more toward the middle or mean of the population. That is, we're much more likely to get samples of 4 that look like (**18**, 12, 8, 10) or (14, 12, **2**, 11), where several more typical scores counteract the influence of one extreme score (noted in bold). Even if we get two extreme scores in a sample (**2**, **16**, 8, 10), if the extreme scores are on opposite ends of the distribution, they balance each other out (e.g., a 2 and 16 would average to a 9). As a result, the distribution of means is taller and skinnier, which also signifies that it has less variability than the population.

In fact, a distribution of a mean's variability is directly related to the N or number of people in each sample. As the number of people in our sample increases, would that make extreme means more or less likely? The answer is that it becomes even harder to get extreme scores. Think about it. If we have a sample of 10 people, to get an extreme sample mean, we would need 10 rare scores to all end up in the same random sample. The chances of that are really low. But if we took a sample of 3 people, it would be much easier for that sample to include three extreme scores. If the sample only had 2 people, getting

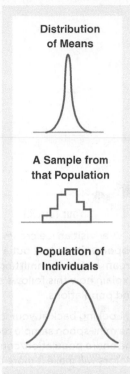

Distribution of Means

A Sample from that Population

Population of Individuals

Figure 5.4 Three Types of Distributions

all extreme scores is even more likely. When we have a small sample, even one extreme score has a big impact because there aren't as many other scores to balance it out. One extreme score has greater impact in a sample of 4 than it would in a sample of 10. *Essentially, as the number of people in the sample increases, the variability in the distribution of means decreases.* Said another way, sample size and variability in distributions of means are inversely related. As we'll see, knowing the distribution of means' characteristics will be important for hypothesis testing later in Chapter 6.

Your Turn 5.1

1. Ever visit an ice cream shop that gives you the opportunity to test out a small spoonful of ice cream before committing to an entire scoop? Explain how this follows a similar logic as samples and populations.

2. Looking back at your ice cream taste test, will the mini-spoon sample really accurately represent the entire population/container? Explain what factors will make it more or less accurate.

3. Taisha believes that Friday is the most fun day of the week. To test this belief, she asks 30 of her friends to rate each day of the week on a 7-point scale ranging from 1 (not at all fun) to 7 (extremely fun). Which type of *sampling technique* did Taisha use?

4. What is the key difference between a frequency distribution (discussed in Chapter 2) and a distribution of sample means?

Sampling and Probability: What You're Trying to Accomplish

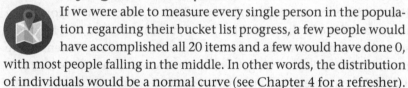

If we were able to measure every single person in the population regarding their bucket list progress, a few people would have accomplished all 20 items and a few would have done 0, with most people falling in the middle. In other words, the distribution of individuals would be a normal curve (see Chapter 4 for a refresher).

Because of this, we also know from working with Z-scores that there are standardized percentages that represent where proportions of scores fall on the distribution. That is, whatever the average or mean number of completed bucket list items happens to be, it is solidly in the middle, which means that 50% of population had accomplished more, while 50% had accomplished less.

What if we took a sample of one person from that population? If we randomly selected one person and determined their bucket list progress, what are the chances that person is below average? Fifty percent. Similarly, what are the chances that our sample of 1 is above average? Again, 50%. In other words, any one person we sample has a 50/50 shot at being below or above average.

Those percentages under the normal curve also represent **probability,** or how likely an event, case, or outcome is to occur relative to all potential outcomes. For example, any person has a 1 in 2 chance of being above the mean. Thinking about *Z*-scores and percentages again, any one person we sample has less than a 1% chance of being more than three standard deviations above or below the mean. Again, extreme scores are infrequent. As a result, the probability or likelihood of sampling one person who is that extreme is really low (specifically less than a 1% chance). Indeed, it's possible to determine the probability for any particular score in a distribution.

Step by Step: Calculating Probability Whether a person is above or below average relative to the normal population will always be a flip of a coin, a 50/50 proposition. But there are going to be plenty of times when we want to determine probabilities with greater specificity. We can do that by following these steps:

Step 1: Determine Potential Outcomes Here we need to figure out all of the possible results. If we're flipping a coin, there are two outcomes (heads or tails). If we are rolling one standard die, there are six possible outcomes (1, 2, 3, 4, 5, 6), whereas rolling a 20-sided die has 20 possible outcomes. If we are measuring human behavior, we can observe all of the behaviors for a group of people and use that information to determine the extent of potential outcomes.

Step 2: Establish What Counts as a Successful Outcome This is entirely up to us, based on what we're looking for. When flipping coins, we could count the number of heads, or just as easily decide to count the number of tails. Once we decide, we'll simply count how many times that successful outcome happened.

Step 3: Divide Successes (Step 2) by Potential Outcomes (Step 1) This step is shown in the figure below. Here we want to see how many successes we had relative to all of the possible outcomes, so we divide the "hits" by all of the potential ways it could have turned out. The chance of getting "heads" is $1/2 = 0.5$. The chance of getting a "4" on a standard dice is $1/6 = 0.17$. The odds of getting that same "4" on a 20-sided die are $1/20 = 0.05$. We should also keep in mind that the probabilities we calculate (0.50, 0.17, 0.05), are also percentages. That is, we have a 50% chance of getting heads on a coin flip, a 17% chance of getting a "4" on a standard die, but only a 5% chance of getting a "4" on a 20-sided die.

$$Probability = \frac{Sucessful\ Outcomes}{Potential\ Outcomes}$$

probability how likely an event, case, or outcome is to occur, relative to all potential outcomes.

"
Statistically Speaking
What's the probability of the Cowboys winning the Super Bowl? Well, it is likely lower than the Patriots' chances.
"

Step 4: Check Yourself . . . Because probabilities (when multiplied by 100) are also percentages, we should never have a probability greater than 1.00 (or 100% chance) or a negative value. It is impossible to have more than a 100% chance of any outcome occurring or less than a 0% chance. Similarly, it is technically impossible to give 110% effort or less than 0%. For the record, that statement is 100% true, but not 120% true.

Thinking Probabilistically Perhaps the most important reason to learn statistics is to help broaden the way you think about the world. Too often we like to simplify our world to make our decisions easier. However, that simplification leaves out a lot of helpful nuance. To capture the subtleties or gray areas in decisions, we should learn to think more in terms of probability and less in terms of absolutes.

For example, suppose someone were to ask, "Will you get married some day?" Chances are that you would answer in absolute terms: yes or no. When you limit your thinking to two options, you're basically saying there is a 50/50 chance. Sorry, but that isn't completely accurate. Your probability of getting married is likely greater than 50%. It would be much more accurate if you gave a percentage likelihood of getting married. Perhaps you are really sure, and are 90% likely. Someone else is a bit less sure, and is perhaps 75% likely, while another person isn't sure at all but thinks marriage is 55% likely. All three people are technically a "yes," but their feelings about getting married are quite different. By thinking in such stark yes/no terms, you're almost inevitably decreasing accuracy.

Now, when you think of your bucket list, what is the likelihood that you'll cross off "See the Northern Lights" from your bucket list? Don't think in terms of absolutes—yes, I will see the Northern Lights, or no, I won't. Like your marriage odds, your chances likely aren't a true 50/50 flip of a coin. Rather, there are factors that tip the likelihood of your visit in one direction or the other. Recall that in Chapter 4, we introduced the normal curve and discussed that there are a multiplicity of factors that contribute to any one outcome. The same is true for your potential Northern Lights visit: interest level, time, proximity, cost, fear of flying, and so on.

If you weigh several of the potential factors involved, it becomes difficult to think confidently in absolutes, because each factor tips the likelihood a bit toward yes or no. Once you start factoring in each of those, it may be that you're much more likely to visit (more like 80% likely and 20% unlikely). Or perhaps upon further consideration you realize that you don't really enjoy the cold and that going somewhere to see the Northern Lights is a long, expensive plane ride away. In that case, your likelihood of visiting may be more like 10% likely and 90% unlikely.

Considering all of the potential factors that can influence an outcome is even more important when thinking about negative events. Are you likely to die of heart disease? Before statistics, the old you might have thought about this in basic yes-or-no terms and optimistically answered "no." But if you consider all of the potential contributing factors such as diet, exercise, sleep, and stress, your probability may still fall on the "no" side (e.g., 20% or 5%). However, if there are certain factors (e.g., you aren't getting enough sleep) that are pushing your probability higher (e.g., your probability is 20% instead of 5%) you can identify areas for improvement. Had you thought simply in terms of yes versus no, you may have missed the opportunity to fully evaluate all of the contributing factors.

Forming a Conclusion/Communicating the Result

So, how does our bucket list progress compare to those of other people? Well, to form a conclusion, we need to know how many items people in the population have completed on average. But, because it would be nearly impossible to actually measure everyone in the population, we are going to rely on a sample of participants to help us estimate the population's characteristics.

As we learned in this section, using a sample to make conclusions about the population can be imperfect. Even when we do our best to get a representative sample, we may or may not get one. As we discussed, there are lots of reasons why a sample may or may not be representative of the population, such as our sampling technique, the population variability, and our sample size. Ultimately, we can never know for sure that a sample will be representative of the population. What we can do, however, is construct a distribution of means, as we discussed earlier. When we look at the means of samples, rather than individual scores, we reduce the impact of extreme scores, so that the mean of our sample is closer, on average, to the population mean. As a result, by considering a distribution of means, we have an easier time of making conclusions about the population.

In the end, whether a particular sample is representative of the population comes down to probability. Samples that are near the population mean are more probable than samples that are far away from the population mean. By knowing about distributions of means, we can determine how probable any sample is, given the characteristics of the population. We will continue to explore these ideas later in this chapter and in the next several chapters.

Your Turn 5.2

1. You attend a magic show where the magician asks you to draw a card from a standard deck of playing cards (note, a deck of cards has 52 total cards). What is the probability that you will draw a king? What is the probability that you will draw a diamond? What is the probability that you will draw a face card?

Statistics for Research

Now that we have some of the basics down, as we've been doing in other chapters, we'll see how these concepts apply to a research context. That'll involve a bit of review, but we'll also introduce some new concepts such as additive and joint probabilities, how probability and distributions work together, sampling errors, and the mathematical properties of distribution of means.

For some people, having their very own dog is a bucket list item. Any dog owner who has tried to train their dog has wondered about its intelligence level. What commands will it understand? Does it respond better to punishment or to rewards? Can it do any tricks? If so, how complex a trick can it do? Questions such as these have led many cognitive psychologists to study animal cognition to understand how animals, such as dogs, process language.

Some researchers have sought to examine just how large the dog vocabulary is, and how large it can get. In one study, researchers taught Chaser, a border collie, to distinguish the words for 1,022 items (Pilley & Reid, 2011). Other studies examine how dogs learn words. For example, researchers sought to test whether, similar to children, dogs use "fast mapping" to learn new words (Kaminski et al., 2004). Fast mapping is a process in which people and animals learn new words by associating unfamiliar words with novel objects. So, if you show a dog three objects (a toy bone, a baseball, and a scarf) two of which are familiar to the dog ("bone" and "baseball") and the other new ("scarf"), the dog will quickly associate the new word ("scarf") with the novel object (the scarf). Based on research such as this, scholars estimate that dogs can understand an average of about 150 words, so we will use this value for our estimate of the population mean.

If we draw a sample of dogs from the population and test each dog's language ability, what is the likelihood that our sample would have an average of 150? If we were to draw multiple samples from the same population, what would the distribution of means look like? Would most of the samples resemble the population in their means and

How many words does this dog understand?

GlobalP/Getty Images

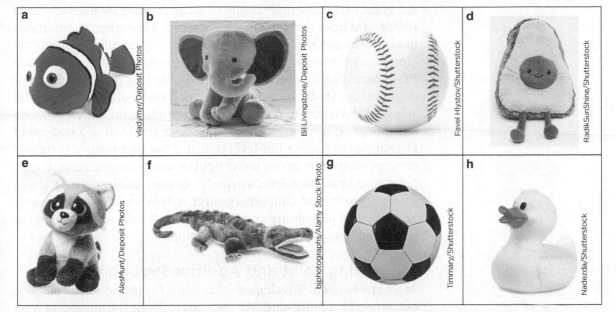

Researchers studying animal cognition need to be creative when measuring what animals understand. Here we might measure a dog's vocabulary size by training it to identify various objects and then testing its ability to fetch particular items.

standard deviations? To answer these questions, we need to further develop our understanding of probability and distributions of sample means that we started to explore in the first half of this chapter.

Where Do the Data Come From?

To study dogs' vocabulary size, we might employ an experimental procedure from previous research (Pilley & Reid, 2011). In particular, we could recruit a sample of dogs and measure their vocabulary size by arranging familiar toys in a row. Using this "Dog Vocabulary Test," we would ask the dog to fetch a particular object and count the number of successful trials. For example, we might arrange a toy orange fish, a gray elephant, a white baseball, a green avocado, a brown raccoon, a green alligator, a soccer ball, and a rubber duckie in a row.

If the dog can correctly retrieve each object by name, we could change out the objects for new objects and repeat the test until the dog is no longer able to correctly retrieve the correct items at a better than chance level. This would give us an estimate of the dog's vocabulary size.

What We're Trying to Accomplish

Once we have data for a sample of dogs, we will use that sample to make estimates of the population's parameters (i.e., the mean and standard deviation). When doing so, we need to recognize that our sample is one of many possible samples we could have drawn from the distribution of means. Remember, distributions of sample means reflect the idea that from any population, there are almost an infinite number of different samples that we could obtain when recruiting a random sample. So, if we had recruited different dogs into our study, we would have calculated a different mean and standard deviation for our sample. Depending on which dogs we select, we might have a sample that does a good job or a bad job of estimating the population-level statistics. For that reason, there will be some probability of our being right or wrong associated with each possible sample. Therefore, we need to develop our understanding of how probability and sampling connect, so that we can use our general knowledge of probability and sampling distributions when trying to make conclusions about a particular sample.

Calculating Joint and Additive Probability

As we saw earlier in this chapter, calculating the probability of any one outcome is straightforward. We just need to divide the number of ways that a successful outcome can occur by the total number of possible outcomes. For example, if we laid out eight different toys and asked the dog to fetch the orange fish, the probability that the dog successfully responds would be the number of correct outcomes, 1 (fetching the orange fish) out of the 8 possible outcomes. Thus, the probability for that single outcome is 1/8, or 0.125, or a 12.5% likelihood of being correct. However, sometimes we want to determine the probability of two outcomes occurring together, or any one of several possible outcomes occurring. In these situations, we need to calculate the joint and additive probabilities.

joint probability describes the probability that two or more events occur simultaneously, or successively.

Joint Probability **Joint probability** describes the likelihood of multiple events occurring at the same time, or successively (see **Figure 5.5**). The hallmark of joint probability is the word "and." We are looking to find the probability that one outcome *and* another outcome occurs. For example, we might want to determine the probability of a dog correctly fetching the orange fish *and then* correctly fetching the brown raccoon.

To solve this type of problem, where we are calculating the probability of successive events, we will multiply the probabilities for each task together. Thus, if the probability of correctly picking the fish is 1/8, and then we replace the orange fish and ask the dog to select the brown raccoon, which itself has a probability of 1/8, the overall probability of both events happening would be equal to $(1/8) \times (1/8) = 1/64 = 0.016$. In other words, there would be a 0.016 probability of the dog correctly

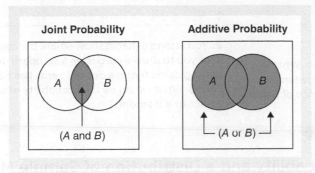

Figure 5.5 Venn Diagrams for Joint and Additive Probability

identifying two toys in a row by chance. It makes sense that the probability for correctly solving two tasks (0.016) should be lower than the probability of correctly solving any one task (1/8 or 0.125).

Additive Probability Additive probability describes the likelihood that any one of several possible outcomes occurs (again, see Figure 5.5). The hallmark of additive probability is the word "or." We are looking for one outcome *or* another outcome to occur. For example, we might be interested in estimating the likelihood that a dog selects an animal *or* a green toy as the outcome of a trial.

To calculate additive probability, we will add the probabilities of both outcomes independently and then subtract their joint probability. To understand how this works, let's look more closely at the probabilities involved in this problem. The probability of a dog selecting a toy animal from our Dog Vocabulary Test is 4 out of 8 (the orange fish, gray elephant, brown raccoon, and green alligator would all be successful outcomes). The probability of a dog selecting a green toy is 2 out of 8 (the green avocado and green alligator would be successful outcomes).

Notice, though, that we've double-counted the green alligator. It occurs in both the animal list and the green list. So, we need to subtract the probability of selecting the green alligator from our total probability, because it can occur only once as the result of a single trial. So, to find the probability of selecting an animal *or* a green toy, we would add the probability of selecting an animal (4/8) to the probability of selecting a green toy (2/8), and subtract the joint probability of the green alligator (1/8).

Thus, the overall probability of selecting an animal or a green toy is equal to 4/8 + 2/8 – 1/8 = 5/8, or 0.625.

additive probability the probability that any one of several events occurs as the result of a trial.

Your Turn 5.3

1. Kai and Sophia are expecting twins. What is the probability that both babies will be female (assuming each baby has a 0.50 chance of being female)?

2. You attend a magic show where the magician asks you to draw a card from a standard deck of playing cards (note, a deck of cards has 52 total cards). What would be the probability of drawing an ace or a diamond?

Probability and a Distribution of Sample Means

We saw in Chapter 2 that we could learn a lot about a distribution of scores by plotting those scores in a frequency distribution. By doing so, we could determine the shape of the distribution (such as whether it was symmetrical or skewed), determine the number of modes for the distribution, and identify the type of kurtosis for the distribution.

A key difference between a frequency distribution and the distribution of sample means is that a frequency distribution presents individuals' scores, while a distribution of sample means presents the means for a group of individuals. A second difference is that the y-axis for a frequency distribution presents the frequency of certain observations, while the y-axis for a distribution of sample means presents the probability of obtaining a particular sample's mean. In other words, a distribution of means is a type of **probability distribution,** which presents all the possible outcomes of an experiment and their associated likelihoods.

Earlier in the Statistics for Life section, we learned how we create a distribution of sample means. Now we're going to see what that distribution tells us about how frequently outcomes occur.

As you can see in **Figure 5.6,** when we draw a sample from the population, we have a high probability of drawing samples with

probability distribution
a probability distribution is a listing of all possible outcomes of an experiment and their associated probabilities.

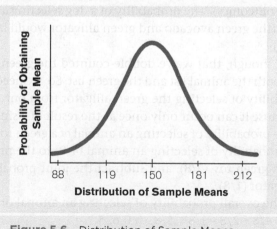

Figure 5.6 Distribution of Sample Means

means around 150, and a low probability of drawing samples that have means that are either much lower or much higher than 150 (i.e., near 88 or 212). For example, let's say we collect a random sample of dogs for our study. There is some chance that we will obtain a sample comprised mostly of border collies and poodles, which are among the smartest breeds of dogs. If that happens, our sample's mean may be higher than the mean for all dogs in the population. Of course, there is also a chance that we will obtain a sample comprised of less intelligent breeds (we'll leave it up to you to decide which those are), and so our sample's means will be lower than the population's mean. This idea that our sample's mean might be slightly higher or lower than the population's mean is called **sampling error** and reflects the idea that any time we draw a sample from a population, there is some probability that the sample's mean will not match the population's mean.

sampling error the difference between a sample statistic and the population, caused by analyzing a subset of the population.

The key question for us to evaluate is how much sampling error we will have when taking a sample from a population. How much do samples tend to vary from the population? Luckily, there is an answer to this question. Now that you know where distributions of means come from and what they can show us, you're ready for a deeper understanding of their mathematical properties.

Mathematical Properties of the Distribution of Sample Means To understand sampling distributions, we need to compare them to regular frequency distributions. Let's start by imagining that we were interested in determining the vocabulary size of dogs living on our street. After canvasing the houses on the street, we identify four dogs (i.e., the full population of dogs that live on this street) and run them through a Dog Vocabulary Test. **Figure 5.7** presents the number of items correctly identified by each dog.

Dog Name	Number of Items Correctly Identified
Macy	128
Patches	111
Utley	184
Finn	177
Mean = 150 **Standard Deviation = 31.18**	

Figure 5.7 Number of Items Correctly Identified by Four Dogs

For the sake of keeping the numbers manageable, let's consider this our population. Using what we learned in Chapter 3, the mean vocabulary size of the population of dogs living on our street is

$$M = (128 + 111 + 184 + 177)/4 = 150$$

and the standard deviation is

$$SD = \sqrt{\frac{(128-150)^2 + (111-150)^2 + (184-150)^2 + (177-150)^2}{4}}$$
$$= 31.18$$

Now, what happens if we were to draw samples from this population? How close would the means of these samples be to the actual population mean? Let's say that we decide to collect samples of two dogs out of the population of four dogs. We will draw every possible combination of two dogs, including the situation where we sample a dog, put it back into the population, and sample it again. This approach is called **sampling with replacement** because we are replacing each individual observation to the population after we sample it. **Figure 5.8** presents every possible sample with a sample size of two.

Notice that most of our samples' means (e.g., 152.50, 147.50) are pretty close to the population's mean (150), while just a few sample means are much lower (e.g., 111.00) or much higher (184.00) than the population mean. To learn more about this distribution of sample means, we need to plot all of the means from our samples to create the sampling distribution. By doing so, we can see just how much each sample differs from the population mean. In other words, we can find the mean and standard deviation of our sampling distribution.

The Mean of the Distribution of Means Take another look at Figure 5.8 and notice that when we calculate the mean of all of the possible sample means from the population, we get an overall mean of 150.00. This mean of the samples' means is equal to the population's mean of the four dogs. We noted this idea earlier in this chapter, but now we can see that it is true. No matter how large the population, whether it is a population of four dogs or 7.5 billion people, the sampling distribution's mean will always equal the population's mean.

At some level, this makes intuitive sense. A sampling distribution is just a collection of all possible samples. The sample means that are greater than the population's mean cancel out the sample means that are less than the population's mean, and as a result when we combine them all together, they equal the mean of the population. We can express this

sampling with replacement a sampling technique in which individuals included in a sample are replaced in the population such that they could be sampled again.

Sample	Scores for Sample	Mean of Sample
Macy, Macy	128, 128	128.00
Macy, Patches	128, 111	119.50
Macy, Utley	128, 184	156.00
Macy, Finn	128, 177	152.50
Patches, Macy	111, 128	119.50
Patches, Patches	111, 111	111.00
Patches, Utley	111, 184	147.50
Patches, Finn	111, 177	144.00
Utley, Macy	184, 128	156.00
Utley, Patches	184, 111	147.50
Utley, Utley	184, 184	184.00
Utley, Finn	184, 177	180.50
Finn, Macy	177, 128	152.50
Finn, Patches	177, 111	144.00
Finn, Utley	177, 184	180.50
Finn, Finn	177, 177	177.00
	Mean of all Samples (μ_M) = 150.00 **Standard Deviation of All Samples (SE) = 22.11**	

Figure 5.8 Number of Items Correctly Identified by a Sample of Two Dogs

idea symbolically by stating, $\mu_M = \mu$, where μ_M indicates the mean of all of the possible sample means, and μ represents the population mean.

The Standard Deviation of the Distribution of Means Look back at the population's standard deviation (in Figure 5.7) and the standard deviation of the distribution of means (in Figure 5.8). Unlike the means, which are equal for the population and the distribution of means, the standard deviations are not equal.

Recall that earlier in this chapter, we said that the distribution of means is taller and skinnier than the population distribution and gets narrower as the sample size increases. This is really important. It tells us that as our sample size increases, there is less variation in our sample means. In other words, the standard deviation of our distribution of means gets smaller as the sample size gets bigger. Indeed, the standard deviation of our distribution of means is the way that we can quantify our sampling error. It captures just how much difference we should observe between a sample and the population, on average. In fact, this idea is so important that we give the distribution of means' standard deviation its own name. It is called the standard error of the mean, or just **standard error (SE)**, and captures the amount of sampling error that we get when we take samples of a certain size.

To calculate the standard deviation of a distribution of means, aka standard error, we will take variance of the population, σ^2, divided by N, or σ^2 / N, which essentially reports the variance of the distribution of means. To get the standard deviation, we will take the square root of the variance. Thus, a formula for the standard error is $\sigma_M = \sqrt{\dfrac{\sigma^2}{N}}$, where σ_M is the symbol representing the sampling distribution's standard deviation. We can also express this using an alternative formula: $\sigma_M = \dfrac{\sigma}{\sqrt{N}}$.

These two equations are mathematically equivalent, but it is more common to use the second one because it's slightly faster to calculate.

Let's look at the formula for standard error a bit more closely. Notice that the standard deviation of the population is in the numerator. This tells us that the standard error will get larger when there is more variability in the population. We mentioned this idea earlier in the chapter, and now we see it play out mathematically. When there is a lot of variation in the population, it is more likely that we will get samples that are different from the population mean, so the distribution of means will have a larger standard deviation. Where there is little variation in the population, we are more likely to get samples that are close to the population mean, so the distribution of means will have a smaller standard deviation. Notice also that the sample size is in the denominator of our equation for standard error. This tells us that our distribution of means' standard deviation will get smaller when the sample size gets larger.

To see how this formula works in practice, let's return to the data for our population of dogs in Figure 5.7. We know from Figure 5.7 that the standard deviation of the population is 31.18. If we calculate the standard deviation of all of the samples of $N = 2$, listed in Figure 5.8, we get a value of 22.11. Now, knowing about how standard error works, we should be able to take the population standard deviation divided by the square root of the sample size and get the standard error. Let's see if it works:

$$\sigma_M = \frac{\sigma}{\sqrt{N}}$$

$$\sigma_M = \frac{31.18}{\sqrt{2}} = 22.11$$

Yep! So, this means that if we were to draw a sample of 2 dogs from the population, they would, on average, vary by 22.11 words from the true population mean. This is really useful information.

Why is it so useful? Well, remember that all research relies on samples, rather than populations. We must understand how close sample means are to the population mean in order to confidently use our sample means to make conclusions about the population's mean. The standard error allows us to quantify how close or far any particular sample is likely to be from the population mean. But we can get even more precise. Remember that a distribution of means is a probability distribution that looks like a bell curve. This implies that we are more likely to observe some sample means more than others.

But just how probable are some means compared to others? To answer this question, we need to know more about the distribution of means' overall shape. By knowing the shape of the sampling distribution, plus the mean and standard error, we will be able to make conclusions about the population mean, based on a sample. Once we can estimate the mean of the population, we can test all sorts of research hypotheses.

The Shape of the Distribution of Means and the Central Limit Theorem Now, we might imagine that the distribution of means could take on all different shapes (e.g., positively skewed, bimodal, etc.), but this is not the case. The distribution of means' shape is governed by the **Central Limit Theorem,** which states that only two things affect its shape: the population distribution's shape, and the sample size. In particular, if the population is normally distributed, the distribution of means will always be normally distributed. However, if the population is not normally distributed, the distribution of means will still approximate a normal curve so long as the sample size of samples that comprise the sampling distribution is greater than or equal to 30. This tells us that even if the population is skewed (e.g., there are lots of dogs that know only a few words, but some that know a ton of words), the sampling distribution will still be normally distributed so long as we have samples that have 30 or more dogs.

The Central Limit Theorem is incredibly important because we already know the mathematical properties of the normal curve. If our distribution of means takes the shape of a normal curve, then we automatically know that 68% of all samples will fall within + / − 1 standard deviation of the population mean, 95% of all samples will fall within + / − 2 standard deviations of the population mean, and 99% of all samples will fall within + / − 3 standard deviations of the population mean. In other words, if we were to collect a random sample of 30 dogs, we can be almost certain (99%) that our sample's mean will be within 3 standard errors of the true population mean. This is true for

Central Limit Theorem a statistical concept describing the shape of a distribution of sample means. As the sample size increases, the distribution of sample means more closely resembles a normal distribution, even if the original population is not normally distributed.

Want a refresher on characteristics of normal curves and the 68–95–99 approximation? SEE CHAPTER 4.

a normally shaped distribution of means because this is true for all normally shaped distributions.

So in the case of dog vocabularies, if we were to collect a random sample of dogs, we would know that 68% of the time, our sample mean would be within 1 standard error of the true population mean; 95% of the time, our sample mean would be within 2 standard errors; and 99% of the time, our sample mean would be within 3 standard errors.

The implications of this idea are bigger than we need to consider for now. We will base almost all of the statistical tests that we learn in the following chapters on this premise. But let's not get ahead of ourselves. The main thing to take away at this point is that the Central Limit Theorem ensures that the sampling distribution approximates a normal curve, even when the population doesn't, so long as we have a sufficiently large sample size.

Forming a Conclusion/Communicating the Result

In this section, we wanted to study animal cognition by measuring dogs' vocabulary size. We realized that it would be impossible to study every single dog in the population, and so we needed to rely on a sample. We considered the impact of working with means from samples rather than individual scores from the population. We also recognized that whenever we draw a sample, there is some probability that the sample will have a mean that is greater than or less than the mean of the population, which we called sampling error.

To understand how much sampling error will be present for any study, we learned about the concept of a sampling distribution. Specifically, we found that if we combine the results from lots of samples, the resulting sampling distribution will have the same mean as the population, and the distribution of means' standard deviation (σ_M) will be equal to the square root of the population variance divided by the sample size $\left(\sqrt{\dfrac{\sigma^2}{N}}\right)$, or to the population's standard deviation divided by the square root of the sample size $\left(\dfrac{\sigma}{\sqrt{N}}\right)$.

Moreover, the sampling distribution's shape (determined by the Central Limit Theorem) will resemble a normal curve, so long as our population was normally distributed or our sample size is at least 30 observations. Because we know that our sampling distribution is a normal curve, we know that most of our sample means will be close to the population mean because this is true for all normal distributions. So, if we collect a sample of dogs and measure their vocabulary size, then our sample's mean should be pretty close to the population of all dogs' mean.

Your Turn 5.4

1. A population of woodchucks can chuck 700 lbs of wood on average, with a standard deviation of 50 lbs. If you were to construct a sampling distribution for all possible samples, with *N* = 100, what would be the mean and sampling distribution's standard deviation?

2. Identify whether the following statements are true or false:

a. Sampling distributions always take on the same shape as the population distribution.

b. Sampling distributions are approximately normally distributed, so long as the sample size of each sample is sufficiently large (*N* > 30).

c. The standard deviation of a sampling distribution is equal to the standard deviation of the population.

d. The mean of a sampling distribution is always equal to the mean of the population.

Focus on Open Science: Computational Reproducibility

When researchers discover something using statistics, such as how many bucket list items a person has completed or the average size of a dog's vocabulary, other researchers may be interested in their findings. They may even want to conduct additional studies on the topic. To make that process easier, open science ensures that study materials are readily available for other researchers to use. For example, if we wanted to conduct a new study of dog vocabulary, it would speed up the scientific process if we had access to all of the study materials that other scholars used in their research.

It would also help us conduct our analyses if we had access to other scholars' data sets. If another scholar found that the average dog has a vocabulary of 1,000 words, we might want to look at their data and double-check to see if we get the same surprising results. This idea is called **computational reproducibility,** and it describes the ability for various researchers to perform analyses on a data set and obtain the same results.

Surprisingly, when different researchers analyze the same data set, they sometimes come to different conclusions about what the data show. Why is this the case? Well, think about it this way: Imagine that we gave two people the ingredients to make chocolate chip cookies, but we did not give them the recipe. Would they be able to make cookies? Probably. Would their cookies taste exactly the same? Probably not. The same is true for data analysis. If we were to give two scholars the same data set, but no instructions for how to code the variables or which analyses to perform, they might choose to focus on different variables, combine the variables in different ways, or perform different analyses, and as a result they might reach different conclusions overall. It's also

computational reproducibility describes the extent to which different researchers are able to reach the same statistical conclusions when analyzing the same data set.

important to realize that even if everyone uses the exact same recipe, subtle differences in technique, imprecise measurements, or errors (scientists are human after all) could produce different-tasting cookies.

Because computational reproducibility can be difficult to achieve, advocates for open science now advise researchers to provide additional instructions with their data set. Call this the "analysis recipe." These instructions detail each of the steps necessary for others to recreate the analyses that are reported in a published research study. How do we generate an analysis recipe? SPSS, like other statistical software packages, records the analyses that we perform in a **syntax file** (see **Figure 5.9**). A syntax file doesn't track the actual results of our analyses, just the list of analyses that we perform. This makes it really useful information when we, or other researchers, try to reproduce our analyses.

syntax file the file generated by statistical software programs that records the set of data analyses that a researcher performs, rather than the results of those analyses.

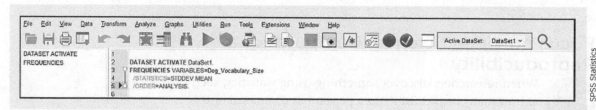

Figure 5.9 SPSS Syntax File

To have SPSS generate a syntax file, all we have to do is, instead of clicking OK, click the Paste button when performing any aspect of data analysis (see **Figure 5.10**).

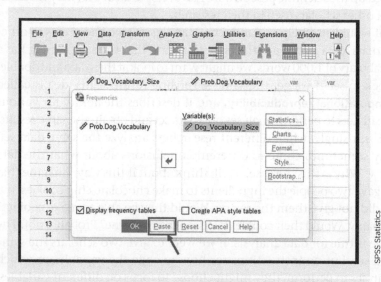

Figure 5.10 Generating Syntax File Using SPSS Paste Button

Become a Better Consumer of Statistics

Having a basic understanding of probability is extremely helpful in everyday life. We need to be able to accurately assess whether it's safer to drive in a car or fly in an airplane, determine whether it's safe to be out on the beach without sunscreen, and determine our level of risk when investing in the stock market.

When it comes to understanding probability, a particularly important idea to keep in mind is the **law of large numbers,** which states that the observed probability for a particular outcome matches its expected probability only over the long term. For example, when flipping a coin 10 times, we don't always see half of the outcomes be heads and the other half tails. Sometimes, we might get 7 heads and 3 tails. Sometimes, all 10 flips might be heads. With only 10 trials, we may see the observed probabilities of a random event diverge from the expected probabilities. However, if we were to flip a coin 1,000 or 10,000 times, we should see that approximately 50% of the outcomes will be heads and 50% of the outcomes will be tails. This is the law of large numbers in action.

Yet, most people fail to appreciate how they are expecting their small sample (a few coin flips) to produce results that would happen only in a much larger sample (a few thousand flips). That is, they misapply the law of large numbers and believe that the observed frequencies for a random event should match their expected frequencies no matter how large the sample size. This idea is sometimes called the **gambler's fallacy,** because gamblers often mistakenly decide to bet large amounts of money when they notice outcomes that diverge from their expected values. For example, if you were to flip a coin four times and each time the outcome was tails, you might think that the next flip is more likely to be heads. You might even be willing to bet money on it. But, this would be a bad idea. Each flip of a coin is an **independent event,** meaning that the result of one trial has no impact on the probability of a subsequent trial. So, even though it feels to us like the probability of the next flip has changed (to increase the odds of a heads coming up), it hasn't. Don't fall victim to the gambler's fallacy!

Statistics on the Job

We tend to associate probability with gambling, but in fact, many professions require employees to have a keen understanding of probability. Epidemiologists, physicians, meteorologists, economists, and (of course) psychologists use probability to understand the world and human behavior.

law of large numbers in random sequences, observed probabilities match expected frequencies only over a large number of trials.

gambler's fallacy the mistaken belief that random sequences will match their expected probabilities over the short term.

independent events two events are independent when the occurrence of one event does not impact the probability of the other.

Probability plays an especially important role in **actuarial science**, which is a field of science devoted to understanding risk in everyday life through the use of probabilities. Actuaries use probability and statistics to help set home, auto, and life insurance premiums (among other duties). To do their jobs, actuaries use probabilities to calculate the risks and benefits associated with a variety of demographic and behavioral variables. For example, an actuary would consider how installing smoke detectors in a house or living closer to a fire hydrant decreases the probability that the homeowner will file a claim for fire damage. Because the probability of filing a claim is lower, the cost of their insurance is lower. Similarly, an actuary may examine the impact of driving a sports car on car insurance costs. They may decide that increased driving speed or a thrill-seeking driver increases the likelihood of a claim, and consequently raises the cost of coverage. For each insurance policy, an actuary must determine the probability of various outcomes, the likelihood of a claim, and the resulting payouts that insurance companies will likely make, and make sure that the rates charged to customers cover their costs.

Because statistics and probability are such a central part of actuarial science, students training to become actuaries must complete advanced training in statistics. Indeed, before they can become certified actuaries, students must first pass Exam P, a three-hour exam that tests their knowledge of probability. Whether you become an actuary or not, we think that you can benefit from having a general knowledge of probability and statistics.

Review Questions

1. You are sitting at the dinner table discussing sampling techniques with your father. He is a forester who studies tree diseases.
   a. When he takes a sample of trees, he randomly selects which trees to evaluate, and he maintains that he uses _____.
   b. He wonders about the statistical and methodological implications of _____, which is the method you are more likely to use as a psychologist.
   c. What impact does your methodology as a psychologist have on the representativeness of your sample?
   d. How might your father's sample be more like the samples you use than he realizes?

2. The variable you are interested in varies a lot from person to person in your population, and you will need to use convenience sampling. How might you increase the representativeness of your sample? Why would this affect the representativeness of your sample?

3. A frequency distribution presents the _____ of a variable and how often they occur. A _____ presents the means for all possible _____ of a certain size from a _____ and the _____ of their occurrence.

4. Describe the following mathematical properties of the distribution of sample means:
   a. Mean
   b. Standard deviation
   c. Shape

5. According to the Central Limit Theorem, under what situations will the sampling distribution approximate a normal curve? Why is it important that the sampling distribution be normally distributed?

6. In a survey of 25 grade-one students, there are 16 students with siblings and 9 students who are only children. Also, 14 of the students have no pets, and 10 of the students with a sibling do not have a pet. If we randomly select a student from this group, then what is the probability of selecting a student with:
   a. A student with a pet?
   b. A student with no siblings?
   c. A student with a pet but no siblings?
   d. A student with a pet or a sibling?
   e. A student with a pet and then a student with no siblings?

7. A popular brand of chocolate chip cookies states that there are an average of 20 chocolate chips per cookie, with a standard deviation of 4 chocolate chips.
   a. If you were to construct a sampling distribution for all possible samples, with $N = 4$, what would the mean (μ_M) and standard error of the mean (σ_M) be for the sampling distribution?
   b. If the sample size was increased to $N = 16$, what would the μ_M and σ_M be for the sampling distribution?
   c. What impact does the sample size have on the μ_M and σ_M of a sampling distribution?

8. Which combination of values will result in the smallest standard error of the mean?
   a. $\mu = 42$, $\sigma = 15$, $N = 25$
   b. $\mu = 37$, $\sigma = 15$, $N = 36$
   c. $\mu = 42$, $\sigma = 7$, $N = 25$
   d. $\mu = 37$, $\sigma = 7$, $N = 36$
   e. Cannot be determined from the information given

 Key Concepts

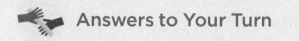

Answers to Your Turn

Your Turn 5.1

1. To know if you're going to like the new bacon caramel maple ice cream, you don't need to taste the entire population (i.e., the entire container). Rather, you taste a small sample based on the assumption that the mini-spoonful represents the rest of the container. In other words, however your sample tastes is what you should expect from a scoop (i.e., a larger sample), and from the population (i.e., the entire container) if you happened to taste it all.

2. If the person is scooping samples only from the container edges, it is less random, making the sample less likely to represent the whole container (i.e., there may be a less of a mixture of ingredients at the edges). Samples of flavors with more things mixed in (e.g., rocky road) will be less likely to represent the population because it will be hard to get an even mixture (too many or too few marshmallows) in the sample due to the variability of the ice cream's make-up. However, a flavor that is more uniform (e.g., vanilla) will have less variability and help the sample more accurately represent the population. Finally, the bigger the sample, the more likely it will be to represent the whole container. More ice cream means a greater chance of getting the full flavor experience, while a smaller taste may miss out on getting all of the ingredients.

3. Convenience sample

4. A frequency distribution presents the scores of a variable and the frequency of their occurrence. A distribution of sample means presents the means for all possible samples of a certain size from a population and the probability of their occurrence.

Your Turn 5.2

1. There are four kings in a deck of cards, so the probability of drawing a king is 4/52 or 1/13, which is 0.08 or 8%. There are 13 diamonds in a deck of cards, so the probability of drawing a diamond is 13/52 or 1/4, which is 0.25 or 25%. There are 12 face cards in a deck of cards, so the probability of drawing a face card is 12/52, which is 0.23 or 23%.

Your Turn 5.3

1. Because we are looking to calculate the probability of two outcomes happening successively (one baby being female and a second baby being female), we need to calculate the joint probability. Thus, we would multiply the probabilities for each outcome together: $0.50 \times 0.50 = 0.25$.

2. Because we are looking for one of several possible outcomes, we will calculate the additive probability. In this case, the probability of drawing an ace is 4/52, because there are four aces in the deck. The probability of drawing a diamond is 13/52, because there are 13 diamonds. To find the additive probability, we need to add these probabilities together and then subtract out their joint probability (because the ace of diamonds is counted twice). Thus, the additive probability equals $4/52 + 13/52 - 1/52 = 16/52$, or 0.31.

Your Turn 5.4

1. The mean of the sampling distribution would be 700, because the mean of the sampling distribution always equals the mean of the population. The sampling distribution's standard deviation, also called standard error, would equal the population's standard deviation, 50, divided by the square root of the sample size. In other words: $50 / \sqrt{100}$, or 5. So, the sampling distribution would have a mean of 700 and a standard error of 5.

2. (a) False. Sampling distributions do not necessarily resemble the population distribution. (b) True. According to the Central Limit Theorem, a sampling distribution will be approximately normally distributed when the sample size is large. (c) False. The sampling distribution's standard deviation, called standard error, is equal to the population's standard deviation divided by the square root of the sample size. (d) True. The sampling distribution's mean is always equal to the population's mean.

Answers to Review Questions

1. **a.** Random sampling
   b. Convenience sampling
   c. It may not be representative of the sample.
   d. His method may also be a convenience sample; not all trees in the population have an equal chance of being selected, as some are inaccessible without days or weeks of travel. Note that his sample will not be affected by volunteer bias.

2. You could increase the size of your sample. This would reduce the impact of extreme scores and make it less likely that all scores in the sample are extreme.

3. scores; distribution of sample means; samples; population; probability

4. **a.** The mean of the sampling distribution is equal to the population mean ($\mu_M = \mu$).
   b. The standard deviation of the distribution of sample means (standard error of the mean) is the population standard deviation divided by the square root of the sample size.
   c. The shape of the distribution is normal if the shape of the population is normal, or if the sample size is greater than or equal to 30.

5. The sampling distribution will approximate a normal curve if the population it comes from is normally distributed or the sample size is greater than or equal to 30. This is important because the mathematical properties of a normal curve are known.

6. **a.** $11/25 = 0.44$ or 44%
   b. $9/25 = 0.36$ or 36%
   c. $5/25 = 0.25$ or 25%
   d. $11/25 + 16/25 - 6/25 = 21/25 = 0.84$ or 84%
   d. $(11/25) \times (9/25) = 0.44 \times 0.36 = 0.1584$ or 15.84%

7. **a.** $\mu_M = 20$, $\sigma_M = 2$
   b. $\mu_M = 20$, $\sigma_M = 1$
   c. As the sample size increases, the μ_M does not change and the σ_M decreases.

8. d

Sharpen your statistics skills with real-life data! Check out OpenStatsLab.com, created by coauthor Kevin McIntyre, to practice running analyses for real published research studies.

6

Introduction to Hypothesis Testing

Can you tell how cool
someone is based on
their number of Instagram
followers?

Learning Outcomes

After reading this chapter, you should be able to:

- Explain the overall rationale and logic behind hypothesis testing.

- List the steps of hypothesis testing.

- Distinguish between research and null hypotheses.

- Create and label a comparison distribution.

- Find the critical values for any alpha level.

- Conduct a hypothesis test using the *p*-values approach.

- Explain the ethical implications of establishing hypotheses and critical values before obtaining results.

We all like to think we're better than average. Smarter, funnier, kinder, and just generally more awesome than others. But have you ever put any of it to the test?

Take, for example, your coolness. Quantifying coolness isn't terribly straightforward. First, you have to figure out what it means to be "cool." Don't worry, the research has you covered. A set of three studies, focused on empirically investigating the definition of coolness, found that "ratings of coolness are primarily about peer-relevant social desirability" (Dar-Nimrod et al., 2012, p. 182). In other words, how much your friends find you socially valued and want to hang out with you. Based on that definition, the best strategy for assessing coolness is probably tapping into a person's social media reach. For better or worse, social media connections paint a pretty good picture of "peer-relevant social desirability"—aka coolness.

Instagram is popular among young people. In fact, most users on Instagram are between 18 and 29 years of age, with college students comprising a third of all users (Lister, 2022). If Instagram is a go-to app among college peers, we can learn a lot about a person's coolness by examining their Instagram profile. Let's focus on one peer group in particular: our statistics classmates. How cool are they? We will find out in this edition of Statistics for Life.

Statistics for Life

At this point in the semester, you've gotten to know a lot of people in your stats class. From what you can tell, they're fairly tuned in to social media and seem to have a lot of followers. But what constitutes a lot, or at least enough to be cool? Clearly, 10 followers is extremely low and 100,000 is incredibly high, but it is less obvious what numbers between these two extremes might indicate. To really gain any insight into their coolness, we really need to know how their follower count compares to others. To do that, we need to figure out how many followers everyone else outside of statistics class has.

Can you tell how cool someone is based on their number of Instagram followers?

Where Do the Data Come From?

As we learned in Chapter 3, we don't really want to know every person's individual follower count because having thousands, or millions, of individual numbers would be impossible to manage. Instead, it is much more useful to find out the central tendency, or what the average Instagram user's followers numbers look like. But we're not going to lie—finding good data for Instagram users' average number of followers was surprisingly difficult.

After some digging, we uncovered a blog describing a study that sampled 21,239 Instagram users (Byrne, 2014). They concluded that the average number of followers was 843. However, and importantly for statistics-savvy people like us, the median number of followers was 194. We know that when the mean and median are so different, the distribution isn't normal, and that outliers are likely to blame for the skew. In fact, that was exactly the case, as one user had over a million followers and five had over a quarter million followers. A different data set from 2015 reported that a U.S. teenager's average number of followers was 150 (Statista.com, 2015), which aligns fairly closely with the median to our initial data set.

Because these data sets are several years old, however, we should be careful about relying on these numbers too much. This is especially true because we also found data showing that, since 2015, the number of Instagram users has increased by 250%, from 400 million in 2015 to 1.21 billion in 2021 (Statista.com, 2022). With Instagram's increasing popularity, it is likely that users average more followers than they did several years ago. Thus, for the purposes of the chapter's example, we will use fictional data that is a bit of a guesstimate based on what we were able to find, and say that the average Instagram user in the general population has 250 followers with a standard deviation of 50 ($\mu = 250$; $\sigma = 50$).

Hypothesis Testing: What We're Trying to Accomplish

Life is full of questions. Many of those questions are about the world around us (e.g., "When the sun is out, are people happier?"), many focus specifically on our own behavior (e.g., "What motivates you to vote?"), and of course, on other people's behavior (e.g., "Are your classmates cooler than most other people?"). With all these questions, we naturally take an educated guess about what we believe the correct answer might be. In other words, we form a hypothesis that makes a prediction, or guess about what will happen in the future regarding a particular question.

So let's form a hypothesis right now in relation to our current question: Are our stats classmates cooler than most other college students? Our hypothesis: Of course they are! And their number of Instagram followers just might show it. But how will we figure out if our hypothesis is correct? Through **hypothesis testing,** which is a procedure that helps us determine whether the evidence (a sample's results) is convincing enough to support a hypothesis that we formulate. In other words, our key question is whether our sample comes from the same population as our comparison, or from a different population.

Before describing the details of hypothesis testing, we want to give an analogy that should help us better understand the overall approach that we will take. One way to think about hypothesis testing is that it resembles a jury trial. As the decision-makers, jurors don't go into a trial blindly. Rather, they begin with a standard conclusion that nothing happened. Believing that the person on trial is innocent is the default starting point. It is then up to the prosecution to provide evidence "beyond a reasonable doubt" that would make jurors reject the default of innocence. If someone isn't innocent, they're guilty. Similarly, in hypothesis testing, we start with the assumption that nothing is happening, or that there is no difference between our sample and population. We change that assumption only if the weight of the evidence (provided by our sample data) is overwhelming and exceeds a predetermined standard.

Before continuing, it's worth a reminder here: It is extremely rare for some of these complex ideas to make complete sense the first time you read about them. These ideas were tough for us at first as students too! Like us, you'll probably have to review these concepts a few times. The key is to stick with it! We have kept that in mind while writing this chapter, so rather than throw ourselves immediately into full-fledged hypothesis testing, we're going to start off simple and build some repetition and review as we go.

hypothesis testing a sequence of steps that help us to determine whether the evidence (a sample's results) support the hypothesis for the population.

Hypothesis Testing Logic: Embrace the Double Negative Understanding hypothesis testing requires that we master double negatives, or those tricky types of statements with two negative aspects, that cancel each other out and end up positive. We don't not want to understand double negatives. Which is to say, we want to understand double negatives. Confusing, right? The key to unlocking the double negative is realizing that two negatives result in a positive. For example, if a teacher says "Avery wasn't absent," it is like saying Avery was there.

Or take another example. Imagine that you hear a noise outside that sounds like a bear. You ask your friend to investigate, and upon returning, your friend proclaims that, "there isn't nothing there." Would you go outside? No! Because if there isn't nothing, there must be something. (Possibly something very bear-like.)

Though this feels a bit convoluted (it is), hypothesis testing essentially works this way. Rather than see if some effect is there, we instead assume nothing is there (i.e., no effect) and try to disprove it (i.e., there isn't nothing there). If we can say there isn't nothing there, then we conclude there is an effect or that something is happening (like a bear snacking in the trash). It takes a bit of mental gymnastics, but if you don't get it at first, remember: Do not think that you will not get it.

Hypothesis Testing Logic: Real or Fake? The discussion of whether something happens, or if there is an effect, may make it sound like a simple yes-or-no proposition. Either that noise you heard outside is a bear, or it isn't. But as you'll recall from Chapter 5, when thinking statistically, we focus on probabilities rather than absolutes, continuums rather than either/or. Rather than deciding if some outcome will or won't happen, we instead focus on as many contributing factors as possible and arrive at a probabilistic conclusion. There was a noise, but it probably isn't a bear because you don't live in the woods, it's winter, and you live on a busy street. But you can't be 100% sure there isn't a bear because weird things can happen, so it isn't impossible that a bear could be out there. But based on all the evidence, you might feel 95% or 99% sure that the noise isn't real, and your yard is bear-free.

The same mental approach is true with hypothesis testing. We want to know if what we find is real, or if it is fake (i.e., happened by chance). This is a key piece of logic that is helpful well beyond statistics. It is important to be able to spot the fakes in our everyday lives, whether it's a fake diamond engagement ring, a knockoff purse, an imitation pair of sunglasses, or an insincere friend.

LumiNola/E+/Getty Images

If your friend gives you a compliment, how do you know they are sincere?

Again, in each case we can't be 100% certain if something isn't real, but we can establish criteria ahead of time to help us make our "real or fake" decision. If we wanted to decide "real or fake" on a pair of sunglasses, we could look at the labels, lenses, frames, and packaging. By doing so, we're creating a set of rules to follow that will help us to have more confidence in our conclusion. This is exactly like what we do in hypothesis testing.

Your Turn 6.1

1. Interpret the following double-negative statement: Upon seeing the results, the doctor declared that the results were not inconclusive.

2. Pay someone a compliment using a double negative.

3. When trying to determine whether something is real or fake, can you ever be 100% sure? Why?

Hypothesis Testing: How Does It Work?

At its heart, hypothesis testing helps us learn about populations by studying samples. Remember from Chapter 5 that we need to study samples because an entire population's data is hard to obtain and difficult to use. We then rely on what we learn from a sample to provide insights into the population. In the case of your statistics class's coolness, rather than collect data from everyone in the entire class (i.e., the population), we're going to keep it simple and rely on sampling one person. (To be clear, in research we would never actually use a sample with just one person. We're doing it here only because it simplifies the process your first time through.) We will randomly select one person and see how that person compares to the population in general. The process by which we make that comparison is hypothesis testing. It is a series of consistent steps that we follow throughout the book that provides us with a roadmap to get us to where we want to go: an answer we can believe in.

Step by Step: Hypothesis Testing We're going to be honest here. These steps may seem a bit tedious and unnecessarily drawn out at times. But, by going through these steps slowly, we promise that it will be easier to master. It's worthwhile because these ideas also serve as the foundation for lots of what we do later in the book.

Step 1: Population and Hypotheses Because we are interested in our statistics classes' coolness, our first population is everyone in our statistics class. The second population is who we want to compare our class to, or people in general. To make it perfectly clear, get in the habit of writing out populations as follows:

Population of Interest: Students in our statistics course.
Comparison Population: People in general.
Sample: A single student from the class.

Next, we must state our hypothesis regarding what we think is going to happen. Importantly, you'll notice that we are doing this early in the process (Step 1), and not formulating hypotheses only after seeing what the results are. More specifically, our **research hypothesis** should state how we believe the populations will compare to each other, or how the populations will differ. In this case, we believe that students in our statistics course are cooler than people in general. Or more formally, Population of Interest > Comparison Population, which we can convey symbolically as: $\mu_1 > \mu_2$.

Remember, hypothesis testing is built on double negatives. That is, we don't directly test that there is an effect. Instead, we test whether we can reject the idea that there is no effect. To do that, we need a hypothesis that essentially states there is nothing there or no effect. The **null hypothesis** is a declaration that counters the research hypothesis by stating there is no effect or no difference, and that the populations are the same. Or more formally, Population of Interest ≤ Comparison Population, which we can convey symbolically as: $\mu_1 \leq \mu_2$. Again, to make it perfectly clear, let's write out our hypotheses as follows:

Research Hypothesis (H_1): Students in our statistics course are cooler than people in general ($\mu_1 > \mu_2$).
Null Hypothesis (H_0): Students in our statistics course are equally cool (or less cool) than people in general ($\mu_1 \leq \mu_2$).

Step 2: Build Comparison Distribution The null hypothesis is our benchmark. To see if the null hypothesis is correct, we need to

---

research hypothesis (H_1) states how we believe the populations will compare to each other or how the populations will differ.

null hypothesis (H_0) a declaration that counters the research hypothesis by stating there is no effect or difference, and that the populations are the same.

establish what that looks like. That is, if everything is status quo and there is really no difference between the populations, what would the characteristics of that distribution be? In other words, the **comparison distribution** is a distribution we compare our sample to that depicts the population's characteristics if the null hypothesis is true.

Importantly, the sample size depicted in our comparison distribution should always match the size of our actual sample. That is, because our sample is one person from the class, the comparison distribution is comprised of single scores. The comparison distribution shows what all of the scores in the population would look like if we randomly selected one person at a time, noted their number of Instagram followers, and plotted it in a histogram. If we repeated that over and over, a normal curve would emerge.

We build the comparison distribution using the information available to us. We'll start with a basic normal distribution with Z-scores labeled, as shown in **Figure 6.1**.

comparison distribution
a distribution we use to compare a sample to that depicting the population's characteristics if the null hypothesis is true.

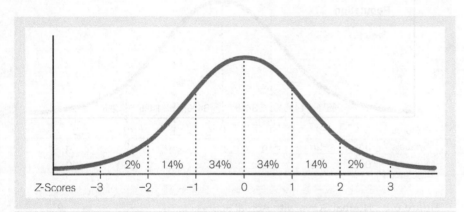

Figure 6.1 Normal Curve with Z-Scores and Percentages Under the Curve

As a visual reminder, we'll add in the symbols for population mean and standard deviation, as shown in **Figure 6.2**. We won't do this each time, but the first time through it helps emphasize what we're doing.

Next, we'll add in actual scores based on the population's mean (μ_2) and standard deviations (σ_2). Note that we're using a subscript "2" to indicate that it is a comparison population. The procedure for adding in actual scores is exactly how we created a number line in Chapter 4 (see **Figure 6.3**).

Step 3: Establish Critical Value Cutoff We want to have the fairest and most ethical test possible by establishing ahead of time the type of evidence we need to feel confident in our results. That is, we want to hold ourselves to a pre-established standard or threshold

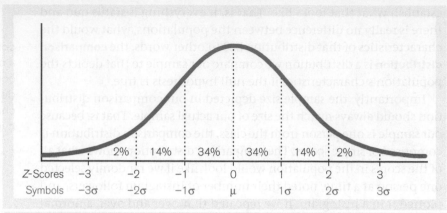

Figure 6.2 Normal Curve with Population Mean and Standard Deviation Symbols

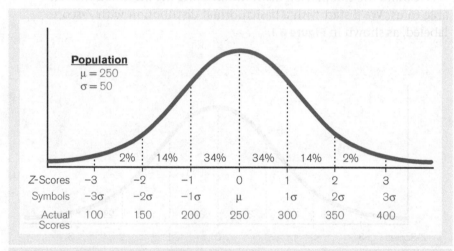

Figure 6.3 Normal Curve with Actual Scores

that allows us to be confident that what we found is real. Contrast this with an unethical and unscientific approach where you decide what counts as "real" only after you know the results. That's bad science that leads to faulty conclusions.

If we want to see if someone is really cool, the target value we're aiming for should be high. Think of it this way: When you're taking a test, you don't want to simply pass with a 60%. You want to pass with an A, and in the most ideal world, you want a really solid A, like a 95% or a 98%. With those grades, it puts you in the top 5% or top 2% of the class. Those types of grades make it super clear that you truly mastered the material—that it's not just random luck.

The same way of thinking guides our choice of a **critical value,** or the cutoff point on the comparison distribution at which we can reject the

critical value the cutoff point on the comparison distribution at which we are able to reject the null hypothesis.

null hypothesis. Because of this process, this type of hypothesis testing is often called the "critical values approach." When establishing our cutoff, we want a number that leaves very little possibility that the result could have happened by luck or chance. We don't want to be "kind of sure" that our statistics class is cool, we want to know for sure.

The best way to do that is to see whether our class falls within the top 2% of the comparison distribution. Identifying where the top 2% falls sound complicated, but we can quickly look back to Figure 6.1. Because we plotted out our comparison distribution so thoroughly in Step 2, we see that the top 2% equates to a Z-score of +2.00. Now that we've established our critical value, we'll add that to our comparison distribution (see **Figure 6.4**).

Want to review ↗
Z-scores and the empirical rule? SEE CHAPTER 4.

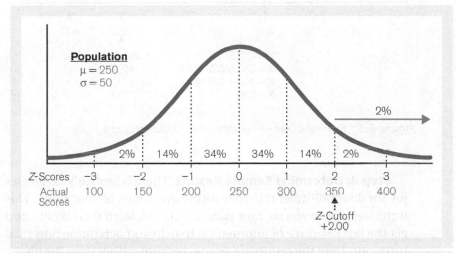

Figure 6.4　Normal Curve with Critical Value Cutoff

It's also helpful to see what the cutoff would be in terms of the actual score (i.e., the actual number of Instagram followers). Again, because we did such a great job in Step 2, we can see that a Z-score of +2.00 equates to an actual score of 350 Instagram followers.

We intentionally kept it simple this first time, but it won't always work out this neatly, so let's look at the underlying math. You'll recall from Chapter 4 that the formula for finding an actual score when you know the Z-score, standard deviation, and mean is:

$$X = (Z)(SD) + M$$
$$X = (2.00)(50) + 250$$
$$X = (100) + 250$$
$$X = 350$$

Check yourself, this should be exactly what we can see on the comparison distribution we created (see **Figure 6.5**).

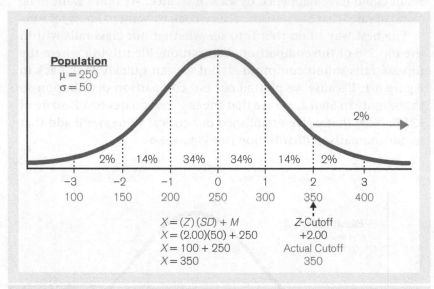

Figure 6.5   Normal Curve with Calculation of Cutoff Score

Step 4: Determine Sample Results   There is probably no greater joy (or disappointment) than learning the results of your study. This is the step where you see how your sample did, learn their results, and get the last key piece of information to help you determine how it all turns out. Here the results are simple because, rather than running a full study, we're interested only in our sample's (one person's) number of Instagram followers. When we randomly select one classmate, that person had 433 followers ($X = 433$).

Because we are thinking in terms of percentages and wanting to get into the top 2% in order to conclude that our class is cooler, we need to convert the sample's number of followers to a Z-score. Again, as you'll recall from Chapter 4, there is a formula that helps us do that: $Z = \dfrac{X - M}{SD}$. Next, we plug in the corresponding values: $Z = \dfrac{433 - 250}{50}$, do a little math: $Z = \dfrac{183}{50}$, and with just a bit more math, we have our result: $Z = 3.66$. This number is called our **test statistic,** because we will use this number to make a decision about whether to reject or fail to reject the null hypothesis. Next, we should show where this falls on the comparison distribution (see **Figure 6.6**).

test statistic the computed statistic used to evaluate the null hypothesis.

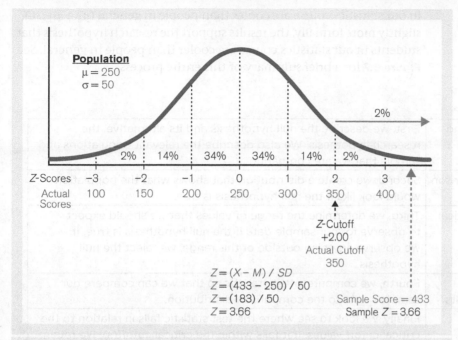

Figure 6.6 Sample Results on the Comparison Distribution

Within the figure:

Population
$\mu = 250$
$\sigma = 50$

2%

2%   14%   34%   34%   14%   2%

Z-Scores −3   −2   −1   0   1   2   3
Actual   100 150 200 250 300 350 400
Scores

Z-Cutoff
+2.00
Actual Cutoff
350

$Z = (X - M) / SD$
$Z = (433 - 250) / 50$
$Z = (183) / 50$
$Z = 3.66$

Sample Score = 433
Sample $Z = 3.66$

Step 5: Decide and Interpret The moment of truth. At this point we have all of the pieces in place. Now we simply need to make sense of the results and interpret what they do (and don't) tell us. Our goal? Reject or fail to reject the null hypothesis. If our result from Step 4 exceeds the critical value's cutoff point from Step 3, we reject the null. If the results in Step 4 fall short of Step 3's cutoff, we fail to reject the null. There are several ways for us to make the exact same decision.

First, we know that our sample score of 433 is greater than (>) the critical value actual score of 350. Similarly, we know that our sample Z-score of 3.66 is greater than (>) the critical value Z-score of 2.00. In other words, Sample > Critical Value, so we made the cutoff. We also know we exceeded the critical value because our sample score falls to the right of the cutoff point. When this happens, we say that the score is in the **critical region,** or the part of the comparison distribution where a score must fall in order to reject the null hypothesis.

Decision time: Because our sample's results (Step 4) exceed the critical value (Step 3), we are able to reject the null hypothesis (H_0) that students in our statistics course are equally cool (or less cool) than people in general ($\mu_1 \leq \mu_2$). If we are able to reject the null that says our class isn't equally as cool as everyone else, we can now say that we found support for the research hypothesis (H_1) that students

For a review of how to convert a sample score to a Z-score, see Chapter 4.

critical region the part of the comparison distribution where a score must fall in order to reject the null hypothesis.

in our statistics course are cooler than people in general ($\mu_1 > \mu_2$). Or, slightly more formally, the results support the research hypothesis that students in our statistics course are cooler than people in general. See **Figure 6.7** for a brief summary of this entire process.

Step 1	Population and Hypotheses	First, we describe the null hypothesis and its alternative, the research hypothesis. We also describe the relevant populations and sample that we are comparing.
Step 2	Build Comparison Distribution	Second, we create a distribution that shows what the population would look like if the null hypothesis is true.
Step 3	Establish Critical Value Cutoff	Third, we determine the range of values that we should expect to observe for our sample data if the null hypothesis is true. If we observe anything outside of this range, we reject the null hypothesis.
Step 4	Determine Sample Results	Fourth, we compute a test statistic so that we can compare our sample's data to the comparison distribution.
Step 5	Decide and Interpret	Finally, we look to see where the test statistic falls in relation to the critical cutoff values. If it falls within the critical cutoff(s), we retain the null hypothesis; if the test statistic falls outside of the critical cutoffs, we reject the null hypothesis. We then interpret our results in the context of our variables.

Figure 6.7 Hypothesis Testing Step by Step Summary

Communicating the Result

Although the basis of hypothesis testing revolves around testing the null hypothesis, when communicating the result, we don't talk about it again. Much like published research articles don't explicitly state that they got informed consent or conducted a debriefing, the null hypothesis receives no mention because it is automatically assumed. Instead, researchers focus exclusively on the research hypothesis and whether the data support it, even though anyone who knows statistics realizes that they actually tested the null. (Yeah, it seems almost unfair to the poor null given that it plays such a critical role in formulating a valid hypothesis, but such is life in the cutthroat world of statistics!)

Forming a Conclusion

Our hypothesis testing steps reveal that our statistics class is pretty cool, specifically cooler than people in general. But is this absolutely definitive? We did everything exactly right, we didn't make any mistakes, and the data allowed us to reject the null. Yet, it is important to realize that those numbers only help us answer our question as we originally conceived it: Is our stats class cooler than the general population when we define coolness as number of Instagram followers? To that question, we can now definitively answer yes! But we have to be careful not to generalize beyond the parameters we set in our research design when we communicate the results. Research design, statistics, and communication of results are intertwined.

For that reason, we have to be careful to not go beyond what our data can actually tell us. If we had decided to define coolness by TikTok followers, Twitter followers, or number of Snapchat streaks, our results (and conclusion) could have been different. Remember, although numbers are objective, interpretation of what those numbers tell us can be subject to bias or misinterpretation.

Your Turn 6.2

1. a. What is the ultimate goal of hypothesis testing?

   b. What are you trying to rule out?

2. a. Can you accept the null?

   b. How about the research hypothesis?

It's hard not to love dogs. But dogs come in a variety of shapes and sizes which can make it difficult to make broad generalizations. For example, are all dogs cute, or are some cuter than others? You think that Labrador retrievers are the cutest type of dog and want to test it with your own Lab. Answer questions 3 and 4.

3. For the research hypothesis "My Labrador retriever is cuter than dogs in general," what would the populations and sample be?

4. My Labrador retriever is cuter than dogs in general. What would the null hypothesis be?

5. Assume that you found a research paper showing that on a 10-point cuteness scale, the average dog is a 7 with a standard deviation of 1 ($\mu = 7; \sigma = 1$). What would the comparison distribution look like if the null hypothesis is true? Follow the procedure outlined in Step 2 of the Hypothesis Test procedure to construct the comparison distribution.

6. a. If you wanted your critical value to be at least 3 standard deviations above the mean, what would your sample's Z-score have to be, at minimum, to reject the null?

   b. What if you wanted the critical value cutoff to be two standard deviations below the mean?

7. I have my chocolate Labrador retriever Finn rated for cuteness, and he scores a 9.75 out of 10. Assume that the cutoff was the top 2%, what is the proper conclusion? Be sure to include a fully labeled diagram depicting the comparison distribution, cutoff, and where the sample's score falls.

Statistics for Research

Fun fact: You're a little bit older now than you were when you first started reading this sentence. Funner fact: You're always your oldest self. (Or, in double negative terms: You're never not your oldest self.)

Of course, these fractional advances in age aren't even a blip on our radar, but, over time, our bodies and brains can yield to the possibility of decline. Fortunately, researchers examine different psychological and physiological interventions designed to keep our bodies and our minds sharp. One area of research that shows promise is the impact of exercise and physical activity on reducing cognitive declines among older adults. For example, research reveals that both aerobic exercise (e.g., Miyazaki et al., 2022) and resistance training (e.g., Landrigan et al., 2020) can slow cognitive decline in older adults.

But what about yoga? Yoga is becoming increasingly popular, with surveys conducted by the U.S. Centers for Disease Control and Prevention indicating that approximately 14% of the population practices yoga in some form (Centers for Disease Control and Prevention, 2018), and some practitioners claim that yoga helps improve both the body and the mind (Birdee et al., 2008). So, as researchers, we might wonder whether yoga affects cognitive functioning among seniors. How could we test this important research question?

One option would be to recruit a sample of older adult participants, teach them yoga, and then determine whether their cognitive functioning differs from a sample of different participants who do not learn yoga. A second option could measure the cognitive functioning of a group of older adult participants, teach them yoga, and then measure this same group of participants again after they have been practicing yoga for a while. Although both of these approaches would be feasible, they would take some time to complete (we would need to train people how to practice yoga and then allow them a long enough period of practicing such that they might start to show differences in cognitive functioning from a control group of people who do not practice yoga).

A third possible research design is to recruit a group of senior yoga practitioners and determine whether their cognitive functioning differs from the population average. Although this approach has its own limitations (e.g., participants are not randomly assigned to condition), we could gather our data quickly and provide an initial test of our research question, before we invest the time needed to conduct a more rigorous study. Importantly, each different research design would require a different statistical technique, so we'll want to be sure to use the test that matches how we set up our study.

Here in the Statistics for Research section, we're going to explore what hypothesis testing looks like using a research-based example. Along the way, we'll dive deeper into the idea of alpha significance levels, and learn a slightly different approach to hypothesis testing known as the "p-value approach."

Does yoga improve cognitive performance? Hypothesis testing allows us to answer research questions such as this one.

Ridofranz/iStock/Getty Images

Where Do the Data Come From?

To measure whether yoga affects cognitive functioning, we need some benchmarks for what constitutes normal cognitive functioning at different ages. Luckily, other researchers have already completed much of the work for us, creating neuropsychological tests designed to measure various cognitive functions (e.g., memory, language, attention, executive functioning; Franzen et al., 2020). These researchers have also established performance standards on these tests that characterize normal and impaired functioning.

One such test is the Boston Naming Test, which presents participants with 60 pictures of objects that are either common words (e.g., pencil) or rarer words (e.g., escalator). Participants get 20 seconds to identify the object depicted in the picture (Spreen & Strauss, 1991). According to previous research, the established average performance on the Boston Naming test for someone 70–74 years old is 54.50 items correct ($SD = 5.10$), with scores below 44 suggesting cognitive impairment (Van Gorp et al., 1986). So, one way to answer our question would be to go to various yoga studios around town and recruit a sample of 100 senior yoga practitioners into our study. With each participant, we could administer the Boston Naming Test. We could then compare the mean of this group to our estimate for the population's mean to test whether yoga changes performance on a measure of cognitive performance.

Hypothesis Testing: What We're Trying to Accomplish

Earlier in this chapter, we said that we wanted to ease into our exploration of hypothesis testing by examining a single person's Instagram account. We're going to take the same approach here. We want to be clear that this is not the approach we will take in actual research. But just as we need training wheels before we learn to ride a bike, we want to take a simple approach before we make things more complicated. We'll add in that complexity in Chapter 7.

With this in mind, imagine that we collect data from lots of people, but randomly select one senior yoga practitioner to be our sample who will represent everyone else in the senior yoga practitioner population. We find that our randomly selected participant scores a 58.20 on the Boston Naming Test (recall that the average score for people in this age group is 54.50). And 58.20 is greater than 54.50. So does this tell us that performing yoga changes cognitive functioning among older adults? Not necessarily.

Although the score for our yoga practitioner is higher than the national average for this age group, our participant's score might be greater than the population mean due to sampling error (i.e., the person we picked just happened to be better at the test). As we saw in Chapter 5, every time we draw a sample from the population, the sample's mean might be greater or less than the actual population's mean based simply on whom we recruited into the study. The point of hypothesis testing is to determine whether the difference between our participant and the population mean is likely due to sampling error or a true effect of yoga.

Another way of saying this is: If yoga has no effect on cognitive functioning, then our sample yoga practitioner essentially comes from the same population as everyone else (i.e., everyone is the same). Therefore, we should expect to see the same variability that exists in the population. If, however, yoga has an effect, we should see evidence that yoga practitioners differ from the general population and essentially comprise an entirely different population.

This is the core question that hypothesis testing answers: Is our sample from the same, or a different, population?

Hypothesis Testing: Establishing the Significance Level

Hypothesis testing answers this question by establishing the probability of our sample if it comes from the population as described in the null hypothesis. Because of sampling error, a range of values will be possible. If the sample mean that we observe falls in that range of typical sampling error values, we will conclude that yoga likely has no effect. However, if our observed sample falls outside of this expected range of values, then we have reason to believe our sample does not come from the same population. In other words, yoga has an effect.

Earlier in this chapter we said that we can choose "critical values" that represent the cutoff points in our comparison distribution that reveal when our data is so unlikely, given the null hypothesis being true, that we should reject the null hypothesis. These critical values help us make our decision about whether the sample is unique from the comparison population. If we fail to reject the null hypothesis, we conclude that our sample is from the same population as our comparison population. If we reject the null, we conclude that our sample is from a different population.

We convey our choice of exactly where we set these critical values with our **alpha level** (also called our *significance level;* the symbol for alpha is α). This specifies just how different the sample mean needs to be from the comparison population mean in order for us to reject the null hypothesis, and to state that the two groups are different from each other. If our observed data fall outside our significance level's critical values, we reject the null hypothesis and can state that our sample mean is "significantly different" from the population mean.

Common or conventional alpha levels are .05 and .01, and reflect the probabilities we consider unlikely to occur if the null hypothesis is true. Note that we can also multiply our alpha levels by 100 to think about these values as percentages (which might be an easier way to think about it). A .05 alpha thus tells us that we would need to observe data that should occur only 5% of the time or less for us to reject the null hypothesis. A .01 alpha, similarly, tells us that we would need to observe data that should occur only 1% of the time or less for us to reject the null hypothesis.

Dividing Our Alpha In our study, we are testing whether performing yoga has an effect on cognitive functioning among older adults. Notice that there are two ways that yoga could affect cognitive functioning: It could be that yoga helps the mind and body and therefore leads to an increase in cognitive functioning. However, it could also be that performing yoga, instead of spending time on more cognitive tasks like reading or doing crossword puzzles, leads to a *decrease* in cognitive functioning. If we leave the direction of the effect open, as we have here, we'll call our test "two-tailed" because we will have two critical regions where we might detect significant effect. If we specify the direction of the effect (e.g., yoga will improve cognitive

alpha (α) level (also called the *significance level*) establishes the value of *p* that, when observed, determines when the null hypothesis should be rejected.

performance), we call our test "one-tailed," because there is only one critical region. We'll learn more about one-tailed and two-tailed tests in Chapter 7.

Because our study of yoga is two-tailed, we will make an adjustment to our alpha level, which indicates how different our sample needs to be from the population for us to reject the null hypothesis. We'll start by setting our overall alpha to be .05 (or 5%), which is the level that most researchers use. Because we acknowledge that yoga may increase or decrease abilities, we need to adjust our alpha accordingly. That is, rather than set our alpha to be one number, reflecting one possible significant outcome, we will split our alpha into two equal parts, reflecting the two possible ways that we could find significant results. We split the alpha, rather than double it, because we still want to set a high standard or threshold for our sample's mean to surpass in order to rule out that yoga has no effect.

Let's see how we would do this. An overall alpha of 0.05 tells us that we would need to observe results that should occur less than 5% of the time if the null hypothesis is true. Next, we need to split our alpha in half, expressed symbolically as $\frac{\alpha}{2}$, because we have two possible significant outcomes (i.e., yoga helping vs. yoga hurting). In this case, because we set our overall alpha to be 0.05, we would divvy the .05 up into two parts, each one set at .025 $\left(\text{because } \frac{0.05}{2} = 0.025 \right)$. So, for our study results to be significant, we will need to find a sample mean that occurs less than 2.5% of the time, if the null is true.

Finding the Critical Values for Any Alpha Level Once we have established our alpha levels, we need to get our critical values. To do this, we will use our Z-table (Appendix C) to find the two Z-scores that correspond to our alpha when divided in half. Thus, we need to find the Z-scores that correspond to a probability of .025 to the left of our first Z-score and .025 to the right of our second Z-score. Remember that our Z-table gives us only the probability to the left of any particular Z-score, so to find the probability to the right of a Z-score, we need to take one minus the probability, in this case 1 – .025, or .975.

Let's use the Z-table to find the critical values associated with the probabilities of .025 and .975.

To find the first critical value, we look in the body of the table for the value of .025. As shown in **Figure 6.8**, the probability of .025 corresponds to a Z-score of −1.96. We next need to find the critical value associated with the probability of .975.

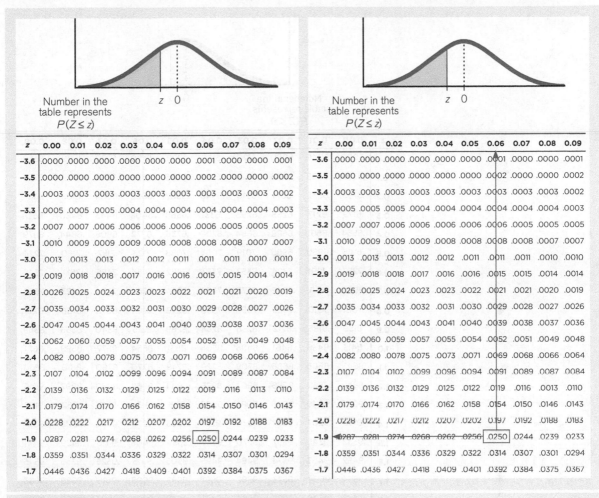

Figure 6.8 Using the Z-Table to Find Critical Values

As shown in **Figure 6.9,** the probability of .975 corresponds to a Z-score of +1.96. Notice that these two critical values are the same in magnitude, but different in sign. This occurs because the normal curve is symmetric. In practice, once you identify one cutoff, you know that the other one is the same magnitude.

Luckily, because researchers typically use alphas of .05 and .01, we can simply commit their corresponding Z-scores to memory instead of looking them up each time. The Z-scores that correspond to an alpha of .05 (.025 when divided in half) are +/−1.96 and the Z-scores that correspond to an alpha of .01 (.005 when divided in half) are +/−2.58.

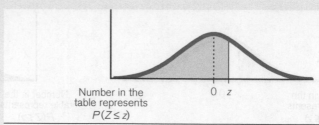

Number in the
table represents
$P(Z \leq z)$

z	0.00	0.01	0.02	0.03	0.04	0.05	0.06	0.07	0.08	0.09
0.0	.5000	.5040	.5080	.5120	.5160	.5199	.5239	.5279	.5319	.5359
0.1	.5398	.5438	.5478	.5517	.5557	.5596	.5636	.5675	.5714	.5753
0.2	.5793	.5832	.5871	.5910	.5948	.5987	.6026	.6064	.6103	.6141
0.3	.6179	.6217	.6255	.6293	.6331	.6368	.6406	.6443	.6480	.6517
0.4	.6554	.6591	.6628	.6664	.6700	.6736	.6772	.6808	.6844	.6879
0.5	.6915	.6950	.6985	.7019	.7054	.7088	.7123	.7157	.7190	.7224
0.6	.7257	.7291	.7324	.7357	.7383	.7422	.7454	.7486	.7517	.7549
0.7	.7580	.7611	.7642	.7673	.7704	.7734	.7764	.7794	.7823	.7852
0.8	.7881	.7910	.7939	.7967	.7995	.8023	.8051	.8078	.8106	.8133
0.9	.8159	.8186	.8212	.8238	.8264	.8289	.8315	.8340	.8365	.8389
1.0	.8413	.8438	.8461	.8485	.8508	.8531	.8554	.8577	.8599	.8621
1.1	.8643	.8665	.8686	.8708	.8729	.8749	.8770	.8790	.8810	.8830
1.2	.8849	.8869	.8888	.8907	.8925	.8944	.8962	.8980	.8997	.9015
1.3	.9032	.9049	.9066	.9082	.9099	.9115	.9131	.9147	.9162	.9177
1.4	.9192	.9207	.9222	.9236	.9251	.9265	.9279	.9292	.9306	.9319
1.5	.9332	.9345	.9357	.9370	.9382	.9394	.9406	.9418	.9429	.9441
1.6	.9452	.9463	.9474	.9484	.9495	.9505	.9515	.9525	.9535	.9545
1.7	.9554	9564	.9573	.9582	.9591	.9599	.9608	.9616	.9625	.9633
1.8	.9641	.9649	.9656	.9664	.9671	.9678	.9686	.9693	.9699	.9706
1.9	.9713	.9719	.9726	.9732	.9738	.9744	.9750	.9756	.9761	.9767
2.0	.9772	.9778	.9783	.9788	.9793	.9798	.9803	.9808	.9812	.9817

Figure 6.9 Using the Z-Table to Find Critical Values

Your Turn 6.3

1. What would be the critical values if we set our alpha as .001?

Hypothesis Testing: Determining Significance Using the *p*-Value Approach

The hypothesis testing approach we used in Statistics for Life was the "critical values approach" because our significance level establishes critical values or thresholds for how improbable our observed data need to be in order to reject the null hypothesis. In our earlier Instagram example, our test statistic exceeded the critical value, which suggested that our data was very improbable if the null hypothesis was true. Consequently, we rejected the null hypothesis.

For our investigation into the efficacy of yoga, we will use a second approach to hypothesis testing, called the **p-value approach,** in which we will find the exact probability of our test statistic, called the **p-value,** assuming our null hypothesis is true. Once we know the *p*-value, we can compare it directly to our alpha. If our *p*-value is less than alpha, we will reject the null hypothesis. If the *p*-value is greater than alpha, we will fail to reject the null hypothesis.

In future chapters, we will use both of the critical values and *p*-value approaches. Typically, we will use the critical values approach when conducting a hypothesis test by hand (that is, when hand calculating the test statistics), and we will use the *p*-value approach when conducting a hypothesis test using a computer. So, let's explore the *p*-value approach in greater detail.

p-value approach approach to hypothesis testing that calculates the exact probability of the test statistic and compares that to alpha.

p-value probability of obtaining sample data (e.g., sample mean) if the null hypothesis is true.

Step by Step: Hypothesis Testing Using *p*-Values Most of the steps using the *p*-value approach are the same as when using the critical values approach that we learned earlier in this chapter. The main difference comes in Steps 3 and 5. Rather than finding a critical region, and examining whether our test statistic falls within it, we will set our target significance level and then determine the exact probability of the *Z*-score associated with our sample results.

Step 1: Population and Hypotheses The first thing we always do in a hypothesis test is establish our population and hypotheses. In this case, our population of interest is senior yoga practitioners. The comparison population is the general population of people aged 70–74 years, because we know the average score on the Boston Naming Test for this group of older adults. As we did in the first half of this chapter, we're going to start simply by having a sample of one older adult yoga practitioner. We'll cover how to run this analysis with a larger sample in the next chapter (Chapter 7).

Population of Interest: Older adult yoga practitioners.
Comparison Population: Older adults aged 70–74.
Sample: One older adult yoga practitioner.

Having established our population of interest and our comparison population, we need to specify our hypothesis for how these two groups will differ. First, we need to establish the null hypothesis. Remember, the null hypothesis always states that there is no effect or no difference, and that the population of interest is the same as the comparison population. Our null hypothesis for this type of test is always the same; in this case it would be that the senior yoga practitioners have the same mean on the Boston Naming Test as the general population. Symbolically, we can state this null hypothesis as $\mu_1 = \mu_2$, where μ_1 is the mean for yoga practitioners and μ_2 is the mean for the population of older adults in general. Next, we establish our research hypothesis: We predict that older adults who practice yoga will perform differently on the Boston Naming Test than seniors in general. Expressed symbolically, we would write the research hypothesis as $\mu_1 \neq \mu_2$. As mentioned earlier, this is a two-tailed test.

Step 2: Build Comparison Distribution What would our sampling distribution look like if the null hypothesis is true? We can sketch our sampling distribution in the shape of a standard normal curve, with Z-scores indicating the number of standard deviations above or below the mean (see **Figure 6.10**).

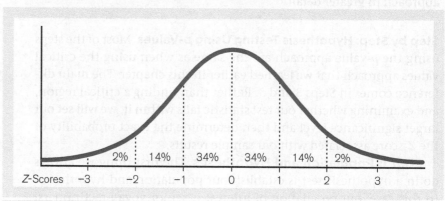

Figure 6.10 Normal Curve with Z-Scores and Percentages Under the Curve

Next, we'll add in the actual scores based on the population's mean (μ_2) and standard deviations (σ_2). Recall that the average performance on the Boston Naming Test for someone 70–74 years old is 54.50 items correct ($SD = 5.10$; Van Gorp et al., 1986), so we can add this information to our comparison distribution. We can also add the score for our sample participant (see **Figure 6.11**).

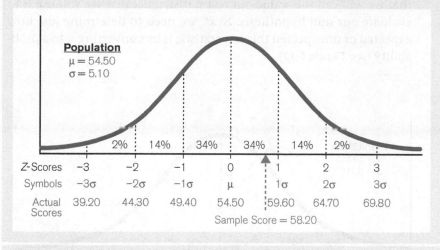

Population
μ = 54.50
σ = 5.10

	2%	14%	34%	34%	14%	2%	

Z-Scores	−3	−2	−1	0	1	2	3
Symbols	−3σ	−2σ	−1σ	μ	1σ	2σ	3σ
Actual Scores	39.20	44.30	49.40	54.50	59.60	64.70	69.80

Sample Score = 58.20

Figure 6.11   Normal Curve with Symbols and Actual Scores

Step 3: Set the Significance Level (α) Using the critical values approach, we next found two cutoff points that were the critical values of Z that we needed to observe in order to reject the null hypothesis. Using the p-value approach, we set a significance level, alpha. Alpha represents the value that the probability of our test statistic (our p-value) must be less than in order for us to reject the null hypothesis. As we noted earlier, by convention most researchers set alpha to be either .05 or .01. However, because our research hypothesis is that yoga practitioners will perform differently than the general population of older adults on the Boston Naming Test, we need to divide our alpha in half, so that we have two possible outcomes for our test: the score for yoga practitioners is greater than the mean of the population and the score for yoga practitioners is less than the mean of the population. Thus, if our overall alpha is .05, our significance level divided in half is .025.

Step 4: Determine Sample Results Our next step is to convert our sample score into a Z-score, so that we can see where it falls in our comparison distribution. We use the same formula as we did earlier: $Z = \dfrac{(X - M)}{SD}$. The score of our sample yoga practitioner (X) was 58.20, the mean of the population (M) was 54.50, and the standard deviation of the population (SD) was 5.10. So, the Z-score for our sample practitioner is $\dfrac{58.20 - 54.50}{5.10}$, which comes out to be 0.72. Remember that we will call this value our test statistic, because we will use it to evaluate our null hypothesis. Next, we need to determine just how expected or unexpected this test statistic is by converting it to a probability (see **Figure 6.12**).

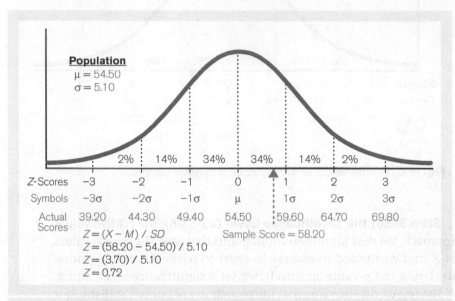

Figure 6.12   Sample Results on the Comparison Distribution

Step 5: Find the Probability of Our Sample Results   Because the normal curve is a probability distribution, we can find the probabilities for any value of Z. This is the information that a Z-table provides, which we first discussed in Chapter 4. To find the probability for our sample results, we simply look up the probability associated with the Z-score that we calculated in Step 3. Remember that to look up the probability for a Z-score, we locate the value of Z to the first decimal place in the first column of the table and then the value of Z to the second decimal in the appropriate column. In this case, because we calculated our Z-score to be 0.72, we would scroll down the first column until we get to 0.7 and then scroll across the columns until we get to 0.02 (see **Figure 6.13**).

According to the Z-table, a Z-score of 0.72 has a probability of .7642, which we can round to .76 because we typically round numbers to two decimals when using APA Style. Because our table tells us only the probability to the left of a particular Z-score, we need to subtract the tabled value from 1 to find the probability to the right of this value

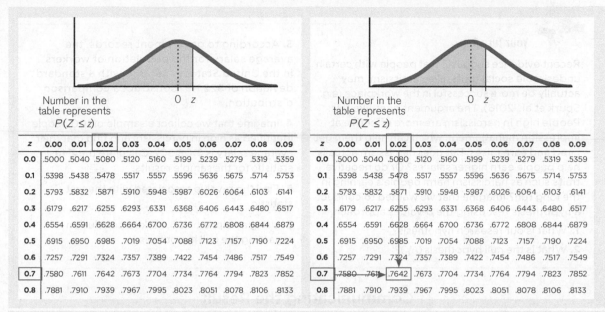

Figure 6.13 Finding the Probability of Our Sample Results Using the Z-Table

(we will need to do this for any Z-score that is greater than 1). Thus, if the probability to the left is .76, the probability to the right is $1 - .76$, or .24. This number is our p-value, which tells us the probability of observing our sample data, if the null hypothesis is true.

Step 6: Decide and Interpret To make our decision regarding whether we should reject or fail to reject the null hypothesis using the p-value approach, we need to compare our p-value to our significance level, set by alpha. If our p-value is greater than alpha, we will fail to reject the null hypothesis. If our p-value is less than alpha, we will reject the null hypothesis.

Recall that in Step 3 we set alpha to be .05, and we divided it in half because we had two possible outcomes for our study (i.e., yoga enhancing cognitive performance and yoga impairing cognitive performance), so our comparison alpha is .025. In this case, our p-value of .24 is greater than our alpha of .025. Therefore, we must *fail* to reject the null hypothesis ($\mu_1 = \mu_2$).

In other words, based on our sample of one yoga practitioner, we do not have enough evidence to claim that yoga changes performance on the Boston Naming Test. Our sample score is too likely, given the comparison distribution assumed under the null hypothesis, to claim that it is different from the population mean.

Your Turn 6.4

Recent evidence suggests that people with certain undesirable social traits, like narcissism, may actually be more successful in the workplace (e.g., Spurk et al., 2016). The argument goes like this: People high in narcissism are more effective at impression management, which can help them get hired and earn raises. But does narcissism actually help people earn higher salaries? Or do negative traits such as narcissism harm people's earning in the long run? Imagine that we wanted to conduct a hypothesis test using the p-values approach.

1. What is our research hypothesis?

2. What is the null hypothesis (H_0)?

3. According to government records, the average salary for the population of workers in the United States is $61,858 with a standard deviation of $22,119. Construct a comparison distribution.

4. Imagine that we collect a sample of 100 people identified as high in narcissism and find that their average salary is $108,307. Calculate the Z-test statistic for the sample results.

5. Find the p-value associated with the test statistic.

6. Using an alpha of .05, make a conclusion regarding the null hypothesis.

Communicating the Result

In formal research settings, a key part of hypothesis testing is communicating our finding in a results paragraph. We always want to start by indicating the type of hypothesis test that we are reporting. As we move through this textbook, we will learn a variety of hypothesis tests, including the independent samples t-test, the one-way ANOVA, and the chi-square test of independence. Because there are so many different versions of hypothesis test, we should explain which one we used in a clear statement, such as "We conducted a one-sample Z-test."

After indicating which test was performed, we want to describe the research hypothesis that we tested in our hypothesis test. For example, "We conducted a one-sample Z-test to examine if yoga affects cognitive functioning among older adults." Note that we want to describe only our research hypothesis; we never describe our null hypothesis, as we said earlier.

Once we have described our research hypothesis, we want to present the result of the hypothesis test. Because there are two possible outcomes for a hypothesis test (either we reject the null or fail to reject the null), we will pick one of the following two options:

- If we rejected the null hypothesis, we should say that the results were "significant" and provide the numeric value of the test statistic and the p-value. For example, we might say that "The results were significant, $Z = 3.66$, $p < .001$." A couple of notes about this.
  - First, by convention, we use the word "significant" to indicate that we rejected the null hypothesis. In everyday usage, the word

significant is synonymous with "meaningful" or important. However, this is not the case in statistics. It is possible for a significant result to be not important. We'll discuss this issue more in Chapter 8. For now, just realize that the term "significance" indicates only that we rejected the null.

o Second, we never want to say that the results "prove" an effect is true or not. Remember, we are making our decision based on the fact that our data are improbable, not impossible. So, while our results allow us to make a decision regarding the null, they don't remove any possibility that we made the wrong decision. Again, we'll talk more about this issue in Chapter 8.

- If we failed to reject the null hypothesis, we will indicate that the results were "nonsignificant." Note that we use the word "nonsignificant," rather than insignificant, to describe this situation. The reason for this is that we don't know exactly why we failed to reject the null hypothesis. Maybe there is no effect. Maybe we conducted a bad study. We don't know for sure. All we know is that in the current study, the results were not significant.

Finally, we want to explain how the population and comparison group means were different (or not) by providing the means and standard deviations for these groups. For example, we might say, "yoga practitioners did not differ on the Boston Naming Test ($M = 58.20$) relative to the general population ($M = 54.50$, $SD = 5.10$)."

So, putting this altogether, our results paragraph would look something like this:

> We performed a one-sample Z-test to examine whether yoga reduces cognitive decline among a sample of older adult participants. The results were nonsignificant, $Z = 0.72$, $p = .24$, such that a sample yoga practitioner did not differ on the Boston Naming Test ($M = 58.20$) relative to the general population ($M = 54.50$, $SD = 5.10$).

Forming a Conclusion

In the first half of this chapter, we learned how to determine whether we should reject or fail to reject a null hypothesis using the critical values approach. Using our knowledge of how Z-scores work, we specified a critical value that indicated the threshold our sample would need to surpass for us to deem our sample significantly different from the population. If our results fell short (i.e., in the nonrejection region), that signified the null hypothesis is true; if our results fell beyond the threshold (i.e., in the critical region), that signified that we could reject the null hypothesis.

In this part of the chapter, we learned a different approach, called the p-value approach, to test whether yoga improves performance on a test of cognitive abilities. The results of our hypothesis test reveal that we did not have enough evidence to show that yoga changes performance on the Boston Naming Test. Of course, we have to remember the limitations of our test. We operationally defined "cognitive functioning" as performance on the Boston Naming Test, which is one of many possible tests of cognitive ability. Perhaps if we had measured a different cognitive ability, using the Stroop test, for example, we might have found an effect of yoga. Another potential problem is that we used only a single yoga practitioner in our sample. Perhaps the yoga practitioner that we selected is representative of the population, but perhaps not. In the next chapter, we will learn how to use a larger sample of scores when conducting a hypothesis test, in order to provide a more rigorous test of the null hypothesis.

Your Turn 6.5

1. If your study results are not significant, this means there is no difference. True? Why or why not?

2. a. Can your study results ever prove something? Why or why not?

b. Give an example of something you might see on TV or read somewhere that shows a person not understanding this idea.

3. Imagine you did a study to determine if people like music better when listening to it on vinyl. You have someone listen to the song on vinyl and rate it, then compare that rating to the average rating on Spotify. You hypothesize that people will like the song better if they hear it on vinyl. Explain each of the following outcomes using everyday language:

a. We are able to reject the null.

b. We fail to reject the null.

Become a Better Consumer of Statistics

One of the key ideas that we should take away from our discussion of hypothesis testing is that just because a sample mean is different from a population value, it doesn't indicate that it is significantly different. We might simply see a difference between our sample and the population due to sampling variation.

This is important to keep in mind when assessing advertisements' claims. For example, perhaps you are in the market for mouthwash.

Advertisers often use research to make claims about their products. Knowing statistics can help you separate fact from fiction.

One ad may claim that, according to research, their mouthwash keeps your mouth feeling fresh for 3 hours, whereas a competitor keeps your mouth feeling fresh for only 2.75 hours. An extra 15 minutes of freshness might seem like a compelling reason to buy the seemingly longer-lasting mouthwash.

But, do we really know that it is really longer lasting? Just because the means are different does not automatically indicate that this is a significant difference. Rather, the difference in means could be due to sampling variation. Perhaps in reality the two mouthwash brands are equally good at keeping your mouth feeling fresh. Without knowing the results of a hypothesis test, we can't be certain. Similar types of advertising claims rely on one person's experience to represent a product's effectiveness (e.g., a certain brand of shampoo resulting in particularly full-bodied hair). Again, though that one person may have authentically noticed an improvement, it's just one person.

Focus on Open Science: Preregistration

If we accurately predicted the outcome of the flip of a coin 10 times in a row, that would be very impressive. Indeed, the odds of that happening are 0.5^{10} or 0.0009765625. However, if we were to flip a coin 10 times, each time looking to see what the outcome is, and then claim that we had correctly predicted the outcome, that wouldn't be impressive at all.

The same is true for predicting an experiment's outcome. If, based on prior research, we predict that yoga improves cognitive functioning among older adults, and then our experiment supports that prediction,

For predictions to be useful, they have to be done before we learn the outcome.

it lends credibility to the rationale we used to derive our hypothesis. If, however, we can make an accurate prediction only after we have seen our study's results, then it really doesn't suggest that our rationale is correct at all. It merely suggests that we are good at explaining how the results of my experiment fit within our rationale. In this case we are essentially retrofitting our prediction to what we already found.

Making a hypothesis only after knowing the results is called **HARKing** (*H*ypothesizing *A*fter *R*esults *K*nown). Surprisingly, in many areas of science, HARKing has been fairly common. According to one study, 27% of psychologists indicated that they had reported a surprising finding as expected in the past (John et al., 2012). Similar problems in medical research prompted the U.S. Food and Drug Administration to create ClinicalTrials.gov, a website concerning research on experimental drugs that requires researchers to specify their hypotheses in advance, preventing them from changing their hypotheses to fit their results.

To combat HARKing in psychology and other sciences, open science advocates promote the **preregistration of hypotheses.** Preregistration involves specifying a study hypothesis in such a way that it is clearly stated prior to any data collection or analyses and cannot be changed. Websites such as osf.io, aspredicted.org, and ClinicalTrials.gov allow researchers to date and time stamp their hypotheses so that they can prove definitively that they stated their hypotheses prior to knowing what the data reveal. This way researchers will not be tempted to retrofit their hypotheses to their findings.

Statistics on the Job

Hypothesis testing is useful for answering research questions, but it can also be useful on the job. Many businesses want to make informed decisions when it comes to developing and marketing new products. Rather than merely relying on their gut instincts, hypothesis testing allows companies to quantitatively evaluate the impact of corporate decisions.

One common methodology that businesses use is called **A/B Testing,** which compares two conditions or versions of a variable to determine which level is superior. For example, imagine a business is considering updating their website to increase their product sales. They only want to switch to the new webpage if it actually increases sales. So, using A/B Testing, the business may have some customers go to the older webpage (version A), and other customers go to the new webpage (version B). The business could then compare the overall sales numbers for each of the two versions of the webpage. If the new

HARKing describes the questionable research practice where researchers make their predictions only after analyzing their data.

preregistration of hypotheses a procedure to increase research transparency where researchers post their predictions in a public forum, such that they can later prove that they made these predictions before analyzing their data.

A/B Testing a method used in business where two versions of a product or message are used simultaneously until hypothesis testing reveals one version to be superior to the other.

Companies use hypothesis testing in many ways, including how to determine what the best new flavors of ice cream might be.

webpage (version B) generates more sales, they can then decide to have all of their customers use the new webpage.

To analyze their data, companies that employ A/B Testing use the same hypothesis-testing approaches that we have explored in this chapter (and those that we will explore in the next several chapters). So, whether a company is trying to figure out which of two webpage designs to roll out, or which of two spokespeople to hire, or which of two new flavors to bring to market, A/B Testing and hypothesis testing can help.

Review Questions

1. In your own words, describe the purpose and logic of hypothesis testing.

2. Interpret the following double-negative statements:
   a. I don't not want chocolate ice cream.
   b. My cat doesn't dislike watching birds.
   c. I promise I won't not try to make a mess.

3. Create a double-negative statement and then interpret it to remove the double negative.

4. Put the steps of the hypothesis-testing procedure (critical value approach) in the correct order:
   a. Build the comparison distribution
   b. Determine the sample results
   c. Decide and interpret the results
   d. Determine the population and hypotheses
   e. Establish the critical value cutoff

5. How does the critical value approach to hypothesis testing differ from the *p*-value approach?

6. Why do researchers avoid using the word "prove" when describing the results of their study?

7. In your own words, describe the null hypothesis and the research hypothesis.

8. If our alpha was .005, what would our critical value(s) be if
   a. we had a one-tailed hypothesis (predicting an increase).
   b. we had a one-tailed hypothesis (predicting a decrease).
   c. we had a two-tailed hypothesis.

9. You have been tasked with developing a new procedure to improve the accuracy of eyewitness testimony because it is estimated that one in three (33%) eyewitnesses make an error in identification (so 67% correct identifications; Wright & McDaid, 1996).
   a. Would your hypothesis test be one or two tailed? Why?
   b. What would the population of interest be? What would the comparison population be?
   c. What is the research hypothesis?
   d. What is the null hypothesis?
   e. Assume that you found a research paper showing that the standard deviation of eyewitness identification errors was 7%. What would the comparison distribution look like?
   f. If you wanted your critical value to be at least 3 standard deviations above or below the mean, what would your sample's Z-score have to be, at a minimum, to reject the null?
   g. You develop your new procedure and find that the eyewitness accuracy is now 85%. What is the proper conclusion? Be sure to include a fully labeled diagram depicting the comparison distribution, the cutoff, and where the sample's score falls.

10. You are interested in whether a group of children that have had restricted language input have normal language skills. You decide to use their productive vocabulary (the number of words they say) as a measure of their language skills. Let's say you found a research paper stating that at 24 months old, most typically developing children are saying an average of 250 words with a standard deviation of 83 words. Based on past research, you believe that the children with restricted language input will have lower than normal language skills.

   a. Would your hypothesis test be one- or two-tailed? Why?

   b. What would the population of interest be? What would the comparison population be?

   c. What is the research hypothesis?

   d. What is the null hypothesis?

   e. What would the comparison distribution look like?

   f. Imagine you measure the productive vocabulary of a single child with restricted language input to be 102 words (note that you'd typically collect data from more than one participant; however, for the purposes of this chapter, we're only using data from one child). Calculate the Z-test statistic for this child.

   g. Find the p-value associated with the test statistic

   h. Using an alpha of .05, make a conclusion regarding the null hypothesis.

11. Why is preregistration of hypotheses and critical values becoming more common in the field of psychology and other sciences?

 Key Concepts

Answers to Your Turn

Your Turn 6.1

1. The doctor is saying the test was conclusive (i.e., there was something there).

2. You are not unintelligent. You are certainly not awful at statistics.

3. Though you can be reasonably/mostly sure, you can never be 100% sure. That's because there are always many factors that contribute an outcome that there is always a slight possibility that you're missing some vital piece of information, measured something inaccurately, or that there was some other type of error that led to an incorrect conclusion.

Your Turn 6.2

1. (a) Reject the null. (b) That there isn't no effect or that there isn't no difference.

2. (a) No. You can only reject it. (b) You can support or accept the research hypothesis.

3. Population of Interest: Labrador retrievers. Comparison Population: Dogs in general. Sample: My Labrador retriever.

4. My Labrador retriever is equally cute as dogs in general.

5.

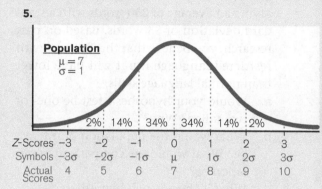

6. (a) +3.01; (b) −2.01.

7. We can reject the null hypothesis (H_0) that my Labrador retriever is equally cute as dogs in general ($\mu_1 = \mu_2$). The results support the research hypothesis that my Labrador retriever is cuter than dogs in general ($\mu_1 > \mu_2$).

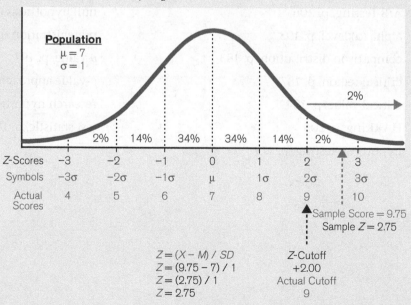

$Z = (X − M) / SD$
$Z = (9.75 − 7) / 1$
$Z = (2.75) / 1$
$Z = 2.75$

Z-Cutoff
+2.00
Actual Cutoff
9

Your Turn 6.3

1. We first divide our alpha in half, .001/2 = .0005, because we want two critical values. Next, we look this value up in the body of our Z-table and find the corresponding Z-score, which reveals the critical value to the left to be –3.29. Because the normal curve is symmetric, we know that the critical value to the right must be +3.29.

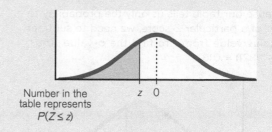

Number in the table represents $P(Z \leq z)$

z	0.00	0.01	0.02	0.03	0.04	0.05	0.06	0.07	0.08	0.09
-3.6	.0000	.0000	.0000	.0000	.0000	.0000	.0001	.0000	.0000	.0001
-3.5	.0000	.0000	.0000	.0000	.0000	.0000	.0002	.0000	.0000	.0002
-3.4	.0003	.0003	.0003	.0003	.0003	.0003	.0003	.0003	.0003	.0002
-3.3	.0005	.0005	.0005	.0004	.0004	.0004	.0004	.0004	.0004	.0003
-3.2	.0007	.0007	.0006	.0006	.0006	.0006	.0006	.0005	.0005	.0005
-3.1	.0010	.0009	.0009	.0009	.0008	.0008	.0008	.0008	.0007	.0007
-3.0	.0013	.0013	.0013	.0012	.0012	.0011	.0011	.0011	.0010	.0010
-2.9	.0019	.0018	.0018	.0017	.0016	.0016	.0015	.0015	.0014	.0014

Your Turn 6.4

1. The mean salary for narcissists is different from the mean salary for the general population.

2. The mean salary for narcissists is equal to the mean salary for the population, $\mu_{\text{Narcissists}} = \mu_{\text{General Population}}$.

3.

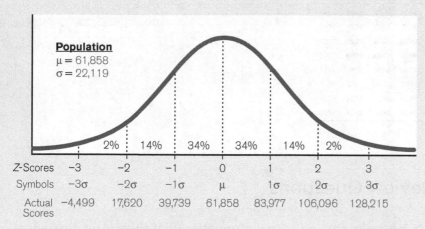

Population
$\mu = 61,858$
$\sigma = 22,119$

	2%	14%	34%	34%	14%	2%	

Z-Scores	–3	–2	–1	0	1	2	3
Symbols	-3σ	-2σ	-1σ	μ	1σ	2σ	3σ
Actual Scores	–4,499	17,620	39,739	61,858	83,977	106,096	128,215

4. $Z = (108,307 - 61,858)/22,119 = 2.10$

5. Because our table tells us only the probability to the left of a particular Z-score, we need to subtract the tables value from 1 to find the p-value. Thus, $p = (1 - .9821) = .018$

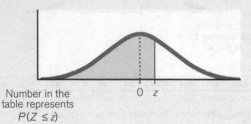

Number in the table represents $P(Z \leq z)$

z	0.00	0.01	0.02	0.03	0.04	0.05	0.06	0.07	0.08	0.09
0.0	.5000	.5040	.5080	.5120	.5160	.5199	.5239	.5279	.5319	.5359
0.1	.5398	.5438	.5478	.5517	.5557	.5596	.5636	.5675	.5714	.5753
0.2	.5793	.5832	.5871	.5910	.5948	.5987	.6026	.6064	.6103	.6141
0.3	.6179	.6217	.6255	.6293	.6331	.6368	.6406	.6443	.6480	.6517
0.4	.6554	.6591	.6628	.6664	.6700	.6736	.6772	.6808	.6844	.6879
0.5	.6915	.6950	.6985	.7019	.7054	.7088	.7123	.7157	.7190	.7224
0.6	.7257	.7291	.7324	.7357	.7389	.7422	.7454	.7486	.7517	.7549
0.7	.7580	.7611	.7642	.7673	.7704	.7734	.7764	.7794	.7823	.7852
0.8	.7881	.7910	.7939	.7967	.7995	.8023	.8051	.8078	.8106	.8133
0.9	.8159	.8186	.8212	.8238	.8264	.8289	.8315	.8340	.8365	.8389
1.0	.8413	.8438	.8461	.8485	.8508	.8531	.8554	.8577	.8599	.8621
1.1	.8643	.8665	.8686	.8708	.8729	.8749	.8770	.8790	.8810	.8830
1.2	.8849	.8869	.8888	.8907	.8925	.8944	.8962	.8980	.8997	.9015
1.3	.9032	.9049	.9066	.9082	.9099	.9115	.9131	.9147	.9162	.9177
1.4	.9192	.9207	.9222	.9236	.9251	.9265	.9279	.9292	.9306	.9319
1.5	.9332	.9345	.9357	.9370	.9382	.9394	.9406	.9418	.9429	.9441
1.6	.9452	.9463	.9474	.9484	.9495	.9505	.9515	.9525	.9535	.9545
1.7	.9554	.9564	.9573	.9582	.9591	.9599	.9608	.9616	.9625	.9633
1.8	.9641	.9649	.9656	.9664	.9671	.9678	.9686	.9693	.9699	.9706
1.9	.9713	.9719	.9726	.9732	.9738	.9744	.9750	.9756	.9761	.9767
2.0	.9772	.9778	.9783	.9788	.9793	.9798	.9803	.9808	.9812	.9817
2.1	.9821	.9826	.9830	.9834	.9838	.9842	.9846	.9850	.9854	.9857
2.2	.9861	.9864	.9868	.9871	.9875	.9878	.9881	.9884	.9887	.9890

6. Because our p-value is less than .025 ($\alpha/2$), we can reject the null hypothesis. Our sample of narcissists earns a significantly higher salary than the general population.

Your Turn 6.5

1. False. Not significant does not conclusively indicate no difference. Rather, the results are inconclusive, which means we can not definitively say if there is a difference or not.

2. (a) No. When we draw conclusions from hypothesis tests, we are making our decision to retain or reject the null hypothesis based on the probability that we observed the data presuming that the null hypothesis is true. Unlikely events, although improbable, do occur sometimes. For this reason, we can never use hypothesis testing to "prove" anything. (b) Answers will vary.

3. (a) When listening to the song on vinyl, our participant liked the song significantly more than those who listened to it on Spotify. (b) The results were nonsignificant. We were not able to find a difference between song ratings on vinyl versus Spotify.

Answers to Review Questions

1. When we conduct research, we make predictions (hypotheses) about what we expect to find. The process of hypothesis testing allows us to determine if there is support for our hypothesis. We always start with the assumption that there is no difference between the populations being compared; as a result, we always evaluate the null hypothesis.

2. **a.** I want chocolate ice cream
   b. My cat likes to watch birds.
   c. I promise I will try to make a mess.

3. Answers will vary.

4. **a.** Determine the population and hypotheses
   b. Build the comparison distribution
   c. Establish the critical value cutoff
   d. Determine the sample results
   e. Decide and interpret the results

5. In the critical value approach, we choose critical values and compare the sample results to that value. If the sample results are more extreme than the cutoff values, we reject the null hypothesis. In contrast, with the *p*-value approach we set a significance level (alpha level) and compare the probability of the sample results to the alpha level. If the probability is lower than the significance level, we reject the null hypothesis.

6. Our decisions are related to whether the data are unlikely (improbable), not whether they are impossible.

7. The null hypothesis states that there is no difference between the populations being compared. The research hypothesis states how the populations being compared are expected to be different from each other.

8. **a.** 2.57 (or 2.58)
   b. −2.57 (or −2.58)
   c. ±2.81

9. **a.** Because you are developing a new procedure, your test will be two-tailed. There are two ways that the procedure could affect eyewitness testimony.
   b. Population of interest = participants using your new procedure, comparison population = eyewitnesses in the general population.
   c. Research hypothesis — participants using your new procedure will perform differently than the general population of eyewitnesses ($\mu_1 \neq \mu_2$).
   d. Null hypothesis — participants using your new procedure will not perform differently than the general population of eyewitnesses ($\mu_1 = \mu_2$).
   e.

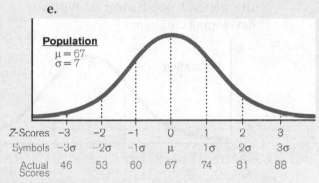

   f. ±3.01
   g. Sample *Z*-score is 2.57. We fail to reject the null hypothesis that the new procedure results in the same performance as the general population. The results are nonsignificant and suggest that the procedure does not impact (increase or decrease) accuracy.

10. a. Because there is past research on the topic, your hypothesis will be one-tailed. You expect your group will be lower than the general population.

b. Population of interest = children with restricted language input, comparison population = typically developing children in the general population.

c. Research hypothesis—children with restricted language input will have lower productive vocabularies than the general population of typically developing children.

d. Null hypothesis—children with restricted language input will not have different productive vocabularies than the general population of typically developing children.

e.

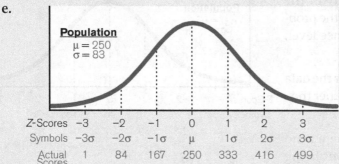

Z-Scores	−3	−2	−1	0	1	2	3
Symbols	−3σ	−2σ	−1σ	μ	1σ	2σ	3σ
Actual Scores	1	84	167	250	333	416	499

Population
μ = 250
σ = 83

f. −1.78

g. 0.0375

h. Because our *p*-value is less than .05, we can reject the null hypothesis. Our child with restricted language input has a significantly smaller productive vocabulary.

11. In many areas of science, making a hypothesis after analyzing the data is quite common, including in psychology. Retrofitting the hypotheses to the results makes it seem like the experiment supports the prediction when the researcher is simply good at explaining the results of a study.

Hypothesis Testing with a Distribution of Means

Learning Outcomes

After reading this chapter, you should be able to:

- Identify the key characteristics of a distribution of means and how we use it for hypothesis testing.

- Explain when it is appropriate to use a Z-test.

- Describe the difference between a directional and nondirectional research hypothesis.

- Use the appropriate language when failing to reject the null hypothesis.

- Summarize the assumptions of the Z-test.

- Create a bar graph that includes error bars.

It starts innocently enough. You wake up with a scratchy throat and promptly drink a glass of water. Still hurts. Uh-oh. Finals week is just days away now, so you don't have time to get sick. Why does it always feel like you get a cold at the worst times?

But it's not just you. As you head out into your suite's common area, you hear coughing and sneezing from two of your other suitemates' rooms. Still another is sleeping on the couch hugging a box of tissues like a teddy bear. All of you are sick. And it's not a coincidence. The end-of-semester chaos leads to a combination of stress, not eating right, not exercising, and not getting enough sleep—the perfect storm for sickness.

But none of you are deterred for long. An hour later, everyone is up and feeling motivated to get better as soon as possible. You don't have time to make an appointment at the health center—besides, half the campus is there right now. Instead, you're going to take matters into your own hands. You all share your ideas for potential cold remedies: eating a raw onion, taking a tablespoon of hot sauce each day, putting mentholated ointment on your feet, drinking hot chocolate made with honey and cinnamon. These all sound a bit crazy, but you're desperate.

Of these options, the one that sounds most palatable (to no one's surprise) is the honey-infused hot chocolate. In fact, everyone feels confident it will be a cure. So that's the plan. All four suitemates will drink three cups of honey-cinnamon hot chocolate for the next three days. But, you wonder, will it actually work, and if so, will it be better than if you had done nothing at all?

Statistics for Life

The thing about catching a common cold is that it's all too common. So common, in fact, that there is a litany of potential "cures." Your suite's proposed elixir has a lot of positive elements going for it. Honey seems healthy, cinnamon feels potentially helpful, a hot liquid has to soothe your throat, and

How could you test remedies for the common cold?

Krakenimages.com/Shutterstock

chocolate to raise your spirits. But, to know if the combination really works, you have to decide what you mean by "works." If you feel better in a week, is that good? To know for sure, you need to figure how long colds typically last for most people.

Where Do the Data Come From?

It's a fairly straightforward question: How long does the common cold last? A quick Internet search reveals a few key sources that address the duration of a cold. A paper that reviewed 40 studies on children's recovery from the cold and other illnesses reported that for most children (90%), cold symptoms dissipated after 15 days (Thompson et al., 2013). An individual study of 1,314 German children reported that the average cold duration was 1.8 weeks or about 13 days, with a standard deviation of 1.30 weeks (Gruber et al., 2008). Finally, a literature review of numerous studies across many different samples (e.g., children and adults) found that the cold peaks at 1–3 days, and typically lasts 7–10 days, with some lasting up to 3 weeks (Allan & Arroll, 2014).

One thing to note about the data is that the large reviews included studies with different designs. In particular, some studies looked at naturally occurring colds, others purposefully exposed participants to the cold virus. Some studies measured people before they had symptoms and then closely tracked duration, others relied on participant self-report. These types of factors contribute to the discrepancies between studies. That said, there does appear to be some consensus. Thus, for the purposes of this chapter's example, we will say the average duration of the common cold among the general population is 9 days with a variance of 5 ($\mu = 9$; $\sigma^2 = 5$).

Hypothesis Testing with a Distribution of Means: What We're Trying to Accomplish

Essentially, our goal here is the exact same as it was when we introduced hypothesis testing in the previous chapter. We want to see if one population is decidedly different from another population. In Chapter 6, we were trying to see if one population was cooler than another—that is, if stats students were cooler than the general population. To measure coolness, we kept it very simple, focusing on only one person's Instagram followers as an indication of how many followers the entire class had. Now that we understand the basic process, we'll focus on the more typical situation where we have information from more than one person.

For our purposes now, we want to look at the experience of our group of four suitemates, and not just one of them. Through our hypothesis test, we're seeking to determine if a group or sample of people is basically the same as the rest of the population. That is, we want to determine if the home remedy of drinking honey-cinnamon infused hot chocolate will reduce the length of time it takes to recover from a cold as compared to the general population, who are not drinking the same hot chocolate home remedy.

To answer this question, we need to introduce a few small wrinkles. First, in order to easily use information from more than one person, we still need one number to represent everyone in the group. That is, instead of looking at each person's individual cold duration, we will use the mean of all four suitemates' cold duration to see what is most typical for the hot chocolate group. Because we will be using a sample mean (i.e., our four suitemates) to represent our population of interest (i.e., people who drink honey-cinnamon hot chocolate), our comparison distribution needs to match that. Think of it this way: As our sample size gets larger, our sample mean is reflecting more and more information, even though it is still just a single number. Because of this, we need to change the way we construct our comparison distribution so that it reflects how much information is going into our sample mean. If we use a sample of four people, the comparison distribution of means should match that and reflect means from samples of four people as well.

So, to perform our hypothesis test based on a sample, we need to combine the ideas that we learned in Chapters 5 and 6. In particular, we need to take the idea of distribution of sample means from Chapter 5, and put it to use by implementing the idea of hypothesis testing and comparison distributions from Chapter 6. In essence, to conduct a hypothesis test when we are comparing a sample mean to the population mean, we will always need to build a comparison distribution that reflects the probability of observing different sample means if the null hypothesis is true. However, unlike in Chapter 6, where our comparison distribution was a typical normal curve of individual scores, our comparison distribution here will be a distribution of sample means.

Hypothesis Testing with a Distribution of Means: How Does It Work?

 Hypothesis testing, at its core, is always the same. Now with a distribution of means, we're comparing groups of people to see if one subset of people is unique or different from everyone else.

Step by Step: Hypothesis Testing with a Distribution of Means These steps should feel familiar. They're exactly the same five steps from Chapter 6. A few of the details will be different because of the type of information we have (i.e., we are dealing with data from a sample. In this case the 4 suitemates), but the basic steps of hypothesis testing will remain the same.

Step 1: Population and Hypotheses We start with populations because ultimately the focus of hypothesis testing is comparing a population of interest (i.e., honey-cinnamon hot chocolate–drinking people) to a comparison population (i.e., people in general). In other words:

Population of Interest: People who drink honey-cinnamon hot chocolate.
Comparison Population: People in general.
Sample: 4 suitemates.

Now that we know who we're comparing, we must state what we expect to happen. Remember, we don't do this in any old haphazard fashion. Rather, we state how we believe the populations will compare to each other in our research hypothesis. We won't test that directly, but will instead test whether the opposite is true. That is, we test the null hypothesis that there is no effect or no difference, and that the populations are the same. Here are our hypotheses:

Research Hypothesis (H_1): The four suitemates who are drinking honey-cinnamon hot chocolate will have colds that are shorter in duration than people in general ($\mu_1 < \mu_2$). (Note here that we are expecting μ_1 to be less than μ_2 because we expect the colds to have a shorter duration.)
Null Hypothesis (H_0): The four suitemates who are drinking honey-cinnamon hot chocolate will have colds that are longer than or equal in duration compared to people in general ($\mu_1 \geq \mu_2$).

Step 2: Build the Comparison Distribution As always, the comparison distribution reflects what things look like when the null hypothesis is correct and there is no effect—in this case, when drinking honey-cinnamon hot chocolate has no effect on cold duration or makes them last longer. Because our population of interest uses a mean from a sample of our 4 suitemates, our comparison distribution needs to match that and should use means from samples of 4 people as well.

We build the comparison distribution of means using the information available to us. First, we start with a basic normal distribution with Z-scores labeled, as seen in **Figure 7.1**.

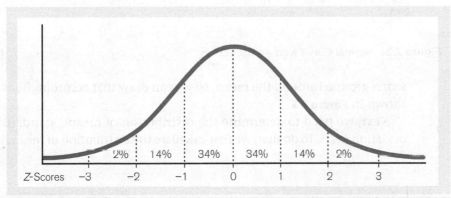

Figure 7.1 Normal Curve with Z-Scores and Percentages Under the Curve

Next, we'll add in actual scores based on the population's mean (μ_2) and standard deviation (σ_2). Note that we're using a subscript "2" in order to indicate that it is Comparison Population. The procedure for adding in actual scores is exactly how we created a number line in Chapter 4 and how we built a comparison distribution in Chapter 6.

We know based on our research that the average duration of the common cold among the general population is 9 days with a variance of 5 ($\mu = 9; \sigma^2 = 5$). To build our distribution, we need to find the standard deviation, not the variance. Converting from σ^2 to σ is as simple as taking the square root, $\sigma = \sqrt{\sigma^2} = \sqrt{5} = 2.24$, or $\sigma = 2.24$ (see **Figure 7.2**).

In Chapter 6, we stopped there because we were dealing with a population of interest that had one person. This time, however, our Population of Interest uses a mean from a sample of 4 people. Our comparison distribution must match that, so we need a distribution of means from our Comparison Population.

First, as we learned in Chapter 5, we know the mean of the distribution of means (μ_M) always matches the population's mean. We also know the distribution of means' shape will be narrower with more

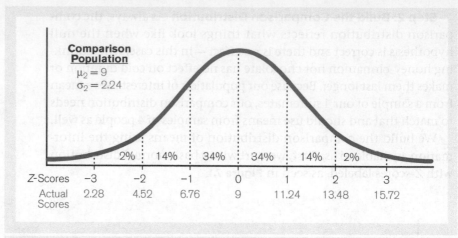

Figure 7.2 Normal Curve with Actual Scores

scores grouped around the mean, so we can draw that accordingly, as shown in **Figure 7.3**.

Next, we need to determine the distribution of means' standard deviation (σ_M). To do that, we first calculate the distribution of means'

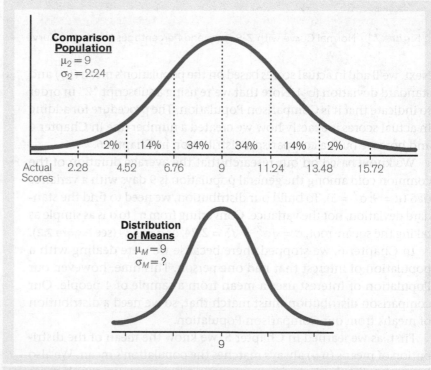

Figure 7.3 Normal Curve and Distribution of Means

variance (σ_M^2). Notice that when talking about variance and standard deviations for the distribution of means, we add the subscript M to indicate the type of distribution (see **Figure 7.4**).

	Sample	Population	Distribution of Sample Means
Mean	M	μ	μ_M
Variance	SD^2	σ^2	σ_{M^2}
Standard Deviation	SD	σ	σ_M

Figure 7.4 Keeping Track of Symbols

We learned earlier that variance in a distribution of means was directly influenced by the size of the sample (larger samples produce less variance because extreme scores are less likely).

$$\sigma_M^2 = \frac{\sigma^2}{N}$$

In our case, population variance (σ^2) = 5 and our sample size equals 4. The calculation of our distribution of means' variance (σ_M^2) would be:

$$\sigma_M^2 = \frac{\sigma^2}{N} = \frac{5}{4} = 1.25$$

But, we actually need to calculate the standard deviation. As before, to get the standard deviation, we take the square root of the variance, or in symbols $\sigma_M = \sqrt{\sigma_M^2}$. In our case, $\sigma_M^2 = 1.25$, so

$$\sigma_M = \sqrt{\sigma_M^2} = \sqrt{1.25} = 1.12$$

Of course, you can also get the distribution of means' standard deviation more directly: $\sigma_M = \sqrt{\dfrac{\sigma^2}{N}}$. If you already know the population's standard deviation, you can also calculate it as $\sigma_M = \dfrac{\sigma}{\sqrt{N}}$. As we mentioned in Chapter 5, other names for the distribution of means' standard deviation are the standard error (*SE*) or standard error of the mean (*SEM*). Don't let the different names trip you up; the concepts are exactly the same, and we will use these names interchangeably.

$$\sigma_M = \sqrt{\sigma_M^2} = \sqrt{\frac{\sigma^2}{N}} = \frac{\sigma}{\sqrt{N}}$$

With that information, we can now finalize our comparison distribution of means using its mean (μ_M) and standard deviation (σ_M). This comparison distribution represents all possible sample means for random samples of $n = 4$ people from a population that averages 9 days to recover from a cold (see **Figure 7.5**).

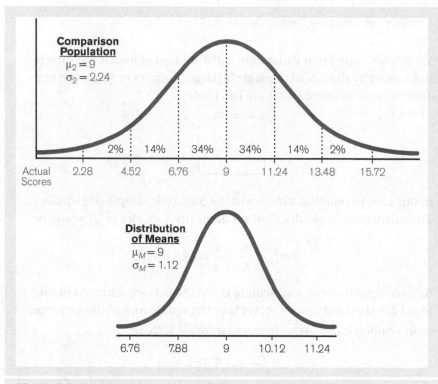

Figure 7.5 Normal Curve and Distribution of Means with Actual Scores

Step 3: Establish Critical Value Cutoff How short do our suitemates' colds have to be in order for us to conclude that honey-cinnamon hot chocolate is a viable cold remedy? That's the key question we need to answer when determining our standard of proof, or critical value. In order to confidently reject the null, we would want our suitemates' colds to fall well below the typical average. Our cutoff point should leave very little doubt that our result happened by accident.

The alpha level (or level of significance) sets the threshold for how probable (or improbable) our data need to be for us to reject the null hypothesis. The most typical alpha cutoff points are 1% and 5%. However, we don't always have to adhere to those and can conduct hypothesis testing using other alpha levels. To show you how that's done and to avoid unnecessary complications in this example while you're still mastering the steps, we've used an unconventional alpha level in this example.

To be sure our cold remedy works, we decide that we want the mean of our suitemates' colds to be shorter than 98% of the possible sample means taken from the population if the null hypothesis is true. That also means that there would be only about 2% of colds that are briefer on average than our suitemates' colds mean. Our 2% cutoff level is essentially our alpha level, which this case would be 0.02.

Remember, since we're focusing on our result less than average (colds will be shorter than they typically are), our critical region falls to the left of the mean on our comparison distribution. That 2% cutoff should sound familiar as it corresponds to a Z-score of -2.00. Because we're focused on the left side of the distribution (the side less than the mean), our Z-score needs to be negative. We know from Chapter 4 that a Z-score of -2.00 is the same as saying 2 standard deviations to the left of the mean (see **Figure 7.6**). Because of that we can simply look at our comparison distribution, count over 2 standard deviations to the left, and see the corresponding score that we already put in from Step 2. With our critical value established, we can add those notations to our comparison distribution.

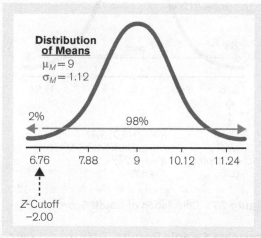

Figure 7.6 Normal Curve with Critical Value Cutoff

Thinking ahead, in order to reject the null, our sample score needs to fall within the 2% part of our comparison distribution and not within the 98%. In other words, we want our population of interest to be distinct, and not like the vast majority (98%) of means that are possible if the null is true.

It's also helpful to see what the cutoff would be in terms of the actual score (i.e., number of days that a person's cold lasts). Again, because we did such a great job in Step 2, we can see that a Z-score of −2.00 equates to a cold duration of 6.76 days. We can see it easily on our comparison distribution, but let's double-check ourselves with the math.

The formula for finding an actual score when you know the Z-score, standard deviation, and mean is:

$$X = (Z)(SD) + M$$
$$X = (-2.00)(1.12) + 9$$
$$X = (-2.24) + 9$$
$$X = 6.76$$

That should sound and look familiar (see **Figure 7.7**). But check for yourself; 6.76 should match up exactly with the number that is 2 standard deviations to the left of the mean on the comparison distribution we created.

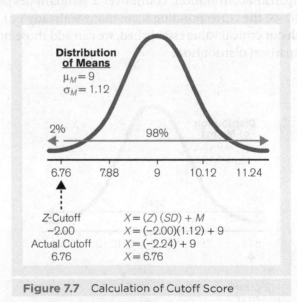

Figure 7.7 Calculation of Cutoff Score

Step 4: Determine Sample Results Time to see how our sample of 4 suitemates did with their colds. Each tracked their symptoms using a daily diary approach where they noted each day (e.g., Day 1, Day 2, etc.)

how they felt. You keep track for an entire month, after which time you want to go back and see how long everyone's colds lasted. To be as fair and unbiased as possible when making the determination about cold duration, you go to the student health center on campus and ask a doctor to review the diaries and determine for each person when their cold ended. The doctor has the following results: 14, 11, 6, 13. Knowing that we want one number to represent the whole group, we quickly calculate the mean $(14 + 11 + 6 + 13)/4 = 44/4 = 11$ days.

Because we are thinking in terms of percentages and wanting to make sure our suitemates' cold duration is shorter than 98% of the comparison population, we need to convert the sample's cold duration to a Z-score. We did this exact procedure in Chapter 6 and used this formula: $Z = \dfrac{X - M}{SD}$. However, that formula is for a single person. We now have the mean from a sample of 4 people. The exact same logic still applies, but the symbols change to reflect the difference. Instead of an individual person's score X, we're using the mean of our sample, so an M is the appropriate symbol. We're comparing that to the mean of the comparison distribution, which is a distribution of means, so our mean symbol needs to change from M to μ_M. Similarly, because we're working with a distribution of means, our standard deviation symbol needs to change from SD to σ_M. With the changes in place, the resulting formula is $Z = \dfrac{X - \mu_M}{\sigma_M}$. We call this the **one-sample Z-test**, because it is a statistical test that lets us determine if a single sample is different from a population when we have continuous (interval or ratio) data.

In our example, our $M = 11$, $\mu_M = 9$, and $\sigma_M = 1.12$. If we plug in the corresponding values:

$$Z = \frac{X - \mu_M}{\sigma_M} = \frac{11 - 9}{1.12} = 1.79$$

We have our result: $Z = 1.79$. Next, we should show where our sample results fall on the comparison distribution, as in **Figure 7.8**.

Step 5: Decide and Interpret Now we can see where our sample falls on the comparison distribution and whether it is different from the majority of the population. That is, does our sample mean fall in the critical region where we can reject the null hypothesis (the 2%), or within the rest of the distribution (the 98%)? It is easy to see that our score of 11 not only falls outside the critical region, but our sample's cold duration of 11 days is actually above the population's mean.

We can make the same conclusion another way. Our sample's mean of 11 days was not lower than the critical value actual score

one-sample Z-test a type of hypothesis test used to compare a single sample mean to a population mean.

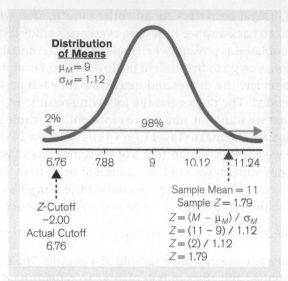

Figure 7.8 Sample Results on the Comparison Distribution

of 6.76. Similarly, we know that our sample Z-score of 1.79 was not below the critical value Z-score of -2.00. In other words, our sample was not more extreme than the critical value. Remember, because we wanted a cold duration that was shorter than everyone else, we needed our sample to fall to the left of the cutoff and be lower than the critical value.

Decision time. Because our sample's results (Step 4) do not exceed the critical value (Step 3), we are unable to reject the null hypothesis (H_0) that our hot chocolate–drinking suitemates' cold durations are longer than or equal to cold durations among people in general ($\mu_1 \geq \mu_2$). If we are unable to reject the null, we must also say that we failed to find support for the research hypothesis (H_1) that our suitemates who drink honey-cinnamon hot chocolate have shorter cold durations than people in general ($\mu_1 > \mu_2$). Remember, this does not mean that we accept the null, only that we don't have enough evidence to reject it.

Directional Hypothesis Testing: One-Tailed Hypothesis Testing

directional hypothesis a type of research hypothesis that specifies whether the sample mean will be less than or greater than the population mean.

To properly conduct hypothesis tests and interpret the results, we need to consider how focused we want to be in our predictions. That is, in Step 1 of hypothesis testing, when we state our hypotheses, we can actually word them in two different ways. The first is a **directional hypothesis,** where we make a prediction about exactly how samples will differ in a positive or negative way. Any time we describe potential differences between samples with words like more or less, larger or smaller, greater or fewer, or stronger or weaker, we're using a directional hypothesis.

For example, in testing the effects of drinking hot chocolate on cold duration, we predicted that hot chocolate would decrease the length of cold duration. The implication here is that we are testing only one direction. Similarly, in Chapter 6, we predicted that "Students in our statistics course are cooler than people in general." This is also a directional hypothesis because we say our fellow students will be cooler than others.

Our hypothesis's direction has implications for the cutoffs we establish in Step 3 of hypothesis testing. If we specify a direction, we focus on only one side or tail of the comparison distribution. In the hot chocolate example, because we predicted that our suitemates would have shorter colds than the general population, we focused on the left side of the distribution. In Chapter 6, because we wanted to see if our classmates were cooler than the population, we focused on the right side of the distribution. We refer to cases like these with directional hypotheses as **one-tailed** tests because the critical region falls on only one of the distribution's tails. In other words, we only look in one direction, as shown in Figure 7.9.

one-tailed a comparison distribution that has a single critical region within only one of the distribution's tails.

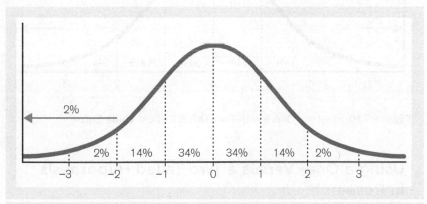

Figure 7.9 Normal Curve with One-Tailed Critical Value Cutoff

Nondirectional Hypothesis Testing: Two-Tailed Hypothesis Testing

The second way that we can state our research hypothesis is as a **nondirectional hypothesis,** where we don't specify the direction or nature of the difference, just that the sample mean will be different from the population mean. In the hot chocolate example, we could have decided to not state a direction and simply said, "The four

nondirectional hypothesis a type of research hypothesis that predicts that the sample mean will be different from the population mean, but does not state the direction of the difference.

suitemates who are drinking honey-cinnamon hot chocolate will have colds that are different in duration than people in general ($\mu_1 \neq \mu_2$)." This would be a nondirectional hypothesis because our predication states only that we expect the groups to differ, and does not state how they may differ. We saw an example of this type of research hypothesis in Chapter 6, where we predicted that elderly people who practice yoga would perform differently on a test of cognitive functioning than the population. This is a nondirectional hypothesis because we aren't stating exactly how the sample will be different from the population, just that they won't be equal.

With a nondirectional hypothesis, we would have to focus on both sides or tails of the distribution because the hypothesis does not specific if the difference is positive of negative. We refer to cases like these with nondirectional hypotheses as **two-tailed** tests because the critical region falls on both of the distribution's tails (see **Figure 7.10**).

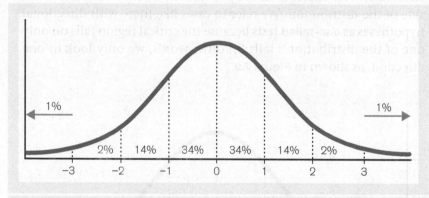

Figure 7.10   Normal Curve with Two-Tailed Critical Value Cutoff

Using a One- Versus a Two-Tailed Hypothesis in Research

An important feature to notice when going from a one-tailed test to a two-tailed test is that the overall size of the critical region remains the same. In this case, the cutoff was set so that the sample score would have to be in the top 2% of cases. As you can see in Figure 7.9, when we have a one-tailed test, the entire 2% falls on one side or tail of the distribution. However, when we have a two-tailed test, we have the same 2% to work with, but now that there are two tails to consider, we need to split the critical region in half and divide by 2. As you can see in Figure 7.10, we now have 1% of the critical region in each tail.

For Step 3 of hypothesis testing, we first establish our cutoff either in terms of conventional levels of significance (e.g., whether we want top 5% or 1%) or based on our research question. Then, based on the hypothesis, we focus the critical region in one tail (directional hypothesis) or split the critical region across two tails (nondirectional hypothesis). Indeed, we already saw this play out in Chapter 6's yoga example, when we needed to divide our alpha in half to reflect the fact that we were making a nondirectional hypothesis.

However, the reality of how researchers use one- and two-tailed tests in their research is different. In practice, even though we typically have directional hypotheses in mind when we conduct a study, which would call for a one-tailed test, researchers rarely actually perform one-tailed significance tests. That's because researchers want to exercise an abundance of caution and help increase the confidence in the conclusions. If you look back to Figure 7.10, the two critical regions are each narrower than the one critical region displayed in Figure 7.9. Thus, it's slightly harder to reject the null hypothesis when we run a nondirectional hypothesis test or a two-tailed test compared to a directional one-tailed test.

Another way of saying this is that, all else being equal, when we perform a two-tailed significance test, our sample mean needs to be even more different from the population mean in order to reject the null hypothesis. Basically, as researchers, even though we could justify using a one-tailed test, we use a two-tailed test to stack the deck against ourselves to make getting significance more difficult. If the sample results fall in the narrower critical region, we are more confident that we did not get the results by chance. We'll address the issue of false positive findings in greater detail in Chapter 8.

Your Turn 7.1

1. Look back at the example from Chapter 6, where we used one classmate's number of Instagram followers to represent the entire class. What would need to be different in order for us to need a distribution of means?

2. For each population of interest, what would the comparison distribution be?

   a. A sample of 10 preschoolers enrolled in a special art program.

   b. A case study of one person who eats a special diet to improve memory.

3. Describe the underlying logic for why a distribution of means has less variance than a distribution of the raw scores.

Communicating the Result

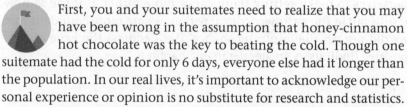 As we did in Chapter 6, we need to carefully consider how we communicate our results. When thinking about the results of our hot chocolate study, we know that we have failed to reject the null hypothesis. However, when communicating results to others, we don't specifically reference the null hypothesis because it is always assumed. In other words, the null hypothesis is always the same for the single-sample Z-test, so we don't need to mention it. Instead, we only need to focus on what our results mean for our research hypothesis. If we fail to reject the null, as we did here, we say that our research hypothesis was not supported. Those familiar with statistics and research will know that is saying the same thing as if we stated that we failed to reject the null.

Also, when communicating with those who don't know statistics as well, the logic of hypothesis testing and rejecting the null can be tough. By not referencing the null, we can save those with less statistics knowledge from potential confusion by focusing only on whether our hypothesis was supported. It is important that, even though we cannot support our research hypothesis, we do not say that honey-cinnamon hot chocolate has no effect on cold duration. We use this specific language to indicate that while our study did not find conclusive evidence, other studies might.

Forming a Conclusion

First, you and your suitemates need to realize that you may have been wrong in the assumption that honey-cinnamon hot chocolate was the key to beating the cold. Though one suitemate had the cold for only 6 days, everyone else had it longer than the population. In our real lives, it's important to acknowledge our personal experience or opinion is no substitute for research and statistics.

That stated, no one study can be the basis for forming a conclusion with absolute certainty. It could be that a different set of four suitemates following the same hot chocolate regimen would have shorter colds—that is, it could be that our sample size was simply too small to capture the true effects of the hot chocolate remedy. Or it could be that this hot chocolate remedy works only in young children, and not college-aged adults. It could also be a process issue, that having the four suitemates record their own symptoms in their daily diary was not as accurate as it needed to be or how we gauged the start and end of the cold wasn't consistent.

Ultimately, we cannot know from just one study if we failed to reject the null because honey-cinnamon hot chocolate really has no effect on colds, or if some aspect of our study made it difficult for us to find accurate results.

Your Turn 7.2

1. Inspired by your question about the common cold, a friend who majors in health studies wants to know the typical duration of the flu and finds that it has a mean duration of 14 days with a standard deviation of 4 days. Answer each of the following without doing any math:

  a. What is the mean of the comparison distribution?

  b. Which of these is the standard deviation of the comparison distribution? (5, 6, 2, 8, 7.5)

2. Convert the following symbols into words:

$$\sigma_M = \sqrt{\sigma_M^2} = \sqrt{\frac{\sigma^2}{N}} = \frac{\sigma}{\sqrt{N}}$$

3. A researcher conducts a study in which the Z-test produces the following results: +0.43. Assuming the critical value was +1.96, please communicate the results.

4. A writer from a popular magazine hypothesized that female contestants on *The Bachelor* have better relationships after leaving the show than people in general. She has data from 20 former contestants to help test this.

  a. What would the populations be?

  b. What would the null hypothesis be?

  c. What is the research hypothesis?

  d. Is the research hypothesis a directional hypothesis or a nondirectional hypothesis?

5. Assume that the writer found a research paper showing that on a 10-point relationship quality scale, the average relationship is an 8 with a variance of 0.25 ($\mu = 8$; $\sigma^2 = 0.25$). What would that distribution look like?

6. Conduct Step 2: Build a Comparison Distribution.

  a. What type of comparison distribution do you need?

  b. What are the three key pieces of information that you need?

  c. What will be the mean (μ_M)?

  d. What will be the shape?

  e. What will be the variance? (σ_M^2)

  f. What will be the standard deviation? (σ_M)

  g. What does the comparison distribution look like?

7. For Step 3: Establish Critical Value Cutoff, in order to believe *Bachelor* contestants have better relationships, you want to be sure they score in the top 2% of the population.

  a. What is the cutoff score associated with that?

  b. What sample score is associated with the cutoff?

  c. Show this on the comparison distribution.

8. For Step 4: Determine Sample Results, the writer measures all contestants' relationships on the 10-point relationship quality scale. She gets the following results: 5, 8, 9, 7, 6, 3, 10, 9, 5, 9, 8, 4, 7, 8, 9, 9, 8, 10, 8, 6.

  a. What test does she need to run?

  b. What are the results?

  c. Show this on the comparison distribution.

9. For Step 5: Decide and Interpret, what is the appropriate conclusion?

Statistics for Research

Our memories can be a curious thing. Sometimes, we can remember the lyrics of songs we haven't heard in years. Other times, we can't remember the standard deviation formula we studied two hours ago. Sometimes, we can remember every detail of a meal that we had four summers ago, but can't remember anything we had for lunch yesterday. Perhaps this is why our memory process and capacity have been the topic of so much extensive scientific research.

One particular aspect of memory that researchers examine is working memory—that is, how much information can people hold in mind at any one time (Cowan, 2010). One popular estimate suggests that our working memory can hold somewhere between 5 and 9 items in mind at any time (Miller, 1956). A question that we might ask is, what variables affect short-term working memory?

Nothing seems to affect our ability to hold information in mind quite like sleep. When we get a full night of sleep, our minds are sharp and quick. When we are sleep deprived, our minds are dull and sluggish. But does sleep deprivation affect working memory capacity? If we wanted to answer this question, one approach would be to collect a sample of sleep-deprived participants, measure their working memory capacity, and then evaluate their data against normative data for the population using the one sample Z-test.

Here in the Statistics for Research section, we're going to explore what hypothesis testing with a distribution of means looks like using a research-based example. Along the way, we'll dive deeper into the idea of the assumptions or prerequisites of hypothesis tests, the *p*-value approach to hypothesis testing with distributions of means, as well as the interpretation and construction of bar graphs with error bars.

Where Do the Data Come From?

To conduct our study of sleep deprivation and working memory, we first need to operationalize working memory capacity. Researchers have developed several tasks to measure working memory. One such measure is called the Corsi block-tapping task (Corsi, 1972). In this task, participants view nine squares on a computer screen. During each trial of the task, a certain number of the squares change color in a specific order. Participants must remember the order in which the squares change color, and respond by clicking on each block in the correct order. Each trial gets progressively harder until the participant can no longer solve the problems correctly. Researchers use the "Corsi span," or number of squares that the participant can reliably solve correctly, as a measure of a person's working memory capacity. (You can easily find several versions of the Corsi block-tapping task online to try yourself.)

How long of a sequence can you remember on the Corsi block-tapping task?

We also need to gather normative data for the population. That is, we need to see how most people do on this task by finding a good estimate of the population's average Corsi span. A quick search of psychology research databases reveals that the mean Corsi span for college-aged adults is 7.10, with a standard deviation of 1.00 (Farrell Pagulayan et al., 2006).

What We're Trying to Accomplish

With our measure of working memory and our population data in hand, imagine that we recruit 50 college students to participate in our study of sleep deprivation and working memory capacity. We ask each participant to come to the lab at 8 P.M. and pull an all-nighter by staying awake until 8 A.M. the following morning. At that time, we administer the Corsi block-tapping task to each participant. We calculate the mean for this sleep-deprived group to be 6.70 with a standard deviation of 1.40. Obviously, 6.70 is less than 7.10. But is this enough evidence to conclude that sleep-deprivation reduces working memory capacity? Or is this within the typical range of sample means that we should expect due to sampling variation?

To answer these questions, we need to use hypothesis testing to compare a sample mean to a population mean. For this type of research design, we'll use a one-sample Z-test. In future chapters, we will discuss other types of hypothesis tests, which are each appropriate for a particular research design.

Assumptions of the One-Sample Z-Test Before we conduct a one-sample Z-test, we need to determine whether we satisfy the assumptions of the test. The **assumptions of a hypothesis test** describe the preconditions that we must meet for the test results to be valid. Assumptions are sort of like prerequisites that you need to satisfy in order to enroll in a class. You can't enroll if you don't meet the prerequisites. Well, the same is true for hypothesis tests. The results will be correct only if we satisfy the assumptions first. For the one-sample Z-test, we must satisfy three key assumptions:

assumptions of a hypothesis test the preconditions that must be satisfied for the results of a hypothesis test to be valid.

1. *The sample must be drawn for a population with a normal distribution, or we must have a sufficiently large sample.* For the one-sample Z-test to work, we must know that the distribution of means takes the shape of a normal curve. Recall from Chapter 5 that the Central Limit Theorem states that the distribution of means will be normal under two situations: If the population is normally distributed, or if each sample in the sampling distribution has at least 30 observations.
2. *The standard deviation of the population (σ) is known.* We must know the standard deviation of the population in order to use the one sample Z-test. The standard deviation of the population is critical information in our calculation of the standard error (which is the standard deviation of the distribution of means). Without this, we can't determine how much

variability there is from sample to sample in our distribution of means, and so we can't determine whether our sample mean is likely or unlikely, given the null hypothesis.

3. *The dependent variable is interval or ratio.* Remember back in Chapter 1 where we distinguished between four different levels of measurement—nominal, ordinal, interval, and ratio? Well, in order for us to conduct a one-sample Z-test, our dependent variable must be either interval or ratio.

Step by Step: Hypothesis Testing with a Distribution of Means Using the *p*-Values Approach To determine whether our sample of sleep-deprived participants performs differently on the Corsi block-tapping task, we need to conduct a hypothesis test. This time, we will use the *p*-value approach that we introduced in the previous chapter.

Step 1: Population and Hypotheses A hypothesis test always pits two competing hypotheses against each other: the null hypothesis and our research hypothesis. To construct these hypotheses, we need to first establish our populations.

Population of Interest: Sleep-deprived adults.
Comparison Population: All adults.
Sample: 50 college students.

So, we want to compare the working memory capacity for sleep-deprived adults to the overall population. Further, we are using a sample of 50 college students to estimate the mean for our population of interest.

Research Hypothesis (H_1): For our research hypothesis, we need to determine what possible outcomes of our study would be scientifically interesting. If sleep-deprived people do worse on our test of working memory capacity, would that be interesting? Yes, because we will learn about the consequences of sleep-deprivation on memory. If sleep-deprived people somehow do better than the population on our test of working memory capacity, would we also find that result interesting? Yes! That surprising result would have implications for many college students who want to perform well on tests.

Both of these results would have the potential to inform the literature on how sleep relates to memory. Therefore, our research hypothesis states that there will be a difference between the population of interest's mean and the comparison population's mean. As we learned earlier in this chapter, this type of research hypothesis is called a nondirectional or two-tailed hypothesis, because we aren't specifying the direction of the effect. In symbol form, our research hypothesis is: $\mu_1 \neq \mu_2$, where μ_1 is the mean for sleep-deprived adults and μ_2 is the mean for the population in general.

Null Hypothesis (H_0): The null hypothesis for this type of hypothesis test is always the same: There is no difference between our population of interest and the comparison population. In other words, $\mu_1 = \mu_2$.

Step 2: Build the Comparison Distribution Next, we need to sketch out what the comparison distribution would look like if the null hypothesis was true. As a starting point, we can determine that the shape of our sampling distribution should be a normal curve, as shown in **Figure 7.11**. Whether our distribution of means actually resembles a normal curve depends on if we have satisfied the assumptions of the test. We will examine this in Step 4.

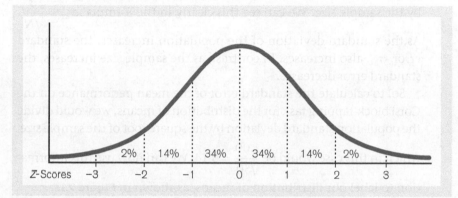

Figure 7.11 Normal Curve with *Z*-Scores and Percentages Under the Curve

Now let's label our comparison distribution with the mean (μ_2) and standard deviation (σ_2) for the population that we have established based on our normative data. Recall that the mean for the population is 7.10 and the standard deviation of the population is 1.00 (Farrell Pagulayan et al., 2006) (see **Figure 7.12**).

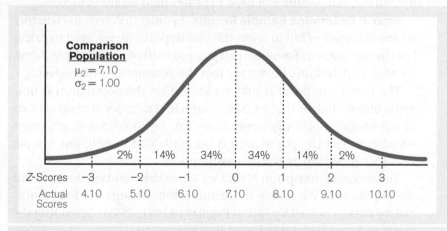

Figure 7.12 Normal Curve with Corresponding Scores on the Corsi Block-Tapping Task

Next, we need to construct our distribution of means by determining its mean and standard deviation. As we noted earlier, the mean of the distribution of means (μ_M) always matches the population's mean. So, just like the comparison population, the mean of the distribution of means is 7.10. The standard error (which reflects the distribution of means' standard deviation), however, is *not* equal to the population's standard deviation. Remember (as we learned in Chapter 5), the standard error reflects the average difference between any sample mean and the population mean. Standard error is partly determined by the standard deviation of the population and partly determined by the sample size. We can see this clearly in the formula: $\sigma_M = \dfrac{\sigma}{\sqrt{N}}$.

As the standard deviation of the population increases, the standard error, σ_M, also increases. In contrast, as the sample size increases, the standard error decreases.

So, to calculate the standard error of the mean performance on the Corsi block-tapping task for the distribution of means, we would divide the population standard deviation by the square root of the sample size, which in this case would be $\dfrac{1.00}{\sqrt{50}} = 0.14$. We can now use this information to label our distribution of means, as shown in **Figure 7.13**.

Step 3: Set the Significance Level (α) Let's set alpha to be .05, because this is the conventional level for alpha set by most researchers. Also, because our research hypothesis (set in Step 1) is a nondirectional hypothesis, we need to divide our alpha in half to reflect the notion that there are two possible results of interest (i.e., that sleep-deprivation could increase or decrease working memory capacity). Thus, .05/2 = .025. The main consequence of this is that in order for us to reject the null hypothesis, our *p*-value will need to be less than an alpha of .025.

Step 4: Determine Sample Results In order to determine whether we should reject or fail to reject the null hypothesis, we need to calculate the test statistic. Before we can proceed with our one-sample *Z*-test, we need to determine if we have met the assumptions of the test.

The first assumption is that we know that the population is normally distributed, or that we have a sufficient number of observations in our sample (typically larger than 30). Although we don't know whether or not the population is normally distributed, our sample size is 50, so we satisfy the first assumption.

The second assumption is that we know the standard deviation of the population. We satisfy this assumption, because we found normative data (reported by Farrell Pagulayan et al., 2006) describing the mean and standard deviation of the population.

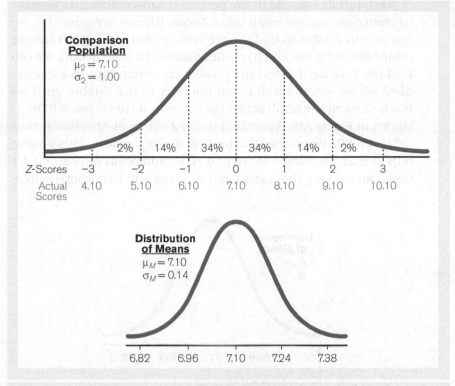

Figure 7.13   Normal Curve and Distribution of Means

Finally, the third assumption is that our dependent variable is interval or ratio. We satisfy this assumption because the Corsi span is a ratio variable (i.e., has a meaningful zero and we can calculate meaningful ratios of scores). So, we have satisfied all three assumptions of the hypothesis test.

As we learned earlier in this chapter, the formula for the test statistic for the one-sample Z-test is $Z = \dfrac{X - \mu_M}{\sigma_M}$. For our working memory capacity study, we found a mean performance on the Corsi block-tapping for our sample of 50 sleep-deprived participants to be 6.70. We can enter this value into our equation for M, along with the mean of the population, 7.10, and the standard error for the distribution of means, 0.14. Thus, we can calculate the Z-test statistic:

$$Z = \frac{M - \mu_M}{\sigma_M} = \frac{6.70 - 7.10}{0.14} = -2.86$$

Next, just like we did in the previous chapter, now that we have converted our sample mean into a Z-score (shown in **Figure 7.14**), we can use our Z-table to find the probability of observing our sample mean, assuming the null hypothesis is true. In other words, we can find our p-value. To find the p-value corresponding to a Z-score of -2.86, we would scroll down the rows of the Z-table until we reach -2.8 and the scroll across the columns until we reach 0.06, as shown in **Figure 7.15**. According to the Z-table, our p-value is thus .0021, or .002 when rounded to three decimal places. This p-value tells us that our sample mean of 6.70 should occur only about 2.1 times out of every thousand samples, if the null hypothesis is true.

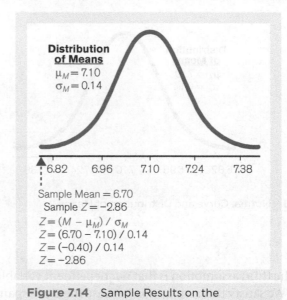

Distribution of Means
$\mu_M = 7.10$
$\sigma_M = 0.14$

6.82   6.96   7.10   7.24   7.38

Sample Mean $= 6.70$
Sample $Z = -2.86$

$Z = (M - \mu_M) / \sigma_M$
$Z = (6.70 - 7.10) / 0.14$
$Z = (-0.40) / 0.14$
$Z = -2.86$

Figure 7.14   Sample Results on the Comparison Distribution

Step 5: Decide and Interpret So, should we reject or fail to reject the null hypothesis? Remember that to make our decision using the p-value approach, we need to compare our p-value to our significance level, set by alpha. In this case, because the p-value provided in the table is less than alpha ($0.002 < 0.05$), we will reject the null hypothesis and conclude that sleep deprivation reduces working memory capacity.

Communicating the Result

To communicate our result, we will prepare a results paragraph using the approach described in Chapter 6. The general idea of this approach is that we need to specify the type of hypothesis test we are performing and the research hypothesis in

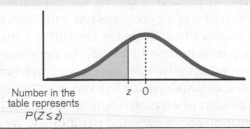

Number in the table represents $P(Z \le z)$

z	0.00	0.01	0.02	0.03	0.04	0.05	0.06	0.07	0.08	0.09
-3.6	.0000	.0000	.0000	.0000	.0000	.0000	.0001	.0000	.0000	.0001
-3.5	.0000	.0000	.0000	.0000	.0000	.0000	.0002	.0000	.0000	.0002
-3.4	.0003	.0003	.0003	.0003	.0003	.0003	.0003	.0003	.0003	.0002
-3.3	.0005	.0005	.0005	.0004	.0004	.0004	.0004	.0004	.0004	.0003
-3.2	.0007	.0007	.0006	.0006	.0006	.0005	.0006	.0005	.0005	.0005
-3.1	.0010	.0009	.0009	.0009	.0008	.0008	.0008	.0008	.0007	.0007
-3.0	.0013	.0013	.0013	.0012	.0012	.0011	.0011	.0011	.0010	.0010
-2.9	.0019	.0018	.0018	.0017	.0016	.0016	.0015	.0015	.0014	.0014
-2.8	.0026	.0025	.0024	.0023	.0023	.0022	.0021	.0021	.0920	.0019
-2.7	.0035	.0034	.0033	.0032	.0031	.0030	.0029	.0028	.0927	.0026
-2.6	.0047	.0045	.0044	.0043	.0041	.0040	.0039	.0038	.0037	.0036
-2.5	.0062	.0060	.0059	.0057	.0055	.0054	.0052	.0051	.0049	.0048

Figure 7.15 Finding the *p*-Value for a *Z* Statistic

the first sentence. Then, in the second sentence, we provide the test statistic and *p*-value, and an interpretation of how the sample's mean compared to the population's mean. Here's what it should look like:

> We performed a one-sample *Z*-test to examine whether sleep deprivation would affect performance on a test of working memory capacity. The results were significant, $Z = -2.86$, $p = .002$, such that sleep-deprived participants performed worse on the Corsi block-tapping task ($M = 6.70$, $SD = 1.40$) compared to the general population ($M = 7.10$, $SD = 1.00$).

In addition to writing a results paragraph, we may also decide to depict our results graphically in a bar graph. A bar graph is a type of figure that provides the means of our study conditions or groups, along with the standard error. We previously discussed how to create a bar graph for a frequency distribution in Chapter 2, but we will now describe how to create a bar graph to depict the results of a one-sample *Z*-test.

error bars lines added to the bars in a bar graph that express the amount of variability in a variable. Error bars may represent the standard deviation, standard error, confidence interval, or any other measure of variability.

The difference between a generic bar graph and a bar graph used to depict the results of a hypothesis test is the inclusion of error bars. **Error bars** graphically indicate the amount of variability associated with a group or condition in a study. In some cases, error bars can simply provide descriptive information, such as when they are used to indicate the standard deviation of a variable (Cumming et al., 2007). But in the context of a hypothesis test, we can use error bars to provide information about statistical significance. We do this by using error bars to indicate the standard error of a variable, or the amount of sampling error that we get when we take samples of a certain size.

To make conclusions about statistical significance using error bars, we look to see whether the error bars overlap (when presenting the standard error). As you can see in **Figure 7.16**, if the error bars for one group (i.e., the sample) overlap the error bars for the other group (i.e., the population), we can conclude that the groups are not significantly different from one another. If the error bars do not overlap, we can't necessarily conclude that the groups are significantly different.

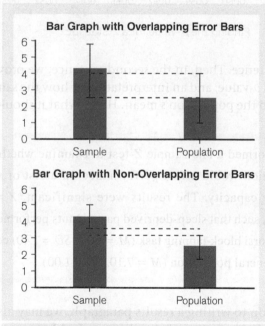

Figure 7.16 Bar Graphs with Overlapping and Non-Overlapping Error Bars

Step by Step: Creating a Bar Graph with Error Bars Although we can create a bar graph using statistical software, such as SPSS, it's just as easy to create one using a word processing program, such as Microsoft Word or Google Docs. You can see an example in **Figure 7.17**.

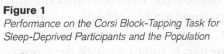

Figure 1

Performance on the Corsi Block-Tapping Task for Sleep-Deprived Participants and the Population

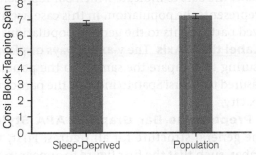

Note: Error bars represent +/–1 standard error of the mean.

Figure 7.17 Bar Graph Formatted in APA Style

Step 1: Create a Column Graph/Chart Most word processing programs offer the option to insert a chart into a document. To edit the information presented in the bar graph, these programs link to a spreadsheet program, such as Microsoft Excel or Google Sheets. By default, these programs may display more than two bars, and so our first step will be to delete the unneeded bars. The one-sample Z-test presents only two means, so we only need two bars in our bar graph.

Step 2: Enter the Means Next, we want to replace the sample values that are provided by default with the mean we observed for our sample and the mean of the population.

Step 3: Create Error Bars Our bar graph should also include error bars that extend one standard error above and below the mean. Each word processing program will have a different method for creating error bars. The important thing to remember is that you must enter the value of the standard error that you calculated (i.e., the denominator of the test statistic). Some word processing programs will generate default values for the standard error, but these are not the values associated with your data set. In Microsoft Word, you will need to use the Custom error bars option to enter the values for the standard error. In Google Docs, use the chart editor to add error bars, and the Constant option to specify the exact value of the standard error.

Step 4: Label the X-Axis The x-axis always displays the groups that we are comparing in a hypothesis test. In the context of a one-sample Z-test, we are comparing a sample to a population. So, we need to label the bars to indicate which bar represents the sample and which represents the population. In this case, we are comparing sleep-deprived participants to the general population.

Step 5: Label the Y-Axis The y-axis always displays the variable we are measuring to compare the sample to the population. In this case, we measured the Corsi Span to indicate the participants working memory capacity.

Step 6: Prepare the Bar Graph in APA Style APA Style describes the general structure for all figures. First, we give each figure a number, such that the first figure to appear in a manuscript is called Figure 1. Under the figure number, we provide a figure title (in italic font). Next, we provide the body of the figure, which in this case is a bar graph with error bars. Finally, below the body of the figure, we should include a figure note, which explains any information that is not readily interpretable. For a bar graph with error bars, we must indicate what information the error bars present, because some error bars may represent standard deviation as opposed to standard error.

Your Turn 7.3

1. Previous research indicates that children who grow up in chaotic households (i.e., those characterized by high noise levels, overcrowding, and a lack of predicable routines) have lower IQs than children who grow up in less chaotic households (Deater-Deckard et al., 2009). Imagine that you want to conduct a study examining whether children growing up in chaotic households are also more likely to get sick (measured by the number of visits to the doctor that a child makes in a year). You know from government statistics that the average child makes 2.13 visits to the doctor per year with a standard deviation of the population of 0.34. You collect data on doctor's visits from 100 children raised in chaotic homes and find the mean number of doctor's visits to be 2.21. What are the population of interest, the comparison population, and sample?

2. State the null and research hypotheses for this research problem.

3. What are the assumptions of the one-sample Z-test? Does this research study satisfy the assumptions?

4. Using the information provided, construct a comparison distribution.

5. What would the distribution of means look like?

6. Determine the sample results by calculating the one-sample Z-test statistic.

7. What is the p-value for the test statistic?

8. Based on the p-value you found, and using an alpha of .05, what should you decide regarding the null hypothesis? What is your interpretation of the results?

Forming a Conclusion

The results of our study suggest that sleep deprivation reduces working memory capacity. Our sample of sleep-deprived participants had a mean that was very unlikely to occur, if the null hypothesis is true. To make this conclusion, we conducted a one-sample Z-test using the p-value approach. We chose the one-sample Z-test because we were comparing a single sample mean to a population mean, and we knew the standard deviation of the population. In future chapters, we will learn alternative hypothesis tests that we will conduct when we want to compare multiple sample means to each other, or if we do not know the standard deviation of the population.

Focus on Open Science: One- Versus Two-Tailed Tests

The downside to the one-tailed research hypothesis is that some of the most important findings are the ones that are unexpected. Sometimes, we may conduct a study with a clear research hypothesis, only to find that the opposite outcome actually occurs. For example, throughout the 1980s and 1990s, tens of thousands of schoolchildren took part in Project DARE, a program designed to reduce drug use among children and teens. If we were researchers examining the program's effectiveness, we might decide to use a one-tailed research hypothesis, with the expectation that participation in Project DARE would reduce drug use relative to the population. If we did so, however, we might miss the surprising finding that participation in Project DARE sometimes backfires, leading children who go through the program to be actually more likely to use drugs (e.g., Lilienfeld, 2007; Werch & Owen, 2002). This surprising effect would have been missed if the scholars proposed a one-tailed research hypothesis.

Kuttig - People/Alamy Stock Photo

Rigorous research is integral to creating—and refining—public policy that can have major health impacts to vulnerable populations, like at-risk teens.

Unfortunately, sometimes the fact that it is easier to reject the null hypothesis when conducting a one-tailed hypothesis test leads researchers to engage in questionable research practices. In particular, when researchers discover that they have failed to reject the null hypothesis for a two-tailed research hypothesis, some researchers may retroactively change their research hypothesis to a one-tailed hypothesis, thus making it easier to find statistically significant results. The impact of this deceitful practice is twofold:

- First, it increases the number of false positive findings (i.e., concluding there is an effect when there actually isn't) that get published, which can impede the progress of science.
- Second, it makes the use of one-tailed research hypotheses suspicious, because we as evaluators of research must determine whether a scholar actually predicted a one-tailed research hypothesis, or did so only after looking at their results.

Luckily, open science helps solve both of these problems via preregistration. When scholars preregister their hypotheses, they must decide ahead of time whether they are making a one- or two-tailed research hypothesis. This eliminates the temptation to switch from a two-tailed to a one-tailed test after conducting data analyses. It also eliminates the suspicion that scholars engaged in this questionable research practice, because they can use their preregistered hypothesis to prove that they actually made a one-tailed prediction.

Become a Better Consumer of Statistics

To make a decision regarding the null hypothesis, we need to know both the means of the sample and population, and the standard error. This information allows us to compute the test statistic and find the p-value. Importantly, just knowing the means is not enough to determine statistical significance. We must know the standard error as well.

Often in media reports of scientific findings, however, bar graphs depicting the results of experiments do not include error bars. Instead, these reports reveal only the differences between means. As a savvy consumer of statistics, we need to be wary of the bar graphs we are most likely to see in the popular press and on the Internet that do not contain error bars. Without the error bars, we may focus only on the means, and overlook the variability that may exist within groups. As a consequence, we may make conclusions that the data do not justify. For example, we may assume that there is a difference between the sample and the population, when in fact there is no difference. So, whenever we see a bar graph without error bars, we should be more skeptical and cautious with our interpretation.

Interpreting Graphs and Charts from Research Articles

In addition to sleep being a possible factor in working memory capacity, previous research has also examined the role of age. For example, a study examining memory for faces reveals that younger participants perform better on the working memory task compared to older participants (Gazzaley et al., 2005). In the article describing these effects, the authors present to us the following bar graph, as shown in **Figure 7.18**.

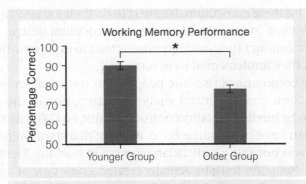

Figure 7.18 Bar Graph Comparing Memory of Faces Between Younger and Older Participants (Data from Gazzaley et al., 2005)

As we can see, the authors provide labels for the two groups that they are comparing in their study. They also clearly label the y-axis as indicating the percentage correct on the memory task. Importantly, they include information that helps readers interpret the differences between the conditions. First, they provide error bars that represent one standard error of the mean. We know that if the error bars overlap, we can conclude that the results are not statistically significant. Here, the error bars do not overlap, so there may be a significant difference between conditions. The authors also include a star above the means, which indicates that the difference between the means is statistically significant. One feature here that is problematic is that the y-axis starts at 50 percent instead of 0, which makes the differences between the groups appear larger.

Statistics on the Job

Many jobs require people to have a basic understanding of statistics in order to be maximally effective in the workplace. Medical doctors, for example, must keep up with the scientific literature so that they know which treatments to prescribe to patients. Medical journals report the results of studies, which typically use hypothesis tests such as the one-sample Z-test. Thus, for doctors to read papers and implement their findings into their practices, they must understand how hypothesis tests work.

Similarly, educational curriculum designers need to be able to conduct and interpret statistical tests when designing and evaluating new curricula. For example, a curriculum designer may need to help a school district develop a method to better teach students certain mathematical skills that will be tested on a state proficiency exam. In order for these curriculum designers to do their job effectively, they not only need to read the literature on curriculum design, but they also must conduct their own hypothesis tests to evaluate whether the changes they implemented were successful.

Many corporations also hire people with statistical knowledge to help perform quality control analyses. Indeed, one of the very first people to be hired as a quality control specialist was William Gossett, a statistician hired by Guinness & Co. Brewery, makers of Guinness beer. Gossett was not just a statistician who could read the literature and conduct statistical tests; he actually created a new type of hypothesis test, called the t-test, that we will learn about in Chapter 9.

CHAPTER 7 > Review

Review Questions

1. After spending time at a friend's cabin, you come home covered in mosquito bites. You wonder how long they will itch, and a quick unscientific search of the Internet tells you that they'll likely itch for 4 days. Without doing any calculations, answer the following:

   a. What is the mean of the comparison distribution?

   b. If the standard deviation of the comparison distribution is 1.5, which of these is the population standard deviation? (0.5, 1, 1.25, 1.5, 2.5)

   c. You find 10 more mosquito bites, so your sample size increases. Which of these is the standard deviation of the new comparison distribution? (1.45, 1.5, 2, 2.25, 2.5)

2. When is it appropriate to use a Z-test?

3. In your own words, explain what statistical assumptions are and why it is important to determine whether they are met before running a statistical test.

4. A positively skewed population has a mean of 39 and a standard deviation of 12. What is the probability of obtaining a sample mean of 56 for a sample of 15 students?

5. A researcher analyzes the study results with a Z-test and finds the following result: −2.18.

   a. If $\alpha = .05$, and she uses a one-tailed test (predicting a decrease), what decision and conclusion does the researcher make?

   b. If instead she uses a two-tailed test, does the decision and conclusion change? Why or why not? If it changes, what is the new decision and conclusion?

   c. If she changes her α to be .01, using a one-tailed test, does the decision and conclusion change? Why or why not? If it changes, what is the new decision and conclusion?

6. Explain what happens to the critical value(s) and the likelihood of rejecting the null hypothesis if the alpha level of a hypothesis test is changed from .05 to .01.

7. Explain what happens to the critical value(s) and the likelihood of rejecting the null hypothesis if the hypotheses are changed from nondirectional to directional.

8. A researcher conducts a study to evaluate the effect of a new method of teaching children to read. A sample of $n = 16$ kindergarten students participate. Each student is taught to read with the new method, and the number of lessons it takes for them to learn to read is recorded. For the population, children typically need $\mu_2 = 90$ lessons and have a $\sigma_2 = 24$. It is normally distributed. The sample of 16 children had a mean score of $M = 77.5$.

   a. What are the population of interest, the comparison population, and the sample?
   b. What would the null hypothesis and research hypothesis be?
   c. Does this research satisfy the assumptions of the one-sample Z-test?
   d. Using the information provided, construct a comparison distribution.
   e. You set the alpha level to be .03. Establish the critical value cutoff(s).
   f. Determine the sample results by calculating the one-sample Z-test.
   g. What is the appropriate conclusion?

9. Create a bar graph with error bars for Question 8. Be sure to include a figure caption.

10. Although you normally check a bag when flying, you wonder if you should travel with just a carry-on when you go on vacation next month. A news report stated that over the past few years an average of 880 bags are lost or delayed per day at your local airport and that the population is normally distributed. For this example, the population standard deviation is 100. Tracking the data for the next 7 days on the airport website, you find that the average number of lost bags per day is 964. You decide you'll take only a carry-on bag if the results are unlikely to have happened by chance, with an alpha level of .05 (use a one-tailed test).

    a. What is the population of interest, the comparison population, and the sample?
    b. What would the null hypothesis and research hypothesis be?
    c. Using the information provided, construct a comparison distribution.
    d. Determine the sample results by calculating the one-sample Z-test.
    e. What is the p-value for the test statistic?
    f. Based on the p-value you found, what should you decide regarding the null hypothesis?
    g. Will you check a bag or only take a carry-on with you on your upcoming trip?

11. Create a bar graph with error bars for Question 10. Be sure to include a figure caption.

Key Concepts

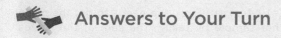
Your Turn 7.1

1. Rather than looking at one person, we should look at everyone from class and take their mean. Since we would have a mean of a sample, our comparison distribution (i.e., the distribution of means) needs to match our population of interest.

2. (a) A distribution of sample means of 10 preschoolers in regular preschool curriculums. (b) A distribution of individuals from the general population who eat a regular diet.

3. The explanation needs to address the likelihood of randomly selecting a score near the mean (high likelihood) versus randomly selecting a more extreme score far from the mean (low likelihood). You should also discuss how multiple rare/low-likelihood events become increasing unlikely with larger samples (it is easier to get 2 rare scores than 5 rare scores). For that reason, when you take means of samples and plot them on a distribution, there are fewer means out on the extreme tails, making the distribution narrower and with lower variability.

Your Turn 7.2

1. (a) The mean is 14, because the mean of the distribution of means (the comparison distribution) is always identical to the population; (b) it has to be 2, because the standard deviation of the distribution of means (the comparison distribution) is always lower than the population standard deviation.

2. The distribution of means' standard deviation is equal to the square root of the distribution of means' variance, which is equal to the square root of the population variance divided by the number of people in the sample, which is equal to the population standard deviation divided by the square root of the number of people in the sample.

3. The researcher fails to reject the null hypothesis. The study did not find evidence to suggest that the sample mean was different from the population mean.

4. (a) Population of Interest: Contestants on *The Bachelor*. Comparison Population: People in general. Sample: 20 previous *Bachelor* contestants. (b) Contestants on *The Bachelor* have equal quality relationships as people in general. (c) Contestants on *The Bachelor* have better relationships than the population. (d) The research hypothesis is directional, because the researcher specifies the direction of difference between *Bachelor* contestants and the population.

5. Note that we first need to convert population variance to population standard deviation by taking the square root of the variance, or $\sqrt{.25} = .50$

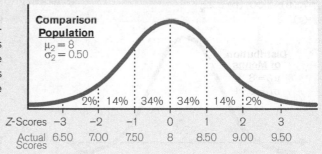

Comparison Population
$\mu_2 = 8$
$\sigma_2 = 0.50$

	2%	14%	34%	34%	14%	2%	
Z-Scores	−3	−2	−1	0	1	2	3
Actual Scores	6.50	7.00	7.50	8	8.50	9.00	9.50

6. (a) A distribution of sample means with a sample size of 20; (b) mean, standard deviation, and shape; (c) 8 (same as the population); (d) more narrow, taller, and skinnier than a normal distribution; (e) $\sigma_M^2 = \sigma^2/N = .25/20 = .0125$; (f) $\sigma_M = \sqrt{\sigma_M^2} = \sqrt{.0125} = .11$ or $\sigma_M = \sigma/\sqrt{N} = .50/\sqrt{20} = .50/4.47 = .11$.

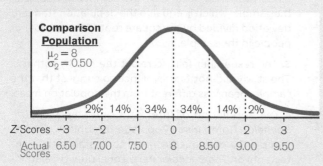

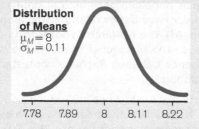

7. (a) +2.00; (b) 8.22; (c)

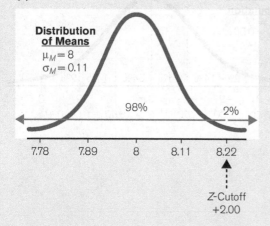

8. (a) Z-test. (b) First, she needs to get the mean of her sample by taking the sum of the scores (148) and dividing by 20, or $148/20 = 7.4$. Next, she must complete the Z-test, $Z = (M - \mu_M)/\sigma_M$ $Z = (7.4 - 8)/.11 = (-.06)/.11 = -5.45$; (c)

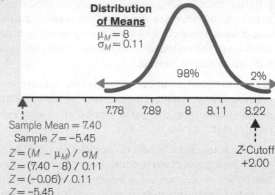

Sample Mean = 7.40
Sample $Z = -5.45$
$Z = (M - \mu_M) / \sigma_M$
$Z = (7.40 - 8) / 0.11$
$Z = (-0.06) / 0.11$
$Z = -5.45$

Z-Cutoff +2.00

9. Be careful here. Even though the resulting Z-score is large, the number is negative (−5.45), so it falls within the 98% of the distribution and does not exceed the cutoff of (+2.00). In other words, the writer's sample was not more extreme than the critical value.

Because our sample's results (Step 4) do not exceed the critical value (Step 3) we are unable to reject the null hypothesis (H_0) that *Bachelor* contestants have the same relationship quality as people in general ($\mu_1 = \mu_2$). If we are unable to reject the null, we must also say that we failed to find support for the research hypothesis (H_1) that *Bachelor* contestants have better relationship quality than people in general ($\mu_1 < \mu_2$).

Your Turn 7.3

1. The population of interest is children raised in chaotic households. The comparison population is all children. The sample is the 100 participants in the study.

2. The null hypothesis is that children raised in chaotic households visit the doctor at the same rate as the general population, $\mu_1 = \mu_2$. The research hypothesis is that growing up in a chaotic household will differ from the population in terms of the number of visits to the doctor, $\mu_1 \neq \mu_2$.

3. The one-sample Z-test assumes that the population is normally distributed or that the sample size is larger than 30 observations, and that the standard deviation of the population is known. This study does satisfy these assumptions, because the sample size is larger than 30 (N = 100) and the population standard deviation is known to be 0.34.

4.

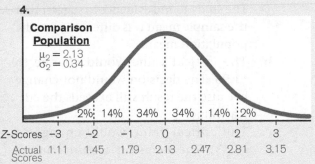

5.

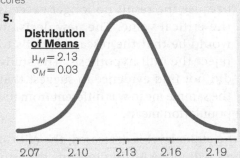

6. To calculate the Z-test, we use the formula $Z = (M - \mu_M)/\sigma_M$. Using the information provided, $Z = (2.21 - 2.13)/0.03 = (0.08)/0.03 = 2.67$.

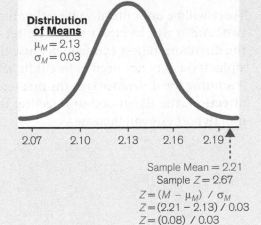

Sample Mean = 2.21
Sample Z = 2.67
$Z = (M - \mu_M) / \sigma_M$
$Z = (2.21 - 2.13) / 0.03$
$Z = (0.08) / 0.03$
$Z = 2.67$

7. To find the p-value for a test-statistic of 2.67, we scroll down the rows of our Z-table until we reach 2.6 and scroll across the columns until we reach 0.07. This reveals that the probability to the left of 2.67 is .9962. Of course, we need the probability to the right of our test-statistic, when it is greater than 0. Thus, we would take 1 minus the tabled value: 1 – .9962 = .0038.

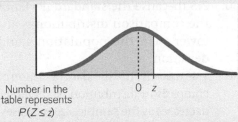

Number in the table represents
$P(Z \leq z)$

z	0.00	0.01	0.02	0.03	0.04	0.05	0.06	0.07	0.08	0.09
0.0	.5000	.5040	.5080	.5120	.5160	.5199	.5239	.5279	.5319	.5359
0.1	.5398	.5438	.5478	.5517	.5557	.5596	.5636	.5675	.5714	.5753
0.2	.5793	.5832	.5871	.5910	.5948	.5987	.6026	.6064	.6103	.6141
0.3	.6179	.6217	.6255	.6293	.6331	.6368	.6406	.6443	.6480	.6517
0.4	.6554	.6591	.6628	.6664	.6700	.6736	.6772	.6808	.6844	.6879
0.5	.6915	.6950	.6985	.7019	.7054	.7088	.7123	.7157	.7190	.7224
0.6	.7257	.7291	.7324	.7357	.7380	.7422	.7454	.7486	.7517	.7549
0.7	.7580	.7611	.7642	.7673	.7704	.7734	.7764	.7794	.7823	.7852
0.8	.7881	.7910	.7939	.7967	7995	.8023	.8051	.8078	.8106	.8133
0.9	.8159	.8186	.8212	.8238	.8264	.8289	.8315	.8340	.8365	.8389
1.0	.8413	.8438	.8461	.8485	.8508	.8531	.8554	.8577	.8599	.8621
1.1	.8643	.8665	.8686	.8708	.8729	.8749	.8770	.8790	.8810	.8830
1.2	.8849	.8869	.8888	.8907	.8925	.8944	.8962	.8900	.8997	.9015
1.3	.9032	.9049	.9066	.9082	.9099	.9115	.9131	.9147	9162	.9177
1.4	.9192	.9207	.9222	.9236	.9251	.9265	.9279	.9292	.9306	.9319
1.5	.9332	.9345	.9357	.9370	.9382	.9394	.9406	.9418	.9429	.9441
1.6	.9452	.9463	.9474	.9484	.9495	.9505	.9515	.9525	.9535	.9545
1.7	.9554	.9564	.9573	.9582	.9591	.9599	.9608	.9616	.9625	.9633
1.8	.9641	.9649	.9656	.9664	.9671	.9678	.9686	.9693	.9699	.9706
1.9	.9713	.9719	.9726	.9732	.9738	.9744	.9750	.9756	.9761	.9767
2.0	.9772	.9778	.9783	.9788	.9793	.9798	.9803	.9808	.9812	.9817
2.1	.9821	.9826	.9830	.9834	.9838	.9842	.9846	.9850	.9854	.9857
2.2	.9861	.9864	.9868	.9871	.9875	.9878	.9881	.9884	.9887	.9890
2.3	.9893	.9896	.9898	.9901	.9904	.9906	.9909	.9911	.9913	.9916
2.4	.9918	.9920	.9922	.9925	.9927	.9929	.9931	.9932	.9934	.9936
2.5	.9938	.9940	.9941	.9943	.9945	.9946	.9948	.9949	.9951	.9952
2.6	.9953	.9955	.9956	.9957	.9959	.9960	.9961	.9962	.9963	.9964
2.7	.9965	.9966	.9967	.9968	.9969	.9970	.9971	.9972	.9973	.9974

8. Because the null hypothesis is two-tailed, you need to observe a p-value of less than .025 in order to reject the null hypothesis. In this case, the p-value of .0038 is less than .025, so you should reject the null hypothesis. Thus, you should conclude that children living in chaotic households visit the doctor significantly more often than average for the population.

Answers to Review Questions

1. **a.** 4 (because the mean of the comparison distribution is always identical to the population)
   b. 2.5 (because the standard deviation of the comparison distribution is always lower than the population standard deviation)
   c. 1.45 (because the standard deviation of the comparison distribution (standard error) decreases as the sample size increases)

2. We use a one-sample Z-test when the population mean and standard deviation are known, the population is normal (or we have a sample ≥ 30), and the dependent variable is interval or ratio.

3. Assumptions are a set of conditions that must be met for the results of a statistical test to be valid. If the assumptions are not met, then the results will be erroneous or misleading.

4. This data cannot be analyzed with a Z-test because the assumption of normality has not been met. The population is skewed and the sample size is too small.

5. **a.** The critical value would be −1.65. The researcher rejects the null hypothesis and accepts the research hypothesis. The study found evidence to suggest that the sample mean was different from the population mean.
   b. The critical value would change to ±1.96. The decision would not change because the result still exceeds the critical value.
   c. The critical value would change to −2.33. The decision would change because the result no longer exceeds the critical value. The new decision would be that the researcher fails to reject the null hypothesis. The study did not find evidence to suggest that the sample mean was different from the population mean.

6. As the alpha level is decreased, the critical values will move further towards the tails of the distribution (more extreme) and the likelihood of rejecting the null hypothesis will decrease.

7. There will be one critical value rather than two, and it will be closer to the center of the distribution (less extreme) because the alpha level does not need to be cut in half. Assuming the difference is in the predicted direction, the likelihood of rejecting the null hypothesis will increase.

8. a. The population of interest is children learning to read using the new method, the comparison population is children learning to read in general, and the sample is the 16 children.

b. Null hypothesis: Children learning to read with the new method will require the same number of lessons as the general population of children ($\mu_1 = \mu_2$). Research hypothesis: Children learning to read with the new method will differ from the population in terms of the number of lessons required ($\mu_1 \neq \mu_2$).

c. The assumptions are met because the population is normally distributed, the standard deviation of the population is known, and the scale of measurement is ratio.

d.

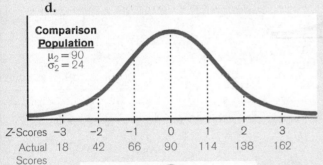

Z-Scores	−3	−2	−1	0	1	2	3
Actual Scores	18	42	66	90	114	138	162

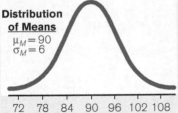

e. ±2.17

f. $\sigma_M = 6$, $z = -2.08$

g. Fail to reject the null hypothesis. Children learning to read using the new method require the same number of lessons as children in the general population.

9.

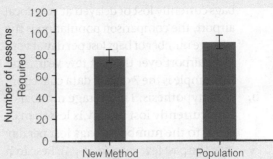

Average number of lessons required to learn to read for the New Method of teaching and the population. Error bars represent +/−1 standard error of the mean.

10. a. The population of interest is the number of bags currently lost or delayed at your local airport, the comparison population is the average number of bags lost per day at your local airport over the past few years, and the sample is the 7 days of data collection.

b. Null hypothesis: The average number of bags currently lost per day is less than or equal to the number of bags lost per day over the past few years ($\mu_1 \leq \mu_2$). Research hypothesis: The average number of bags currently lost per day is greater than the number of bags lost per day over the past few years ($\mu_1 > \mu_2$).

c.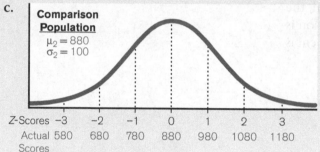

Comparison Population
$\mu_2 = 880$
$\sigma_2 = 100$

Z-Scores	−3	−2	−1	0	1	2	3
Actual Scores	580	680	780	880	980	1080	1180

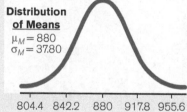

Distribution of Means
$\mu_M = 880$
$\sigma_M = 37.80$

804.4 842.2 880 917.8 955.6

d. $\sigma_M = 37.80$, $z = 2.22$

e. 0.0136

f. Reject the null hypothesis and accept the research hypothesis. The current number of bags lost per day is greater than the number lost over the past few years.

g. You decide that you will only take a carry-on bag on your upcoming trip.

11.

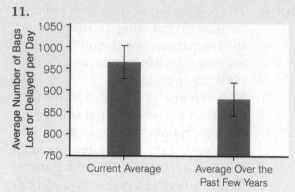

Current average number of bags lost or delayed per day and the average number lost or delayed per day over the past few years. Error bars represent +/−1 standard error of the mean.

Statistical Significance, Confidence Intervals, Effect Size, and Power

Learning Outcomes

After reading this chapter, you should be able to:

● Calculate confidence intervals.

● Define statistical significance and discuss its role in research.

● Explain the importance of sample size for statistical significance.

● Identify the types of decision errors we can make when conducting significance tests.

● Distinguish between statistical significance and practical importance.

● Describe the factors that increase or decrease the likelihood of finding a statistically significant effect.

● Describe the concept of effect size.

● Describe the concept of statistical power.

You're only a few weeks into the semester, but it has already caught up to you: sleep deprivation. There just aren't enough hours in the day to do everything you need to get done and still get enough sleep to avoid walking around in a zombie-like fog. There's no doubt what you *should* do: Go to bed each night by 10 P.M. and get a full night's sleep so that you can wake up recharged and ready for your 8 A.M. class. But realistically, you also want to have a social life, which is going to require staying up past 10 P.M.

The solution? Naps! Twenty minutes here, 45 minutes there, each sprinkled around your busy schedule. But you're already doing that and still feel drowsy.

Perhaps it isn't about what time you go to bed, but rather your sleep quality. Right now, even though you're exhausted, when you try to sleep you're either so overtired or overcaffeinated that the sleep you do get doesn't help. Frustrated, you call your mom to vent. She has a suggestion: essential oils. She explains that everyone she knows raves about how well they work not just for sleep, but for everything.

Mom's often right about stuff, you begrudgingly admit to yourself, but, seriously—essential oils? Is this *really* going to solve your sleep issues? Should you jump on the bandwagon and try essential oil aromatherapy, or should you save your money and skip what might just be a passing trend?

Statistics for Life

As much as you love your mom, you know better than to blindly trust anyone's personal opinions or claims. Your mom's friends, neighbors, and coworkers, who all insist essential oils work, may not be the best judges. It simply could be that oils users want to believe the oils work because they've spent money on them. We need to check the research.

A search of the Internet uncovers supportive findings from companies who sell oils. Though they may tout their findings, the companies

Are essential oils a good way to improve sleep? How sure are you?

Martina Hanakova/Alamy Stock Photo

don't share the details of actual studies because their research is proprietary.

When we look at scientific journals, the evidence is mixed. For example, a review of over 200 studies on aromatherapy's effectiveness found no evidence that aromatherapy helped the treatment of pain, anxiety, depression, dementia, or hypertension (Lee et al., 2012). That's not promising, but these studies also didn't study sleep. A review of 8 studies focused on lavender and sleep found that lavender oil users reported benefits and suggested that diffusing lavender while sleeping may help minimize sleep disturbances (Fismer & Pilkington, 2012). However, these studies had small samples and methodological issues. In fact, the review of 200 aromatherapy studies noted that only 10 studies had sufficient scientific rigor to even consider the findings (Lee et al., 2012).

More recently, a study reported that a group of 19 elderly subjects slept longer when they slept with essential oils on their pillow (Takeda et al., 2017). Though that may make us more optimistic about essential oils' potential benefits for college student napping, that study focused on the nighttime sleep of older adults, which may be different.

Where Do the Data Come From?

The next time you talk to your mom, you mention the research you read. She remains convinced that aromatherapy will solve your sleep quality problems. Not only that, but she also says she has proof that she received from the neighborhood essential oil expert. She screenshots the pamphlet she received, which is titled "Essential Oils: Lavender Is Like a Lullaby for Improving Naps."

Looking it over, you notice that the pamphlet cites some of the same research we noted earlier, but conveniently leaves out some of the limitations. The pamphlet also vaguely describes a study they conducted where they had 1,000 people ($N = 1,000$) come to a sleep lab to take a 20-minute mid-afternoon nap while running an essential oil diffuser. The goal was to see who felt more well-rested (defined as more alert and energetic) after their nap. They randomly assigned half of the participants to use a diffuser filled with lavender oil ($N = 500$), while the other half used a diffuser filled with distilled water ($N = 500$). According to the pamphlet, the lavender oil group reported feeling more well-rested ($M = 6.00$; $\sigma^2 = 1.56$) than the distilled water group ($M = 5.85$; $\sigma^2 = 2.10$) and includes the notation that $p < .10$. While all of that looks convincing, it's quite possible that at this point you aren't quite sure.

The pamphlet prominently features their study's evidence to boldly proclaim lavender's ability to improve naps. But, are you convinced that breathing lavender oils improves nap quality? Should you run out and get your own lavender oil diffuser?

Confidence Intervals of the Mean: What We're Trying to Accomplish

Do essential oils work or not? Simple question, but categorical, black/white, either/or type thinking often leaves information out. Instead, we're more likely to accurately capture reality if we think along a continuum, in shades of gray. This is the difference between taking a class pass/fail (categorical approach) versus receiving a grade based on your course percentage (continuum approach). The pass/fail approach lumps everyone who got an A with everyone who got a C. Thus, if we want to convey your course performance more accurately, we should use the continuum approach, where your grade falls on the full continuum of 0% to 100%. With this approach, we can clearly see the substantial performance difference between, say, a 97% and a 73%.

Though hypothesis testing produces reject or fail to reject conclusions, we often want additional information. There is another approach. This is basically the idea behind **confidence intervals** (CIs), which aim to present the range of scores where we're reasonably sure we would find the population's true mean. CIs are like informed guesses or approximations. It is an approach that acknowledges the near impossibility of precision. We will likely never know the population's true mean with absolute certainty. A confidence interval hedges a bit and gives an estimate that basically says, "We can't pinpoint the population mean, but we are reasonably sure it is right around here."

confidence interval a range of scores that likely includes the population's true mean.

How confident are you that the price of the prize falls in this range?

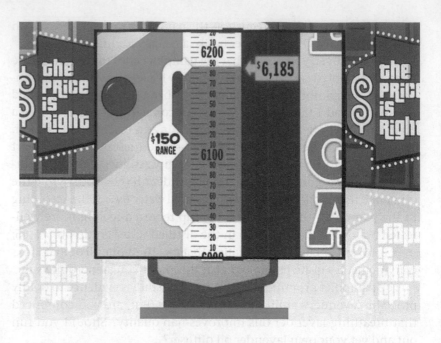

The general idea of confidence intervals is a lot like something you would see on one of the longest running game shows on American television, *The Price Is Right*. Show contestants can play a variety of different games, each with the same goal: to guess the price of a prize. One particular game, Range Finder, presents contestants with a luxurious prize. For this example, let's say the prize is a hot tub. Next, they see a game board that has a wide range of scores (e.g., $6,000–$6,200) with $10 increments. The game board also has a target zone, which is a $150 shaded area that contestants need to move so that the hot tub's actual price falls within the $150 target zone's interval. Of course, *The Price Is Right* keeps the target zone limited to make the game more challenging and force contestants to be more precise. If the target zone was larger (e.g., $1,500) it would require less precision to have the prize's price fall within the range.

 Your Turn 8.1

1. How much will your textbooks cost next semester?

   a. If you made a precise guess for your textbook costs, how likely is that to be correct?

   b. Give a guess for your textbook costs using a confidence interval. Are you more or less likely to include the correct final cost?

   c. If you wanted to be more certain that the true cost of your textbooks fell within your confidence interval, what could you do to the range?

Confidence Intervals of the Mean: How Do They Work?

Granted, thinking about confidence intervals like a game show is an oversimplification, but it is a good starting point. When performing a study, we almost never collect data for the full population, which makes it impossible to know the population's true mean, so we need to estimate it. The best information we have available to us to make an estimate is the sample mean.

Said another way, we have a sample, and now we want to use that to estimate the population from which the sample originated. Is the sample's mean exactly the same as the population? Probably not. But having the sample's mean is better than nothing. Although it's just one sample, we know that it likely falls relatively close to the true population mean (or at least within $+/-3$ standard errors) because, as we learned in Chapter 5, this is true for all distributions of means. So, using our sample mean and our knowledge of how distributions of means work, we will be able to give an estimate or range where we think the population's actual mean is likely to be if we took similar samples (in both who the people are and how many of them there are) to what we currently have.

The essential oils company that authored the pamphlet reported only their *p*-value to indicate significance. However, if they had used confidence intervals, the logic would have looked like this: The pamphlet authors would want to know everyone's nap quality in a population of lavender oil users. Getting information from that entire population is impossible. However, they have a sample of 500 people who used a lavender oil while napping and can use that sample to get an estimate of where the population's mean likely falls. The confidence interval is the range of scores that represents their best guess of where the lavender oils population's actual mean falls.

Confidence Interval Levels Confidence intervals vary in size depending on how sure you want to be. However, much like there are conventional levels of significance, there are a few intervals that are more commonly used in practice. The most typical intervals are 99% and 95% because researchers don't want to be just a little sure, they want to be really (like A/A+) sure. When we construct a 99% confidence interval, we are generating a confidence interval that will include the population's mean 99 times out of 100. In comparison, when we construct a 95% confidence interval, we are generating a confidence interval that will include the population's mean 95 times out of 100.

Another way of thinking about confidence levels is the percentage of times that we will *fail* to capture the mean of the population within the upper and lower limits of the confidence interval. **Figure 8.1** depicts a set of five confidence intervals created from five different samples. As you can see, the mean of the population ($\mu = 3$) falls within the upper and lower limits for four out of the five confidence intervals. Only Sample 4 failed to contain the mean of the population. If we set our confidence level at 95% confidence, we should see 5 out of 100 confidence intervals fail to include the population mean (or an error rate of 5%). If we set our confidence level at 99% confidence, we should see only 1 out of 100 confidence intervals fail to include the population mean (an error rate of 1%).

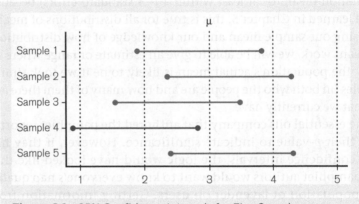

Figure 8.1 95% Confidence Intervals for Five Samples

Because a 99% interval expresses greater confidence that the population mean is included with the range, a 99% confidence interval is wider than a 95% confidence interval. If we want to be more certain, we cast a wider net. When should we choose 99% versus 95% confidence? Well, it is a trade-off. A 99% CI is going to be wider and will almost assuredly contain the population's actual mean, but it is less precise and consequently less informative. You may wonder why we don't have a 100% CI, but for us to be that sure would be like saying the price of a hot tub is between $1 and $1,000,000. We are likely 100% correct, but it isn't terribly helpful when it comes to knowing the average price for a hot tub.

That said, while 99% confidence intervals will always have a wider interval than 95% confidence intervals, ideally a study's 99% CI will still be quite narrow. As we'll learn about more in the next section, a CI's size is the result of the sample, and we know that samples vary (sometimes a lot). As a result, any particular sample's mean may vary widely from the population's mean. However, we also know from previous discussions that our sample is more likely to mimic the population when the sample size is larger. A sample of 3,000 people is more likely to have a mean close to the population than a sample of 3 people. The bigger our sample, the better our population estimate and the narrower our confidence interval.

Your Turn 8.2

1. Here are three confidence intervals each with the same sample size.

    a. Match them to proper percentages.

    b. How were you able to do this without having any additional information?

    _____ 6.56–7.01   (a) 68% confidence interval

    _____ 5.96–7.62   (b) 95% confidence interval

    _____ 6.74–6.98   (c) 99% confidence interval

Step by Step: Calculating Confidence Intervals of the Mean When the Standard Deviation of the Population Is Known In practice, we use confidence intervals to express a margin of error surrounding our estimate of the population mean. Think of it like political polls you've seen. We will have an estimate for the population mean based on our sample, but we will acknowledge that there is a margin of error of +/– a bit above and below the mean. Looking back at our essential oils and napping example, here we'll focus on the 500 people in the lavender group. To calculate those upper and lower limits in our confidence interval, we can follow these steps:

Step 1: Determine the Confidence Interval Level As we stated earlier, the most common CIs are 95% or 99%. We simply need to pick one. The most common is 95%, so we'll work with that. We also need to know the number of tails we're using. Recall that in Chapter 7, we learned that with hypothesis tests we can look at one of the tails, or both. However, confidence intervals are always two-tailed because we always want to determine the upper and lower limits.

As we mentioned earlier, if our confidence level is 95%, this implies that we have an error rate of 5%. However, we don't want all of our errors to be overestimates of the population mean or underestimates. We want an equal chance of making both types of errors. So, we need to split that 5% up between the two tails. In other words, we want to split our error rate into two equal parts of 2.5% (5%/2 = 2.5%). This means that our confidence interval will have a 2.5% error region to the left of the lower limit and a 2.5% error region to the right of the upper limit.

Step 2: Determine the *Z*-Scores for the Upper and Lower Limits With the 2.5% markers in place, we need to find the corresponding *Z*-scores. Just as we did in Chapters 4 and 6, we can use the *Z*-table to identify the *Z*-scores that correspond to 2.5% in tails of the *Z* distribution. To find the *Z*-score that corresponds to the lower limit, we need to first convert the percentage error to a probability and then identify the *Z*-score that corresponds to that probability. For an error of 2.5%, we convert that to a probability by dividing it by 100. So, 2.5% divided by 100 is .0250. Now, we can find the *Z*-score that corresponds to a probability of .0250 in our *Z*-table. Examining Appendix C, we find that a *Z*-score of −1.96 has a probability of .0250. This is the *Z*-score we will need to find our lower limit.

Next, we want to find the *Z*-score for our upper limit. Here, we want the *Z*-score that corresponds to a 2.5% error to the right of the upper limit. As we just discovered, a 2.5% error corresponds to a probability of .0250. However, because our *Z*-table only reports the probability to the left of a particular *Z*-score, and we want the probability to the right to be .0250, we need to subtract our probability from one, 1 − .0250 = .975. This works because the total area under the normal curve equals 1. So, .0250 probability to the right corresponds to 1 − .0250, or .9750 to the left. We can now find the *Z*-score that has a probability of .9750, and if we do, we'll see that it is 1.96. Hopefully, this number sounds familiar, because the *Z*-cutoff for the lower limit was −1.96. The upper and lower *Z*-scores will always have the same absolute value. So for a 95% confidence interval, our *Z*-cutoffs are ±1.96. Realistically, after you check the table the first few times, you'll end up knowing that a *Z*-score of ±1.96 corresponds to the 95% confidence interval, while ±2.58 corresponds to the 99% confidence interval.

Step 3: Convert *Z*-Score Limits to Raw Scores Knowing the *Z*-scores is an important step, but it isn't a valuable end goal because the world works in terms of actual scores, not *Z*-scores. To translate our upper and lower limits into more useful terms, we need to convert the *Z*-score limits to raw scores. We can use the following formulas to convert our *Z*-cutoffs to actual scores:

$$\text{Lower Limit} = (-Z\text{-cutoff})\,(\sigma_M) + M$$
$$\text{Upper Limit} = (+Z\text{-cutoff})\,(\sigma_M) + M$$

Hopefully, this formula feels reminiscent of another formula we've used. It likely brings back fond memories of Chapter 4, when we converted Z-scores to a Raw Score, which follows the exact same principles of what we're doing here. Back then, to find a raw score, we would multiply our Z-score by the standard deviation, then add the mean, or $X = (Z)(SD) + M$. Here, it is much the same. We're converting the Z-score so that it speaks the same language as our measurement scale, but putting it in terms of our scale's mean and standard error (σ_M).

We have the mean from our sample, but still need the standard error (σ_M). As you'll recall, from Chapters 5 and 7, here is the formula: $\sigma_M^2 = \sigma^2 / N$ where σ^2 is the variance of the population and N is our sample size. First, we should gather the key information by looking back at the pamphlet for the lavender oil group: $N = 500$; $M = 6.00$; $\sigma^2 = 1.56$. Now we can plug the numbers into the formula:

$$\sigma_M^2 = \frac{\sigma^2}{N} = 1.56/500 = 0.00312; \sigma_M = \sqrt{\sigma_M^2} = \sqrt{0.00312} = 0.056$$

Now that we have our standard error, we can complete the equation to determine the raw scores of our confidence interval. Lower Limit $= (-1.96)(\sigma_M) + M = (-1.96)(0.56) + 6 = (-1.10) + 6 = 5.89$. The calculation for the upper limit is going to be much the same; the only difference is that the sign of the Z-cutoff is positive. Upper Limit $= (+1.96)(\sigma_M) + M = (1.96)(0.56) + 6 = (1.10) + 6 = 6.11$.

Step 4: Check Yourself . . . The CI calculation inherently relies on the Z-score to set the limits. Because the Z-score's magnitude will always be the same (typically 1.96), the upper and lower limit should always be the same distance from the mean. The only difference is that one is bigger and the other smaller (depending on the sign of the Z-score). As a result, our sample's mean should always fall exactly in the middle of the confidence interval. To be sure, line them up (lower limit, mean, upper limit): 5.89, 6.00, 6.11.

We also notice that the confidence interval is relatively close to the mean (only $+/-0.11$). This is pretty amazing. We are able to be 95% confident that the mean of the population falls within a pretty narrow range of the mean of our sample. We are able to achieve the relatively narrow confidence interval because we had a large sample ($N = 500$), which helps drive down the standard error. When we multiply the confidence limit's Z-score by a lower number, the limits are closer to the mean, which means the CI shrinks and becomes narrower.

We should mention one caveat to what we're doing here. The procedure we've encountered assumes that we already know the variance (or standard deviation) of the population. So, somehow, we know the variance of the population, but not the mean. But, in reality, we almost never know the variance of the population. And even if we did, we need to know the mean of the population in order to calculate the variance of the population. All of this doesn't quite make sense. Rest assured, though, that the fundamentals of the procedure work. In Chapter 9, we will learn a procedure for estimating the variance of the population using the variance of a sample.

When we report confidence intervals in APA Style, the format is as follows: mean, then confidence interval percentage level, then the lower and upper limits. For example, "$M = 6.00$, 95% CI [5.89, 6.11]." One thing to consider when thinking about a confidence interval is what it tells us versus what it doesn't tell us. Remember that a confidence interval represents our estimate of the population's mean. It doesn't tell us anything about the individual scores that make up the confidence interval. So, while it would be appropriate to say, "We are 95% confident that the mean of the population lies somewhere between 5.89 and 6.11," it would *not* be appropriate to say the following: "We are 95% confident that the scores range from 5.89 and 6.11." Again, the confidence interval estimates the population mean, not the scores that go into the population. This is a subtle but important distinction.

Your Turn 8.3

1. Find the confidence intervals for the distilled water group.

Statistical Significance: What We're Trying to Accomplish

To make the sometimes convoluted process of hypothesis testing a bit easier to understand, we introduced several key concepts in the previous two chapters. Now we're going to delve a bit deeper, fill in some blanks, and lay the foundation for concepts that will recur throughout the remaining chapters. We focused a lot in Chapters 6 and 7 on how hypothesis testing involved comparing the sample score (Step 4) to the cutoff or critical value (Step 3).

If our sample exceeded the cutoff, we rejected the null hypothesis and supported the research hypothesis. There's another way to say the exact same thing: the results were **statistically significant**. Stated more formally, results are statistically significant when the outcome is highly unlikely to have happened if, in reality, the null hypothesis is true.

statistically significant
results that are highly unlikely to have happened if in reality the null hypothesis is true.

Remember, as we described in Chapter 6, we can think of this process similarly to how a jury trial works. The jury starts with the assumption that the defendant is innocent. They then hear the evidence. If the evidence is very unlikely to have occurred if the defendant is innocent, the jury switches from not guilty to guilty. In a hypothesis test, we start with the assumption that the null hypothesis is true. We then evaluate how likely it is that we observed the results that we did. If the results are highly unlikely, assuming that the null is true, then we will switch and conclude that the null is false.

Statistical Significance: How Does It Work?

Notice the type of wording we use when discussing statistical significance: "highly unlikely" and "probably." We purposefully avoid stating findings in absolutes or definitively declaring anything as completely sure or true. That's because statistical significance relies on probability.

Ultimately, we determine whether a finding is statistically significant based on a comparison of the alpha level and the p-value, both of which are rooted in probability. As you recall, the alpha level (or level of significance) sets the threshold for how probable (or improbable) our data need to be for us to reject the null hypothesis. The p-value indicates the probability of our data if the null hypothesis is true. So, when our data are more improbable that the level set by the alpha, we reject the null. Let's explore these ideas in a bit more detail.

Significance Levels The alpha level specifies the threshold that we set for significance and represents the probability that we reject the null hypothesis even if it is actually true. In other words, our chances of finding that essential oils are effective is partly determined by the threshold we set our alpha level to be. If we set a lower alpha (e.g., go from .05 to .01), we are making it harder to find statistical significance because we need to observe less probable evidence in the form of our data to reject the null hypothesis. If we set a higher alpha level (e.g., go from .001 to .01), we are making it easier to find statistical significance, because we are setting a less strict threshold.

In hypothesis testing, we get to establish the significance levels and therefore the critical value cutoffs in Step 3. Technically speaking, that significance level is up to the discretion of the researcher. Depending on the particular study, we can decide to have more lenient or stricter cutoff scores. However, to eliminate the guesswork or any potential bias (e.g., a researcher making the cutoff too easy), the field has established **conventional levels of significance,** which are the alphas that researchers most commonly use in hypothesis testing. Those levels are

conventional levels of significance the typical alpha levels that researchers use in hypothesis testing (5% and 1%, or $\alpha = .05$ and $\alpha = .01$).

$\alpha = .05$ and $\alpha = .01$. These alpha levels imply that we need to observe p-values that are less than .05 and .01 (respectively) in order to find statistical significance. Looking back, your mom's essential oils pamphlet indicates that $p < .10$. So, by traditional standards, the evidence presented in support of the effectiveness of essential oils would not be considered statistically significant.

Significance and the Probability of Our Data The other key idea that we need to understand when conducting hypothesis tests is the p-value. We use the letter p when discussing significance because it indicates the probability of our observed results if the null hypothesis is true. Let's pause here for a moment and consider what the previous sentence says. The p-value is the probability of our data assuming the null is true. The p-value *does not* indicate the probability that the null hypothesis, or research hypothesis for that matter, is true. This is a critical distinction that we need to make, and we are going to repeat it: the p-value is the probability of our data (under the assumption that the null is true), not the probability of the null hypothesis itself.

So, if $p = 1.00$, this would mean that our data are exactly what we should expect to observe if the null is true. For example, if we found $p = 1.00$ for our essential oils study, it would imply that there is no difference between the means of the essential oils and distilled water groups in our study (which is precisely what the null hypothesis states).

On the other hand, as p approaches zero (the p-value can never equal zero), there is a smaller and smaller probability of observing the data that we did presuming the null is true. In other words, as p gets smaller, our results become more and more unlikely to have occurred based on what the null hypothesis states. In our essential oils study, as p approaches zero, it implies that it is very improbable that we obtained this data if the null is true. If the p-value is less than alpha, we can conclude that our data are so improbable under the assumption that the null is true that we are going to infer that the null is false.

To help us get a better grip on what a p-value tells us, it can be helpful to multiply our p-value by 100 to determine the number of times out of 100 that we should observe the results that we did, if the null hypothesis is true. For example, if we found that $p = .03$ for the essential oils study, it would reveal that we should observe these results only 3 times out of 100 if the null is true. If, instead, we found $p = .001$ for the essential oils study, it would indicate that we should observe these results only 0.1 times out of 100 (or 1 time out of 1,000) if the null hypothesis is true. In each of these cases, our *p*-value suggests that the results we observed are very unlikely to have occurred if the null was true. Given how unlikely the observed results are, we will decide, using conventional standards of significance, to reject the null hypothesis.

The essential oils pamphlet reported $p < .10$. We now know that we should get results similar to these about 10 out of 100 times when the null is true. Another way of saying this is that there is a 10% chance of observing these results when there is in fact no effect. Something that happens 10% of the time is not typically considered rare enough to reject the null hypothesis. Because of this, we typically would fail to reject the null hypothesis and conclude that we don't have enough evidence to claim that essential oils are effective, using conventional levels of significance.

Statistical Significance: Decisions and Errors

We conduct hypothesis testing and determine significance (i.e., where sample results fall on the comparison distribution) so we can decide whether we can reject the null hypothesis and support the research hypothesis in Step 5. The decision criterion in hypothesis testing is straightforward. If our sample results in Step 4 exceed the cutoff from Step 3, we reject the null.

Even if we do everything correctly in hypothesis testing, however, there is no guarantee that we will make the correct decision. That's because we are attempting to gain insight into something we can't see directly (i.e., the population's true or actual mean). Consequently, we rely on probabilities and express our certainty regarding our conclusion using significance levels. Thus, even when we are really sure about rejecting the null (e.g., $p = .001$), we know that there is still a 1-in-1,000 chance (or a 0.1% chance) that we observed our results and the null is, in fact, true. In other words, there is still a chance (albeit small) that we are wrong to reject the null.

Decision Errors in Hypothesis Testing Most of the time, if we follow the steps of hypothesis testing, our decision regarding the null will match reality. However, there are two main errors that we can make:

1. We can say that something is there when, in fact, it is not.
2. We can say that nothing is there when, in fact, it is.

To understand the basics of the two errors, let's first consider a nonstatistical example. Nearly every college campus has its own ghost story where students believe some part of campus (typically the library) is haunted. Let's say we want to get to the bottom of this and do a little ghost hunting. You and three friends fire up the Mystery Machine 3000 and go looking for ghosts.

Your search can produce two types of correct decisions and two types of incorrect decisions (see **Figure 8.2**). First, you can correctly conclude there are no ghosts when there truly aren't (Box 3), or conclude there are ghosts when there truly are (Box 2). You can also make two incorrect decisions. First, you could say there are ghosts when there really aren't (Box 1). Second, you could mistakenly say there aren't any ghosts when in fact the building is haunted (Box 4).

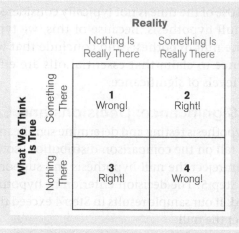

Figure 8.2 Decision Versus Reality

We don't do a lot of ghost-hunting in research, but the same types of outcomes occur with our hypothesis testing decisions. We could correctly conclude that essential oils don't help sleep when they actually don't (Box 3); or, in other words, we correctly fail to reject the null hypothesis. We could also correctly conclude that essential oils help sleep when they actually do (Box 2); or, in other words. we correctly reject the null hypothesis, thus supporting the research hypothesis. Either conclusion of our hypothesis test is great, because we made a correct decision.

Type I Error: Seeing What's Not There Unfortunately, we can also make the wrong decision in two different ways. First, we could say that essential oils help sleep when they actually don't (Box 1 in Figure 8.3). This is a **Type I error,** and describes the situation when we mistakenly reject the null hypothesis when the null hypothesis is actually true. Our conclusion supports the research hypothesis when we shouldn't. In other words, we commit a Type I error when we're gullible. We see ghosts or results that aren't actually there. We're too lenient and mistakenly decide there is a difference when there isn't.

Our chance of making a Type I error is determined by our alpha or significance level. If we set the alpha to be .05, this means that our

Type I error rejecting the null hypothesis when you should not (i.e., saying there is an effect when there is not).

probability of making a Type I error is .05. In other words, when we reject the null hypothesis using an alpha of .05, we will make a Type I error 5% of the time. In contrast, if we set our alpha level to be .01, our probability of making a Type I error is only .01 (meaning that we'll make a Type I error 1% of the time).

Type II Error: Missing What's There The other type of error we could make would be to say that essential oils don't help sleep when they actually do (Box 4 in **Figure 8.3**). This is called a **Type II error** and describes the situation when we mistakenly fail to reject the null hypothesis when the null hypothesis is actually false. In other words, we commit a Type II error when we're oblivious. We're missing the ghosts or results that are actually there, mistakenly deciding there is no difference when there is. It was there, and we missed it.

		Reality				Reality	
		Null Hyp. Is True (Actually No Difference)	Null Hyp. Is False (Actually Is a Difference)			Null Hyp. Is True (Actually No Difference)	Null Hyp. Is False (Actually Is a Difference)
Hypothesis Testing Conclusion	Results Conclusive (Reject the Null Hyp.)	**1** Type I Error (α)	**2** Correct Decision	**Hypothesis Testing Conclusion**	Results Conclusive (Reject the Null Hyp.)	**1** Conclude oils help sleep and they don't.	**2** Conclude oils help sleep and they do.
	Results Inconclusive (Fail to Reject the Null Hyp.)	**3** Correct Decision	**4** Type II Error (β)		Results Inconclusive (Fail to Reject the Null Hyp.)	**3** Conclude oils don't help sleep and they don't.	**4** Conclude oils don't help sleep and they do.

Figure 8.3 Decisions and Errors in Hypothesis Testing

Unlike the probability of making a Type I error, which is easy to figure out, our chance of making a Type II error is impossible to determine for certain (symbolically, we'll use the Greek letter beta, β, to express the probability of making a Type II error). When we fail to correctly reject the null hypothesis, it could be because there really is no effect of our independent variable, or it could be that we simply didn't have enough evidence to reject the null. We'll never know for sure. That said, later in this chapter we'll discuss an idea called statistical **power,** which measures our ability to correctly reject the null hypothesis. As our statistical power increases, our Type II error rate decreases.

Type II error failing to reject the null when you should (i.e., missing an effect that was there).

power the likelihood that a research study can correctly reject the null hypothesis.

In practice, we want our chances of making both types of mistakes to be as low as possible. But if we try to minimize one type of error, we often end up increasing the other type. For example, if we want to be sure that we're not missing ghosts that are actually there (i.e., making a Type II error), we could make our detection equipment hypersensitive. The problem is that overly sensitive equipment can lead to false positives where we say something is there but isn't (a Type I error).

We can minimize false positive/Type I errors by making our detection equipment really picky. The problem with that is that we may miss out on detecting ghosts that are actually there, resulting in a false negative (a Type II error). The key is striking a balance. In practice we do that by adhering to conventional levels of significance. By setting our alpha level at .05, it essentially says that our likelihood of committing a Type I error is 5% (our alpha level is the same as our alpha or Type I error level), which is lenient enough to detect effects when they are there, but strict enough to avoid too many false positives.

How SPSS Reports Statistical Significance

In SPSS, the p-value appears in columns with the heading "Significance" (see **Figure 8.4**). Most often we should report the p-value in the column labeled "Two-Sided p." Note that SPSS doesn't tell us if our p-value is significant or not. To do this, we need to compare the p-value that is reported to our alpha level (typically .05 or .01). If the observed p-value is greater than our alpha, we will fail to reject the null hypothesis. If the observed p-value is less than our alpha, we reject the null hypothesis and conclude that our results are statistically significant.

Significance	
One-Sided p	Two-Sided p
.204	.409

Figure 8.4 SPSS Reporting of p-Values

Communicating the Result

In research articles, significance will appear one of two ways, which has varied over time and according to the specific journal. For many years, we reported significance based on which conventional level of significance the results surpassed. Thus, we would report results as significant and then give levels such as $p < .05$, $p < .01$, or $p < .001$ (e.g., "Results were significant, $p < .05$"). The problem here is that for the lowest level (.05), readers would know that the results made the .05 cutoff, but wouldn't know by how much (e.g., it could have been close—$p = .044$—or far—$p = .0004$). In contrast, if results were not significant, we would either report as *n.s.* (nonsignificant) or give the exact p-value we reached, $p = .65$. It is now more common to give the exact alpha level, regardless of whether the results were significant (e.g., $p = .002$, $p = .64$, or $p = .98$). Giving the exact alpha level is easy to do (statistical programs all provide these numbers), and it is more informative. In addition, we should always assume reported alpha levels are two-tailed, unless noted otherwise (e.g., $p = .044$, one-tailed).

Forming a Conclusion

 Looking back at what the essential oils pamphlet tells us about significance, we can draw a few conclusions. First, we know that the pamphlet reported $p < .10$, which is not a conventional level of significance and is more lenient than what researchers typically use (i.e., alpha levels of .05 or .01). In addition, the pamphlet doesn't specify whether the hypothesis test was a one- or two-tailed test. It could very well be one-tailed, because the most likely hypothesis would have been that the oils would help or improve sleep (i.e., they wouldn't have bothered to do the test if they thought the oils would harm sleep). If it was a one-tailed test, then the hypothesis test is even more lenient. We also know that they obtained a p-value less than .10, but since they do not give the exact p-value level, we don't know if they were close to a significant result according to conventions (e.g., $p = .057$) or further away (e.g., $p = .097$).

Finally, part of being a good consumer of statistical information is realizing that the mere presence of statistics isn't conclusive evidence. That is, for someone who doesn't understand statistics, seeing that a pamphlet provides statistical information (e.g., $p < .10$) might seem impressive or meaningful. Certainly, those numbers must mean something, and if they're included, those statistics probably say something good. However, because we know about statistics, we can interpret that number more accurately and realize that $p < .10$ is not traditionally sufficient to conclude that essential oils are effective. Seeing statistics and assuming they're positive is a potential heuristic or mental shortcut people may use when interpreting information. However, as people who understand what those numbers actually say, we won't be misled.

 Your Turn 8.4

1. A study examining the impact of meditation on stress reports that those who meditated had lower stress than those who sat quietly ($p = .04$). Interpret the alpha level in terms of (a) a percentage; (b) a proportion.

2. A researcher who does a study on the effects of walking listening to the ocean on anxiety, wants to set their cutoff in Step 3 at 5%. Show what that would look like on a comparison distribution for (a) a one-tailed and (b) a two-tailed test.

3. A first-year student in an introduction to psychology class asks you for help with reporting results on a lab report they have to do. The intro student wrote, "The study worked, Sig. < .08." What suggestions do you have for them?

4. Taylor and Jamie are trying to have a baby. Jamie takes a pregnancy test. Explain (a) two ways they could make the correct decision and (b) two ways they could make the incorrect decision, and (c) create a chart to show all potential outcomes.

Statistics for Research

Many psychologists use the science of psychology to help improve their clients' lives. For example, clinical psychologists, counseling psychologists, and therapists use findings from studies related to mental health to help people with a variety of problems, such as depression and anxiety. For each client's unique situation, they must choose among various treatment options and pick the one they think will work best.

One approach that they may consider for their clients is massage therapy. Massage therapy is thought to promote psychological well-being through the manual manipulation of the skin and muscles (Moyer et al., 2004). How would a clinical psychologist evaluate whether massage therapy is an appropriate treatment, compared to other options, for a particular patient in treating a particular disorder? In order to answer this question, we need to know a little more about statistical significance, including common misconceptions that people have about significance. In Statistics for Research, we'll learn about the fallacies that people have regarding significance, and we'll examine several key concepts such as effect size and power.

Where Do the Data Come From?

It can be hard for a clinical psychologist to decide among various treatment options based on any one particular study. Each study may test whether a particular treatment is effective, but to understand the practical meaning of any one

A massage feels nice, but can it also reduce anxiety?

Steve Debenport/E+/Getty Images

finding is difficult. To see the larger pattern of how one treatment compares to others is often necessary to situate a particular finding within a group of similar studies. This is one of the goals of **meta-analysis,** a statistical approach that seeks to combine results from many research studies. So, to evaluate whether massage therapy is an effective treatment, we can look up the effectiveness of other therapeutic techniques reported in a meta-analysis. But to understand why this is necessary, we need to first understand two common misconceptions about hypothesis testing.

meta-analysis a type of research study that combines results from all relevant research.

Statistical Significance Versus Practical Importance

Although hypothesis testing is the backbone of many statistical tests, there are two common fallacies or mistakes that we need to clear up. The first fallacy, sometimes called the **nullification fallacy,** is the mistaken idea that a nonsignificant finding indicates that there is no difference between means (or no relationship between the variables). Here, people mistakenly think that failure to reject the null hypothesis indicates that there is no effect (Kühberger et al., 2015). For example, a study might evaluate the effectiveness of massage therapy by comparing the anxiety levels of people getting massage therapy to a control condition. The study might have 50 participants (25 per condition) and find no significant difference between groups. Though that study failed to find an effect, it doesn't mean we should automatically conclude that massage therapy doesn't work.

nullification fallacy describes the mistaken assumption that nonsignificant findings are caused only by the absence of an effect of the independent variable.

Failing to reject the null hypothesis could be due to two general reasons. First, it's possible that there truly is no effect. If the massage therapy doesn't affect anxiety levels, then the mean for the massage therapy condition shouldn't differ from the control condition, which is exactly what the null hypothesis states. In this case, we fail to reject the null because the null is true. Second, it's possible to fail to reject the null even though the null is false (which we called a Type II error earlier in this chapter). This can happen when we don't have enough statistical power to achieve a significant finding. In other words, massage therapy actually does reduce anxiety, but our study wasn't well suited to capture the effect. We'll talk more about power a bit later in this chapter. For now, we simply need to recognize that there are multiple reasons why our hypothesis test might be nonsignificant, so we need to resist the urge to make unjustified conclusions.

The second fallacy, the **significance fallacy,** is the mistaken idea that a significant finding is an important finding. In other words, we mistakenly conclude that statistical significance (which is what research studies report) equates with practical importance (Kühberger et al., 2015). Just because a finding is significant doesn't necessarily imply

significance fallacy describes the mistaken assumption that statistically significant findings are meaningful or useful in a practical context.

that the finding has real-world implications. For example, a large-scale study of 10,000 people might find that people getting massage therapy have a mean anxiety level of 5.71 (on a 1-to-7 scale), while people in the control condition have a mean anxiety level of 5.82, and conclude, based on their analysis, that the difference is statistically significant.

Though our hypothesis test indicates that there is a significant difference, we need to also consider whether the findings have any real-world implication. In our everyday lives, would we be able to notice such a subtle decrease in anxiety levels (5.71 vs. 5.82)? Perhaps not. Therefore, it's possible for a significant difference to have limited practical or everyday importance.

The significance fallacy's origin is probably the fact that in the English language, the words "significant," "meaningful," and "important" are all synonyms. But, in statistics, we must treat these words as distinct. Statistical significance refers only to whether we are able to reject the null hypothesis. It does not tell us anything about the practical meaningfulness or importance of our findings.

So, to our question of whether a psychologist should start recommending the use of massage therapy to clients, we need to go beyond statistical significance and look at effect size.

Effect Size: Determining a Hypothesis Test's Practical Importance

One of the main reasons researchers collect study results in a meta-analysis is to estimate the size of a treatment's impact on the outcome. But the problem researchers run into is that any group of studies will use a variety of methods and measures and will test distinct treatments. One study could use interviews, another correlations between standardized measures, and still another could use a randomized experiment. Because of these potential differences, making direct comparisons between studies is difficult. To avoid these types of "apples to oranges" comparisons, we need a way to make studies more directly comparable.

The good news is that at the heart of any study is the same basic question: how much does one variable relate to another variable? In other words, what is the size of the link between two variables? In statistics we call this the **effect size,** or the strength of the association between two variables. Put another way, effect size measures a research finding's practical, rather than statistical, importance.

effect size a measure of the strength of an association between two variables; or the practical, rather than statistical, importance of a research finding.

Measures of Effect Size: Calculating Cohen's *d* The best way to determine whether a significant effect is practically meaningful is to calculate its effect size. For each type of hypothesis test, there is a corresponding way to measure effect size. One approach to calculating effect size when comparing two means (such as in the Z-tests that we learned about in Chapters 6 and 7) is called **Cohen's d**. Named after Jacob Cohen, the statistician who developed it, this effect size measure determines the number of standard deviations' difference between the two means that we are comparing. To calculate Cohen's d, we take the mean difference between our sample and population and divide it by the standard deviation.

Cohen's d a measure of effect size used for comparing two means.

$$\text{Cohen's } d = \frac{\mu_1 - \mu_2}{\sigma}$$

Using the results for the massage therapy example presented above, we would calculate the effect size by entering the means for the massage therapy condition ($M = 52.55$, $SD = 6.98$) and the control condition ($M = 52.72$, $SD = 5.14$) into the numerator, and the standard deviation for the population into the denominator. In this case, assume that we know that the standard deviation for the population is 6.17. Thus, the effect size for massage therapy is $d = (52.72 - 52.55)/6.17 = (0.17)/6.17 = 0.03$.

Measures of Effect Size: Interpreting Cohen's d Once we have calculated Cohen's d, we need to interpret it. Recall that Cohen's d reflects the number of standard deviations' difference between our group means. So, finding a Cohen's d of 0.20, as depicted in **Figure 8.5**, would indicate that our study conditions differ by 0.20 standard deviations. If we find a Cohen's d of 0.80, we would conclude that our group means differ by 0.80 standard deviations. Figure 8.5 depicts the difference between conditions for four effect sizes. As you can see, when the effect size increases, the distance between the two group means increases, and the amount of overlap between the distributions decreases.

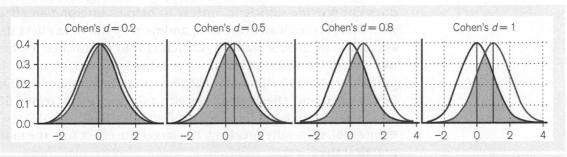

Figure 8.5 Distributions Reflecting Various Cohen's d Effect Sizes

We also need to know how our effect size compares to other similar studies. To evaluate the practical importance of massage therapy, for example, we can compare its effect size to the effect sizes of different types of therapy. For example, one anxiety disorder treatment meta-analysis found that pharmaceutical treatments have Cohen's d effect sizes on average between 2.0 and 2.5 (Bandelow et al., 2015). This tells us that people taking these anti-anxiety medications have anxiety levels that are 2.0 to 2.5 standard deviations below people in the control condition who did not take medications. In contrast, cognitive-behavioral therapy's effect size is approximately 1.20 to 1.30, such that people receiving this type of therapy have levels of anxiety that are 1.20 to 1.30 standard deviations below people in the control condition. When comparing these effect sizes to that of massage therapy's effect size of 0.03, it becomes obvious that anti-anxiety medications and cognitive-behavioral therapy are vastly more effective at reducing anxiety symptoms.

When interpreting Cohen's d, we need to consider the research area in which we are working. Research area impacts effect size interpretations. For some research topics, we may regularly find effect sizes of 2.00 or larger. However, for other areas, effect sizes of 0.50 are more common. As a result, it's difficult to determine what value of Cohen's d constitutes a large, medium, or small effect without having some knowledge of the previous literature that has examined a particular topic. For example, without knowing that cognitive-behavioral therapy and pharmaceutical treatments have much larger effect sizes than massage therapy, we might mistakenly conclude that massage therapy is a reasonable alternative treatment for people dealing with anxiety. But, knowing that the other effect sizes are so large (i.e., so effective), it would be malpractice for a clinical psychologist to prescribe massage therapy, as opposed to other treatments, to people suffering from severe anxiety.

Of course, there are some situations in which the literature does not provide sufficient context to help us interpret an effect size. Some research areas are new, and we may not have effect size estimates. In these situations, Cohen (1988) established a labeling system for when effect sizes are large, medium, or small. In particular, "large" effects are those with a Cohen's d of 0.80 or larger, "medium" effects are those with a Cohen's d of at least 0.50, and "small" effects are those with a Cohen's d of at least 0.20 (see **Figure 8.6**). Generally speaking, the larger the effect size, the more practical the effect.

> **"**
> ## Statistically Speaking
> Chain restaurants' food isn't bad, but when compared to a family-owned restaurant, the effect size is large and clearly noticeable.
> **"**

Cohen's Labeling System for Effect Size	Value of Cohen's *d*
Small	0.20
Medium	0.50
Large	0.80

Figure 8.6 Cohen's Labeling System for Effect Sizes

Your Turn 8.5

1. Imagine you see an advertisement for a website called Gunk, which sells Gunk Tea, an herbal drink that the website claims reduces the duration of headaches. Intrigued, you read a short description of the study that the website uses as evidence for its claims and see that the report makes the following statement: "Participants using Gunk Tea had headaches that were significantly shorter than control participants, $Z = 1.96$, $p = .05$. Thus, Gunk Tea is an important treatment that you can use to shorten your headaches." Is the website justified in making this conclusion?

2. After more research on Gunk Tea, you discover that the mean headache duration for participants using Gunk Tea was 49.66 minutes and the mean for participants in the control condition was 50.04 minutes (the standard deviation for the population is known to be 7.17 minutes). Using Cohen's labeling system for effect size, what is the effect size for Gunk Tea?

3. Study A reports a significant finding at the $p < .001$ level, and Study B also reports a significant finding at the $p = .03$ level. Based on this information alone, which study's results are more likely to have practical importance?

Power: Determining a Hypothesis Test's Sensitivity

Any time we conduct a study, we're hoping to find statistical significance, assuming there is a real association between our variables. However, when it comes to successfully doing that, all studies are not created equal. That is, research studies vary in terms of their statistical power, or ability to correctly reject the null hypothesis. In other words, power is our ability to find a statistically significant result when there truly is an effect in the population (that is, correctly reject a false null hypothesis).

We can think about power in a similar way to the different lenses on a microscope. The smaller the object that we want to see, the stronger the power lens we need to have. For example, if we wanted to see the cells that make up a plant, we need to have a 100X lens. However, if we wanted to see the structures that exist within a cell (e.g., mitochondria), we would need a more powerful 500X lens. To see even smaller structures (e.g., DNA), we need an even more powerful 1000X lens. In each case, there is something there, but to detect it, we need sufficient power.

The same thing is true for statistics. If we want to see large effects, we don't need a lot of power. But, if we want to see small effects, we need more power. In essence, statistical power captures a hypothesis test's sensitivity or probability of detecting an effect, when it actually exists. In this way, power is the opposite of a Type II error, which happens when we missed something that was there or *failed* to reject a false null hypothesis. Power is the idea that we have correctly found something that was there or correctly rejected a false null hypothesis. For this reason, we can think of power as $1 - \beta$ (recall that earlier in the chapter we said β symbolizes our Type II error rate).

What Determines Power? Several factors contribute to our study's power level. The first, and most important, factor is the sample size. The greater the sample size, the more power we have to detect an effect. Sample size increases our power because sample size influences our calculation of the standard error. As the sample size increases, the standard error decreases. As the standard error decreases, our test statistic increases. The larger our test statistic, the easier it is to reject the null hypothesis. Thus, we can say that a study with only 50 participants has lower power than a study with 500 participants.

A second factor is the effect size. As we saw earlier in this section, some effects are larger than others. For example, cognitive-behavioral therapy has a larger effect on anxiety (a Cohen's d of about 1.3) than massage therapy (a Cohen's d of about 0.03). Therefore, it should be easier for researchers to detect a significant effect of cognitive-behavioral therapy relative to massage therapy. When an effect is large rather than small, there will be a larger difference between the means in the Z-test formula's numerator. As the numerator increases, so does the value of the test statistic, which makes it easier to reject the null hypothesis.

A third factor that affects our power level is the population's standard deviation. When the population's standard deviation is small, there is less variability from measurement to measurement. Consequently, it is easy to observe the effect of our independent variable. In contrast, when the population's standard deviation is large, we have to deal with a lot of noise (perhaps due to problems with how we measured a variable or inconsistency in how we collected data), which can obscure our independent variable's effect. Thus, as the population's standard deviation increases, it is more difficult to reject the null hypothesis. Our formula for standard error captures the role of the population's standard deviation. When the standard deviation increases, our standard error also increases. As the standard error increases, our test statistic decreases.

A fourth and final factor in determining power is our alpha. As we learned in Chapter 6, alpha is our significance level, and as we learned earlier in this chapter, it is also our Type I error rate. When we set alpha to be a larger number, such as 0.10 as opposed to 0.05, we gain the ability to find an effect (i.e., increase power) because we only need data that occurs less than 10% of the time under the null hypothesis for us to reject the null. Of course, the flip side of this is that we have increased our chances of making a Type I error (now making one approximately 10% of the time instead of 5%). For this reason, researchers very rarely increase their alpha to gain power. See Figure 8.7 for a summary of these factors.

Factor	Increases Statistical Power	Decreases Statistical Power
Sample Size	Large	Small
Effect Size	Large	Small
Standard Deviation of Population	Small	Large
Alpha (α)	Large	Small

Figure 8.7 Factors That Increase or Decrease Statistical Power

How Do We Know How Many Participants We Need? Conducting a Power Analysis Power is an important consideration when planning a study. If we don't have sufficient power, we are unlikely to find significant results, even when there really is an effect for us to find. To prevent this unfortunate situation and wasting time conducting underpowered studies that have little chance of finding significant effects, most researchers conduct a **power analysis,** which is an analysis conducted prior to the start of a study that determines the sample size needed to achieve a specified level of power based on a researcher's anticipated effect size.

When conducting a power analysis, researchers must input values for three parameters: the alpha, the effect size, and the desired level of power. With respect to alpha, by convention, most researchers set alpha to be .05 or .01. When should researchers set alpha to be .01

power analysis an analysis conducted prior to the start of a study that has the goal of determining the sample size needed to achieve a specified level of power.

as opposed to .05? Well, because alpha is the Type I error rate, we might set alpha to be a lower value if we are particularly concerned about wrongly concluding an effect exists, when it does not (e.g., if we are developing a new drug to treat a disease, we may want to have greater assurance that if we say the drug works, it really does).

With respect to the anticipated effect size, researchers often must estimate the value they expect for a particular study. Although this may seem difficult to do, before conducting a study, we can rely on several sources of information to help. First, we can look to prior studies on similar topics and identify their effect sizes. For example, if we are conducting research on the efficacy of massage therapy on anxiety, we could use the effect size for pharmaceutical and cognitive-behavioral therapies because these are well-established treatments for anxiety.

Second, we can conduct a *pilot test,* which is a small-scale study that we conduct to test the feasibility of our research (Leon et al., 2011). Conducting a pilot test allows us to calculate the effect size observed in the pilot test so that we can use that value in our power analysis for our large-scale study.

Third, if we do not have anything else to go on, we can use Cohen's standards for small, medium, and large effects. For example, we might guess that massage therapy has a small effect, which Cohen equates to an effect size of 0.20 (see Figure 8.6). Thus, we could input 0.20 into our power analysis as our estimate of the effect size.

Finally, with respect to the desired power level, we must determine what we want to achieve. If we set power to be 0.50, this means that we would be able to correctly reject the null hypothesis 50% of the time—basically, the flip of a coin. Hopefully, being right only 50% of the time feels low to you. If our power is only 0.50, it means that half of the time we will fail to reject the null hypothesis, even when there is an effect of our independent variable. The research process is too laborious and time consuming to only have a 50–50 shot of getting a significant result. In contrast, if we set power to 0.90, this means that we would be able to correctly reject the null hypothesis 90% of the time. It also means that we would still fail to reject the null hypothesis about 10% of the time, which means we have only a 1-in-10 chance of missing an effect if it exists. Indeed, most researchers aim for a power of 0.80, which provides them with a sensitivity level that is a reasonable balance between the chance of finding significant results, if they exist, and missing an effect that was there.

Hopefully, it is clear that the more power we have, the better. Of the four factors that determine our power level, as researchers, we really control only one of them: the sample size. We have the ability to collect more data. It may be costly in terms of time and money, but by collecting a larger sample, we make it that much easier to find significant results. This is why it's so important to conduct a power analysis. We must know our target sample size to have a realistic chance of finding significant results, when they exist.

The mathematical formula to determine the sample size needed for a specific level of power changes for each type of analysis that we might conduct, so we will not go into the details here. Instead, we will note that we have several resources to help us conduct a power analysis. First, we can refer to power tables, such as the one in **Figure 8.8** created by Cohen.

two-tailed $\alpha = .05$ or one-tailed $\alpha = .025$

	d										
Power	**0.10**	**0.20**	**0.30**	**0.40**	**0.50**	**0.60**	**0.70**	**0.80**	**1.0**	**1.20**	**1.40**
.25	332	84	38	22	14	10	8	6	5	4	3
.50	769	193	86	49	32	22	17	13	9	7	5
.60	981	246	110	62	40	28	21	16	11	8	6
2/3	1144	287	128	73	47	33	24	19	12	9	7
.70	1235	310	138	78	50	35	26	20	13	10	7
.75	1389	348	155	88	57	40	29	23	15	11	8
.80	1571	393	175	99	64	45	33	26	17	12	9
.85	1797	450	201	113	73	51	38	29	19	14	10
.90	2102	526	234	132	85	59	44	34	22	16	12
.95	2600	651	290	163	105	73	54	42	37	19	14
.99	3675	920	409	231	148	103	76	58	38	27	20

Figure 8.8 Power Tables for Cohen's *d* Effect Size (from Cohen, 1988)

As we can see in Figure 8.8, each row presents varying levels of statistical power, and each column represents different effect sizes that we might observe. The cells of the power table indicate the sample size needed to achieve a particular level of power.

Aside from using power tables, we can also use computer programs to conduct power analyses. A free and popular option is called G*Power, which is available for download online.

Your Turn 8.6

1. Using the power table in Figure 8.8, what sample size would we need to detect a small effect (d = 0.20) 80% of the time?

2. Tyreke is examining a medium-sized effect (d = 0.50). After collecting data all semester long, he is able to get 47 participants to complete his study. Using the power table in Figure 8.8, approximately what is the likelihood that Tyreke will be able to find significant results if there is a true effect of his independent variable?

Communicating the Result

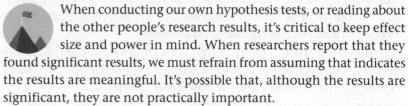

In Chapter 6, we learned how to write a results paragraph. We noted that when reporting the results of a Z-test, we would report the value of the Z-test statistic and the p-value using this format: $Z = \#.\#\#, p = .\#\#\#$). However, as we learned in this chapter, knowing the p-value isn't sufficient to interpret the results of a hypothesis test. We also need to know the effect size. So, researchers must include this information in our results paragraph, typically after reporting the p-value. When reporting Cohen's d, we would use the following approach: $Z = \#.\#\#, p = .\#\#\#, d = \#.\#\#$. We might also see it reported as, $Z = \#.\#\#, p = .\#\#\#$, effect size $(d) = \#.\#\#$. If we were reporting the results for the massage therapy effect size calculated above, we would prepare the following results paragraph:

> We conducted a one-sample Z-test to examine whether massage therapy reduced symptoms of anxiety. The results were significant, $Z = 1.96, p = .049, d = 0.028$, such that those in the massage therapy condition had significantly lower levels of anxiety ($M = 52.55, 6.98$) compared to those in the control condition ($M = 52.72, 5.14$). Despite the results being significant, the effect size of the massage therapy was small relative to other known treatments of anxiety.

Forming a Conclusion

When conducting our own hypothesis tests, or reading about the other people's research results, it's critical to keep effect size and power in mind. When researchers report that they found significant results, we must refrain from assuming that indicates the results are meaningful. It's possible that, although the results are significant, they are not practically important.

Notice that for the massage therapy and anxiety example presented above, if we merely considered the significance of our hypothesis test, we might wrongly conclude that massage therapy is as effective at reducing anxiety as pharmaceutical or cognitive-behavioral interventions. It's only when we compare the effect sizes of these treatments to other approaches that we learn that massage therapy has miniscule effects. For this reason, many scholars have suggested that psychological researchers move away from focusing on *p*-values and statistical significance and instead focus on effect sizes when interpreting findings (Asendorpf et al., 2013).

When making conclusions about an effect, whether it is one of our own findings or one that we read about, we also need to consider power. If researchers report a nonsignificant effect, it could be because there really is no effect, or that the study was underpowered. If the study is underpowered, it is impossible to make definitive conclusions about the presence or absence of an effect. For example, if a paper reports that pharmaceutical therapies significantly reduce anxiety but that cognitive-behavioral therapy does not, it is possible that the effect size of cognitive-behavioral therapy is just smaller than that of pharmaceutical therapy, and that cognitive-behavioral therapy would have been a significant treatment if the study had a larger sample size. See **Figure 8.9** for a summary of how to interpret different combinations of significance and power.

Significance?	Statistical Power	Interpretation
Yes	High	Encouraging, but need to examine the effect size to evaluate practical importance.
Yes	Low	Could suggest a large effect size, but also could be the result of small sample size not accurately representing the population.
No	High	Indicates a small effect size of limited practical importance.
No	Low	Cannot make any definitive conclusion. Need to collect more data.

Figure 8.9   Possible Interpretations for Various Combinations of Significance and Statistical Power

Indeed, historically, research in psychology and other sciences has been underpowered (Maxwell, 2004). Studies estimate that the average power for studies published in psychology journals is only 0.35 (e.g., Bakker et al., 2012). This means that, on average, research studies have only a 35% chance of detecting a statistically significant effect when it actually exists. This is one of the reasons that scholars have called for an increased focus on statistical power when designing research studies.

Focus on Open Science: Effect Size, Power, and Replication

replication (also called *reproducibility*) the notion in science that all findings should survive repeated testing before they are accepted.

One of the hallmarks of science is **replication** (also called *reproducibility*), which describes scientists' ability to get the same results for an experiment across repeated testing (Popper, 1959). If a scientist finds evidence for an effect once but not on subsequent tests, we must conclude that there is likely no effect. Similarly, if one scientist finds evidence for an effect, but no other scientist can reproduce the findings, we must again conclude that there is likely no effect. In both of these cases, the initial findings might have been due to Type I errors, methodological flaws, or some other fluke or random factor. Scientific progress entails keeping only the findings that replicate.

Examples of initially exciting findings that failed to reproduce exist across the sciences. In 1989, chemists Martin Fleischmann and Stanley Pons found evidence for "cold fusion," a type of nuclear reaction that occurs at room temperature. However, other scientists tried to replicate the finding but couldn't (Goodstein, 1994). In psychology, an attempt to replicate the findings reported in 100 published papers found that only 39 replicated (Open Science Collaboration, 2015). The failure to reproduce 61 out of the 100 papers led some psychologists to wonder whether there is a **replication crisis** in psychology. This crisis captures psychological researchers' lack of confidence in published findings that were previously thought to be accurate. As a result, psychologists have started to place greater emphasis on power and replication.

replication crisis a crisis that exists in psychology and other sciences as a result of the failure to replicate findings that were previously accepted.

To help increase the likelihood that study findings replicate, advocates of open science have started emphasizing the importance of power analyses to ensure that studies are properly powered. Many journals and grant funding agencies (such as the National Science Foundation) now require scholars to perform a power analysis prior to conducting a study to ensure that it has a high likelihood of finding an effect if there is one to be found. Peer reviewers are also more critical of underpowered studies now compared to in the past, making it harder for splashy yet unlikely-to-replicate studies to be published. Finally, journals now regularly publish replication studies, enabling researchers to share their results, or lack thereof, and potentially call into question prior findings. In the end, each of these practices helps increase the likelihood that only high-quality research gets published.

Become a Better Consumer of Statistics

One place where you are most likely to see confidence intervals discussed is with political polls. Leading up to an election, news organizations seek insights into which candidate

Pollsters trying to predict elections use representative samples to predict how people will ultimately vote when at the voting booth. Because this process is imperfect, political polls always acknowledge a margin of error.

is in the lead. When they report results, you'll often see something like Candidate X 42%, Candidate Y 38%, Undecided 20%, margin of error +/−2 percentage points. What does that mean? Much like we discussed earlier, the people running the poll don't have access to the entire population of voters. Instead, they use a representative sample that they randomly select. The pollsters then use that sample's information to provide information about the population.

As we know, sampling bias introduces the potential for error. Pollsters acknowledge the amount of imprecision by giving results, along with plus or minus a certain number of percentage points (e.g., "22% approval rating +/− 3%"). Those intervals are typically less than 4 percentage points, and will be lower when the sample size is bigger. Sometimes the news will report the race as a statistical dead heat. That's because the confidence intervals around each candidate overlap. For example, if the poll results are Candidate X 42% +/− 2% and Candidate Y 38% +/− 2%, because Candidate X's 42% could actually be as low as a 40% (42% − 2% margin of error = 40%), while Candidate Y's 38% could actually be as high as 40% (38% + 2% margin of error = 40%), their confidence intervals overlap. Thus, it is possible each candidate actually has the exact same amount of support. For the candidates to be truly different and for one person to have a lead, the margins of error cannot overlap.

Statistics on the Job

Regardless of what career path you choose, decisions are going to be part of your job. For every decision, you should think about how your decision matches up with reality. For example, a decision that is common to nearly every career is picking the right person to hire from job interviews.

Perhaps you're on the committee searching for the newest team member, or you're looking to hire your own assistant. In these cases,

The hiring process generally entails trying to avoid both Type I and Type II errors.

you have to navigate all of the information presented and make the right decision (i.e., hiring a good candidate and rejecting the bad ones) so you can avoid the consequences of a bad decision (i.e., hiring a bad candidate and mistakenly rejecting the good ones). Just as with hypothesis testing, as you can see in **Figure 8.10**, hiring decisions have the same potential to result in Type I or Type II error. The Type I error is hiring someone you think is great, but isn't. The Type II error is missing out on hiring someone who is actually great.

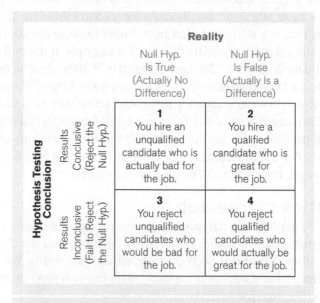

		Reality	
		Null Hyp. Is True (Actually No Difference)	Null Hyp. Is False (Actually Is a Difference)
Hypothesis Testing Conclusion	Results Conclusive (Reject the Null Hyp.)	**1** You hire an unqualified candidate who is actually bad for the job.	**2** You hire a qualified candidate who is great for the job.
	Results Inconclusive (Fail to Reject the Null Hyp.)	**3** You reject unqualified candidates who would be bad for the job.	**4** You reject qualified candidates who would actually be great for the job.

Figure 8.10   Correct and Incorrect Decisions for Hiring Job Candidates

Review Questions

1. In your own words, define and differentiate alpha and *p*-value.

2. If a study reports $p = .038$, would it be considered statistically significant by traditional standards? Why or why not?

3. Here are three *Z*-scores and their associated *p*-values.

   _____ $Z = 2.44, p = .015$ (i) $N = 16$
   _____ $Z = 1.83, p = .067$ (ii) $N = 36$
   _____ $Z = 1.22, p = .222$ (iii) $N = 64$

   a. Without doing any calculations, match them to their sample sizes.

   b. How were you able to do this without having any additional information?

4. If the alpha level is decreased from .05 to .01, what happens to the likelihood of rejecting the null hypothesis? What happens to your Type I error rate?

5. If a researcher writes "The results were statistically significant, $Z = 1.99$, $p = .048$, $d = 0.68$." Could they have made a Type I error? Why or why not? Could they have made a Type II error? Why or why not?

6. If a 99% confidence interval is more likely to capture the mean, why do researchers often choose to report a 95% confidence interval instead?

7. Looking back at the essential oils and napping example, generate a 99% confidence interval for the people in the lavender group. Do the same for the people in the distilled water group.

8. Your city has decided that people are driving too fast in school zones, and it is a public safety hazard that needs to be addressed. They ask you to develop new signage materials, and you place them in 36 randomly selected school zones. For the population, people drive an average of $\mu = 6.2$ miles per hour above the posted speed limit. The shape of the distribution is normal, with a $\sigma_2 = 3.6$ miles per hour. People who saw the new signage materials drove an average of 4.9 miles per hour above the posted speed limit.

   a. Calculate the 95% confidence interval.

   b. Using Cohen's (1988) labeling system for effect size, what is the effect size for the new signage materials?

9. Define and differentiate statistical significance and practical importance in your own words. How is each one measured?

10. What factors influence a study's power level? As a researcher, which of these factors can you most easily control?

11. You are in the planning phase of a new research study. You expect a medium-sized effect ($d = 0.60$) and want your power to be at least 0.80. Using a power table, what is the minimum number of participants you should recruit for your study?

Key Concepts

Cohen's *d*, p. 275

confidence interval, p. 257

conventional levels of significance, p. 265

effect size, p. 274

Answers to Your Turn

Your Turn 8.1

1. (a) This could be anything—$356, $450, etc.—but is likely to be incorrect; (b) this could be anything—it should convey a range of $250-$400 or $375-$575 but is more likely to contain actual cost; (c) make the range larger or wider—if your guess ranges from $200 to $600, it is more likely to include the right answer than if you guessed $350-$400.

Your Turn 8.2

1. (a) b, c, a; (b) as the percentage of the confidence interval increases, the range of the numbers should increase as well. Thus, a 99% CI should be largest and a 68% smallest.

Your Turn 8.3

1. Step 1: Determine the Confidence Intervals—95% confidence interval; two tails

Step 2: Determine the Z-Scores for the Upper and Lower Limits—95% CI = +/– 1.96 for Z-Cutoff

Step 3: Convert Z-Score Limits to Raw Scores—gather the key information by looking back at the pamphlet: $N = 500$; $M = 5.85$; $\sigma^2 = 2.10$. Now we can plug the numbers into the formula: $\sigma^2_M = \sigma^2/N = 2.10/500 = 0.004$; $\sigma_M = \sqrt{\sigma^2 M} = \sqrt{0.004} = 0.06$. Lower Limit = (−1.96) $(\sigma_M) + M = (−1.96)(0.06) + 5.85 = (−0.12) + 5.85 = 5.73$. Upper Limit = $(1.96)(\sigma_M) + M = (1.96)(0.06) + 5.85 = (0.12) + 5.85 = 5.97$.

Step 4: Check Yourself—line up the lower confidence limit, mean, Upper Confidence Limit = 5.73, 5.85, 5.97.

They are sequential with the mean equidistant from the lower and upper limits.

Your Turn 8.4

1. (a) There is a 4% chance that the results could occur if the null hypothesis is true. (b) We would get these results by chance, only 4 times out of 100, and that 96 times out of 100 these results could not happen if the null hypothesis were true.

2. (a)

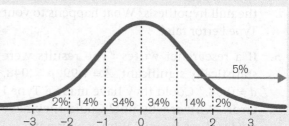

(b)

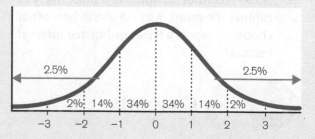

3. First, the student should be clearer about what the variables were (e.g., what "worked"). Instead of saying it "worked," state whether the result was significant (and if the alpha level is above .05, it actually did not work). When reporting, use the symbol p, not Sig. (even though that may be how the statistical program labels it.). Give the exact level rather than use the "<" symbol. Only consider the results significant (or having "worked") if the p-value is less than the alpha level (typically less than .05).

4. (a) They could correctly conclude she is pregnant (the test shows a "+" to indicate pregnant) when in reality she is pregnant, or they could correctly conclude she is not pregnant (the test shows a "−" to indicate not pregnant) when in reality she is not pregnant. (b) They could incorrectly conclude she is pregnant (the test shows a "+" to indicate pregnant) when in reality she is not pregnant (a Type I error or a false positive). They could also incorrectly conclude she is not pregnant (the test shows a "−" to indicate not pregnant) when in reality she is pregnant (a Type II error or a false negative).

(c)

	Reality	
	Null Hyp. Is True (Actually No Difference)	Null Hyp. Is False (Actually Is a Difference)
Hypothesis Testing Conclusion — Results Conclusive (Reject the Null Hyp.)	**1** Wrong! Conclude she is pregnant and she isn't.	**2** Correct Conclude she is pregnant and she really is.
Results Inconclusive (Fail to Reject the Null Hyp.)	**3** Correct Conclude she isn't pregnant and she really isn't.	**4** Wrong! Conclude she isn't pregnant and she really is.

Your Turn 8.5

1. No. The website falls victim to the significance fallacy. Just because the hypothesis test is significant doesn't mean that Gunk Tea has an important effect. For example, it could be that Gunk Tea reduces the duration of headaches by only a few seconds on average. This small difference in headache duration would not justify people spending money on Gunk Tea. Similarly, the effect of Gunk Tea may be much smaller than other treatments, such as over-the-counter pain relievers.

2. $(49.66 - 50.04)/7.17 = 0.05$. Because the effect size is less than 0.20, we can conclude that Gunk Tea has a very small effect size.

3. It's impossible to tell. The p-value does not indicate practical importance, because it is affected by the sample size. We need to calculate the effect size to know whether an effect is meaningful in a practical sense.

Your Turn 8.6

1. $N = 393$

2. Tyreke will have 0.66 power, so he will be able to find significant results about 66% or 2/3 of the time.

Answers to Review Questions

1. The p-value is the probability of obtaining our results if the null hypothesis is true. The alpha level sets the threshold for how probable (or improbable) our data needs to be for us to reject the null hypothesis. If the p-value we obtain is lower than the alpha value we have set, then we will reject the null hypothesis. If the p-value is higher than the alpha level, then we will fail to reject the null hypothesis.

2. Traditional standards set the alpha level of studies at either .05 or .01. If the traditional standard that was used is .05, then the result would be considered statistically significant. If the standard used was .01, then the result would not be considered statistically significant.

3. a. (iii), (ii), (i)
   b. As sample size increases, the estimated standard error will decrease and the Z-score will increase. As the Z-score increases, the p-value will decrease.

4. The likelihood of rejecting the null hypothesis decreases, and the Type I error rate also decreases.

5. The researchers could have made a Type I error because they state that a difference exists (statistically significant), but there is a possibility that a difference doesn't actually exist. The researchers could not have made a Type II error because that type of error involves failing to detect a difference when a difference actually exists, and the researchers have stated that they detected a difference.

6. Although a 99% confidence interval is more likely to capture the mean, it is less precise and therefore less informative than a 95% confidence interval.

7. Lavender group: lower limit = 5.87, upper limit = 6.13. Distilled water group: lower limit = 5.70, upper limit = 6.00

8. a. Lower confidence limit = 3.72, upper confidence limit = 6.08
   b. Cohen's $d = 0.36$, small to medium effect size

9. Statistical significance refers to how likely it is that you would obtain your results if the null hypothesis was true. It is measured with p-values that are then compared to alpha levels.
   Practical importance refers to whether the results have real-world implications or impact. It is measured with effect-size statistics, such as Cohen's d, that can be used when comparing 2 means.

10. Sample size, effect size, the population's standard deviation, and our alpha level. The factor that is most easily controlled is the sample size.

11. $N = 45$

9

Introduction to *t*-Tests: The Single Sample *t*-Test and *t*-Test for Dependent Means

Learning Outcomes

After reading this chapter, you should be able to:

- Identify similarities and differences between a *Z*-test and a *t*-test.

- Explain why an estimate of population variance from a sample is biased.

- Explain how to make an estimate of population variance unbiased.

- Summarize the logic of degrees of freedom.

- Describe the underlying logic for why *t* distribution is different from a normal distribution.

- Use a single sample *t*-test appropriately.

- Find a cutoff score in a *t*-table.

- Use the *t*-test for dependent means appropriately.

- Identify the assumptions of the *t*-test for dependent means.

- Describe the strengths and weaknesses of repeated-measures designs.

It happens every semester. Weeks will go by with nothing due. Then, out of nowhere, you get slammed with three papers all due the same week, almost like your professors are conspiring against you. You should have started weeks ago, but you work better under pressure, right?

The only problem is finding a place where you can actually get things done. Your place isn't great because your roommates are always around and never seem to have any work to do. Other places like the Student Center and the library aren't ideal because there's always a ton of people in both places, which will make you want to hang out, not work.

You decide to go to a coffee shop because there's lots of noise, activity, and a chill atmosphere. Being in public also forces you to stay on task. Because of the catchy name, you settle on going to *Brew Ha Ha's*. You order the "Love Ur Mama" brew, which is basically a vanilla milkshake with three shots of espresso. You find a comfy chair under an antique bird cage and hop on the free Wi-Fi so you can access the school's library. Surely, this will help you be productive.

Or, will you? It could go either way. On the plus side, you're away from friends. On the downside, it could be too noisy. With that in mind, you put on your headphones and the noise mostly fades away. Game on.

Statistics for Life

Solving the puzzle of what makes a person more productive is a million-dollar industry. There are seemingly endless numbers of different to-do list and reminder programs, scheduling apps, and time management strategies with fancy names like "Getting Things Done or GTD," "The Pomodoro Technique," and "The Eisenhower Matrix." But perhaps those systems make productivity

unnecessarily complicated. Maybe it really is as simple as going to a coffee shop. It makes you wonder: Are students who work at a coffee shop more productive than students in general?

Where Do the Data Come From?

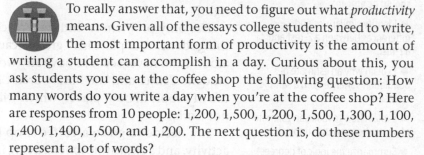

To really answer that, you need to figure out what *productivity* means. Given all of the essays college students need to write, the most important form of productivity is the amount of writing a student can accomplish in a day. Curious about this, you ask students you see at the coffee shop the following question: How many words do you write a day when you're at the coffee shop? Here are responses from 10 people: 1,200, 1,500, 1,200, 1,500, 1,300, 1,100, 1,400, 1,400, 1,500, and 1,200. The next question is, do these numbers represent a lot of words?

To answer this question, we need to know how many words a typical student writes a day. You do a quick Google search but can only find information on established authors. Apparently, Nicholas Sparks and Stephen King manage 2,000 words a day; Maya Angelou wrote 2,500 words, and Anne Rice wrote 3,000 (Patterson, 2015). But, they're pros. You need info on college students in general. That type of information would be hard for you to collect. To find out, you check your school's writing center. The director informs you that based on the thousands of students she has consulted with throughout her career, the average college student writes 750 words a day ($\mu = 750$).

At this point you might be thinking that the "Where Do the Data Come From?" section was a little light on information and doesn't tell you everything you think you might need. You're absolutely right. We're missing one key piece of information that we need to conduct a hypothesis test: the variance of the population. Although we know the mean of the population is 750 words, we don't know the variance. As a result, we won't be able to use the Z-test like we did in Chapter 6, because the *Z*-test requires that we know the population variance. We can work around not having the population variance by instead using the single sample *t*-test (see **Figure 9.1**).

Things We Know	*Z*-Test	*t*-Test
Sample	Single	Single
Population Mean (μ)	Yes	Yes
Population Variance (σ²)	Yes	No
Comparison Distribution	Normal	*t*

Figure 9.1 What We Know: *Z* Versus *t*

Single Sample *t*-Test: What We're Trying to Accomplish

The **single sample *t*-test** (or *one-sample* t-*test*) is a statistic that lets us determine if a single sample is different from a population when we have interval or ratio data and when we don't know the variance.

single sample *t*-test (also called *one-sample* t-*test*) a statistic that lets us determine if a single sample is different from a population when we have continuous (interval or ratio) data and when we don't know the variance.

The *t*-test for a single sample is the first type of *t*-test that we'll discuss, but every type of *t*-test in subsequent chapters has a couple of features in common. They all work with *continuous (interval or ratio) level data,* and all *t*-tests *compare differences between two means.* In our case, we want to compare the mean of our sample of coffee shop writers to the mean of the population of college students at our school, to see if coffee shop writers produce more words a day.

When we say "single sample" that indicates we will compare the mean of one group (our sample's mean) to the mean of the population. We can use a single sample *t*-test in a couple of different situations:

1. Compare a sample mean to a known population mean (e.g., if we wanted to compare people working in a coffee shop to the population of all people)
2. Compare a sample mean to a target value (e.g., if we wanted to determine whether people were above or below the midpoint of a Likert scale)

Your Turn 9.1

1. Give your own example of a research question that would call for a single sample *t*-test.

2. a. Give two ways that the *Z*-test and the *t*-test are similar.

   b. Give two ways they are different.

Finding the Missing Variance In Chapters 6 and 7, we learned how to conduct a one-sample Z-test. A key step in the Z-test (Step 2) is to build a comparison distribution and distribution of means. Creating the distribution of means requires us to know the population's variance so that we can calculate the standard deviation of the distribution of means using the formula $\sqrt{\dfrac{\sigma^2}{N}}$. The takeaway is that to compare our sample to the rest of the population, we need to know the population's variance. The reality, though, is that we almost never know the population's variance. Thus, we can almost never create a distribution of means or perform the rest of the one-sample Z-test. So how are we going to proceed if we don't know the variance of the population?

Well, the good news is that we do know something that gives us important insight into the population's variance: the variance of our sample. Remember that in Chapter 3, we learned that the variance of a sample is a biased estimator of the variance of the population. Essentially, this means that the variance of a sample is, on average, less than the variance of the population. This happens because when we take samples, there is a risk that we're missing the population's extreme scores, or the scores that are out on the tails of the population's distribution. This risk is especially true when our sample size is small. Extreme scores are rare, so when you randomly sample only a few people, there's a high probability we're going miss those few really small or really big scores.

Without those extreme scores, a sample will cluster more around the mean and have less spread or variation in its scores. The result is that a sample's variance, as we said, will be less than that of the population. In other words, the estimate is biased, which means it is systematically wrong. That sounds bad. But the fact that the error is systematic actually helps us quite a bit. Because we know that our estimate is off in a routine and predictable way, we can adjust accordingly.

To make that adjustment, we're going to use some elementary school math. What is 12 divided by 4? Well, 12 / 4 = 3. Now, what happens when the denominator or bottom number is slightly smaller (3 instead of 4)? Then 12 / 3 = 4. The result is slightly larger. This is always true: 100 / 10 = 10, and 100 / 9 = 11.11; 500 / 25 = 20, and 500 / 24 = 20.83. You'll also notice that as the numerator (top number) gets larger (500 instead of 1), the impact of dividing by a smaller denominator decreases. Smaller denominators still produce larger results, but those results are only slightly larger. All of this is true when we use division to determine variance. Typically, we calculate variance of a population (σ^2) as $\dfrac{\Sigma(X - M)^2}{N}$. But if we do it that way, we now know the result is biased and systematically too small. To correct the bias, we need our result to be slightly larger than it would normally. We accomplish this by using a slightly smaller denominator. Instead of dividing by N, we're going to divide by $N - 1$. The resulting formula for the unbiased estimate of population variance (S^2) is $\dfrac{\Sigma(X - M)^2}{N - 1}$.

It is unbiased because we know that the average of all sample variances from a population will equal the variance of the population. We should also notice that the symbol for calculating variance switched from σ^2 to S^2 (or SD^2). The new symbol lets us know that the calculated variance is based on a sample and is an estimate of the population.

$$S^2 = \frac{\Sigma(X - M)^2}{N - 1} = \frac{SS}{N - 1} = \frac{SS}{df}$$

We'd like to pause here to point out something important. Remember back in earlier chapters when we saw formula notations like $\Sigma(X - M)^2$ and felt a little lost and intimidated? Those days are over, and now when we encounter those symbols, we know it's our old friend sum of squares (SS). We also realize that $\dfrac{\Sigma(X - M)^2}{N - 1}$ is the same as saying $\dfrac{SS}{N - 1}$. Sure, it's kind of random to point out here, but we wanted to take a moment to appreciate how far we've come and how well we're doing with understanding statistics and the formulas.

Your Turn 9.2

1. Your lab partner has accidentally calculated both a biased and unbiased estimate of the population variance. They're upset because now they don't know which is which. You promise that just by looking at the numbers, you can tell them which is which. Why would you be able to do that? Explain.

Degrees of Freedom Speaking of formula notations that go by another name, as we learned in Chapter 3, the denominator in the unbiased variance formula $(N - 1)$ is also noted as the degrees of freedom, and we use the notation *df*. The degrees of freedom tell us the number of scores that are able to differ. For example, imagine that our coffee shop has only 10 spots to sit and work. As the first 10 customers filter in, choosing a spot to sit is super easy. The first student, Asia, could sit in any of the 10 spots she wants. In other words, her seat is free to vary. The same is true for students 2–9. Each of their choices has the ability to vary between different options. However, the last student who walks in (Zendaya) cannot vary, she has no freedom to differ (See **Figure 9.2**). Her seat is locked in by virtue of there being only one seat left.

	Seat Location	Customer
1	Window Seat on the Left	Gabriella
2	Window Seat on the Right	Paulo
3	4 Person Work Table - Seat 1	Porcia
4	4 Person Work Table - Seat 2	Demetri
5	4 Person Work Table - Seat 3	Emily
6	4 Person Work Table - Seat 4	
7	Bean Bag	Mathias
8	Single Table & Chair	Wyatt
9	Old Comfy Reading Chair	Asia
10	Recliner	Crystal

Figure 9.2 Degrees of Freedom for Seat Location

The same thing happens mathematically. Say you have a set of five numbers that you know has a mean of 6, and the first four numbers are 5, 8, 10, and 4. The existing numbers sum to 27, so that last one has no freedom to be anything other than a 3 (sum of 30 divided by 5 scores = 6). It can't be anything different. In practice, degrees of freedom are typically the number of cases minus one. Or, as we saw before, $df = (N - 1)$, resulting in an alternate expression of the unbiased estimate of population variance's formula: $S^2 = \dfrac{SS}{df}$.

The *t* Distributions To perform a hypothesis test when we don't know the population's variance, we can substitute in the sample's variance. We can do this because we know that the sample's variance is typically a good (unbiased) estimate of the population's variance. But, good doesn't mean perfect. The reason the one-sample *Z*-test works is that not only can we describe the mean and variance of the distribution of means but we also know because of the central limit theorem that it typically takes on the shape of a normal curve. As a result, we can use the normal curve to determine the probability of our data occurring, assuming that the null is true. We called this probability the *p*-value.

Can we still use the normal curve to determine the *p*-value if we are estimating the population's variance? No. When we estimate the population's variance using the sample's variance, we will observe greater variation in the means of our samples than we would expect using the normal curve. So, our distribution of means will no longer be the shape of a normal curve.

Instead, our distribution of means' shape will match one of the *t* distributions. The *t* distributions look similar to the normal curve in that they are symmetric and bell shaped. However, the *t* distributions are wider and flatter, with thicker tails, than the normal curve. In fact, the exact shape of a *t* distribution changes depending on how much information we have to make the estimate. Consequently, there are actually lots of different *t* distributions, each based on how many degrees of freedom we have.

Why does the shape change? As you can see in **Figure 9.3,** the more information we have to make our estimate, the closer the *t* distribution gets to the normal curve. Just as when you have more pixels an image becomes clearer, when we have more data we get a

> **Statistically Speaking**
>
> "Those profit projections seem a little biased. We want to be as unbiased as possible, so let's adjust by lowering our anticipated sales before giving our report to the board."

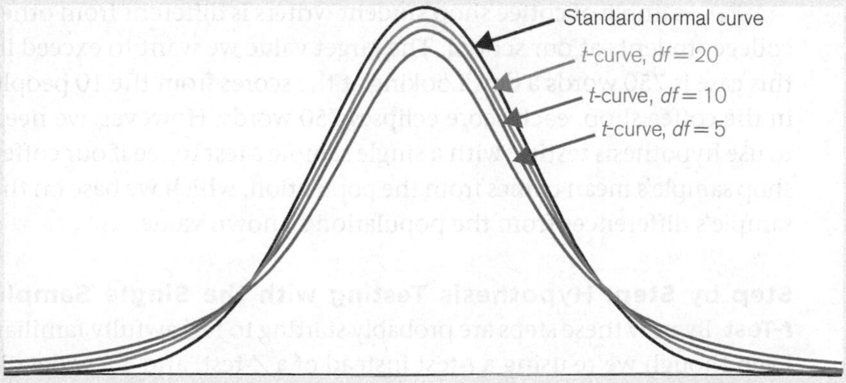

Standard normal curve
t-curve, df = 20
t-curve, df = 10
t-curve, df = 5

Figure 9.3 Comparison of the Normal Distribution to Several *t* Distributions clearer picture of what the population looks like. When we have less information (i.e., a smaller sample), there is a greater chance that we're not capturing the extreme scores. As a result, as the N (and, by extension, df) decreases, the t distribution's shape becomes wider and flatter, and with more observations in the tails. With limited information we can't be sure what the extreme scores might look like, so the distribution has to reflect that. However, as we get more and more information (i.e., a larger sample), we become more certain that we're capturing some of the extreme scores from the population. The t distribution reflects that by narrowing and being more peaked. In other words, it starts looking more like a normal distribution.

Now that we know how to estimate the population's variance using the sample's variance, and that we need to use the t distribution to determine the p-value of our test, we are ready to learn to conduct the single sample t-test.

Your Turn 9.3

1. Convert the following symbols into words:

$$S^2 = \frac{\Sigma(X - M)^2}{N - 1}$$

2. It's the end of the semester and you have only one grade left. You need to get a B+ in the course to stay on the Dean's List, and need a 100% on your final exam to pull it off. How does the concept of degrees of freedom apply here?

Hypothesis Testing with a Single Sample t-Test: How Does It Work?

Remember, hypothesis testing is fundamentally about populations and samples. In our case, we want to know if our sample of coffee shop student writers is different from other college students at our school. The target value we want to exceed in this case is 750 words a day. Looking at the scores from the 10 people in the coffee shop, each score eclipses 750 words. However, we need to use hypothesis testing with a single sample t-test to see if our coffee shop sample's mean comes from the population, which we base on the sample's differences from the population's known value.

Step by Step: Hypothesis Testing with the Single Sample t-Test By now these steps are probably starting to feel awfully familiar. Even though we're using a t-test instead of a Z-test, and a few details are different, the basic steps of hypothesis testing will remain the same. Forever.

Step 1: Population and Hypotheses Even though a single sample *t*-test focuses on a sample, hypothesis testing starts with populations. That's because we are ultimately trying to see if our sample (student coffee shop writers) comes from a different population from our comparison population (i.e., college students in general from our school). In other words:

Population of Interest (μ_1): College students who write at coffee shops.

Comparison Population (μ_2): College students in general from our school.

Sample: The 10 students writing at the coffee shop.

Next, we need to make a prediction about what we think will happen. Our research hypothesis must do this in terms of how the populations compare to each other. The null hypothesis then states there is no effect or no difference and that the populations are the same. Remember, we won't actually test the research hypothesis but will instead test whether we can reject the null hypothesis. Here are our hypotheses:

Research Hypothesis (H_1): Students who write in the coffee shop will differ from college students in general from our school on the number of words they write each day ($\mu_1 \neq \mu_2$). In other words, the Population of Interest's mean is different from the Comparison Population's mean. (Note here that because we could think of reasons why the coffee shop could help or could hurt, we are making a nondirectional prediction.)

Null Hypothesis (H_0): Students who write in the coffee shop will not differ from college students in general from our school on the number of words they write each day ($\mu_1 = \mu_2$). In other words, the Population of Interest's mean is not different from the Comparison Population's mean.

Step 2: Build Comparison Distribution Consistent with what we've been doing with hypothesis testing, the comparison distribution needs to represent how things look when the null hypothesis is correct and there is no effect. In this case, coffee shop writing productivity is no different from other college students' productivity.

Our sample consists of 10 coffee shop writers for whom we have calculated a mean. The comparison distribution needs to reflect that, so we need to construct a distribution of means, based on samples of 10 people. Like we've done before, we will build this distribution by starting with the curve itself. However, because we're using an estimate of the population variance, we cannot be sure that we have a normal distribution. Remember, we need to use a *t* distribution.

We can build the comparison distribution of means just as we've done previously by starting with the curve and scores underneath (see **Figure 9.4**).

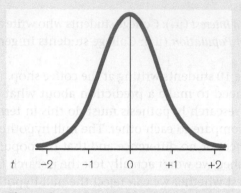

t   -2   -1   0   +1   +2

Figure 9.4   *t* Distribution with *t* Scores

Next, we need to add in the actual scores. To create a comparison distribution, we first need to know what the comparison population looks like based on its mean (μ_2) and standard deviation (σ_2). (Remember, those subscript 2's remind us that the information applies to the comparison population.) Though we know the comparison population's mean ($\mu_2 = 750$) from the writing center director, we don't have the variance. We'll need to estimate it using the following formula:

$$S_2^2 = \frac{\Sigma(X - M)^2}{N - 1} \text{ or } S_2^2 = \frac{SS}{df}.$$

As you can see in **Figure 9.5**, $S_2^2 = \dfrac{201000}{9} = 22333.33$. We know the variance, but to build our distribution, we need the standard deviation. Converting from S_2^2 to S_2 is as simple as taking the square root, $S_2 = \sqrt{S_2^2} = \sqrt{22333.33} = 149.44$, or $S_2 = 149.44$. We use that to fill in the rest of the actual scores (e.g., $750 + 149.44 = 899.44$) as seen in **Figure 9.6**.

We now know what the comparison population looks like based on our estimated standard deviation. We're not quite done, because our Population of Interest is a sample of 10 people, from which we have calculated a mean. Thus, the comparison distribution must be constructed based on means from samples of 10 people.

Coffee Writer	Words Per Day (X)	($X - M$)	($X - M$)^2
1	1,200	−130	16,900
2	1,500	170	28,900
3	1,200	−130	16,900
4	1,500	170	28,900
5	1,300	−30	900
6	1,100	−230	52,900
7	1,400	70	4,900
8	1,400	70	4,900
9	1,500	170	28,900
10	1,200	−130	16,900
ΣX	13,300	SS	201,000
N	10	df	9
M	1,330		

		S^2	SS/df
Comparison Population Characteristics		S^2	22333.33
		S	$\sqrt{S^2}$
		S	149.44
Comparison Distribution Characteristics		S_M^2	S^2/N
		S_M^2	2233.33
		S_M	$\sqrt{S_M^2}$
		S_M	47.26

Figure 9.5 Computations for Single Sample t-Test

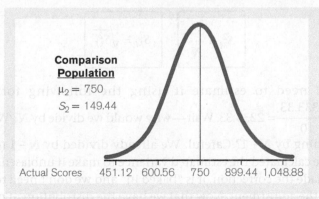

Comparison Population
$\mu_2 = 750$
$S_2 = 149.44$

Actual Scores   451.12   600.56   750   899.44   1,048.88

Figure 9.6 t Distribution with Actual Scores

Remember, we know the mean of the distribution of means (μ_M) matches the Comparison Population's mean ($\mu_2 = 750$) (**Figure 9.7**).

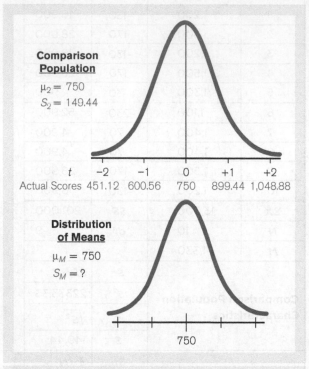

Figure 9.7 *t* Distribution and Mean of Distribution of Means

Next, we need to determine the distribution of means' standard error (S_M). Note that we carry over the *S* symbol to remind ourselves that we're relying on estimates. To do that, we first calculate the distribution of means' variance (S_M^2).

$$S_M^2 = \frac{S^2}{N} \qquad S_M = \sqrt{S_M^2}$$

We'll need to estimate it using the following formula: $S_M^2 = \dfrac{22333.33}{10} = 2233.33$. Wait—why would we divide by *N*? Weren't we dividing by $N-1$? Careful. We already divided by $N-1$ (or *df*) when we calculated the estimated variance to make it unbiased. Once we've made the correction, it is "baked in" and we don't need to keep making the adjustment. Now that we have the distribution of means' variance, we can convert it to a standard deviation using the following formula: $S_M = \sqrt{S_M^2} = \sqrt{2233.33} = 47.26$; $S_M = 47.26$. Now that we have the comparison distribution's mean and standard deviation, we can add in the actual scores (**Figure 9.8**).

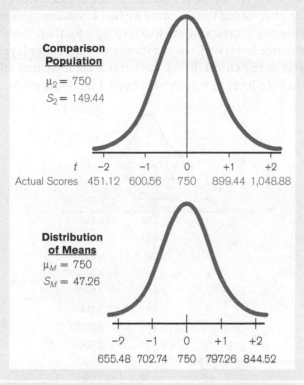

Comparison Population

$\mu_2 = 750$
$S_2 = 149.44$

t	−2	−1	0	+1	+2
Actual Scores	451.12	600.56	750	899.44	1,048.88

Distribution of Means

$\mu_M = 750$
$S_M = 47.26$

−2	−1	0	+1	+2
655.48	702.74	750	797.26	844.52

Figure 9.8 t Distribution and Distribution of Means with Actual Scores

Step 3: Establish Critical Value Cutoff For us to conclude that those who write at a coffee shop are significantly more productive in terms of the number of words they write, how many words do they need? That is the essence of the cutoff, which acts as the threshold we need to surmount in order to have some confidence in rejecting the null. To do that, we need to establish cutoff scores on our comparison distribution.

Our comparison distribution is now t-shaped because we're using estimated population variance. Consequently, the percentages of scores in the tails are different. Those percentages impact where the top or bottom 5% or 2.5% fall in the tails, which results in the cutoff scores being different as well. Not only that but the t distribution's shape depends on the degrees of freedom (df), so cutoff scores will also vary by the number of df. Luckily those cutoff scores are predetermined and available for us to look up in a table.

Here's a bonus, once we know three pieces of information: whether the hypothesis is one or two tailed, the degrees of freedom, and the significance level, determining our cutoff scores on a t distribution is easier than what we did with Z-tables. That's because we first find the section for a two-tailed test (because we had a nondirectional hypothesis), find the row corresponding to our df ($df = 9$), then the column for our significance level (we'll use the standard significance level, $\alpha = .05$), which gives us the cutoff. In our case, it is 2.26. If we had selected the .01 significance level, it would have been 3.25 (**Figure 9.9**).

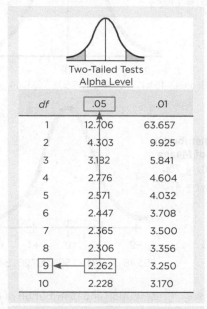

	Two-Tailed Tests Alpha Level	
df	.05	.01
1	12.706	63.657
2	4.303	9.925
3	3.182	5.841
4	2.776	4.604
5	2.571	4.032
6	2.447	3.708
7	2.365	3.500
8	2.306	3.356
9	2.262	3.250
10	2.228	3.170

Figure 9.9 Using the t-Table to Find the Critical Value Cutoffs

Remember our saying earlier that as we have more information (i.e., larger samples / more degrees of freedom), the t distribution becomes increasingly normal? In the table of t-cutoff scores that appears in Appendix C, notice how at the .05 level, as the df increases, the t-cutoff gets closer and closer to the Z-cutoffs of 1.64 (one-tailed) and 1.96 (two-tailed). Cool, right?

Okay, back to hypothesis testing. Our last step is indicating the critical value on our comparison distribution, which you can see in **Figure 9.10**.

Step 4: Determine Sample Results Now we get to see how our coffee shop writing compadres compare to the comparison population. We have data from 10 coffee shop writers, but we need one number to represent that entire group. To accomplish that, we calculate the mean number of words for the coffee shop sample: $(1,200 + 1,500 + 1,200 + 1,500 + 1,300 + 1,100 + 1,400 + 1,400 + 1,500 + 1,200) /10 = 13,300 / 10 = 1,330$ words.

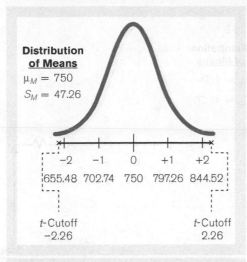

Figure 9.10 Distribution with Critical Value Cutoffs

Next, we want to compare our sample's mean to the Comparison Population's mean ($M - \mu$). But what we really want to know is how the difference between those means compares to the comparison distribution in terms of how far it is in standard units from the mean (S_M). These are the building blocks for calculating a **t-score,** which tells us how many standard errors our sample mean is from the comparison distribution's mean.

$$t = \frac{M - \mu}{S_M}$$

As you can see from the formula, it follows the same logic as the Z-test. The symbols are just slightly different to account for the fact that we estimated the population's variance. Plugging our numbers into the formula $t = (M - \mu)/S_M$ gives us the following: $t = \dfrac{1330 - 750}{47.26} = \dfrac{580}{47.26} = 12.27$. Next, we should show where our sample's t-score falls on the comparison distribution.

Step 5: Decide and Interpret It is clear from **Figure 9.11** that our sample's t-score of 12.27 far exceeds the t-cutoff score of 2.26. We can double-check that by comparing our sample's mean of 1,330 words to the distribution of means' actual scores. Looking at the figure, the word count for a t-score of 2.26 would have been approximately 850 words. Obviously 1,330 is greater than that, which is consistent with our comparison of the t-scores. Though that may feel repetitive, it is always a good idea to double check that our answers make logical sense.

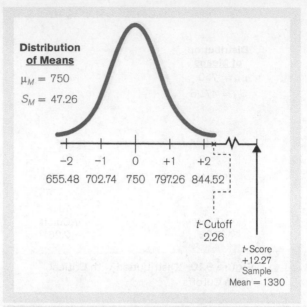

Figure 9.11 Sample Results on the Comparison Distribution

Decision time. Because our sample's results (Step 4) exceed the critical value (Step 3), we are able to reject the null hypothesis (H_0) that students who write in the coffee shop will not differ from college students in general from our school on the number of words they write each day ($\mu_1 = \mu_2$). If we are able to reject the null, we can also say that we are able to support the research hypothesis (H_1) that students who write in the coffee shop will differ from college students in general from our school on the number of words they write each day ($\mu_1 \neq \mu_2$).

 SPSS VIDEO TUTORIAL: To learn more, check out the video tutorial One-Sample t-Test.

 HAND CALCULATION VIDEO TUTORIAL: To learn more, check out the video tutorial Calculating the One-Sample t-test by Hand.

Communicating the Result

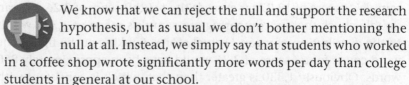 We know that we can reject the null and support the research hypothesis, but as usual we don't bother mentioning the null at all. Instead, we simply say that students who worked in a coffee shop wrote significantly more words per day than college students in general at our school.

Also, when discussing study results that were significant, we must be careful to avoid saying that our results "prove" that coffee shops are the best place to write. Because of the way statistical significance, *p*-values, and hypothesis testing work, we can never be 100% certain of an outcome. Our significant finding could be a Type I error. We also have to recognize that this is only one test of the phenomenon, and one positive result is not absolutely definitive. Consequently, we should use tentative or nuanced language, sometimes called hedge wording, to say that our findings "suggest," "indicate," or "seem to say," then give our conclusion.

Forming a Conclusion

Our data suggest that writing in a coffee shop is associated with greater productivity in terms of words written, compared to college students' typical writing productivity. We need to hedge a bit because the way we answered our research question may not be perfect. In other words, the statistics we calculate are only as a good as the numbers we have and the design we used. To be good consumers of statistics, we need to know not only how to interpret statistics but also where those numbers came from in the first place.

To be honest, the approach we used to answer our research question was not ideal. Some of the problems include the fact that we didn't randomly select our sample, we relied on coffee shop writers' self-report of words per day (which could be inflated), and we relied on the director of the writing center's expertise rather than a more objective measure. To really properly test a coffee shop effect on writing productivity, we would need to correct these flaws and should consider what we did here as merely a pilot test for future research testing coffee shops' effect on productivity. As a result, we should be appropriately skeptical of the current results and temper our conclusions accordingly.

Your Turn 9.4

1. a. When you have more info, is the *t* more or less like the normal curve?

b. Why?

2. Your suitemates are great, in every way but one. As nerdy as it sounds, they don't study enough. They disagree and think they actually study more than the typical college student. To test this your 5 suitemates keep track of their study time for a week. According to your Center for Student Success, the students should study 3 hours for every credit hour. Since your suitemates all take 15 credits that means the typical study time for 15 credits is 45 hours a week (15 credits × 3 hours per credit = 45 hours) of studying outside of class.

Are your suitemates studying enough?

2a. Step 1: Population and Hypotheses. (a) What would the populations be? (b) What would the hypotheses be?

2b. Step 2: Build a Comparison Distribution. Your suitemates all track their study hours for the week and give you the following results: 40, 30, 50, 25, 35. (a) What does the comparison population look like? What shape is it? Why is it a *t* distribution? (b) What will be the comparison population's mean (μ_2)? (c) What will be the comparison population's variance? (S_2^2)? Standard deviation (S_2)? (d) What type of comparison distribution do you need? (e) What will be the mean (μ_M)? (f) What will be the variance (S_M^2)? Standard deviation (S_M)? (g) What does the comparison distribution look like?

2c. Step 3: Establish Critical Value Cutoff. In order to know for sure if you suitemates study significantly more or less than 45 hours a week, you need to establish a cutoff score. (a) What three pieces of information do you need to find the cutoff score on the *t*-table? (b) What is the

t-cutoff associated with this information? (c) Show this on the comparison distribution.

2d. Step 4: Determine Sample Results. (a) What test does she need to run? (b) What are the results? (c) Show this on the comparison distribution.

2e. Step 5: Decide and Interpret. What is the appropriate conclusion?

Statistics for Research

Every January 1, millions of people set New Year's resolutions for themselves. Some people might want to exercise more. Others might want to eat healthier foods. Still others might vow to stop procrastinating on important tasks. Yet, despite these good intentions, most people fail to follow through on their New Year's resolutions. Why? Are people bad at setting goals? Or is there some psychological reason for why people fail to follow through?

A lot of research examines our inability to set goals and follow through on them. Some of this research suggests that people fail to follow their goals because they lack the self-control resources to do so (e.g., Baumeister et al., 1998). Other research suggests that people fail to adequately plan ahead when setting their New Year's resolutions (Gollwitzer, 1999). A third line of research suggests that people simply forget about their goals (Rogers & Milkman, 2016).

According to this research, when people go about their daily lives, they are busy and distracted by the tasks of everyday life, and they just don't remember to work on their New Year's resolution. If this were

Why do so many people fail to follow through on their New Year's resolutions?

andresr/E+/Getty Images

the reason that people fail to meet their New Year's resolutions, could we increase people's abilities to follow through on their resolutions simply by reminding them to do so? How would we test this idea?

One possibility would be to track people's adherence to their goals over time. If people need reminders to pursue their goals, we could compare their goal pursuit before getting reminders to their goal pursuit after getting reminders. If the ability to follow through on goals is better after getting reminders, then it would support the notion that people fail to follow through on their goals because they forget about them.

Here in the Statistics for Research section, we're going to explore a different *t*-test (the *t*-test for dependent means or paired-samples *t*-test) that builds on what we learned with the single sample *t*-test. In this section, you will be introduced to the idea of measuring change via pre- and posttests, using difference scores, and calculating confidence intervals for dependent means.

Where Do the Data Come From?

 To conduct a study on goal reminders, we could ask participants to set a daily goal (e.g., exercise for at least 30 minutes) and then ask them at the end of one week to indicate the number of days that they followed through on their goal. This would be our **pretest** measurement, because it is the measurement we make before implementing our manipulation. We could then ask people to pursue their goal for a second week, but this time we could send them daily reminders. Each day, at a set time, we could send participants text messages reminding them to work on their resolution.

Again, at the end of the week, we could ask the participants to indicate the number of days that they followed through on their goal. This would be our **posttest** measurement. If we observe a change or a difference between the pretest and posttest measurements, it would indicate that the reminders were effective. When participants get both levels of our independent variable (i.e., no-reminders condition vs. reminders condition), this is a **repeated-measures design** (or a *within-subjects design*). It's unique because we measure the same participant twice, once at pretest without reminders and one at posttest after the reminders. By repeating our measurement with each participant, we can see how they change.

Let's imagine that we visit a local gym the first week of January and select 60 new members to be in our study. Each of our participants indicates that they have a goal to exercise. After letting them pursue their goal without any reminders for the first week, we find that people exercise 2.55 days out of the possible 7 on average, with a standard deviation of 1.58. In other words, without getting a reminder, our pretest mean is 2.55 (*SD* = 1.58). During the second week of the study, we

pretest a measurement taken prior to the introduction of the independent variable.

posttest a measurement taken after the introduction of the independent variable.

repeated-measures design (also called *within-subjects design*) study methodology in which each participant is measured twice on the dependent variable: prior to the introduction of the independent variable (called the pretest), and after the introduction of the independent variable (called the posttest).

send all participants a daily reminder that they have a goal to exercise. At the end of the week, we find that people exercise 3.62 days out of the possible 7 on average, with a standard deviation of 1.67. In other words, the posttest mean is 3.62 ($SD = 1.67$).

From this information, it is clear that participants followed through on their goals for more days in the second week of the study compared to the first. But does this represent a significant effect of the reminders? Or, could the difference in pretest and posttest means simply reflect sampling error? We would expect the means to differ somewhat just due to random events that happen in people's lives. Perhaps in the first week, for example, some participants were unusually busy and exercised fewer days compared to the second week.

We need a test that distinguishes the type of fluctuations in scores that we would expect to see due to randomness from the systematic differences that we should observe if there is an effect of our intervention.

t-Test for Dependent Means: What We're Trying to Accomplish

t-test for dependent means (also called *paired samples* t-*test*) a type of hypothesis test used to compare two sets of non-independent scores. Typically used to compare scores measured from the same participants, such as in a repeated measures design.

Unlike the single sample t-test that we learned earlier in this chapter, where we compared a sample to a population value, here we need to compare the pretest measurement to the posttest measurement. The appropriate test for this type of research scenario is the **t-test for dependent means** (or *paired-samples* t-*test*), which is a statistic that lets us determine if two scores from the same sample are significantly different when we have continuous (interval or ratio) data and when we don't know the variance. We call the pretest and posttest measurements "dependent" because how we interpret a posttest score is "dependent" on the value of the person's pretest score. In essence, although we have two distinct scores that we need to evaluate, what's most important is how these scores compare to each other within each participant (**Figure 9.12**).

To understand this idea further, consider two participants from our goal follow-through experiment, Samantha and Alejandro, and their pretest and posttest scores. Samantha has a pretest score of 2 and a posttest score of 5. Alejandro has a pretest score of 5 and a posttest score of 6. For our research question, the key differences are within

Things We Know	Single Sample t-Test	t-Test for Dependent Means
Key Question	Does a sample's mean differ from the population's mean?	Are two scores measured from the same participants different?
Population Mean (μ)	Yes	Unknown
Population Variance (σ²)	Yes	Unknown
Comparison Distribution	t	t

Figure 9.12 What We Know: Single Sample t-Test Versus t-Test for Dependent Means

each participant. That is, it's important to know how Samantha's pretest compares to her posttest, and how Alejandro's pretest and posttest compare. However, it isn't so important that Samantha ended up with a posttest score of 5, which is less than Alejandro's posttest score of 6, because comparing two people doesn't address whether the reminder message helped these participants achieve their goals.

What we need to evaluate is the change in the scores *within* each participant. When we do that, we can see that Samantha had an overall increase in number of days following through on her goals of 3 days (2 vs. 5), and that Alejandro had an overall increase of 1 day (5 vs. 6). In other words, both participants followed through on their goals for more days when getting the reminders. So, to test our hypothesis about daily reminders' effectiveness on goal pursuit, we need to compare the scores within each participant, rather than between the participants. This is why the repeated-measures design is sometimes called *within-subjects*, because we are looking at two scores within the same participants. We'll also note here that the *t*-test for dependent means is sometimes called a *paired-samples t-test,* because we are comparing pairs of scores for each participant.

Hypothesis Testing with a *t*-Test for Dependent Means: What We're Trying to Accomplish

The main idea behind the *t*-test for dependent means is that we will analyze how much people's scores change or differ from pretest to posttest measurements. If there is an effect of our independent variable, then most participants will show similar changes in their scores from the first to the second measurement. If the independent variable has no effect, then these change scores will equal zero (i.e., no change). Thus, the *t*-test for dependent means is concerned with **difference scores** (or change scores), which reflect the numerical discrepancy between pretest and posttest measurements. We'll use the symbol D to indicate that we are measuring a difference score, and the symbol M_D to indicate the mean of the difference scores.

Calculating a difference score is easy: we take the posttest and subtract the pretest score. For example, we would calculate Samantha's difference score by taking her posttest score (5) minus her pretest score (2), which equals 3 (5 – 2 = 3). Similarly, for Alejandro, we would take his posttest score (6) minus his pretest score (5), which equals 1 (6 – 5 = 1). Note that Samantha and Alejandro have positive difference scores, indicating that they followed through on their goals for more days after getting the reminders than before. If they had negative difference scores, it would mean that they followed through on their goals more before getting the reminders than after.

Beyond the fact that we are examining difference scores, the *t*-test for dependent means is actually very similar to the single sample *t*-test

difference score the difference between the pretest and posttest measurements.

that we learned in the first half of this chapter (which is why we are presenting them together). Instead of comparing a single sample mean to the population mean, we will evaluate our difference scores in comparison to the difference scores that we should expect to see if there is no effect of our independent variable. That is, if our manipulation truly has no effect, pretest and posttest scores should be roughly the same, resulting in difference scores that, on average, should equal zero. At the same time, we will recognize that, because of sampling error, we may obtain samples where the mean of the difference scores does not exactly equal zero. This is why we need a new type of comparison distribution: The distribution of means of difference scores.

The Comparison Distribution: The Distribution of Means of Difference Scores The distribution of means of difference scores is not unlike the distribution of sample means that we learned when performing the Z-test or the single sample t-test earlier in this chapter. With a distribution of sample means, we plotted the means of all possible samples of a particular size. Here we do something similar, but instead of plotting sample means, we are plotting the means of difference scores for all possible samples.

For example, we could gather a sample of 60 participants, run them through our procedure, and calculate the difference score (i.e., the posttest score minus the pretest score) for each person in the sample (e.g., 1, 3, 0, 2, 3, 0, 0, 4, −4, etc.), then calculate the mean of those 60 difference scores from the entire sample. Finally, we'd plot that in a distribution. We could then gather another different sample of 60 participants, run them through the same procedure, and plot that sample's mean difference score. We would repeat this process until we had gathered all possible combinations of 60 people from the population. The resulting distribution would be the *distribution of means of difference scores*. Importantly, just like with the distribution of means, where the mean of the distribution of means equals the mean of the population ($\mu_M = \mu$), the mean of the distribution of means of difference scores also equals the mean difference score in the population ($\mu_{M_D} = \mu_D$). Thus, the center of our distribution of means of difference scores will be the mean of the population.

That's how we would theoretically create the distribution. But by now we realize that gathering every possible sample of 60 people from the population is impossible because it's way too time-consuming and costly. Thankfully, there is a simpler way. Instead, we consider what the distribution of means of difference scores would look like *if there were no effect*. Another way of saying this is that we think about what the distribution would look like if the null hypothesis were true. Remember that the null hypothesis always predicts no effect. In the context of a *t*-test for dependent means, if there is no effect, then the pretest scores will equal the posttest scores (if they are both the same, there will be no difference), and the difference scores will equal zero. Therefore, if the null hypothesis is true, then our distribution of means of difference scores will have a mean of zero (**Figure 9.13**).

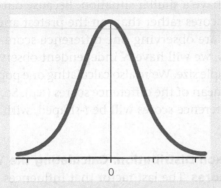

Figure 9.13 Distribution of Means of Difference Scores if the Null Hypothesis is Correct

The Comparison Distribution: *Z* or *t*? So, we will set the mean of our comparison distribution to zero. What about the shape of the distribution? Will it resemble a *Z*-curve or a *t*-curve? As we learned earlier in this chapter, the key to answering these questions is whether or not we know the variance of the population. If we know the population's variance, the Central Limit Theorem states that so long as our sample size is greater than 30, we can use a *Z*-curve to approximate the comparison distribution's shape. But if we don't know the population's variance, or our sample size is less than 30, we should use the *t* distribution.

For our study on goal follow-through, we have 60 participants, so we are good on the sample size front. But, critically, we don't know the variance of the difference scores at the population level. So, the *Z*-curve is out. We must estimate the variance of the difference scores using the variance that we calculate for our sample, so therefore we must use the *t*-curve to approximate the shape of the comparison distribution.

Of course, as we learned earlier, there are actually lots of *t*-curves. Each one is shaped slightly differently based on its degrees of freedom. We need to figure out the number of degrees of freedom that we have when calculating the *t*-test for dependent means. In general, whenever we are contemplating the number of degrees of freedom for any particular hypothesis test, we need to consider the number of independent observations we have made minus the number of population estimates that we have calculated.

In the example using the single sample t-test that we described earlier in this chapter, we made 10 observations of students working in coffee shops and calculated one population estimate. So, we had 10 independent observations minus one population estimate, we had nine degrees of freedom ($10 - 1 = 9$). Here, for the dependent samples t-test, we have a similar situation. Because our analysis focuses on difference scores rather than on the pretest and posttest scores separately, we are observing one difference score per participant. In other words, we will have N independent observations, where N reflects our sample size. We're also calculating one population estimate reflecting the mean of the difference scores (μ_D). So, the distribution of mean of difference scores will be t-shaped, with $N - 1$ degrees of freedom.

The Comparison Distribution: Calculating the Variance of the Difference Scores The last factor that influences the distribution of means of difference scores' shape is the variance of the difference scores. We already said that we don't know the population's variance, so we will have to estimate it using our sample's variance. The main wrinkle here is that our variance captures the difference scores' variance and not the individual pretest and posttest scores' variance. The good news is that, so long as we keep this in mind, the process for calculating the difference scores' variance is very similar to the process we have used in the past.

In general, we are going to calculate how much each individual difference score deviates from the difference scores' mean, $D - M_D$. We will then square these deviations, $(D - M_D)^2$, sum them up to create a sum of squared deviations SS_D, and divide by $N - 1$. The resulting value is the difference scores' variance, S_D^2.

$$S_D^2 = \frac{\Sigma(D - M_D)^2}{N - 1}$$

Let's use this formula to calculate the variance of our sample's difference scores. As we can see in **Figure 9.14,** the sum of squares is 297.73, there are 59 degrees of freedom and so the variance is 5.05. We're going to use this information from our sample to estimate the population's variance. In particular, we will use this information when calculating the standard error, which reflects the comparison distribution's standard deviation.

Participant	Pretest Score (X_1)	Posttest Score (X_2)	Difference Score (D)	Deviation ($D - M_D$)	Squared Deviation ($D - M_D)^2$
1	0.00	1.00	1.00	−0.07	0.00
2	3.00	6.00	3.00	1.93	3.74
3	4.00	4.00	0.00	−1.07	1.14
4	5.00	7.00	2.00	0.93	0.87
5...	1.00	4.00	3.00	1.93	3.74
...58	2.00	3.00	1.00	−0.07	0.00
59	6.00	2.00	−4.00	−5.07	25.67
60	3.00	5.00	2.00	0.93	0.87
		ΣD	64.00	SS	297.73
		N	60	df	59
		M_D	1.07		
Estimated Population Variance from the Sample				s^2	SS/df
				s^2	5.05
Comparison Distribution Variance & Standard Deviation: Distribution of Means				$S_{M_D}^2$	s^2/N
				$S_{M_D}^2$	0.08
				S_{M_D}	$\sqrt{S_M^2}$
				S_M	0.29
t-Score				t	$(M - \mu_{M_D})/S_{M_D}$
				t	3.68

Figure 9.14 Computing the Variance of the Difference Scores

Your Turn 9.5

1. For each of the studies described below, identify the appropriate hypothesis test that the researchers should perform.

a. A sports psychologist wants to determine whether visualizing a positive outcome helps athletes perform under pressure. To test this, she compares the number of free throws that basketball players make prior to and after receiving visualization training.

b. A clinical psychologist wants to examine whether a new treatment for posttraumatic stress disorder eliminates flashbacks. To test this, he records the number of flashbacks that his patients report and tests whether it is different from zero.

c. A personality psychologist wants to determine whether people high in conscientiousness receive fewer speeding tickets on average than the general population. To test this, she compares the driving records of a sample of people who score high in conscientiousness to population statistics (mean and standard deviation) provided by the government.

Hypothesis Testing with a *t*-Test for Dependent Means: How Does It Work?

Now that we have the appropriate comparison distribution, we can conduct our hypothesis test. Although the sequence of steps that we will follow for the *t*-test for dependent means is the same as the other hypothesis tests that we have learned, there are some slight differences in the details. Most of these differences pertain to the fact that we are analyzing difference scores, rather than raw scores.

Assumptions of the *t*-Test for Dependent Means Before we conduct a *t*-test for dependent means, we need to determine whether we satisfy the assumptions of the test. For our results to be valid, we must satisfy three key assumptions:

1. *The dependent variable must be interval or ratio.* Our pretest and posttest measures must be at interval or ratio levels of measurement. If we have a nominal or ordinal dependent variable, we should never conduct a *t*-test for dependent means.

2. *The distribution of difference scores should be approximately normal, or we must have a sufficiently large sample.* At the population level, the distribution of difference scores should be normal in shape. Of course, we typically don't know the shape of the population distribution. However, because of the Central Limit Theorem, we know that the population's shape is less important so long as we have large samples (e.g., greater than 30). Nevertheless, we should be on the lookout for outliers that might increase the chances that we violate this assumption.

3. *The difference scores should be independent.* When we conduct the *t*-test for dependent means, we are assuming that within each person the scores are dependent, but across the participants the scores are independent. That is, the difference scores for one participant do not affect the difference scores for another participant.

Step by Step: Hypothesis Testing with the *t*-Test for Dependent Means

Step 1: Population and Hypotheses We start, as always, by defining our population of interest, our comparison population, and our sample.

Population of Interest (μ_1): People who do get reminders to follow through on their New Year's resolutions.

Comparison Population (μ_2): People who do not get reminders to follow through on their resolutions.

Sample: Sixty participants in the study, measured before getting reminders (pretest measurement) and after getting reminders (posttest measurement).

Next, we need to determine whether our research hypothesis will be one-tailed or two-tailed; that is, directional or nondirectional. Although we might expect that reminders will increase goal adherence, we don't want to take this finding for granted. Although unlikely, it could be the case that giving people reminders has a counterproductive effect (e.g., people don't like being told what to do) and reduces the likelihood that people follow through on their goals. So, let's take the conservative approach used by most researchers and set a two-tailed research hypothesis.

Research Hypothesis (H_1): Giving people reminders about their goals will change the number of days that people follow through on them. The mean difference score will not be zero.

Null Hypothesis (H_0): Reminders will have no effect on people's ability to follow through on their goals. The mean difference score will be zero.

Step 2: Build Comparison Distribution What would the comparison distribution look like if the null hypothesis is true? That's the question we need to answer. To get our answer, we need to specify three bits of information: the mean of the comparison distribution, the standard error, and the specific *t*-curve that approximates the shape of the comparison distribution.

Let's start with the mean. As we learned earlier, we will construct our comparison distribution assuming that the null hypothesis is correct. If the null is true, then the mean of our comparison distribution will be zero, indicating no difference. In other words, the difference scores' mean for the population is zero because our reminders didn't affect whether people follow through on their goals and, therefore, pretest scores will equal posttest scores. So, we can enter zero as the mean of our comparison distribution. We've already determined that our comparison distribution will be *t*-shaped, so we can enter values of *t* under the comparison distribution (**Figure 9.15**).

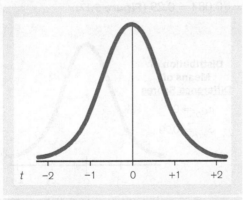

Figure 9.15 *t* Distribution with *t*-Scores

We've got a generic curve so far. Let's adapt it for our current study. First, we will calculate the actual scores of the population that we are estimating using the standard deviation of our sample. Earlier, we calculated the variance of the sample to be 5.05. To calculate the standard deviation, we need to take the square root of the variance, $S_2 = \sqrt{S_2^2} = \sqrt{5.05} = 2.25$. So, our estimate of the population standard deviation is $S_2 = 2.25$. We can now add scores that correspond to each value of t (**Figure 9.16**).

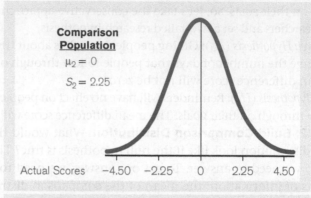

Figure 9.16 Comparison Population with Actual Scores

Now that we have described the comparison population, we can determine the characteristics of the distribution of means of difference scores. Our sample is but one of many possible samples, each with a sample size of 60. So, we need to convert our sample's variance (S^2) to the variance of the distribution of means of difference scores ($S_{M_D}^2$) by dividing our estimate of the population's variance, 5.05, by the sample size, 60: $S_{M_D}^2 = 5.05/60 = 0.084$. By taking the square root of the variance, $\sqrt{S_{M_D}^2}$, we convert the variance to the standard deviation, which in the context of a distribution of means of difference scores is called the standard error of the mean of difference scores, $S_{M_D} = \sqrt{S_{M_D}^2} = \sqrt{0.084} = 0.29$ (**Figure 9.17**).

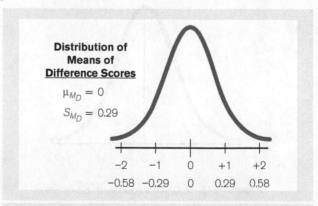

Figure 9.17 Distribution of Means of Difference Scores

Step 3: Establish Critical Value Cutoff Because our comparison distribution is t-shaped, we will use the t distribution to get our critical values. The exact critical values depend on two factors: the significance level (alpha) and the number of degrees of freedom. With respect to alpha, let's set our significance level to be .05, as this is the default level used by most researchers. For degrees of freedom, we will take our overall sample size (N) minus 1, or $N - 1$. For our current study, we had 60 total participants, so we have $60 - 1$, or 59 degrees of freedom. Once we have determined our significance level and degrees of freedom, we can find our critical values in our t-table (**Figure 9.18**).

df	One-Tailed Tests Alpha Level		Two-Tailed Tests Alpha Level	
	0.05	0.01	0.05	0.01
7	1.895	2.998	2.365	3.500
8	1.860	2.897	2.306	3.356
9	1.833	2.822	2.262	3.250
10	1.813	2.764	2.228	3.170
11	1.796	2.718	2.201	3.106
12	1.783	2.681	2.179	3.055
13	1.771	2.651	2.161	3.013
14	1.762	2.625	2.145	2.977
15	1.753	2.603	2.132	2.947
16	1.746	2.584	2.120	2.921
17	1.740	2.567	2.110	2.898
18	1.734	2.553	2.101	2.879
19	1.729	2.540	2.093	2.861
20	1.725	2.528	2.086	2.846
21	1.721	2.518	2.080	2.832
22	1.717	2.509	2.074	2.819
23	1.714	2.500	2.069	2.808
24	1.711	2.492	2.064	2.797
25	1.708	2.485	2.060	2.788
26	1.706	2.479	2.056	2.779
27	1.704	2.473	2.052	2.771
28	1.701	2.467	2.049	2.764
29	1.699	2.462	2.045	2.757
30	1.698	2.458	2.043	2.750
35	1.690	2.438	2.030	2.724
40	1.684	2.424	2.021	2.705
60	1.671	2.390	2.001	2.661
80	1.664	2.374	1.990	2.639
100	1.660	2.364	1.984	2.626
120	1.658	2.358	1.980	2.617
∞	1.645	2.327	1.960	2.576

Figure 9.18 Using the t-Table to Find the Critical Value Cutoffs

Unfortunately, our exact number of degrees of freedom is not included in our t-table. When this happens, we can either round down to the nearest degree of freedom that does appear in the table, which in this case would be 40 degrees of freedom, or we can look up the exact value using critical values calculators that are available online (to do this, enter "critical value calculator t-test"). An online calculator reveals that the exact critical value of t for 59 degrees of freedom is 2.001.

Step 4: Determine Sample Results Before moving forward, we need to check that we've satisfied the t-test for dependent means' assumptions. The first assumption is that we measured our dependent variable at the interval or ratio level. Here, our dependent variable is the number of days that participants follow through on their goal to exercise. Number of days is measured at the ratio level, so we are in the clear.

The second assumption is that the population distribution of difference scores is normal, or we have large samples. Although we don't know the shape of the population, we do have a sufficiently large sample ($N = 60$), so we satisfied this assumption. Also, we can look for outliers by converting all difference scores to Z-scores. If any of the Z-scores are greater than 3 (or less than –3), they are considered outliers. Doing this would reveal that none of the Z-scores are greater than 3 (or less than –3), so we do not have any outliers.

Finally, the third assumption is that the difference scores are independent. Because we made sure that none of the participants had any interactions with each other, we satisfied this assumption. So, we have satisfied all three assumptions of the hypothesis test and can proceed with our test.

We're now ready to convert the sample mean of the difference scores that we observed for our study sample to a t-score (also called the t-test statistic) that we can evaluate relative to our critical value (**Figure 9.19**). As we calculated in Figure 9.14, mean difference score for our sample was 1.07.

Mean Difference Score	M_D	1.07
Estimated Population Variance from the Sample	S^2	SS/df
	S^2	5.05
Comparison Distribution Variance & Standard Deviation: Distribution of Means	$S^2_{M_D}$	S^2/N
	$S^2_{M_D}$	0.08
	S_{M_D}	$\sqrt{S^2_M}$
	S_{M_D}	0.29
	S_{M_D}	1.07
t-Score	t	$(M_D - \mu_{M_D})/S_{M_D}$
	t	3.68

Figure 9.19 Computations for the t-Test for Dependent Means

All we need to do to convert this to a *t*-score is subtract the value of the mean difference score assumed under the null hypothesis (μ_{M_D}), which is zero, and then divide by the standard error: $t = \dfrac{M_D - \mu_2}{S_{M_D}}$, or $(1.07 - 0) / 0.29 = 3.68$. We can now compare the *t*-score to the critical values that we found in the previous step (**Figure 9.20**).

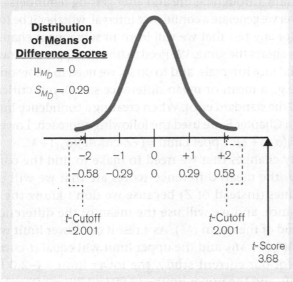

Distribution of Means of Difference Scores

$\mu_{M_D} = 0$

$S_{M_D} = 0.29$

−2	−1	0	+1	+2
−0.58	−0.29	0	0.29	0.58

t-Cutoff −2.001

t-Cutoff 2.001

t-Score 3.68

Figure 9.20 Sample Results on the Comparison Distribution

Step 5: Decide and Interpret Our *t*-score falls outside of the critical value, so we can reject the null hypothesis. In other words, although we don't know our *t*-score's exact *p*-value, it must be less than .05, because this is the threshold we used to find our critical values. Thus, our sample's mean difference of 1.07 days is outside of what we would expect to see due to sampling error, if the null hypothesis is true. We will therefore conclude that sending people reminders did significantly increase the number of days that they followed through on their goals.

Generating a Confidence Interval for the *t*-Test for Dependent Means Hypothesis testing's goal is to make a decision regarding our hypothesis: retain it or reject it. Thus, when we conduct our hypothesis test, if we get a *p*-value of .05 or less, we reject the null hypothesis. But, if we get a *p*-value of .06, we fail to reject the null. Is a *p*-value of .05 that much different from a *p*-value of .06 in terms of evidentiary value? No.

Because of this, some researchers have advocated for the use of confidence intervals for estimating the mean difference score within the population (e.g., Cumming, 2014). The logic for this is very similar to what we encountered when discussing confidence intervals in Chapter 8. A confidence interval of the mean estimates the range of scores that the population's mean is likely to fall within. A confidence interval for the mean difference score estimates the range of mean difference scores that the population's mean difference score is likely to fall within. For example, we might estimate the range of scores that the population's mean difference is likely to fall within, comparing people's follow-through before and after getting reminders.

Whenever we generate a confidence interval, whether it be for a Z-test or a t-test (or any test that we will learn in subsequent chapters), the approach is always the same. We need to find the upper and lower limits of our confidence intervals, and to do so, we need to know our sample estimate (e.g., a mean or mean difference score), our critical cutoff values, and the standard error. When creating a confidence interval for the mean in Chapter 8, we used the following approach: Lower Limit = $(-Z\text{-cutoff})(\sigma_M) + M$; Upper Limit = $(+Z\text{-cutoff})(\sigma_M) + M$.

The only changes that we need to make to find the confidence interval for the mean difference scores are that we will use our t critical values (instead of Z) because we don't know the population's variance, and we will use the mean of the difference scores (M_D) instead of the mean (M). As a result our lower limit will equal $(-t\text{-cutoff})(S_{M_D}) + M_D$, and the upper limit will equal $(t\text{-cutoff})(S_{M_D}) + M_D$. So, for our current study, the lower limit = $(-2.001)(0.29) +1.07 = 0.49$, and the upper limit = $(2.001)(0.29) = 1.07 = 1.65$. This is a 95% confidence interval, because we used an alpha of 0.05 to find our critical values.

What does this tell us? Well, unlike the hypothesis test that only tells us if the effect of reminders is different from zero (which is what we establish under the null hypothesis), the confidence interval estimates what the mean difference is likely to be in the population. Here, we have 95% confidence that the mean difference falls between 0.49 and 1.65 days. That is, if people are trying to set goals and follow through with them, they will complete their goal on average between 0.49 and 1.65 days per week more often if they get daily reminders than if they don't.

Computing the Effect Size for the t-Test for Dependent Means
As we learned in Chapter 8, there is a difference between the statistical significance and practical importance of a hypothesis test. Although we found statistical significance, we can't necessarily conclude that the results are important from a practical perspective. We need to compute the effect size to make this conclusion. The appropriate measure of effect size is Cohen's d, or the number of standard deviations' difference between the pretest and posttest measurements.

To calculate Cohen's *d*, we need to convert our mean difference score (M_D) into standard deviation units, so that we can determine the number of standard deviations' difference between the pretest and posttest scores. We do this by dividing the mean difference by the standard deviation of the difference scores (S_D).

$$d = \frac{M_D}{S_D}$$

In our study examining reminders' effect on the number of days that people follow through on their goals, the mean difference score was 1.07 and the difference scores' standard deviation was 2.25. Our effect size estimate would therefore be determined by the equation $d = 1.07 / 2.25 = 0.48$. An effect size of 0.48 indicates that participants followed through on their goals 0.48 standard deviations more when they received reminders compared to when they did not receive reminders. According to the guidelines described in Chapter 8, a Cohen's *d* of 0.48 represents a medium-sized effect. Of course, as mentioned in Chapter 8, to really understand the magnitude of this effect, we should examine the literature on goals to see whether this effect size is larger than, smaller than, or similar in size to other interventions.

Advantages and Disadvantages of the *t*-Test for Dependent Means One of the main reasons why the *t*-test for dependent means is a popular statistical analysis is because it is very sensitive to changes in participants' scores on our dependent variable over time. Many psychological interventions aim to change people's behaviors and attitudes. By measuring participants before and after an intervention, we can clearly identify any effect of the intervention (e.g., whether clients improved from before to after therapy). If the pretest measurement for a participant equals the posttest measurement, then the intervention had no effect. If the two measurements differ, then it is likely (although not guaranteed) that the intervention did have an effect. It's that simple. Note that this focus on how participants' scores change is not the focus of the single sample *t*-test. In the single sample *t*-test, we are comparing a sample to the population. If we find a difference between the sample and the population, we can only conclude that the sample is different from the population, not that the independent variable changed the participants scores. This is a subtle, but important distinction, and one that we will return to in the next chapter.

Because the *t*-test for dependent means analyzes changes within participants, it is also a very powerful test. Recall that in Chapter 8, we defined power as the ability to reject the null hypothesis, when it is false. So, when we say that the *t*-test for dependent means is a powerful test, we are saying that we have a greater likelihood of rejecting the null—that is, finding significant results—compared to other types of hypothesis tests. Another way that we can think about the power of the *t*-test for dependent means is that we need relatively fewer participants to achieve significant results, compared to other types of hypothesis tests. Again, think back to Chapter 8. We said that statistical power is closely connected to our sample size. Thus, as the power of a hypothesis test increases, the number of participants needed to find a significant effect decreases.

All of this sounds great. The *t*-test for dependent means is a powerful test, and we don't need as many participants to find significance. What's the catch? Why don't we always design studies that allow us to use the *t*-test for dependent means? Well, there is a big potential problem. In particular, because participants are in both conditions of the study, such as in our study examining the effects of reminders, it is possible that the participants figure out what this study is about and change their behavior as a result. Think about it this way: The participants are in a study for one week, and they report the number of days that they followed through on their goal to exercise. Then, during the second week, everything else is the same except that participants receive daily reminders to exercise. It would be easy to realize that the study was examining reminders' effect on exercise. These participants may decide to increase their number of days exercising, not because of the reminder per se, but because they want to show an improvement for the researchers.

participant effect changes in the participants' scores that are due to participants' expectations or beliefs about the purpose of an experiment, rather than the independent variable.

This type of problem is called a **participant effect** and reflects changes in the participants' scores on the dependent variable that are due to participants' beliefs or expectations about the study. The big problem is that, as researchers, we can't tell why participants' scores have changed from pretest to posttest. Their scores could change because of the independent variable or because of the participant effects. Because we can't know for sure why the scores changed, our results' validity may be called into question. Therefore, it's really important for us to consider whether participant effects might be a problem before we conduct our study. If participant effects might be a problem, we should consider using a different type of research design (such as the between-subjects approach that we will learn about in the next chapter).

Other Situations Where We Should Use the *t*-Test for Dependent Means So far in this chapter, we have identified one type of research design where the appropriate hypothesis test is the *t*-test for dependent means: the repeated-measures design. But, in fact, this hypothesis test can be used in other situations as well. Another research scenario where we should use this type of *t*-test is when we have a **matched-samples design.** In a matched-samples design, each participant is matched, or connected with, another participant. It could be, for example, that we are looking at the difference in follow-through on the goal to exercise between married couples. Just as with the repeated-measures design, our focus is on the difference score within each couple. So, even though there are two different people (the two members of the couple), our focus is on the difference score, so we need to treat them as dependent means.

matched-samples design study methodology in which two different participants are matched on the basis of a shared characteristic, which results in their being treated as dependent means.

SPSS VIDEO TUTORIAL: To learn more, check out the video tutorial Paired Sample *t*-Test.

HAND CALCULATION VIDEO TUTORIAL: To learn more, check out the video tutorial Calculating the *t*-Test for Dependent Means by Hand.

Communicating the Result

When communicating our result of a *t*-test for dependent means using APA Style, we always want to include the following information: the type of test that we performed, the research hypothesis, the *t*-score with degrees of freedom in parentheses, the *p*-value, the effect size, and, if the result is statistically significant, an explanation of the direction of the effect. For our current study, our results would look like this:

> We conducted a *t*-test for dependent means to examine the hypothesis that reminders to follow through on their goals would affect the number of days that people exercise. The results of this test were significant, $t(59) = 3.68$, $p = .001$, $d = 0.48$. Participants followed through on their goal to exercise more days on average when getting daily reminders ($M = 3.62$, $SD = 1.67$) than they did when not getting daily reminders ($M = 2.55$, $SD = 1.58$).

Forming a Conclusion

Our goal for this unit was to understand why people fail to follow through on their New Year's resolutions. We tested the possibility that perhaps people simply forget about their goals during the busyness of daily life. To investigate this idea, we conducted a study where we measured the number of days that people follow through on their goals before and after giving them daily reminders. Because this type of study is a repeated-measures design, we conducted a *t*-test for dependent means.

The test results revealed that getting daily reminders significantly increased the number of days that people follow through relative to not getting reminders. Not only was this effect statistically significant but we also found that it had a medium-sized effect.

Of course, there are some disadvantages to the repeated-measures design that could have been at play here. Because they were exposed to both the no-reminders condition and the reminders condition, perhaps participant effects drove the results. If this is the case, how could we reduce or eliminate the possibility of participant effects if we were to conduct a follow-up study? Well, one possibility would be to have different participants in our two conditions. That is, rather than measure people before and after getting reminders, we could give one group of participants reminders and give a different group of participants no reminders. We explore this type of study design in our next chapter.

 Your Turn 9.6

1. Previous research indicates that people have better memories for negative words than they do for neutral words (Kensinger & Corkin, 2003). Imagine that you want to conduct a follow-up study examining whether experiencing fear leads people to have better or worse memories. To test this, you ask 25 participants to listen to an audio clip from a documentary about wildlife while in a neutral mood. Next, you induce fear in the participants by having them watch a 5-minute clip from a horror movie. Finally, you have the participants listen to another segment from the documentary on wildlife. Both documentary segments provided the same number of facts about wildlife. You ask participants to complete a memory test for the facts about wildlife before and after the fear-induction video, and the number of correctly answered questions is the dependent variable. What type of hypothesis test should you conduct?

    1a. Step 1: Population and Hypotheses. What is the population of interest, the comparison population, and sample? State the null and research hypotheses for this research problem.

    1b. Step 2: Build a Comparison Distribution. After conducting initial analyses on your data,

you calculate the mean difference score (M_D) by subtracting the memory scores for fear-induced memories minus the memory scores for neutral memories (with positive scores indicating that memory was enhanced when experiencing fear). You find that the mean difference is 2.84 and the variance (S^2) is 38.14. Based on the information provided, answer the following questions: (a) Is the comparison distribution a normal curve or a *t*-curve? (b) If it is a *t*-curve, how many degrees of freedom are present? (c) What is the mean of the comparison population, assumed by the null hypothesis? (d) What is the standard deviation of the comparison population, estimated using our sample? (e) What is the standard error of the distribution of means of difference scores?

    1c. Step 3: Establish Critical Value Cutoff. If our alpha is .05, what are the critical value cutoffs?

    1d. Step 4: Determine Sample Results. What is the *t*-score? Where does the *t*-score fall in relation to the critical values?

    1e. Step 5: Decide and Interpret. What is the appropriate conclusion?

Focus on Open Science: *p*-Hacking

Imagine that we have spent the last year conducting a research study examining whether reminders help people better pursue their goals. After conducting weeks of planning and months of data collection, we are ready to sit down and analyze our data. After entering our data into SPSS, we perform analyses and find that the *p*-value for our main result is not .05 but is instead .062. In other words, we fell just short of statistical significance. We could call it a day and accept that we do not have enough evidence to claim that reminders help people. Or, we might be tempted to engage in what's known as *p*-hacking.

***p*-Hacking** is the questionable research practice whereby researchers manipulate their data or analyses until they find significant results. For example, perhaps, after looking back through our data, we find a participant whose scores don't seem to make sense to us. We might think that this participant wasn't taking the study seriously and decide to exclude this participant from our analyses. If we run our analyses again, we might now find that the *p*-value for our main result is .04, and suddenly our results are significant! But are they really? Or, did we hack our way to a finding that doesn't really exist (sometimes called a "false positive" finding)?

Unfortunately, many people are tempted to *p*-hack (John et al., 2012). In academic sciences, the way research faculty earn promotions and notoriety is to publish their studies in top journals. Those journals traditionally publish only statistically significant findings, and unethical researchers take shortcuts with their analyses and *p*-hack until they get significant results.

Systemic pressures lead to unethical individual behavior. This is not unlike the problem of performance-enhancing drugs in sports.

***p*-hacking** the questionable research practice whereby researchers manipulate their data until they find significant results.

Not unlike athletes who use performance-enhancing drugs, some researchers engage in *p*-hacking to improve their results.

Richard Levine/Alamy Stock Photo

In order to meet the stringent criteria for top performance in their sport, some athletes decide to take shortcuts in the form of steroids or other drugs. The problem of p-hacking is especially harmful because we trust scientists to uphold the highest of standards in their search for knowledge. When we lose trust in scientists, we lose trust in science.

So what can we do about this? How can we reduce the incidence of p-hacking? To date, researchers have focused their efforts on two approaches. The first is to preregister not only their hypotheses, which we discussed in Chapter 6, but to also preregister their analysis plan. An **analysis plan** is a document describing all of the analyses that a researcher anticipates performing as part of their study. This includes not only decisions about what type of analyses they will perform but also how they will deal with outliers, nonresponses, and other issues that can affect the quality of data. By specifying these choices in advance, researchers can avoid the temptation to run various iterations of analyses with the goal of finding a significant p-value.

The second approach that researchers have advocated is to lower our threshold for the default level of alpha. Historically, researchers have agreed that an alpha of .05 is an appropriate default level for alpha. More recently, though, some researchers have suggested that we should lower the default level of alpha to .005 (Benjamin et al., 2018). If we set alpha to be .005, these researchers argue, it would be much more difficult to find significant results via p-hacking. In essence, an alpha of .005 would require considerably stronger evidence to reject the null hypothesis. Fluke findings that may approach the .05 significance level would be so far away from the .005 criterion that researchers would be less tempted to p-hack. Although the proposal to reduce the default alpha to .005 hasn't yet been enacted as of this writing, it shows that the problem of p-hacking is serious and is something that researchers and consumers of research should recognize.

analysis plan a document that describes how data will be collected, processed, and analyzed.

Become a Better Consumer of Statistics

Late-night infomercials often use questionable methodologies and statistics when trying to convince us to buy their products. For example, infomercials for home gym equipment often tout the results of scientific studies that seem to show that using their product burns more calories or builds more muscle than alternative equipment. They make claims such as "people using the Abdominal Animal lost 10 pounds more than they did through diet alone." These infomercials frequently include before and after pictures that seem to support the amazing benefits of using their products.

However, as we have learned in this chapter, the evidence used to support these products' efficacy may be quite flawed. For example, participants in studies testing the Abdominal Animal's efficacy may believe that the new equipment is special and exciting, and as a result may decide to exercise for 45 minutes per day rather than the 20 minutes that the commercial suggests. These participants may not only use the machine but may decide that, since they are using this new exercise product anyway, they should also eat healthier and start a calorie-restricted diet. As a result, any changes in the participants' weights might not be attributable to the Abdominal Animal, because there are so many other factors at work, such as changes in diet, frequency of use, rigor of workout, and genetics of the individual. Did they lose weight because of the Abdominal Animal? Or because of the restricted-calorie diet? It's impossible to say.

So, as consumers of statistical information, we need to be skeptical of claims made as a result of "before and after" studies. We should ask ourselves, "Did the participants have an expectation of what the study was about?" and "Could those expectations have affected the results?" If the answer to these questions is yes, then we should put away our credit card and go back to sleep, because the evidence isn't strong enough.

There's no substitute for hard work. Be wary of products that promise amazing results by showing differences in before and after results.

Interpreting Graphs and Charts From Research Articles

In our reminder and goal achievement study, we had one primary dependent variable: the number of days that people followed through on their goal in a one-week period. Many studies, however, measure multiple outcomes to determine the effect of the independent variable. When this is the case, it is often helpful to the reader to summarize the results in a table or figure.

For example, a study examining the effects of kidney transplant surgery tested participants' goal disturbance before and after getting the transplant (de Vries et al., 2017). Goal disturbance reflects the degree to which participants' goals are impaired as a result of their kidney failure. The researchers examined various life areas where the participants were likely to experience goal

---

Table 2

Top 10 disturbed goals pre-transplantation and change scores pre/post-transplantation

	N	Goal	T0 Mean (SD)	T1 Mean (SD)	Change T0 – T1	
					t	Effect size (Cohen's d)
1	165	To be able to eat and drink what I like (38.2)	1.96 (1.18)	1.07 (1.06)	8.22*	.64
2	161	To fully enjoy life (31.1)	1.74 (1.32)	1.25 (1.27)	4.17*	.33
3	166	To go on vacation/to travel (36.1)	1.73 (1.38)	1.32 (1.28)	3.30*	.26
4	171	To be able to arrange my time schedule myself (29.2)	1.61 (1.27)	0.98 (1.15)	5.61*	.43
4	163	To decide for myself how to live my life (28.8)	1.61 (1.34)	1.20 (1.30)	3.35*	.26
5	162	To exercise (27.8)	1.53 (1.35)	1.14 (1.17)	3.31*	.26
6	163	To have a good sex life (28.2)	1.51 (1.41)	1.33 (1.39)	1.56	.12
7	167	To follow my own interests (21.6)	1.47 (1.24)	0.99 (1.19)	4.12*	.32
8	165	To support others (24.2)	1.45 (1.31)	1.01 (1.16)	3.96*	.31
9	167	To help people in need (24.0)	1.38 (1.32)	1.01 (1.24)	3.22*	.25

*$p \leq .005$.
Note: Within parentheses the percentage of participants indicating high or very high disturbance at baseline.

Figure 9.21 Sample Table (Data from deVries et al., 2017)

disturbance, and then looked to see if the level of goal disturbance was reduced following the kidney transplant. To present their results, the researchers provided a table (**Figure 9.21**) listing the most disturbed goals, as well as the change from pretest to posttest measurements.

As we can see in the table, the researchers present all of the relevant information for readers to interpret the results. They provide the pretest means (called T0), the posttest means (called T1), the *t*-score, and the effect size. The authors indicate which of the *t*-tests are significant using asterisks next to the *t*-scores. By comparing the pretest and posttest measurements, we can see that participants experienced significantly less goal disruption following transplant for 9 out of the 10 life goals. Only the goal "To have a good sex life" was rated at a similar level of goal disruption before and after kidney transplant.

Statistics on the Job

Imagine that you're a therapist and need to schedule appointments for your clients next week. You have 20 open slots, and exactly 20 clients to schedule. Sounds perfect, right? Not so fast. As you start scheduling everyone based on their preferred times, you'll quickly realize that the first 19 that you try to schedule have a choice. For example, they have the freedom to go at 6 P.M. on Tuesday or 5 P.M. on Wednesday. However, because you have only 20 time slots for 20 clients, the 20th and final client you schedule has no freedom to choose. They get stuck with the only time slot you have left. If you look at this in terms of degrees of freedom, your N is your number of time slots, so your degrees of freedom are $N - 1$, or 19. That is, only 19 clients have the freedom to have their session at different times. That last person is always locked in to the only remaining opening. Knowing this about degrees of freedom, when you find yourself in this situation of trying to schedule multiple people, you'd be wise to either always have more time slots than people needing to fill them, or you should be sure that the 20th person you're trying to schedule has the most availability.

Review Questions

1. For each of the studies described below, identify the appropriate hypothesis test that the researchers should perform.

   a. An educational psychologist wants to evaluate the effect of stimulant medication on disruptive classroom behaviors in children diagnosed with ADHD. To do this, they record the number of times the children get out of their seats without permission. The first day they observe the children without any medication, and the second day they observe the children after they have taken their medication.

   b. A company offers a SAT prep course and states that those who complete the training earn better scores. To evaluate the validity of this statement, you compare the SAT scores of those who complete the prep course to average SAT scores from the general population, and you use the sample standard deviation.

   c. The academic counselors at your college want to evaluate the effect that a new advising protocol has on the time to complete an associate's degree. To test this, they compare the average number of classes a student takes at their college now to the population statistics from the same college over the past 10 years before the new protocol was implemented (mean and standard deviation).

   d. A sports psychologist is interested in the effect of aerobic exercise on lung capacity. To evaluate this, she measures the lung capacity of a sample of people before and after they complete a 3-month training program.

2. Why do we divide the sum of squares (SS) by $N - 1$ when using sample data?

3. You had manually entered 40 data points when your cat bumped your cup of water, and now you cannot read one of your data points. Thankfully, you had already calculated the mean of the sample. Using the concept of degrees of freedom, explain how you can figure out the value that is no longer legible.

4. How and why are the t distributions different from a normal distribution?

5. What are your two options for finding the critical value for a single sample t-test or a t-test for dependent means if your degrees of freedom value isn't listed in the t-test table?

6. A sample of $N = 16$ individuals is selected from a normally distributed general population with $\mu = 35$. After a treatment is administered to the individuals, the sample mean is found to be $M = 30$ and the sum of squares is $SS = 960$. Use a two-tailed test and an $\alpha = .05$

   a. Step 1: Population and Hypotheses. What would the populations be? What would the hypotheses be?

   b. Step 2: Build a Comparison Distribution. What shape is the comparison population? What will the comparison distribution's mean (μ_2) be? What will the comparison population variance (S_2^2) be? Standard deviation (S_2)? What will the mean (μ_M) be? What will the variance (S_M^2) be? Standard deviation (S_M)? Draw what the comparison distribution looks like.

c. Step 3: Establish Critical Value Cutoff. What is the *t*-cutoff associated with this information? Show this on the comparison distribution.

d. Step 4: Determine Sample Results. What are the results of the *t*-test? Show this on the comparison distribution.

e. Step 5: Decide and Interpret. What is the appropriate conclusion?

7. You wonder whether years of inbreeding have changed the food consumption of golden hamsters. You hypothesize that food consumption has increased because food is more consistently and readily available. You know the average food consumption of wild hamsters is $\mu = 7.30$ grams per day. You measure food consumption of 39 hamsters that are currently in your colony, and you analyze the data using SPSS. You obtain the following results:

One-Sample Statistics

	N	Mean	Std. Deviation	Std. Error Mean
food_consumption	39	7.741	1.9398	.3106

One-Sample Test

	Test Value = 7.3						
			Significance		Mean Difference	95% Confidence Interval of the Difference	
	t	df	One-Sided p	Two-Sided p		Lower	Upper
food_consumption	1.420	38	.082	.164	.4410	−.188	1.070

One-Sample Effect Sizes

		Standardier[a]	Point Estimate	95% Confidence Interval	
				Lower	Upper
food_consumption	Cohen's d	1.9398	.227	−.092	.544
	Hedges's correction	1.9792	.223	−.090	.533

[a]The denominator used in estimating the effect sizes.
Cohen's d uses the sample standard deviation.
Hedges's correction uses the sample standard deviation, plus a correction factor.

a. What would the populations be? What would the hypotheses be?
b. What is the appropriate conclusion?
c. Write the results as they would appear in an APA-formatted results section.

8. A researcher was interested in evaluating the impact of a training session about appropriate workplace behavior. Before and after the training session, he evaluated the number of inappropriate workplace behaviors that the participants could identify in fictionalized scenarios. Theoretically, the training could increase or decrease the identification inappropriate workplace behaviors. He obtains the following data from 6 participants. Use an alpha = .01.

Participant	Before Training	After Training
1	12	13
2	11	14
3	9	14
4	18	17
5	12	15
6	8	9

a. Step 1: Population and Hypotheses. What would the populations be? What would the sample be? What would the hypotheses be?

b. Step 2: Build a Comparison Distribution. How many degrees of freedom are there? What is the mean of the comparison population, assumed by the null hypothesis? What is the standard deviation of the comparison population, estimated using our sample? What is the standard error of the distribution of means of difference scores? Draw the comparison distribution.

c. Step 3: Establish Critical Value Cutoff. What is the t-cutoff associated with this information? Show this on the comparison distribution.

d. Step 4: Determine Sample Results. What are the results of the t-test? Where does this score fall in relation to the critical values? Show this on the comparison distribution.

e. Step 5: Decide and Interpret. What is the appropriate conclusion?

f. Calculate Cohen's d. Is the effect small, medium, or large?

g. Calculate a 95% confidence interval.

9. Let's say the researcher in question 8 had been concerned with having insufficient power. Instead of analyzing the data when he had only 6 participants, he collected data from 15 participants and then analyzed the data using SPSS. He obtains the following:

Paired Samples Statistics

		Mean	N	Std. Deviation	Std. Error Mean
Pair 1	Before_Training	11.2000	15	3.07525	.79403
	After_Training	13.4000	15	2.72029	.70238

Paired Samples Correlations

				Significance	
		N	Correlation	One-Sided p	Two-Sided p
Pair 1	Before_Training & After_Training	15	.775	<.001	<.001

Paired Samples Test

		Paired Differences			95% Confidence Interval of the Difference				Significance	
		Mean	Std. Deviation	Std. Error Mean	Lower	Upper	t	df	One-Sided p	Two-Sided p
Pair 1	Before_Training – After_Training	−2.20000	1.97122	.50897	−3.29163	−1.10837	−4.322	14	<.001	<.001

Paired Samples Effect Sizes

		Standardier[a]	Point Estimate	95% Confidence Interval	
				Lower	Upper
Part 1	Before_Training – After_Training	Cohen's d	1.97122	−1.116	−1.775	−.453
		Hedges's correction	2.02606	−1.086	−1.707	−.441

[a]The denominator used in estimating the effect sizes.
Cohen's d uses the sample standard deviation of the mean difference.
Hedges's correction uses the sample standard deviation of the mean difference, plus a correction factor.

a. Would his conclusion be different from what you calculated in the previous question? Why or why not?

b. Write the results as they would appear in an APA-formatted results section.

10. What are the assumptions of a *t*-test for dependent means?

11. You're interested in the effect of background noise on attention spans. You measure the number of questions a person can complete in a silent room, and then you measure how many questions they can complete while watching a TV show. You find that they can complete more when in a silent room and are ready to announce that this proves your hypothesis. Before you do that, one of your classmates mentions that it may be the result of a participant effect. What are they referring to?

12. Your professor tells your class that a strength of the *t*-test for dependent means is that it is a very powerful test, and then they move on to the next topic. Your classmate is confused about what this means and asks you for help. What do you tell them?

Key Concepts

analysis plan, p. 328

difference score, p. 311

matched-samples design, p. 325

p-hacking, p. 327

participant effect, p. 324

posttest, p. 309

pretest, p. 309

repeated-measures design, p. 309

single sample *t*-test, p. 293

Answers to Your Turn

Your Turn 9.1

1. Answers will vary but should all feature the comparison of a sample's mean to a target or expected value from the broader population, or a replication. For example, you could use a single sample *t*-test to see if a company's sales group is meeting a sales target, or to see if an SAT prep program is helping the group do better than a typical high school student who hasn't taken the program.

2. (a) They both use a single sample and you have the population mean. (b) For the *Z*-test, you know the population variance, but you don't for the *t* and need to estimate it from the sample's variance. The *Z*-test's comparison distribution is normal, while the *t*-test uses a *t* distribution.

Your Turn 9.2

1. An unbiased estimate will always be the larger of the two numbers because the denominator is smaller (it uses $N - 1$, instead of N).

Your Turn 9.3

1. The estimated population variance is equal to the sum of squares divided by the degrees of freedom.

2. At the end of the semester, you have already received your grades for all of the other tests, assignments, and papers. In order to get the B+ you need, you

have no choice but to get a 100%. You have run out of degrees of freedom. All of those earlier assignments had some ability to vary and still result in your getting the B+ in the course. But now that you're at the last grade, the final exam, it can't vary. There are no more grades, so you've run out of wiggle room and degrees of freedom.

Your Turn 9.4

1. (a) More. (b) When you have more information (larger sample/more *df*), your estimates are better and will more closely approximate the normal distribution.

2. 2a. (a) Population of Interest: Your suitemates. Comparison Population: College students in general. Sample: Your 5 suitemates. (b) Research: Your suitemates study a different amount of time from that of college students in general. Null: Your suitemates study the same amount of time as college students in general.

2b. (a) It is a *t* distribution, with a shape ultimately determined by the degrees of freedom, because we need to estimate the variance; (b) 45 (same as the population); (c) $S_2^2 = SS/df = 370/4 = 92.50$; $S_2 = \sqrt{S_2^2} = \sqrt{92.50} = 9.62$; (d) a distribution of means of samples with a sample size of 5; (e) 45, same as the population; (f) $S_M^2 = S_2^2/N = 92.50/5 = 18.50$, and $S_M = \sqrt{S_M^2} = \sqrt{18.50} = 4.30$;

(g)

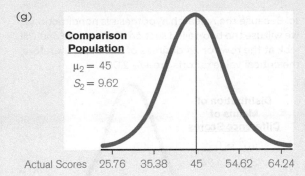

Comparison
Population

$\mu_2 = 45$

$S_2 = 9.62$

Actual Scores   25.76   35.38   45   54.62   64.24

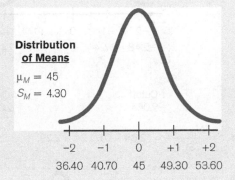

Distribution
of Means

$\mu_M = 45$

$S_M = 4.30$

-2   -1   0   +1   +2

36.40   40.70   45   49.30   53.60

2c. (a) Number of tails (two-tailed test because we had a nondirectional hypothesis), degrees of freedom ($df = 4$), significance level (we'll use the standard significance level, $p = .05$); (b) 2.78;

(c)

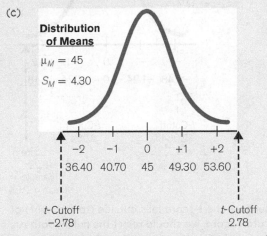

Distribution
of Means

$\mu_M = 45$

$S_M = 4.30$

-2   -1   0   +1   +2

36.40   40.70   45   49.30   53.60

t-Cutoff
-2.78

t-Cutoff
2.78

2d. (a) t-Test; (b) first she needs to get the mean of her sample by taking the sum of the scores (180) and dividing by 5, or 180/5 = 36, then she must complete the t-test:
$t = (M - \mu_M)/S_M = (36 - 45)/4.3 = (-9)/4.3 = -2.09$;

(c)

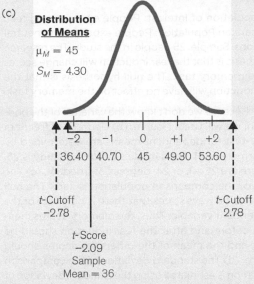

Distribution
of Means

$\mu_M = 45$

$S_M = 4.30$

-2   -1   0   +1   +2

36.40   40.70   45   49.30   53.60

t-Cutoff
-2.78

t-Cutoff
2.78

t-Score
-2.09
Sample
Mean = 36

2e. Our sample's t-score of -2.09 did not exceed the cutoff score of -2.78. Because our sample's results (Step 4) do not exceed the critical value (Step 3), we are unable to reject the null hypothesis (H_0) that your suitemates study the same amount as college students in general ($\mu_1 = \mu_2$). If we are unable to reject the null, we must also say that we failed to find support for the research hypothesis (H_1) that your suitemates study a different amount of time than college students in general. ($\mu_1 \neq \mu_2$). Although our suitemates' mean study hours (36) falls 9 hours below the target value of 45 study hours that a college student with 15 credits should generally study, the difference is not significant. As a result, we cannot be confident that it is a real difference.

Your Turn 9.5

1. (a) The researcher should conduct a t-test for dependent samples, because she used a repeated-measures design. (b) The researcher should conduct a single sample t-test because he is comparing the results of a sample of participants to some specific value but does not know the variance of the population. (c) The researcher should conduct a Z-test because she is comparing a single sample to the population and knows the variance of the population.

Your Turn 9.6

1. You should conduct a t-test for dependent means because the study is analyzing pairs of scores for each participant.

1a. Population of Interest: People experiencing fear. Comparison Population: People experiencing neutral emotions. Sample: 25 people in the study. The research hypothesis is that the fear induction will change scores on the memory task. The null hypothesis is that the fear induction will have no effect on the memory task.

1b. (a) Because we don't know the variance of the population, we will use a t-curve. (b) Degrees of freedom for a t-test for dependent means are determined by the formula $N - 1$. The sample size for the study is 25, so there are $25 - 1$, or 24, degrees of freedom. (c) The mean of the comparison population is zero. The null hypothesis always states that there is no effect of the independent variable. Thus, the memory scores measured before and after the fear induction should be equal, and the mean of the difference scores should be zero. (d) The standard deviation of the comparison population is estimated using the standard deviation of our sample. If the variance of the sample (S^2) is 38.14, then the standard deviation of the sample (S) is equal to $\sqrt{S^2} = \sqrt{38.14} = 6.18$; (e) $S_{M_D} = \sqrt{\left(\dfrac{38.14}{25}\right)} = 1.24$

1c. Because the research hypothesis is nondirectional, we will use the two-tailed section of our t table and will look at the row for 24 degrees of freedom. Therefore, the critical value cutoffs are $+/- 2.064$.

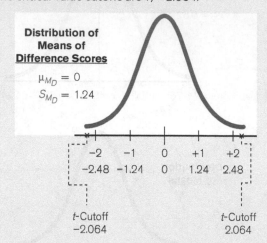

Distribution of
Means of
Difference Scores

$\mu_{M_D} = 0$
$S_{M_D} = 1.24$

| | -2 | -1 | 0 | +1 | +2 |
| | -2.48 | -1.24 | 0 | 1.24 | 2.48 |

t-Cutoff
-2.064

t-Cutoff
2.064

1d. $t = \dfrac{M_D - \mu_2}{S_{M_D}} = (2.84 - 0)/1.24 = 2.29.$

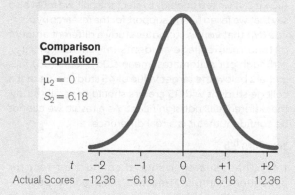

**Comparison
Population**

$\mu_2 = 0$
$S_2 = 6.18$

| t | -2 | -1 | 0 | +1 | +2 |
| Actual Scores | -12.36 | -6.18 | 0 | 6.18 | 12.36 |

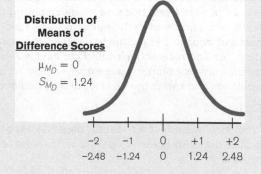

**Distribution of
Means of
Difference Scores**

$\mu_{M_D} = 0$
$S_{M_D} = 1.24$

| -2 | -1 | 0 | +1 | +2 |
| -2.48 | -1.24 | 0 | 1.24 | 2.48 |

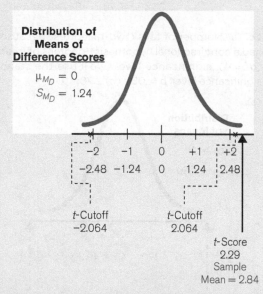

Distribution of
Means of
Difference Scores

$\mu_{M_D} = 0$
$S_{M_D} = 1.24$

| | -2 | -1 | 0 | +1 | +2 |
| | -2.48 | -1.24 | 0 | 1.24 | 2.48 |

t-Cutoff
-2.064

t-Cutoff
2.064

t-Score
2.29
Sample
Mean = 2.84

1e. Because the t-score falls outside (to the right) of the cutoff score, we should reject the null hypothesis and conclude that fear does affect memory. Because the mean difference score was positive, we can state that participants' memory scores were higher after the fear-induction task than they were before the fear-induction task. Thus, fear seems to enhance memory.

Answers to Review Questions

1. a. The researcher should conduct a *t*-test for dependent samples, because she used a repeated-measures design.
    b. The researcher should conduct a single sample *t*-test because he is comparing the results of a sample of participants to some specific value but does not know the variance of the population.
    c. The researcher should conduct a *Z*-test because she is comparing a single sample to the population and knows the variance of the population.
    d. The researcher should conduct a *t*-test for dependent samples, because she used a repeated-measures design.

2. When we use sample data, dividing by *N* systematically underestimates the value of the population variance. This means that if we divide by *N*, we have a biased estimate. This happens because extreme scores are relatively rare and sample variances tend to be closer to the sample mean than the population mean. To correct this bias, we divide the sum of squares (*SS*) by *N* − 1 rather than *N*.

3. Degrees of freedom are the number of values that are free to vary. Since you know the other 39 values and the mean, there is only one value that the missing data point could be. In other words, with the information you still have access to, the degrees of freedom are used up and the final value is locked in place.

4. They are different because we observe greater variation in the means of our samples than we would expect in a normal curve. The distribution of means is no longer a normal curve. The *t* distributions are wider and flatter, with thicker tails. The *t* distributions vary as a function of degrees of freedom and

become more similar to the normal curve as our sample size increases.

5. You can either round down to the nearest degree of freedom that does appear in the table, or you can look up the exact critical value online using a critical value calculator.

6. a. Population of Interest: the individuals who receive the treatment. Comparison Population: the normally distributed general population that the sample was selected from. Research Hypothesis: The sample has a different mean from that of the general population. Null Hypothesis: The sample has the same mean as the general population.
    b. It is a *t* distribution shape, determined by the degrees of freedom; $\mu_2 = 35$; $S_2^2 = 64$; $S_2 = 8$; $\mu_M = 35$ (same as population); $S_M^2 = 4$; $S_M = 2$

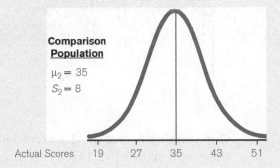

Comparison Population
$\mu_2 = 35$
$S_2 = 8$

Actual Scores   19   27   35   43   51

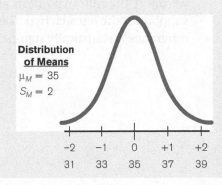

Distribution of Means
$\mu_M = 35$
$S_M = 2$

−2   −1   0   +1   +2
31   33   35   37   39

c. Critical values are ±2.131

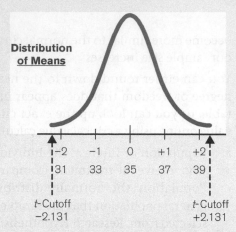

Distribution of Means

| -2 | -1 | 0 | +1 | +2 |
| 31 | 33 | 35 | 37 | 39 |

t-Cutoff −2.131   *t*-Cutoff +2.131

d. $t = (30 - 35)/2 = -5/2 = -2.5$

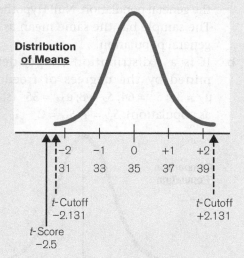

Distribution of Means

| -2 | -1 | 0 | +1 | +2 |
| 31 | 33 | 35 | 37 | 39 |

t-Cutoff −2.131   *t*-Cutoff +2.131

t-Score −2.5

e. Our sample's *t*-score of −2.5 exceeded the cutoff score of −2.131. Therefore, we reject the null hypothesis and find support for the research hypothesis. The difference is statistically significant.

7. a. Population of Interest: the mice in your colony. Comparison Population: wild hamsters. Research Hypothesis: Food consumption of laboratory bred hamsters is higher than wild hamsters. Null Hypothesis: Food consumption of laboratory bred hamsters is the same as that of wild hamsters.

b. The *p*-value of a one-tailed single sample *t*-test is .082, which is more than our alpha (.05). We fail to reject the null hypothesis and conclude that there is no reason to believe that the food consumption of laboratory-bred hamsters is different from that of wild hamsters.

c. A single sample *t*-test was conducted to evaluate whether the food consumption of laboratory-bred hamsters ($M = 7.74$, $SD = 1.94$) was higher than that of wild hamsters ($M = 7.30$). The results were not significant, $t(38) = 1.42$, $p = .082$, $d = 0.23$.

8. a. Population of Interest: people after training. Comparison Population: people before training. Sample: the 6 people in the study. Research Hypothesis: Training will change the identification of inappropriate workplace behaviors. Null Hypothesis: The training will have no effect on the identification of inappropriate workplace behaviors.

b. $df = 5$, mean assumed by null hypothesis $= 0$; $S_2 = 2.10$, $S_{MD} = 0.69$

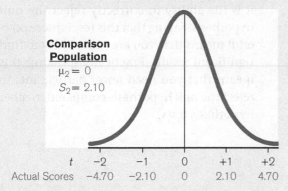

Comparison Population
$\mu_2 = 0$
$S_2 = 2.10$

| t | -2 | -1 | 0 | $+1$ | $+2$ |
| Actual Scores | -4.70 | -2.10 | 0 | 2.10 | 4.70 |

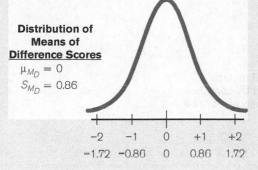

Distribution of Means of Difference Scores
$\mu_{MD} = 0$
$S_{MD} = 0.86$

-2 -1 0 $+1$ $+2$
-1.72 -0.86 0 0.86 1.72

c. cutoff value $= \pm 4.032$

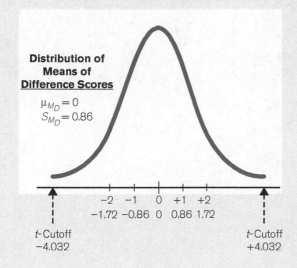

Distribution of Means of Difference Scores
$\mu_{MD} = 0$
$S_{MD} = 0.86$

-2 -1 0 $+1$ $+2$
-1.72 -0.86 0 0.86 1.72

t-Cutoff -4.032

t-Cutoff $+4.032$

d. $t = (2 - 0)/0.86 = 2/0.86 = 2.33$

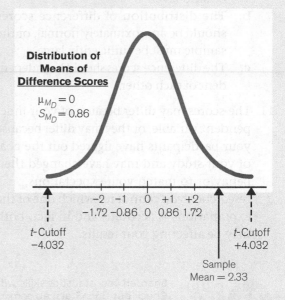

Distribution of Means of Difference Scores
$\mu_{MD} = 0$
$S_{MD} = 0.86$

-2 -1 0 $+1$ $+2$
-1.72 -0.86 0 0.86 1.72

t-Cutoff -4.032

t-Cutoff $+4.032$

Sample Mean $= 2.33$

e. Fail to reject the null hypothesis

f. 0.95 large

g. Lower limit $= -1.47$; upper limit $= 5.47$

9. a. His conclusion now would be that he rejects the null hypothesis and accepts the research hypothesis. There is reason to believe that the training significantly increased the detection of inappropriate workplace behaviors. The conclusion would change because now the *p*-value is less than the alpha cutoff.

b. A *t*-test for dependent means was conducted to evaluate the hypothesis that a training session would affect the detection of inappropriate workplace behaviors in fictionalized scenarios. The results were significant, $t(14) = -4.32$, $p < .001$, $d = 1.12$. Participants detected more inappropriate workplace behaviors after training ($M = 13.40$, $SD = 2.72$) than before training ($M = 11.20$, $SD = 3.08$).

10. **a.** The dependent variable must be interval or ratio level.
b. The distribution of difference scores should be approximately normal, or the sample must be sufficiently large.
c. The difference scores should be independent of each other.

11. The scores may differ because of your independent variable, or they may differ because your participants have figured out the goal of your study and may have changed their behavior to match your expectations. As a researcher, you cannot tell which one of the explanations is accurate, and in fact, both may be affecting your results.

12. Power is the ability to detect a difference when a difference really exists; that is, it is the ability to correctly reject the null hypothesis. Saying that this test is more powerful means that you are more likely to find significant results. Practically speaking, this means that you need fewer participants to reject the null hypothesis compared to other hypothesis tests.

OPEN STATS LAB

Sharpen your statistics skills with real-life data! Check out OpenStatsLab.com, created by coauthor Kevin McIntyre, to practice running analyses for real published research studies.

10

t-Test for Two Independent/ Unrelated Samples

Learning Outcomes

After reading this chapter, you should be able to:

● Explain the key question that a *t*-test for two independent samples seeks to answer.

● Identify similarities and differences between a *t*-test for two independent samples and other *t*-tests.

● Describe the underlying logic for calculating a pooled estimate of the population variance.

● Identify when it is appropriate to use a *t*-test for two independent samples.

● Find a cutoff score in a *t*-table.

● Describe the underlying logic for combining the variances from both distribution of means when calculating a variance for the distribution of differences between means.

● Calculate the *t*-score for the *t*-test for two independent samples.

● Describe the assumptions of the *t*-test for two independent samples.

As any college student would tell you, high school was easy compared to the requirements, classes, and assignments in college. It's not like you weren't warned. When your high school teachers weren't focused on telling you to put your phone away, they were trying to scare you into getting prepared for college. Because college influences your career success, the appeal of being better, faster, stronger, and smarter is real. And even though you're in college, it's never too late to start flexing those cognitive muscles. After all, we exercise to make our body stronger. Perhaps we need to do the same for our brain as well. Work smarter, not harder.

As it turns out, there's an app for that. There are many brain-training apps available now that promise to enhance mental abilities, sharpen cognition, and boost IQ by doing fun games. Allegedly.

The question is, do they really work? Well, there are several signs that the brain-training app's claims are legitimate. For example, when you go to brain-training sites, they give a lot of supporting information about their millions of users, a board of credentialed scientists, research partners, and pervasive use of the word "science." But is it really science? Part of being psychologically literate and a good consumer of scientific information is knowing what type of evidence is necessary to be truly convinced. You need to test it out.

Statistics for Life

First, you've been a behavioral science student long enough to know that checking the existing literature is always a good idea. When you do, there's an article, "Do 'Brain-Training' Programs Work?" that reviews brain-training research (Simons et al., 2016), and another, "Toward a Science of Effective Cognitive Training" (Smid et al., 2020), both of which cast serious doubt on programs' claims. However, one study with a large sample of 4,715 people found that brain-training, when compared to completing crossword puzzles, had a range of benefits such as quicker

Brain-training apps are popular. But can they help you succeed in college?

processing speeds, better memory, and problem solving (Hardy et al., 2015). That sounds promising, but a brain-training company funded the study and also happened to employ the study's authors. However, another study found that training memory had benefits, but mainly for subsequent tasks that were more similar to the training (Gathercole et al., 2019). Now you aren't sure what to think. To really be convinced, you need to answer a key question: Does brain-training improve college performance?

Where Do the Data Come From?

According to a social butterfly friend of yours, he has 12 friends who are using brain-training and 13 who aren't, and you're curious to know if you could actually see any differences between the two sets of people.

To see brain-training's potential for improving college performance, the exercises would need to improve outcomes on a task that college students typically have to do. College students' most common course-related task is still studying notes and taking a test on that material. You ask your friend if his acquaintances are up for a little challenge. You take a section of notes from your first-year history course, and the 10-question multiple-choice weekly quiz that went with it. You give your participants 15 minutes to study the notes, then they take the quiz. You note their scores along with whether they had been doing brain-training (see **Figure 10.1**).

Brain-Training Friends	Quiz Score	Non-Brain-Training Friends	Quiz Score
Alyssia	5	Sacha	3
Selma	8	Tiegan	5
Andy	7	Jordon	8
Jessica	9	Marley	4
Layton	4	Ally	2
Jameson	3	Clinton	9
Debora	6	Carson	10
Zaiden	8	Niamh	10
Charley	10	Jen	4
Malloy	7	Hassan	7
Baylee	10	Candice	5
Harleen	4	Brinley	5
		Bryce	6

Figure 10.1 Participants' Scores on History Quiz

t-Test for Two Independent Samples: What We're Trying to Accomplish

The key question for us to answer is whether the two groups (brain-training and no brain-training) are different, or if they are the same. In more statistical terms, we want to see if the two samples/groups/conditions come from two different populations, or if both samples come from the same population. We can test this idea using the **t-test for two independent (or unrelated) samples** (also known as *independent samples* t-*test*), which is a statistic that lets us determine if two samples are from different populations when we have a continuous (interval or ratio) dependent variable and when we don't know the population's variance. In other words, the *t*-test for two independent samples allows us to see if means from two samples, or groups of different people, are different enough to have not happened by chance.

Outside of statistics and brain-training, you've probably heard the expression, "there are two kinds of people." There are cat people and dog people, night owls and morning people, people who have dozens of red notifications all over their phone and those who have none. In each case, we assume the two "types" differ from each other in some

t-test for two independent samples (also called *independent samples* t-*test*) a statistical test that lets us determine if two samples are from different populations when we have a continuous (interval or ratio) dependent variable and when we don't know the population variance.

meaningful way. If there are truly two different types of people, they would theoretically have come from two different populations (see **Figure 10.2**). Similarly, we might expect that those who do brain-training will be a different kind of person from those who don't.

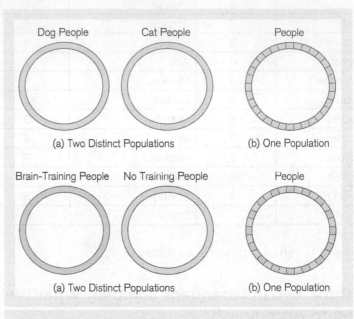

Figure 10.2 Two Kinds of People? Dog vs. Cat People

Of course, if the two groups aren't really different on a given dimension, it suggests that there is really only "one kind of person," and that everyone comes from the same population. Essentially with the *t*-test for two independent samples we want to see if two groups have real differences between them. We can use a *t*-test for two independent samples in two different situations:

1. Compare means of two randomly assigned groups from a two-group experiment (e.g., Who has higher life satisfaction—those randomly assigned to complete a gratitude journal, or those assigned to keep a regular journal?)

2. Compare means of two naturally occurring (i.e., nonrandomly assigned) groups (e.g., Who does better on the SAT—those who went to public school, or those who attended private school?)

Let's stop for a moment to contrast *t*-tests for dependent and independent samples (see **Figure 10.3**). There are several distinctions, but the most notable is that with dependent samples in the previous chapter, we had two scores (how well participants followed through with their goal before and after reminders) from the same person. Scores for dependent samples are often of the pre–post or before–after variety, and we focused on differences between those pretest and posttest scores to see if there was change over time. With independent samples we have two means, each from a unique sample, and we focus on comparing the mean from each group to see if they are different.

	t-Test for dependent samples	*t*-Test for two independent samples
Key Concept	Change; Comparing Matched Groups	Comparing Different Groups
Key Question	Are the two scores different over time?	Are the two groups different from each other?
Where to Look for Differences?	Within Subjects	Between Subjects
Typical Research Design	Pre-Post; Matched	Two-Group
Compare Two Means?	Yes	Yes
Population Mean (μ)	Unknown (assume 0)	Unknown (assume 0)
Population Variance (σ^2)	Unknown	Unknown
Comparison Distribution	Distribution of Means of Difference Scores	Distribution of Differences Between Means
Comparison Distribution Shape	*t*	*t*
Comparison Distribution Mean	0 (i.e., no change/ difference)	0 (i.e., no difference)
Comparison Distribution Variance	$S^2_{M_D}$	S^2_{Pooled}

Figure 10.3 What We Know: *t*-Test Comparison

As with the other types of *t*-tests we've discussed, the *t*-test for two independent samples compares differences between two means, requires that we estimate population variance, and requires that our outcome or dependent variable is continuous (interval or ratio) level data across all *t*-tests. In our case, we want to compare friends who have done brain-training to friends who haven't, to see if brain-training improves performance on a history quiz. We can test this question with the independent-samples *t*-test; let's see how.

Your Turn 10.1

1. Please give your own example of a research question that would call for a *t*-test for two independent samples.

2. a. Give three ways the *t*-test for dependent means and *t*-test for independent means are distinct.

   b. Give three things all *t*-tests have in common.

The Comparison Distribution: Distribution of Differences Between Means With each statistical test we encounter, a key difference is the comparison distribution. That's because as the nature of our data changes, the comparison distribution must change to match our data. When we were interested in difference scores with the *t*-test for dependent samples, our comparison distribution was a Distribution of Means of Difference Scores. Now, with the *t*-test for two independent samples, we are interested in the difference between means of two groups (brain-training and no brain-training). As a result, we need to have a comparison distribution that matches our data, so we would need a Distribution of Differences Between Means.

To visualize where this distribution comes from, imagine (a) two distinct populations (shown in **Figure 10.4**). These are the two populations where each sample could have originated. Because we are working with means from each of our samples, our comparison distribution

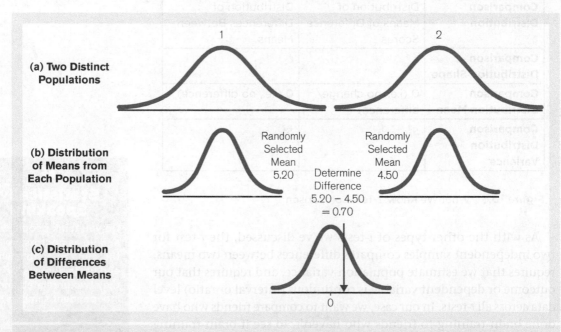

Figure 10.4 Comparison Distribution: Creation of the Distribution of Differences Between Means

will involve means (rather than scores), so we need to create (b) distributions of means based on each population. These distributions of means originate from the same process we've seen in the past: pull a random sample from the population, calculate the mean, plot it, and repeat an infinite number of times.

In the past, a single distribution of means has been sufficient to conduct our analyses because we've always worked with a single sample. However, we now have two samples, so we need a distribution of means from each sample. Our research question focuses on the differences between means, so we'll need a comparison distribution that does the same. To get (c) a Distribution of Differences Between Means, we would theoretically need to randomly select a mean from sample 1's distribution of means (e.g., 5.20), then randomly select a mean from sample 2's distribution of means (e.g., 4.50), and determine the difference (i.e., subtract them; 5.20 – 4.50). We would then plot the result (e.g., 0.70). Now imagine doing this over and over. That creates the Distribution of Differences Between Means.

The Comparison Distribution: Finding the Missing Mean Creating our comparison distribution requires a mean and variance, ideally from the population. Similar to the situation we encountered with the *t*-test of dependent samples, we don't have any concrete information about the population's means. In fact, we technically aren't sure if our participants come from one big population or from two distinct populations. Without that information, we must again rely on the null hypothesis' logic to determine the mean of our comparison distribution.

Remember, a *t*-test for two independent samples tests whether there are two different kinds of people. If there are, the two groups should have different means. In this context, the null hypothesis, or opposite of what we expect, would be that the two groups have the same mean. When we have any two identical means (e.g., 2.50 and 2.50, or 4.23 and 4.23), the difference between them (e.g., 2.50 – 2.50, or 4.23 – 4.23), the result is a score of 0, signifying no difference. Thus, because our comparison distribution represents what the world looks like when the null hypothesis is true, our Distribution of Differences Between Means has a mean of 0 that represents that our two groups are the same.

This, of course, is the general logic of hypothesis testing. In real-life data collection, even when the null is true, it's unlikely our mean difference score will be exactly 0. Instead, due to sampling error, the groups' means will be slightly different. So, we also need to specify the amount of difference between our groups' means that we would expect to see if the null is true, and by extension, the amount of difference that would be big enough for us to reject the null. Thus, we also need to specify the variance of the comparison distribution.

The Comparison Distribution: Finding the Missing Variance Once again, to get to where we want to go (our comparison distribution's standard error), we first have to determine the population's variance. As with other *t*-tests, we will use what we know about the sample to estimate the population. The wrinkle this time is that we have information from two samples instead of just one. Now, we have a decision. Do we use just one sample, and if so, which one? Or, do we use both? Generally speaking, we want to combine the estimates from both samples because the more information you have, the better the estimate. The same is true for population estimates; using both samples gives us more information, which will produce a more accurate estimate.

However, each sample may not have the same amount of information (i.e., participants/sample size). To account for this, we do what the U.S. House of Representatives does: We give more influence to the groups that have more people. This is why more populous states like Texas and New York have more representatives, which gives them greater influence, than less populous states like Montana and North Dakota. By allotting influence proportionally based on the number of people, the logic is that it gives the best estimate of how most people feel.

We follow the same logic when estimating the population variance from our samples. To give each sample their fair share of influence over the population estimate, we pool or combine (i.e., S^2_{Pooled}) the samples' variance estimates (i.e., S^2_1 and S^2_2). But to keep it fair and to give more weight to larger groups, we adjust each sample's estimate by the sample's degrees of freedom (i.e., df_1 and df_2; recall that $df = N - 1$), relative to the total degrees of freedom from both samples combined (i.e., $df_{Total} = df_1 + df_2$). The result is $S^2_{Pooled} = (df_1 / df_{Total})(S^2_1) + (df_2 / df_{Total})(S^2_2)$. If this formula feels familiar, it's because we used a very similar approach in Chapter 3 when pooling together the means from different samples.

By following the process described in this formula, we're essentially creating an average of the two samples' estimates that weights each estimate according to how much information it provides. For example, let's say we have a study where 20 of our participants come from Sample 1 and 30 come from Sample 2. When we combine them together, our formula would weight the Sample 1's variance by 20/50 (or two-fifths), while weighting Sample 2's variance by 30/50 (or three-fifths). Remember, when interpreting symbols, the numerical subscript 1's and 2's indicate which sample the information comes from. Also, note that we're using degrees of freedom instead of number of participants. That's because we are using samples to estimate the population's variance, and we need to make sure our estimate is unbiased.

$$S^2_{Pooled} = \frac{df_1}{df_{Total}}(S^2_1) + \frac{df_2}{df_{Total}}(S^2_2)$$

Your Turn 10.2

1. Your lab partner calculated a pooled estimate of the population variance (S^2_{Pooled}) of 27.39 from two sample estimates, $S^2_1 = 22.25$ and $S^2_2 = 26.99$, and checks with you to see if their calculation is correct. Without doing any math, and without any additional information, you immediately know that your partner's calculation is wrong. Why?

2. Your lab partner gives it another try, and this time correctly calculates the population variance (S^2_{Pooled}) as 26.39 from the sample estimates $S^2_1 = 22.25$ and $S^2_2 = 26.99$. Without doing any math, and without any additional information, which sample was larger? Explain.

Hypothesis Testing with a *t*-Test for Two Independent Samples: How Does It Work?

Hypothesis testing helps us know if any differences we see matter. That is, we might observe differences in our world, such as those who do brain-training seem mentally sharper and quicker. But just because we notice that difference, it does not guarantee it is real. Some differences between groups simply happen by chance, or more technically, due to sampling error. To know if a difference we're seeing is an actual difference, we need to use hypothesis testing. Doing so makes sure we establish clear criteria for what would qualify as a large enough difference to convince us (with 95% certainty) that the difference we see is authentic.

Step by Step: Hypothesis Testing with the *t*-Test for Two Independent Samples Any time we have two samples that don't have the exact same mean, there is a difference between them. What we need to determine is whether that difference is large enough to be relatively certain that it is a real difference and didn't happen by chance. To do that, we need hypothesis testing.

Step 1: Population and Hypotheses As always, we start by outlining who we are studying and what we expect to find.

Population of Interest (μ_1): People who do brain-training.

Comparison Population (μ_2): People who don't do brain-training.

Sample: 25 college-bound friends, 12 who do brain-training and 13 who do not.

Next, we need to make a prediction about how the populations compare to each other, and include a null hypothesis that states the opposite of our prediction. Here are our hypotheses:

Research Hypothesis (H_1): People who do brain-training will have higher history quiz scores than those who don't do brain-training ($\mu_1 > \mu_2$). In other words, we are making a directional hypothesis that the Population of Interest's mean will be greater than the Comparison Population's mean.

Null Hypothesis (H_0): People who do brain-training will have the same (or lower) history quiz score as those who don't do brain-training ($\mu_1 \leq \mu_2$). In other words, the Population of Interest's mean is either the same or lower than the Comparison Population's mean.

Step 2: Build Comparison Distribution As before, our sampling or comparison distribution should represent no effect or the null hypothesis, which in this case is no difference between the brain-training groups. Because we are interested in differences between means of groups, our comparison distribution will be a *t*-shaped Distribution of Differences Between Means.

Mean of the Distribution of Differences Between Means: To build our comparison distribution, we first need the mean. We do not have any direct information about the population, so we will rely on the logic of hypothesis testing with the null hypothesis. Our comparison distribution represents the null, and our null states that there is no difference between the groups, which would make the typical or mean difference 0.

Population Variance: Next, we need to find our comparison distribution's variance. However, we need some other information in order to find that. First, we need to estimate the population's variance (see **Figure 10.5**). To do that, we will take the information we have from our samples and combine it. Specifically we will use each sample's estimate of the population variance (S_1^2 and S_2^2) to create the pooled estimate of population variance (S_{Pooled}^2). To do that we first calculate the samples' estimated variances,

$$S_1^2 = \frac{SS_1}{df_1} = \frac{62.22}{11} = 5.66$$

$$S_2^2 = \frac{SS_2}{df_2} = \frac{82.00}{12} = 6.83$$

Brain-Training Friends	Quiz Scores (X_1)	($X_1 - M$)	($X_1 - M$)^2	Non-Brain-Training Friends	Quiz Score (X_2)	($X_2 - M$)	($X_2 - M$)^2
Alyssia	5	−1.75	3.06	Sacha	3	−3.00	9.00
Selma	8	1.25	1.56	Tiegan	5	−1.00	1.00
Andy	7	0.25	0.06	Jordon	8	2.00	4.00
Jessica	9	2.25	5.06	Marley	4	−2.00	4.00
Layton	4	−2.75	7.56	Ally	2	−4.00	16.00
Jameson	3	−3.75	14.06	Clinton	9	3.00	9.00
Debora	6	−0.75	0.56	Carson	10	4.00	16.00
Zaiden	8	1.25	1.56	Niamh	10	4.00	16.00
Charley	10	3.25	10.56	Jen	4	−2.00	4.00
Malloy	7	0.25	0.06	Hassan	7	1.00	1.00
Baylee	10	3.25	10.56	Candice	5	−1.00	1.00
Harleen	4	−2.75	7.56	Brinley	5	−1.00	1.00
				Bryce	6	0.00	0.00

ΣX	81	SS	62.22	ΣX	78	SS	82.00
N	12	df_1	11	N	13	df_2	12
M_1	6.75			M_2	6.00		

Estimated Population Variance from the Sample	S_1^2	SS/df		Estimated Population Variance from the Sample	S_2^2	SS/df
	S_1^2	5.66			S_2^2	6.83

	df_{Total}	$df_1 + df_2$
	df_{Total}	23

Pooled Estimate of the Population Variance	S_{Pooled}^2	$\dfrac{df_1}{df_{Total}}\left(S_1^2\right) + \dfrac{df_2}{df_{Total}}\left(S_2^2\right)$
	S_{Pooled}^2	6.27

Variance of the Distribution of Means	$S_{M_1}^2$	S_{Pooled}^2/N_1	Variance of the Distribution of Means	$S_{M_2}^2$	S_{Pooled}^2/N_2
	$S_{M_1}^2$	0.52		$S_{M_2}^2$	0.48

Comparison Distribution: Distribution of Differences Between Means	$S_{Difference}^2$	$S_{M_1}^2 + S_{M_2}^2$
	$S_{Difference}^2$	1.00
	$S_{Difference}$	$\sqrt{S_{Difference}^2}$
	$S_{Difference}$	1.00

t-Score	t	$(M_1 - M_2)/S_{Difference}$
	t	0.75

Figure 10.5 Computations for t-Test for Two Independent Samples

Next, we take the sample variances and pool them while weighting each estimate based on the sample's degrees of freedom, using this formula:

$$S^2_{Pooled} = \frac{df_1}{df_{Total}}(S^2_1) + \frac{df_2}{df_{Total}}(S^2_2) = \frac{11}{23}(5.66) + \frac{12}{23}(6.83)$$

$$= 2.71 + 3.56 = 6.27$$

Distribution of Means' Variance: With the estimated population variance in place, we need to determine the variance of the distribution of means for each sample. Though we have two samples, we only have one estimate of the population variance (S^2_{Pooled}), so we will need to use that to calculate the variance of both distributions of means. In formula form, the estimated variance for the distribution of means for the brain-training sample is:

$$S^2_{M_1} = \frac{S^2_{Pooled}}{N_1}$$

$$S^2_{M_1} = \frac{6.27}{12} = 0.52$$

Now we need to do the same for the no brain-training sample,

$$S^2_{M_2} = \frac{S^2_{Pooled}}{N_2}$$

$$S^2_{M_2} = \frac{6.27}{13} = 0.48$$

Note that here we are dividing by the sample size and not by degrees of freedom. That's because a distribution of means' variance depends on the sample size.

$$S^2_{M_1} = \frac{S^2_{Pooled}}{N_1}$$

$$S^2_{M_2} = \frac{S^2_{Pooled}}{N_2}$$

Want to review the logic behind the distribution of means' variance? SEE CHAPTER 7.

Distribution of Differences Between Means' Variance and Standard Deviation: As we've done with other hypothesis testing examples, we need the standard error to build a comparison distribution. To get the standard error, we first calculate the comparison distribution's variance. With two distributions of means, we need to account for both samples' variation. Greater variation in either sample will create greater variation in the differences.

Here's what we mean: If we subtract two numbers (e.g., 5 − 2), the difference is 3. If either the 5 or the 2 change (i.e., vary), the outcome of the difference (3), changes as well. For example, if the 5 becomes a 6, the difference between the numbers changes (6 – 2 = 4). Similarly, if we vary the 2 and make it a 3, the difference score changes again (5 – 3 = 2). In other words, when calculating differences, variation in either number coincides with greater variation in the difference score. For that reason, when we look at two samples, each sample's variation impacts variation in the differences between them.

What that means for our calculation is that we have to add the sample distribution of means' variances together as follows:

$$S^2_{Difference} = S^2_{M_1} + S^2_{M_2}$$

$$S^2_{Difference} = 0.52 + 0.48$$

$$S^2_{Difference} = 1.00$$

Ultimately, we want the comparison distribution's standard error of the difference, so we take the square root of the variance, or

$$S_{Difference} = \sqrt{S^2_{Difference}} = \sqrt{1.00} = 1.00.$$

$$S^2_{Difference} = S^2_{M_1} + S^2_{M_2}$$
$$S_{Difference} = \sqrt{S^2_{Difference}}$$

Now we can build the comparison distribution of means just as we've done previously drawing a t distribution, plugging in the mean (0) and indicating the numbers that correspond to 1 and 2 standard errors above and below the mean. In this case, our standard deviation ($S_{Difference}$) is 1.00, so our numbers are +/–1.00 and +/–2.00. You can see the entire process mapped out in **Figure 10.6**.

Step 3: Establish Critical Value Cutoff To determine whether any difference we find between our two groups is a real difference, we want to be sure it is large enough so that we are reasonably sure that the difference is not a fluke. We achieve this by establishing a cutoff that we need to surpass in order to reject the null, or the idea there is no difference.

As with other t-tests, our comparison distribution is a t distribution, so we will use a t-table to determine where our cutoff falls. To use that table, we need three pieces of information: number of tails, significance level, and degrees of freedom. We have a directional hypothesis

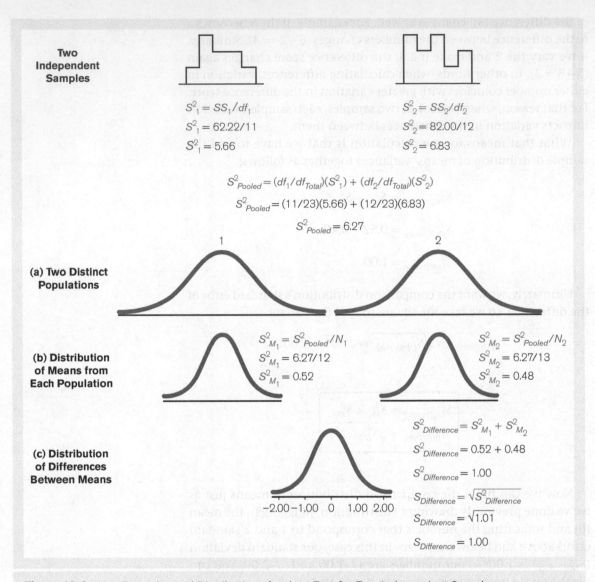

Figure 10.6   Key Formulas and Distributions for the *t*-Test for Two Independent Samples

(we expect brain-training to do better) so we have a one-tailed test and will use the conventional level of significance (*p* = .05). Our degrees of freedom when we have two samples needs to account for all of the degrees of freedom (not just those from one sample or the other), so we will use the total degrees of freedom (*df*$_{Total}$ = 23). We identify each piece of information in the *t*-table to find the proper row and column, and where they intersect is our *t*-cutoff, 1.714 (shown in **Figure 10.7**).

	One-Tailed Tests Alpha Level		Two-Tailed Tests Alpha Level	
df	0.05	0.01	0.05	0.01
8	1.860	2.897	2.306	3.356
9	1.833	2.822	2.262	3.250
10	1.813	2.764	2.228	3.170
11	1.796	2.718	2.201	3.106
12	1.783	2.681	2.179	3.055
13	1.771	2.651	2.161	3.013
14	1.762	2.625	2.145	2.977
15	1.753	2.603	2.132	2.947
16	1.746	2.584	2.120	2.921
17	1.740	2.567	2.110	2.898
18	1.734	2.553	2.101	2.879
19	1.729	2.540	2.093	2.861
20	1.725	2.528	2.086	2.846
21	1.721	2.518	2.080	2.832
22	1.717	2.509	2.074	2.819
23	1.714	2.500	2.069	2.808
24	1.711	2.492	2.064	2.797
25	1.708	2.485	2.060	2.788

Figure 10.7   Using the *t*-Table to Find the Critical Value Cutoffs

Finally, we should indicate where our cutoff falls on our comparison distribution (see **Figure 10.8**). Remember, because we are expecting our population of interest (brain-trainers) to perform better on the quiz, the cutoff is a positive number that goes to the right of the mean.

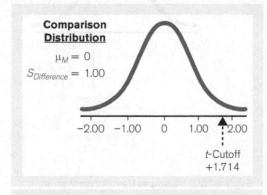

Figure 10.8   *t* Distribution with Critical Value Cutoff

Step 4: Determine Sample Results At this point we have collected data from both groups including whether they have engaged in brain-training or not, and their score on the history quiz. In order to see if there are differences between groups, we must determine the mean quiz score for the 12 people in the brain-training group and for the 13 people in the no brain-training group. Doing those calculations reveals that the mean scores are 6.75 for the brain-training group and 6.00 for the no brain-training group.

Next, we want to compare our two sample's mean to see if they are different by subtracting them ($M_1 - M_2$). Those two number are different, but what we really want to know is how the difference between those means compares to how much the differences between means in the comparison distribution typically differ ($S_{Difference}$). These pieces allow us to calculate our t-score, with the following formula:

$$t = \frac{M_1 - M_2}{S_{Difference}} = \frac{6.75 - 6.00}{1.00} = \frac{0.75}{1.00} = 0.75$$

$$t = \frac{M_1 - M_2}{S_{Difference}}$$

Next, we should show where our sample's t-score falls on the comparison distribution (see **Figure 10.9**).

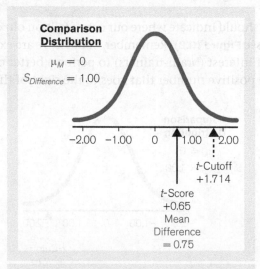

Comparison Distribution

$\mu_M = 0$
$S_{Difference} = 1.00$

−2.00   −1.00   0   1.00   2.00

t-Cutoff
+1.714

t-Score
+0.65
Mean
Difference
= 0.75

Figure 10.9   Sample Results on the Comparison Distribution

Step 5: Decide and Interpret It is clear from Figure 10.9 that our sample's t-score of 0.75 is far below the t-cutoff score of 1.714. We can also see that our difference in means between our samples of 0.75 is very close to 0.

Time to make our decision. Because our sample's results (Step 4) do not exceed the critical value (Step 3), we fail to reject the null hypothesis (H_0) that people who do brain-training will have the same history quiz score as those who don't do brain-training ($\mu_1 \leq \mu_2$). If we fail to reject the null, we must also say that our research hypothesis (H_1) that people who do brain-training will have higher history quiz scores than those who don't do brain-training ($\mu_1 > \mu_2$) was not supported, because we found no evidence to support the notion that brain-training resulted in significantly higher test scores. In other words, we must conclude that these data do not suggest that brain-training significantly increases history quiz scores.

Hopefully, with the concepts and skills that we have learned in this chapter, performing the t-test for independent means is relatively straightforward. Before reading on, watch the video associated with this chapter.

 HAND CALCULATION VIDEO TUTORIAL: To learn more, check out the video tutorial *Performing the t-Test for Independent Means.*

Communicating the Result

 When we fail to reject the null hypothesis, we should say that our results were "nonsignificant." We should *not* say that the results were "insignificant," because this term typically refers to the effect size (which we will talk about in the Statistics for Research portion of this chapter).

Also, when we fail to reject the null, we have to be careful not to word things too harshly. That is, we should not say that our study failed, or that there is no effect, or that brain-training does not work. The fact is, we still do not know if brain-training has an impact on college studying and quiz scores. We have a small piece of evidence that brain-training does not work, but it is far from definitive. So, much like we avoid being overly bold in saying things worked when we get statistical significance, we also avoid beating ourselves up too much when we fail to reject the null.

Forming a Conclusion

The results of our t-test were nonsignificant. That is, we didn't find that our brain-training group performed differently from the non-brain-training group. Now, before we read too much into this, we need to consider that nonsignificant findings are "inconclusive" because there are lots of reasons why we might fail to find an effect. First is the possibility that the effect doesn't exist (i.e., brain-training doesn't really work). Second, as we learned in Chapter 8, our study could be underpowered, with the sample size not large enough to detect an effect. Thus, our nonsignificant finding could be a Type II error. Third, it is also possible that our study was not done well enough to properly test for the effect. If the study design is substandard, statistical conclusions from that design are suspect.

In our case, we did not even run a proper study. Having a particular friend group do a task and answer some questions does not qualify as a scientific study. For a proper study, we would ideally have a random sample of people with no connection at all to the researcher. We also should have recruited participants who had never used brain-training, then randomly assigned half to do the brain-training. This would rule out the possibility that those who were already using brain-training were in some way different from the start. To give any possible effect a fair test, we should also include more participants so we have 80 degrees of freedom total or more (because at the point and beyond, the cutoff scores are virtually identical). Finally, any quality study of brain-training would closely monitor how much participants use the training and would make sure everyone used it frequently to optimize any potential benefit. It's clear that our study had a lot of shortcomings, which is why we cannot draw any definite conclusions based on what we did.

Your Turn 10.3

1. When calculating the variance for the distribution of differences between means, why do we add the variances from both distributions of means?

2. As part of a health studies minor you're completing, you need to take a nutrition class. Last month following a discussion on the benefits of clean eating, the class decided to test clean eating's benefits by seeing if increases energy. Using a random number generator, everyone was assigned a number. Those who got an even number ate clean for a month, while those with an odd number ate normally. At the end of the month, everyone took an assessment of mental energy where 1 = Low Energy and 7 = High Energy. Everyone in your nutrition class follows their randomly assigned diet and gets a mental energy score. Here are the scores for the groups: Clean Eating (7, 7, 6, 5, 7) and Non-Clean Eating (3, 7, 6, 5, 4, 4, 6).

a. Step 1: Population and Hypotheses. (1) What would the populations be? (2) What would the hypotheses be?

b. Step 2: Build a Comparison Distribution. (1) What is the comparison distribution? What shape is it? (2) What will be the comparison distribution's mean be? Why? (3) What will be the estimate of the population variance? (4) What is the variance of the two distributions of means? (5) What is the variance ($S^2_{Difference}$) and standard deviation ($S_{Difference}$) of the comparison distribution?

c. Step 3: Establish Critical Value Cutoff. In order to know for sure if the group who ate clean had more mental energy, you need to establish a cutoff score. (1) What three pieces of information do you need to find the cutoff score on the t-table? (2) What is the t-cutoff associated with this information?

d. Step 4: Determine Sample Results. (1) What test does she need to run? (2) What are the results? (3) Show Steps 2, 3, and 4 of hypothesis testing on a diagram.

e. Step 5: Decide and Interpret: What is the appropriate conclusion?

Statistics for Research

Advances in technology have made our lives easier in many respects (e.g., GPS helps us avoid getting lost; texting makes it easy to connect with others). Yet, people seem more stressed out than ever. Recent surveys of stress in the United States reveal that stress levels are at historic highs, with 2 out of 3 American adults reporting increased stress over the pandemic (APA, 2020). Symptoms include "snapping" (i.e., becoming easily angered), greater body tension, mood swings, and lashing out at a loved one. To help reduce their stress, some people turn to mindfulness meditation to help them cope.

Mindfulness-based stress reduction is a psychotherapeutic technique that increases the extent to which people are consciously aware of their surroundings and are sensitive to their inner thoughts and emotions (Woods & Rockman, 2021). In particular, when performing mindfulness meditation, people sit with their eyes closed and focus on the present moment, noticing the sounds and smells of their environment.

Does mindfulness meditation reduce stress?

E+/Getty Images

Although there is a growing literature examining the benefits of mindfulness meditation (Harp et al., 2022; Howarth et al., 2019; Ito et al., 2022), some scholars argue that there are limitations to this research (Van Dam et al., 2018). Notably, these scientists suggest that some past work on mindfulness has been conducted without adequate rigor (e.g., failure to use adequate control conditions). Based on these limitations, imagine that we wanted to conduct a study to test this question: Does mindfulness meditation effectively reduce college students' stress?

How should we design such a study? An important consideration to start with is which type of study design is best: repeated measures or between subjects? In Chapter 9, we learned about the repeated-measures study design, which is essentially a before and after type of study. We measure each participant before our intervention and again afterwards. So, one option would be to measure the stress levels of our participants, have them engage in mindfulness meditation, and then measure their stress levels again. Although this option would be okay, as we learned in the last chapter, this type of design is prone to participant effects. Our participants may want to feel lower stress, and so they may look for ways in which the mindfulness meditation helped them. Given this potential drawback, we probably shouldn't choose the repeated-measures design.

independent groups design (also called a *between-subjects design*) a type of study where different groups of participants experience the different levels of the independent variable.

Instead, we may want to go with an **independent groups design** (also called a *between-subjects design*), which is a type of study where different groups of participants experience the different levels of the independent variable. Thus, in this type of design, we would have one group of participants undergo mindfulness meditation, while a second group of different participants serves as our control condition. In general, we are much less likely to observe participant effects in independent groups designs, because participants in one condition don't know what participants in the other condition are doing. Thus, it is more difficult for them to guess what the study is about overall. Because we have different people in our two conditions, we need to use the *t*-test for independent samples that we learned about in the first half of this chapter.

Here in the Statistics for Research section, we're going to focus more on the type of research design that a *t*-test for independent means analyzes, discuss the assumptions for running this test (and how to test them), and how to determine confidence intervals and effect sizes with the *t*-test for independent means.

Where Do the Data Come From?

To conduct our study of mindfulness meditation, we decide to have participants in the mindfulness condition watch a 30-minute video each day for one month. In the video, an expert therapist guides participants through a mindfulness exercise.

For participants in the control condition, we have them watch a similar-length video featuring brown noise. To measure our dependent variable, we have all participants complete the Perceived Stress Scale (Cohen et al., 1983), which asks participants to respond to items such as, "In the past month, how often have you felt nervous and 'stressed'?" Participants respond to each item on a 5-point scale, with 0 indicating that they never feel a certain way and 4 indicating that they feel that way very often. (If you want to test your own stress level, enter the search terms Perceived Stress Scale to access the measure.)

Now that we have our study design, imagine that we recruit 80 participants, half of which we randomly assign to the mindfulness condition and half of which we randomly assign to the control condition. After completing the intervention phase of the study, we measure our two groups' stress level and find that the mindfulness condition's mean is 2.56 ($SD = 1.08$), while the control condition's mean is 3.148 ($SD = 0.93$), with higher scores indicating that participants are experiencing higher levels of stress. From this information, does mindfulness meditation reduce stress? Well, we don't know yet. Although the mindfulness mean is lower, it could be that the differences between the two groups' means are due to sampling error. In order to say that there is an effect of mindfulness meditation, we need to conduct the t-test for two independent samples.

t-Test for Two Independent Samples: What We're Trying to Accomplish

Our research goal is to determine if participants who engage in mindfulness meditation represent a different population from, or the same population as, people who don't engage in mindfulness meditation. If the mindfulness sample represents a different population, they should report significantly lower stress levels than participants in the control condition. To test this, we will build a comparison distribution starting with the hypothesis that mindfulness meditation has no effect. We will then evaluate just how probable it would be for us to observe a difference between the means, if mindfulness has no effect (this is what the p-value tells us). Thus, the key question we will evaluate is whether the difference between means that we observe in our study is expected or unexpected, assuming the null is true.

Hypothesis Testing with a t-Test for Two Independent Samples: How Does It Work?

To conduct our hypothesis test, we need to see where our study results fall on the distribution of differences between means. Before we get to this step, though, we need to start by making sure we meet the assumptions of the test.

Assumptions of the *t*-Test for Two Independent Samples The *t*-test for independent samples works only if we satisfy the following four assumptions:

1. *The dependent variable must be interval or ratio.* We must measure our outcome variable at interval or ratio levels of measurement, and we cannot use nominal- or ordinal-level data.

2. *The scores for participants must be independent.* This assumption states that the scores for one participant do not influence the scores for another participant. To satisfy this assumption, we should carefully consider our study design. Is it possible for the participants to interact with each other such that their scores are no longer independent? If, for example, we run our study in groups, is it possible for one participant to affect another? If so, we should redesign our study so that the scores are independent, or we should perform a different analysis.

3. *The population's scores on the dependent variable are normally distributed, or we have large samples.* To satisfy this assumption, we need either to know that our dependent variable is normally distributed within the population or to have sufficiently large samples so that the distribution of means is approximately normal. Recall that the Central Limit Theorem states that the shape of the distribution of means will be approximately normal as the sample size increases ($N > 30$). Note that a sample size of 30 is not large or sufficient with respect to statistical power. It is merely the sample size at which our distribution of means approaches normality, even if the population is non-normal in shape.

4. *The variances of our two populations are equal.* This assumption is called the **equality of variances assumption** (also called the *homogeneity of variances assumption*) and reflects the fact that our independent variable should affect our groups' means, but not their variances. For this reason, we can pool our two samples' variances together when we estimate the populations' variance. Now, we should point out that it is unlikely that our two samples will have exactly equal variances. This fact can make it hard sometimes to determine whether we have satisfied or violated this assumption. We will come back to this issue in a moment. For now, we just need to know that we are going to assume that the variances of our samples are equal to each other.

equality of variances assumption (also called the *homogeneity of variances assumption*) an assumption that two population variances are equal. Used in the *t*-test for independent samples to justify the pooling of samples' variances to estimate the population's variance.

Step by Step: Hypothesis Testing with the *t*-Test for Two Independent Samples We are now ready to conduct our formal hypothesis test.

Step 1: Population and Hypotheses To determine if mindfulness meditation has an effect, we need to establish our populations and predictions.

Population of Interest (μ_1): People who engage in mindfulness meditation.

Comparison Population (μ_2): People who do not engage in mindfulness meditation.

Sample: Consists of 80 participants, half of whom complete the mindfulness meditation intervention and half of whom are in the control condition.

Next, we need to establish our research and null hypotheses. Our main decision here is whether or not we want to make a directional or nondirectional research hypothesis. Although we might believe that mindfulness meditation will reduce stress, it may not. Potentially, while meditating, people might start to ruminate on their problems, leading them to experience an increase in stress. Because this outcome would also be interesting to us, we will set up a nondirectional, two-tailed research hypothesis.

Research Hypothesis (H_1): Participants in the mindfulness meditation condition will report different stress levels from those of the participants in the control condition ($\mu_1 \neq \mu_2$).

Null Hypothesis (H_0): Participants in the mindfulness and control conditions will report the same average stress levels ($\mu_1 = \mu_2$).

Step 2: Build Comparison Distribution What would the comparison distribution look like if mindfulness meditation has no effect on stress? That's the question we need to answer to construct our comparison distribution. As we learned in the first half of this chapter, we need to determine the mean of the distribution of differences between means, the pooled estimate of the population's variance, and the standard error of the difference (which, remember, is the standard deviation of our distribution of differences between means).

Let's start with the easy one. The mean of the distribution of differences between means assumes that the null is true. If the null is correct, then the mean for our two groups will be equal, which means that the difference between the two means must be zero. So, our comparison distribution has a mean of zero.

Next, we need to calculate the pooled estimate of the population's variance (see **Figure 10.10**). Because we have a large sample size (overall $N = 80$), we are not going to compute the sum of squares for each condition. Instead, we already know that the standard deviation for the mindfulness condition is 1.08 and the standard deviation for the control condition is 0.93, so we can square these numbers to get their

Mindfulness Condition	Stress (X_1)	($X_1 - M$)	($X_1 - M$)^2	Control Condition	Stress (X_2)	($X_2 - M$)	($X_2 - M$)^2
1	2.98	0.42	0.18	41	3.82	0.67	0.45
2	4.68	2.12	4.49	42	4.18	1.03	1.06
3	2.52	−0.04	0.00	43	4.03	0.88	0.77
⋮	⋮	⋮	⋮	⋮	⋮	⋮	⋮
40	3.17	0.61		80	3.69	0.54	0.29

N	40	df_1	39	N	40	df_2	39
M_1	2.56	SD_1	1.08	M_2	3.148	SD_1	0.93

Estimated Population Variance from the Sample	S_1^2	SD^2		Estimated Population Variance from the Sample	S_2^2	SD^2	
	S_1^2	1.17			S_2^2	0.86	

		df_{Total}	$df_1 + df_2$
		df_{Total}	78

Pooled Estimate of the Population Variance	S_{Pooled}^2	$\dfrac{df_1}{df_{Total}}(S_1^2) + \dfrac{df_2}{df_{Total}}(S_2^2)$
	S_{Pooled}^2	1.015

Variance of the Distribution of Means	$S_{M_1}^2$	S_{Pooled}^2 / N_1	Variance of the Distribution of Means	$S_{M_2}^2$	S_{Pooled}^2 / N_2
	$S_{M_1}^2$	0.02538		$S_{M_2}^2$	0.02538

Comparison Distribution: Distribution of Differences Between Means	$S_{Difference}^2$	$S_{M_1}^2 + S_{M_2}^2$
	$S_{Difference}^2$	0.05076
	$S_{Difference}$	$\sqrt{S_{Difference}^2}$
	$S_{Difference}$	0.2253

t-Score	t	$(M_1 - M_2)/S_{Difference}$
	t	−2.61

Figure 10.10 Computations for *t*-Test for Two Independent Samples

associated variances. Thus, the variance for the mindfulness condition is 1.08^2 or 1.17, and the variance for the control condition is 0.93^2 or 0.86. Now, we want to pool these together. To pool these together, we use the formula, $S_{Pooled}^2 = (df_1 / df_{Total})(S_1^2) + (df_2/df_{Total})(S_2^2)$. Granted, when both groups have the same N, pooling in this way isn't technically necessary. However, we're going to stick with this approach to keep things simple. Using the variances and degrees of freedom for our current study,

$$S^2_{Pooled} = \frac{39}{78}(1.17) + \frac{39}{78}(0.86) = 0.585 + 0.43 = 1.015$$

This result makes sense, because our pooled variance is halfway between our two sample variances, which have an equal number of degrees of freedom.

Now that we have calculated the pooled estimate of the population's variance, we can compute the variance of the distribution of means. To do this, we divide the pooled variance by the degrees of freedom for each sample separately. For the mindfulness condition,

$$S^2_{M_1} = \frac{S^2_{Pooled}}{N_1} = \frac{1.015}{40} = 0.0254$$

For the control condition,

$$S^2_{M_2} = \frac{S^2_{Pooled}}{N_2} = \frac{1.015}{40} = 0.0254$$

Last, to calculate the standard error of the difference, we will sum the two variances and then convert them to a standard deviation by taking the square root. Thus,

$$S^2_{Difference} = S^2_{M_1} + S^2_{M_2}$$

$$S^2_{Difference} = 0.0254 + 0.0254$$

$$S^2_{Difference} = 0.0508$$

$$S_{Difference} = \sqrt{S^2_{Difference}} = \sqrt{0.0508} = 0.2253$$

Remember, the standard error is always the denominator of our test statistic, so we will need this number when we compute the t-score in Step 4. You can see the entire process in **Figure 10.11**.

Step 3: Establish Critical Value Cutoff When conducting an independent samples t-test by hand, we will need to use the critical value approach. Why? Because, as we learned in Chapter 9, the t-curve's shape changes based on the number of degrees of

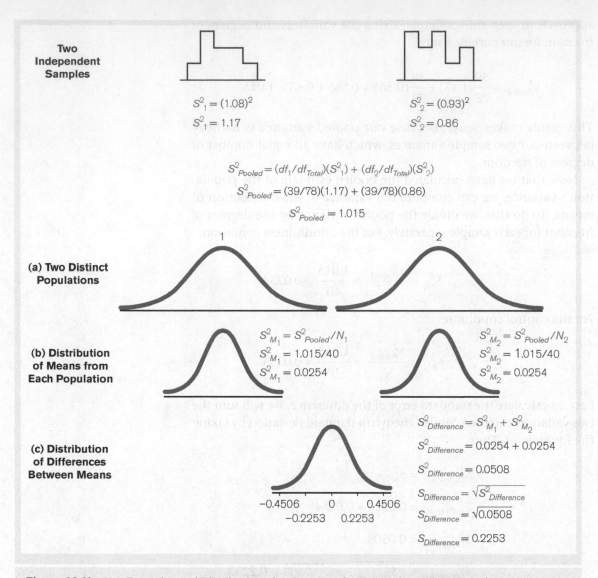

Two Independent Samples

$S^2_1 = (1.08)^2$
$S^2_1 = 1.17$

$S^2_2 = (0.93)^2$
$S^2_2 = 0.86$

$$S^2_{Pooled} = (df_1/df_{Total})(S^2_1) + (df_2/df_{Total})(S^2_2)$$
$$S^2_{Pooled} = (39/78)(1.17) + (39/78)(0.86)$$
$$S^2_{Pooled} = 1.015$$

1   2

(a) Two Distinct Populations

(b) Distribution of Means from Each Population

$S^2_{M_1} = S^2_{Pooled}/N_1$
$S^2_{M_1} = 1.015/40$
$S^2_{M_1} = 0.0254$

$S^2_{M_2} = S^2_{Pooled}/N_2$
$S^2_{M_2} = 1.015/40$
$S^2_{M_2} = 0.0254$

(c) Distribution of Differences Between Means

-0.4506 0 0.4506
-0.2253 0.2253

$S^2_{Difference} = S^2_{M_1} + S^2_{M_2}$
$S^2_{Difference} = 0.0254 + 0.0254$
$S^2_{Difference} = 0.0508$
$S_{Difference} = \sqrt{S^2_{Difference}}$
$S_{Difference} = \sqrt{0.0508}$
$S_{Difference} = 0.2253$

Figure 10.11   Key Formulas and Distributions for the *t*-Test for Two Independent Samples

freedom. Thus, there are an infinite number of different possible *t*-curves. So, instead of giving us every possible value of *t* and its associated *p*-value, our *t*-table gives us only the values of *t* when our *p*-value is exactly .05 or .01. This works because all we need to do to reject the null hypothesis is to show that our *p*-value is less than alpha.

To find our critical value cutoffs, we need to know our total degrees of freedom. In Chapter 9, we said degrees of freedom are the number of scores that are free to differ, and that we generally calculate them by taking the number of independent observations minus the number of population estimates. For the independent samples *t*-test, we have

N independent observations, because we get a score for each participant in the study. We are also estimating two population means, one for each of our two conditions. So, our total degrees of freedom are $N - 2$ (another way of thinking about this is that we are finding the degrees of freedom for each sample and adding them together: $N_1 - 1 + N_2 - 1 = N - 2$).

In the case of our mindfulness meditation study, we had 80 total observations, so we have 78 degrees of freedom. Another way to think about this is to break our degrees of freedom down by condition, as we did earlier in the chapter. Within each condition, we have 40 observations and one mean. So, each condition has 39 degrees of freedom, which, when added together, totals 78.

Given that we have 78 degrees of freedom, what are our critical values? We need to go to our t-table. Remember that we set our research hypothesis to be two-tailed, so the only other thing we need to determine is our alpha level. Let's follow the conventions and set alpha to be .05 (see **Figure 10.12**).

	One-Tailed Tests Alpha Level		Two-Tailed Tests Alpha Level	
df	0.05	0.01	0.05	0.01
1	6.314	31.821	12.706	63.657
2	2.920	6.965	4.303	9.925
3	2.353	4.541	3.182	5.841
4	2.132	3.747	2.776	4.604
5	2.015	3.365	2.571	4.032
6	1.943	3.143	2.447	3.708
7	1.895	2.998	2.365	3.500
8	1.860	2.897	2.306	3.356
9	1.833	2.822	2.262	3.250
10	1.813	2.764	2.228	3.170
15	1.753	2.603	2.132	2.947
20	1.725	2.528	2.086	2.846
25	1.708	2.485	2.060	2.788
30	1.698	2.458	2.043	2.750
40	1.684	2.424	2.021	2.705
60	1.671	2.390	2.001	2.661
80	1.664	2.374	1.990	2.639
100	1.660	2.364	1.984	2.626

Figure 10.12 *t*-Table Preview

Because our *t*-table doesn't include 78 degrees of freedom exactly, we should round down to the next available degrees of freedom, which in this case is 60. Therefore, our critical value cutoffs are +/–2.001. Let's include these cutoffs in our comparison distribution (see **Figure 10.13**).

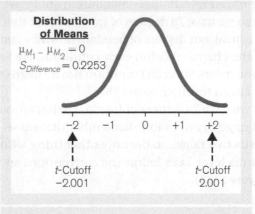

Distribution of Means

$\mu_{M_1} - \mu_{M_2} = 0$
$S_{Difference} = 0.2253$

t-Cutoff
–2.001

t-Cutoff
2.001

Figure 10.13 *t* Distribution with Critical Value Cutoff

Step 4: Determine Sample Results We're almost ready to convert our sample results into a *t*-score. Before we do that, we need to make sure that we've satisfied the four assumptions for the independent samples *t*-test. The first of these assumptions says that the dependent variable must be measured on the interval or ratio level. For our current study, we must measure stress using the Perceived Stress Scale, which qualifies as an interval-level variable, so we satisfied the first assumption. The second assumption says that participants' scores are independent observations. We had participants complete the study individually, so their scores are independent. Check. The third assumption says that the population is normally distributed, or we have large samples. For our current study, we recruited 40 participants per condition (for a total of 80 participants), thus we should have a sufficiently large sample such that we don't need to worry about violating this assumption.

Testing the fourth assumption of the independent samples *t*-test is a bit more complicated. Recall that the fourth assumption is the equality of variances assumption, which states that the variances of our two conditions should be approximately equal. Looking at our current study results, we can see that the variance for the mindfulness condition is 1.17 and the variance for the control condition is 0.86.

Obviously, these two numbers aren't equal. But, as it turns out, we don't know yet if they are different. We can't say that these two numbers are truly different because both samples are subject to sampling error. It's possible that these two groups have equal variances at the population level, but because we measured samples, we happened to get variances that are slightly different from each other. So, how do we evaluate whether these variances are equal or not equal? Well, we will take the same approach to determine if the variances are equal that we take to determine if the means are equal: we are going to conduct a hypothesis test.

The particular hypothesis test is called **Levene's Test for Equality of Variances,** which is a variant of the F-test that we will learn in Chapter 11. But even without knowing the details, we should be able to follow the general idea of this hypothesis test thanks to our general understanding of how hypothesis tests work. The null hypothesis for Levene's Test says that the variances of the two groups are equal. The research hypothesis states that they are not equal. Note that we *want* the variances to be equal, which is what the null hypothesis says. So, this is an odd type of hypothesis test, because we want to fail to reject the null. Most of the time, of course, we want to reject the null hypothesis and retain the research hypothesis.

Because we'll talk about the math needed to calculate the F-score in the next chapter, we are going to skip it for now and let SPSS calculate the Levene's Test F-score and p-value. Let's take a look at the relevant SPSS output in **Figure 10.14**.

Levene's Test for Equality of Variances a statistical analysis used to test the equality of variances assumption.

		Levene's Test for Equality of Variances	
		F	Sig.
Stress	Equal variances assumed	3.397	.069
	Equal variances not assumed		

Figure 10.14 SPSS Output for Levene's Test

We can see from this output that the F statistic is 3.397 and the p-value is .069. Because our p-value (.069) is greater than alpha (.05), or .069 > .05, we fail to reject the null hypothesis. In other words, our variances are not significantly different. Thus, we conclude that we have satisfied the equality of variances assumption. Note that if our results reveal that Levene's Test is significant (i.e., if the *p*-value for Levene's Test is less than .05), it tells us that we have violated the equality of variances assumption. If this happens, we should perform alternative hypothesis tests that don't have the equality of variances assumption, such as Welch's *t* or the **Mann–Whitney *U*.** These hypothesis tests are similar to the *t*-test for independent means in that they compare two groups of participants on a dependent variable, but neither assumes equal variances. We're not going to go into detail on these tests now, but it is important to know that there are options should we violate the assumption.

Mann–Whitney *U* a statistical test that compares two independent samples for a dependent variable that is ordinal.

Now that we have satisfied the assumptions, it's time to put mindfulness meditation to the test. Does it reduce stress relative to our control condition? To compute our *t*-score, we calculate the difference between our two group means and divide by the standard error of the difference:

$$t = \frac{M_1 - M_2}{S_{Difference}} = \frac{2.56 - 3.148}{0.2253} = \frac{-0.588}{0.2253} = -2.46$$

Comparing our *t*-score to our critical values, we see that our *t*-score falls outside of the critical value (see **Figure 10.15**).

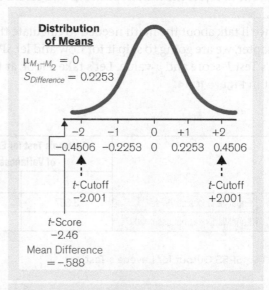

Distribution of Means

$\mu_{M_1-M_2} = 0$
$S_{Difference} = 0.2253$

	-2	-1	0	+1	+2
	-0.4506	-0.2253	0	0.2253	0.4506

t-Cutoff
-2.001

t-Cutoff
+2.001

t-Score
-2.46
Mean Difference
= -.588

Figure 10.15 Sample Results on the Comparison Distribution

Step 5: Decide and Interpret Because our *t*-score falls outside the critical value cutoffs, we can reject the null hypothesis (H_0). Although we don't know the exact *p*-value for our *t*-test statistic, it must be less than .05, because this is how we determined where the cutoffs would be.

We can conclude, therefore, that mindfulness meditation significantly changes stress levels. Also, because the mindfulness condition's mean was less than the control condition's mean, we can conclude that mindfulness meditation reduces stress levels, compared to a control ($\mu_1 < \mu_2$).

Generating a Confidence Interval for the Differences Between Two Independent Samples So what is the mean difference between the mindfulness condition and the control condition in the population? We don't know yet. The hypothesis test that we just performed merely tells us that the data we observed were improbable assuming the null is true. From this, we infer that there is a nonzero effect of mindfulness meditation. But knowing that something is not zero doesn't really tell us what it is. If we want to estimate the mean difference at the population level, we need to generate a confidence interval.

To find the upper and lower limits for the confidence interval for the differences between two independent means, we need to slightly modify the formula for confidence intervals that we learned in Chapter 8 and used in Chapter 9. In particular, we are estimating a difference between two means ($M_1 - M_2$), rather than the value of a single mean, so we will substitute this for the mean.

$$\text{Lower Limit} = (-t\text{-cutoff})(S_{Difference}) + (M_1 - M_2)$$
$$\text{Upper Limit} = (+t\text{-cutoff})(S_{Difference}) + (M_1 - M_2)$$

Thus, to find the lower limit, we calculate $(-t\text{-cutoff})(S_{Difference}) + (M_1 - M_2)$ and to find the upper limit, we calculate $(-t\text{-cutoff})(S_{Difference}) + (M_1 - M_2)$. Using our current results, the lower limit would be $(-2.001)(0.2253) + (2.56 - 3.148) = -0.4508 + -0.588 = -1.04$, and the upper limit would be $(2.001)(0.2253) + (2.56 - 3.148) = 0.4508 + -0.588 = -0.14$. Therefore, the 95% confidence interval for the difference between means would range from -1.04 to -0.14. This tells us that the population's average perceived stress reduction from mindfulness meditation (relative to our control condition) falls somewhere between 0.14 and 1.04 units on the Perceived Stress Scale.

Computing the Effect Size for the *t*-Test for Two Independent Samples We found a significant effect of mindfulness, but is it a practically meaningful effect? We need to compute the effect size to answer this question. Just as it was for the *t*-test for dependent means in Chapter 9, the appropriate measure of effect size for the *t*-test for independent means is Cohen's *d*, which tells us the number of standard deviations' difference between the two study conditions. To compute Cohen's *d*, we need to take the difference between means that we calculated in the numerator of our t-score and divide that by the pooled standard deviation. Why does this work? Well, the pooled standard deviation isn't affected by our study's sample size, while sample size does affect the standard error we use to calculate the t-score. Because of this, Cohen's d is immune to the effects of very large samples, which can make trivial differences between our means become statistically significant.

$$d = \frac{M_1 - M_2}{S_{Pooled}}$$

As part of our calculation of the t-score, we already calculated the difference between means, $(M_1 - M_2)$. We also calculated the pooled variance, S^2_{Pooled}, so all we need to do to calculate Cohen's d is to convert the pooled variance to the pooled standard deviation, by taking the square root of the variance $\left(\sqrt{S^2_{Pooled}}\right)$, and then enter these numbers into our equation. The pooled standard deviation is equal to $\sqrt{S^2_{Pooled}} = \sqrt{1.015} = 1.01$. Thus, our effect size is

$$d = \frac{M_1 - M_2}{S_{Pooled}} = \frac{2.56 - 3.148}{1.01} = \frac{-0.588}{1.01} = -0.58$$

An effect size of 0.58 (when reporting d, we disregard the sign and focus solely on the value for determining the size of the effect) indicates that participants in the mindfulness meditation condition reported just over one-half standard deviations less stress than the control condition. Using Cohen's guidelines for interpreting effect size, which we first discussed in Chapter 8, this would qualify as a medium-sized effect. Of course, to get a clearer sense of the magnitude of this effect, we should look to the stress literature and compare this effect size to other interventions designed to reduce stress.

experiment a type of research study that compares at least two groups of participants that are equivalent in every way, except on the independent variable. The goal of an experiment is to show that changes in the independent variable cause changes to the dependent variable.

Advantages and Disadvantages of the t-Test for Two Independent Samples The independent samples t-test is one of the most commonly performed statistical analyses in science. One of the reasons for this is that it is perfectly suited to test **experiments.** In an experiment, a researcher compares at least two groups of participants that are equivalent in every way, except on the independent variable. Many experiments compare an experimental condition to a control condition, as we did in our test of mindfulness mediation. The goal of an experiment is to be able to show that changes in the independent variable cause changes in the dependent variable. We can make a cause-and-effect conclusion if we have manipulated the independent variable (i.e., determined the conditions of the study) and randomly assigned participant to condition (i.e., assigned participants to either the experimental condition or control condition on the basis of a random number generator).

Despite this, there are a couple of drawbacks to this approach. First, the independent groups design requires that there be different people in each of the two groups that we are comparing. Thus, we need to have a much larger sample size to make meaningful conclusions, relative to the single sample t-test or the t-test for dependent groups. Unfortunately, getting a large sample can be challenging. In our mindfulness meditation study, we indicated that participants would spend one month engaging in mindfulness meditation (or the control activity). Getting 80 people to do this will already be difficult, so recruiting even more participants becomes even harder. To increase their motivation, we might need to pay our participants to complete the study. The larger the sample size we need to perform our analyses, the more money we need to cover our expenses. So, the need for a large sample size can be an expensive downside of the independent groups design.

A second limitation of the t-test for independent samples is that we can examine only two groups at a time. What if we want to perform an experiment that compares mindfulness meditation to a control condition and a third condition where people perform physical exercise? As we will see in the next chapter, the t-test for independent samples is inappropriate to use when comparing more than two conditions at a time. For that, we would need to use a statistical technique called *Analysis of Variance*, or *ANOVA* for short (discussed in Chapter 11).

SPSS Video Tutorial: *t*-Test for Independent Means

Hopefully, performing the t-test for independent means seems pretty straightforward. We learned the fundamentals of the analysis in the Statistics for Life portion of this chapter, and we learned some additional details here in the Statistics for Research part of the chapter. Now, let's see how we would perform this analysis using SPSS. Watch this SPSS video for this chapter, which demonstrates the steps to conduct the t-test for independent means in SPSS.

> **SPSS VIDEO TUTORIAL:** To learn more, check out the video Independent Samples *t*-Test.

Communicating the Result

When writing our results paragraph, we should describe the type of hypothesis test that we conducted, the research hypothesis, the t-score with degrees of freedom in parentheses, the p-value, the effect size, the 95% confidence interval of the difference, and an explanation of the direction of the effect. For our study of mindfulness meditation, our results paragraph would look something like this:

> We conducted a *t*-test for independent means to examine the hypothesis that mindfulness meditation would affect stress levels, relative to a control condition. The results of this test were significant, $t(78) = -2.61, p = .011, d = 0.58$, 95% CI [$-1.04, -0.14$], such that participants in mindfulness condition reported significantly less stress ($M = 2.6, SD = 1.1$) compared to participants in the control condition ($M = 3.2, SD = 0.9$).

When writing our results sections, there are two APA Style rules to keep in mind:

1. We round means and standard deviations to one decimal when a variable is discrete (i.e., measured in whole numbers), such as with surveys and questionnaires. We round all other numbers, except *p*-values, to two decimals. We can round *p*-values to two or three decimals.
2. We italicize all statistical symbols (such as *t, M,* and *p*), except for statistical letters that are Greek letters (such as α).

An APA-Style figure would look like this (**Figure 10.16**):

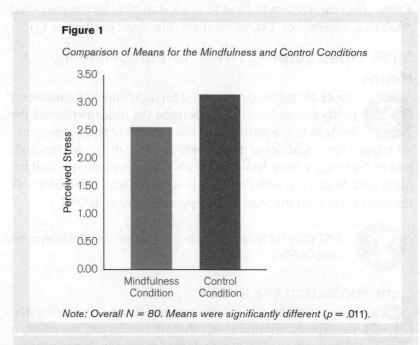

Figure 1

Comparison of Means for the Mindfulness and Control Conditions

Note: Overall N = 80. Means were significantly different (p = .011).

Figure 10.16 APA-Style Results: Bar Graph

Forming a Conclusion

Our goal was to evaluate the mindfulness meditation's efficacy to determine if it reduces stress. To do that, we used an independent groups research design in which we had some participants complete a mindfulness meditation intervention and others complete a control task. Because we have different people in these two conditions, we performed the *t*-test for two independent samples.

Our test results revealed that mindfulness meditation does reduce stress levels, relative to a control group. Moreover, we found a medium-sized effect, with mindfulness meditation reducing stress by just over half a standard deviation. As always, though, we want to think critically about the strengths and weaknesses of our study. Though one month of mindfulness meditation reduces perceived stress, how long does this effect last? If we waited another month to measure stress levels, would participants still have lower stress? Also, we compared the efficacy of mindfulness to a control condition in which people watched videos with brown noise. Would mindfulness meditation be more or less effective if we compared it to other stress-reducing treatments? We always want to keep limitations such as these in mind when both conducting our own research and reading about the results of others' research.

Your Turn 10.4

1. You develop a new type of therapy called mindlessness meditation, which is like mindfulness meditation except that instead of thinking about the present moment, you ask people to think about absolutely nothing. You are able to recruit only 8 people into your exploratory research study. Can you use an independent groups research design? Why or why not?

2. During the winter months, when the sky is gray and the sun rarely shines, the prevalence of seasonal affective disorder increases. To treat seasonal affective disorder, many clinical psychologists recommend light therapy, a form of therapy where patients sit in front of a light box that exposes them to bright lights that cause their bodies to release beneficial hormones. A clinical psychologist wants to examine the effectiveness of light therapy for treating seasonal affective disorder, relative to the drug *Upify,* a common (and fictional) antidepressant. To test this, he recruits 30 people with seasonal affective disorder and assigns 15 to complete a light therapy regimen for two months and 15 to take *Upify.* After two months, participants complete a depression questionnaire. Results reveal that participants in the light therapy condition have a mean level of depression of 11.90 (**SD** = 6.33) while participants in the *Upify* condition have a mean level of depression of 12.90 (**SD** = 7.10). Conduct a hypothesis test to determine whether light therapy is more or less effective than *Upify*.

2a. Step 1: Population and Hypotheses. What is the population of interest, the comparison population, and the sample? State the null and research hypotheses for this research problem.

2b. Step 2: Build a Comparison Distribution. What is the mean of the comparison distribution? What is the pooled estimate of the population's variance? What is the variance and standard error of the distribution of means?

2c. Step 3: Establish Critical Value Cutoff. How many degrees of freedom total are there? Is the research hypothesis one-tailed or two-tailed? What are the critical value cutoffs for an alpha = .05?

2d. Step 4: Determine Sample Results. Solve for the *t*-score.

2e. Step 5: Decide and Interpret. Compare the *t*-score you computed to the critical values. What is your conclusion regarding the null hypothesis?

Focus on Open Science: Exploratory Versus Confirmatory Research

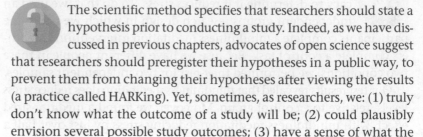 The scientific method specifies that researchers should state a hypothesis prior to conducting a study. Indeed, as we have discussed in previous chapters, advocates of open science suggest that researchers should preregister their hypotheses in a public way, to prevent them from changing their hypotheses after viewing the results (a practice called HARKing). Yet, sometimes, as researchers, we: (1) truly don't know what the outcome of a study will be; (2) could plausibly envision several possible study outcomes; (3) have a sense of what the outcome might be, but the best way to analyze the data is ambiguous.

For these reasons we need to be able to distinguish between exploratory and confirmatory research. Scientists conduct **exploratory research** when they cannot state the specific analysis that they will conduct to test a specific hypothesis at the outset of the study (Simmons et al., 2017). For example if researchers aren't quite sure what makes people optimistic, they may study several variables at once to identify which relates to optimism. Scientists conduct **confirmatory research** when absolutely all the key aspects of the study, from design to analysis, are determined before the researchers have inspected the data (Wagenmakers et al., 2012). For example, if researchers wanted to see if writing in a gratitude journal three times a week increases optimism compared to no writing, they would have all aspects planned before conducting the study.

The distinction between exploratory and confirmatory research is very important for scientific progress. First, historically, journals have been more likely to publish confirmatory studies. This has led some researchers to conduct exploratory analyses, but then write up the results as if they were confirmatory. Second, exploratory analyses are more likely to results in false positive findings. Often, researchers conducting exploratory research may run dozens or hundreds of analyses. We know that when we set alpha to .05, we will falsely reject the null hypothesis 5 times out of every 100 analyses. Remember from Chapter 8 that alpha is our Type I error rate. So, when conducting exploratory research, we may be at greater risk of finding significant results that aren't real.

From this discussion, it might seem like confirmatory research is far and away superior to exploratory research. This isn't necessarily the case. Sometimes confirmatory research becomes exploratory research as a result of unanticipated challenges that researchers face (Nosek et al., 2018). For example, let's say that we set out to test the hypothesis that mindfulness mediation helps reduce stress, relative to a control

exploratory research
research that is not intended to test a particular hypothesis, but rather to learn more about a psychological phenomenon.

confirmatory research
research that is intended to test a particular hypothesis, using a specific methodology and analysis.

condition. Although, based on our power analysis, we hoped to have 200 participants, we were able to collect data from only 125 participants. The study, though underpowered, is still an adequate test of our predictions. Yet, due to the potential lack of power, we may find nonsignificant results due to Type II errors (see Chapter 8 for a discussion of Type I and Type II errors), which impacts our ability to make strong conclusions. We should also recognize that some of the most important scientific findings started out as exploratory findings (Tukey, 1980). The first antidepressant drugs, for example, were originally designed to treat tuberculosis, and their impact on mood was unexpected (López-Muñoz & Alamo, 2009). So, we can learn a lot by keeping an open mind when we conduct exploratory research.

There are at least two solutions to improve psychological science with respect to the distinction between exploratory and confirmatory research. First, researchers should explicitly identify exploratory studies and analyses in their publications. When writing up the results of a study, we should indicate to the reader those tests and results that were planned in advance, and those that we conducted as a result of the practical issues that arose during the study. Second, we should make exploratory research a standard phase of the research process (Sakaluk, 2016). According to this approach, all research should start with an exploratory phase, where researchers conduct studies with relatively small sample sizes in order to develop their predictions and methods, followed by a confirmatory phase where researchers conduct studies with large samples and preregistered hypotheses. By making exploratory research a standard part of the research process, scientists should have less pressure to masquerade exploratory research as confirmatory research.

"
Statistically Speaking

I need to find the best place to get a taco. To figure it out, I could do some exploratory work and test out all the taco places, or I could take the confirmatory route and ask for a recommendation from my chef friend and then see what I think of that place.

"

Become a Better Consumer of Statistics

Back in Chapter 8, we learned about the "significance fallacy," which describes the mistaken notion that statistically significant results are meaningful in a practical sense. As we learned, effect size is a much better indicator of practical importance. Another aspect of statistical significance that we should be wary of is the idea that significant results are also "real" or "true."

According to this way of thinking, because we are able to reject the null hypothesis, it must be the case that the effect or relationship we are studying actually exists. Unfortunately, this is also a fallacy. When researchers conduct poorly designed studies, or use sloppy methods, it is still possible to find statistical significance. In such cases, we need to worry about **confounds,** which are variables other than the independent variable that can cause changes in the dependent variable.

confounds variables that vary along with the independent variable that can cause changes in the dependent variable.

When investigating the effects of hiking on a person's mood, what confounds might be present?

Czech Evgenia/Shutterstock

CONSORT diagram a figure included in research articles that documents the flow of participants in a study from recruitment to data analysis.

For example, imagine that we wanted to determine the impact of hiking on a person's positive mindset. As part of a study, we could have one group go hiking in the woods while the other does nothing. If we find a significant difference between these two groups, we wouldn't necessarily know whether participants' increased positivity in the hiking condition was from hiking, or simply because they went outdoors (which is a confound). The main idea is that statistical significance does not tell us anything about the methodology of the study, and that as consumers of statistics, we need to consider all of the possible reasons why a study found significant (or nonsignificant) results.

Interpreting Graphs and Charts from Research Articles

When conducting research, we have to deal with the fact that the research process can be messy. We might perform random selection to help increase the chances that our sample is representative of the population, only to have participants drop out of the study, potentially resulting in a biased sample. We might meticulously plan our study and create materials to capture our variables of interest, only to have participants who don't read the instructions or answer "7" to every question. We might have a rigorous data analysis protocol set up, only to find that we have a skewed distribution and our protocol is inappropriate. Because scientists in the real world can face challenges such as these, scholars have created a type of figure called a **CONSORT diagram** that graphically tracks the participants throughout the duration of the study and provides reasons why participants were excluded from data analyses.

Figure 10.17 is a CONSORT diagram for a study comparing a brain-training program called Brain Age to the non-brain-training game Tetris (Nouchi et al., 2013). As we can see in the diagram, the authors recruited 41 participants, but 9 declined to participate, leaving 32 in the sample. These participants were then randomized into one of two conditions, the Brain Age intervention condition or the Tetris Intervention condition. Of the 16 participants in the Brain Age intervention, all completed the study and had analyzable results. Of the 16 participants in the Tetris intervention, one participant discontinued their participation due to being in a traffic accident.

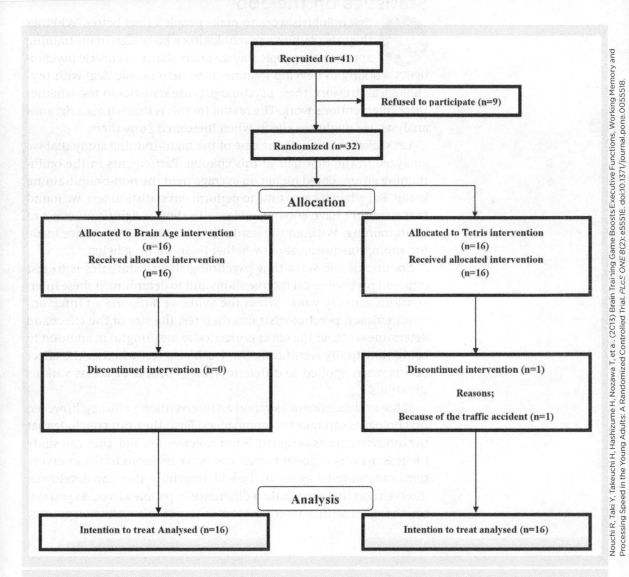

Figure 10.17 CONSORT Diagram from Nouchi et al., 2013

Nouchi R, Taki Y, Takeuchi H, Hashizume H, Nozawa T, et al. (2013) Brain Training Game Boosts Executive Functions, Working Memory and Processing Speed in the Young Adults: A Randomized Controlled Trial. *PLoS ONE* 8(2): e55518. doi:10.1371/journal.pone.0055518.

By examining the CONSORT diagram of an article such as this one, we can have greater insight into the methodological problems that may have increased the likelihood of biased results.

Although most psychology journals do not require authors to include CONSORT diagrams, some do. We are most likely to see CONSORT diagrams in clinical psychology journals, health psychology journals, as well as neurology and psychiatry journals.

Statistics on the Job

Psychologists work to make people's lives better. Whether they are cognitive psychologists who design brain-training apps to help people stay mentally sharp, or clinical psychologists working to develop treatments to help people deal with psychological stressors, these psychologists use statistics to test whether these interventions work. The reason for this is that without rigorous analyses, we might see effects when there aren't any there.

Let's take for example the case of the brain-training study that we analyzed in the first half of this chapter. Participants in the brain-training group scored higher on average than the non-brain-training group. But when it came time to perform our statistical test, we found that we didn't have enough evidence to show a significant effect of brain-training. Without the results of this test, we might have made the wrong conclusion about whether brain-training helps.

So, one of the ways that psychologists use statistics is to test different psychological interventions and to determine if these interventions actually work. When the evidence supports an intervention's efficacy, psychologists can then test the size of the effect and determine whether the effect is practically meaningful in addition to being statistically significant. They can also test whether the effect occurs when applied to different types of people or across various situations.

If the evidence doesn't support an intervention's efficacy, however, psychologists can take two approaches. First, they can conclude that the intervention, as designed, is not effective. Second, they can study the reasons why it doesn't work, can make revisions to the intervention, and can test it again. In the end, hopefully, they can develop an intervention that does make a difference in people's lives. As you can see, though, statistics are critical at each step of this evaluation process.

Review Questions

1. Select the most appropriate statistical test for each of the following:
   a. An elementary school teacher is interested in seeing how the color used to make edits on students' work affects self-esteem. For $n = 13$ children the edits are made in red ink, and for $n = 12$ children the edits are made in green ink.
   b. Researchers demonstrated that Tai Chi can significantly reduce symptoms for individuals with arthritis. Self-reports of pain and stiffness were measured at the beginning of an 8-week Tai Chi course and again at the end.
   c. You want to scientifically evaluate your Nonna's claim that drinking chamomile tea before going to sleep reduces sleep latency. You recruit 46 people with sleep problems and match them into pairs. Then you randomly assign one person from each pair to drink chamomile tea at bedtime (experimental group) and the other to go to sleep without drinking tea (control group). You measure sleep latency with an EEG.
   d. You are a member of your community college's Psi Beta chapter (national honors society for psychology majors), and you wonder whether students who are members of an honors society feel more connected to their college than those who aren't. You collect data from students who are members of an honors society at your college and compare it to the average connectedness score that your college recently published.
   e. A demographer wants to compare the salaries of primary care physicians who live in rural areas to those living in urban centers. They get a sample of $n = 34$ physicians living in rural areas, and a sample of $n = 45$ physicians living in urban centers.

2. True or False (if false, correct the statement):
   a. All t-tests require estimating the population variance using the sample variance
   b. A t-test for independent samples can be used with a pre-post design.
   c. All t-tests focus on differences between two means.
   d. All t-tests require two groups of participants.
   e. A t-test for dependent samples requires dependent variables that are continuous (interval or ratio) level data but a t-test for independent samples does not.
   f. The t-test for dependent samples focuses on within-subjects comparisons while the t-test for independent samples focuses on between-subjects comparisons.
   g. Only the t-test for dependent samples requires that the variances of the two samples are equal.
   h. The t-test for independent samples, but not the t-test for dependent samples, requires that the population's scores on the dependent variable be normally distributed, or that we have large samples.

3. Look at the following SPSS output and answer the following questions
   a. Has the assumption of equality of variances been met? How do you know?
   b. Which row of the output should we use?

Independent Samples Test

| | | Levene's Test for Equality of Variances | | t-test for Equality of Means | | | | | 95% Confidence Interval of the Difference | |
| | | | | | | Significance | | | | | |
		F	Sig.	t	df	One-Sided p	Two-Sided p	Mean Difference	Std. Error Difference	Lower	Upper
Amount_of_Food_Eaten	Equal variances assumed	5.647	.025	1.003	28	.162	.325	.6200	.6184	–.6467	1.8867
	Equal variances not assumed			1.003	17.006	.165	.330	.6200	.6184	–.6847	1.9247

4. In what way is calculating the pooled variance similar to the calculation of a weighted mean?

5. You are completing a worksheet in class and have calculated a pooled estimate of the population variance (S^2_{Pooled}) of 8.32 from the following two sample estimates $S^2_1 = 12.48$ and $S^2_2 = 18.20$.
   a. Without doing any additional math, you know that you need to go back and check your work because something is wrong. How do you know?
   b. You give it another try (using the same sample estimates), and this time your answer is 15.34. This matches the answer key. Which sample was larger? Explain.

6. You're feeling a different level of motivation to study in the classes that directly relate to your major relative to courses not related to your major. You wonder if this is true for other students, so you survey 24 of your classmates. You ask them to rate how motivated they are to study in the course (on a scale from 1 to 10, where 1 is very low motivation and 10 is very high motivation) as well as whether the course is related to their major. You find that there are 12 students whose major is related to the class, their average motivation is 8.1 ($SD = 3.2$). The course is unrelated to their major for the remainder of the students, and their average motivation is 5.3 ($SD = 3.8$).
   a. What is the population of interest, the comparison population, and the sample? State the null and research hypotheses for this research problem.
   b. Build the comparison distribution. What is the mean of the comparison

distribution? What is the pooled estimate of the population's variance? What is the variance and standard error of the distribution of means?

c. Establish the critical value cutoff. How many total degrees of freedom total are there? Is the research hypothesis one tailed or two tailed? What are the critical value cutoffs for an alpha = .01?

d. Determine sample results. Solve for the t-score.

e. Decide and interpret. Compare the t-score you computed to the critical values. What is your conclusion regarding the null hypothesis?

f. What is the mean difference between the students whose major is related to the course and the students whose major is unrelated to the course? Calculate the 95% confidence interval.

7. Your cheer coach used to emphasize how important cross-training was in terms of performance and injury prevention. You decide to compare the number of injuries experienced by cheerleaders to those who cross-train versus those who don't. To test this, you recruit 25 people who state that they consistently cross-train and 20 people who state that they don't consistently cross-train, and you have them report how many injuries they've experienced in the past 5 years that resulted in their not being able to participate in their main sport for 1 or more weeks. Results reveal that participants in the cross-training group had an average of 2.4 injuries (SD = 0.32), and participants in the no-cross-training group had an average of 2.7 injuries (SD = 0.54). Conduct a hypothesis test to determine whether those who cross-train experience fewer injuries than those who don't. Assume that all assumptions have been met.

a. What is the population of interest, the comparison population, and the sample? State the null and research hypotheses for this research problem.

b. Build the comparison distribution. What is the mean of the comparison distribution? What is the pooled estimate of the population's variance? What is the variance and standard error of the distribution of means?

c. Establish the critical value cutoff. How many degrees of freedom total are there? Is the research hypothesis one-tailed or two-tailed? What are the critical value cutoffs for an alpha = .05?

d. Determine sample results. Solve for the t-score.

e. Decide and interpret. Compare the t-score you computed to the critical values. What is your conclusion regarding the null hypothesis?

f. Is the result a practically meaningful difference? Calculate Cohen's d. According to the guidelines, is this a small, medium, or large effect?

8. Why do we need to combine the variances of each sample in a t-test for two independent/unrelated samples when we are calculating the variance for the distribution of differences between means?

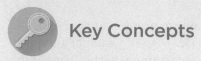

Key Concepts

confirmatory research, p. 378

confounds, p. 379

CONSORT diagram, p. 380

equality of variances assumption, p. 364

experiment, p. 374

exploratory research, p. 378

independent groups design, p. 362

Levene's Test for Equality of Variances, p. 371

Mann–Whitney U, p. 372

t-test for two independent samples, p. 345

Answers to Your Turn

Your Turn 10.1

1. Answers will vary but should all feature the comparison of means from two distinct samples/groups/conditions. For example, you could use a t-test for two independent samples to determine if those who do yoga experience less stress compared to those who go running.

2. (a) (1) The t-test for two independent samples focuses on differences between means of two samples, while the t-test for dependent samples focuses on differences between two scores from the same person. (2) The t-test for two independent samples is used with a two-group design, while the t-test for dependent samples is used with a pre-post design. (3) The t-test for two independent samples focuses on between-subjects comparisons, while the t-test for dependent samples focuses on within-subjects comparisons. The t-test for two independent samples comparison distribution is a Distribution of Differences Between Means, while the t-test for dependent samples comparison distribution is a Distribution of Means of Difference Scores.

(b) (1) All t-tests require estimating the population variance. (2) All t-tests have a t-shaped comparison distribution. (3) All t-tests focus on differences between two means. (4) All t-tests require dependent variables that are continuous (interval or ratio)-level data.

Your Turn 10.2

1. Because a pooled estimate is essentially a weighted average of the two samples' variance estimate, the pooled estimate must fall in between the two sample estimates. It is impossible for an average to fall outside of the top and bottom numbers being averaged.

2. The pooled estimate gives greater weight or influence to the larger sample. Because the pooled estimate is so much closer to sample 2, it suggests that sample 2 had more people, which gave its estimate of 26.99 greater influence over the final pooled estimate.

Your Turn 10.3

1. When calculating the difference between two numbers, changes or variation in either number will influence the result. In the context of our comparison distribution, variation in each distribution of means contributes to the amount of variation in the difference between the means. If both distributions of means have a lot of variance, means selected from them would vary more. If both means vary a lot, the resulting differences between those means will also vary more. Because each sample contributes to the variance in differences between means, we add the variances together to account for both distributions of means' variance.

2. (a) (1) Population of Interest: People who eat clean. Comparison Population: People who don't eat clean (and eat normally), Sample: Five classmates who eat clean and seven classmates who do not eat clean; (2) Research: Those who eat clean will have more mental energy than those who do not eat clean. Null: Those who eat clean will have the same amount (or less) mental energy than those who do not eat clean.

(b) (1) It is a distribution of differences between mean and has a t distribution shape that is ultimately determined by the degrees of freedom; (2) 0 because it reflects the null hypothesis that there is no difference between the samples mean; (3) $S_1^2 = 0.80$; $S_2^2 = 2.00$, $df_1 = 4$, $df_2 = 6$, $df_{Total} = 10$, $S_{Pooled} = 1.52$; (4) $S_{M1}^2 = 0.30$, $S_{M2}^2 = 0.22$; (5) $S_{Difference}^2 = 0.52$; $S_{Difference} = 0.72$.

(c) (1) Number of tails (one-tailed test, because we had directional hypothesis), degrees of freedom ($df_{Total} = 10$), significance level (we'll use the standard significance level, $p = .05$); (2) 1.813.

(d) (1) t-test for two independent samples; (2) $t = 1.94$; (3)

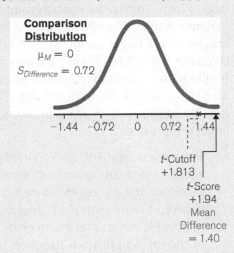

Comparison Distribution

$\mu_M = 0$

$S_{Difference} = 0.72$

−1.44 −0.72 0 0.72 1.44

t-Cutoff +1.813

t-Score +1.94 Mean Difference = 1.40

(e) Our t-score of 1.94 exceeded the cutoff score of 1.813. Because our sample's results (Step 4) exceeded the critical value (Step 3), we are able to reject the null hypothesis (H_0) that those who eat clean will have the same amount (or less) mental energy than those who do not eat clean ($\mu_1 = \mu_2$). If we are able to reject the null, we can say that we support the research hypothesis (H_1) that those who eat clean will have more mental energy than those who do not eat clean ($\mu_1 > \mu_2$).

Your Turn 10.4

1. If you were to use an independent groups design, you would only have four participants per condition. Though a statistics program like SPSS would provide the analysis, there aren't enough participants to satisfy the assumption of normality. In general, the independent groups design requires a larger sample size.

2. (a) The population of interest is people with seasonal affective disorder who use light therapy. The comparison population is people with seasonal affective disorder who take *Upify*. The sample is the 30 participants, half of whom use light therapy and half of who use *Upify*. The research hypothesis is that light therapy will have a different effect on depression symptoms, compared to *Upify*. The null hypothesis is that the two forms of therapy will not differ in their effectiveness.

(b) The mean of the comparison distribution is 0, because we construct the comparison distribution assuming the null hypothesis is true. The pooled estimate of the population variance, $S_{Pooled}^2 = (df_{Total}/df_{Total})(S_1^2) + (df_2/df_{Total})(S_2^2) = (14/28)(6.33^2) + (14/28)(7.10^2) = 20.03 + 25.20 = 45.23$. The variance of the distribution of means, $S_{Difference}^2 = S_{M_1}^2 + S_{M_2}^2$, where $S_{M_1}^2 = S_{Pooled}^2/N_1$ and $S_{M_2}^2 = S_{Pooled}^2/N_2$. $S_{M_1}^2 = 45.23/15 = 3.02$. $S_{M_2}^2 = 45.23/15 = 3.02$. $S_{Difference}^2 = 3.02 + 3.02 = 6.04$. The standard error, $S_{Difference} = \sqrt{S_{Difference}^2} = \sqrt{6.04} = 2.46$.

2c. There are 28 degrees of freedom total. The research hypothesis is two-tailed. The critical values are −2.048 and +2.048.

2d. Using the means of the two conditions, we can solve for t using the equation $t = (M_1 - M_2)/S_{Difference} = (11.90 - 12.90)/2.46 = -0.41$.

2e. The t-score did not exceed the critical values, so we fail to reject the null hypothesis. We cannot conclude that light therapy is more or less effective than *Upify*.

Answers to Review Questions

1. a. *t*-test for two independent/unrelated samples
    b. *t*-test for dependent means
    c. *t*-test for matched samples or dependent means
    d. single sample *t*-test
    e. *t*-test for two independent/unrelated samples

2. a. True
    b. False; a *t*-test for dependent samples can be used with a pre-post design, but a *t*-test for independent samples cannot.
    c. True
    d. False; the *t*-test for two independent samples requires two groups of participants, while a *t*-test for dependent samples and a single sample *t*-test require only one.
    e. False; all types of *t*-tests require continuous (interval or ratio) level data.
    f. True
    g. False; all *t*-tests require that the population scores on the dependent variable are normally distributed, or that we have large samples.
    h. True

3. a. The assumption has not been met. Levene's Test for Equality of Variances is statistically significant ($p = .025$). The null hypothesis associated with the Levene's Test is that the variances are equal, the research hypothesis is that they are not equal. Since the test is statistically significant, it means that we reject the null hypothesis and find support for the research hypothesis.
    b. We should use the second row of the table, the one labeled "Equal variances not assumed."

4. When we calculate the pooled variance, we give more weight to the sample that has a larger group. That is, the pooled (combined) variance is more heavily influenced by the sample with a larger sample size. When we calculate a weighted mean, we give more weight to the sample that has a larger group. That is, the overall (combined) mean is more heavily influenced by the sample with a larger sample size.

5. a. The pooled estimate is a weighted average of the two sample variance estimates; therefore, the pooled estimate must be between the two sample estimates. It is impossible for an average to be outside of the top and bottom numbers being averaged.
    b. Since the average is exactly halfway between the two sample estimates, the sample sizes must have been identical.

6. a. The population of interest is students whose major is related to the course. The comparison population is students whose major is unrelated to the course. The sample is the 24 participants, 12 with a major related to the course and 12 with a major unrelated to the course. The research hypothesis is that those with a major related to the course have a different motivation level than those whose major is unrelated to the course. The null hypothesis is that those with a major related to the course will be the same as those with a major unrelated to the course.

b. The mean of the comparison distribution is 0. The pooled estimate of the population variance, $S^2_{Pooled} = 12.34$. The variance of the distribution of means, $S^2_{Difference} = 2.06$. The standard error, $S_{Difference} = 1.43$.

c. There are 22 degrees of freedom total. The research hypothesis is two-tailed. The critical value is 2.819.

d. The sample results, $t = 1.96$.

e. The t-score does not exceed the critical value, so we fail to reject the null hypothesis. Our research hypothesis was not supported.

f. Upper limit = 6.83, lower limit = −1.23.

7. a. The population of interest is people who cross-train. The comparison population is people who don't cross-train. The sample is the 45 participants, 25 of whom cross-train and 20 who don't cross-train. The research hypothesis is that those who cross-train will have fewer injuries than those who don't cross-train. The null hypothesis is that those who cross-train will have the same amount (or more) of injuries as those who don't cross-train.

b. The mean of the comparison distribution is 0. The pooled estimate of the population variance, $S^2_{Pooled} = 0.19$. The variance of the distribution of means, $S^2_{Difference} = 0.017$. The standard error, $S_{Difference} = 0.13$.

c. There are 43 degrees of freedom total. The research hypothesis is one-tailed. The critical value is −1.684.

d. The sample results, $t = -2.31$.

e. The t-score exceeded the critical value, so we reject the null hypothesis and find support for the research hypothesis that those who cross-train have fewer injuries than those who don't.

f. Cohen's $d = 0.70$, a medium effect.

8. Variation in either one of the samples contributes to the variation in the differences. An increase in the variation of one or both samples will result in an increase in the variation of the differences between the samples.

Sharpen your statistics skills with real-life data! Check out OpenStatsLab.com, created by coauthor Kevin McIntyre, to practice running analyses for real published research studies.

11

One-Way Analysis of Variance (ANOVA)

Learning Outcomes

After reading this chapter, you should be able to:

● Explain the key question that a one-way analysis of variance seeks to answer.

● Identify similarities and differences between a *t*-test for two independent samples and a one-way analysis of variance.

● Explain when it is appropriate to use a one-way analysis of variance.

● Describe the underlying logic for calculating within-groups estimate of variance.

● Identify chance factors that contribute to within-groups variation.

● Describe the underlying logic for calculating between-groups estimate of variance.

● Find a cutoff score in an *F*-table.

● Interpret what one-way analysis of variance results can and cannot tell us.

● Describe the underlying logic for conducting post hoc tests and how they are different from a *t*-test for independent samples.

● Determine the size of a between-subjects effect.

The senior talent show. It's an annual rite of passage across many schools in the country. Talent shows build a sense of community and school spirit, put students' nonacademic skills on display, and, most importantly, get students out of class for an hour or so. The principal starts the show. The first student gets up with her guitar and sings a song she wrote. Someone else performs a magic trick. A guy from your chemistry class then performs a surprisingly solid dance routine.

Next up is Kai. He's your sister's friend, so you don't know him that well, but well enough to be surprised that he's in the show for any type of talent. On the PowerPoint slide above his name it simply says "Shock & Awe."

The music starts. The audience stares at a small lonely table, with a solitary water bottle on top. The music's intensity builds. Kai emerges from behind the curtain, slowly walking back and forth, stalking the table. He picks up the bottle in a dramatic motion, steps back, fakes left like he's doing a basketball jump shot, spins, and puts his left hand over his eyes as the music suddenly stops. He then flips the water bottle almost impossibly high in the air. The bottle twirls like a baton, hurdling back down toward the table. Everyone is dead silent awaiting the finish.

And . . . the bottle sticks the landing, without even a wobble! The music thunders back to life! Kai bows and slowly walks off. The crowd goes wild. No one could believe what they just witnessed.

Now in college, as you sit around with your friends from stats class studying for an upcoming exam, the conversation wanders into the topic of social media "challenges." When someone mentions the water bottle flip challenge, you share the legend of Kai's senior talent show performance and wonder aloud how he pulled it off. You all start flipping water bottles and quickly realize that doing it successfully is nowhere near as easy as Kai made it look. What's his secret?

CamN/Shutterstock

What is the secret to mastering the art of the bottle flip?

Statistics for Life

Each of your friends has a guess. One person suggests it was a special type of bottle with a wide base. Nope—it was the standard bottle everyone got from the vending machine. Perhaps it was the type of table. Nope—it was a basic table from the media center. Maybe Kai just practiced a ridiculous amount to become such a flipping expert. But you assure everyone that if they knew the guy, the "tons of practice" hypothesis was impossible. The only reasonable explanation anyone came up with was that Kai figured out that the water level influenced how easy it was to flip and land a bottle. Only one way to know: We need to test it.

Where Do the Data Come From?

First, we need to determine which water levels to test. Everyone seems to agree that a nearly empty bottle will have a hard time standing up, and that they've never seen anyone attempt it with a completely full bottle. After some debate, there seems to be consensus around three water levels: 1/3, 1/2, and 1/4. Of course, we could try to test lots of other possibilities, but those three are a good place to start for our first study.

A fellow student messages the class and asks everyone who's interested in showing up to Monday's class 30 minutes early for a "fun challenge." From your statistics class of 75, 27 people show up early enough to participate. Everyone gets randomly assigned to a group (Group 1 = 1/3 full; Group 2 = 1/2 full; Group 3 = 1/4 full) using a random number generator. Each group grabs their assigned bottle, then each individual person in that group flips the bottle until they get it to land. One person catalogs everyone's results and group number (**Figure 11.1**). As your classmates filter in to start class, someone asks, "What are you guys doing?" Science. That's right, we're doing science.

Group 1 (1/3 Full)		Group 2 (1/2 Full)		Group 3 (1/4 Full)	
Participant Name	**Number of Flips**	**Participant Name**	**Number of Flips**	**Participant Name**	**Number of Flips**
Emilia	11	Brett	17	Ladonna	15
Jarrod	8	Saul	14	Kyung	7
Renay	3	Nilan	18	Leah	18
Robinson	2	Maxine	24	Rajneesh	20
Kumari	13	Sung-Hyun	6	Brooklyn	22
Shelly	17	Saburo	21	Rufus	17
Genna	1	Sherika	5	Calandra	18
Serena	1	Xiaomeng	17	Thompson	19
Daisuke	4	Lupe	16	Mariko	7

Figure 11.1   Water Bottle Flip Challenge Results

One-Way Analysis of Variance (ANOVA): What We're Trying to Accomplish

The key question we need to answer is whether all three groups are the same, or if they are actually different from each other in some way. In more statistical terms, we are trying to determine if our groups come from different populations or the same one. We can test that question using the **one-way analysis of variance** (also known as **ANOVA**), which is a statistic that lets us determine if three or more samples are from different populations, when we have continuous (interval or ratio) data (we explain more about why that is in the Statistics for Research section). In other words, the one-way analysis of variance allows us to see if means from our three samples or groups are different enough to not to have happened by chance.

Though ANOVA focuses on group differences and not individuals, we can think of the general logic this way: If we have three animals (like we see in **Figure 11.2**), an ANOVA can tell us if all three animals are from the same population, or if they come from different populations. Importantly, by itself the one-way analysis of variance cannot tell us which specific animals are different from one another. For example,

one-way analysis of variance (or ANOVA) a hypothesis test that lets us determine if three or more samples are from different populations when we have continuous (interval or ratio) data.

Figure 11.2 Same or Different?

an ANOVA can't reveal if the first animal is different from the second or third, or if the second and third are different from each other. In other words, ANOVA lets us know if there's a difference, but not where it is.

When we want to compare three or more groups, it may seem logical to run a series of *t*-tests on each possible pairing (group 1 vs. group 2, 2 vs. 3, 1 vs. 3). We discuss this possibility in depth later on, but for now we'll note that this approach is problematic and that ANOVA is a superior approach (in short, running multiple *t*-tests results in greater likelihood of committing a Type I error, relative to ANOVA).

We can use a one-way analysis of variance in a few different situations:

1. Compare means of three randomly assigned groups from a multigroup experiment (e.g., Who has higher life satisfaction — those randomly assigned to complete a gratitude journal, those assigned to keep a regular journal, or those who do nothing?)

2. Compare means of three or more naturally occurring (i.e., nonrandomly assigned) groups (e.g., Who does better on the SAT — those who went to public school, those who attended private school, or those who were home schooled?)

In each case the independent or grouping variable is nominal (categorical) with at least three levels, and the dependent or outcome variable is interval or ratio.

Let's stop for a moment to contrast the *t*-test for two independent samples with the one-way ANOVA. There are several distinctions, but the most notable is that with an ANOVA we focus on three or more groups, whereas with a *t*-test for two independent samples we only looked at two groups. The tests also estimate population variance using different techniques (more on how that works in the next section).

Beyond that, the tests' goals are largely the same: see if groups come from the same, or different, populations (**Figure 11.3**).

	t-Test for Two Independent Samples	**One-Way Analysis of Variance**
Key Concept	Compare Groups	Compare Groups
Number of Groups	2	3 or More
Key Question	Are the two groups different from each other?	Are the three+ groups different from each other?
Where Are We Looking for Differences?	Between-Subjects	Between-Subjects
Typical Research Design	Two-Group	Multigroup
Comparison Distribution Shape	*t*	*F*
Estimate Population Variance?	Yes	Yes
Basis for Population Variance Estimate	Pooled estimate from two samples	Between-group and within-group estimates
Controls Experimentwise Error?	No	Yes

Figure 11.3 What We Know: *t*-Test Versus ANOVA Comparison

As with the *t*-tests we've discussed, one-way analysis of variance compares differences between means, requires that we estimate population variance, and requires that our outcome or dependent variable is continuous (interval or ratio) level data. In our case, we want to compare three different water levels to determine which one leads to the most flipping success.

Your Turn 11.1

1. Please give your own example of a research question that would call for a one-way analysis of variance.

2. To identify potential differences between four groups of student-athletes (men's lacrosse, women's lacrosse, men's soccer, women's soccer), the athletics department conducts an ANOVA.

    a. What can that test tell them?

    b. What can't it tell them?

3. a. Give three ways the *t*-test for independent means and one-way analysis of variance are distinct.

    b. Give three ways they are similar.

Partitioning the Variance: Two Key Sources Ultimately, we want to see if our three water levels produce different mean numbers of flips. To do this, we are going to take a different approach than what we did with the *t*-tests that we learned in the previous chapters. Instead of comparing a bunch of group means to each other separately as would happen if we conducted *t*-tests for each pair of conditions, ANOVA allows us to examine all of the conditions simultaneously. Doing so gives us the best chance of finding a difference between the groups, if one exists.

The first wrinkle in an ANOVA is that we now have two different ways to estimate population variance. One is the *within-groups estimate of population variance,* where we look at how much scores vary among participants within the same condition or group. Here we would focus on how much people in the 1/3 full group differ from each other, then look at how the people in the 1/2 full group differ from each other, and finally how those in the 1/4 group vary from each other. This is essentially the type of variation we have focused on in previous tests up to this point. When we calculated *t* tests for two independent samples and needed to pool variance estimates, we had an estimate from each condition that focused on variation from within each group.

In ANOVA, we have a second variance source. Since more information is always better, we're going to use this as well. The *between-groups estimate of population variance* looks at how much scores vary across groups or conditions. Here we focus on how much people in a group (e.g., 1/3 full) differ from people in the other two groups (e.g., the 1/2 and 1/4).

Think of it this way: If you saw a picture of 5 cats, it would be easy to identify the entire group as being cats. However, *within* that group of cats, there is inevitable variation in the cats' size, coloring, eye color, fur type, and demeanor. Similarly, if you had a second picture of 5 dogs, the same would be true. They're all dogs, but there is considerable variation *within* the group of dogs (really, it is amazing how different dogs can be!). We can also identify how much the group of cats on average differs from the group of dogs on average. That is, we can identify the variation *between* the two groups. Later, we will then compare the between-groups variance to the within-groups variance to see if differences between our conditions are sufficiently larger than the difference we typically see within the groups.

The Within-Groups Estimate: Quantifying Error Variance For scientific purposes, ideally study participants would be clones who are identical in every possible way. That isn't possible, so our participants come to our studies as unique and different individuals. In other

How much variation do you notice within each group? How much variation do you notice between the groups?

Kasefoto/Shutterstock

Dora Zett/Shutterstock

words, they have a lot of **error variance,** or variations in scores due to extraneous variables, measurement error, or random error (e.g., luck or chance factors). Those chance factors come from previous experiences, personality, mood, skills/abilities, attributes, and luck, all of which contribute to differences within a group.

That is, even though two people get the exact same treatment (both flip the same 1/3-full water bottle), their scores will likely be different due to chance factors. How so? Those two people could differ in previous experience flipping water bottles, natural hand-eye coordination, competitiveness, need for achievement, how they feel that day (e.g., happy, tired, stressed, etc.), and just how lucky they get.

This happens within every group in a study. Each water-level group will have error variance within it that has nothing to do with the independent variable of water level. It is merely the result of participants' unavoidable individual differences. Because this type of variation is inescapable, it serves as a baseline. That is, error variance tells us how much variation we can typically expect. There's always some variation, so what does a standard level look like?

In order to estimate population variance from inside our groups, we will use our samples' variance, much like we did for *t*-tests for two independent samples. As before, we will use information about each groups' variation and combine that by averaging all of the groups' information together to calculate the *within-groups population variance estimate* (S^2_{Within} also called the mean square within). We calculate this by taking the variance estimate from each sample, adding them together, then dividing the sum by the number of groups, or $S^2_1 + S^2_2 + S^2_3 / N_{Groups}$. Note that this formula is for three groups; if we had more groups, we would have added those variance estimates in the numerator (e.g., S_4^2, S_5^2, etc.) and adjusted the denominator accordingly.

$$S_{Within}^2 = \frac{S_1^2 + S_2^2 + \dots + S_{Last}^2}{N_{Groups}}$$

The Between-Groups Estimate: Quantifying the Effect When we run a study with several groups, we make sure each group gets a slightly different experience to determine whether those experiences create different outcomes. In other words, we want to see if our treatment, manipulation, or intervention creates differences between the groups, or *systematic variance*. Ideally, every difference we see between our groups is from systematic variance. But it isn't. Even if there were no treatment at all, simply by having three separate groups there will be sampling variation (i.e., people in the three groups are different). The result is we have the same type of error variance between our groups that we had for our within-groups estimates.

Ultimately, we're hoping systematic variance from our treatment exceeds the naturally occurring error variance. In our study, we're looking to determine whether water level (our treatment) has a systematic effect on number of flips it takes to successfully land the water bottle. To figure that out, we have to use the information available to us. In this case, the best information we have to see differences between groups are the groups' means. Consider these sets of hypothetical means:

Set 1 Group 1 = 3.45; Group 2 = 6.98; Group 3 = 1.09
Set 2 Group 1 = 5.65; Group 2 = 6.02; Group 3 = 5.91

Which set has more variation? Clearly, Set 1's means are less similar than Set 2's which are all fairly close. Now, if the null hypothesis is true (which is our working assumption), all three samples are from the same population, which should lead to group means that are more similar. We might wonder, then, why the means aren't identical if they're all coming from the same place. Due to sampling variation, each group has a unique set of people who are different themselves due to error variance. However, there is another reason why the scores might differ.

If samples reflect their populations (which they should), scores with greater variability (like Set 1) are more likely to be sampled from populations with greater variability. Here's why.

First, notice how all three distributions on each side of **Figure 11.4** line up perfectly. That's because we're assuming that each set of three samples is from the same population with the same mean. In other words, this depicts the situation when the null hypothesis is true and that there is no difference between the samples. As you can see in Figure 11.4a on the left, when we draw samples from populations with higher variability (i.e., distributions that are more spread out), the scores we randomly select are less similar (i.e., it's easier to pick scores that are further from the mean). The resulting means from those samples will be more different from each other, resulting in greater variability in our three means.

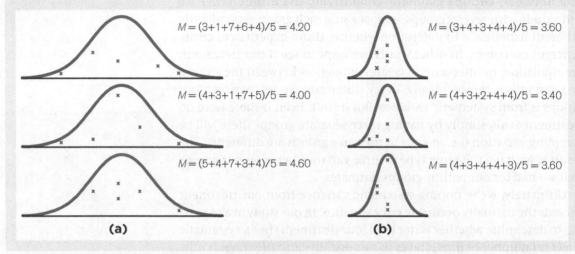

$M = (3+1+7+6+4)/5 = 4.20$

$M = (3+4+3+4+4)/5 = 3.60$

$M = (4+3+1+7+5)/5 = 4.00$

$M = (4+3+2+4+4)/5 = 3.40$

$M = (5+4+7+3+4)/5 = 4.60$

$M = (4+3+4+4+3)/5 = 3.60$

(a) **(b)**

Figure 11.4 The Link Between Population Variability and Mean Variability

The opposite is also true. In Figure 11.4b on the right, when we randomly select samples from populations with low variability (i.e., distributions that are less spread out), the scores we randomly select are likely to be closer together (i.e., there is a much lower probability for us to select the more extreme scores). The resulting means from those samples will be more similar, resulting in lower variability. Said another way, when there is more population variance, there will be more variance in sample means. Consequently, we can infer that when sample means vary more, there is more variance in the population. Remember, samples mirror populations.

This bit of logic gives us a second way to estimate population variance. If we can calculate how much the samples' means vary, it provides some insight into the population variance. To determine the differences in sample means, we use the same procedure we used when we wanted to see how much individual scores vary. First, we calculate the mean of our scores (which in this case are group means). Because we're dealing with means, the calculation produces a mean of means ($\Sigma M/N$), otherwise known as the **grand mean (GM).** The grand mean is the overall mean of everyone in the study. Next, we determine how much each group's mean deviates from the grand mean. Then, we

grand mean (GM) a mean calculated from a group of other means.

square that difference for all of the same reasons we discussed in Chapter 3. Finally, we add up all of the squared differences to get the sum of squared deviation from the grand mean (**Figure 11.5**).

Group	Sample Means (*M*)	Deviation from Grand Mean (*M* − *GM*)	Squared Deviation from Grand Mean (*M* − *GM*)²
Group 1			
Group 2			
Group 3			
Σ =		SS =	
N_{Groups} =		df =	
GM =			

Figure 11.5 Calculating Group Means' Differences From the Grand Mean

Now that we know how much variation we have between our samples' means, we can estimate the variance of the distribution of means (S_M^2), which we do using the standard logic of dividing the sum of squares (*SS*) by the degrees of freedom (*df*). In this case, the relevant degrees of freedom is the $df_{Between}$ or the number of groups minus 1 ($N_{Groups} - 1$), for a final formula of $S_M^2 = SS/df_{Between}$.

Next we would calculate the *between-groups population variance estimate* ($S_{Between}^2$) also called the mean square between by using the information we have about means from samples (S_M^2) to make inferences about the population of individuals. If all of this feels a bit backwards, that's because it is essentially the opposite of what we were doing.

Want to review degrees of freedom? SEE CHAPTER 9.

Then (*t*-test for two independent samples):

$$\text{Individuals} \rightarrow \text{Means } S_M^2 = \frac{S^2}{N}$$

Now (analysis of variance):

$$\text{Means} \rightarrow \text{Individuals } S^2 = S_M^2 \times (N)$$

Because the processes are parallel, we use the same equation from the *t*-test with a mathematical tweak. To make the equation suit our needs, we multiply each side by *N* so that we're solving for S^2 instead of S_M^2. Because it is the between-groups estimate, we add a subscript, making the final formula:

$$\boxed{S_{Between}^2 = S_M^2 \times (N)}$$

Statistically Speaking

People like to think that people who live in a particular residence hall are weird compared to students from other residence halls. But what we need to realize is that the differences among the students living in each hall are likely greater than the overall differences between the halls.

Remember, if the null is true, the between-groups estimate of the population variance will be small because our samples all originate from the same population. However, when the null hypothesis is not true, our samples don't come from the same population, the populations would have different means, and they wouldn't line up.

As you can see in **Figure 11.6,** when populations differ, the samples' means have greater variance between them. That's because the group differences are due to systematic variance from the treatment (i.e., water level), in addition to some error variance. In other words, when the null isn't true, the samples' means would vary because water level has an effect, which suggests that our samples come from different populations. All of which makes our between-groups estimate of population variance larger.

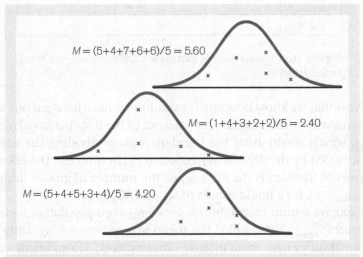

$M = (5+4+7+6+6)/5 = 5.60$

$M = (1+4+3+2+2)/5 = 2.40$

$M = (5+4+5+3+4)/5 = 4.20$

Figure 11.6 The Link Between Population Variability and Mean Variability

What's the _F_? Computing the _F_-Ratio But, how big does the between-groups estimate have to be for us to be sure it's more than just error variance? To answer that, first let's think about systematic variance relative to the null. If the null is true and the water level has no impact on flipping ability, there should be no systematic variation. Conversely, if the null is false and water level has an effect, systematic variation should be greater than 0 (**Figure 11.7**).

On the other hand, error variance is always present. So, when the null is true, any differences we see are due to error variance in both between-groups and within-groups estimates. However, when the null isn't true, systematic variance makes our between-groups larger. But how large does it need to be in order for us to conclude it is a real difference?

$$\frac{\text{Between-Groups Estimate}}{\text{Within-Groups Estimate}} = \frac{\text{Systematic Variance} + \text{Error Variance}}{\text{Error Variance}}$$

When the Null Is True

$$\frac{\text{Between-Groups Estimate}}{\text{Within-Groups Estimate}} = \frac{(0) + \text{Error Variance}}{\text{Error Variance}}$$

When the Null Is False

$$\frac{\text{Between-Groups Estimate}}{\text{Within-Groups Estimate}} = \frac{(>0) + \text{Error Variance}}{\text{Error Variance}}$$

Figure 11.7   Variance Estimates and Sources of Variance

To put our between-groups estimate of variance in context, we need something to compare it to that represents how much people typically vary in our samples. Conveniently, we already have that information from our within-groups estimate of population variance. That is, we can think of the within-groups estimate as the baseline of how much natural variation our samples have. In our case, the real effect that we're looking for is whether water level produces systematic variance in flipping success above and beyond typical error variance.

To make these types of determinations in an analysis of variance, we want to see how our between-groups estimate of population variance compares to our within-groups estimate of population variance. In other words, we want to see if the difference between our groups is greater than the difference within our groups. We call that comparison an **F-ratio**, or score representing how the between-groups estimate of population variance compares to the within-groups estimate of population variance ($F = S^2_{Between}/S^2_{Within}$). When the between-groups and within-groups estimates are similar, the F-ratio is close to 1, but as the between-groups estimate exceeds the within-groups estimate, the F-ratio will exceed 1.

F-ratio score representing how the between-groups estimate of population variance compares to the within-groups estimate of population variance ($F = S^2_{Between}/S^2_{Within}$).

$$F = \frac{S^2_{Between}}{S^2_{Within}}$$

The logic here is parallel to what we do perceptually when trying to focus on one conversation in a noisy and crowded environment. There is a lot of sound variation, but we want to isolate the key sound or effect that's of interest. Similarly, when scientists deploy tsunami detectors in the ocean, the device needs to discern the difference between regular everyday variations in wave activity from atypical wave heights that might indicate a dangerous tsunami. In simplified terms, that device would need to constantly compare the variations it's measuring against the baseline standard to see if the difference in a potential tsunami wave is different enough to classify as a real effect.

Essentially, the *F*-ratio tells us whether the differences we think exist between groups are really different from how much people in those groups typically vary. Really, this asks a profound question: Are the differences between us greater than the differences within us? We ask versions of this question all of the time in our everyday lives. Are men and women really that different? Do liberals and conservatives really look at the world in opposite ways? Do groups of people from other countries really want to do anything in life different from what we do?

Testing these types of questions with statistics is important because in our everyday lives, we're bad at making this judgment ourselves. We mess this up because we generally focus too much on differences between groups and too easily overlook differences within those groups. Take a look back at our picture of cats and dogs. Are those groups different? Sure, there are differences, but are those groups really that different? By looking at the groups, it is apparent that each set of animals has considerable variation within their group. When making our cat-and-dog comparison, we conveniently ignore that and simply focus on variation between the two groups. When we do that, we're not being as thoughtful in our comparison as we could be. However, when we think statistically, we'll find that the answer to questions like, "Are we actually that different?" is "No." The analysis of variance's logic forces us to think more deeply by considering potential between-groups differences' size relative to the within-groups differences that naturally exist. This is not only a nice statistical principle, but a pretty solid life lesson as well.

Your Turn 11.2

1. a. Which of the following sets of means, comes from populations with greater variance? (Set 1: 2.23, 2.56, 1.99; Set 2: 4.45, 4.98, 6.57)

b. How can you tell?

2. a. Draw three distributions that show between-groups estimation of population variance when the Null = True.

b. Draw another three distributions that show when the Null = Not true.

3. How is the process we're following for calculating the between-groups estimate of the population variance the opposite of what we did with the *t*-test for two independent samples?

4. Your lab partner has calculated an *F*-ratio of 5.29, but isn't sure if there is any systematic variance.

a. Without doing any calculations, is there systematic variance?

b. How do you know?

5. Give your own example of how thinking about the world in terms of within- and between-groups variance is helpful.

Hypothesis Testing with a One-Way Analysis of Variance (ANOVA): How Does It Work?

When conducting an analysis of variance, our goal is to see whether our samples are different from one another. The problem is that any three groups of people are going to be at least a little different, even if they all come from the same population. To account for this, similar to hypothesis testing with other statistical tests, we need a predetermined threshold that our results need to exceed in order for us to conclude that our samples are actually different.

Want to review the steps of hypothesis testing? SEE CHAPTER 6. ↗

Step by Step: Hypothesis Testing with the One-Way Analysis of Variance (ANOVA) Despite the one-way analysis of variance looking for differences among three or more groups, the fundamentals of hypothesis-testing remain the same.

Step 1: Population and Hypotheses Once again, our first step is to establish our populations and make a prediction about what we expect to find.

Population 1 (μ_1): People who flip a bottle that is 1/3 full.

Population 2 (μ_2): People who flip a bottle that is 1/2 full.

Population 3 (μ_3): People who flip a bottle that is 1/4 full.

Whereas previous statistics that used hypothesis testing designated a population of interest, we aren't doing that here. That's because we are interested in potential differences among all of the groups, not how a particular group compares to a comparison population. Because of that, our hypotheses for a one-way ANOVA are fairly standard, and admittedly, somewhat generic. Here are our hypotheses:

Research Hypothesis (H_1): The population means are not equal ($\mu_1 \neq \mu_2 \neq \mu_3$). Essentially, we expect the three populations will have different means because we expect our treatment (i.e., water level) to create systematic variance between the groups. By necessity, our hypothesis is nondirectional because we are predicting a difference without stating what that difference may be.

Null Hypothesis (H_0): The population means are equal ($\mu_1 = \mu_2 = \mu_3$). In other words, the three populations will have the same mean.

Step 2: Build Comparison Distribution Compared to the *t*-test for two independent samples' Step 2, our life for ANOVA just got a whole lot easier. Remember, when there is no effect, the *F*-ratio is very close to 1. That's because only error variance is influencing both the between-groups and within-groups estimates of variance. When we have systematic variance, it makes the between-groups estimate larger, producing an *F*-ratio greater than 1.

Because this is always the case, we will need to compare our study's *F*-ratio to a distribution of all possible *F*-ratios, known as the **F distribution.** The *F* distribution's shape is a bit different from the *Z* and *t* distributions. First of all, we should notice that the *F* distribution starts at zero and takes on only positive values. This is because variances can never be negative, so the two variances can never be a negative number. Second, the *F* distribution is positively skewed, with a mode around 1. When the null hypothesis is true, the amount of between-groups variance will be approximately the same as the within-groups variance, so the *F*-ratio will be very close to one, with large *F*-ratios being increasingly rare (**Figure 11.8**).

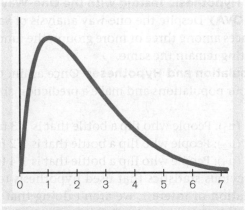

Figure 11.8 *F* Distribution

Similar to the *t* distribution, the *F* distribution's exact shape depends on the degrees of freedom in the study. Because we have two estimates of variance (between-groups and within-groups), we have degrees of freedom for each. We've already discussed how the between-groups degrees of freedom are the number of groups minus 1 ($df_{Between} = N_{Groups} - 1$). Similar to what we did in the *t*-test for two independent samples, our within-groups degrees of freedom are the combination or sum of each group's degrees of freedom ($df_{Within} = df_1 + df_2 + df_3$).

$$df_{Between} = N_{Groups} - 1$$
$$df_{Within} = df_1 + df_2 + df_3$$

Step 3: Establish Critical Value Cutoff Like we've done with other tests, we need to establish a cutoff to determine if our *F*-ratio is large enough to decide that the differences between our groups are real.

Within-Groups df	Significance (Alpha) Level	Between-Groups Degrees of Freedom					
		1	2	3	4	5	6
1	0.01	4052	5000	5404	5625	5764	5859
	0.05	162	200	216	225	230	234
2	0.01	98.50	99.00	99.17	99.25	99.30	99.33
	0.05	18.51	19.00	19.17	19.25	19.30	19.33
3	0.01	34.12	30.82	29.46	28.71	28.24	27.91
	0.05	10.13	9.55	9.28	9.12	9.01	8.94
4	0.01	21.20	18.00	16.70	15.98	15.52	15.21
	0.05	7.71	6.95	6.59	6.39	6.26	6.16
5	0.01	16.26	13.27	12.06	11.39	10.97	10.67
	0.05	6.61	5.79	5.41	5.19	5.05	4.95
6	0.01	13.75	10.93	9.78	9.15	8.75	8.47
	0.05	5.99	5.14	4.76	4.53	4.39	4.28
7	0.01	12.25	9.55	8.45	7.85	7.46	7.19
	0.05	5.59	4.74	4.35	4.12	3.97	3.87
8	0.01	11.26	8.65	7.59	7.01	6.63	6.37
	0.05	5.32	4.46	4.07	3.84	3.69	3.58
10	0.01	10.05	7.56	6.55	6.00	5.64	5.39
	0.05	4.97	4.10	3.71	3.48	3.33	3.22
12	0.01	9.33	6.93	5.95	5.41	5.07	4.82
	0.05	4.75	3.89	3.49	3.26	3.11	3.00
14	0.01	8.86	6.52	5.56	5.04	4.70	4.46
	0.05	4.60	3.74	3.34	3.11	2.96	2.85
16	0.01	8.53	6.23	5.29	4.77	4.44	4.20
	0.05	4.49	3.63	3.24	3.01	2.85	2.74
18	0.01	8.29	6.01	5.09	4.58	4.25	4.02
	0.05	4.41	3.56	3.16	2.93	2.77	2.66
20	0.01	8.10	5.85	4.94	4.43	4.10	3.87
	0.05	4.35	3.49	3.10	2.87	2.71	2.60
22	0.01	7.95	5.72	4.82	4.31	3.99	3.76
	0.05	4.30	3.44	3.05	2.82	2.66	2.55
24	0.01	7.82	5.61	4.72	4.22	3.90	3.67
	0.05	4.26	3.40	3.01	2.78	2.62	2.51
26	0.01	7.72	5.53	4.64	4.14	3.82	3.59
	0.05	4.23	3.37	2.98	2.74	2.59	2.48

Figure 11.9 *F*-Table Preview

As before, we will rely on a table to determine where our cutoff falls. To use the F-table, we need three pieces of information: significance level, between-groups degrees of freedom, and within-groups degrees of freedom. F-tables typically feature the two conventional levels of significance (i.e., .01 and .05). We'll use the default p-level of .05 for our study.

We have three groups, so we calculate our between-groups degrees of freedom as follows: $df_{Between} = N_{Groups} - 1 = 3 - 1 = 2$. Each of our individual groups has 9 participants, so each group has 8 degrees of freedom because $df = N - 1$. To get the within-groups degrees of freedom, we add all three groups together as follows: $df_{Within} = df_1 + df_2 + df_3 = 8 + 8 + 8 = 24$.

We now use the degrees of freedom to locate our cutoff on the F-table. First we identify our $df_{Between}$ across the top and our df_{Within} down the left-side column. Where that row and column meet is our F-cutoff, making sure to focus on the .05 significance level. (Note that sometimes there will be separate F-tables for the .01 and .05 significance levels, while at other times both levels will appear within the same table.) For our study, the cutoff is 3.40 (**Figure 11.9**).

Finally, we should indicate where our cutoff falls on our comparison distribution (**Figure 11.10**).

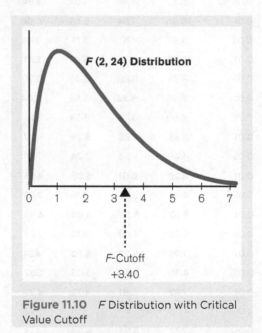

Figure 11.10 *F* Distribution with Critical Value Cutoff

Step 4: Determine Sample Results We've run the study by having participants in all three water level groups flip their water bottles

Group 1 (1/3 Full)				Group 2 (1/2 Full)				Group 3 (1/4 Full)			
PartNum	(X_1)	$(X_1 - M)$	$(X_1 - M)^2$	PartNum	(X_2)	$(X_2 - M)$	$(X_2 - M)^2$	PartNum	(X_3)	$(X_3 - M)$	$(X_3 - M)^2$
Emilia	11	4.33	18.78	Brett	17	1.67	2.78	Ladonna	15	−0.89	0.79
Jarrod	8	1.33	1.78	Saul	14	−1.33	1.78	Kyung	7	−8.89	79.01
Renay	3	−3.67	13.44	Nila	18	2.67	7.11	Leah	18	2.11	4.46
Robinson	2	−4.67	21.78	Maxine	24	8.67	75.11	Rajneesh	20	4.11	16.90
Kumari	13	6.33	40.11	Sung–Hyun	6	−9.33	87.11	Brooklyn	22	6.11	37.35
Shelly	17	10.33	106.78	Saburo	21	5.67	32.11	Rufus	17	1.11	1.23
Genna	1	−5.67	32.11	Sherika	5	−10.33	106.78	Calandra	18	2.11	4.46
Serena	1	−5.67	32.11	Xiaomeng	17	1.67	2.78	Thompson	19	3.11	9.68
Daisuke	4	−2.67	7.11	Lupe	16	0.67	0.44	Mariko	7	−8.89	79.01
ΣX	60	SS	274.00	ΣX	138	SS	316.00	ΣX	143	SS	232.89
N	9	df_1	8	N	9	df_2	8	N	9	df_3	8
M_1	6.67			M_2	15.33			M_3	15.89		

N_{Groups}	3	$df_{Between}$	$N_{groups} - 1$				df_{Within}	$df_1 + df_2 + df_3$	
		$df_{Between}$	2				df_{Within}	24	
Estimated Population Variance		S_1^2	SS/df	Estimated Population Variance		S_2^2	SS/df	Estimated Population Variance	S_3^2	SS/df
		S_1^2	34.25			S_2^2	39.50		S_3^2	29.11

Within-Groups Estimate of the Population Variance

$S_{Within}^2 = (S_1^2 + S_2^2 + S_3^2) / N_{Groups}$	34.29

Between-Groups Estimate of the Population Variance

Sample Means (M)		Deviation from Grand Mean $(M - GM)$	Squared Deviation from Grand Mean $(M - GM)^2$
6.67		−5.96	35.56
15.33		2.70	7.31
15.89		3.26	10.62
ΣM	37.89		
N	3		SS	53.49
Grand Mean	(GM)	$(\Sigma M) / N_{Groups}$	12.63
Est. Variance Dist. Of Means	(S_M^2)	SS/$df_{Between}$	26.74

$S_{Between}^2 = S_M^2 \times (N)$	240.70

F-Ratio

F-Ratio (F)	$S_{Between}^2 / S_{Within}^2$	7.02

Figure 11.11 Computations for One-Way Analysis of Variance (ANOVA)

to see how many attempts it took before they landed it upright. To determine whether the three groups are different, we need to get our two estimates of population variance (**Figure 11.11**).

First we'll calculate the within-groups estimate with the following formula, $S^2_{Within} = S^2_1 + S^2_2 + S^2_3 / N_{Groups} = (34.25 + 39.50 + 29.11)/3 = (102.86)/3 = 34.29$. Next, we use the variation between sample means to estimate the distribution of means' variance with the following formula, $S^2_M = SS/df_{Between} = 53.49/2 = 26.74$. Now, we can determine our between-subjects estimate of population variance using this formula, $S^2_{Between} = S^2_M (N) = 26.74 (9) = 240.70$. Remember, in this equation N stands for the number of people in each group (in this study, each group had 9 people).

These pieces allow us to calculate our F-ratio, with the following formula, $F = \dfrac{S^2_{Between}}{S^2_{Within}} = \dfrac{240.70}{34.29} = 7.02$.

Essentially, this indicates that the variance between our groups (240.70) was large compared to how much participants in this sample typically varied (34.29). Next, we should show where our F-score falls on the comparison distribution.

Step 5: Decide and Interpret It is clear from **Figure 11.12** that our sample's F-ratio of 7.02 exceeds the F-cutoff score of 3.40. Time to make our decision. Because our sample's results (Step 4) surpass the critical

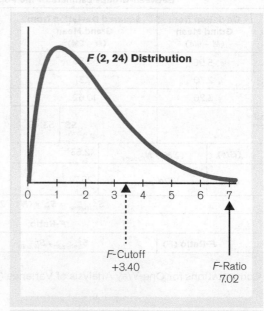

Figure 11.12 Sample Results on the Comparison Distribution

value (Step 3), we reject the null hypothesis (H_0) that the population means are equal ($\mu_1 = \mu_2 = \mu_3$). If we reject the null, we have found support for the research hypothesis (H_1) that the population means are not equal ($\mu_1 \neq \mu_2 \neq \mu_3$).

For a demonstration of the hand calculations involved in the one-way ANOVA, watch the video associated with this chapter.

 HAND CALCULATION VIDEO TUTORIAL: To learn more, check out the video Performing the One-Way ANOVA.

Communicating the Result

 When communicating one-way analysis of variance findings, we need to be careful not to overstate our data when our findings support the research hypothesis. That is, the ANOVA tests only to see if there is a difference among the groups. For this reason, we have to describe our conclusion in a way that conveys that there is a general difference in our groups without any further speculation about the nature of those differences. In our study we can say that different water levels appear to create differences in flipping success, but we can't say exactly where any specific differences may be.

Forming a Conclusion

 As exciting as it can be to find significant results, we always have to look at the study design with a critical eye. Because it's our own study, and we found significant results, it's easy to not evaluate it too much. After all, it worked, so why question it?

There's utility in looking back at the study. First, we can note strengths that lead us to feel better about our results or may help us generate ideas for future studies. Of course, we may also identify issues that are easily solvable with further study. In the case of our water bottle study, our sampling was problematic. Although we randomly assigned our classmates to conditions, those classmates all had an idea of our study's goal. Ideally, when we run a study, the participants are naïve to the study's purpose and hypotheses, so their inside knowledge doesn't affect the results. Before getting too excited about our flipping results, we should probably run additional studies to try to replicate the finding, this time with a less knowledgeable sample.

Your Turn 11.3

1. a. What causes the F distribution to have its shape?

   b. What does this suggest about the world we live in?

2. The athletic director at your school wants your help testing various visualization techniques to help athletes' confidence. She recruits 12 student-athletes from the women's soccer team, and you randomly assign them to one of three conditions: (1) Visualize their previous best performance. (2) Visualize 10 different plays or specific movements they will need to do. (3) Visualize the future outcome they most desire. After a session where athletes engage in visualization for 20 minutes, you give participants a measure of their sport-related confidence heading into their next practice. You end up with 4 soccer players in each visualization condition. Here are the scores for the groups: Best Performance (6.33, 4.59, 4.88, 6.92), Specific Moves (6.99, 5.81, 6.79, 4.76), and Ideal Future (5.74, 4.53, 6.98, 5.11). In the 12 player participants, you have 4 seniors, 6 juniors, and 2 sophomores.

   a. Step 1: Population and Hypotheses. (1) What would the populations be? (2) What would the hypotheses be?

   b. Step 2: Build a Comparison Distribution. What is the comparison distribution? What shape is it?

   c. Step 3: Establish Critical Value Cutoff. In order to know for sure there are differences between the visualization exercises, you need to establish a cutoff score. (1) What three pieces of information do you need to find the cutoff score on the F-table? (2) What is the F-cutoff associated with this information?

   d. Step 4: Determine Sample Results. (1) What test does she need to run? (2) What are the results? (3) What should you do with the information about class level? (4) Show Steps 2, 3, and 4 of the hypothesis testing on a diagram.

   e. Step 5: Decide and Interpret. What is the appropriate conclusion?

Statistics for Research

When people learn new skills, what happens to their brains? Do certain brain structures grow? Or, do new skills promote reconfiguration of existing neural connections? Questions such as these have inspired neuropsychologists to study how learning changes the brain's anatomy (Steele & Zatorre, 2018). For example, previous research reveals that learning to juggle for the first time can increase the thickness of the gray matter in the brain's cortex (Draganski et al., 2004) and brain plasticity, or ability to change neuron connectivity to improve brain functioning (Gerber et al., 2014). Other research shows that learning a foreign language (Mårtensson et al., 2012), studying for medical school exams (Draganski et al., 2006), and learning to play a musical instrument (Schneider et al., 2002) also relate to similar increases in the brain's gray matter thickness. Recent research also found that ice skaters who had long-term training exhibited greater brain plasticity compared to those who did not have the skill training (Zhang et al., 2021). But what about learning statistics? Does learning how to conduct a t-test or a one-way ANOVA also increase gray matter thickness?

Imagine that we conduct a study to answer that question. How would we conduct such a study? One option would be to measure the gray matter thickness of people after they learn statistics. But, even when they aren't learning statistics, people are learning how to do a new dance on TikTok or learning about the characters in a new show that they are binging. So, we need to have a control group that doesn't learn statistics, but goes about their everyday lives. We may also want to see if learning other things results in different changes from learning statistics. So, we could have a third group learn a non-statistics skill, like a foreign language. By including this group, we could see whether the potential brain changes that occur because of learning statistics differ from the changes that occur as a result of learning a language.

Here in the Statistics for Research section, we're going to learn about why we use ANOVA instead of running multiple *t*-tests, how to partition variance with sums of squares, and how to use mean squares to calculate the *F*-ratio. We'll also learn the assumptions of the one-way ANOVA, how to conduct post hoc tests, how to calculate effect sizes, and, finally, how to create an ANOVA summary table.

Where Do the Data Come From?

We need to recruit participants that are equivalent in every way, except for their learning experience (statistics, foreign language, or control). Let's imagine that we are able to collect a sample of 45 participants and randomly assign 15 to each condition. Both the statistics and the foreign language group complete a 6-week intensive training course, while the control condition doesn't take any class and goes about their daily lives. At the end of the 6-week period, we scan all participants in an MRI machine to measure the gray matter thickness of the brain area known for mathematical and language processing called the left inferior frontal gyrus. Our results reveal that participants in the statistics condition have a mean gray matter thickness of 3.09 mm ($SD = 0.04$), those in the foreign language condition have a mean gray matter thickness of 3.11 mm ($SD = 0.04$), and participants in the control condition have a mean gray matter thickness of 3.05 mm ($SD = 0.04$). Does statistical training increase gray matter thickness, relative to learning a foreign language or control condition?

One-Way Analysis of Variance (ANOVA): What We're Trying to Accomplish

Because we are comparing more than two conditions for one independent variable, we need to conduct a one-way analysis of variance. Indeed, the term "one-way" simply refers to the fact that we are assessing the impact of *one* **factor** (which

factor the independent variable in an analysis of variance. Typically, a factor has three or more levels.

level a condition of a factor.

is the terminology used in the context of ANOVA to refer to our independent variable) on the dependent variable. Typically, a factor in one-way ANOVA has three or more **levels,** which are factor's groups. In the context of our current study, we have one factor, which we can call Condition and which contains three levels (statistics condition, foreign language condition, and control condition).

So, we use ANOVA to look for differences between three or more levels of a factor. Now, one question we could ask is whether ANOVA is superior to running multiple *t*-tests. That is, couldn't we use a series of *t*-tests to compare the statistics condition to the foreign language condition, the statistics condition to the control condition, and the foreign language condition to the control condition and get an equivalent set of results? Well, we could, but there's an important reason why we shouldn't: When we perform multiple hypothesis tests, we increase the chances of making a Type I error. A Type I error, remember, occurs when the null hypothesis is true, but we falsely reject it.

Why We Don't Run Multiple *t*-Tests Our Type I error rate always matches our alpha, so if we run one hypothesis test with alpha set to .05, our Type I error rate for that hypothesis test is .05. The problem is that if we run multiple hypothesis tests, even though each test has an alpha set to .05, our overall Type I error rate increases in a predictable way. The key here is that we need to distinguish between our **testwise error rate** (which reflects the probability of making a Type I error for any particular test) and our **experimentwise error rate** (which reflects the overall Type I error rate when conducting multiple hypothesis tests). The reason why we don't want to perform multiple *t*-tests is that even though the testwise error rate for each *t*-test is equal to alpha (say .05), our experimentwise error rate increases by at least $1 - (1 - \alpha)^k$, where k is the number of hypothesis tests that we perform. **Figure 11.13** depicts the changes in the experimentwise error rate as we increase the number of comparisons we make using the *t*-test, each with an alpha of .05.

testwise error rate the probability of making a Type I error for any particular hypothesis test.

experimentwise error rate the overall Type I error rate for an experiment when conducting multiple hypothesis tests.

Number of Tests	Testwise Error Rate	Experimentwise Error Rate
1	.05	.05
2	.05	.0975
3	.05	.1426
4	.05	.1855
5	.05	.2263

Figure 11.13 Testwise Versus Experimentwise Error

As we can see, if we perform three *t*-tests (each with an alpha of .05), our overall Type I error rate (i.e., the experimentwise error) would be equal to $1 - (1 - .05)^3 = 1 - .95^3 = 1 - 0.8574 = .1426$, or 14.26%. That's a high error rate and would lead to a lot of false positive findings. In contrast, if we use ANOVA, because we are running only one hypothesis test, our testwise and experimentwise error rates will both be equal to .05 (or whatever we set alpha to be). This is the key reason why we will conduct a one-way ANOVA: Using one-way ANOVA limits our experimentwise error rate no matter how many levels we have for our factor.

Partitioning the Variance As we learned in the first half of this chapter, the one-way analysis of variance works by comparing the amount of between-groups variation ($S^2_{Between}$) to the amount of within-groups variation (S^2_{Within}). Because of this, we focused on the concepts and formulas designed to measure these two sources of variation so that we could calculate the *F*-ratio. Here, we'll explore these ideas again and develop our understanding a bit more, too.

The general idea of the analysis of variance is that we want to "partition" or divide up the total variance of the dependent variable into its subcomponent sources. For example, we can consider the total amount of variation in gray matter thickness for all our participants, regardless of condition. We can measure the total amount of variation in gray matter thickness using a metric that we encountered back in Chapter 3 called the sum of squares. The sum of squares reflects the sum of the squared deviation scores, and back in Chapter 3 we expressed this using the formula $SS = \Sigma(X - M)^2$. In ANOVA, we calculate the total variation of the dependent variable (which we'll call the **sum of squares total,** or SS_{Total}) in the same way, $SS_{Total} = \Sigma(X - GM)^2$ (**Figure 11.14**). The only difference between these formulas is that in ANOVA we note that we are looking at each score (X) relative to the grand mean (GM), just so that we don't confuse ourselves (there are multiple means to consider in an ANOVA after all).

Once we have quantified the total variation in the dependent variable, we can consider the sources of this variation. One source of the total variation is the between-groups variation, which reflects how much the condition means differ from the grand mean ($M - GM$). To calculate the total amount of between-groups variation, we square these deviations (to avoid them summing to zero) and then add them up. Also, because each mean is made up of a certain number of scores, we need to multiply each between-groups deviation score by its respective sample size (which we symbolize as N_k). So, our measure of the total between-groups variation is the sum of squared deviation scores,

sum of squares total (SS_{Total}) the difference between each score and the grand mean.

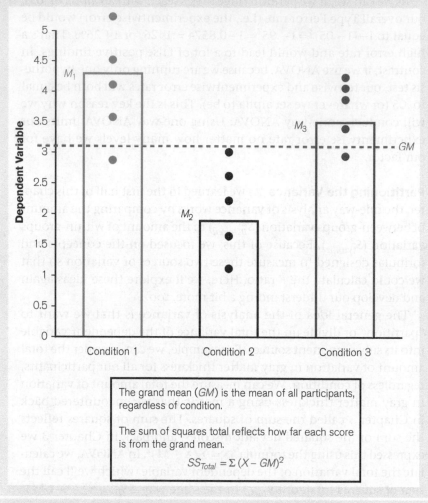

The grand mean (*GM*) is the mean of all participants, regardless of condition.

The sum of squares total reflects how far each score is from the grand mean.

$$SS_{Total} = \Sigma (X - GM)^2$$

Figure 11.14 Understanding ANOVA: Sum of Squares Total

sum of squares between (*SS*_{Between}) the sum of squared deviation scores, which measures the total between-groups variation.

$\Sigma N_k (M - GM)^2$, which is also called the **sum of squares between,** or **$SS_{Between}$** (Figure 11.15). As the effect of our manipulation gets larger, the sum of squares between gets larger as well.

A second source of the total variation is the within-groups variation, which reflects how much each score differs from its group mean $(X - M_{Group})$. To calculate the total of these deviations, we need to first square them, otherwise they would always sum to zero and thus wouldn't reveal how much variability exists within the groups. So, our measure of the total amount of within-groups variation is the sum of

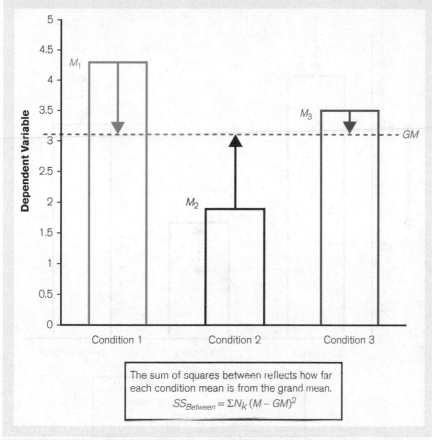

The sum of squares between reflects how far each condition mean is from the grand mean.
$$SS_{Between} = \Sigma N_k (M - GM)^2$$

Figure 11.15 Understanding ANOVA: Sum of Squares Between

squared deviation scores, $\Sigma(X - M_{Group})^2$, which is also called the **sum of squares within,** or SS_{Within}. When the scores within a condition are relatively consistent, they will be close to the group mean, and the sum of squared deviation scores will be small. When there is a lot of variation in the scores, reflecting measurement or random error, the sum of the squared deviation scores will be large (**Figure 11.16**).

So, of all the variation in gray matter thickness, some can be attributed to the differences between the conditions and some can be attributed to the differences within the conditions. We can express this idea mathematically, using the equation $SS_{Total} = SS_{Between} + SS_{Within}$.

Based on this conceptualization, we might consider why ANOVA is the analysis of *variance*, not the analysis of the sum of squares. Well,

sum of squares within (SS_{Within}) the sum of squared deviation scores, which measures the total within-groups variation.

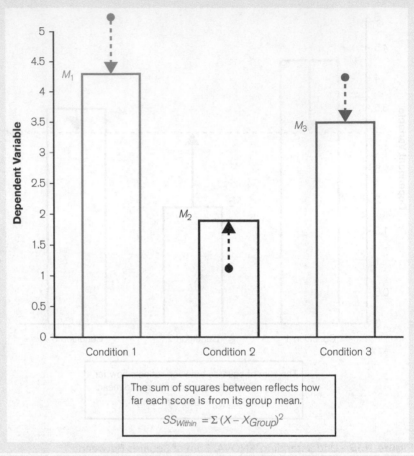

The sum of squares between reflects how far each score is from its group mean.

$$SS_{Within} = \Sigma (X - X_{Group})^2$$

Figure 11.16   Understanding ANOVA: Sum of Squares Within

there's a good reason. Just as we learned in Chapter 3, the sum of squares has a fatal flaw as a measure of variability. The sum of squares (whether it's measuring the sum of squares total, within, or between) is affected not only by the amount of variation, but the sample size. As we gather larger and larger samples, our sums of squares increase, even if the proportion of total, between, and within variation remains the same. For this reason, we need to divide each of the sums of squares by their relevant degrees of freedom before we can compute the F-ratio.

We learned how to calculate the degrees of freedom in the Statistics for Life portion of this chapter, but here we will develop our understanding a bit further. With degrees of freedom, the overall consideration is the number of independent observations minus the number of estimated population parameters. Let's start with the **degrees of freedom total (df_{Total})**. For our entire data set, we have N independent

degrees of freedom total (df_{Total}) the sample size minus 1, or the sum of the between and within degrees of freedom.

observations and one estimated population parameter (the grand mean). So, we determine the number of degrees of freedom total by taking the overall sample size minus 1 ($N - 1$).

For the degrees of freedom between, we said earlier that we determine this with the formula $N_{Groups} - 1$. This makes sense because the sum of squares between compares each group mean to the grand mean, so we are using the number of group means as the independent observations and we are estimating one population parameter (the grand mean).

For the degrees of freedom within, earlier we expressed this using the formula, $df_1 + df_2 + \ldots + df_{Last}$. Another way to think about this calculation is that we are taking the overall sample size minus the number of groups or conditions in our study. Again, this should make sense because in the calculation of the sum of squares within, we have N independent observations and we are estimating three population parameters (one mean for each of the three conditions). So, an equivalent way of expressing the formula for the degrees of freedom within is $N - N_{Groups}$, where N_{Groups} is the number of groups or conditions in our study.

Now that we have calculated the sums of squares and their relevant degrees of freedom, we can convert them to between and between-groups variances, and therefore the F-ratio. To calculate the between-groups variance, we divide the sum of square between by the degrees of freedom between. This essentially converts the total amount of between-groups variation to a measure of variance, or $S^2_{Between}$. This value is also called the **mean square between (MS_B)**, because it captures the mean amount of squared deviation between the study groups (the amount of deviation per df).

To calculate the within-groups variances, we simply divide the sum of squares within by the degrees of freedom within. This converts the within-groups sum of squares to the within-groups variance (S^2_{Within}). This value is also called the **mean square within (MS_W),** because it is the mean of the squared variation within groups.

Conceptualizing analysis of variance in this way allows us to present a new equation for the F-ratio that is mathematically equivalent to the one that we learned in the Statistics for Life portion of the chapter. The F-ratio equals the mean square between divided by the mean square within. Let's now use this approach to determine whether learning statistics leads to an increase in gray matter, relative to learning a foreign language or control condition.

mean square between (MS_B) the mean amount of squared deviation between the groups.

mean square within (MS_W) the mean of the squared variation within groups.

$$F = \frac{S^2_{Between}}{S^2_{Within}} = \frac{MS_B}{MS_W}$$

Your Turn 11.4

1. Which sum of squares (total, between, or within) measures the squared difference between each score and the grand mean?

2. Which sum of squares (total, between, or within) measures the squared difference between each score and the mean of the group to which it belongs?

3. True or False: Each additional analysis we do on a data set increases the experimentwise error.

4. A clinical psychologist wants to test the potential of everyday activities to reduce depression. She randomly assigns participants to one of four conditions. In the first condition, participants spend 4 weeks gardening. In the second condition, participants spend 4 weeks walking. In the third condition, participants spend 4 weeks performing yoga. The fourth condition is a control condition. After the 4 weeks, participants' depression levels are measured.

    a. When analyzing the data, the clinical psychologist decides to perform a series of *t*-tests to compare each condition to each other. Is this an appropriate analytic strategy?

    b. What is the factor for this experiment?

    c. How many levels does the factor have?

Hypothesis Testing with a One-Way Analysis of Variance (ANOVA): How Does It Work?

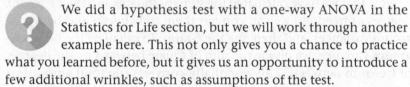

We did a hypothesis test with a one-way ANOVA in the Statistics for Life section, but we will work through another example here. This not only gives you a chance to practice what you learned before, but it gives us an opportunity to introduce a few additional wrinkles, such as assumptions of the test.

Assumptions of the One-Way ANOVA Like the other hypothesis tests we have learned so far, the one-way ANOVA has a set of assumptions that we must satisfy in order for the test to work properly. Assumptions are like prerequisites. Just as we can't register for a class unless we have satisfied the prerequisites, we can't complete an ANOVA unless we have satisfied the following assumptions:

1. *The dependent variable must be interval or ratio.* Our outcome variable must be measured at interval or ratio levels of measurement, and cannot be nominal or ordinal.

2. *Participants' scores must be independent.* The observations for each population are independent of one another. The score for each participant does not affect the score for any another participant.

3. *The populations' scores on the dependent variable are normally distributed, or we have large samples.* To satisfy this assumption, we either need to know that the populations' distributions are normally distributed, or we need to have a large enough sample to ensure that their sampling distributions are normally distributed due to the Central Limit Theorem.

4. *Our populations' variances are equal.* We assume that our populations have the same variances, and that our independent

variable affects their means, but not their variances. Thus, if the populations start with equal variances, and our manipulation does not affect those variances, then the populations should end with equal variances.

Step by Step: Hypothesis Testing with the One-Way Analysis of Variance (ANOVA)

Step 1: Population and Hypotheses For this analysis, we are going to compare three populations on our dependent variable, gray matter thickness of the left inferior frontal gyrus:

Population 1 (μ_1): People who learn statistics.

Population 2 (μ_2): People who learn a foreign language.

Population 3 (μ_3): People who do not learn statistics or a foreign language, our control group.

We next need to establish our research and null hypotheses.

Research Hypothesis (H_1): When performing a hypothesis test, like the one-way ANOVA, we might be tempted to specify exactly how the means will differ. But, sometimes in science, the results surprise us. To allow for this possibility, we will state a nondirectional research hypothesis and simply predict that the population means will not be not equal ($\mu_1 \neq \mu_2 \neq \mu_3$). In other words, our research hypothesis is that the gray matter thickness will not be the same across our three conditions.

Null Hypothesis (H_0): The null hypothesis for one-way ANOVA is always the same: there will be no differences between the populations. In other words, the population means are equal ($\mu_1 \neq \mu_2 \neq \mu_3$). Each of our three conditions will have the same gray matter thickness on average.

Step 2: Build Comparison Distribution The comparison distribution is an F distribution based on the degrees of freedom between the groups and the degrees of freedom within groups. For our current study, we have three conditions, so our degrees of freedom between is $df_{Between} = N_{Groups} - 1 = 3 - 1 = 2$. To get the degrees of freedom within, we first calculate the degrees of freedom for each of our three conditions: each condition has 15 participants, so the degrees of freedom is $15 - 1$, or 14. Therefore, our degrees of freedom within is $df_{Within} = N - N_{Groups} = 45 - 3 = 42$. Note that if we add the between and within degrees of freedom, they should equal degrees of freedom total, $df_{Total} = 45 - 1 = 44$.

Step 3: Establish Critical Value Cutoff Now we are almost ready to find our cutoff critical value. We just need to set our significance level first. Let's set our significance level to .05, meaning that our data needs to occur 5% of the time or less, in order for us to reject the null hypothesis. With a significance level of .05, we can refer to our F-table to find our critical value. As we just determined, our $df_{Between} = 2$, so we will scroll across to the second column of our table, and our $df_{Within} = 42$, so we will scroll down to the appropriate row (**Figure 11.17**).

Within-Groups df	Significance (Alpha) Level	Between-Groups Degrees of Freedom					
		1	2	3	4	5	6
1	0.01	4052	5000	5404	5625	5764	5859
	0.05	162	200	216	225	230	234
5	0.01	16.26	13.27	12.06	11.39	10.97	10.67
	0.05	6.61	5.79	5.41	5.19	5.05	4.95
10	0.01	10.05	7.56	6.55	6.00	5.64	5.39
	0.05	4.97	4.10	3.71	3.48	3.33	3.22
15	0.01	8.68	6.36	5.42	4.89	4.56	4.32
	0.05	4.54	3.68	3.29	3.06	2.90	2.79
20	0.01	8.10	5.85	4.94	4.43	4.10	3.87
	0.05	4.35	3.49	3.10	2.87	2.71	2.60
25	0.01	7.77	5.57	4.68	4.18	3.86	3.63
	0.05	4.24	3.39	2.99	2.76	2.60	2.49
30	0.01	7.56	5.39	4.51	4.02	3.70	3.47
	0.05	4.17	3.32	2.92	2.69	2.53	2.42
35	0.01	7.42	5.27	4.40	3.91	3.59	3.37
	0.05	4.12	3.27	2.88	2.64	2.49	2.37
40	0.01	7.32	5.18	4.31	3.83	3.51	3.29
	0.05	4.09	3.23	2.84	2.61	2.45	2.34
45	0.01	7.23	5.11	4.25	3.77	3.46	3.23
	0.05	4.06	3.21	2.81	2.58	2.42	2.31
50	0.01	7.17	5.06	4.20	3.72	3.41	3.19
	0.05	4.04	3.18	2.79	2.56	2.40	2.29
55	0.01	7.12	5.01	4.16	3.68	3.37	3.15
	0.05	4.02	3.17	2.77	2.54	2.38	2.27
60	0.01	7.08	4.98	4.13	3.65	3.34	3.12
	0.05	4.00	3.15	2.76	2.53	2.37	2.26
65	0.01	7.04	4.95	4.10	3.62	3.31	3.09
	0.05	3.99	3.14	2.75	2.51	2.36	2.24
70	0.01	7.01	4.92	4.08	3.60	3.29	3.07
	0.05	3.98	3.13	2.74	2.50	2.35	2.23
75	0.01	6.99	4.90	4.06	3.58	3.27	3.05
	0.05	3.97	3.12	2.73	2.49	2.34	2.22
80	0.01	6.96	4.88	4.04	3.56	3.26	3.04
	0.05	3.96	3.11	2.72	2.49	2.33	2.22

Figure 11.17 *F*-Table Preview

Unfortunately, as we can see, our *F*-table doesn't include a row for exactly 42 degrees of freedom within. Luckily, there are several internet-based critical values calculators that can tell use the exact critical value for 2 degrees of freedom between and 42 degrees of freedom within. An online critical values calculator tells us our precise cutoff is 3.22. So, we will need to observe an *F*-ratio that is greater than 3.22 in order for us to reject the null hypothesis (**Figure 11.18**).

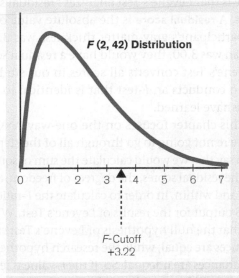

F (2, 42) Distribution

F-Cutoff
+3.22

Figure 11.18 *F* Distribution with Critical Value Cutoff

Step 4: Determine Sample Results Does learning statistics affect brain thickness differently from learning a foreign language, or learning nothing in particular (our control condition)? To answer this question, we need to calculate the *F*-ratio. Before we do that, we need to make sure that we've satisfied the four assumptions of the *F*-test.

The first assumption is that the dependent variable is interval or ratio. For the current study, we measured gray matter thickness in millimeters, which is a ratio variable. So, we have satisfied this assumption. The second assumption is that the scores are independent. The gray matter thickness for any one participant would not affect the gray matter thickness for any other participant, so we have satisfied the second assumption. The third assumption is that our population's scores on the dependent variable are normally distributed or that our samples are large. Well, in our current study, our overall sample size is 45, which should be large enough to ensure that we have satisfied this assumption.

The fourth assumption is that our populations have equal variances. Just like with the independent samples *t*-test, we assume that our manipulation affects the means of our populations, but not their variances. If this is the case, then our populations' variances should be equal because we recruited participants into the study from the same overall population.

To make sure, just like we did in Chapter 10 (you can find more about Levene's Test there), we can conduct Levene's Test for Equality of Variances, which is a modification of the one-way ANOVA. The main difference is that Levene's Test analyzes "residual scores" rather than raw scores. A **residual score** is the absolute value of a deviation score. So, if a participant's gray matter thickness was 3.50 and their condition's mean was 3.00, they would have a residual score of 3.50 – 3.00 = .50. Levene's Test converts all scores in our study to residual scores, and then conducts an *F*-test that is identical to the one-way ANOVA that we have learned.

residual score the absolute value of a deviation score $(x - M)$.

Given that this chapter focuses on the one-way ANOVA and not Levene's Test, we're not going to go through all of the steps of Levene's Test. Suffice it to say that we would calculate the sum of squares between and within for the residual scores, the degrees of freedom, and the mean square between and within, in order to calculate the *F*-ratio. Instead, we will look at SPSS output for the results of Levene's Test. What's important to know is that the null hypothesis of Levene's Test states that the condition variances are equal, while the research hypothesis states that the condition variances are unequal. So, if the *p*-value is less than alpha (say .05), then we will have violated the assumption. If the *p*-value is greater than alpha, we have satisfied the assumption. **Figure 11.19** presents the SPSS output for Levene's Test for our current study.

Test of Homogeneity of Variances		Levene Statistic	df1	df2	Sig.
Cortical_Thickness	Based on Mean	.035	2	42	.966
	Based on Median	.022	2	42	.978
	Based on Median and with adjusted df	.022	2	40.39	.978
	Based on trimmed mean	.034	2	42	.966

Figure 11.19 SPSS Output for Levene's Test

Based on this output, we can see that the *p*-value for Levene's Test is .97, which is greater than .05. Thus, we should fail to reject the null hypothesis that the variances are equal. In other words, we have satisfied the equality of variances assumption. If the *p*-value was less than .05, we wouldn't be able to perform the one-way ANOVA. Instead, we could run alternative tests, such as Welch's ANOVA or the Kruskal–Wallis test. Neither of these tests requires the equality of variance assumption.

Now that we have satisfied all four assumptions, we can calculate the F-ratio. The approach we take here is based on the logic we developed in this portion of the chapter, but leads to the same result as the one we encountered in the Statistics for Life portion of the chapter. In both approaches, the F-ratio is the ratio of the between-groups variance divided by the within-groups variance.

We start by calculating the sum of squares between, using the equation $\sum N_k(M - GM)^2$. For our current study, $SS_{Between} = 15(3.087 - 3.08)^2 + 15(3.107 - 3.08)^2 + 15(3.05 - 3.08)^2 = 15(.000049) + 15(.000729) + 15(.001024) = .00074 + .01094 + .01535 = .027$.

Next, we calculate the sum of squares within, using the equation $\sum(X - M_{Group})^2$. Using the data for the current study, $SS_{Within} = (3.11 - 3.09)^2 + \cdots + (3.04 - 3.05)^2 = .077$. Note that **Figure 11.20** presents all of the calculations needed to calculate the sum of squares within. If we add the sum of squares between and sum of squares within, we get the sum of squares total.

Now that we have the sum of squares, we want to determine the degrees of freedom. To calculate the degrees of freedom between, we take the number of groups minus 1. For our current data, $N_{Groups} - 1 = 3 - 1 = 2$. To calculate the degrees of freedom within, we take our overall sample size minus the number of groups. For our current data, $N - N_{Groups} = 45 - 3 = 42$. If we add the degrees of freedom between and the degrees of freedom within, we get the degrees of freedom total.

We're now ready to calculate the mean square between and mean square within, which are the last bits of information we need to calculate the F-ratio. To calculate the mean square between, we take the sum of squares between and divide by the degrees of freedom between. Using our current data, $MS_{Between} = \dfrac{.027}{2} = .014$. To calculate the mean square within, we take the sum of squares within and divide by the degrees of freedom within. For our current data, $MS_{Within} = \dfrac{.077}{42} = .002$.

Now that we have calculated the measures of the between and within variation, we can calculate the F-ratio, $F = S^2_{Between}/S^2_{Within} = MS_B/MS_W = 0.014/0.002 = 7.38$. So, our average difference between groups is about seven times larger than the average difference within groups. That seems like a lot, but is it big enough evidence to reject the null hypothesis? Exactly how surprising are these data?

Figure 11.20 Computations for One-Way Analysis of Variance (ANOVA)

Participant Number	Group 1 (Statistics)			Participant Number	Group 2 (Foreign Language)			Participant Number	Group 3 (Control)		
	(X_1)	$(X_1 - M_{Group})$	$(X_1 - M_{Group})^2$		(X_2)	$(X_2 - M_{Group})$	$(X_2 - M_{Group})^2$		(X_3)	$(X_3 - M_{Group})$	$(X_3 - M_{Group})^2$
1	3.11	0.02	0.00	16	3.09	−0.02	0.00	31	3.03	−0.02	0.00
2	3.04	−0.05	0.00	17	3.07	−0.04	0.00	32	3	−0.05	0.00
3	3.11	0.02	0.00	18	3.11	0.00	0.00	33	3.1	0.05	0.00
4	3.09	0.00	0.00	19	3.14	0.03	0.00	34	3.09	0.04	0.00
5	3.1	0.01	0.00	20	3.08	−0.03	0.00	35	3.06	0.01	0.00
6	3.06	−0.03	0.00	21	3.18	0.07	0.01	36	3.08	0.03	0.00
7	3.01	−0.08	0.01	22	3.05	−0.06	0.00	37	2.96	−0.09	0.01
8	3.05	−0.04	0.00	23	3.05	−0.06	0.00	38	3.06	0.01	0.00
9	3.07	−0.02	0.00	24	3.13	0.02	0.00	39	3.08	0.03	0.00
10	3.07	−0.02	0.00	25	3.13	0.02	0.00	40	3.02	−0.03	0.00
11	3.06	−0.03	0.00	26	3.04	−0.07	0.00	41	3.11	0.06	0.00
12	3.11	0.02	0.00	27	3.11	0.00	0.00	42	3.06	0.01	0.00
13	3.17	0.08	0.01	28	3.16	0.05	0.00	43	2.98	−0.07	0.00
14	3.09	0.00	0.00	29	3.14	0.03	0.00	44	3.05	0.00	0.00
15	3.16	0.07	0.01	30	3.13	0.02	0.00	45	3.04	−0.01	0.00
ΣX 46.3			**SS** 0.03	ΣX 46.61			**SS** 0.03	ΣX 45.72			**SS** 0.03
N_1 15			df_1 14	N_2 15			df_2 14	N_3 15			df_3 14
M_1 3.09				M_2 3.11				M_3 3.05			

N_{Groups} 3

$N_{Groups} - 1$ $df_{Between}$ $df_{Between}$ 2

$N - N_{Groups}$ df_{Within} df_{Within} 42

$Grand\ Mean = \dfrac{(\Sigma X_1) + (\Sigma X_2) + (\Sigma X_3)}{N} = 3.08$

ANOVA Table

Source	Sum of Squares	df	Mean Square	F
Between Groups	$\Sigma N_k (M - GM)^2$ 0.027	$N_{Groups} - 1$ 2	$SS_{Between}/df_{Between}$ 0.014	$MS_{Between}/MS_{Within}$ 3.08
Within Groups	$\Sigma(X - M_{Group})^2$ 0.077	$N - N_{Groups}$ 42	SS_{Within}/df_{Within} 0.002	
Total	$\Sigma(X - GM)^2$ 0.105	44		

Step 5: Decide and Interpret As we can see in **Figure 11.21**, our F-ratio of 7.38 is greater than our critical value of 3.22.

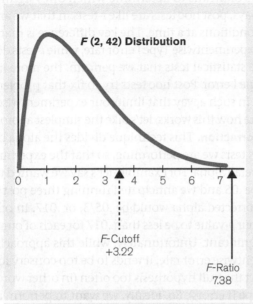

F (2, 42) Distribution

F-Cutoff
+3.22

F-Ratio
7.38

Figure 11.21 Sample Results on the Comparison Distribution

Thus, we can reject the null hypothesis, and conclude that our population means are not equal. In other words, the mean gray matter thickness for our statistics learning condition, foreign language learning condition, and control condition are not equal.

Post Hoc Tests: Where Is the Difference? Let's take a step back and think about what a significant F statistic tells us: the condition means are not all equal. Another way of saying this is that there is a significant difference between at least two of our study conditions. However, we don't know exactly which conditions differ, or by how much. That may not seem like a big deal, but there are actually lots of possibilities to consider. It could be that the foreign language condition has the thickest gray matter, the statistics condition is second thickest, and the control condition is the least thick. Or, it could be that both the foreign language and statistics conditions are not different from each other, but both of these conditions are significantly thicker than the control condition. Or, there could be some other pattern of differences.

For us to be able to interpret our findings, knowing where the differences are is crucial. To get that, we need to perform an additional set of tests to identify the differences between the conditions. These tests are called **post hoc tests.** The term "post hoc" translates

post hoc tests statistical analyses performed after rejecting the null hypothesis of an ANOVA and used to identify specific differences between pairs of groups.

to "after this" and reflects the idea that these are statistical tests that we conduct only *after* we obtain a significant *F*-test to compare all possible pairs of means to determine which ones significantly differ.

In some ways, post hoc tests are like *t*-tests in that we are always comparing two conditions at a time. The key difference is that post hoc tests control our experimentwise Type I error rate, while *t*-tests do not. Remember, the more statistical tests that we perform, the more likely we are to commit a Type I error. Post hoc tests try to fix that problem by divvying up our alpha in such a way that limits our experimentwise error rate.

To illustrate how this works, let's take the simplest approach, called the **Bonferroni correction.** This technique divides the alpha by the number of hypothesis tests we are performing, so that the experimentwise alpha equals the overall alpha. For example, let's say we wanted to set our overall alpha to be .05 and we anticipated running three post hoc tests. Our Bonferroni corrected alpha would be .05/3, or .017. In other words, we would need our *p*-value to be less than .017 for each of our three post hoc tests to be significant. Unfortunately, while this approach does control our experimentwise error rate, it tends to be too conservative, leading us to fail to reject the null hypothesis too often (in other words, we commit too many Type II errors). So, ideally, we want to perform a post hoc test that doesn't lead us to commit too many Type I or Type II errors.

Over the years, many such post hoc tests have been developed, each one differing in how it controls the experimentwise error rate. Some post hoc tests, like Scheffé, are conservative and maintain tight control over the experimentwise error rate, making it very hard to find differences between our study conditions. Other post hoc tests, like Fisher's LSD, are more liberal and have looser control over the experimentwise error rate, making it easier to find differences between our study conditions (**Figure 11.22**).

"
Statistically Speaking

An article in the student paper reports that students have different opinions about which local pizza place has the best food. Knowing that people have different preferences isn't very useful. Now, they need to do some post hoc head-to-head comparisons to see which ones are truly different from each other.

"

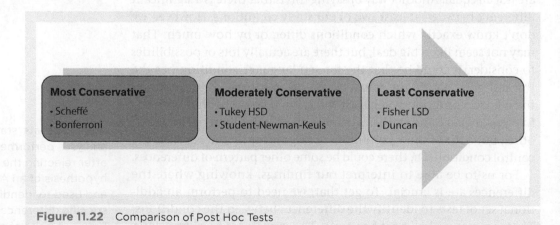

Figure 11.22 Comparison of Post Hoc Tests

Picking a post hoc test often comes down to a balance: We want to control our experimentwise error, while still having adequate power to find differences when they exist. Because of this, we are going to focus on a moderately conservative test called **Tukey's Honestly Significant Difference (HSD),** which is a post hoc test that seeks to identify the smallest difference (called the HSD) between any pair of means that would be significant at a specific level of alpha. We can think of the HSD as similar to the critical value cutoffs in our F-test because we must observe a difference that is larger than the HSD to obtain significance. That is, if differences between pairs of our means exceed the HSD, there is a significant mean difference. Overall, this approach does a good job of controlling our experimentwise error, but is also powerful enough to find differences between our study conditions, which is why it is a moderately conservative post hoc test.

Tukey's Honestly Significant Difference (HSD) a post hoc test that seeks to identify the smallest difference (called the HSD) between any pair of means that would be significant at a specific level of alpha.

Step by Step: Conducting the Tukey Post Hoc Test Returning to our research study example comparing gray matter thickness among our three conditions, we know that there is a significant effect of our independent variable because our one-way ANOVA was significant, but we don't yet know which conditions differ from each other. We need to conduct a post hoc. To perform the Tukey HSD, there are four steps that we must complete.

Step 1: Calculate the Differences Between Each Pair of Condition Means To complete this step, we subtract each mean from every other condition's mean. **Figure 11.23** presents all of the pairs of conditions, along with the condition means and the difference between each pair of means.

Which Pair of Conditions Are We Testing?		What Is the Difference Between the Means of Each Pair?
Condition 1	Condition 2	$M_{\text{Condition 1}} - M_{\text{Condition 2}} =$ **Mean Difference**
Foreign Language	Statistics	$3.11 - 3.09 =$ **0.02**
Foreign Language	Control	$3.11 - 3.05 =$ **0.06**
Statistics	Control	$3.09 - 3.05 =$ **0.04**

Figure 11.23 Calculation of Differences

Step 2: Establish the Critical Value Cutoff The Honestly Significant Difference (HSD). Now that we know the mean differences between our study conditions, we need to determine the HSD. Remember, the HSD is the critical value. We need our mean differences in Figure 11.23 to be larger than the HSD in order for us to conclude that the means are significantly different. However, unlike most critical values that we look up in a table (e.g., the F distribution), determining the HSD is a bit more involved. We calculate HSD using the following formula: $HSD = q_k \sqrt{\dfrac{MS_w}{n}}$, where q_k is the **Studentized Range statistic,** MS_w is the mean square within from our F-test, and n is the sample size in each of the conditions.

We start our calculation of the HSD by looking up the value of q in the Studentized Range Table. The Studentized Range statistic is the way that the HSD controls the experimentwise Type I error. The more groups we compare, the more we need to worry about Type I errors. Similarly, the smaller our sample size (captured by the degrees of freedom within), the more we need to worry about Type I error. So, the Studentized Range statistic q adjusts by getting larger when we have more groups to compare and smaller samples.

Thus, to find the value of q for our gray matter thickness experiment, we would go across the various columns until we reach k, which represents the number of conditions in our study ($k = 3$), because we are comparing three conditions. Then we go down the various rows until we reach the degrees of freedom within (df) from our F-test ($df = 42$). Note that our table does not contain a row for 42 degrees of freedom, so we will use the closest value, which is 40. As we can see, our q_k is 3.44.

Once we have found q_k, we are ready to calculate the HSD. Recall, that we calculated the mean square within to be .002 and have 15 participants per condition. Thus, our HSD is the following: $HSD = 3.44 \sqrt{\dfrac{.002}{15}} = 3.44 \times 0.012 = 0.04$, meaning that we need to observe differences between our condition means that are equal to or larger than 0.04 in order for us to conclude that the conditions significantly differ.

Step 3: Compare the Mean Differences to the HSD We can now look back at the differences between our condition means that we calculated in Step 1 to see if any are equal to or larger than the HSD. As we can see in **Figure 11.24**, two of the three differences equal or exceed 0.04. From this, we can conclude that the foreign language condition had a significantly larger mean gray matter thickness than the control condition, because the mean difference between this pair of means is 0.06, which is larger than the HSD. Similarly, we can conclude that the statistics condition had a significantly larger mean gray matter thickness than the control condition, because the mean difference between this pair of means is 0.04, which is equal to the HSD. The foreign language condition's mean gray matter thickness does not significantly differ from the statistics condition, because the mean difference is 0.02, which is smaller than the HSD.

Within-Groups df	Significance (Alpha) Level	k = Number of Treatments (Levels)										
		2	3	4	5	6	7	8	9	10	11	12
4	0.05	3.93	5.04	5.76	6.29	6.71	7.05	7.35	7.60	7.83	8.03	8.21
	0.01	6.51	8.12	9.17	9.96	10.58	11.10	11.54	11.92	12.26	12.57	12.84
6	0.05	3.46	4.34	4.90	5.30	5.63	5.90	6.12	6.32	6.49	6.65	6.79
	0.01	5.24	6.33	7.03	7.56	7.97	8.32	8.61	8.87	9.10	9.30	9.48
8	0.05	3.26	4.04	4.53	4.89	5.17	5.40	5.60	5.77	5.92	6.05	6.18
	0.01	4.75	5.64	6.20	6.62	6.96	7.24	7.47	7.68	7.86	8.03	8.18
10	0.05	3.15	3.88	4.33	4.65	4.91	5.12	5.30	5.46	5.60	5.72	5.83
	0.01	4.48	5.27	5.77	6.14	6.43	6.67	6.87	7.05	7.21	7.36	7.49
12	0.05	3.08	3.77	4.20	4.51	4.75	4.95	5.12	5.27	5.39	5.51	5.61
	0.01	4.32	5.05	5.50	5.84	6.10	6.32	6.51	6.67	6.81	6.94	7.06
14	0.05	3.03	3.70	4.11	4.41	4.64	4.83	4.99	5.13	5.25	5.36	5.46
	0.01	4.21	4.89	5.32	5.63	5.88	6.08	6.26	6.41	6.54	6.66	6.77
16	0.05	3.00	3.65	4.05	4.33	4.56	4.74	4.90	5.03	5.15	5.26	5.35
	0.01	4.13	4.79	5.19	5.49	5.72	5.92	6.08	6.22	6.35	6.46	6.56
18	0.05	2.97	3.61	4.00	4.28	4.49	4.67	4.82	4.96	5.07	5.17	5.27
	0.01	4.07	4.70	5.09	5.38	5.60	5.79	5.94	6.08	6.20	6.31	6.41
20	0.05	2.95	3.58	3.96	4.23	4.45	4.62	4.77	4.90	5.01	5.11	5.20
	0.01	4.02	4.64	5.02	5.29	5.51	5.69	5.84	5.97	6.09	6.19	6.28
24	0.05	2.92	3.53	3.90	4.17	4.37	4.54	4.68	4.81	4.92	5.01	5.10
	0.01	3.96	4.55	4.91	5.17	5.37	5.54	5.69	5.81	5.92	6.02	6.11
30	0.05	2.89	3.49	3.85	4.10	4.30	4.46	4.60	4.72	4.82	4.92	5.00
	0.01	3.89	4.45	4.80	5.05	5.24	5.40	5.54	5.65	5.76	5.85	5.93
40	0.05	2.86	3.44	3.79	4.04	4.23	4.39	4.52	4.63	4.73	4.82	4.90
	0.01	3.82	4.37	4.70	4.93	5.11	5.26	5.39	5.50	5.60	5.69	5.76
60	0.05	2.83	3.40	3.74	3.98	4.16	4.31	4.44	4.55	4.65	4.73	4.81
	0.01	3.76	4.28	4.59	4.82	4.99	5.13	5.25	5.36	5.45	5.53	5.60

Figure 11.24 Studentized Range Statistic Table

Computing the Effect Size for the One-Way ANOVA Our results suggest that there is an overall significant effect of condition, with the foreign language and statistics conditions not differing from each other in terms of gray matter thickness, but with both conditions significantly thicker than the control. However, just as with other hypothesis tests, statistical significance does not imply that the effect is large or important. We need to calculate a measure of effect size for the one-way ANOVA to make this determination.

Remember that the effect size measure we used for the *t*-test is called Cohen's *d*, and it measures the number of standard deviations difference between our study conditions. Recall from Chapter 10 that we calculated Cohen's *d* by dividing the difference between means $(M_1 - M_2)$ by the total variance, which we estimated using the pooled standard deviation (S_{Pooled}). For one-way ANOVA, we will use a similar conceptual approach: We will take the overall amount of difference between the means, this time measured by the sum of squares between $(SS_{Between})$, and divide that by the total amount of variability in the dependent variable as measured by the sum of squares total (SS_{Total}). This effect size measure is called **eta squared (or η^2).**

eta squared (or η^2) measure of effect size used in one-way ANOVA. Helps researchers determine the practical or meaningfulness of a significant result and is measured by dividing sum of squares between $(SS_{Between})$ by the sum of squares total (SS_{Total}).

$$\eta^2 = \frac{SS_{Between}}{SS_{Total}}$$

Our current study's $SS_{Between}$ is 0.027. As mentioned earlier, we can calculate the total sum of squares using the equation $SS_{Total} = \Sigma(X - GM)^2$ or by adding the sum of squares between plus the sum of squares within $(SS_{Total} = SS_{Between} + SS_{Within})$, which is $SS_{Total} = 0.027 + 0.077 = 0.105$. Plugging this into our equation for eta squared, $\eta^2 = SS_{Between}/SS_{Total} = 0.027/0.105 = 0.26$.

Eta squared indicates what proportion of the dependent variable's total variance is accounted for by the independent variable (i.e., the group to which a particular score belongs). In terms of the result, we want to interpret whether this is a large or small effect size. Like all effect size measures, there is some degree of subjectivity. What we consider a large or small effect changes by research discipline and by topic. As a result, the best way to evaluate effect size is by comparing the effect size that we observed to other effect sizes reported in the scientific literature.

If we don't have a robust literature to rely upon, we can refer to the following conventional standards: An eta squared of 0.01 is considered small, a 0.06 is medium, and a 0.14 or larger is considered large. Thus, the eta squared that we observed in our study of 0.26 corresponds to a large effect. In other words, learning statistics or a foreign language has a large effect on gray matter thickness, relative to our control condition. One last thing to note here is that eta squared goes by a different name when performed in the context of regression. When calculated for the purposes of measuring the linear association between two variables in a regression, we call eta squared R^2. We'll encounter R^2 in Chapter 15.

SPSS Video Tutorial: One-Way ANOVA

Now that we understand the steps of the one-way ANOVA, and are able to compute the F-ratio by hand, let's see how we would perform this analysis using SPSS. Watch this SPSS video for this chapter, which demonstrates how to perform the one-way ANOVA in SPSS.

> **Σ** SPSS VIDEO TUTORIAL: To learn more, check out the SPSS video tutorial One-Way ANOVA.

Communicating the Result

To communicate the results of a one-way ANOVA, we need to describe not only the F-test results, but also the post hoc test results. Typically, when reporting the results of the F-test, researchers create an *ANOVA summary table*, which is a standardized way to organize and present the results of a one-way ANOVA analysis.

Creating an ANOVA Summary Table As we have seen throughout this chapter, several values go into the one-way ANOVA. We must calculate the sum of squares between and within, the degrees of freedom between and within, the mean squares between and within, and, of course, the F-ratio. An ANOVA summary table simply presents all of this information in one place. Indeed, this summary table is identical to the output that SPSS provides in the output for a one-way ANOVA.

As you can see in **Figure 11.25,** the first column is called "Source" and indicates where the variance comes from. Recall that earlier in this chapter, we said that the key idea of ANOVA is that we partition the variance of our dependent variable into two sources: between-groups variation and within-groups variation. In addition to these two sources of variation, we have a third row that captures the dependent variable's total variability.

Source	Sum of Squares	df	Mean Square	F	p
Between Groups	$SS_{Between}$	$N_{Groups} - 1$	$MS_{Between}$	$MS_{Between} / MS_{Within}$	
Within Groups	SS_{Within}	$N - N_{Groups}$	MS_{Within}		
Total	SS_{Total}	$N - 1$			

Figure 11.25 Generic ANOVA Summary Table

The remainder of the table presents the numerical information for calculating the *F*-ratio. The second column in our ANOVA summary table lists the sum of squares, the third column lists the degrees of freedom (*df*), the fourth column lists the mean squares, the fifth column provides the *F*-ratio, and the final column provides the *p*-value.

For our current results, we calculated the sum of squares between ($SS_{Between}$) to be 0.027, so we would enter that value in the first column's first row. We had 2 degrees of freedom between and would enter that value in the second column's first row. We would continue entering all of the relevant values until the final **Figure 11.26** looks like this:

Source	Sum of Squares	df	Mean Square	F	p
Between Groups	0.027	2	0.014	7.38	.002
Within Groups	0.077	42	0.002		
Total	0.105	44			

Figure 11.26   ANOVA Summary Table

Writing an ANOVA Results Section In addition to preparing an ANOVA summary table, we will also communicate our results in a results paragraph. The general approach is similar to what we have used in other analyses. We state the type of test we performed, the specific hypotheses we tested, and the results of our *F*-test and post hoc tests. For the *F*-test results, we need to report the degrees of freedom between and within, the *F* statistic that we observed, the *p*-value, and the eta squared. In generic form, it will look like this: $F(df_{Between}, df_{Within}) = \#.\#\#, p = .\#\#, \eta^2 = .\#\#.$

Thus, a results paragraph for our current results would look something like this:

> We performed a one-way ANOVA to determine if there was an effect of condition on gray matter thickness. The results revealed a significant effect of condition, $F(2, 42) = 7.38, p = .002, \eta^2 = .26$. We followed up this significant result by conducting Tukey HSD post hoc tests, which revealed that participants in both the statistics condition ($p = .046$) and the foreign language condition ($p = .001$) had significantly thicker gray matter than participants in the control condition. Participants in the statistics condition did not differ from participants in the foreign language condition ($p = .39$).

Forming a Conclusion

We sought to test whether learning about statistics affects the thickness of the gray matter in the brain. We decided to compare the gray matter thickness of participants who learned statistics to participants who learned a foreign language, or nothing in particular. Because we compared three conditions, rather than two, we used a one-way ANOVA. The results of our one-way ANOVA revealed that there was a significant effect of condition. Unfortunately, the ANOVA results don't tell us which conditions differ. So, we also learned how to conduct post hoc tests to identify which conditions differ, and we found that learning statistics or a foreign language both increased cortical size and increased gray matter thickness compared to the control condition, but also that statistics and foreign language learning did not differ from each other.

Your Turn 11.5

1. Based on what you know about calculating an ANOVA, fill in the missing values:

Source	Sum of Squares	df	Mean Square	F
Between Groups	8	2	_____	_____
Within Groups	_____	_____	2	
Total	_____	20		

2. Using the ANOVA table that you just completed, calculate the value of eta squared (η^2).

Focus on Open Science: Conflicts of Interest

As researchers, we often spend a lot of time, energy, and money studying a particular topic. When a study "works," we may obtain various benefits, such as recognition as a top scholar, promotions, or financial benefits. As such, we can be susceptible to a **conflict of interest,** which, the U.S. government's Office of Research Integrity says, occurs "when an investigator's relationship to an organization affects, or gives the appearance of affecting, his/her objectivity in the conduct of scholarly or scientific research" (Office of Research Integrity, 2017).

One common conflict of interest occurs when a researcher has a financial stake in a study's outcome. Imagine a researcher works for a pharmaceutical company that is developing a new drug that could potentially be worth millions of dollars. When they test the efficacy of the drug, the company and the researcher have extra incentive to show

conflict of interest
occurs when a researcher is motivated to find a particular outcome for a study.

Due to multiple conflicts of interest, among many other ethically problematic scientific practices, the biotech company Theranos ultimately collapsed and its CEO, Elizabeth Holmes (pictured here), was sentenced to 11 years in prison for fraud.

Karl Mondon/MediaNews Group/Bay Area News/Getty Images

the drug works. This motivation to show an effect can compromise the integrity of the research. For example, it may lead some researchers to engage in previously discussed questionable research practices, such as HARKing and *p*-hacking. Because conflicts of interest are often problematic, most academic journals now require that scholars disclose potential conflicts of interest.

Become a Better Consumer of Statistics

As savvy statistics consumers, we need to be on the lookout for potential conflicts of interest. When we read about a new intervention, a new drug, or a new finding, we need to consider the information's source. We need to be on the lookout for conflicts of interest in our daily lives as well. For example, when we go to purchase a new smartphone, we may read reviews. We could find that information on leading tech websites that critique key features, on YouTube channels that compare phones, or read reviews on consumer websites. Whatever our approach, we need to consider the reviewer's authenticity and potential conflict of interest. For example, when people give paid reviews, could that be a conflict of interest that impacts their review?

Generally speaking, the more information we have, the better. Often we hear a finding like "children who participate in team sports have greater brain plasticity." That sounds like an intriguing finding, but should you rush to sign your children up for every team sport you can find? As consumers of statistical information, a question we need to ask ourselves when evaluating research is "compared to whom/what?" Who were the team sports kids compared to? Kids doing

FatCamera/iStock/Getty Images

Do team sports really increase brain plasticity? Smart consumers of statistics should be skeptical — and know what questions to ask.

nothing, or kids playing a solo sport (like golf), or kids playing board games together? The answer matters for how we interpret the statistical finding. Thus, when we hear a news report touting some research finding, we need to think about which groups of participants were evaluated, and whether the study had adequate comparison groups to make the claims that it is making.

Interpreting Graphs and Charts from Research Articles

When presenting the results of a one-way ANOVA, we not only need to present the means and standard deviations of the various study conditions, but we also need to indicate which of the conditions significantly differ. In other words, we need to convey the results of our post hoc results. One way that we can do this is through the use of subscripts. Subscripts allow us to indicate whether the means are significantly different from one another, or not. When two means share the same subscript, they do not significantly differ. When two means have different subscripts, they are significantly different.

Let's take a look at an example. In a study examining the effectiveness of electronic response devices (e.g., Clickers) on student participation, researchers divided students up into four conditions (Stowell & Nelson, 2007). Each condition heard the same 30-minute lecture, but the researchers manipulated how students could participate. In the standard lecture condition, the instructor periodically posed questions to students. In the hand-raising condition, the instructor provided students a series of multiple-choice questions for students to respond to by raising their hands. In the response card condition, students used cards to indicate their response to multiple choice questions. Finally, in the Clickers condition, students responded to the instructor's questions using an electronic device. The researchers recorded both the rate of participation among students and their performance on review questions and a quiz.

To present their results, the researchers provided the following table (**Figure 11.27**):

Table 1. Participation Rates and Learning Performance by Assessment Technique

Group	Informal Participation Ratio*	% Formal Participation	% Correct, Formal Review Questions	% Correct, Postlecture Quiz
Standard lecture	1.00	–	–	57_a
Hand-raising	1.20	76_a	98_a	60_a
Response cards	1.21	97_b	$92_{a,b}$	52_a
Clickers	1.11	100_b	82_b	60_a

Note: Means with different subscripts are significantly different from each other at $p < .05$ in a Tukey post hoc comparison.
*Ratio of number of responses received to the number of informal questions asked.

Figure 11.27 Sample Table (Data from Stowell & Nelson, 2007)

Within each column, the authors used subscripts to indicate which conditions were significantly different, according to a Tukey post hoc test. For example, for the variable % Formal Participation, both the response card condition and the Clickers condition had significantly higher rates of participation than the hand-raising condition. Without this information, readers couldn't determine which groups were significantly different (e.g., does the 97% participation rate in the response card differ from the 100% participation rate in the Clickers condition?). So, when we are interpreting tables from papers reporting ANOVA, we need to pay attention to subscripts.

Statistics on the Job

 To be successful in virtually any job, you need to be a problem-solver. The funny thing about problems is that there are often more than a couple of possible solutions. Which employee incentive program is best? Which treatment program is most helpful for your clients? Which marketing strategy will be most effective? There are many answers to each of these questions.

If you want to be good at your job, you have a vested interest in determining which solution is best. Even if they're all equally good

Companies like Apple will conduct multiple ad campaigns to determine which is most effective with consumers, similar to how and why we conduct ANOVA tests.

at producing a desired outcome, you'd want to go with the one that is most cost effective or least time-consuming. Making that determination is easier if you think about comparing a set of three or more possible solutions as an ANOVA problem. By trying several ways of tackling a problem, you can see if there is a difference among them. More importantly, if you find differences, you can systematically compare the solutions to each other to determine where the key benefits occur.

For example, a market researcher may run three different advertisement campaigns (print magazine, podcast, and social media) for a company to determine which is most effective, similar to how and why we conduct ANOVA tests. They would then track sales increases resulting from each type of ad. If they find an overall difference, identifying the exact format that was most effective would allow them to deploy their advertising budget most effectively.

Review Questions

1. What is the key question that an ANOVA seeks to answer? How is this represented in the research hypothesis and the null hypothesis?

2. Fill in the following table to compare and contrast the *t*-test for two independent samples and the one-way analysis of variance

	t-Test for Two Independent Samples	One-Way Analysis of Variance
Key concept		
Number of groups		
Where are we looking for differences		
Typical research design		
Comparison distribution shape		
Basis for population variance estimate		
Measurement level of the independent variable		
Measurement level of the dependent variables		
Distribution of population scores on the dependent variable		
Independent or dependent populations		

3. Which is the appropriate statistical test?
   a. A marketing executive wants to compare three types of consumer reward programs to see which one increases brand loyalty the most.
   b. A researcher wants to compare weight gain in mice when fed a new high-fat diet versus the standard laboratory diet.
   c. A speech language pathologist wants to compare the number of reading errors made by teenagers diagnosed with dyslexia when they use a standard font to the number of errors made when the same teens use a font labeled as dyslexia friendly.

4. What does the within-groups estimate of variance represent, and how is it calculated?

5. What are two chance factors that contribute to within-groups variation?

6. What does the between-groups estimate of variance represent, and how is it calculated?

7. Your friend Russel calculates an *F*-ratio of $F(2, 12) = 3.35$.
   a. What should he conclude?
   b. If instead of 5 participants per group he had 15, what would he conclude?
   c. Did his conclusion change? Why or why not?

8. One of the most common study strategies used by college students is rereading their notes even though it has been consistently found to be one of the least effective strategies for learning information (Kaminske, 2020). A professor decides to do a small demonstration to illustrate this for a class, dividing the class into 4 equal groups of 6 and assigning the groups to one of the following conditions: rereading notes, spaced practice, retrieval practice, or a combination method that involved both spaced practice and retrieval practice. The data from this experiment are presented below. Assume $\alpha = .05$.

	Reread Method	Spaced Practice Method	Retrieval Practice Method	Combination Method
Mean	63	80	79	87
Standard deviation	12.99	9.12	10.66	11.28
Sample size	6	6	6	6

a. What are your populations?
b. What is your null hypothesis? What is your research hypothesis?
c. What are your $df_{Between}$, df_{Within}, and df_{Total}?
d. Establish your critical value cutoff.
e. Determine your sample results. Assume that all assumptions for the analysis have been met.
f. What is the appropriate conclusion?
g. Calculate the value of eta squared (η^2). By conventional standards, is this effect small, medium, or large?
h. Conduct the Tukey post hoc test if it is appropriate and indicate which, if any, comparisons are statistically significant. If it is not appropriate, explain why.

9. A psychologist would like to examine the effects of sugar consumption on the activity level of preschool children. Three samples of children are selected with $n = 5$ in each sample. One group gets no sugar, one group gets a small amount, and the third group gets a large amount. The psychologist records the activity level for each child. The data from this experiment are presented below. Assume $\alpha = .01$.

No Sugar	Small Amount	Large Amount
4	5	5
2	4	8
6	5	4
2	1	2
1	5	6

a. What are your populations?
b. What is your null hypothesis? What is your research hypothesis?
c. What are your $df_{Between}$, df_{Within}, and df_{Total}?
d. Establish your critical value cutoff.
e. Determine your sample results. Assume that all assumptions for the analysis have been met.
f. What is the appropriate conclusion?
g. Calculate the value of eta squared (η^2). By conventional standards, is this effect small, medium, or large?
h. Conduct the Tukey post hoc test if it is appropriate. If it is not appropriate, explain why.

10. Define both testwise error rate and experimentwise error rate. How does conducting multiple t-tests to compare 3+ groups affect these error rates? How does an ANOVA address this issue?

11. Researchers were interested in determining whether participants with better sleep hygiene experienced higher levels of sleep quality. They measured participants' sleep quality (poor, fair, moderate, and excellent) and then measured their sleep quality using the Pittsburgh Sleep Quality Index (PSQI). Scores on the index range from 0 to 21, with lower scores indicating a healthier sleep quality.

a. What are your populations?
b. What is your null hypothesis? What is your research hypothesis?
c. Based on the SPSS output, is the homogeneity of variances assumption met?
d. Based on the SPSS output, what is the appropriate conclusion? Use an $\alpha = .05$.
e. Interpret the Tukey post hoc tests. Which conditions, if any, are different from each other? Again, use an $\alpha = .05$.

Descriptives								
PSQI								
			Std.	Std.	95% Confidence Interval for Mean			
					Lower	Upper		
	N	Mean	Deviation	Error	Bound	Bound	Minimum	Maximum
Poor	10	15.80	2.898	.917	13.73	17.87	11	20
Fair	10	13.50	2.677	.847	11.58	15.42	10	18
Moderate	10	9.60	2.221	.702	8.01	11.19	5	12
Excellent	10	7.10	2.331	.737	5.43	8.77	4	11
Total	40	11.50	4.200	.664	10.16	12.84	4	20

Tests of Homogeneity of Variances					
		Levene Statistic	df1	df2	Sig.
PSQI	Based on Mean	.575	3	36	.635
	Based on Median	.522	3	36	.670
	Based on Median and with adjusted df	.522	3	35.461	.670
	Based on trimmed mean	.591	3	36	.625

ANOVA

PSQI					
	Sum of Squares	df	Mean Square	F	Sig.
Between Groups	454.600	3	151.533	23.373	<.001
Within Groups	233.400	36	6.483		
Total	688.000	39			

Post Hoc Tests

Multiple Comparisons

Dependent Variable: PSQI
Tukey USD

(I) Sleep_hygiene	(J) Sleep_hygiene	Mean Difference (I − J)	Std. Error	Sig.	95% Confidence Interval	
					Lower Bound	Upper Bound
Poor	Fair	2.300	1.139	.200	−.77	5.37
	Moderate	6.200*	1.139	<.001	3.13	9.27
	Excellent	8.700*	1.139	<.001	5.63	11.77
Fair	Poor	−2.300	1.139	.200	−5.37	.77
	Moderate	3.900*	1.139	.008	.83	6.97
	Excellent	6.400*	1.139	<.001	3.33	9.47
Moderate	Poor	−6.200*	1.139	<.001	−9.27	−3.13
	Fair	−3.900*	1.139	.008	−6.97	−.83
	Excellent	2.500	1.139	.144	−.57	5.57
Excellent	Poor	−8.700*	1.139	<.001	−11.77	−5.63
	Fair	−6.400*	1.139	<.001	−9.47	−3.33
	Moderate	−2.500	1.139	.144	−5.57	.57

*.The mean difference is significant at the 0.05 level.

12. Based on what you know about calculating an ANOVA, fill in the missing values and then answer the following questions:

Source	Sum of Squares	df	Mean Square	F
Between Groups	17.34		5.78	
Within Groups		24		
Total	83.34			

a. How many groups were there?
b. How many participants per group were there?
c. If this was a research study, would you reject or fail to reject the null hypothesis? Assume $\alpha = .05$.
d. Calculate the value of eta squared (η^2). By conventional standards, is this effect small, medium, or large?

Key Concepts

Bonferroni correction, p. 426

conflict of interest, p. 433

degrees of freedom total (df_{Total}), p. 416

error variance, p. 396

eta squared (or η^2), p. 430

experimentwise error rate, p. 412

F distribution, p. 404

F-ratio, p. 401

factor, p. 411

grand mean (GM), p. 398

level, p. 412

mean square between (MS_B), p. 417

mean square within (MS_W), p. 417

one-way analysis of variance (or ANOVA), p. 392

post hoc tests, p. 425

residual score, p. 422

Studentized Range statistic (q_k), p. 428

sum of squares between ($SS_{Between}$), p. 414

sum of squares within (SS_{Within}), p. 415

sum of squares total (SS_{Total}), p. 413

Tukey's Honestly Significant Difference (HSD), p. 427

testwise error rate, p. 412

Answers to Your Turn

Your Turn 11.1

1. Answers will vary but should all feature the comparison of means from three or more distinct samples/groups/conditions. For example, you could use a one-way analysis of variance to determine if how people listen to music (vinyl, CD, phone) influences enjoyment.

2. (a) If the groups are likely to be from different populations or if they are likely from the same population (i.e., if there is a difference overall). (b) An ANOVA can't tell them which groups/sports are different from each other (e.g., are the soccer teams different?). It can only reveal if there are differences overall among all the groups.

3. (a) Any three of the following: The *t*-test focuses on two groups, ANOVA focuses on three or more. The *t*-test is used with a two-group design, the ANOVA with a multigroup design. The comparison distributions are different: *t* for *t*-test, *F* for ANOVA. The methods for estimating variance also differ with the *t*-test pooling variance estimates from the two samples, while the ANOVA uses a combination of within- and between-groups estimates.

(b) Both tests focus on comparing groups, use between-subjects designs, and need to estimate population variance.

Your Turn 11.2

1. (a) Set 2 would have come from populations with greater variance. (b) The sample means are more different from each other. Because samples reflect the populations they're drawn from, greater differences in means of samples suggests greater difference in the populations.

2. (a) The distributions should look identical and the means should all line up. (b) The distributions should not overlap.

3. With the *t*-test of two independent samples, we had information about individuals and used that to make inferences about a distribution of means. In the one-way analysis of variance, we instead have information about means and want to make inferences about the population of individuals.

4. (a) When an *F*-ratio is greater than 1, there is some treatment effect. (b) The between-groups estimate of variance is the combination of systematic and error variance, while the within-groups estimate includes only error variance. Because the error variance would be roughly equal, for the *F*-ratio to exceed 1, there has to be some systematic variance.

5. These will vary but should focus on how we tend to overemphasize between-groups variation and overlook within-groups variation. It should also be in clear in the example how it focuses on the question, "Are the differences between us greater than the differences within us?"

Your Turn 11.3

1. (a) The *F* distribution's shape indicates that for most comparisons, the *F*-ratio will be very close to one, with large *F*-ratios being increasingly rare. (b) This also points out something important about our world. Most of the time, groups of people are much more similar than they are different, and that systematic differences are fairly rare.

2. (a) (1) Population 1: Athletes who visualize their previous best performance. Population 2: Athletes who visualize 10 different plays or specific movements they will need to do. Population 3: Athletes who visualize the future outcome they most desire. (2) Research: The population means are not equal. Null: The population means are equal.

(b) (1) *F* distribution with a shape that ultimately depends on the between-groups and within-groups degrees of freedom.

(c) (1) Significance level (we'll use the standard significance level, $p = .05$), degrees of freedom between-groups ($df_{Between} = 2$), and degrees of freedom within-groups ($df_{Within} = 9$); (2) 4.26.

(d) (1) One-way analysis of variance. (2) $F = 0.25$ (Key Calculations: $GM = 5.79$, $S^2_{Within} = 1.14$, $S^2_M = .07$, $S^2_{Between} = .28$). (3) Nothing. That information should be ignored because it does not relate to the research hypothesis.

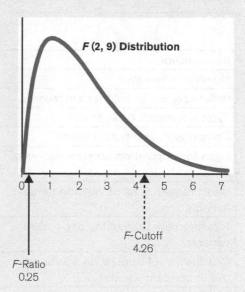

F (2, 9) Distribution

F-Cutoff
4.26

F-Ratio
0.25

(e) Our *F*-ratio of 0.25 failed to exceed the cutoff score of 4.26. Because our sample's results (Step 4) did not surpass the critical value (Step 3), we are not able to reject the null hypothesis (H_0) that the population means are equal. If we are unable to reject the null, the research hypothesis (H_1) that the population means are not equal is inconclusive.

Your Turn 11.4

1. Sum of squares total

2. Sum of squares within

3. True

4. (a) No. Running multiple *t*-tests would increase the experimentwise error rate, making it more likely to commit a Type I error. (b) The factor is the condition to which participants were assigned. (c) The factor has four levels, representing the four conditions.

Your Turn 11.5

1.

Source	Sum of Squares	*df*	Mean Square	F
Between Groups	8	2	__4__	__2__
Within Groups	__36__	__18__	2	
Total	__44__	20		

2. $\eta^2 = \dfrac{SS_{Between}}{SS_{Total}} = \dfrac{8}{44} = .18.$

Answers to Review Questions

1. The key question is whether all of the groups come from the same population or if the populations differ from each other in some way. The research hypothesis is that at least one of the groups comes from a different population than the others ($\mu_1 \neq \mu_2 \neq \mu_3$). The null hypothesis is that all the population means are the same ($\mu_1 = \mu_2 = \mu_3$).

2.

	t-Test for Two Independent Samples	One-Way Analysis of Variance
Key concept	Compare groups	Compare groups
Number of groups	2	3 or more
Where are we looking for differences	Between-subjects	Between-subjects
Typical research design	Two-group	Multigroup
Comparison distribution shape	*t*	*F*
Basis for population variance estimate	Pooled estimate from two samples	Between-group and within-group estimates
Measurement level of the independent variable	Nominal	nominal
Measurement level of the dependent variables	Interval or ratio	Interval or ratio
Distribution of population scores on the dependent variable	Normal or large sample size	Normal or large sample size
Independent or dependent populations	Independent	Independent

3. **a.** One-way analysis of variance
   b. t-Test for two independent samples
   c. t-Test for dependent means

4. The within-groups estimate of variance represents error variance. It includes measurement error, individual differences, and random error. It is also referred to as mean square within (MS_{Within}). To calculate it, you add the variance from each group ($s_1^2 + s_2^2 + \ldots$) and then divide by the number of groups (N_{Groups}). Alternatively, you can add the sums of squares for each group ($SS_1 + SS_2 + \ldots$) and divide by the degrees of freedom within (df_{Within}).

5. Answers will vary but could include extraneous variables, measurement error, random error, and individual differences.

6. The between-groups estimate of variance represents the systematic variance that is the result of our treatment/manipulation/intervention as well as error variance (the same as in our within-groups estimate of variance). It is calculated by adding up the squared deviation of each group mean from the grand mean (s_m^2), dividing by the degrees of freedom between ($df_{Between}$) and then multiplying by the number of participants per group (N). Alternatively, if the groups differ in size, you can multiply each group squared deviation score by its sample size ($SS_{Between}$) and then dividing by the degrees of freedom between ($df_{Between}$).

7. **a.** Russel should fail to reject the null hypothesis because the sample results do not exceed the critical value of 3.89.
   b. Russel should reject the null hypothesis and accept the research hypothesis because the sample results exceed the critical value of 3.23.

c. His conclusion changed. The df_{within} increased from 12 to 42, which means that the critical value changed from 3.89 to 3.23. The value Russel calculated went from being below the critical value to above the critical value.

8. **a.** Population 1 (μ_1): rereading method
   Population 2 (μ_2): spaced practice method
   Population 3 (μ_3): retrieval practice method
   Population 4 (μ_4): combination method
   b. Null hypothesis: the population means are equal ($\mu_1 = \mu_2 = \mu_3 = \mu_4$).
   Research hypothesis: the population means are not equal ($\mu_1 \neq \mu_2 \neq \mu_3 \neq \mu_4$).
   c. $df_{Between} = 3$; $df_{Within} = 20$, $df_{Total} = 23$
   d. critical value = 3.10
   e. $s_{Within}^2 = 123.2$, $s_m^2 = 102.92$, $s_{Between}^2 = 617.5$, $F = 5.01$
   f. Reject the null and accept the alternate; our population means are not equal.

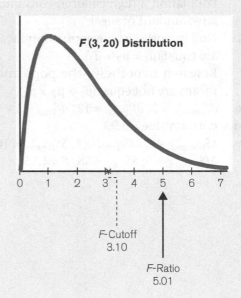

F (3, 20) Distribution

F-Cutoff
3.10

F-Ratio
5.01

g. $SS_{Between} = 1852.5$, $SS_{Within} = 2464$, $SS_{Total} = 4316.5$, $\eta^2 = 0.43$, large effect size

h. $q_k = 3.58$, $HSD = 16.22$

*mean difference reread method versus spaced practice method = 17

mean difference reread method versus retrieval practice method = 16

*mean difference reread method versus combination method = 24

mean difference spaced practice method versus retrieval practice method = 1

mean difference spaced practice method versus combination method = 7

mean difference retrieval practice method versus combination method = 8

(Comparisons with a * beside them are significantly different from each other at the $\alpha = .05$ level.)

9. a. Population 1 (μ_1): children consuming no sugar

Population 2 (μ_2): children consuming small amount of sugar

Population 3 (μ_3): children consuming large amount of sugar

b. Null hypothesis: the population means are equal ($\mu_1 = \mu_2 = \mu_3$).

Research hypothesis: the population means are not equal ($\mu_1 \neq \mu_2 \neq \mu_3$).

c. $df_{Between} = 2$, $df_{Within} = 12$, $df_{Total} = 14$

d. critical value = 6.93

e. $SS_{Within} = 48$, $MS_{Within} = 4$, $SS_{Between} = 10$, $MS_{Between} = 5$; $SS_{Total} = 58$, $F = 1.25$

f. Fail to reject the null; there is no reason to believe that the groups differ in terms of activity levels.

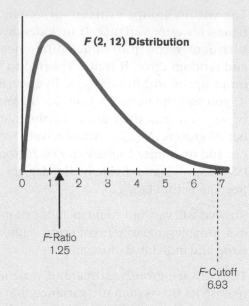

g. $\eta^2 = 0.17$, large effect (by conventional standards)

h. Post hoc tests are not appropriate because the F-test was not significant.

10. The testwise error rate is the probability of making a Type I error on any given test. The experimentwise error rate is the overall probability of making a Type I error when we conduct multiple hypothesis tests on a set of data. If we perform multiple t-tests, then the testwise error rate remains equal to alpha, but the experimentwise error rate increases as the number of tests is increased. The ANOVA compares all of the groups in a single hypothesis test, and therefore experimentwise error rate is not affected regardless of how many groups we have.

11. a. Population 1 (μ_1): poor sleep quality
Population 2 (μ_2): fair sleep quality
Population 3 (μ_3): moderate sleep quality
Population 4 (μ_4): excellent sleep quality

b. Null hypothesis: the population means are equal ($\mu_1 = \mu_2 = \mu_3 = \mu_4$)
Research hypothesis: the population means are not equal ($\mu_1 \neq \mu_2 \neq \mu_3 \neq \mu_4$)

c. The *p*-value for Levene's Test is 0.635, which is greater than .05, so we fail to reject the null hypothesis and can conclude that the variances of our conditions are not significantly different. We have satisfied the assumption.

d. Because the *p*-value is less than alpha, we conclude that there is a significant effect of sleep hygiene.

e. Participants who had poor sleep hygiene differed from both those who had moderate sleep hygiene ($p < .001$) and excellent sleep hygiene ($p < .001$) but not from those who had fair sleep hygiene ($p = .200$). Participants who had fair sleep hygiene differed from those who had moderate sleep hygiene ($p = .008$) and excellent sleep hygiene ($p < .001$). Participants who had moderate sleep hygiene did not differ from those who had excellent sleep hygiene ($p = .144$).

12.

Source	Sum of Squares	df	Mean Square	F
Between Groups	17.34	3	5.78	2.10
Within Groups	66	24	2.75	
Total	83.34	27		

a. There were 4 groups ($df_{Between} = N_{Groups} - 1$).

b. There was a total of 28 participants ($df_{Total} = N - 1$); therefore, there were 7 participants per group.

c. Critical value = 3.01, fail to reject the null hypothesis because the *F* is 2.10.

d. $\eta^2 = 0.21$, large

Sharpen your statistics skills with real-life data!
Check out OpenStatsLab.com, created by coauthor Kevin McIntyre, to practice running analyses for real published research studies.

Repeated-Measures Analysis of Variance (RM ANOVA)

E ver wonder how certain songs become hits? Every once in a while, a so-so-at-best song becomes a smash hit. Songs like "MMMBop" by Hanson, "Who Let the Dogs Out" by Baha Men, "Gangnam Style" by Psy, "Friday" by Rebecca Black, "Watermelon Sugar" by Harry Styles, and "Havana" by Camila Cabello manage somehow to be uber popular without being a lyrical or melodic masterpiece. More like "Havana ooh naa no thanks." So what gives?

As much as how we listen to music has evolved over the past few decades, radio has remained a steady influence. Music executives know that radio still has trend-setting power and that getting a lot of airplay is the key to having a hit song. To increase their songs' play numbers, the music labels make requests, do showcase shows for radio station program managers, and spend promotion dollars. Stations play certain songs more than others, those songs move up the charts, become hits, and some even become Baby Shark-like earworms that you can't get out of your head.

Essentially, this is how much of advertising works. Marketing professionals find ways to constantly expose us to their products. Whether it's through roadside billboards, internet pop-ups, in-app ads, or product placement in TV shows and movies, advertisers know that seeing things more builds connections to their products. It makes you think about how much control you have over the songs you like. Do our individual preferences really dictate our musical tastes, or are we being manipulated into liking certain tunes?

Statistics for Life

Granted, it is not surprising that music companies would try to create hits. However, as listeners, we must have some say over which songs we like. What we don't have is complete control over how much we hear a song on the radio. That matters because we know from previous psychology classes that "mere exposure effect" states that we like things more when we see them more or are more familiar with them (Zajonc, 1968). This is why

How do songs (especially bad ones) get so popular?

advertisements are a ubiquitous presence in our lives. The mere exposure effect also helps explain why the person you routinely see on your way to your afternoon class looks increasingly attractive.

If what we encounter more becomes more familiar, which increases liking, the same thing may happen with music. Perhaps the first time you hear a song, you're indifferent. You may even think a song about "MMMbopping" or "letting dogs out" is weird. But, after hearing it several more times, it worms its way into your head. Later in the day while walking or sitting in class, you can't help but hum it to yourself. It's catchy, so it must be good. Let's put the song exposure idea to the test.

Where Do the Data Come From?

First, we need to find a song and artist that is completely unfamiliar to people. This is critical because if we believe hearing a song more makes it more likeable, we want to be sure no one gets a head start by having heard the song previously. For popular music on the radio, people aged 18–34 are a key target demographic, so we'll want to recruit participants in that age range. Given that age, we'll pick a song from a new hip-hop artist Statistico who just signed a deal with Uncommon Deviation Records. We've settled on the new song, "Can't Beat My Beta (Alpha Dawg Remix)." Sound ridiculous? Maybe. But if exposure effects are real, then simply hearing this song several times should make it more likeable.

To see if this is the case, we go to where we know there will be a lot of 18- to 34-year-olds: the mall. There, we recruit people we see wearing headphones or air pods to participate in the "Immerse Yourself in Music" study. After making sure they are 18 and have provided informed consent, we play the song 5 times. Following the first, third, and fifth times listening to it, we ask each participant to rate "How much do you like the song?" using the following 1–10 scale where, "1 = Not at All, 5 = Moderately, 10 = Extremely." During one sunny Saturday afternoon at the mall, we manage to collect data from only 5 people. Everyone's ratings appear in **Figure 12.1**.

Participant	Conditions		
	First Listen (X_1)	Third Listen (X_2)	Fifth Listen (X_3)
Sharon	7	8	10
Greer	1	4	9
Ella	1	2	3
Raleigh	3	4	8
Jarron	2	6	5

Figure 12.1 Immerse Yourself in Music Results

Repeated-Measures Analysis of Variance (ANOVA): What We're Trying to Accomplish

Our key question is, "Does the song become more likeable after being exposed to it several times?" In other words, we need to answer whether the three measurements (i.e., after the first, third, and fifth listens) differ in some way, or if they are all the same. In more statistical terms, we are trying to determine if the three levels (first, third, fifth listen) of our independent variable (exposure) are the same (i.e., indicate no change), or if the levels vary enough to indicate a significant change or difference.

We can test that using the **repeated-measures analysis of variance** (also known as *one-way within-groups ANOVA*), which is a statistic that lets us determine if three or more scores from the same sample are significantly different when we have interval or ratio data and when we don't know the population's variance. We use repeated-measures ANOVA for within-subjects or repeated-measures designs when we measure each participant several times on the same dependent variable. This probably sounds a bit familiar because it closely parallels what we did with the *t*-test for dependent means (or paired samples *t*-test). The only difference is that back when we did the *t*-test, we only had two levels of the independent variable, and now with the repeated-measures ANOVA we have three or more.

We can use a repeated-measures analysis of variance in a few different situations:

1. Compare measurements for three or more levels of an independent variable from a repeated-measures design (e.g., What

repeated-measures analysis of variance (also known as *one-way within-groups ANOVA*) a statistic that lets us determine if three or more scores from the same sample are significantly different when we have continuous (interval or ratio) data and when we don't know the variance.

Want to review the repeated-measures designs and the *t*-test for dependent means? SEE CHAPTER 9.

flavor of ice cream—chocolate, vanilla, or strawberry—tastes best?).

2. Compare measurements from the same person over time (e.g., How do students' anxiety levels compare from the beginning, middle, and end of the semester?).

In each case the independent variable changes slightly, while the dependent variable remains exactly the same for each measurement. We treat the levels of the independent variable as categorical, while the dependent or outcome variable must be continuous (i.e., not categorical).

When comparing the one-way between-subjects analysis of variance (ANOVA) with a repeated-measures analysis of variance, nearly every feature is the same (see **Figure 12.2**). The only exception is that repeated measures focuses on within-subjects differences, while the between-groups ANOVA focuses on differences between different groups of people.

	Between-Groups Analysis of Variance	Repeated-Measures Analysis of Variance
Key Concept	Compare groups	Compare groups
Number of Groups	3 or more	3 or more
Key Question	Are the three+ groups different from each other?	Are the three+ levels different from each other?
Where Are We Looking for Differences?	Between-groups	Within-groups
Typical Research Design	Multigroup	Multigroup
Number of Factors	1 ("one-way")	1 ("one-way")
Comparison Distribution Shape	F	F
Estimate Population Variance?	Yes	Yes
Basis for Population Variance Estimate	Within-group and between-group estimates	Within-group and between-group estimates

Figure 12.2 What We Know: Between-Groups ANOVA Versus Repeated-Measures ANOVA Comparison

Your Turn 12.1

1. Provide your own example of a research question that would call for a repeated-measures analysis of variance.

2. A movie company wants to see which of their three summer movies is best, so they randomly assign 300 people to watch one of three movies and report how much they enjoy the film.

    a. Would we test this data using a between-groups or a repeated-measures ANOVA?

    b. How can we test a similar research question using the other type of ANOVA (i.e., whichever one we didn't use in Part A)?

Partitioning the Variance: Total In the previous chapter, we learned the foundational logic for the between-subjects analysis of variance and how we partition or divide up the dependent variables' variance to different sources (e.g., between, within). Here, we're going to use the same approach but modify it a bit for the within-subjects nature of our data.

Any time we collect a bunch of ratings from people, their responses will vary. Not only will there be differences between each person, but each individual will also give different ratings. For example, some people may like jazz music more than others, and some people may like jazz at certain times more than others. In statistical terms, we have many different sources of variance, some between people and some within. What we need to figure out is how much of the total variance comes from each particular source.

First, we figure out how much variability we have overall. When we did this for one-way, between-subjects ANOVA, we calculated the sum of squares total. For repeated measures, we're going to take the same approach. We want to know how much each score, from every participant, differs from the overall mean of everyone's scores (which we call the grand mean). To calculate the sum of squares total (SS_{Total}), we take each participant's score (X) in every condition, subtract the grand mean, square it, and then sum it all up $\Sigma(X - GM)^2$. Now, let's see where that total variance comes from and how much each source contributes.

$$SS_{Total} = \Sigma(X - GM)^2$$
$$SS_{Between} = \Sigma(M - GM)^2$$
$$SS_{Participants} = \Sigma(M_{Participants} - GM)^2$$
$$SS_{Within} = SS_{Total} - SS_{Between} - SS_{Participants}$$

Partitioning the Variance: Between-Groups Ultimately, to test our exposure hypothesis we need to focus on the between-groups or treatment effect (also called the "factor"), because that tells us whether our independent variable's levels had different effects on the dependent variable.

To find the between-groups sum of squares ($SS_{Between}$), we need to determine how much the mean for each level of the independent variable differs from the mean of all scores (i.e., the grand mean). Note that we're calling it between-groups to mimic what we did with one-way ANOVA, but in reality everyone is from one group, and what we're looking at is variance between the levels or conditions of our independent variable.

To calculate the between-groups sum of squares, we take each condition's mean, subtract the grand mean, square it, and then sum it all up: $\Sigma(M - GM)^2$. Pause for a second. This likely sounds similar to what we did for the SS_{Total}, but note that this time we calculate the deviation between the conditions means and the grand mean $(M - GM)$ instead of what we did for the total sum of squares, which was the deviation of the scores and the grand mean $(X - GM)$.

Partitioning the Variance: Within-Groups As with between-subjects ANOVA in Chapter 11, our end goal is to see if the variation from our independent variable exceeds the naturally occurring variation among our participants. In other words, we're comparing our between-groups variance to the within-groups variance. Though the between-groups variance calculation is similar for both between-groups and repeated-measures ANOVA, determining within-groups variance is a bit different.

In a between-groups ANOVA, any differences from a particular individual would affect one condition, because each participant gets only one level of the independent variable. That is, if a participant who always gives high ratings ends up in the study's first condition, that condition's mean would get inflated. That's a major problem, because our statistics cannot determine if the high score is from something about the participant, or from our treatment. A repeated-measures study minimizes this problem because any participant's uniqueness influences all conditions. In other words, that person who always gives high ratings now affects every level of the independent variable.

Within-groups variability comes from two sources: individual differences, called participant variance, and error. Participant variance reflects the differences in our individual participants. In our study of music exposure, we need to determine how much each participant is different from the other participants. For example, perhaps Sharon is a music aficionado who enjoys any new music, while Raleigh needs some time to warm up to a new song, and Ella dislikes most music most of the time. In practice, we can measure this by seeing how much each individual participant differs from the overall or grand mean. To do that, we first need to get each participant's personal average by taking the mean of their scores from all three conditions. For example, Sharon's personal average or mean $(M_{Participants})$ would be $(7 + 8 + 10)/3 = 25/3 = 8.33$. Raleigh's person mean is $(3 + 4 + 8)/3 = 15/3 = 5.00$. Ella's personal mean is $(1 + 2 + 3)/3 = 6/3 = 2.00$.

As we can see, a participant's mean (i.e., their personal average rating across all conditions) will deviate from the grand mean. Looking at subject or participant means helps us see if anyone generally gives high or low ratings, relative to the grand mean (or what everyone typically gives). In our study, participant means could vary based on how much a participant likes music in general, or hip-hop music in particular. It's also possible that some participants are more agreeable and generally give high ratings to anything (e.g., Sharon with a mean of 8.33), while others are perpetually harder to please and routinely give low ratings to most things (e.g., Ella with a mean of 2.00). In those cases, both are quite different from the grand mean (4.87). To calculate variance from participants or the participants sum of squares ($SS_{Participants}$ or $SS_{Subjects}$), we take each participant's overall mean ($M_{Participants}$), subtract the grand mean, square it, and then sum it all up $\Sigma(M_{Participants} - GM)^2$.

With individual differences accounted for, we're ready to calculate the within-groups sum of squares (SS_{Within}, sometimes called SS_{Error}). Because every participant is in every condition, we need to account for how participant variance impacts all conditions. For that reason, in repeated-measures ANOVA our within-groups variance (SS_{Within}) is actually an interaction between participants variance and condition (Participants × Condition). This allows us to look at participant patterns across levels of the independent variable. Calculating this, however, is a process of elimination. At this point we know how much variance there is overall (SS_{Total}), how much comes from between the conditions ($SS_{Between}$), and how much is due to participants' individual differences ($SS_{Participants}$). The only piece remaining is the within-subjects variances. Now, if $SS_{Total} = SS_{Between} + SS_{Participants} + SS_{Within}$, we can take the SS_{Total} and subtract out $SS_{Between}$ and $SS_{Participants}$ to give us SS_{Within} or ($SS_{Total} - SS_{Between} - SS_{Participants}$).

Your Turn 12.2

1. How is the process for calculating the between-groups sum of squares different in repeated-measures ANOVA from what we did with the between-groups ANOVA?

2. Why are participant's individual differences less problematic in repeated-measures ANOVA than in between-groups ANOVA?

Hypothesis Testing with a Repeated-Measures Analysis of Variance (ANOVA): How Does It Work?

Does hearing a song a lot make us like it more? When conducting a repeated-measures analysis of variance, our goal is to see whether our participants' scores vary across the different measurements of our dependent variable. Granted, any time we measure something several times, our measurements will vary a little bit. For our hypothesis test, the key will be whether the differences that are due to our independent variable are sufficiently large to consider them as not happening by chance.

Step by Step: Hypothesis Testing with the Repeated-Measures Analysis of Variance (ANOVA) As you will see, the steps here are nearly identical to what we did for the between-groups analysis of variance.

Step 1: Population and Hypotheses We first establish our populations and make a prediction about what we expect to find.

Population 1 (μ_1): People who hear a song one time.

Population 2 (μ_2): People who hear a song three times.

Population 3 (μ_3): People who hear a song five times.

Sample: Five people aged 18–34 who listen to music.

Similar to the between-groups ANOVA, we aren't designating a population of interest or comparison population. That's because we are interested in potential differences among all the groups. Consequently, our hypotheses for a between-groups ANOVA are fairly standard, and admittedly, somewhat generic:

Research Hypothesis (H_1): The population means are not equal ($\mu_1 \neq \mu_2 \neq \mu_3$). Essentially, we expect the three populations will have different means because we expect our treatment (i.e., exposure) to create systematic variance between the groups. We are using a non-directional hypothesis because, although we suspect that greater exposure will increase liking, it is also possible that greater exposure could decrease liking (i.e., hearing a bad song more makes it more annoying). In repeated-measures ANOVA, we also use nondirectional hypotheses because the *F*-test can't be directional (it tests only for overall difference). Therefore, we are going to predict a difference without stating what direction that difference may be.

Null Hypothesis (H_0): The population means are equal ($\mu_1 = \mu_2 = \mu_3$). In other words, the three populations will have the same mean.

Step 2: Build Comparison Distribution In ANOVA, Step 2 is straightforward because we will compare the *F*-ratio we get in Step 4 to a distribution of all possible *F*-ratios, known as the *F* distribution. Remember, our study's degrees of freedom dictate the *F* distribution's shape. Our key *F*-ratio will compare the between-groups variance to the within-groups variance, so we will need an *F* distribution based on those degrees of freedom.

We calculate our between-groups degrees of freedom as follows: $df_{Between} = N_{Groups} - 1 = 3 - 1 = 2$. To get the within-subjects degrees of freedom, we need the participants degrees of freedom ($df_{Participants}$). We calculate that by taking our total number of participants (n) and subtracting 1, as follows: $df_{Participants} = N - 1 = 5 - 1 = 4$. To calculate the within-groups degrees of freedom, we multiply the between and participants degrees of freedom as follows: $df_{Within} = (df_{Between})(df_{Participants}) = (2)(4) = 8$. Finally, the total degrees of freedom is the sum of all degrees of freedom, as follows: $df_{Total} = df_{Between} + df_{Participants} + df_{Within} = 2 + 4 + 8 = 14$.

Within-Groups df	Significance (Alpha) Level	Between-Groups Degrees of Freedom					
		1	2	3	4	5	6
1	0.01	4052	5000	5404	5625	5764	5859
	0.05	162	200	216	225	230	234
2	0.01	98.50	99.00	99.17	99.25	99.30	99.33
	0.05	18.51	19.00	19.17	19.25	19.30	19.33
3	0.01	34.12	30.82	29.46	28.71	28.24	27.91
	0.05	10.13	9.55	9.28	9.12	9.01	8.94
4	0.01	21.20	18.00	16.70	15.98	15.52	15.21
	0.05	7.71	6.95	6.59	6.39	6.26	6.16
5	0.01	16.26	13.27	12.06	11.39	10.97	10.67
	0.05	6.61	5.79	5.41	5.19	5.05	4.95
6	0.01	13.75	10.93	9.78	9.15	8.75	8.47
	0.05	5.99	5.14	4.76	4.53	4.39	4.28
7	0.01	12.25	9.55	8.45	7.85	7.46	7.19
	0.05	5.59	4.74	4.35	4.12	3.97	3.87
8	0.01	11.26	8.65	7.59	7.01	6.63	6.37
	0.05	5.32	4.46	4.07	3.84	3.69	3.58
9	0.01	10.56	8.02	6.99	6.42	6.06	5.80
	0.05	5.12	4.26	3.86	3.63	3.48	3.37
10	0.01	10.05	7.56	6.55	6.00	5.64	5.39
	0.05	4.97	4.10	3.71	3.48	3.33	3.22
11	0.01	9.65	7.21	6.22	5.67	5.32	5.07
	0.05	4.85	3.98	3.59	3.36	3.20	3.10
12	0.01	9.33	6.93	5.95	5.41	5.07	4.82
	0.05	4.75	3.89	3.49	3.26	3.11	3.00
13	0.01	9.07	6.70	5.74	5.21	4.86	4.62
	0.05	4.67	3.81	3.41	3.18	3.03	2.92
14	0.01	8.86	6.52	5.56	5.04	4.70	4.46
	0.05	4.60	3.74	3.34	3.11	2.96	2.85
15	0.01	8.68	6.36	5.42	4.89	4.56	4.32
	0.05	4.54	3.68	3.29	3.06	2.90	2.79
16	0.01	8.53	6.23	5.29	4.77	4.44	4.20
	0.05	4.49	3.63	3.24	3.01	2.85	2.74
17	0.01	8.40	6.11	5.19	4.67	4.34	4.10
	0.05	4.45	3.59	3.20	2.97	2.81	2.70

Figure 12.3 *F*-Table Preview

Because the *F*-ratio will be comparing the amount of variability between the groups to the amount of variability within, we only need the $df_{Between}$ and df_{Within} to determine our *F* distribution's shape. Thus, we will use an *F* (2, 8) distribution. Note that we calculate the other degrees of freedom because we will eventually need those for our ANOVA table, as well as for future calculations.

$$df_{Participants} = N - 1$$
$$df_{Between} = N_{Groups} - 1$$
$$df_{Within} = (df_{Between})(df_{Participants})$$
$$df_{Total} = df_{Participants} + df_{Between} + df_{Within}$$

Step 3: Establish Critical Value Cutoff We will use our comparison *F* distribution to determine if where our *F*-ratio falls. That will allow us to see if our *F*-ratio is large enough to surpass the cutoff. To use the *F*-table to find our cutoff, we need three pieces of information: significance level, between-groups degrees of freedom, and within-groups degrees of freedom. We'll use the standard .05 significance level, and we already know that our between-groups degrees of freedom was 2 and our within-groups degrees of freedom was 8. Looking at the table (**Figure 12.3**), the cutoff for our study is 4.46.

Finally, we should indicate where our cutoff falls on our comparison distribution (**Figure 12.4**).

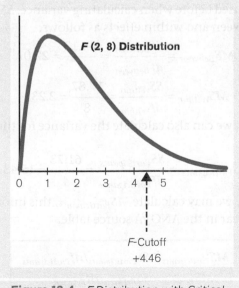

F (2, 8) Distribution

F-Cutoff
+4.46

Figure 12.4 *F* Distribution with Critical Value Cutoff

Step 4: Determine Sample Results We've run the study by having each of our 5 participants listen to the song "Can't Beat My Beta (Alpha Dawg Remix)" by Statistico, and indicate how much they enjoyed it after the first, third, and fifth times hearing it. To determine if greater exposure (i.e., hearing the song more), influences enjoyment of the song, we need to compare the between-groups variance to the within-groups variance. Note that we performed all calculations using a computer to ensure accuracy. Hand calculations may vary slightly due to differences in rounding.

As we can see in the computations (**Figure 12.5**), we calculate the total sum of squares with the following formula, $SS_{Total} = \Sigma(X - GM)^2 = 123.73$. How much of this variation is due to the number of times participants listened to the song (our independent variable)? That's what we need to figure out next. To find the variation between the conditions (i.e., the between sum of squares) we use the following formula, $SS_{Between} = \Sigma(M - GM)^2 = 44.13$.

Now that we know the amount of variation between the conditions, we need to find the variation due to individual differences, or the participants sum of squares, with the following formula: $SS_{Participants} = \Sigma(M_{Participants} - GM)^2 = 61.73$. Finally, we find the within-groups sum of squares with the following formula: $SS_{Within} = SS_{Total} - SS_{Between} - SS_{Participants} = 17.87$.

Because ANOVA focuses on variance, we now need to calculate the variance from each of our main sources (Participants, Between, and Within). We call this our mean squares (MS) and follow the general formula we've used before when calculating variance: SS/df. We tailor that to the between and within effects as follows:

$$MS_{Between} = \frac{SS_{Between}}{df_{Between}} = \frac{44.13}{2} = 22.07$$

$$MS_{Within} = \frac{SS_{Within}}{df_{Within}} = \frac{17.87}{8} = 2.23.$$

If we're curious, we can also calculate the variance for the participants as follows:

$$MS_{Participants} = \frac{SS_{Participants}}{df_{Participants}} = \frac{61.73}{4} = 15.43.$$

Note that while we may calculate $MS_{Participants}$, this information does not always appear in the ANOVA source table.

$$MS_{Participants} = SS_{Participants}/df_{Participants}$$
$$MS_{Between} = SS_{Between}/df_{Between}$$
$$MS_{Within} = SS_{Within}/df_{Within}$$

Participant	Conditions			$(M_{Participants})$
	First Listen (X_1)	Third Listen (X_2)	Fifth Listen (X_3)	
Sharon	7	8	10	8.33
Greer	1	4	9	4.67
Ella	1	2	3	2.00
Raleigh	3	4	8	5.00
Marron	2	6	5	4.33
Condition Means	2.80	4.80	7.00	Grand Mean (GM) 4.87

Participant	Condition	Score (X)	$(M_{Participants})$	SS_{Total}		$SS_{Between}$		$SS_{Participants}$	
				$(X - GM)$	$(X - GM)^2$	$(M - GM)$	$(M - GM)^2$	$(M_{Part} - GM)$	$(M_{Part} - GM)^2$
Sharon	First Listen (X_1)	7	8.33	2.13	4.55	−2.07	4.27	3.47	12.02
Greer		1	4.67	−3.87	14.95	−2.07	4.27	−0.20	0.04
Ella		1	2.00	−3.87	14.95	−2.07	4.27	−2.87	8.22
Raleigh		3	5.00	−1.87	3.48	−2.07	4.27	0.13	0.02
Marron		2	4.33	−2.87	8.22	−2.07	4.27	−0.53	0.28
Cond. 1 Mean		2.80							
Sharon	Third Listen (X_2)	8	8.33	3.13	9.82	−0.07	0.00	3.47	12.02
Greer		4	4.67	−0.87	0.75	−0.07	0.00	−0.20	0.04
Ella		2	2.00	−2.87	8.22	−0.07	0.00	−2.87	8.22
Raleigh		4	5.00	−0.87	0.75	−0.07	0.00	0.13	0.02
Marron		6	4.33	1.13	1.28	−0.07	0.00	−0.53	0.28
Cond. 2 Mean		4.80							
Sharon	Fifth Listen (X_3)	10	8.33	5.13	26.35	2.13	4.55	3.47	12.02
Greer		9	4.67	4.13	17.08	2.13	4.55	−0.20	0.04
Ella		3	2.00	−1.87	3.48	2.13	4.55	−2.87	8.22
Raleigh		8	5.00	3.13	9.82	2.13	4.55	0.13	0.02
Marron		5	4.33	0.13	0.02	2.13	4.55	−0.53	0.28
Cond. 3 Mean		7.00							

Grand Mean (GM) = 4.87			SS_{Total} = 123.73		$SS_{Between}$ = 44.13		$SS_{Participants}$ = 61.73	
$N_{Conditions}$ = 3		$n = 5$	$SS_{Within} =$	$SS_{Total} - SS_{Between} - SS_{Participants}$	17.87			
$df_{Participants}$	$n - 1$		4	$MS_{Participants} = SS_{Participants}/df_{Participants}$		15.43		
$df_{Between}$	$N_{Conditions} - 1$		2	$MS_{Between} = SS_{Between}/df_{Between}$		22.07		
df_{Within}	$(df_{Between})(df_{Participants})$		8	$MS_{Within} = SS_{Within}/df_{Within}$		2.23		
df_{Total}	$df_{Between} + df_{Participants} + df_{Within}$		14	$F_{Participants} = MS_{Participants}/MS_{Within}$		6.91		
				$F_{Between} = MS_{Between}/MS_{Within}$		9.88		

Figure 12.5 Computations for Repeated-Measures Analysis of Variance (ANOVA). (Hand calculations may vary slightly from the numbers reported due to rounding.)

As in the between-subjects ANOVA, the F-ratio tells us whether there is greater variance between the conditions than in how much people in those groups typically vary (e.g., within-groups). The most important F-ratio for answering our research question is the $F_{Between}$, because that tells us how variance from our independent variable compares to variance from within the group. We calculate that as follows:

$$F_{Between} = \frac{MS_{Between}}{MS_{Within}} = \frac{44.13}{2.23} = 9.88.$$

Again, if we're curious, we can also calculate the variance for the participants as follows: $F_{Participants} = \frac{MS_{Participants}}{MS_{Within}} = \frac{15.43}{4} = 6.91$. Note again that while we may calculate $F_{Participants}$, this information does not always appear in the ANOVA source table.

$$F_{Participants} = MS_{Participants}/MS_{Within}$$
$$F_{Between} = MS_{Between}/MS_{Within}$$

Next, we should show where our $F_{Between}$ score falls on the comparison distribution (**Figure 12.6**).

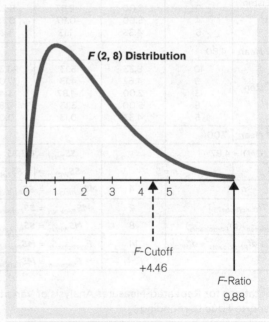

Figure 12.6 Sample Results for the Repeated-Measures ANOVA on the Comparison Distribution

We can also easily display our key calculations in an ANOVA source table (**Figure 12.7**).

Source	SS	df	MS	F
Participant	61.73	4		
Between	44.13	2	22.07	9.88
Within	17.87	8	2.23	
Total	123.73	14		

Figure 12.7 ANOVA Source Table

Step 5: Decide and Interpret It is clear from Figure 12.7 that our sample's F-ratio of 9.88 exceeds the F-cutoff score of 4.46. Time to make our decision. Because our sample's results (Step 4) surpass the critical value (Step 3), we reject the null hypothesis (H_0) that the population means are equal ($\mu_1 = \mu_2 = \mu_3$). Because we rejected the null, we have found support for the research hypothesis (H_1) that the population means are not equal ($\mu_1 \neq \mu_2 \neq \mu_3$).

For a step-by-step explanation of the hand calculations involved in the repeated-measures ANOVA, watch the video "Performing the RM ANOVA."

HAND CALCULATION VIDEO TUTORIAL: To learn more, check out the video tutorial Performing the Repeated-Measures ANOVA.

Communicating the Result

We have found support for our hypothesis that exposure influences song enjoyment. But the F-ratio does not tell us if exposure generally helped or hurt. To determine that, we can look at the means of the conditions. There, we see that the average rating after hearing the song once was 2.80, while the means after hearing it a third time (4.80) and fifth time (7.00) were progressively higher.

However, we have to be careful. That's because our F-ratio tells us only if conditions differ overall, and not if one condition is significantly different from the other (i.e., does hearing it 5 times make the song significantly more enjoyable than hearing it 3 times?). That's why, for now, our conclusion has to be general: we can say that greater exposure from hearing a song more produces higher ratings of enjoyment. In the next part of this chapter, Statistics for Research, we will learn how to determine if our conditions are significantly different from one another.

Forming a Conclusion

Before we make too much of a result and form a conclusion, we must always critically evaluate our methods to get a sense of the potential strengths and limitations. The biggest potential red flag in our study is that we had only 5 participants. As we know, such a low N can hurt both our ability to generalize and our power. Yet, one of the repeated-measures design's main benefits is that it compares participants to themselves, which limits within-groups variability. The result is a boost to power, allowing us to more easily find significant effects with smaller sample sizes.

That said, we still only had 5 participants from a local mall, so we should be careful about drawing any strong conclusion or generalizing too broadly. In addition, our study may be limited because we focused on hip-hop music. Thus, it is possible that greater exposure does not have the same effect on classic rock, folk, country, or rap music. Also, we studied the effects of listening to a song only up to 5 times. It is possible that exposure's effects are different after hearing a song 10 or 20 times. All of which suggests that further study is a good idea.

Your Turn 12.3

1. To help students plan for college, the school guidance counselor at North Shore High School, Ms. Actsat, will tour three colleges with students. On the trip, the seven students who signed up will visit Strawgoh University, Shermer University, and Bayside University. To help them avoid forgetting how they felt about each visit, immediately after each school, Ms. Actsat has students rate their interest in attending on a 1–7 scale (1 = Not at All Interested; 7 = Extremely Interested). Though Ms. Actsat won't say, she believes clear differences will emerge because she believes one of the schools has a "magical impact on students."

    a. Step 1: Population and Hypotheses. (1) What would the populations be? (2) What would the hypotheses be?

    b. Step 2: Build Comparison Distribution. What is the comparison distribution? What shape is it?

    c. Step 3: Establish Critical Value Cutoff. In order to know for sure there are differences

between the visualization exercises, you need to establish a cutoff score. (1) What three pieces of information do you need to find the cutoff score on the F-table? (2) What is the F-cutoff associated with this information?

    d. Step 4: Determine Sample Results. Each of the seven students on the trip gave 3 ratings, all in the same order (Strawgoh U, Shermer U, Bayside U). Here are each student's scores: Denzil (7, 2, 2); Ava (6, 6, 4); Rob (5, 2, 4); Vena (7, 3, 2); Daniilu (4, 5, 5); Izzy (6, 2, 3); Harshad (5, 1, 1). All of the students are 17 except for Vena, who is 18, and Daniilu, who is 16. (1) What test does Ms. Actsat need to run? (2) What are the results? (3) What should you do with the information about age? (4) Show Steps 2, 3, and 4 of hypothesis testing on a diagram.

    e. Step 5: Decide and Interpret. What is the appropriate conclusion?

2. Create an ANOVA source table to display the results.

Statistics for Research

Memories for most events fade over time. Some events, however, are so important that they seem to be frozen in our memories. These types of memories are called flashbulb memories. For example, lots of people report remembering exactly where they were and what they were doing when they learned about the attacks of September 11, 2001, in New York City. Events such as these, and the ultra-vivid memories that seem to be associated with them, have led researchers to investigate whether some events are less vulnerable to forgetting than typical memories. But are flashbulb memories actually long lasting and resistant to forgetting? Or do these memories fade over time too?

Well, research examining flashbulb memories suggests that people don't necessarily retain more information for flashbulb memories, but they do have a greater sense of vividness and a stronger belief that these memories are accurate (Talarico & Rubin, 2003). Perhaps one reason for this is that although people experience a lot of forgetting in the first year following a flashbulb memory event, they can maintain some detail of these memories for up to a decade later (Hirst et al., 2015). Overall, flashbulb memories seem pretty similar to everyday memories, and people merely perceive them to be "frozen" in time.

One commonality among flashbulb memory research is a focus on negative societal events, such as terrorist attacks, the assassination of political leaders, or tragic accidents like the 1986 space shuttle *Challenger* explosion. Could it be that flashbulb memories for negative events are subject to forgetting, while flashbulb memories for positive events are more robust? Let's imagine that we wanted to examine people's memories following a positive event, such as after a university's football team wins a national championship. How likely are people to incorrectly remember the details of where they were and what they were doing months or years later following a positive flashbulb event?

Here in the Statistics for Research section, we're going to learn about assumptions of the repeated-measures ANOVA (including sphericity), conducting a repeated-measures ANOVA with four conditions, conducting Mauchly's Test of Sphericity, conducting post hoc tests (e.g., Tukey HSD), and constructing a line graph to depict the results.

Where Do the Data Come From?

Every January, one lucky campus will experience the joys of their college football team winning the national championship. If we wanted to study flashbulb memories for positive events, we could contact students at the championship-winning

Reed Hoffmann/AP Photo

university and ask them to answer a series of questions about their
experiences immediately following the game. For example, we could
ask them about where they were, who they were with, and what they
were doing during the game. We could also ask participants to describe
different parts of the game itself. Who was leading at the end of each
quarter? What big plays occurred?

Given that these experiences had just occurred, we would treat these
responses as "correct" answers. We could then track our participants
for several months. After six months, we could contact our participants
and ask them to complete the same memory quiz again. Any deviation
in response could be treated as an incorrect answer, and participants'
number of incorrect answers would be our dependent variable. We
could do the same procedure again after 12 months, 24 months, and
36 months to test whether participants' memories for this positive
event stay the same or change over time. Essentially, do participants
have more incorrect answers on our memory quiz as time goes by?

Repeated-Measures Analysis of Variance
(RM ANOVA): What We're Trying to Accomplish

Let's imagine that we perform our study on 12 participants
and find that after six months, the participants provide an
average of 10.67 (SD = 3.08) incorrect answers on the memory quiz (that is, they provide responses that differ from what they said
immediately after the game). Further, after 12 months, we measure
the participants again and find that they provide 10.25 (SD = 2.42)
incorrect answers. At 24 months, the participants provide 14.17 (SD =
2.40) incorrect answers. Finally, at 36 months after the championship

game, participants provide 15.58 (SD = 2.74) incorrect answers to the memory quiz.

What does this tell us about the nature of flashbulb memories for positive events? Well, not much yet. It does appear that participants' memories for the flashbulb event is getting worse over time. But, we need to determine whether we have evidence that these means are greater than what we would expect due to sampling variation if the population mean is actually zero (i.e., no difference over time).

We also want to consider the differences among the participants. One of the main advantages of the repeated-measures ANOVA is that we can calculate the amount of variability in our dependent measurements due to differences among our participants and then remove this extra source of variability from our analyses. For example, imagine that some participants in our flashbulb memory study are big-time football fanatics, while others aren't that much into sports. The football fans may have a distinct advantage when it comes to remembering certain aspects of the game, and therefore they may be more able to remember these details over time, compared to the nonfans.

When we are conducting our analysis of the effect of time on memory for a flashbulb event, we don't want a participant's fanship level affecting our conclusions. So, the repeated-measures ANOVA helps us remove this unwanted source of variation in participants' scores, which earlier in this chapter we called the sum of squares participants ($SS_{Participants}$), so that we are examining only the effects of our independent variable (time) on the dependent variable (number of incorrect responses on the memory quiz).

Hypothesis Testing with a Repeated-Measures Analysis of Variance (RM ANOVA): How Does It Work?

The main idea behind repeated-measures ANOVA is that we will identify where the variance in participants' memory scores comes from. Does the variance come from the independent variable? If so, we should observe a relatively large value for the sum of squares between ($SS_{Between}$). Does the variance come from the differences between participants? If so, we should observe a large value for the sum of squares participants ($SS_{Participants}$). Is there a lot of variability that is not due to our independent variable or differences between participants? If so, we should observe a large value for the sum of squares within (SS_{Within}). Of course, to make our final conclusion about significance, we will need to compare these numbers to each other, which is what we do when we calculate the F-ratio.

Assumptions of the Repeated-Measures ANOVA The repeated-measures ANOVA has several assumptions that we must satisfy in order for it to work properly. If we don't satisfy these assumptions, we may lose our ability to determine the probability (i.e., *p*-value) for the *F* statistic that we calculate. If we can't determine the *p*-value, we can't make a decision regarding the null hypothesis. So, it's essential that we satisfy the following assumptions:

1. *The dependent variable must be interval or ratio.* We must measure our outcome variable at interval or ratio levels of measurement, and we cannot use nominal- or ordinal-level data.

2. *The sample is randomly selected from the population, and the scores are independent between participants.* To satisfy this assumption, the participants must be selected at random from the population, and the scores of any one participant may not affect the scores of any other participant.

3. *The dependent variable for each level of the repeated measure must be normally distributed, or the sample must be sufficiently large.* Remember that according to the Central Limit Theorem, a distribution of means will be normal if the population is normally distributed or if we have a large sample. Because it's difficult to know the population distribution's shape, most researchers try to obtain large samples in order to satisfy this assumption.

4. *The variances of the difference scores for all possible pairs of measurements within participants are equal.* This is called the **sphericity assumption.** This assumption is similar to the equality of variances assumption that we discussed in Chapter 11, but instead of assuming that each condition's variances are equal, we are assuming that the difference scores from each pair of measurements have equal variances. This means that if we were to compute a difference score between one pair of measurements (say, Time 1 vs. Time 2) and then calculate the variance ($S^2_{Time-Time\ 2}$) of those difference scores, we should get approximately the same amount of variance for any other pair of measurements (say, Time 1 vs. Time 3).

sphericity assumption assumption of repeated-measures ANOVA that states that all pairs of difference scores should have equal variances.

Your Turn 12.4

1. In a study of political advertisements' effectiveness, a researcher asks probable voters to rate a political candidate. The voters then watch a new campaign ad and once again rate the candidate. The voters then discuss their perceptions as a group and re-rate the candidate one final time. What assumption of repeated-measures ANOVA would this violate?

2. How is the sphericity assumption similar to the equality of variances assumption? How is it different?

Step by Step: Hypothesis Testing with the Repeated-Measures Analysis of Variance (RM ANOVA) As we saw in the first half of this chapter, conducting a repeated-measures ANOVA is pretty straightforward. We need to start by defining our populations and establishing the null and research hypotheses.

Step 1: Population and Hypotheses For our study of flashbulb memories, we will compare the number of incorrect answers to our memory quiz at four different time points. Thus, even though we are measuring the same people multiple times, we are using their data to represent four distinct populations:

Population 1 (μ_1): People's memory errors after 6 months.

Population 2 (μ_2): People's memory errors after 12 months.

Population 3 (μ_3): People's memory errors after 24 months.

Population 4 (μ_4): People's memory errors after 36 months

Sample: Twelve college students whose university just won the national championship.

Research Hypothesis (H_1): Our expectation is that people will have more incorrect answers to the memory quiz as time goes on. That is, their memories for the flashbulb event will get worse over time. However, because it's possible that flashbulb memories work differently from most memories, we will set a nondirectional research hypothesis: the population means are not equal ($\mu_1 \neq \mu_2 \neq \mu_3 \neq \mu_4$).

Null Hypothesis (H_0): The population means are equal ($\mu_1 = \mu_2 = \mu_3 = \mu_4$). In other words, the number of incorrect answers to the memory quiz will be the same over time.

Step 2: Build Comparison Distribution We need to know what values of the F-ratio we should expect to see when the null hypothesis is true. So, we need to determine our degrees of freedom because this will determine the exact shape of the F distribution that we will use to establish our critical value.

As we learned in the first half of this chapter, we calculate the between-groups degrees of freedom using the formula $N_{Groups} - 1$. Because our flashbulb memory study had four measurements, our degrees of freedom between is $df_{Between} = N_{Groups} - 1 = 4 - 1 = 3$. To calculate the participants degrees of freedom, we use the formula $N - 1$. For our current study, we had 12 participants, so our degrees of freedom participants is $df_{Participants} = N - 1 = 12 - 1 = 11$. Next, we need to calculate the within-groups degrees of freedom using the formula $(df_{Between})(df_{Participants})$. So, for the current study, our degrees of freedom within $= df_{Within} = (df_{Between})(df_{Participants}) = (3)(11) = 33$. Finally, to calculate the total degrees of freedom, we just add up all of the values we just calculated: $df_{Total} = df_{Between} + df_{Participants} + df_{Within} = 3 + 11 + 33 = 47$.

Within-Groups df	Significance (Alpha) Level	Between-Groups Degrees of Freedom					
		1	2	3	4	5	6
18	0.01	8.29	6.01	5.09	4.58	4.25	4.02
	0.05	4.41	3.56	3.16	2.93	2.77	2.66
19	0.01	8.19	5.93	5.01	4.50	4.17	3.94
	0.05	4.38	3.52	3.13	2.90	2.74	2.63
20	0.01	8.10	5.85	4.94	4.43	4.10	3.87
	0.05	4.35	3.49	3.10	2.87	2.71	2.60
21	0.01	8.02	5.78	4.88	4.37	4.04	3.81
	0.05	4.33	3.47	3.07	2.84	2.69	2.57
22	0.01	7.95	5.72	4.82	4.31	3.99	3.76
	0.05	4.30	3.44	3.05	2.82	2.66	2.55
23	0.01	7.88	5.66	4.77	4.26	3.94	3.71
	0.05	4.28	3.42	3.03	2.80	2.64	2.53
24	0.01	7.82	5.61	4.72	4.22	3.90	3.67
	0.05	4.26	3.40	3.01	2.78	2.62	2.51
25	0.01	7.77	5.57	4.68	4.18	3.86	3.63
	0.05	4.24	3.39	2.99	2.76	2.60	2.49
26	0.01	7.72	5.53	4.64	4.14	3.82	3.59
	0.05	4.23	3.37	2.98	2.74	2.59	2.48
27	0.01	7.68	5.49	4.60	4.11	3.79	3.56
	0.05	4.21	3.36	2.96	2.73	2.57	2.46
28	0.01	7.64	5.45	4.57	4.08	3.75	3.53
	0.05	4.20	3.34	2.95	2.72	2.56	2.45
29	0.01	7.60	5.42	4.54	4.05	3.73	3.50
	0.05	4.18	3.33	2.94	2.70	2.55	2.43
30	0.01	7.56	5.39	4.51	4.02	3.70	3.47
	0.05	4.17	3.32	2.92	2.69	2.53	2.42
35	0.01	7.42	5.27	4.40	3.91	3.59	3.37
	0.05	4.12	3.27	2.88	2.64	2.49	2.37
40	0.01	7.32	5.18	4.31	3.83	3.51	3.29
	0.05	4.09	3.23	2.84	2.61	2.45	2.34
45	0.01	7.23	5.11	4.25	3.77	3.46	3.23
	0.05	4.06	3.21	2.81	2.58	2.42	2.31
50	0.01	7.17	5.06	4.20	3.72	3.41	3.19
	0.05	4.04	3.18	2.79	2.56	2.40	2.29

Figure 12.8 *F*-Table Preview

Step 3: Establish Critical Value Cutoff To find our critical value of F, we need to first establish our significance level of alpha because this determines which F-table we will use. Let's set alpha to be .05. Next, we need to look across the columns of the F-table to find our $df_{Between}$ and look down the rows to find our df_{Within}. For our current data, we determined that we have 3 degrees of between and 33 degrees of freedom within. As we can see in **Figure 12.8,** although our F-table does have a column for 3 degrees of freedom between, it does not have a row for exactly 33 degrees of freedom within.

The closest value included in the table is for 30 degrees of freedom within, which has a critical value of 2.92. The critical value for 33 degrees of freedom within must be slightly smaller than this, because the critical value goes down as the degrees of freedom go up. Our best approach for determining the exact critical value for 33 degrees of freedom within is to use an online critical value calculator. Taking this approach, the exact critical value for 3 degrees of freedom between and 33 degrees of freedom within is 2.89. In other words, for the F distribution depicted in **Figure 12.9,** we must observe an F-ratio that is greater than 2.89 in order for us to reject the null hypothesis and conclude that flashbulb memories for positive events change over time.

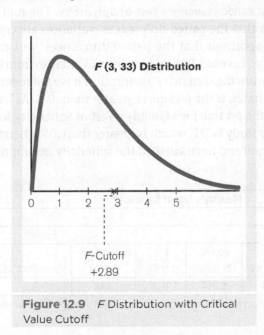

Figure 12.9 F Distribution with Critical Value Cutoff

Step 4: Determine Sample Results Do memories for positive flashbulb events fade over time? Or do they stay accurate? To answer these questions, we will conduct a repeated-measures ANOVA. In order for our results to be valid, we first need to make sure that we have satisfied the four assumptions of the repeated-measures ANOVA.

The first assumption is that our dependent variable is measured at the interval or ratio level of measurement. Here, our dependent variable is the number of incorrect responses to the memory quiz, which is a ratio-level measurement and satisfies the first assumption. The second assumption is that our sample is randomly selected from the population and the scores of each participant must be independent from one another. Well, we recruited participants from the university of the championship-winning football team, so we did not use random selection. This may be problematic and is a potential limitation of our study. Nevertheless, we did satisfy the second part of this assumption, because participants' responses were independent from one another. The third assumption is that the distributions of our dependent variables must be normal or we have large samples. Our sample size is only 12, which may not be large enough to ensure that the sampling distributions are normal. This could be a potential limitation of our study.

Finally, the fourth assumption is the sphericity assumption, which states that the variances of the difference scores for all possible pairs of scores are equal. To evaluate this assumption, we are going use SPSS to conduct a test called **Mauchly's Test of Sphericity.** The null hypothesis for this test is that the paired differences' variances are equal and the alternative hypothesis that the paired differences' variances are not equal. Similar to Levene's Test for Equality of Variances from Chapters 10 and 11, we satisfy the sphericity assumption if we *fail* to reject the null hypothesis (that is, if the p-value is greater than .05). As we can see in **Figure 12.10,** the p-value for Mauchly's Test of Sphericity for our flash-bulb memory study is .31, which is greater than .05. Therefore, we fail to reject the null and have satisfied the sphericity assumption.

Mauchly's Test of Sphericity
a hypothesis test used to assess the sphericity assumption of repeated-measures ANOVA.

Mauchly's Test of Sphericity[a]							
Measure: MEASURE_1							
					Epsilon[b]		
Within Subjects Effect	Mauchly's W	Approx. Chi-Square	df	Sig.	Greenhouse-Geisser	Huynh-Feldt	Lower-bound
TIME	.539	6.014	5	.307	.748	.949	.333

Tests the null hypothesis that the error covariance matrix of the ortho normalized transformed dependent variables is proportional to an identity matrix.

a. Design: Intercept
   Within Subjects Design: TIME

b. Maybe used to adjust the degrees of freedom for the averaged tests of significance. Corrected tests are displayed in the Tests of Within-Subjects Effects table.

Figure 12.10 Mauchly's Test of Sphericity SPSS Output

Now that we have addressed our assumptions, we are ready to calculate the *F*-ratio. Note that the values reported below may differ slightly from what you get when calculating the *F*-ratio by hand, but this is likely due to rounding differences.

The first step is to calculate the sum of squares total, which tells us the overall amount of variability in our dependent variable. As depicted in **Figure 12.11,** we calculate the sum of squares total using the following approach:

$$SS_{Total} = \Sigma(X - GM)^2 = 562.67.$$

Now that we know how much total variation there is to work with, we want to divide it up (or, to say it more formally, "partition the variance") into its subcomponent sources. The first source we want to measure is the sum of square between ($SS_{Between}$), which will tell us how much of the dependent variable's variation is attributable to our independent variable, Time. To calculate the sum of squares between, we use the formula

$$SS_{Between} = \Sigma(X - GM)^2 = 247.17$$

You can see all of the computation in Figure 12.11. Next, we can partition out any variability in participants' memories due to individual differences, using the formula:

$$SS_{Participants} = \Sigma(M_{Participants} - GM)^2 = 80.35.$$

Finally, whatever variability is left from the total is the sum of squares within, so we can figure that out using the formula:

$$SS_{Within} = SS_{Total} - SS_{Between} - SS_{Participants} = 562.67 - 247.17 - 80.35 = 235.15.$$

Of course, our sample's size affects the sums of squares that we just calculated (i.e., the sum of squares total will get larger as the sample size gets larger, which affects all the other sums of squares as well). To account for that, we need to divide each sum of squares (Between, Participants, and Within) by its relevant degrees of freedom. Remember that whenever we divide the sum of squares by its degrees of freedom, the resulting value is called variance. But, dividing a sum by how many numbers go into it is also how we calculate means. So, the variances in this context are called the mean squares, because they tell us the average amount of squared variation due to each source. Thus, to calculate the mean square between, we divide the sum of squares between by the degrees of freedom between,

$$MS_{Between} = SS_{Between}/df_{Between} = 247.17/3 = 82.39.$$

We take the same approach to calculate the mean square participants,

$$MS_{Participants} = SS_{Participants}/df_{Participants} = 80.35/11 = 7.30.$$

Participant	Conditions				
	Incorrect Answers at 6 Months (X_1)	Incorrect Answers at 12 Months (X_2)	Incorrect Answers at 24 Months (X_3)	Incorrect Answers at 36 Months (X_4)	($M_{Participants}$)
1	11	7	15	21	13.50
2	7	9	13	14	10.75
3	10	11	12	18	12.75
4	16	8	15	19	14.50
5	9	8	13	16	11.50
6	14	7	15	15	12.75
7	13	13	14	16	14.00
8	9	13	11	13	11.50
9	14	10	18	15	14.25
10	6	13	12	12	10.75
11	8	11	13	16	12.00
12	11	13	19	12	13.75
Condition Means	10.67	10.25	14.17	15.58	Grand Mean (*GM*) 12.67

Participant	Condition	Score (*X*)	($M_{Participants}$)	SS_{Total}		$SS_{Between}$		$SS_{Participants}$	
				$(X - GM)$	$(X - GM)^2$	$(M - GM)$	$(M - GM)^2$	$(M_{Part} - GM)$	$(M_{part} - GM)^2$
1		11	13.50	–1.67	2.78	–2.00	4.00	0.83	0.69
2		7	10.75	–5.67	32.11	–2.00	4.00	–1.92	3.67
3		10	12.75	–2.67	7.11	–2.00	4.00	0.08	0.01
4		16	14.50	3.33	11.11	–2.00	4.00	1.83	3.36
5	Incorrect Answers at 6 Months (X_1)	9	11.50	–3.67	13.44	–2.00	4.00	–1.17	1.36
6		14	12.75	1.33	1.78	–2.00	4.00	0.08	0.01
7		13	14.00	0.33	0.11	–2.00	4.00	1.33	1.78
8		9	11.50	–3.67	13.44	–2.00	4.00	–1.17	1.36
9		14	14.25	1.33	1.78	–2.00	4.00	1.58	2.51
10		6	10.75	–6.67	44.44	–2.00	4.00	–1.92	3.67
11		8	12.00	–4.67	21.78	–2.00	4.00	–0.67	0.44
12		11	13.75	–1.67	2.78	–2.00	4.00	1.08	1.17
	Cond. Mean	10.67							
1		7	13.50	–5.67	32.11	–2.42	5.84	0.83	0.69
2		9	10.75	–3.67	13.44	–2.42	5.84	–1.92	3.67
3		11	12.75	–1.67	2.78	–2.42	5.84	0.08	0.01
4		8	14.50	–4.67	21.78	–2.42	5.84	1.83	3.36
5	Incorrect Answers at 12 Months (X_2)	8	11.50	–4.67	21.78	–2.42	5.84	–1.17	1.36
6		7	12.75	–5.67	32.11	–2.42	5.84	0.08	0.01
7		13	14.00	0.33	0.11	–2.42	5.84	1.33	1.78
8		13	11.50	0.33	0.11	–2.42	5.84	–1.17	1.36
9		10	14.25	–2.67	7.11	–2.42	5.84	1.58	2.51
10		13	10.75	0.33	0.11	–2.42	5.84	–1.92	3.67
11		11	12.00	–1.67	2.78	–2.42	5.84	–0.67	0.44
12		13	13.75	0.33	0.11	–2.42	5.84	1.08	1.17
	Cond. Mean	10.25							

(Continue

#	Condition								
1		15	13.50	2.33	5.44	1.50	2.25	0.83	0.69
2		13	10.75	0.33	0.11	1.50	2.25	−1.92	3.67
3		12	12.75	−0.67	0.44	1.50	2.25	0.08	0.01
4		15	14.50	2.33	5.44	1.50	2.25	1.83	3.36
5	Incorrect	13	11.50	0.33	0.11	1.50	2.25	−1.17	1.36
6	Answers at	15	12.75	2.33	5.44	1.50	2.25	0.08	0.01
7	24 Months	14	14.00	1.33	1.78	1.50	2.25	1.33	1.78
8	(X_3)	11	11.50	−1.67	2.78	1.50	2.25	−1.17	1.36
9		18	14.25	5.33	28.44	1.50	2.25	1.58	2.51
10		12	10.75	−0.67	0.44	1.50	2.25	−1.92	3.67
11		13	12.00	0.33	0.11	1.50	2.25	−0.67	0.44
12		19	13.75	6.33	40.11	1.50	2.25	1.08	1.17
	Cond. 3 Mean	14.17							
1		21	13.38	8.33	69.44	2.92	8.51	0.71	0.50
2		14	10.63	1.33	1.78	2.92	8.51	−2.04	4.17
3		18	12.63	5.33	28.44	2.92	8.51	−0.04	0.00
4		19	14.38	6.33	40.11	2.92	8.51	1.71	2.92
5	Incorrect	16	11.38	3.33	11.11	2.92	8.51	−1.29	1.67
6	Answers at	15	12.63	2.33	5.44	2.92	8.51	−0.04	0.00
7	36 Months	16	13.88	3.33	11.11	2.92	8.51	1.21	1.46
8	(X_4)	13	11.38	0.33	0.11	2.92	8.51	−1.29	1.67
9		15	14.13	2.33	5.44	2.92	8.51	1.46	2.13
10		12	10.63	−0.67	0.44	2.92	8.51	−2.04	4.17
11		16	11.88	3.33	11.11	2.92	8.51	−0.79	0.63
12		12	13.63	−0.67	0.44	2.92	8.51	0.96	0.92
	Cond. 3 Mean	15.58							

Grand Mean (GM) = 12.67			$SS_{Total} = 562.67$	$SS_{Between} = 247.17$		$SS_{Participants} = 80.35$
$N_{Conditions} = 4$		$n = 12$	$SS_{Within} = SS_{Total} - SS_{Between} - SS_{Participants}$			235.15
$df_{Participants}$	$n - 1$	11	$MS_{Participants} = SS_{Participants}/df_{Participants}$		7.30	
$df_{Between}$	$N_{Conditions} - 1$	3	$MS_{Between} = SS_{Between}/df_{Between}$		82.39	
df_{Within}	$(df_{Between})(df_{Participants})$	33	$MS_{Within} = SS_{Within}/df_{Within}$		7.13	
df_{Total}	$df_{Between} + df_{Participants} + df_{Within}$	47	$F_{Participants} = MS_{Participants}/MS_{Within}$		1.03	
			$F_{Between} = MS_{Between}/MS_{Within}$		11.56	

Figure 12.11 Computations for Repeated-Measures Analysis of Variance (ANOVA)

Finally, we use this approach once again to calculate the mean square within:

$$MS_{Within} = SS_{Within}/df_{Within} = 235.15/33 = 7.13.$$

Now that we have calculated our means squares, we are ready to compute the F-ratio, which is the ratio of the mean square between to the mean square within:

$$F_{Between} = MS_{Between}/MS_{Within} = 82.39/7.13 = 11.56.$$

To determine if this value of F is large enough to reject the null hypothesis, we need to compare it to our critical cutoff value (**Figure 12.12**).

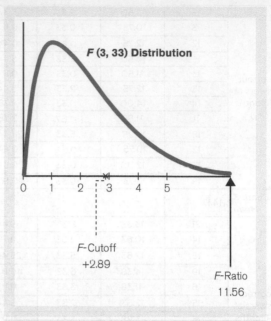

Figure 12.12 Sample Results on the Comparison Distribution

Step 5: Decide and Interpret Because the value of the F-ratio that we calculated for our data is greater than the critical cutoff value, we can reject the null hypothesis, H_0. Participants' memories for positive flashbulb events do change over time.

Post Hoc Tests: Where Is the Difference? Just like in one-way between-subjects ANOVA, a significant F-ratio merely tells us that at least two of the measurements are significantly different from one another. The F-test, however, does not identify which of the within-participants' levels are different. Thus, after finding significant results for our repeated-measures ANOVA, we need to conduct post hoc tests.

Now, one approach we could potentially take is to use the Tukey HSD technique that we learned in Chapter 11. In this approach, we calculate the smallest difference between two means that would be significant at a given level of alpha (which we call the honestly significant difference, or HSD) using the formula. $HSD = q_k \sqrt{\dfrac{MS_W}{n}}$, where q_k is the studentized range statistic based on k conditions (a value we look up in a table), MS_W is the mean square within from our F-test, and n is the sample size in each of the conditions. Once we know the value of the HSD, all we need to do is calculate the differences between the means for each pair of time points. If the difference that we observe is larger than the HSD, we can conclude that the difference is significant.

$$HSD = q_k \sqrt{\frac{MS_W}{n}}$$

Thus, for our current study, we would start our Tukey post hoc analysis by calculating the differences for each pair of condition means, which in this case are the various times that we measured participants' memories (see **Figure 12.13**).

Which Pair of Means Are We Testing?		What Is the Difference Between Each Pair of Means?
Incorrect Answers at 6 Months	Incorrect Answers at 12 Months	$10.67 - 10.25 = 0.42$
Incorrect Answers at 6 Months	Incorrect Answers at 24 Months	$10.67 - 14.17 = -3.50$
Incorrect Answers at 6 Months	Incorrect Answers at 36 Months	$10.67 - 15.58 = -4.91$
Incorrect Answers at 12 Months	Incorrect Answers at 24 Months	$10.25 - 14.17 = -3.92$
Incorrect Answers at 12 Months	Incorrect Answers at 36 Months	$10.25 - 15.58 = -5.33$
Incorrect Answers at 24 Months	Incorrect Answers at 36 Months	$14.17 - 15.58 = -1.41$

Figure 12.13 Calculation of Differences for Each Pair of Means

Now that we know by how much each pair of means differs, we need to compute the HSD. To do this, we first look up the studentized range statistic (q_k) from the table presented in **Figure 12.14**.

Because the table does not have our exact degrees of freedom within value, we can interpolate a value based on the information available, or we can use an online resource. According to an online calculator for the studentized range statistic, when k (the number of levels of our repeated-measure factor) = 4 and df_{Within} = 33, the q statistic is 3.83. Plugging this number into our formula reveals the following:

$$HSD = 3.83\sqrt{\frac{7.13}{12}} = 2.95.$$

So, in order for a pair of means to be significantly different, the difference needs to be greater than 2.95.

Within-Groups df	Significance (Alpha) Level	k = Number of Treatments (Levels)										
		2	3	4	5	6	7	8	9	10	11	12
12	0.05	3.08	3.77	4.20	4.51	4.75	4.95	5.12	5.27	5.39	5.51	5.61
	0.01	4.32	5.05	5.50	5.84	6.10	6.32	6.51	6.67	6.81	6.94	7.06
13	0.05	3.06	3.73	4.15	4.45	4.69	4.88	5.05	5.19	5.32	5.43	5.53
	0.01	4.26	4.96	5.40	5.73	5.98	6.19	6.37	6.53	6.67	6.79	6.90
14	0.05	3.03	3.70	4.11	4.41	4.64	4.83	4.99	5.13	5.25	5.36	5.46
	0.01	4.21	4.89	5.32	5.63	5.88	6.08	6.26	6.41	6.54	6.66	6.77
15	0.05	3.01	3.67	4.08	4.37	4.59	4.78	4.94	5.08	5.20	5.31	5.40
	0.01	4.17	4.84	5.25	5.56	5.80	5.99	6.16	6.31	6.44	6.55	6.66
16	0.05	3.00	3.65	4.05	4.33	4.56	4.74	4.90	5.03	5.15	5.26	5.35
	0.01	4.13	4.79	5.19	5.49	5.72	5.92	6.08	6.22	6.35	6.46	6.56
17	0.05	2.98	3.63	4.02	4.30	4.52	4.70	4.86	4.99	5.11	5.21	5.31
	0.01	4.10	4.74	5.14	5.43	5.66	5.85	6.01	6.15	6.27	6.38	6.48
18	0.05	2.97	3.61	4.00	4.28	4.49	4.67	4.82	4.96	5.07	5.17	5.27
	0.01	4.07	4.70	5.09	5.38	5.60	5.79	5.94	6.08	6.20	6.31	6.41
19	0.05	2.96	3.59	3.98	4.25	4.47	4.65	4.79	4.92	5.04	5.14	5.23
	0.01	4.05	4.67	5.05	5.33	5.55	5.73	5.89	6.02	6.14	6.25	6.34
20	0.05	2.95	3.58	3.96	4.23	4.45	4.62	4.77	4.90	5.01	5.11	5.20
	0.01	4.02	4.64	5.02	5.29	5.51	5.69	5.84	5.97	6.09	6.19	6.28
24	0.05	2.92	3.53	3.90	4.17	4.37	4.54	4.68	4.81	4.92	5.01	5.10
	0.01	3.96	4.55	4.91	5.17	5.37	5.54	5.69	5.81	5.92	6.02	6.11
30	0.05	2.89	3.49	3.85	4.10	4.30	4.46	4.60	4.72	4.82	4.92	5.00
	0.01	3.89	4.45	4.80	5.05	5.24	5.40	5.54	5.65	5.76	5.85	5.93
40	0.05	2.86	3.44	3.79	4.04	4.23	4.39	4.52	4.63	4.73	4.82	4.90
	0.01	3.82	4.37	4.70	4.93	5.11	5.26	5.39	5.50	5.60	5.69	5.76

Figure 12.14 Studentized Range Statistic Table

As we can see in Figure 12.13, the differences between memory at 6 months versus 24 months, 6 months versus 36 months, 12 months versus 24 months, and 12 months versus 36 months all have paired differences that are larger than 2.95. Thus, each of these means are significantly different from one another. The differences between memory at 6 months versus 12 months and 24 months versus 36 months have paired differences that are less than 2.95, so these differences are nonsignificant.

An important caveat is that this approach is very sensitive to violations of the sphericity assumption. Recall that the sphericity assumption says that the variances of the difference scores for all pairs of conditions must be equal. If we violate this assumption, it means that the variances are not equal. This is a problem for the Tukey HSD because the formula uses the mean square within MS_W, which reflects the overall error term computed from all of the groups to test the differences for each pair of means. If a particular pair of means does not have the same variance as the other pairs, then it wouldn't be appropriate to use the MS_W, and the resulting analysis may not yield an appropriate test of significance. Thus, many people hesitate to use this Tukey HSD as a post hoc for repeated-measures ANOVA.

Indeed, SPSS does not even offer us the option to use the Tukey approach. Instead, SPSS offers alternative approaches that are less sensitive to violations of sphericity. One of these approaches is to conduct a series of paired-samples t-tests, but with a corrected level of alpha, called a *Bonferroni correction,* to reduce our experimentwise Type I error rate. In essence, the Bonferroni correction works by recognizing that the more hypothesis tests we perform, the more likely we are to make a Type I error. The Bonferroni correction sets the significant level for each of our t-tests equal to α/c, where α is our overall alpha and c is the number of mean comparisons we are evaluating. By correcting our significance level in this way, the Bonferroni correction counteracts the increase in Type I error rate.

$$Bonferroni\ p = \alpha/c$$

For our current data, we want to compare four means (the four times we measured each participant's flashbulb memories), which results in six possible comparisons (as illustrated in Figure 12.13). So, if our overall alpha = .05 and we have six comparisons, that tells us that our Bonferroni corrected significance level p = .05/6 = .008. In other words, we need our p-value for any paired-samples t post hoc to have a p-value less than .008 for us to consider it a significant difference. We will see output from SPSS showing what this looks like later in the chapter.

Computing the Effect Size for the Repeated-Measures ANOVA
A significant repeated-measures ANOVA merely tells us that we rejected the null hypothesis. It does not imply that our results are

important or meaningful. To help us make these conclusions, we should calculate a measure of effect size. For one-way ANOVA, we learned to compute eta squared (η^2), and we could use eta squared again here, but it wouldn't accurately reflect the effect size. Remember from Chapter 11 that we calculate eta squared by taking the sum of squares between ($SS_{Between}$) divided by the sum of squares total (SS_{Total}). In a repeated-measures ANOVA, we are able to remove additional variation from the sum of squares total due to our ability to measure differences within individuals, which we called the sum of squares participants ($SS_{Participants}$). So, it doesn't make sense to add this source of variation back into our effect size calculation (which would happen if we use the sum of squares total to calculate eta squared).

Instead, we will divide our sum of squares between ($SS_{Between}$) by the sum of squares total minus the sum of squares participants ($SS_{Total} - SS_{Participants}$). We call this way of calculating effect size **partial eta squared (η_p^2)** because we are we are removing a part of the total amount of variability from our dependent variable that is attributable to some other source (in this case the sum of squares participants). Thus, we calculate partial eta squared as follows:

partial eta squared (η_p^2) an effect size measure. In repeated-measures ANOVA, it indicates the amount of variation in the dependent variable attributable to the differences between condition means, after removing the participant variance.

$$\eta_p^2 = SS_{Between}/(SS_{Total} - SS_{Participants})$$

To find partial eta squared for our study of flashbulb memories, we would perform the following calculations:

$$\eta_p^2 = SS_{Between}/(SS_{Total} - SS_{Participants}) = 247.17/562.67 - 80.35$$
$$= 247.17/482.32$$
$$= 0.51$$

Alternatively, because the sum of squares total minus the sum of squares participant ($SS_{Total} - SS_{Participants}$) equals the sum of squares between plus the sum of squares within ($SS_{Between} + SS_{Within}$), we can calculate partial eta squared using the formula:

$$\eta_p^2 = SS_{Between}/(SS_{Between} + SS_{Within})$$

and get the same result:

$$\eta_p^2 = 247.17/247.17 + 235.15$$
$$= 247.17/482.32$$
$$= 0.51$$

To interpret this effect size, we would first want to compare it to other studies of flashbulb memories to see if it is larger or smaller than the typical effect. Beyond that, we can use generic standards of what constitutes small, medium, and large effects, which would reveal that this is a large effect (see Chapter 8).

Your Turn 12.5

1. In a study of the effects of smell on memory, participants wrote about the memories evoked by three different scents: apple pie, bar soap, and wet dog. The researchers then counted the number of details included in each memory to test the hypothesis that social memories (such as those evoked by apple pie) should be more detailed than nonsocial memories (such as those evoked by the scent of bar soap or wet dog). The data from 5 participants are provided below:

Participant	Apple Pie	Bar Soap	Wet Dog
1	18	9	17
2	14	7	12
3	17	14	11
4	20	4	14
5	15	11	15

a. Step 1: Population and Hypotheses. (1) What would the populations be? (2) What would the hypotheses be?

b. Step 2: Build Comparison Distribution. What is the comparison distribution? What shape is it?

c. Step 3: Establish Critical Value Cutoff. Given alpha of .05, what is the F critical value?

d. Step 4: Determine Sample Results. (1) SPSS output reveals that the p-value for the sphericity assumption is .514. What does this tell us about whether we have satisfied the sphericity assumption? (2) If the sphericity assumption is satisfied, conduct the repeated-measures ANOVA and find the value of the F-ratio.

e. Step 5: Decide and Interpret. What is the appropriate conclusion?

2. Calculate the effect size using partial eta squared.

3. To determine which conditions are significantly different, the researcher conducts post hoc analyses using paired-samples t-tests with Bonferroni corrections. Interpret the results presented in the SPSS output below:

Pairwise Comparisons						
Measure: MEASURE_1						
(I) Condition	(J) Condition	Mean Difference (I – J)	Std. Error	Sig.[a]	95% Confidence Interval for Difference[a]	
					Lower Bound	Upper Bound
1	2	7.800	2.311	.084	−1.353	16.953
	3	3.000	1.265	.230	−2.010	8.010
2	1	−7.800	2.311	.084	−16.953	1.353
	3	−4.800	2.223	.291	−13.603	4.003
3	1	−3.000	1.265	.230	−8.010	2.010
	2	4.800	2.223	.291	−4.003	13.603

Based on estimated marginal means
a. Adjustment for multiple comparisons: Bonferroni.

SPSS Video Tutorial: Repeated-Measures ANOVA

 As we've seen, performing the repeated-measures ANOVA by hand can be time consuming. That's why most researchers use software to perform analyses. Let's see how we would perform this analysis using SPSS. Watch this SPSS video, which demonstrates how to perform the repeated-measures ANOVA in SPSS.

> **SPSS VIDEO TUTORIAL: To learn more, check out the video tutorial Repeated-Measures ANOVA.**

Communicating the Result

Our approach for communicating the repeated-measures ANOVA results will not be that different from what we did in Chapter 11 for the one-way ANOVA. In particular, we will typically prepare a results section that describes the overall results of our analysis and an ANOVA summary table that provides all of the numbers needed for calculating the F-ratio. We might describe the results this way:

> We conducted a repeated-measures ANOVA to determine if the number of incorrect responses to the memory quiz changed over time. The test results were significant, $F(3, 33) = 11.56$, $p < .001$, $\eta_p^2 = .51$. Post hoc tests reveal that although participants' memories did not get worse between 6 and 12 months ($p > .05$), participants did have significantly more incorrect answers on the memory quiz at 24 months ($p < .05$) and at 36 months ($p < .05$), compared to 6 months following the positive flashbulb event.

Our ANOVA summary table would include the following information:

Source	Sum of Squares	df	Mean Square	F	p
Between Groups	247.17	3	82.39	11.56	<.001
Participants	80.35	11			
Within Groups	235.33	33	7.13		
Total	562.67	47			

Creating a Line Graph When reporting descriptive statistics (i.e., means and standard deviations), researchers typically use bar graphs. However, when reporting the results of a study with repeated measures, it is common for researchers to use a **line graph.** A line graph presents the means (and error bars) for each repeated measurement, with lines that connect the measurements. Although the information presented in a line graph is the same as what appears in a bar graph, by connecting the measurements with lines, the graph communicates that it reflects change over time.

line graph a type of graph where means are connected by lines. Used to depict the results of repeated-measures analyses.

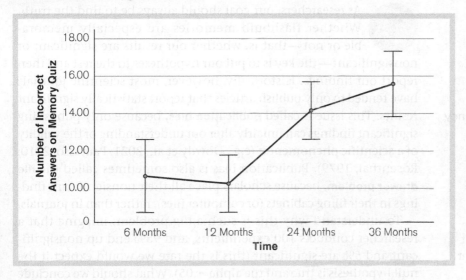

To create a line graph, we can use SPSS or a word processing program. In SPSS, when performing the repeated-measures ANOVA, we can click on the option called "Plots," which will create a line graph. We then just need to select the independent variable and move it to the box called "horizontal axis."

Forming a Conclusion

Some research questions examine how participants change over time. For our test of flashbulb memories, we wanted to determine whether participants reported incorrect details of a positive flashbulb event over time, which would indicate that these memories are not more robust that other memories. Because we measured the same participants multiple times, we determined that the repeated-measures ANOVA was the most appropriate analysis because it measures how time affects participants on our dependent variable, and also considers an additional source of variation in participants' scores: differences in individual participants.

Overall, our repeated-measures ANOVA was significant, suggesting that the mean number of incorrect answers to the memory quiz changed over time. In order to determine the exact nature of these changes, we then conducted post hoc analyses and found that participants' memories were not significantly different between 6 and 12 months, but did show significant increases in incorrect answers between 12 and 24 months. Finally, we computed the effect size for this finding, which revealed a large effect.

Focus on Open Science: The File Drawer Problem

As researchers, our goal should always be to find the truth. Whether flashbulb memories are especially memorable or not—that is, whether our results are significant or nonsignificant—the key is to put our hypotheses to the test and then report our findings. Historically, however, most scientific journals have tended to only publish articles that report statistically significant results. This issue is called **publication bias,** because only publishing significant findings can unfairly alter our understanding of the validity of a scientific phenomenon (e.g., Dowdy et al., 2021; Pautasso, 2010; Rosenthal, 1979). Publication bias is also sometimes called the **file drawer problem,** because scholars place all their nonsignificant findings in their filing cabinets (or computer files), rather than in journals.

To understand why this is such a big problem, imagine that a researcher conducts 100 experiments, and 95% end up nonsignificant and 5% are significant (this is the rate we would expect if the null hypothesis is true and the alpha = .05). What should we conclude about the phenomenon? We should conclude that the null hypothesis is correct: there is no effect of the independent variable. However, if a scientific journal publishes only the 5% of the findings that are

publication bias tendency for scholarly journals to publish only papers that report statistically significant findings.

file drawer problem problem arising when scholars do not attempt to publish nonsignificant findings.

The file drawer problem is similar to if scientists decided to simply bury all their nonsignificant findings. This will ultimately skew the conclusions we can draw from research studies and leads to bad science.

avoodin/Deposit Photos

statistically significant, and not the 95% that were nonsignificant, then readers of the journal may mistakenly believe that the phenomenon is real when it is not.

The file drawer problem is also an issue for researchers trying to conduct meta-analyses. Remember in Chapter 8 we discussed a type of analysis called a meta-analysis in which researchers combine the results of many studies on a particular phenomenon and then conduct additional analyses on this larger data set. Unfortunately, if journals publish only significant results, then the studies that go into the meta-analyses are biased to begin with, and so the meta-analysis results will likely be biased as well.

To combat the file drawer problem, proponents of open science have developed several approaches. First, they have created publication outlets for both significant and nonsignificant findings. For example, PsyArXiv (https://psyarxiv.com/) is a repository that allows scholars to submit papers regardless of whether they report significant or nonsignificant results. Second, scholars have created a new type of publication called a **registered report** (see Chambers, 2019). In a registered report, the researcher submits a literature review and research hypothesis, as well as a proposed methodology to test this hypothesis. Before actually conducting the study, the research proposal and plan gets submitted for peer review. If the peer reviewers deem the question worthy of investigation, and the methodology appropriate to address the hypothesis, then the journal agrees to publish the paper after the researcher collects and analyzes the data, regardless of whether the findings are significant. Because the paper is essentially accepted for publication, the researcher is not pressured in any way to present the results in a biased manner.

registered report type of scholarly article that is accepted for publication prior to collection of data, based on the importance of the hypothesis it is testing and the procedures used to test the hypothesis.

Become a Better Consumer of Statistics

Repeated-measures ANOVA is an excellent technique for examining changes in participants over time. Whether people like a song more the more often they hear it, or remember details for certain events, repeated-measures ANOVA helps us identify just how much participants change, and in what direction they change. Still, when we read about studies that use this type of analysis, we need to carefully consider whether the changes that the studies report are meaningful.

In Chapter 2, we learned about ceiling and floor effects. Recall that ceiling effects occur when almost all of the participants start at the extreme positive end of the scale that we are measuring, while floor effects occur when almost all participants start at the extreme negative end of the scale. For example, if we were to measure how

Asking a just-divorced couple how they feel about each other might not lead to the most accurate evaluations, as their responses will likely be influenced by floor effects.

Dmytro Zinkevych/Shutterstock

much two newlyweds love each other, they would almost certainly exhibit ceiling effects because they would answer at the upper end of the measurement scale (e.g., a 7 on a 1–7 love scale). In contrast, two recently divorced people would likely exhibit floor effects if we were to ask them how much they loved each other (e.g., a 1 on a 1–7 scale). If we followed newlywed or recently divorced participants over time, we might observe changes in their ratings for their partners (or former partners). However, because ceiling effects can only go down and floor effects can only go up, we should be wary of overinterpreting these findings.

Let's take another example to understand why this can be potentially problematic. Imagine that we see an advertisement for a new cold remedy. The ad states that participants taking the medicine felt significantly better afterward. Does this mean that the remedy is effective? Well, imagine that the researchers testing this medicine started their investigation by measuring participants when their symptoms were most extreme (people responded "1" on a 1–7 scale measuring how healthy they feel). The researchers measured the participants again after a week of treatment with the cold remedy, and they found that the participants' responses were significantly better (perhaps they're now a 4 or 5), indicating that they were feeling better. But can we necessarily attribute these changes to the cold remedy? Or is it possible that they got better because they started at the extreme end of the scale and there was only one direction they could go? Unfortunately, a repeated-measures ANOVA won't tell us why participants change, only if they do, so we need to carefully consider whether ceiling or floor effects may be present when interpreting the results of longitudinal studies.

Interpreting Graphs and Charts from Research Articles

As we learned earlier, when reporting the results of a repeated-measures ANOVA, most researchers present their findings in a line graph. To see what this looks like, take a look at **Figure 12.15**, which is a line graph from a paper investigating flashbulb memories (Talarico & Rubin, 2003). This line graph presents the results for participants on four dependent measures (e.g., vividness), two for everyday memories and two for flashbulb memories, each of which were measured four times (7, 42, and 224 days after the initial measurement).

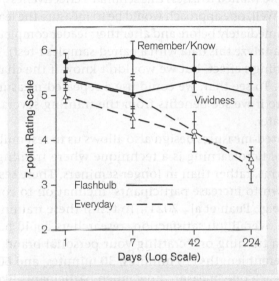

Figure 12.15   Line Graph (Data from Talarico & Rubin, 2003)

This line graph depicts the difference between everyday memories and flashbulb memories on the four dependent variables. For flashbulb memories (the two solid lines at the top of the graph), participants believed they remembered the flashbulb event at the same level up to 224 days later. Similarly, participants' perceptions of their memory's vividness remained at a very high level. In contrast, we can see that for an everyday memory, participants' recollection and memory's vividness ratings steadily decreased over time. We can also see that the authors included error bars, so that we can get a sense of the amount of variability at each measurement.

Statistics on the Job

Many workplaces employ people with training in industrial and organizational psychology (also called I/O psychology) to teach their workforce. For example, these psychologists may hold seminars that teach employees to work in teams, improve productivity, or practice effective leadership strategies. Of course, for each of these types of interventions, it's important to demonstrate that they are effective and have long-lasting effects.

Let's imagine that an I/O psychologist hosts a leadership seminar designed to improve leaders' ability to effectively communicate with their direct reports (or the employees who work under their supervision). If we wanted to assess this seminar's effectiveness, how would we do so? Well, one approach would be to measure the leader's direct reports immediately before and after their leader completes the seminar (and analyze this data with a paired-samples t-test). That might show training's effect, but we wouldn't know if the changes lasted over time. To see that, we could use a repeated-measures ANOVA to measure if we see benefits from the training several weeks, or months, later.

A repeated-measures design also allows us to test multiple interventions. Microlearning is a technique where training occurs in short lessons, rather than in longer seminars. These sessions have been shown to increase participants' inclination to complete the training (e.g., Puah et al., 2021). To test if these trainings increase employee overall job satisfaction, researchers could have participants do a training on "crafting your personal brand," but have three different lengths (10 minutes, 30 minutes, and 60 minutes), and after each one, measure how much participants like their job. This can tell us if the short 10-minute session is most effective. Of course, the order in which participants receive these trainings may matter. How one condition or treatment may impact subsequent conditions (i.e., an *order effect*) is a common issue with repeated measurements that should be accounted for by randomizing the order over participants.

CHAPTER 12 Review

Review Questions

1. What is the key question that a repeated-measures ANOVA seeks to answer? How is this represented in the research hypothesis and the null hypothesis?

2. The repeated-measures ANOVA looks for differences _____ while the between-subjects ANOVA looks for differences _____.

3. How are the assumptions of a repeated-measures ANOVA like those of a between-subjects ANOVA? How are they different?

4. What is the appropriate statistical test?
   a. A researcher wants to compare the reaction time of a person before and after they consume 6 ounces of alcohol. The researcher measures participants' reaction times before the alcohol consumption, as well as 30 and 60 minutes after.
   b. A researcher in circadian rhythms measures the impact of a light pulse on the activity patterns of $5\text{-}HT_{1A}$ receptors in knockout mice by comparing a group of mice who receive the pulse to a control group who does not.
   c. A student is interested in children's understanding of opposites. She compares 3-, 4-, and 5-year-old children.
   d. A clinician wants to measure the impact of divorce on externalizing behavior in youth. They intend to contact families for 3 consecutive years, starting within 3 months of the divorce.
   e. A graduate student wants to measure the impact of explicitly teaching children about sarcasm. She measures their understanding before and after reading the book with the children.

5. In a repeated-measures analysis of variance, individual differences affect _____ levels of an independent variable and _____ be partitioned out of (removed from) the overall error variance (SS_{Within}).

6. Label each formula with the correct variance:

Variance	Formula
	$SS_{Total} - SS_{Between} - SS_{Within}$
	$\Sigma(M - GM)^2$
	$\Sigma(M_{Participants} - GM)^2$
	$\Sigma(X - GM)^2$

7. Label each formula with the degrees of freedom:

Degrees of Freedom	Formula
	$(df_{Between})(df_{Participants})$
	$N_{Groups} - 1$
	$N - 1$
	$df_{Within} + df_{Between} + df_{Participants}$

8. How does SPSS label SS_{Within} in the output?

9. Can you calculate SS_{Total} or $SS_{Participants}$ from a standard SPSS output? Why or why not?

10. Can a repeated-measures analysis of variance have directional null and research hypotheses? Why or why not?

11. Why are post hoc tests, such as the Bonferroni correction, necessary? When should post hoc tests be conducted?

12. You have been contracted by a company to evaluate the effects of a leadership seminar that they are hosting that is designed to improve the participant's ability to effectively communicate (like the example in Statistics on the Job). You decide to measure participants immediately before and after the seminar, as well as 3 months and 6 months after the seminar ends). You obtain the following data from 4 participants. Note that higher scores reflect greater effectiveness in communication.

a. What are your populations?
b. What is your null hypothesis? What is your research hypothesis?
c. What are your $df_{Between}$, df_{Within}, $df_{Participants}$, and df_{Total}?
d. Establish your critical value cutoff.
e. Determine your sample results. Assume that all assumptions for the analysis have been met.
f. What is the appropriate conclusion?
g. Calculate the value of eta squared (η^2). By conventional standards, is this effect small, medium, or large?

	Conditions			
Participant	Before Seminar	Immediately After Seminar	3 Months After Seminar	6 Months After Seminar
Liu	50	55	64	62
Aracely	47	54	68	60
Preeti	34	45	65	62
George	54	60	73	68

Key Concepts

file drawer problem, p. 482

line graph, p. 481

Mauchly's Test of Sphericity, p. 470

partial eta squared (η_p^2), p. 478

publication bias, p. 482

registered report, p. 483

repeated-measures analysis of variance, p. 450

sphericity assumption, p. 466

Your Turn 12.1

1. Answers will vary but should all feature the comparison of measurements from three or more distinct levels of an independent variable. For example, you could use a repeated-measures analysis of variance to determine if how people listen to music (vinyl, CD, phone) influences enjoyment.

2. (a) Between-groups analysis of variance. (b) The ANOVA we didn't use in Part A is repeated measures. In order to implement that, we would have to have all 300 participants watch all three movies as part of a within-subjects or repeated-measures design.

Your Turn 12.2

1. The process is largely the same (determining the difference between the condition mean and the grand mean). The key difference is that we have to calculate it for each participant. For example, if we have 10 participants, we need to calculate it 10 times for each condition.

2. In a between-groups ANOVA, individual differences impact only one condition/group/level of the independent variable. Because it influences only one condition, it mimics the between-groups effect we're hoping to find in a between-groups ANOVA. Individual differences in repeated measures are less problematic because they impact all levels of the independent variable, so their effects are approximately even across conditions.

Your Turn 12.3

1. (a) (1) Population 1: Students who visit Strawgoh University. Population 2: Students who visit Shermer University. Population 3: Students how visit Bayside University. Sample: The 5 high school students on Ms. Actsat's trip. (2) Research: The population means are not equal. Null: The population means are equal.

(b) F distribution with a shape that ultimately depends on the between-groups and within-groups degrees of freedom.

(c) (1) Significance level (we'll use the standard significance level, $p = .05$), degrees of freedom

between-groups ($df_{Between} = 2$), and degrees of freedom within-groups ($df_{Within} = 12$); (2) 3.89.

(d) (1) Repeated-measures analysis of variance. (2) Key Calculations: $GM = 3.90$; $SS_{Total} = 73.81$; $SS_{Between} = 34.38$; $SS_{Participants} = 15.81$; $SS_{Within} = 23.62$; $MS_{Between} = 17.19$; $MS_{Within} = 1.97$; $F_{Between} = 8.73$. (3) Nothing. That information should be ignored because it does not relate to the research hypothesis. (4)

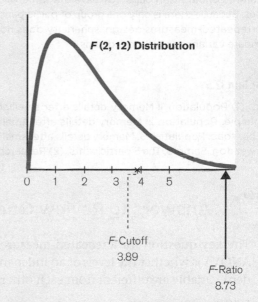

F (2, 12) Distribution

F-Cutoff
3.89

F-Ratio
8.73

(e) Our F-ratio of 8.73 exceeded the cutoff score of 3.89. Because our sample's results (Step 4) surpassed the critical value (Step 3), we are able to reject the null hypothesis (H_0) that the population means are equal. If we are able to reject the null, the research hypothesis (H_1) that the population means is supported.

2.

Source	SS	df	MS	F
Participant	15.81	6		
Between	34.38	2	17.19	8.73
Within	23.62	12	1.97	
Total	73.81	20		

Your Turn 12.4

1. This research design violates the assumption that scores are independent between participants, because the participants discuss the candidate with each other, which could affect their scores on the final rating.

2. Both the sphericity assumption and the equality of variances assumption concern the variances of dependent measures. The sphericity assumption states that the difference scores for each pair of dependent variables have the same variance. The equality of variances assumption states that the dependent variable for the different conditions in our study have the same variances. Because there is only one group of participants in a repeated-measures design, sphericity does not compare variances across conditions.

Your Turn 12.5

1. (a) (1) Population 1: Memory details after smelling apple pie. Population 2: Memory details after smelling bar soap. Population 3: Memory details after smelling wet dog. Sample: The 5 participants. (2) Research:

The population means are not equal. Null: The population means are equal.

(b) F distribution with a shape that has 2 degrees of freedom between and 8 degrees of freedom within.

(c) 4.46.

(d) (1) Because the p-value for Mauchly's Test of Sphericity is greater than .05, we can conclude that the sphericity assumption is satisfied. (2) $F = 7.82$ (Key Calculations: $GM = 13.20$, $SS_{Total} = 258.40$; $SS_{Between} = 154.80$; $SS_{Participants} = 24.40$; $SS_{Within} = 79.20$; $MS_{Between} = 77.40$; $MS_{Within} = 9.90$; $F_{Between} = 7.82$).

(e) Because our F-ratio of 7.82 is greater than the critical value of 4.46, we can reject the null hypothesis (H_0) that the population means are equal. In other words, the mean number of details evoked by different scents is different across the three scents.

2. $\eta_p^2 = SS_{Between}/(SS_{Total} - SS_{Participants}) = 154.80/(258.40 - 24.40) = 154.80/234.00 = 0.66$.

3. Although the overall repeated-measures ANOVA is significant, none of the post hoc analyses reveals a significant difference between any of the conditions.

 # Answers to Review Questions

1. The key question for a repeated-measures ANOVA is whether the levels of an independent variable are different from each other.

2. Within subjects; between subjects.

3. In both types of ANOVA, the dependent variable must be interval or ratio, the samples must be randomly selected from the population, and the scores between participants are independent; the dependent variable must be normally distributed or the sample must be sufficiently large. In the repeated-measures ANOVA, the variances of the difference scores for all possible pairs of measurements within participants must be equal (sphericity). In the between-subjects ANOVA, the population variances must be equal (homogeneity of variances).

4. Repeated-measures ANOVA
   a. Repeated-measures ANOVA
   b. Should be t-test for independent samples
   c. Between-groups ANOVA
   d. Repeated-measures ANOVA
   e. t-test for dependent samples

5. All; can.

6.

Variance	Formula
SS_{Within}	$SS_{Total} - SS_{Between} - SS_{Within}$
$SS_{Between}$	$\Sigma(M - GM)^2$
$SS_{Participants}$	$\Sigma(M_{Participants} - GM)^2$
SS_{Total}	$\Sigma(X - GM)^2$

7.

Degrees of freedom	Formula
df_{Within}	$(df_{Between})(df_{Participants})$
$df_{Between}$	$N_{Groups} - 1$
$df_{Participants}$	$N - 1$
df_{Total}	$df_{Within} + df_{Between} + df_{Participants}$

8. Error.

9. No, you cannot. SPSS provides you only with $SS_{Between}$ and SS_{Within}. Since you have only 2 out of the 4 sums of squares, you cannot use them to calculate the missing ones.

10. No, it cannot. The ANOVA tests whether any of the means differs, but a significant F-ratio does not tell us which ones differ. As a result, the hypotheses are not directional.

11. Post hoc tests are necessary because the ANOVA indicates whether one or more of the means differ from the others; however, it does not tell us which ones differ. Post hoc tests should be conducted only after a significant F-ratio is found in the ANOVA.

12. a. Population 1 (μ_1): scores before training
Population 2 (μ_2): scores immediately after training
Population 3 (μ_3): scores 3 months after training
Population 4 (μ_4): scores 6 months after training

b. Null hypothesis: the population means are equal ($\mu_1 = \mu_2 = \mu_3 = \mu_4$)
Research hypothesis: the population means are not equal ($\mu_1 \neq \mu_2 \neq \mu_3 \neq \mu_4$)

c. $df_{Between} = 3$; $df_{Within} = 9$; $df_{Participants} = 3$; $df_{Total} = 15$

d. Critical value = 3.96

e. $SS_{Between} = 1091.19$; $SS_{Within} = 126.06$; $SS_{Participants} = 300.69$; $SS_{Total} = 1517.94$; $MS_{Between} = 363.73$; $MS_{Within} = 25.96$; $F = 10.89$

f. Reject the null and accept the alternate; our population means are not equal.

g. $\eta^2 = 0.90$, large effect size

OPEN STATS LAB

Sharpen your statistics skills with real-life data! Check out OpenStatsLab.com, created by coauthor Kevin McIntyre, to practice running analyses for real published research studies.

13 > Factorial Analysis of Variance (ANOVA)

Learning Outcomes

After reading this chapter, you should be able to:

● Explain the key question that a factorial analysis of variance seeks to answer.

● Identify similarities and differences between a one-way analysis of variance and a factorial analysis of variance.

● Explain when it is appropriate to use a factorial analysis of variance.

● Explain the advantages of factorial analysis of variance.

● Describe the underlying logic for calculating the total, between, and within sum of squares.

● Summarize what factorial analysis of variance results can and cannot tell us.

● Describe different types of interaction effects and identify an interaction by examining a graph.

W̲e all have friends who are social media all-stars, constantly posting visually stunning pictures, cute selfies, and a few clever hashtags to boot—#meIRL. In an image-obsessed world, selfies are the front line of our impression management efforts. Whether it's on TikTok, Instagram, Snapchat, VSCO, Twitter, LinkedIn, Facebook, or any other social media page, our profile picture shapes others' first impressions of us. We need to get this right.

That's especially true in the dating world. As potential partners flip, scroll, click, or swipe through profiles looking for a match, that first picture is everything. Absent a photo shoot, selfies are the way to go. But, what makes for a killer selfie? Based on the profiles out there, the favorite strategies seem to be clever camera angles, making pouty-lipped duck faces, flashing hand signs around the face, or using filters. Clearly the assumption is that these tactics make you look more appealing. However, just because a lot of people do something and believe it works, doesn't mean it actually does. It makes you wonder: Is there a strategy people can use to really make them look the most attractive?

Statistics for Life

With selfies, we have complete control over everything. Don't like something? Take another one. Do we get obsessive sometimes? Sure, but the stakes are high, so we leave nothing to chance. At the same time, in our quest to craft the perfect selfie, we don't want to seem like a try-hard. If we go too far, selfies look fake and narcissistic. This makes selfies a bit of a double-edged sword that could help or hurt dating prospects. Not to mention that taking selfies may contribute to social anxiety (Liu et al., 2022).

When there are several plausible outcomes like this, we get to put them to the test by researching what's really best. For example, one study found that men tend to shoot their selfies from a low angle to look taller, while women use a high angle (Sedgewick et al., 2017).

Hero Images Inc./Alamy Stock Photo

Would this person look better or worse with a filter added?

For dating purposes, however, men and women both rotate their head a bit and avoid low angles (Gale & Lewis, 2019). Based on this, it would be interesting to test whether a natural straightforward angle or a high angle makes a person look more attractive.

When touching up photos, filters are the way to go. We can add extra swag like puppy dog ears, cat whiskers, or flower crowns. Or we can use face tuning to make more subtle enhancements like whitening our teeth, shrinking our nose, smoothing out spots, and enlarging our eyes. Sure, those touch-ups create a bit of an unrealistic look, but they help, right? Curious, we do a quick Google search, which reveals conflicting opinions. Some suggest filters hurt self-esteem and make us forget what we really look like, while several try to explain why filters help.

Unfortunately, the one thing missing from the internet articles is empirical research to back up their claims. Here's our chance. Because those cartoony animal-ear type filters are so obvious, it's more interesting to see if it's better to use a face tuning filter or nothing at all. Ultimately, to see what optimizes a selfie's attractiveness, we have two possibilities we want to check out: the photo's angle and filter use. We could run two separate studies to look at each one at a time, but that is awfully time-consuming. Instead, we need to figure out a way to test both of these at once.

Where Do the Data Come From?

To crack the code, we're going to need some selfies. We could scour social media for the selfies we require. We have two variables (pose and filter), each with two levels: pose (high angle vs. no angle) and filter (face tuning vs. no filter). To save time, we want to test all of this together, which means we need

Michael Simons/Pocstock

Does the angle at which a selfie is taken really change how attractive the image is?

selfies that combine these levels. That means we should find four types of selfies:

- high angle/face tuning;
- high angle/no filter;
- no angle/face tuning;
- no angle/no filter.

Though people post a lot of selfies, finding those exact combinations, all taken by the same person in the same setting, might be impossible. Instead, we can ask our friend if she'd be willing to take the exact selfies we want, and let us use them. She agrees, and after a few retakes to get them exactly right, we have our four pictures.

We could do the same and get a set of selfies from a guy friend, but we decide to stick with female selfies because so much of the research finds that females take them more often (e.g., Stuart & Kurek, 2019; Veldhuis et al., 2018).

Since we're only doing this for fun and to satisfy our own curiosity, we'll ask a few friends for their reaction. We'll show each person only one of the selfies (i.e., it will be between-subjects), because if anyone sees more than that, they'll quickly catch on to what we're trying to do. We put the photos in random order and show them to people only when they are alone, so that others don't influence their answer. After they look at the photo, we ask, "Using a 1–10 scale where 1 = Not at All, 5 = Moderately, and 10 = Extremely, how attractive is the person in the picture?" We end up getting ratings from only 16 people, but the good news is that we have 4 people for each of our combinations. Everyone's ratings appear in **Figure 13.1,** along with the mean for each group.

	Group 1	Group 2	Group 3	Group 4
	High Angle/ Face Tuning	**High Angle/ No Filter**	**No Angle/ Face Tuning**	**No Angle/ No Filter**
	3	1	5	6
	7	4	7	9
	6	5	8	10
	5	3	6	8
Group Mean	**5.25**	**3.25**	**6.50**	**8.25**

Figure 13.1 Super Selfie Results

factor a term synonymous with independent variable in the context of factorial ANOVA.

Want to review the one-way analysis of variance? SEE CHAPTER 11. ↗

Factorial Analysis of Variance (ANOVA): What We're Trying to Accomplish

When we have two independent variables, we call this a "two-way" factorial ANOVA, because we have two **factors** (another name for independent variables) and because we can consider each score in two ways. We can consider each score based on its level on pose variable (high angle or no angle), and we can consider its level on the filter variable (face tuning or no face tuning). Note that if we added a third factor, we would call this a "three-way" factorial design because we have three independent variables and can consider each score in three different ways.

The key difference with factorial analysis of variance and a one-way between-groups ANOVA is the possibility of combinations. We're blending two (or more) different independent variables or factors (pose and filter) to determine how they both influence our dependent variable (attractiveness). That's different, because the one-way between-groups ANOVA and repeated-measures ANOVAs could handle only one factor or independent variable at a time, which also eliminated the potential for combinations.

With two independent variables, we have at least two key questions we can answer: "Do selfie poses influence how attractive a person looks?" and "Do selfie filters influence how attractive a person looks?" However, we can also look at another possibility: "Does the

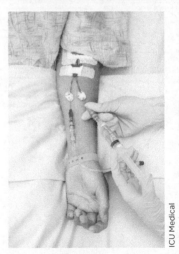

ICU Medical

Just as the use of two IVs in a medical procedure delivers specific medicine combinations to a patient, two IVs (independent variables) in a research design allow us to determine which two or more variables interact.

factorial analysis of variance (ANOVA) (also known as *factorial ANOVA* when there are two factors) a statistic that lets us determine if two or more categorical or nominal independent variables influence a continuous (interval or ratio) dependent variable.

combination of selfie pose and filter influence how attractive a person looks?" We can test these questions using the **factorial analysis of variance (ANOVA),** which is a statistic that lets us determine if two or more nominal independent variables influence an interval- or ratio-dependent variable. We can use a factorial analysis of variance in a few different design situations:

1. A factorial design in which the researcher manipulates two or more independent variables to determine their effect on the dependent variable (e.g., How does eye contact and touch impact flirtation effectiveness?).

2. A hybrid design in which the researcher has two or more independent variables, with a mixture of manipulated and quasi-independent (i.e., measured) variables, to determine their effect on the dependent variable (e.g., How does men and women's use of touch [on the arm vs. on the back] impact flirtation effectiveness?).

Strictly speaking, we use a factorial ANOVA hypothesis test any time we have more than one independent variable, regardless of how many levels those variables have, or whether we have a between- or within-subjects design.

Getting to Know a Factorial ANOVA When we have two independent variables, each with two levels, we can also call this a two-by-two (i.e., 2×2) ANOVA. If we happened to have a third independent variable with two levels, we would call it a two-by-two-by-two or $2 \times 2 \times 2$ ANOVA. If that third independent variable had four levels, we would call it a two-by-two-by-four or $2 \times 2 \times 4$ ANOVA. In other words, when deciphering ANOVA notations, the number of numbers indicates how many independent variables there are (e.g., a $2 \times 2 \times 4$ has three numbers in it, so there are three factors). The numbers themselves indicate how many levels that particular independent variable has. For example, in a 3×4 ANOVA, the first independent variable has three levels, while the second independent variable has four levels. For now, we will focus on the simplest form with two factors, each with two levels.

Looking back at Figure 13.1, let's transform that into a 2×2 table that better shows our design and how our independent variables combine. First, let's chart out our independent variables and levels (see **Figure 13.2**).

Where each independent variable goes in terms of row or column is somewhat arbitrary, but you will notice our defaulting to putting the

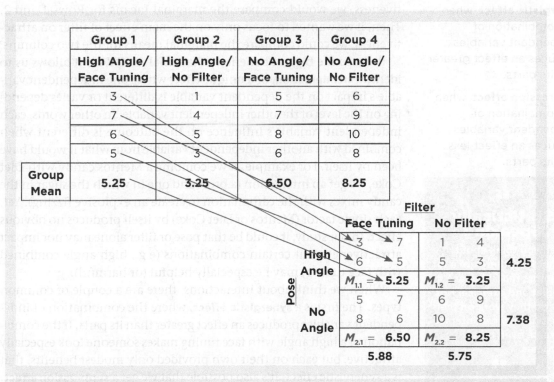

Figure 13.2 shows a 2×2 table with "Filter" heading, columns "Face Tuning" and "No Filter", and rows "Pose" with "High Angle" and "No Angle".

Figure 13.2 2 × 2 Table — Super Selfie Study

first independent variable in the rows. Next, we have to fill the boxes in with our data. As you can see in **Figure 13.3**, the data in Group 1's combination goes into the upper left box (Row 1, Column 1) showing the High Angle/Face Tuning combination. Group 2's data would then go into the upper right box (Row 1, Column 2), Group 3's into the lower left (Row 2, Column 1) and Group 4's into the lower right (Row 2, Column 2).

	Group 1	Group 2	Group 3	Group 4
	High Angle/ Face Tuning	High Angle/ No Filter	No Angle/ Face Tuning	No Angle/ No Filter
	3	1	5	6
	7	4	7	9
	6	5	8	10
	5	3	6	8
Group Mean	5.25	3.25	6.50	8.25

Filter

		Face Tuning		No Filter		
High Angle		3	7	1	4	
		6	5	5	3	4.25
		$M_{1.1} =$ 5.25		$M_{1.2} =$ 3.25		
No Angle		5	7	6	9	
		8	6	10	8	7.38
		$M_{2.1} =$ 6.50		$M_{2.2} =$ 8.25		
		5.88		5.75		

Pose

Figure 13.3 2 × 2 Table of Means — Super Selfie Study

cell mean the mean of all scores for a particular combination of the independent variables' levels.

marginal mean the mean of all scores in a single row or column.

main effects how different levels of one independent variable compare, ignoring any other independent variables.

interaction a unique effect where one independent variable's impact on the dependent variable is different or varies depending on the level of the other independent variable.

synergistic effect when the combination of independent variables produces an effect greater than its parts.

suppression effect when the combination of independent variables produces an effect less than its parts.

It's the exact same information, but in a new format. First, what had been a Group Mean, we now call a **cell mean,** or the mean of all scores for a particular combination of the independent variables' levels. For example, Group 1's mean now becomes $M_{1.1}$, to note that it is the mean for the combination of each independent variable's first level. We use this notation for each cell: $M_{1.1}$, $M_{1.2}$, $M_{2.1}$, $M_{2.2}$. We can also find the mean attractiveness rating for any one level of an independent variable. That is, if we only want to know about attractiveness ratings for high-angle selfies, we can find that by looking only at the first/topmost row ($M_{1.1}$ and $M_{1.2}$).

The number outside of the box is a **marginal mean,** which is the mean of all scores in a single row or column. Looking at Figure 13.3, 4.25 is the average of all scores in Row 1, 7.38 is the mean of all scores in Row 2 ($M_{2.1}$ and $M_{2.2}$), 5.88 is the mean of Column 1's scores ($M_{1.1}$ and $M_{2.1}$), and 5.75 is the mean of Column 2's scores ($M_{1.2}$ and $M_{2.2}$).

The marginal means allow us to detect **main effects,** or how the different levels from one independent variable (e.g., Level 1 vs. Level 2) compare to each other, ignoring any other independent variables. For example, if we want to focus only on the main effect of pose on attractiveness, we would compare the marginal means for Rows 1 and 2. Then, if we wanted to focus only on the main effect of filter on attractiveness, we could compare the marginal means for the two columns.

Perhaps the biggest benefit of a factorial ANOVA is it allows us to identify an **interaction,** or a unique effect where one independent variable's impact on the dependent variable is different or varies depending on the level of the other independent variable. In other words, each independent variable's influence on the outcome is different when combined with another independent variable from what it would have been by itself. For example, if we combine a Mentos candy with Diet Coke, we get an interaction (a profound one in which the sugar in the candy mixes with the carbonation to create an explosive fizzing). Yet, each single factor (Mentos or Diet Coke) by itself produces no obvious effect. In our study, it could be that pose or filter alone may not impact attractiveness, but certain combinations (e.g., high angle combined with face tuning) may be especially helpful (or harmful).

When we think about interactions, there are a couple of common types. The first is a **synergistic effect,** where the combination of independent variables produces an effect greater than its parts. If the combination of a high angle with face tuning makes someone look especially attractive, but each on their own provided only modest benefits, that is a synergistic effect. It's also possible that we get a **suppression effect,** where the combination of independent variables produces an effect less than the sum of its parts. If the combination of a high angle with face tuning makes someone look especially unattractive, even though both variables on their own provided modest benefits, that is a suppression effect. Being able to identify main and interaction effects is helpful when reading and interpreting journal articles.

Your Turn 13.1

1. A senior thesis student does a study looking at how a person's handshake firmness and style influences perceptions of their charisma. They've accidentally set up their data as a one-way ANOVA. Transform it into a 2 × 2 table format:

	Group 1	Group 2	Group 3	Group 4
	One Hand/ Strong	One Hand/ Weak	Two Hands/ Strong	Two Hands/ Weak
	10	2	7	1
	9	3	5	2
	7	5	4	3
Group Mean	8.67	3.33	5.33	2.00

2. You read a study that describes a 2 × 3 × 4 ANOVA.

a. How many independent variables are there?

b. How many levels does the first independent variable have?

c. How many levels does the second independent variable have?

3. For each of the following, indicate the design, and the appropriate statistic.

a. A teacher wants to see if 1st or 3rd graders learn vocabulary better by taking weekly quizzes or reading the words in stories.

b. A researcher wants to see how manipulating a person's group status (part of the in group or not) and feeling ostracized (left out or included) impacts creativity.

c. A baker wants to see which type of cupcake people like the best and has customers rate each of the following: red velvet, devil's food, wedding cake, pound cake.

4. For each item below, identify the type of interaction that occurs.

a. A normally outstanding student, who effectively studies for tests, does a worse job studying when studying along with classmates.

b. A band with 4 members enjoys a ton of success, leading individual members to attempt solo careers, but each person by themselves is unsuccessful.

Partitioning the Variance: Total Fair warning: This section is a bit technical. But, it really all comes back to the same idea we've encountered in Chapters 11 and 12, which is figuring out how much scores differ from what is typical or average (i.e., sums of squares). To do this, we will determine the total or overall variability that we have, which we call the sum of squares total, or SS_{Total}. We want to see how much each participant's score within each cell (X) differs from the overall grand mean ($X - GM$). We then square it and sum those up across all the cells to get the overall total, $\Sigma(X - GM)^2$. Now that we have the total variances, we can see how much each source (between and within groups) contributes to the overall variance.

Partitioning the Variance: Between-Groups A factorial ANOVA's between-group sum of squares helps us see our treatment or independent variable's influence on the dependent variable. In previous ANOVAs (one-way and repeated-measures), we had a single independent variable, and therefore had a single between-groups sum of squares. Now, with more than one independent variable, we will need to find the between-groups effect for each independent variable along with how the independent variables combine or interact.

Let's take this one variable at a time. The first independent variable and between-groups sum of squares is the Pose Effect. This is also the main effect for row (because of how we set up the variables in the 2×2 box diagram). The Main Effect (Pose) or Main Effect (Row) focuses on how much scores from cells in our top row ($M_{Row\ 1.1}$ and $M_{Row\ 1.2}$), each differ, on average, from the grand mean.

For example, $SS_{Row\ 1.1} = \Sigma(M_{Row\ 1.1} - GM)^2$. We'd do the same for ($M_{Row\ 1.2}$), since the 1.2 cell is also in that top row, $SS_{Row\ 1.2} = \Sigma(M_{Row\ 1.2} - GM)^2$. We do the same for scores in Row 2 (No Angle), using the cell means for Row 2, ($M_{Row\ 2.1}$ and $M_{Row\ 2.2}$). Finally, we would sum across all four cell's row sum of squares ($SS_{Row\ 1.1} + SS_{Row\ 1.2} + SS_{Row\ 2.1} + SS_{Row\ 2.2}$) to give us the overall SS_{Row}. That's a lot to digest, so it's worth going back and rereading that paragraph so you can see the pattern and logic behind what we're doing.

Next, we'll look at the other independent variable, or the Filter Effect, which is also the main effect for columns. The Main Effect (Column) or Main Effect (Filter) focuses on how much scores from Column 1 (Face Tuning), on average ($M_{Column\ 1.1}$ and $M_{Column\ 2.1}$), differ from the mean of all scores (i.e., the grand mean, or GM). For example, $SS_{Column\ 1.1} = \Sigma(M_{Column\ 1.1} - GM)^2$. This parallels what we did for rows, so we also do this using the cell means for Column 2, ($M_{Column\ 1.2}$ and $M_{Column\ 2.2}$). Finally, to give us the overall SS_{Column}, we again sum across all four cells' column sum of squares ($SS_{Column\ 1.1}$ + $SS_{Column\ 1.2}$ + $SS_{Column\ 2.1}$ + $SS_{Column\ 2.2}$).

Finally, we have to determine the between-subjects sum of squares for the Pose × Filter interaction effect. The good news is that we don't need to do a bunch of new calculations. We can use the fact that the SS_{Total} is the sum of SS_{Row}, SS_{Column}, $SS_{Interaction}$, and SS_{Within} to help us determine the $SS_{Interaction}$. In other words, we can find all of the other sum of squares first, then subtract them from SS_{Total}, which will give us $SS_{Interaction}$. Expressed as a formula, $SS_{Interaction} = SS_{Total} - SS_{Row} - SS_{Column} - SS_{Within}$. Note that if we want to take this approach, we need to calculate SS_{Within} before attempting to calculate $SS_{Interaction}$. We'll take a different (and more precise) approach to calculating the $SS_{Interaction}$ in the Statistics for Research portion of this chapter.

Partitioning the Variance: Within-Groups Like other ANOVAs, the ultimate goal is to determine if variation from our independent variables (between-subjects) exceeds the naturally occurring variation among our participants (within-subjects). In other words, we're comparing our three sources of between-groups variance to the typical variance within our participants. Whereas the repeated-measures ANOVA had the same participants in every group, with the factorial ANOVA we have different participants in each combination. As a result, we calculate a within-groups sum of squares (SS_{Within}) instead of a participant sum of squares.

To calculate the within-groups sum of squares (SS_{Within}), we take each participant's score (X), subtract the cell's mean ($M_{1.1}$), square it, and then sum it all up, $\Sigma(X - M_{1.1})^2$. Note that this is for a person in the upper left cell, who received the first level of each independent variable (High Angle/Face Tuning). For a score in the upper right cell (High Angle/No Filter), we would find the scores' deviation from that cell's mean ($M_{1.2}$), and so on. After finding the sum for each cell, we would then sum all four cells ($SS_{Within\ 1.1}$ + $SS_{Within\ 1.2}$ + $SS_{Within\ 2.1}$ + $SS_{Within\ 2.2}$) to give us the overall within-groups sum of squares (SS_{Within}).

$$SS_{Total} = \Sigma(X - GM)^2$$
$$SS_{Row} = \Sigma(M_{Row} - GM)^2$$
$$SS_{Column} = \Sigma(M_{Column} - GM)^2$$
$$SS_{Interaction} = SS_{Total} - SS_{Row} - SS_{Column} - SS_{Within}$$
$$SS_{Within} = \Sigma(X - M_{Cell})^2$$

Your Turn 13.2

1. How is the logic we're following for calculating the between-groups sum of squares different in a factorial ANOVA from what we did with the one-way between-groups ANOVA?

Hypothesis Testing with a Factorial Analysis of Variance (ANOVA): How Does It Work?

You've reached a major milestone: Factorial ANOVA is the most complicated analysis that we will encounter in this textbook. But, by this point, you're virtually an expert at hypothesis testing, so you'll be happy to know that hypothesis testing with factorial ANOVA follows the same steps we've been using all along and is very similar to what we did with the one-way between-groups ANOVA. The only wrinkle is that we have a few additional effects to test (our second independent variable and the interaction).

Step by Step: Hypothesis Testing with the Factorial Analysis of Variance (ANOVA) As always, our first step is to establish the populations.

Step 1: Population and Hypotheses Although we have multiple independent variables, we set this up as if there are four groups, similar to what we did for the one-way analysis of variance. In parentheses after each population, we note the cell that corresponds to each cell.

Population 1 (μ_1; 1.1): People who take selfies at a high angle and use face tuning.

Population 2 (μ_2; 1.2): People who take selfies at a high angle and don't use any filter.

Population 3 (μ_3; 2.1): People who take selfies at no angle and use face tuning.

Population 4 (μ_4; 2.2): People who take selfies at no angle and don't use any filter.

Sample: Sixteen people who attended a fraternity-sorority mixer.

With our populations established, next we make predictions about what we expect to find. Because we have two independent variables (i.e., two main effects), we will need a hypothesis for each one, as well as one for the interaction. Here are the three hypotheses:

Research Hypothesis 1—Main Effect (Row/Pose) (H_1): People who take selfies with a high angle and people who take selfies with no angle will have different levels of attractiveness ($\mu_1 + \mu_2 \neq \mu_3 + \mu_4$). Looking at the symbol notation, we're essentially saying that both populations associated with high angle poses (μ_1 and μ_2) will differ from both populations associated with no angle selfies (μ_3 and μ_4). We use a nondirectional hypothesis because it isn't clear how pose might affect attractiveness. It could be that high angle makes people look better, or it could be that high angle hurts attractiveness because it looks less natural. Therefore, we are going to predict a difference without stating what that difference may be.

Null Hypothesis 1: The population means are equal ($\mu_1 + \mu_2 = \mu_3 + \mu_4$). In other words, the high angle selfie populations will have the same mean as the no angle selfie populations.

Research Hypothesis 2—Main Effect (Column/Filter) (H_2): People who take selfies with a face tuning filter and people who take selfies with no filter will have different levels of attractiveness ($\mu_1 + \mu_3 \neq \mu_2 + \mu_4$). Looking at the symbol notation, we're suggesting that both populations associated with face tuning filters (μ_1 and μ_3) will differ from both populations associated with no filter selfies (μ_2 and μ_4). We use a nondirectional hypothesis because it isn't clear how filter might affect attractiveness. It could be that face tuning enhances attractiveness, or it could make people look worse.

Null Hypothesis 2: The population means are equal ($\mu_1 + \mu_3 = \mu_2 + \mu_4$). In other words, the face tuning selfie populations will have the same mean as the no filter selfie populations.

Research Hypothesis 3—Interaction Effect (Row × Column) (H_3): For people who take selfies at a high angle, filter's effect on their attractiveness will be different than how filter affects people who take selfies with no angle. ($\mu_1 - \mu_2 \neq \mu_3 - \mu_4$). Looking at the symbol notation, we're suggesting that the pattern in Row 1/High Angle across the filter levels ($\mu_1 - \mu_2$) will be different from the pattern in Row 2/No Angle across the filter levels ($\mu_3 - \mu_4$).

Null Hypothesis 3: The population means are equal ($\mu_1 - \mu_2 = \mu_3 - \mu_4$). In other words, pose's effect on attractiveness does not rely on filter's effect, meaning that Row 1/High Angle's pattern across the filter levels ($\mu_1 - \mu_2$) will be the same as Row 2/No Angle's pattern across the filter levels ($\mu_3 - \mu_4$).

Step 2: Build Comparison Distribution As with previous ANOVAs, to determine if our main effects or interaction effect is significant, we need to compare *F*-ratios that we observe in our data to the *F* distribution, which provides the likelihood of observing different values of *F* if the null hypothesis is true. So, before we move on, we need to specify the comparison distribution first. As before, our degrees of freedom dictate the *F* distribution's shape. The key difference with a factorial ANOVA is that we have degrees of freedom for each between-groups effect.

Within-Groups df	Significance (Alpha) Level	Between-Groups Degrees of Freedom					
		1	2	3	4	5	6
1	0.01	4052	5000	5404	5625	5764	5859
	0.05	162	200	216	225	230	234
2	0.01	98.50	99.00	99.17	99.25	99.30	99.33
	0.05	18.51	19.00	19.17	19.25	19.30	19.33
3	0.01	34.12	30.82	29.46	28.71	28.24	27.91
	0.05	10.13	9.55	9.28	9.12	9.01	8.94
4	0.01	21.20	18.00	16.70	15.98	15.52	15.21
	0.05	7.71	6.95	6.59	6.39	6.26	6.16
5	0.01	16.26	13.27	12.06	11.39	10.97	10.67
	0.05	6.61	5.79	5.41	5.19	5.05	4.95
6	0.01	13.75	10.93	9.78	9.15	8.75	8.47
	0.05	5.99	5.14	4.76	4.53	4.39	4.28
7	0.01	12.25	9.55	8.45	7.85	7.46	7.19
	0.05	5.59	4.74	4.35	4.12	3.97	3.87
8	0.01	11.26	8.65	7.59	7.01	6.63	6.37
	0.05	5.32	4.46	4.07	3.84	3.69	3.58
9	0.01	10.56	8.02	6.99	6.42	6.06	5.80
	0.05	5.12	4.26	3.86	3.63	3.48	3.37
10	0.01	10.05	7.56	6.55	6.00	5.64	5.39
	0.05	4.97	4.10	3.71	3.48	3.33	3.22
11	0.01	9.65	7.21	6.22	5.67	5.32	5.07
	0.05	4.85	3.98	3.59	3.36	3.20	3.10
12	0.01	9.33	6.93	5.95	5.41	5.07	4.82
	0.05	4.75	3.89	3.49	3.26	3.11	3.00
13	0.01	9.07	6.70	5.74	5.21	4.86	4.62
	0.05	4.67	3.81	3.41	3.18	3.03	2.92
14	0.01	8.86	6.52	5.56	5.04	4.70	4.46
	0.05	4.60	3.74	3.34	3.11	2.96	2.85
15	0.01	8.68	6.36	5.42	4.89	4.56	4.32
	0.05	4.54	3.68	3.29	3.06	2.90	2.79
16	0.01	8.53	6.23	5.29	4.77	4.44	4.20
	0.05	4.49	3.63	3.24	3.01	2.85	2.74
17	0.01	8.40	6.11	5.19	4.67	4.34	4.10
	0.05	4.45	3.59	3.20	2.97	2.81	2.70

Figure 13.4 *F*-Table Preview

We calculate the between-groups (Row) degrees of freedom as follows: $df_{Row} = N_{Rows} - 1 = 2 - 1 = 1$. We get the between-groups (Column) degrees of freedom as follows: $df_{Column} = N_{Columns} - 1 = 2 - 1 = 1$. Our between-groups (Interaction) degrees of freedom is: $df_{Interaction} = (df_{Rows})(df_{Columns}) = (1)(1) = 1$. Finally, we calculate our within-subjects degrees of freedom as the sum of each cell's degrees of freedom (i.e., the number of scores in each cell – 1):

$$df_{Within} = df_{1.1} + df_{1.2} + df_{2.1} + df_{2.2} = 3 + 3 + 3 + 3 = 12.$$

The total degrees of freedom is the sum of all the others:

$$df_{Rows} + df_{Columns} + df_{Interaction} + df_{Within} = 1 + 1 + 1 + 12 = 15.$$

We can also calculate the degrees of freedom total (df_{Total}) by taking the overall sample size minus 1: $df_{Total} = 16 - 1 = 15$.

Want to review degrees of freedom? SEE CHAPTER 9.

$$df_{Row} = N_{Rows} - 1$$
$$df_{Column} = N_{Columns} - 1$$
$$df_{Interaction} = (df_{Rows})(df_{Column})$$
$$df_{Within} = (df_{1.1} + df_{1.2} + df_{2.1} + df_{2.2})$$
$$df_{Total} = df_{Row} + df_{Column} +$$
$$df_{Interaction} + df_{Within}$$

Step 3: Establish Critical Value Cutoff To use the F-table to find our cutoff, we still need the same three pieces of information: significance level, between-groups degrees of freedom, and within-groups degrees of freedom. We'll use the standard .05 significance level, each of our between-subjects effects (Row, Column, Interaction) have the same degrees of freedom (1), and our within-groups degrees of freedom was 12. Looking at the table (**Figure 13.4**), the cutoff for an $F(1, 12)$ comparison distribution is 4.75.

Finally, we should indicate where our cutoff falls on our comparison distribution (**Figure 13.5**).

Step 4: Determine Sample Results We've run the study by having 16 participants each look at one selfie featuring one pose and filter combination, then let us know how attractive they thought the person was. To determine if Pose (high angle vs. no angle), Filter (face tuning vs. no filter), as well as the interaction of both (Pose × Filter) influence attractiveness ratings, we need to compare each effect's between-groups variance to the within-groups variance.

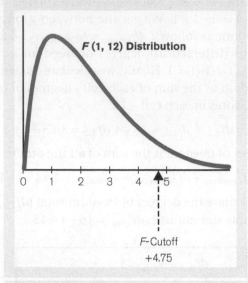

Figure 13.5 *F* Distribution with Critical Value Cutoff

First, we'll calculate the total sum of squares with the following formula for each cell's score: $\Sigma(X - GM)^2$. Then, to get the overall total, we'll sum across all the cells, for each cell:

$$SS_{Total} = 10.016 + 35.016 + 6.891 + 32.516 = 84.439$$

Next, we'll calculate the within-groups sum of squares with the following formula in each cell, $\Sigma(X - M_{Cell})^2$. Then, to get the overall within-groups sum of squares we'll sum across all the cells:

$$SS_{Within} = 8.75 + 8.75 + 5.00 + 8.75 = 31.25$$

Note that we're doing this right after the SS_{Total} so that we can calculate the $SS_{Interaction}$ with the simpler formula.

Next, we'll calculate the between-groups sum of squares for Row/Pose with the following formula in each cell, $(M_{Row} - GM)^2$. Then, to get the overall row sum of squares, we'll sum across all the cells $\Sigma(M_{Row} - GM)^2$:

$$SS_{Rows} = 9.766 + 9.766 + 9.766 + 9.766 = 39.064$$

Next, we'll calculate the between-groups sum of squares for Column/Filter with the following formula in each cell, $(M_{Column} - GM)^2$. Then, to get the overall column sum of squares, we'll sum across all the cells $\Sigma(M_{Column} - GM)^2$:

$$SS_{Column} = 0.016 + 0.016 + 0.016 + 0.016 = 0.06$$

High Angle/Face Tuning (Row 1/Column 1)

PartNum	(X)	$(X - GM)^2$	$(X - M_{1.1})^2$	$(M_{Row\,1} - GM)^2$	$(M_{Col\,1} - GM)^2$
1	3	7.910	5.063	2.441	0.0039
5	7	1.410	3.063	2.441	0.0039
9	6	0.035	0.563	2.441	0.0039
13	5	0.660	0.063	2.441	0.0039
$M_{1.1}$ 5.25		10.016	8.750	9.766	0.016
N 4		SS_{Total}	$SS_{Within\,1.1}$	$SS_{Row\,1.1}$	$SS_{Column\,1.1}$
$df_{1.1}$ 3		Sums from Cell 1.1			

High Angle/No Filter (Row 1/Column 2)

PartNum	(X)	$(X - GM)^2$	$(X - M_{1.2})^2$	$(M_{Row\,1} - GM)^2$	$(M_{Col\,2} - GM)^2$
2	1	23.160	5.063	2.441	0.0039
6	4	3.285	0.563	2.441	0.0039
10	5	0.660	3.063	2.441	0.0039
14	3	7.910	0.063	2.441	0.0039
$M_{1.2}$ 3.25		35.016	8.750	9.766	0.016
N 4		SS_{Total}	$SS_{Within\,1.2}$	$SS_{Row\,1.2}$	$SS_{Column\,1.2}$
$df_{1.2}$ 3		Sums from Cell 1.2			

$M_{Row\,1}$ 4.250

No Angle/Face Tuning (Row 2/Column 1)

PartNum	(X)	$(X - GM)^2$	$(X - M_{2.1})^2$	$(M_{Row\,2} - GM)^2$	$(M_{Col\,1} - GM)^2$
3	5	0.660	2.250	2.441	0.0039
7	7	1.410	0.250	2.441	0.0039
11	8	4.785	2.250	2.441	0.0039
15	6	0.035	0.250	2.441	0.0039
$M_{2.1}$ 6.50		6.891	5.000	9.766	0.016
N 4		SS_{Total}	$SS_{Within\,2.1}$	$SS_{Row\,2.1}$	$SS_{Column\,2.1}$
$df_{2.1}$ 3		Sums from Cell 2.1			

No Angle/No Filter (Row 2/Column 2)

PartNum	(X)	$(X - GM)^2$	$(X - M_{2.2})^2$	$(M_{Row\,2} - GM)^2$	$(M_{Col\,2} - GM)^2$
4	6	0.035	5.063	2.441	0.0039
8	9	10.160	0.563	2.441	0.0039
12	10	17.535	3.063	2.441	0.0039
16	8	4.785	0.063	2.441	0.0039
$M_{2.2}$ 8.25		32.516	8.750	9.766	0.016
N 4		SS_{Total}	$SS_{Within\,2.2}$	$SS_{Row\,2.2}$	$SS_{Column\,2.2}$
$df_{2.2}$ 3		Sums from Cell 2.2			

$M_{Row\,2}$ 7.375

$M_{Column\,1}$ 5.875 $M_{Column\,2}$ 5.750

	GM	$(\Sigma M)/N_{Groups}$	5.813

Sums of Squares	84.438	31.250	39.063	0.063	14.063	84.438
	SS_{Total}	SS_{Within}	SS_{Row}	SS_{Column}	SS_{Int}	Check. Within + Row + Column + Int, should match SS_{Total}
	Sums combining Cell 1.1, Cell 1.2, Cell 2.1, Cell 2.2					

Degrees of Freedom	df_{Row}	$N_{Rows} - 1$	1.00	df_{Int}	$(df_{Rows})(df_{Columns})$	1.00
	df_{Column}	$N_{Columns} - 1$	1.00	df_{Within}	$df_{1.1} + df_{1.2} + df_{2.1} + df_{2.2}$	12.00

Mean Squares	MS_{Row}	SS_{Row}/df_{Row}	39.063
	MS_{Column}	SS_{Column}/df_{Column}	0.063
	$MS_{Interaction}$	$SS_{Interaction}/df_{Interaction}$	14.063
	MS_{Within}	SS_{Within}/df_{Within}	2.604

F-Scores	F_{Row}	MS_{Row}/MS_{Within}	15.00
	F_{Column}	MS_{Column}/MS_{Within}	0.02
	$F_{Interaction}$	$MS_{Interaction}/MS_{Within}$	5.40

Figure 13.6 Computations for a Factorial Analysis of Variance (ANOVA)

Finally, we'll calculate the between-groups sum of squares for the Interaction (Pose × Filter), with the following formula, $SS_{Interaction} = SS_{Total} - SS_{Row} - SS_{Column} - SS_{Within} = 84.44 - 31.25 - 39.06 - 0.06 = 14.06$. (Note that we are rounding to two decimal places here to simplify the calculation. **Figure 13.6** shows the numbers rounded to four decimals.)

Because ANOVA focuses on variance, using the sums of squares, we now need to calculate the variance from each of our main sources (Between and Within). We call this our mean squares (MS) and follow the general formula we've used before when calculating variance: SS/df. We tailor that to each effect as follows:

$$MS_{Row} = SS_{Row}/df_{Row} = 39.06/1 = 39.06$$

$$MS_{Column} = SS_{Column}/df_{Column} = 0.06/1 = 0.06$$

$$MS_{Interaction} = SS_{Interaction}/df_{Interaction} = 14.06/1 = 14.06$$

$$MS_{Within} = SS_{Within}/df_{Within} = 31.25/12 = 2.60$$

$$MS_{Row} = SS_{Row} / df_{Row}$$
$$MS_{Column} = SS_{Column} / df_{Column}$$
$$MS_{Interaction} = SS_{Interaction} / df_{Interaction}$$
$$MS_{Within} = SS_{Within} / df_{Within}$$

$$F_{Row} = MS_{Row} / MS_{Within}$$
$$F_{Column} = MS_{Column} / MS_{Within}$$
$$F_{Interaction} = MS_{Interaction} / MS_{Within}$$

As in the one-way between-groups ANOVA, the F-ratio tells us whether variance from a between-groups source differs from how much people typically vary (i.e., the within-groups variance). We determine this by comparing variance or mean squares from the relevant sources. We tailor that to each effect as follows:

$$F_{Row} = MS_{Row}/MS_{Within} = 39.06/2.60 = 15.00$$

$$F_{Column} = MS_{Column}/MS_{Within} = 0.06/2.60 = 0.02$$

$$F_{Interaction} = MS_{Interaction}/MS_{Within} = 14.06/2.60 = 5.40$$

Next, we should show where our F-score falls on the comparison distribution to see if each effect's F exceeds the cutoff (**Figure 13.7**). Note that we can place them all on the same distribution because all three effects had the same degrees of freedom. If our effects had different degrees of freedom, we would need to plot them on different comparison distributions.

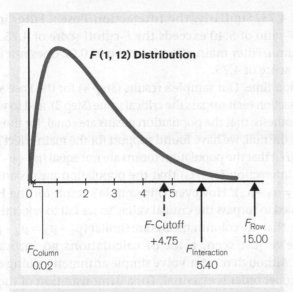

Figure 13.7 Sample Results on the Comparison Distribution

We can also easily display all of our key calculations in an ANOVA source table.

Step 5: Decide and Interpret It is clear from **Figure 13.8** that the Row/Pose main effect's F-ratio of 15.00 exceeds the F-cutoff

Source	SS	df	MS	F
Between				
Row	SS_{Row}	df_{Row}	MS_{Row}	F_{Row}
Column	SS_{Column}	df_{Column}	MS_{Column}	F_{Column}
Interaction	$SS_{Interaction}$	$df_{Interaction}$	$MS_{Interaction}$	$F_{Interaction}$
Within	SS_{Within}	df_{Within}	MS_{Within}	
Total	SS_{Total}	df_{Total}		

Source	SS	df	MS	F
Between				
Row	39.06	1	39.06	15.00
Column	0.06	1	0.06	0.02
Interaction	14.06	1	14.06	5.40
Within	31.25	12	2.60	
Total	84.44	15		

Figure 13.8 Factorial ANOVA Source Table: What Goes Where

score of 4.75. Similarly, the Interaction/Pose × Filter interaction effect's F-ratio of 5.40 exceeds the F-cutoff score of 4.75. However, the Column/Filter main effect's F-ratio of 0.02 does not exceed the F-cutoff score of 4.75.

Decision time. Our sample's results (Step 4) for the Pose Main Effect and Interaction each surpass the critical value (Step 3), and so we reject the null hypothesis, that the population means are equal, for those effects. If we reject the null, we have found support for the main effect hypothesis for pose (H_1) that the population means are not equal ($\mu_1 + \mu_2 \neq \mu_3 + \mu_4$), and the interaction for (H_3) that the population means are not equal ($\mu_1 - \mu_2 \neq \mu_3 - \mu_4$). However, our sample's result for the Filter Main Effect failed to surpass the critical value, so we fail to reject the null and conclude that the column means are similar ($\mu_1 + \mu_3 = \mu_2 + \mu_4$).

As we've just seen, a lot of calculations go into a factorial ANOVA. Although most involve simple arithmetic, doing everything in the proper order is essential. For a demonstration of the hand calculations involved in the factorial ANOVA, watch the video associated with this chapter.

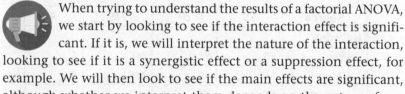

HAND CALCULATION VIDEO TUTORIAL: To learn more, check out the video Performing Factorial ANOVA.

Communicating the Result

 When trying to understand the results of a factorial ANOVA, we start by looking to see if the interaction effect is significant. If it is, we will interpret the nature of the interaction, looking to see if it is a synergistic effect or a suppression effect, for example. We will then look to see if the main effects are significant, although whether we interpret them depends on the nature of our research question. If the interaction is nonsignificant, then we will look at, and interpret, the main effects in detail.

Because we found a significant interaction between pose and filter, we will start our interpretation of the results there. To understand our interaction, we need to look at the cell means, specifically the pattern of Row 1/High Angle's cell means across the columns, compared to Row 2/No Angle's cell means across the columns. There we see that when taking a selfie with a high angle, using face tuning results in higher attractiveness ratings than using no filter. However, when taking a selfie with no angle, filter has the opposite effect, with face tuning resulting in lower attractiveness ratings compared to no filter.

Next, we can look at the main effects. We found that there was a nonsignificant effect of filter. Essentially, this tells us that there was no difference for Column/Filter, suggesting that face tuning ($M = 5.88$) produced similar attractiveness ratings as using no filter ($M = 5.75$). The main effect of pose was significant, although the F-ratio by itself does not tell us the effect's direction (i.e., which level of the independent variable was more attractive). To determine that, we must look at the marginal means for Row 1/High Angle and Row 2/No Angle. There we see that participants rated selfies taken with no angle ($M = 7.38$) as more attractive than those taken at a high angle ($M = 4.25$).

Note that although we have been mentioning rows and columns, it was only to make it easier to understand the steps while learning them the first time. When communicating a factorial ANOVA result, we should focus on the effects using variable and level labels, rather than naming them as rows and columns. To see how to report these findings in APA Style, see the Statistics for Research section in this chapter.

Forming a Conclusion

Now we need to figure out what all of these results tell us. Before doing that, we must acknowledge a major caveat: our results are based on only 16 people. Not only that, it means that only 4 people saw each combination, not to mention the fact that everyone rated attractiveness while at a mixer. That is not an ideal setting, and it does not give us the most representative sample. For those reasons, our study is best considered a **pilot test**, or a trial run that allows us to refine the study prior to running a full-scale study.

With that in mind, our results suggest that the highest attractiveness ratings came from the combination of no angle and no filter. In other words, selfies look better when they look more natural. This is consistent with research showing that observers prefer candid photos of others, despite people believing that they look better in posed shots (Berger & Barasch, 2015). This also runs counter to the stereotypes of what people think looks more attractive on social media. In other words, natural is better, and artificial poses or face-tuning actually make you look less attractive. Not only do candid photos evoke a more positive perception from others, but they are better for your own self-image. Research finds that those who did more editing of their selfies also reported more body dissatisfaction (Tiggemann et al., 2020).

Though it's possible that we failed to find an effect for filter because of low power, due to low sample size, null results can also suggest that we should consider a different independent variable. Given that we found an effect for pose, we may want to try a new variable that interacts with pose or emphasizes more natural pictures. For example, we could try different settings like a house versus a park, or a flirty face versus a basic smile.

pilot test a trial run that allows us to refine the study prior to running a full-scale study.

Your Turn 13.3

Dr. Dormir is a sleep researcher who wants to determine the best conditions for falling asleep. She believes the key is sleep environment, and that music and room temperature are key factors in that. In terms of music, she wants to test classical music and smooth jazz. For room temperature, she wants to see if it's better when the room is cool (62 degrees Fahrenheit) or warm (72 degrees Fahrenheit). To test out the procedure, Dr. Dormir has a small group of participants come to the sleep lab on campus and randomly assigns them to one of four groups. After lying in bed for 10 minutes, Dr. Dormer has participants rate their drowsiness on a 1–7 scale (1 = Not at All Drowsy; 7 = Extremely Drowsy). Though she may not have enough data to tell for sure, Dr. Dormir believes classical is the best music, and low temperatures are ideal for sleeping. She also thinks low temperatures are especially helpful when listening to classical.

1. a. Based on what you know about these designs, what will the four groups be?

   b. What would the basic table look like?

Conduct the Steps of Hypothesis Testing for This Study

2. Step 1: Population and Hypotheses.

   a. What would the populations be?

   b. What would the hypotheses be?

3. Step 2: Build Comparison Distribution. What is the comparison distribution? What shape is it?

4. Step 3: Establish Critical Value Cutoff. In order to know for sure there are differences between the visualization exercises, you need to establish a cutoff score.

   a. What three pieces of information do you need to find the cutoff score on the F-table?

   b. What is the F-cutoff associated with this information?

5. Step 4: Determine Sample Results. Each of the 12 students who came to the sleep center were evenly assigned to combination, resulting in 3 participants per combination. Here are the scores for each combination: Classical/62 Degrees (7, 7, 6); Classical/72 Degrees (4, 2, 3); Smooth Jazz/62 Degrees (3, 3, 2); Smooth Jazz/72 Degrees (2, 1, 2). Each person also indicates the size of their own bed at home (4 people have a twin, 5 have a queen, 3 have a king).

   a. What test does she need to run?

   b. What are the results?

   c. What should you do with the information about bed size?

   d. Show Steps 2, 3, and 4 of hypothesis testing on a diagram.

6. Step 5: Decide and Interpret. What is the appropriate conclusion?

7. Create an ANOVA source table to display the results.

8. a. Show scores, cell means, and marginal means in a table.

   b. Using this table, along with our hypothesis testing results, what can we determine about the direction of our effects?

Statistics for Research

Many of the world's greatest artists have suffered from emotional disturbances. Emily Dickinson, Vincent van Gogh, and Kurt Cobain, for example, all suffered from depression. Similarly, other artists report having bursts of creativity following the experience of negative emotional events, such as the death of a loved one or divorce. This link between negative emotions and creativity has been supported in research studies, which reveal, for example, that creative people tend to suffer from higher rates of emotional problems than the general public (Akinola & Mendes, 2008). Based on this information, we might predict that negative emotions increase creativity.

Still other evidence seems to support the opposite conclusion: positive emotions increase creativity. For example, the broaden-and-build theory (Fredrickson, 2001) suggests that positive emotions broaden people's perspectives and allow them to be more creative. In support of this idea, past research reveals that people experiencing positive emotions demonstrate more flexible and creative thinking (Isen et al., 1987).

Which of these hypotheses is true? Do negative emotions or positive emotions increase creativity? One possibility is that they are both true. That is, in certain situations, or for certain people, negative emotions increase creativity, while in other situations, or for different people, positive emotions increase creativity. For example, it could be that when people are under high levels of stress they become more creative when experiencing negative emotions, while people who are not stressed become more creative when experiencing positive emotions. Because we are predicting that the effect of stress changes depending on the type of emotion, we are predicting an interaction. For this reason, we need to use the factorial analysis of variance (ANOVA), because factorial ANOVA allows us to test for interactions.

Here in the Statistics for Research section, we're going to learn about common patterns of results and what they imply for main effects and interactions, advantages of factorial ANOVA, assumptions of the factorial ANOVA, using Levene's Test, calculating the $SS_{Interaction}$ directly, handling simple main effects, measuring effect size, and constructing a bar graph.

Where Do the Data Come From?

How could we test our hypothesis that stress levels change positive and negative emotions' effect on creativity? One option would be to manipulate stress levels by having some participants go through a stressful situation while others go through a non-stressful situation. For example, we could recruit 40 participants and randomly assign half of the participants to complete the Trier Social Stress Test, where participants believe they have five minutes to prepare a presentation for a group of judges, as if they are going on a job interview (Kirschbaum et al., 1993). Participants can write down notes, but at the last second the participants learn that they may not use their notes for the presentation. This situation induces high levels of stress in most people, and so we could have our high-stress condition complete this task. In contrast, we could randomly assign the other half of the participants to a low-stress condition. We could give these participants as much time as they want to prepare for a presentation and that they will give their presentation, with notes, to an empty room.

To manipulate positive and negative emotions, we could tell half of the participants that research reveals that people perform better when they experience negative emotions. For these participants, we could tell them that before they complete the job interview presentation (either the high or low stressful version) that they should think about a memory that is associated with negative emotions, such as after the death of a loved one. This would be our negative emotion condition. For the other half of the participants, we could tell them that research reveals that people perform better when they experience positive emotions. For these participants, we could tell them to think about a positive memory before performing the job interview presentation. Thus, we would have 10 participants in each of the four conditions: positive emotions/low stress, positive emotions/high stress, negative emotions/low stress, negative emotions/high stress.

Finally, if stress and/or emotions affect creativity, we need some way of determining how creative people are. One option to measure creativity is the alternative uses test (Guilford et al., 1958). In this test, participants are asked to think of as many uses for everyday objects like paper clips or bricks. We then determine creativity by the number of unique uses that the person develops for the object. For example, a person might list using a paper clip to hold paper together, pick a lock, open the SIM card door on their smartphone, or weigh down the nose of a paper airplane. Because this person came up with four unique uses of a paper clip, their score would be 4.

How creative are you? ↗
Try to think of as many uses of a brick as possible.

Factorial Analysis of Variance (ANOVA): What We're Trying to Accomplish

As we learned in the first half of this chapter, we conduct factorial ANOVA when we have more than one independent variable. Doing so allows us to look not only at the effect of each independent variable separately, which we call the main effects, but also at their combined effect, which we call an interaction effect. Although it might seem like there are infinite possibilities for how a factorial ANOVA might turn out, there are only a handful of common patterns. Let's look at each of these in more detail.

Pattern 1: A Main Effect of Only One Factor The first pattern is where we see an effect for only one of the factors. For example, if we find that positive emotions lead participants to have more creative responses on the alternative uses test than negative emotions, regardless of whether people were stressed or not, we would say that there is a main effect of emotions. **Figure 13.9** illustrates what this might look like. The left panel of the figure lists hypothetical means for our four conditions. The right panel displays those means in a bar graph.

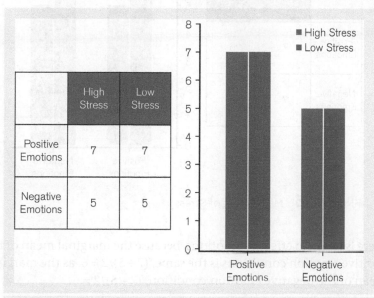

Figure 13.9 Main Effect of Emotions

We can determine that there is a main effect of emotions by looking at the marginal means. If we average the two positive emotion conditions $(7 + 7)/2$, the marginal mean is 7. If we average the two negative emotion conditions $(5 + 5)/2$, the marginal mean is 5. Because the marginal mean for the positive emotion conditions is greater than the marginal mean for the negative emotion conditions, we can conclude that there is a main effect of emotions. However, for stress, this isn't the case. When we average the two high-stress conditions $(5 + 7)/2 = 6$, we get the same marginal mean as when we average the two low-stress conditions $(5 + 7)/2 = 6$.

Alternatively, perhaps we don't find that emotions affect creativity at all, but stress does. Perhaps we find that if people are stressed, they produce more creative responses on the alternative uses test, regardless of their emotions. In this case, we would say that there is a main effect of stress. **Figure 13.10** depicts what this might look like.

We know that there is a main effect of stress because the marginal mean for the high-stress conditions $(7 + 7)/2 = 7$ is greater than the marginal mean for the low-stress conditions $(5 + 5)/2 = 5$. In comparison,

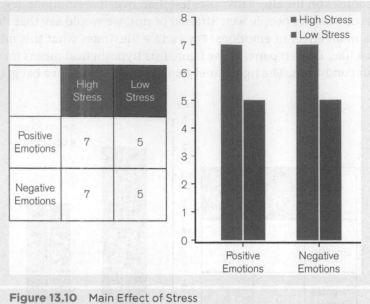

	High Stress	Low Stress
Positive Emotions	7	5
Negative Emotions	7	5

Figure 13.10 Main Effect of Stress

there is no main effect of emotions, because the marginal mean of the positive emotion conditions is the same, $(7 + 5)/2 = 6$, as the marginal mean of the negative emotion condition, $(7 + 5)/2 = 6$.

Pattern 2: Two Main Effects Of course, it's possible that we could find that both emotions and stress have main effects on creativity but do not interact. For example, we might find that people are more creative when they experience positive emotions compared to when they experience negative emotions. Moreover, people are more creative when they have high stress relative to low stress. **Figure 13.11** shows what this might look like.

Again, we determine whether there is a main effect by looking at the marginal means. Let's start with the main effect of emotions. The marginal mean for the positive emotion conditions, $(9 + 5)/2 = 7$, is greater than the marginal mean for the negative em0tion conditions $(5 + 1)/2 = 3$, supporting the conclusion that there is a main effect of emotions. Next, we evaluate the main effect of stress. The marginal mean for the high stress conditions, $(9 + 5)/2 = 7$, is greater than the marginal mean for the low stress conditions, $(5 + 1)/2 = 3$.

Pattern 3: Synergistic Interaction An interaction occurs when the effect of one independent variable changes across the levels of the other independent variable. That is, if the effects of emotions on creativity changes depending on whether people are stressed or not. As we

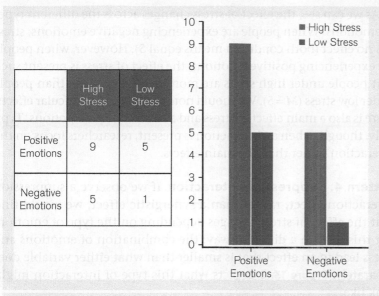

Figure 13.11   Main Effects of Stress and Emotion, but No Interaction

mentioned earlier in the chapter, there are many types of interactions, such as synergistic effects and suppression effects. Let's imagine that emotions and stress have a synergistic interaction effect; that is, the combination of emotions and stress lead to an effect that is larger than either emotions or stress do individually. **Figure 13.12** shows what that may look like.

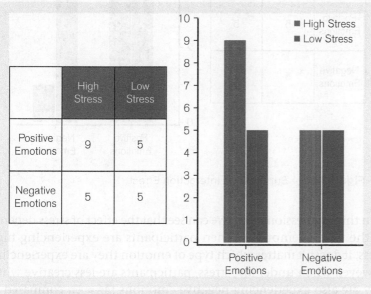

Figure 13.12   Synergistic Interaction Effect

As we can see, the effect of stress changes across the different types of emotions. When people are experiencing negative emotions, stress has no effect (both condition means equal 5). However, when people are experiencing positive emotions, the effect of stress is present such that people under high stress are more creative ($M = 9$), than people under low stress ($M = 5$). We should note that in these particular effects, there is also a main effect of stress and a main effect of emotions. Typically, though, when an interaction is present, researchers focus on the interaction rather than the main effects.

Pattern 4: Suppression Interaction If we observe a suppression interaction effect, rather than a synergistic effect, we would find that the effect of stress changes depending on the type of emotion, but this time in a different way; the combination of emotions and stress lead to an effect that is smaller than what either variable does separately. **Figure 13.13** depicts what this type of interaction might look like.

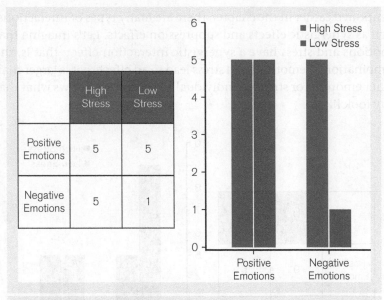

Figure 13.13   Suppression Interaction Effect

In this suppression effect, we can see that the effect of stress depends on the type of emotion. When participants are experiencing high stress, it doesn't matter which type of emotion they are experiencing. However, when under low stress, participants are less creative when they are also experiencing negative emotions ($M = 1$), compared to when they are under high stress ($M = 5$).

Pattern 5: Crossover Interaction There is another common type of interaction effect that we did not discuss in the first half of this chapter but is relevant to our current hypothesis, and that is called a **crossover effect.** In a crossover effect, the effect of one independent variable produces the opposite effect across the levels of the other independent variable.

Recall that our original hypothesis for the effects of emotions and stress was that people would be highly creative when experiencing positive emotions and low stress, or negative emotions and high stress. In other words, stress doesn't make everything better or everything worse. Instead, the effects of stress are completely different for each type of emotion. That makes the effects of emotion flip, such that they cross over to be the opposite of one another, leading to the most creativity occurring when stress is low with positive emotions, and high stress with negative emotions. **Figure 13.14** depicts what this might look like.

crossover effect a type of interaction that occurs when the effect of one independent variable produces the opposite effect across the levels of the other independent variable.

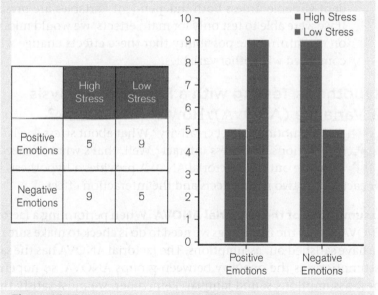

Figure 13.14   Crossover Interaction Effect

In this crossover effect interaction, we can see that the effect of stress completely reverses when we consider the type of emotion. When stress is high, people are more creative when they are experiencing negative emotions ($M = 9$) than when they are experiencing positive emotions ($M = 5$). When stress is low, people are more creative when they are experiencing positive emotions ($M = 9$) than when they are experiencing negative emotions ($M = 5$).

Advantages of the Factorial ANOVA Because factorial ANOVA allows us to test for different patterns in our data (i.e., main effects and interactions), it has several advantages compared to one-way between-groups ANOVA. Here are a few of these advantages:

1. Factorial designs are more efficient. Rather than conducting two separate studies, each investigating one independent variable at a time, we can conduct one study that investigates two independent variables simultaneously. This, potentially, saves us time and resources.

2. Life is rarely simple. When we study what makes people creative (or any other type of multifaceted outcome), it's almost never one variable. So, factorial designs allow us to capture more complexity in our research by looking at multiple independent variables.

3. Most importantly, factorial designs, and the factorial ANOVA, allow us to test for interactions. As we noted earlier (using the example of Mentos candy and Coke), it's possible for neither of two independent variables to have an effect on the dependent variable unless both independent variables are present. If we were able to test only for main effects, we would miss out on examining the possibility that these effects change when combined with other variables.

Hypothesis Testing with a Factorial Analysis of Variance (ANOVA): How Does It Work?

? Do emotions affect creativity? What about stress levels? Do emotions and stress interact? Well, that's what we need to figure out. The factorial ANOVA provides a hypothesis test for each of the two main effects and the interaction effect.

Assumptions of the Factorial ANOVA When performing a factorial ANOVA, one of the first things we need to do is check to make sure that we have satisfied our assumptions. The factorial ANOVA has the same assumptions as the one-way between-groups ANOVA, so hopefully these assumptions sound familiar. Remember, we must satisfy these assumptions in order for our results to be valid (or accurate).

1. *The dependent variable must be interval or ratio.* As with the other hypothesis tests we have learned so far, we must measure our dependent variable at interval or ratio levels of measurement. In other words, if we have a nominal- or ordinal-level dependent variable, we need to conduct a different test.

2. *Participants' scores must be independent.* The observations for each population are independent of one another. None of our independent variables can be within-subjects.

3. *The population's scores on the dependent variable are normally distributed, or we have large samples.* This assumption states that either we know that the populations' distributions are normally distributed, or we have a large enough sample to ensure that their sampling distributions are normally distributed, as a result of the Central Limit Theorem.

4. *The populations' variances are equal.* We assume that our populations start out with the same variances, and that our independent variable affects only the means of the conditions and not their variances. Thus, if the populations start with equal variances, and our manipulation does not affect those variances, then the populations should end with equal variances.

Step by Step: Hypothesis Testing with the Factorial Analysis of Variance (ANOVA) As with any hypothesis test, our first step is to specify the populations and hypotheses we are testing.

Step 1: Population and Hypotheses Ultimately, our study of the effects of emotions and stress on creativity is a test of four populations, each one defined by the combination of our two independent variables:

Population 1 (μ_1; 1.1): People experiencing positive emotions and low stress.

Population 2 (μ_2; 1.2): People experiencing positive emotions and high stress.

Population 3 (μ_3; 2.1): People experiencing negative emotions and low stress.

Population 4 (μ_4; 2.2): People experiencing negative emotions and high stress.

Sample: Forty participants randomly assigned to one of each of the four conditions ($N = 10$ per condition).

Research Hypothesis 1—Main Effect of Emotion: This main effect test is examining whether people experiencing positive emotions differ in their creativity from people experiencing negative emotions, regardless of their level of stress. Our hypothesis is two-tailed, meaning that we don't know for sure whether positive or negative emotions will lead to more creativity overall, just that the positive emotion conditions will differ from the negative emotion conditions, ($\mu_1 + \mu_2 \neq \mu_3 + \mu_4$).

Null Hypothesis 1: The population means are equal ($\mu_1 + \mu_2 = \mu_3 + \mu_4$); there is no effect of emotions on creativity.

Research Hypothesis 2—Main Effect of Stress: This main effect is testing whether people differ in their levels of creativity based on whether they are in a high stress or low stress condition. That is, regardless of their emotions (positive or negative), this main effect is looking to see if high stress or low stress people are more creative. Because we don't know whether high or low stress will lead to more creativity, we will make this a two-tailed research hypothesis, $(\mu_1 + \mu_3 \neq \mu_2 + \mu_4)$.

Null Hypothesis 2: The null hypothesis is that all of the means will be equal $(\mu_1 + \mu_2 = \mu_3 + \mu_4)$; there is no effect of stress on creativity.

Research Hypothesis 3—Interaction Effect (Row × Column) (H_3): As we stated earlier, we expect that people will be more creative when experiencing positive emotions and low stress or negative emotions and high stress, but will be less creative when experiencing positive emotions and high stress or negative emotions and low stress $(\mu_1 - \mu_4 \neq \mu_2 - \mu_3)$. This is a crossover effect. However, despite the specificity of our research hypothesis, we are going to leave open the possibility of observing any type of interaction (e.g., synergistic, suppression).

Null Hypothesis 3: The null hypothesis is that all of the means will be equal $(\mu_1 - \mu_4 = \mu_2 - \mu_3)$; there is no interaction of emotions and stress on creativity.

Step 2: Build Comparison Distribution To evaluate the null hypotheses (and by extension the research hypotheses) that we just described, we need to build a comparison distribution. The shape of the F distribution changes based on the degrees of freedom between and the degrees of freedom within. In some situations (such as when we have a differing number of conditions for each of the independent variables), our critical values will be different for the main effects and interaction. In this case, we have two independent variables, each with two conditions, so the critical values will be the same. Nevertheless, we should calculate the degrees of freedom carefully and methodically.

To calculate the degrees of freedom for the main effect of the first independent variable (the row variable), we take the number of conditions minus 1. Why is this how we determine the degrees of freedom for the main effect? Well, remember that in Chapter 9 we said that degrees of freedom are determined by the number of independent observations minus the population parameters we have calculated. When we calculate the sum of squares for the main effect of an independent variable, we compare the mean for each condition to its marginal mean. In the case of factorial ANOVA, the independent observations are the condition means, and the population parameter is the marginal mean. Thus, we take the number of conditions minus 1. For our creativity study, emotion was the row variable, and there are two emotion conditions (positive and negative), so the main effect of emotion has $df_{Row} = N_{Rows} - 1 = 2 - 1 = 1$ degree of freedom.

Similarly, to calculate the degrees of freedom for the main effect of the second independent variable (the column variable), we take the number of conditions minus 1. For our creativity study, stress was the column variable and there were two conditions (high stress and low stress). So, the main effect of stress has $df_{Column} = N_{Columns} - 1 = 2 - 1 = 1$ degree of freedom.

Next, to calculate the degrees of freedom for the interaction term, we multiply the degrees of freedom for the row variable by the degrees of freedom for the row variable. For our creativity study, we had one degree of freedom for emotion and one degree of freedom for stress; thus, our interaction effect has $df_{Interaction} = (df_{Rows})(df_{Columns}) = (1)(1) = 1$ degree of freedom.

Finally, we need to calculate the degrees of freedom within. To do this, we take the sample size per cell in our table minus 1. This is the case because to calculate the sum of squares within, we took each score minus the cell mean. So, we had the number of scores in each cell as independent observations and the cell mean as the population parameter. We did this for each cell, so we need to add the degrees of freedom per cell to find our overall degrees of freedom within:

$$df_{Within} = df_{1.1} + df_{1.2} + df_{2.1} + df_{2.2} = 9 + 9 + 9 + 9 = 36.$$

Although it's not necessary for the construction of the comparison distribution, we can calculate the degrees of freedom total by summing all of the degrees of freedom that we have found so far:

$$df_{Rows} + df_{Columns} + df_{Interaction} + df_{Within} = 1 + 1 + 1 + 36 = 39.$$

This value should equal the overall sample size minus 1 because we calculate the sum of squares total by taking each score in our distribution minus the grand mean. Thus, we have N independent observations and one population parameter.

Step 3: Establish Critical Value Cutoff Now that we know the number of degrees of freedom for each main effect, the interaction, and the within effect, we can determine the critical value(s) for the main effects and interaction effect. Because both the main effects and the interaction effects have the same degrees of freedom between (1) and within (36), all three effects will have the same critical value. To find the critical value(s), we will refer to our F-table (**Figure 13.15**).

Unfortunately, our exact number of degrees of freedom within is not provided in our table. So, we can either round down to the closest value that is provided in our table (in this case, 35 degrees of freedom within), or we can use an online critical value calculator. If we round down to 35 degrees of freedom within, our critical value is 4.12. If we use an online calculator for 36 degrees of freedom within, our critical value is 4.11. Hopefully, we can see that these critical values are really

Within-Groups df	Significance (Alpha) Level	Between-Groups Degrees of Freedom					
		1	2	3	4	5	6
1	0.01	4052	5000	5404	5625	5764	5859
	0.05	162	200	216	225	230	234
2	0.01	98.50	99.00	99.17	99.25	99.30	99.33
	0.05	18.51	19.00	19.17	19.25	19.30	19.33
4	0.01	21.20	18.00	16.70	15.98	15.52	15.21
	0.05	7.71	6.95	6.59	6.39	6.26	6.16
6	0.01	13.75	10.93	9.78	9.15	8.75	8.47
	0.05	5.99	5.14	4.76	4.53	4.39	4.28
8	0.01	11.26	8.65	7.59	7.01	6.63	6.37
	0.05	5.32	4.46	4.07	3.84	3.69	3.58
10	0.01	10.05	7.56	6.55	6.00	5.64	5.39
	0.05	4.97	4.10	3.71	3.48	3.33	3.22
12	0.01	9.33	6.93	5.95	5.41	5.07	4.82
	0.05	4.75	3.89	3.49	3.26	3.11	3.00
14	0.01	8.86	6.52	5.56	5.04	4.70	4.46
	0.05	4.60	3.74	3.34	3.11	2.96	2.85
16	0.01	8.53	6.23	5.29	4.77	4.44	4.20
	0.05	4.49	3.63	3.24	3.01	2.85	2.74
18	0.01	8.29	6.01	5.09	4.58	4.25	4.02
	0.05	4.41	3.56	3.16	2.93	2.77	2.66
20	0.01	8.10	5.85	4.94	4.43	4.10	3.87
	0.05	4.35	3.49	3.10	2.87	2.71	2.60
25	0.01	7.77	5.57	4.68	4.18	3.86	3.63
	0.05	4.24	3.39	2.99	2.76	2.60	2.49
30	0.01	7.56	5.39	4.51	4.02	3.70	3.47
	0.05	4.17	3.32	2.92	2.69	2.53	2.42
35	0.01	7.42	5.27	4.40	3.91	3.59	3.37
	0.05	4.12	3.27	2.88	2.64	2.49	2.37
40	0.01	7.32	5.18	4.31	3.83	3.51	3.29
	0.05	4.09	3.23	2.84	2.61	2.45	2.34
45	0.01	7.23	5.11	4.25	3.77	3.46	3.23
	0.05	4.06	3.21	2.81	2.58	2.42	2.31
50	0.01	7.17	5.06	4.20	3.72	3.41	3.19
	0.05	4.04	3.18	2.79	2.56	2.40	2.29

Figure 13.15 *F*-Table Preview

close to each other and likely would lead us to make the same decision regarding the null regardless of which approach we took. In this case, because the online calculator critical value is more accurate, we will adopt a critical value of 4.11 (**Figure 13.16**).

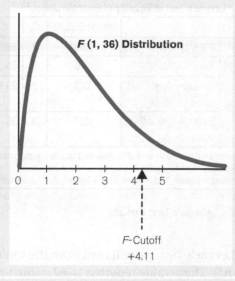

Figure 13.16 F Distribution with Critical Value Cutoff

Step 4: Determine Sample Results We're now ready to calculate the F-ratios for our two main effects and interaction. Before we do, though, we need to start by checking to see if we have satisfied the assumptions of factorial ANOVA.

The first assumption is that the dependent variable is interval or ratio. For our current study, score on the alternative uses test is our dependent variable, and it is a ratio variable. So we have satisfied the first assumption. The second assumption is that participants' scores are independent. Let's assume that we tested participants individually and so participants could not affect each other's performance, which means that we satisfy the second assumption. The third assumption states that participants' scores on the dependent variable are normally distributed or our samples are large. For our study, we only have 40 participants overall (and 10 per condition). This could potentially be a limitation of our study, so we would likely want to replicate our findings with a larger sample. Finally, the fourth assumption is the equality of variance assumption. As with one-way between-groups ANOVA, we can have SPSS conduct Levene's Test for Equality of Error Variances. The null hypothesis for Levene's Test is that the variances are equal. Thus, to satisfy the assumption, we want to fail to reject the null hypothesis. In other words, we want the p-value to be greater than .05. SPSS output for Levene's Test is displayed in **Figure 13.17**.

Levene's Test of Equality of Error Variances[a,b]					
		Levene Statistic	df$_1$	df$_2$	Sig.
Creativity_Score	Based on Mean	.239	3	36	.869
	Based on Median	.240	3	36	.868
	Based on Median and with adjusted df	.240	3	29.825	.868
	Based on trimmed mean	.237	3	36	.870

Tests the null hypothesis that the error variance of the dependent variable is equal across groups.
  a. Dependent variable: Creativity_Score
  b. Design: Intercept + Emotion_Type + Stress_Level + Emotion_Type * Stress Level

Figure 13.17   Levene's Test Results

To interpret Levene's Test, we will read from the top row of output ("Based on Mean"). The p-value reported is .87, which is greater than .05. Thus, we have satisfied the assumption.

Given that we have satisfied the assumptions, we are ready to calculate the F-ratio. Remember that the whole idea of analysis of variance is that we're going to find the total amount of variance in the dependent variable (SS_{Total}) and then partition that variance into its sources: the within-groups variation (SS_{Within}), the main effect of the first independent variable (SS_{Rows}), and the main effect of the second independent variable (SS_{Column}). We can attribute any remaining variance to the interaction effect ($SS_{Interaction}$).

Let's start by calculating the total sum of squares. To do this, as always, we calculate the difference between each score and the grand mean, square the result, and add up all of the values: $\Sigma(X - GM)^2$. As you can see in **Figure 13.18,** we found the sum of squares total for each of the conditions first and then summed these across the four conditions:

$$SS_{Total} = 29.56 + 28.66 + 65.11 + 33.66 = 158.98$$

Next, we calculate the within-groups sum of squares. Note that software packages (such as SPSS) call this the sum of squares error, because it captures the variability in the dependent variable that is not due to the independent variables (main effects or interaction). Because the condition mean changes across the four conditions, we will compute

Positive Emotions/Low Stress (Row 1/Column 1)

Part Num	(X)	$(X-GM)^2$	$(X-M_{1.1})^2$	$(M_{Row\,1}-GM)^2$	$(M_{Col\,1}-GM)^2$
1	17	0.00	1.21	0.05	0.11
2	20	9.15	3.61	0.05	0.11
3	16	0.95	4.41	0.05	0.11
4	19	4.10	0.81	0.05	0.11
5	20	9.15	3.61	0.05	0.11
6	18	1.05	0.01	0.05	0.11
7	18	1.05	0.01	0.05	0.11
8	17	0.00	1.21	0.05	0.11
9	17	0.00	1.21	0.05	0.11
10	19	4.10	0.81	0.05	0.11
$M_{1.1}$ 18.10		29.56	16.90	0.51	1.06
N 10		SS_{Total}	$SS_{Within\,1.1}$	$SS_{Row\,1.1}$	$SS_{Column\,1.1}$
$df_{1.1}$ 9		Sums from Cell 1.1			

Positive Emotions/High Stress (Row 1/Column 2)

Part Num	(X)	$(X-GM)^2$	$(X-M_{1.2})^2$	$(M_{Row\,1}-GM)^2$	$(M_{Col\,2}-GM)^2$
11	16	0.95	0.09	0.05	0.11
12	17	0.00	0.49	0.05	0.11
13	17	0.00	0.49	0.05	0.11
14	18	1.05	2.89	0.05	0.11
15	19	4.10	7.29	0.05	0.11
16	17	0.00	0.49	0.05	0.11
17	16	0.95	0.09	0.05	0.11
18	14	8.85	5.29	0.05	0.11
19	14	8.85	5.29	0.05	0.11
20	15	3.90	1.69	0.05	0.11
$M_{1.2}$ 16.30		28.66	24.10	0.51	1.06
N 10		SS_{Total}	$SS_{Within\,1.2}$	$SS_{Row\,1.2}$	$SS_{Column\,1.2}$
$df_{1.2}$ 9		Sums from Cell 1.2			

$M_{Row\,1}$ 17.20

Negative Emotions/Low Stress (Row 2/Column 1)

Part Num	(X)	$(X-GM)^2$	$(X-M_{2.1})^2$	$(M_{Row\,2}-GM)^2$	$(M_{Col\,1}-GM)^2$
21	11	35.70	17.64	0.05	0.11
22	18	1.05	7.84	0.05	0.11
23	15	3.90	0.04	0.05	0.11
24	14	8.85	1.44	0.05	0.11
25	17	0.00	3.24	0.05	0.11
26	16	0.95	0.64	0.05	0.11
27	15	3.90	0.04	0.05	0.11
28	14	8.85	1.44	0.05	0.11
29	16	0.95	0.64	0.05	0.11
30	16	0.95	0.64	0.05	0.11
$M_{2.1}$ 15.20		65.11	33.60	0.51	1.06
N 10		SS_{Total}	$SS_{Within\,2.1}$	$SS_{Row\,2.1}$	$SS_{Column\,2.1}$
$df_{2.1}$ 9		Sums from Cell 2.1			

Negative Emotions/High Stress (Row 2/Column 2)

Part Num	(X)	$(X-GM)^2$	$(X-M_{2.2})^2$	$(M_{Row\,2}-GM)^2$	$(M_{Col\,2}-GM)^2$
31	19	4.10	0.49	0.05	0.11
32	18	1.05	0.09	0.05	0.11
33	18	1.05	0.09	0.05	0.11
34	18	1.05	0.09	0.05	0.11
35	19	4.10	0.49	0.05	0.11
36	16	0.95	5.29	0.05	0.11
37	19	4.10	0.49	0.05	0.11
38	20	9.15	2.89	0.05	0.11
39	16	0.95	5.29	0.05	0.11
40	20	9.15	2.89	0.05	0.11
$M_{2.2}$ 18.30		35.66	18.10	0.51	1.06
N 10		SS_{Total}	$SS_{Within\,2.2}$	$SS_{Row\,2.2}$	$SS_{Column\,2.2}$
$df_{2.2}$ 9		Sums from Cell 2.2			

$M_{Row\,2}$ 16.75

$M_{Column\,1}$ 16.65 $M_{Column\,2}$ 17.30

GM $(\Sigma M)/N_{Groups}$ 16.98

Sums of Squares	158.98	92.70	2.03	4.23	60.03	158.98
	SS_{Total}	SS_{Within}	SS_{Row}	SS_{Column}	SS_{Int}	Check: Within + Row + Column + Int, should match SS_{Total}

Sums combining Cell 1.1, Cell 1.2, Cell 2.1, Cell 2.2

Degrees of Freedom	df_{Row}	$N_{Rows}-1$		1.00	df_{Int}	$(df_{Rows})(df_{Columns})$	1.00
	df_{Column}	$N_{Columns}-1$		1.00	df_{Within}	$df_{1.1} + df_{1.2} + df_{2.1} + df_{2.2}$	36.00

Mean Squares	MS_{Row}	SS_{Row}/df_{Row}	2.03
	MS_{Column}	SS_{Column}/df_{Column}	4.23
	$MS_{Interaction}$	$SS_{Interaction}/df_{Interaction}$	60.03
	MS_{Within}	SS_{Within}/df_{Within}	2.58

F-Scores	F_{Row}	MS_{Row}/MS_{Within}	0.79
	F_{Column}	MS_{Column}/MS_{Within}	1.64
	$F_{Interaction}$	$MS_{Interaction}/MS_{Within}$	23.31

Figure 13.18 Computations for a Factorial Analysis of Variance (ANOVA)

the sum of squares within for each condition first, and then combine across the four conditions:

$$SS_{Within} = \Sigma(X - M_{Cell})^2 = 16.90 + 24.10 + 33.60 + 18.10 = 92.70.$$

We're now ready to calculate the two main effects. For the main effect of the first independent variable, Row/Emotion, we focus on the difference between the row marginal means and the grand mean:

$$SS_{Row} = \Sigma(M_{Row} - GM)^2 = 0.51 + 0.51 + 0.51 + 0.51 = 2.03.$$

For the main effect of the second independent variable, Column/Stress, we focus on the difference between the column marginal means and the grand mean:

$$SS_{Column} = \Sigma(M_{Column} - GM)^2 = 1.06 + 1.06 + 1.06 + 1.06 = 4.23.$$

Finally, we learned in the Statistics for Life portion of this chapter that we can determine the sum of squares for the interaction (Emotion × Stress) by figuring out how much variation in the dependent variable is left unaccounted for (whatever is left must be due to the interaction):

$$SS_{Interaction} = SS_{Total} - SS_{Row} - SS_{Column} - SS_{Within}$$
$$= 158.98 - 2.03 - 4.23 - 92.70 = 60.03.$$

We can also calculate the $SS_{Interaction}$ directly. To do so, we will compute a deviation score that examines the difference between each cell mean and the grand mean ($M_{Cell} - GM$) because an interaction examines how the pattern of cell means changes as we change the levels of the factors. We will square these deviations so that they don't sum to zero, and we also need to weight them by the sample size per cell, N_{Cell}, in the event that we have different sample sizes per condition. Lastly, because the main effects influence the scores that occur in each cell, we need to subtract out their influences. This leaves us with the formula for the sum of squares interaction, $SS_{Interaction} = \Sigma N_{Cell}(M_{Cell} - GM)^2 - SS_{Row} - SS_{Column}$. Using this equation with our current data,

$$SS_{Interaction} = 10(18.10 - 16.975)^2 + 10(16.30 - 16.975)^2 + 10(15.20$$
$$- 16.975)^2 + 10(18.30 - 16.975)^2 - 2.03 - 4.23$$
$$= 12.66 + 4.56 + 31.51 + 17.56 - 2.03 - 4.23$$
$$= 66.29 - 2.03 - 4.23$$
$$= 60.03$$

As we noted earlier, ANOVA focuses on variances rather than the sum of squares. Why? Because the sample size affects the sum of squares, such that the larger the sample, the larger the sum of squares will be. So, we calculate the mean of each source of variation by dividing each sum of squares by its relevant degrees of freedom. Doing so converts each into a measure of variance, but in the context of ANOVA, these are called the Mean Squares (in that they are the mean of the squared deviation scores).

To find the mean square for our first independent variable, we use the following formula:

$$MS_{Row} = SS_{Row}/df_{Row} = 2.03/1 = 2.03.$$

To find the mean square for our second independent variable, we use the formula

$$MS_{Column} = SS_{Column}/df_{Column} = 4.23/1 = 4.23.$$

To find the mean square for the interaction, we use the formula

$$MS_{Interaction} = SS_{Interaction}/df_{Interaction} = 60.03/1 = 60.03.$$

Finally, the mean square for the within-groups variation is determined by the formula

$$MS_{Within} = SS_{Within}/df_{Within} = 92.70/36 = 2.58.$$

We're almost there. Our last step is to calculate our F-ratios. We need to do this for the two main effects and the interaction:

$$F_{Row} = MS_{Row}/MS_{Within} = 2.03/2.58 = 0.79$$
$$F_{Column} = MS_{Column}/MS_{Within} = 4.23/2.58 = 1.64$$
$$F_{Interaction} = MS_{Interaction}/MS_{Within} = 60.03/2.58 = 23.31.$$

To determine whether these effects are significant, we will compare each F-ratio to the critical values we found in Step 3.

Step 5: Decide and Interpret As we can see in **Figure 13.19,** only one of the F-ratios is greater than the critical value. This is the F-ratio

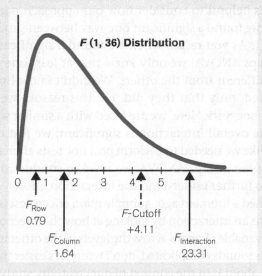

Figure 13.19 Sample Results on the Comparison Distribution

for the interaction term. This tells us that the interaction of emotion and stress on creativity is statistically significant (23.31 > 4.11). However, neither of the main effects are significant because both of these F-ratios are less than the critical value.

Simple Main Effects Tests: What Are They? How Do They Work?

The results we found from our factorial ANOVA suggest that we have a significant interaction. But, unfortunately, they don't tell us anything else about the interaction's pattern. We don't know, for example, whether it's a synergistic, suppression, or crossover effect. So, whenever we find a significant interaction, we need to perform follow-up tests to investigate the nature of the interaction. These tests are called **simple main effects tests,** and their goal is to break down the interaction by looking at how the effect of one independent variable changes across the levels of the other independent variable. In other words, we look at how the effect changes one row or one column at a time.

Before we go further in describing simple main effects tests, it's important to clarify two points. First, even though these follow-up tests are called simple "main effects" tests, they are different from the tests of the main effects that we learned earlier. The main effects tests that we have described previously examine each independent variable's effect without taking into account the other independent variable. Simple main effects tests, in contrast, take both independent variables into account at the same time. So, even though the names of these tests sounds similar, we need to keep them separate in our minds.

Second, it's helpful to consider how our approach parallels what we did when we found a significant one-way between-groups ANOVA in Chapter 11. As you recall, when we found a significant one-way between-groups ANOVA, we only knew that at least one of the conditions was different from the others. We didn't know how the conditions differed, only that they did. For this reason, we needed to conduct post hoc tests. Here, we are faced with a similar scenario. We know that the overall interaction is significant; we just don't know why. So, just like we needed to perform post hoc tests after a significant one-way between-groups ANOVA, we need to conduct simple main effects tests to further understand the interaction effect.

As mentioned a moment ago, a simple main effects test breaks down or deconstructs an interaction by looking at how the effect of one of the independent variable changes across the levels of the other independent variable. If this sounds complicated, don't worry; it's easier than it seems.

Let's think about it in the context of our creativity study. We expect to find two simple main effects: (1) when stress is low, positive emotions will lead to more creativity than negative emotions; (2) when

simple main effects tests hypothesis tests that help us understand why an interaction is significant. Simple main effects tests examine how the effect of one independent variable changes across the levels of the other independent variable.

Want to review post hoc tests and the one-way analysis of variance? SEE CHAPTER 11.

stress is high, negative emotions will lead to more creativity than positive emotions. In other words, we expect the effect of emotions (our first independent variable) to change depending on the levels of stress (our second independent variable).

Of course, this is not the only way we could conceptualize simple main effects. We could also consider the effect of stress within emotion by testing these two simple main effects: (1) when emotions are positive, low stress will lead to more creativity than high stress; (2) when emotions are negative, high stress will lead to more creativity than low stress. So, our first task when conducting simple main effects is to determine how to frame the simple main effects. Do we want to look at how the levels of the first independent variable compare within the levels of the second independent variable? Or do we want to look at how the levels of the second independent variable compare within the levels of the first independent variable? There is no right or wrong answer. We should use past research and our study rationale to help us decide which approach to take.

Given that our original research question focused on the effects of emotion within stress, let's start by focusing on the first simple main effect listed above (on the left side of **Figure 13.20**), which compares the positive and negative emotions conditions when stress is low. Essentially, what we have now is a one-way between-groups ANOVA, with the marginal mean acting as the grand mean. So, just like with one-way between-groups ANOVA, we're going to partition the variance into

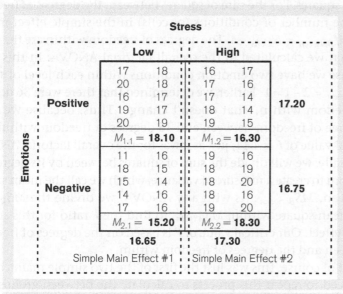

Figure 13.20   Simple Main Effects 1 and 2

two key sources: the between-groups variance and the within-groups variance. For the between-groups variance, the simple main effects focus on the difference between the condition means (M_{Cell}) and the relevant marginal mean, which in this case is the column marginal (M_{Column}). We then square these differences and sum them up for each score within the cell: $\Sigma(M_{Cell} - M_{Column})^2$. Alternatively, because all of the scores within a cell will have the same difference between the condition mean and the marginal mean, we can use the following formula: $\Sigma n_{Cell}(M_{Cell} - M_{Column})^2$, where n is the sample size for the cell.

$$SS_{Row\ (Column\ 1)} = \Sigma n_{cell}(M_{Cell} - M_{Column\ 1})^2$$
$$SS_{Row\ (Column\ 2)} = \Sigma n_{cell}(M_{Cell} - M_{Column\ 2})^2$$

For the within-groups variance, rather than recalculate the sum of squares within, we will use the value that we already calculated in the factorial ANOVA. Now, this may seem odd because the overall sum of squares within is based on all of the conditions and not just the ones that make up the first simple main effect. This is true, but it is actually a strength of the simple main effects approach. By using the sum of squares within from the overall ANOVA, we will gain statistical power, making it easier to reject the null hypothesis when it is false.

After we calculate the sum of squares between and within, we will divide each by their relevant degrees of freedom to convert them to mean squares. For the sum of squares between, the degrees of freedom are the number of conditions (or cells) in the simple effect minus one, $df_{Between} = N_{Cells} - 1$. The degrees of freedom within are the same as what we calculated in the overall factorial ANOVA. In this case, because we have two emotion conditions within each level of stress, $df_{Between} = 2 - 1 = 1$. Earlier, we determined that there were 36 degrees of freedom within. That doesn't change. Thus, because we have 1 degree of freedom between and 36 degrees of freedom within, our critical value of F is 4.11, just as it was for the overall factorial ANOVA.

Finally, we will divide the sum of squares between by its degrees of freedom to create a measure of variance, which we call the mean square between, $MS_{Between}$. As with any ANOVA, we divide the $MS_{Between}$ the mean square within, MS_{Within}, to find the F-ratio for this simple main effect. Our critical value of F is based on the degrees of freedom between and the degrees of freedom within.

But of course, this was just the first of the two simple main effects. We need to repeat this process to calculate the between-groups sum of squares for the second simple main effect (on the right side of

Figure 13.20), which compares the positive and negative emotion conditions when stress is high.

Calculating the Simple Main Effects Let's now calculate the simple main effect of emotion within stress, first for low stress and second for high stress.

1. *Simple main effect of emotion within low stress:* $SS_{Between} = \Sigma n(M_{Cell} - M_{Column})^2 = 10(18.10 - 16.65)^2 + 10(15.20 - 16.65)^2 = 10(1.45)^2 + 10(-1.45)^2 = 21.02 + 21.02 = 42.04$. $SS_{Within} = 92.70$ (from overall ANOVA). $MS_{Between} = SS_{Between}/df_{Between} = 42.04/1 = 42.04$. $MS_{Within} = 2.58$ (from overall ANOVA). $F = MS_{Between}/MS_{Within} = 42.04/2.58 = 16.29$. Because this F-ratio is greater than our critical value of 4.11, we can conclude that the simple main effect of emotion within low stress is significant at the alpha = .05 level.

2. *Simple main effect of emotion within high stress:* $SS_{Between} = \Sigma n(M_{Cell} - M_{Column})^2 = 10(16.30 - 17.30)^2 + 10(18.30 - 17.30)^2 = 10(-1.00)^2 + 10(1.00)^2 = 10.00 + 10.00 = 20.00$. $SS_{Within} = 92.70$ (from overall ANOVA). $MS_{Between} = SS_{Between}/df_{Between} = 20.00/1 = 20.00$. $MS_{Within} = 2.58$ (from overall ANOVA). $F = MS_{Between}/MS_{Within} = 20.00/2.58 = 7.75$. Because this F-ratio is greater than our critical value of 4.11, we can conclude that the simple main effect of emotion within high stress is significant at the alpha = .05 level.

Interpreting the Simple Main Effects Now that we know that each of the simple effects are significant, we can interpret them. All we need to do is compare the means. When stress is low, the mean for the positive emotions condition ($M = 18.10$) is greater than the mean for the negative emotions condition ($M = 15.20$). However, when stress is high, the mean for the positive emotions condition ($M = 16.30$) is less than the mean for the negative emotions condition ($M = 18.30$). Thus, in line with our predictions, the simple main effect tests confirm that people are more creative when they experience low stress and positive emotions, or high stress and negative emotions, relative to when they experience low stress and negative emotions or high stress and positive emotions.

Measuring Effect Size As with all hypothesis tests, a significant result is not only a function of the effect size, but the sample size too. Thus, a significant effect is not necessarily an important effect. For this reason, we need to compute a measure of effect size for each main effect and the interaction when conducting a factorial ANOVA. In other words, we need to compute three measures of effect size.

The measure that we will use for effect size is partial eta squared (η_p^2), which we learned to conduct in Chapter 12. We calculate partial eta squared using the following formula: $\eta_p^2 = SS_{Effect}/(SS_{Effect} + SS_{Within})$, where SS_{Effect} is either the main effect or interaction effect of interest and SS_{Within} is the sum of squares within for the overall ANOVA. Note that because we have three effects (two main effects and one interaction), we will need to calculate partial eta squared three times. Here are the relevant calculations:

1. *Main effect of emotion type:*

$$\eta_p^2 = SS_{Effect}/(SS_{Effect} + SS_{Within}) = 2.02/(2.02 + 92.70) = 2.02/94.72 = 0.021$$

2. *Main effect of stress level:*

$$\eta_p^2 = SS_{Effect}/(SS_{Effect} + SS_{Within}) = 4.22/(4.22 + 92.70) = 4.22/96.92 = 0.044$$

3. *Emotion × Stress interaction:*

$$\eta_p^2 = SS_{Effect}/(SS_{Effect} + SS_{Within}) = 60.02/(60.02 + 92.70) = 60.02/152.72 = 0.39$$

Want to review effect size? SEE CHAPTER 8.

As we can see, both of the main effects have very small effect sizes, whereas the interaction effect is medium sized.

SPSS Video Tutorial: Factorial ANOVA

 Most researchers learn to compute factorial ANOVA while taking a class in statistics, but they use computers to do all of the calculations after that. So, let's see how we would perform this analysis using SPSS. Watch this SPSS video for this chapter, which demonstrates how to perform factorial ANOVA using SPSS.

> **SPSS VIDEO TUTORIAL: To learn more, check out the video Factorial ANOVA.**

Communicating the Result

Now that we've interpreted our output, it's time to write up our results. When reporting the results of our factorial ANOVA, we start by reminding the reader of the design of the study (that is, the number of levels for each of the independent variables) and the hypotheses. We will then report the results of the two main effects and the interaction effect. If the interaction is significant, we will report simple main effects tests. If the interaction is nonsignificant, we will focus on the main effects. Thus, a results paragraph for the current findings would look something like this:

We performed a 2 (emotion type: positive vs. negative) × 2 (stress level: low vs. high) factorial ANOVA to test the hypothesis that participants' creativity would change depending on whether they were experiencing positive or negative emotions under conditions of high or low stress. The results revealed a nonsignificant main effect of emotion, $F(1, 36) = 0.77, p = .38, \eta_p^2 = .02$, as well as a nonsignificant main effect of stress, $F(1, 36) = 1.64, p = .21, \eta_p^2 = .04$. The results revealed a significant emotion × stress interaction effect, $F(1, 36) = 23.31, p < .001, \eta_p^2 = .39$. Simple main effects tests further revealed that when stress was low, participants had higher creativity scores when experiencing positive emotions ($M = 18.10, SD = 1.37$) than when experiencing negative emotions ($M = 15.20, SD = 1.93$), $F(1, 36) = 16.33, p < .001$. In contrast, when stress was high, participants had higher creativity scores when experiencing negative emotions ($M = 18.30, SD = 1.42$) than when experiencing positive emotions ($M = 16.30, SD = 1.64$), $F(1, 36) = 7.77, p < .001$.

Creating a Clustered Bar Graph When reporting the results of a factorial ANOVA, researchers often present their results in a **clustered bar graph**, which is a type of bar graph that depicts the results when our research has more than one nominal independent variable. These bar graphs make it easy to interpret the nature of the main effects and interaction. Word processing programs, such as Microsoft Word and Google Docs, offer us easy ways to insert clustered bar graphs into our documents. Take a look at the clustered bar graph in **Figure 13.21,** depicting our current results.

As we see, the bars are clustered so that the results of similar conditions for one of the independent variables (stress) are clustered along the x-axis, and the similar conditions for the other independent variable (emotion) are presented in the same color. We also want to include error bars, so that the reader can assess the amount of variability in each condition.

Interpreting a Clustered Bar Graph When looking at a clustered bar graph, we can make broad conclusions regarding the presence of main effects and interactions using a simple technique. We are going to connect (in our minds) the bars from the same conditions with a line, such as we do here in **Figure 13.22.** Here, we have connected the

clustered bar graph a bar graph used to depict the results of a factorial ANOVA.

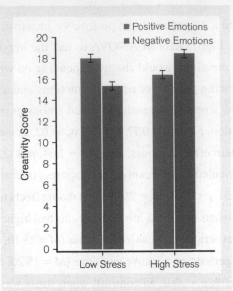

Figure 13.21 Clustered Bar Graph

two positive emotions conditions and the two negative emotion conditions with lines. If the two lines are parallel, we know that there is no interaction effect. If the two lines are not parallel, it suggests that there may be an interaction. Looking at Figure 13.22, we can see that the lines are not parallel, and instead form an X. This suggests that an interaction is present.

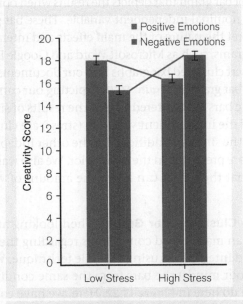

Figure 13.22 Clustered Bar Graph with Lines Connecting Bars

Forming a Conclusion

By running a factorial ANOVA, we were able to look at the two independent variables' effects on one dependent variable. In this case, we could look at how positive and negative emotions, as well as high and low levels of stress, affect creativity. Importantly, testing these independent variables in the same analysis, rather than in two separate one-way ANOVAs, allowed us to look for interaction effects. Our results revealed only an interaction effect, meaning that the effects of positive and negative emotions on creativity changes when people are under high or low stress. To further understand our interaction, we learned to compute simple main effects tests.

Your Turn 13.4

1. Describe at least two reasons why it's better to run a factorial ANOVA, rather than two separate one-way ANOVAs.

2. What is a simple main effect test? How does it differ from a main effect?

3. A forensics psychologist is interested in studying the accuracy of eyewitness memories. In particular, she wants to determine whether hypnosis can be used to retrieve details for a crime that an eyewitness doesn't initially remember. In addition, the researcher wants to test whether the potential effects of hypnosis work immediately or after a delay. To test this, she asks participants to watch a video of a crime. She then has half of the participants complete a memory task in which they try to remember as many details of the crime as possible while under hypnosis or not under hypnosis. The other half of the participants complete the memory task (while under hypnosis or not) two weeks after watching the crime video.

What might the results look like if there is:

    a. a significant main effect of test timing (immediate vs. delayed),

    b. a significant main effect of hypnosis (hypnosis vs. no hypnosis), and

    c. a significant test timing by hypnosis interaction?

4. After collecting her data (shown in the chart on the next page), the researcher makes the following computations.

Based on these calculations, the researcher concludes that there is a significant main effect of hypnosis, $F(1, 16) = 9.96$, $p = .006$, a nonsignificant main effect of test timing, $F(1, 16) = 0.84$, $p = .37$, and a significant hypnosis by test timing interaction, $F(1, 16) = 7.55$, $p = .014$.

    a. What is the effect size of the main effect of hypnosis (partial eta squared, η_p^2)?

    b. Conduct simple main effects tests to examine the simple main effect of hypnosis within each level of test timing (critical value = 4.49).

5. A researcher is investigating variables that may improve psychological well-being. In particular, she tests the effects of exercise (high or low) and social support (high support or low support). After performing her factorial ANOVA, she reports her findings in the following clustered bar graph:

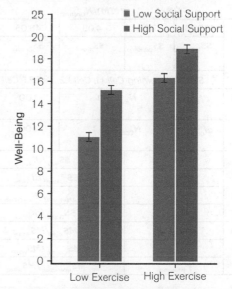

Based on this clustered bar graph:

    a. Is there a main effect of exercise?

    b. Is there a main effect of social support?

    c. Is there an exercise × social support interaction?

(Continued)

Immediate Memory Test/No Hypnosis (Row 1/Column 1)

Part Num	(X)	$(X-GM)^2$	$(X-M_{1.1})^2$	$(M_{Row\,1}-GM)^2$	$(M_{Col\,1}-GM)^2$	INT^2
1	12	10.56	6.76	0.20	2.40	1.82
2	16	0.56	1.96	0.20	2.40	1.82
3	16	0.56	1.96	0.20	2.40	1.82
4	15	0.06	0.16	0.20	2.40	1.82
5	14	1.56	0.36	0.20	2.40	1.82
$M_{1.1}$ 14.60		13.313	11.200	1.013	12.013	9.113
N 5		SS_{Total}	$SS_{Within\,1.1}$	$SS_{Row\,1.1}$	$SS_{Column\,1.1}$	$SS_{Int\,1.1}$
$df_{1.1}$ 4						

Sums from Cell 1.1

Immediate Memory Test/Hypnosis (Row 1/Column 2)

Part Num	(X)	$(X-GM)^2$	$(X-M_{1.2})^2$	$(M_{Row\,1}-GM)^2$	$(M_{Col\,2}-GM)^2$	INT^2
6	16	0.56	1.00	0.20	2.40	1.82
7	15	0.06	0.00	0.20	2.40	1.82
8	13	5.06	4.00	0.20	2.40	1.82
9	16	0.56	1.00	0.20	2.40	1.82
10	15	0.06	0.00	0.20	2.40	1.82
$M_{1.1}$ 15.00		6.313	6.000	1.013	12.013	9.113
N 5		SS_{Total}	$SS_{Within\,1.1}$	$SS_{Row\,1.1}$	$SS_{Column\,1.1}$	$SS_{Int\,1.1}$
$df_{1.2}$ 4						

Sums from Cell 1.1

$M_{Row\,1}$ 14.80

Delayed Memory Test/No Hypnosis (Row 2/Column 1)

Part Num	(X)	$(X-GM)^2$	$(X-M_{2.1})^2$	$(M_{Row\,2}-GM)^2$	$(M_{Col\,1}-GM)^2$	INT^2
11	17	3.06	17.64	0.20	2.40	1.82
12	12	10.56	0.64	0.20	2.40	1.82
13	9	39.06	14.44	0.20	2.40	1.82
14	12	10.56	0.64	0.20	2.40	1.82
15	14	1.56	1.44	0.20	2.40	1.82
$M_{2.1}$ 12.80		64.813	34.800	1.013	12.013	9.112
N 5		SS_{Total}	$SS_{Within\,2.1}$	$SS_{Row\,2.1}$	$SS_{Column\,2.1}$	$SS_{Int\,2.1}$
$df_{2.1}$ 4						

Sums from Cell 2.1

Delayed Memory Test/Hypnosis (Row 2/Column 2)

Part Num	(X)	$(X-GM)^2$	$(X-M_{2.2})^2$	$(M_{Row\,2}-GM)^2$	$(M_{Col\,2}-GM)^2$	INT^2
16	18	7.56	0.36	0.20	2.40	1.82
17	19	14.06	0.16	0.20	2.40	1.82
18	22	45.56	11.56	0.20	2.40	1.82
19	15	0.06	12.96	0.20	2.40	1.82
20	19	14.06	0.16	0.20	2.40	1.82
$M_{2.2}$ 18.60		81.312	25.200	1.013	12.013	9.113
N 5		SS_{Total}	$SS_{Within\,2.2}$	$SS_{Row\,2.2}$	$SS_{Column\,2.2}$	$SS_{Int\,2.2}$
$df_{2.2}$ 4						

Sums from Cell 2.2

$M_{Row\,2}$ 15.70

$M_{Column\,1}$ 13.70 $M_{Column\,2}$ 16.80

GM	$(\Sigma M)/N_{Groups}$				15.25
Sums of Squares	165.75	77.20	4.05	48.05	36.45
	SS_{Total}	SS_{Within}	SS_{Row}	SS_{Column}	SS_{Int}

165.75 — *Check:* Within + Row + Column + Int, Should match SS_{Total}

Sums combining Cell 1.1, Cell 1.2, Cell 2.1, Cell 2.2

Degrees of	df_{Row}	$N_{Rows}-1$	1.00	df_{Int}	$(df_{Rows})(df_{Columns})$	1.00
	df_{Column}	$N_{Columns}-1$	1.00	df_{Within}	$df_{1.1}+df_{1.2}+df_{2.1}+df_{2.2}$	16.00

Mean Squares		
MS_{Row}	SS_{Row}/df_{Row}	4.05
MS_{Column}	SS_{Column}/df_{Column}	48.05
$MS_{Interaction}$	$SS_{Interaction}/df_{Interaction}$	36.45
MS_{Within}	SS_{Within}/df_{Within}	4.83

F-Scores		
F_{Row}	MS_{Row}/MS_{Within}	0.84
F_{Column}	MS_{Column}/MS_{Within}	9.96
$F_{Interaction}$	$MS_{Interaction}/MS_{Within}$	7.55

Focus on Open Science: Distributed Research Networks

One of the biggest advances to emerge in psychology as a result of the development of open science is the creation of **distributed research networks.** These networks involve dozens or sometimes hundreds of scholars across the globe working to address similar research questions. In contrast to a single researcher working for decades to answer a particular research question, distributed researcher networks allow researchers to divvy up projects, so that no one scholar has a lot of work. This allows the overall research project to occur much more quickly.

For example, the Many Labs 2 project attempted to replicate 28 findings in psychology by bringing together hundreds of scholars so that they could measure 15,305 participants in 36 countries (Klein et al., 2018). Similarly, the Psychology Science Accelerator is a collection of over 500 scholars who select projects, collect data, and publish their results as a collaborative team.

The goal of distributed research networks such as these is to get researchers to work together to produce the best, highest-quality research. By working together, these researchers can collect large samples, which have the ability to both reduce Type I errors, but also have the ability to reduce Type II errors. Moreover, these distributed research networks must share information across many people to work properly, thus ensuring that scientists follow open science practices such as sharing their data and research materials.

distributed research network a team of scholars working across the globe on the same research project.

Become a Better Consumer of Statistics

Critiques of psychological science often involve the notion that most researchers rely on convenience samples of college students that are not representative of the population as a whole. More broadly, research across the sciences often relies on **WEIRD samples,** which are samples of individuals from Western, Educated, Industrialized, Rich, and Democratic countries. As we read about the latest scientific findings on Twitter, or see new reports of cutting-edge research on television, we need to ask ourselves several important questions. Who were the participants that this research studied? Are the participants representative of the general population? If the participants are not representative, how much importance should we attribute to the results?

Let's take an example. Imagine that we conducted the study on selfies described in the Statistics for Life portion of this chapter. We said earlier that we gathered our data by asking our friends to rate

WEIRD samples acronym that describes samples from Western, Educated, Industrialized, Rich, and Democratic cultures.

How generalizable are results found in WEIRD populations, such as college students, to society more broadly?

iStock/Getty Images

selfies that differed based on the type of pose and whether a filter was used. Yet, our friends are unlikely to be a representative sample of the population. This fact would obviously temper our excitement if we found significant results. Yet, most research in the social sciences suffers from similar problems. Most psychology research, for example, relies on convenience samples of students enrolled in introductory psychology classes. This practice oversamples people from WEIRD cultures. Indeed, one study found that 80% of all research participants are from cultures that make up only 12% of the world's population (Henrich et al., 2010). So, when we are reading about various research findings, we need to consider the sample and whether we can extend the findings across the population.

Interpreting Graphs and Charts from Research Articles

The typical way to graphically report the results of a factorial ANOVA is the clustered bar graph. Let's take a look at an example from a paper that investigated the effects of response method and working memory capacity on creativity (Hao et al., 2015). In this study, researchers divided participants into two groups based on their working memory capacity or their ability to hold multiple items in mind. Participants then completed the alternative uses task with one of two response methods: Half of the participants spoke their responses out loud, whereas the other half wrote their responses. The researchers presented their results in the clustered bar graph shown in **Figure 13.23**.

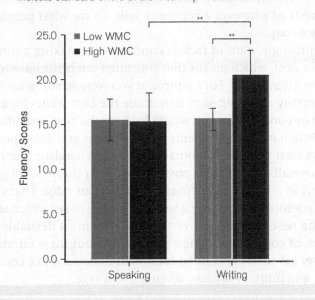

FIGURE 1 | Alternative Uses Task (AUT) fluency scores of participants with higher or lower working memory capacity (WMC) in the speaking and writing conditions. Error bars indicate standard errors of the mean. **$p < 0.01$.

Figure 13.23 Clustered Bar Graph (Data from Hao et al., 2015)

Based on this clustered bar graph, we can easily see that the researchers found an interaction effect. If we connect the two gray bars and the two black bars with lines, we see that the lines are not parallel, suggesting there is an interaction. When it comes to determining what type of interaction effect is present, it looks to be a synergistic interaction. Participants high in working memory capacity and in the written response condition produced more responses on the creativity measure, compared to the other three conditions. The study's results paragraph, where the researchers indicate that the interaction is significant, supports our "eyeballed" conclusion. The main effect of working memory capacity was also significant. We can see this in the graph by averaging (in our minds) the two black bars and comparing that to the average of the two gray bars. Similarly, the main effect of response type was significant. We can see this in the graph by averaging the two speaking conditions and comparing that to the average of the two writing conditions.

Statistics on the Job

The great thing about building your research and statistics skills is that they apply in a wide range of settings. Often those skills help students who graduate with a bachelor's degree in psychology get jobs you would not typically associate with a psychology major. For example, one of the careers you could pursue is an associate scientist or scientific liaison for a consumer product company. That sounds fancy, but it essentially means someone who conducts tests of whatever a company sells, to see what people are most likely to buy.

Not surprisingly, a lot of factors contribute to making a product desirable (or not), which means that consumer scientists have to pay attention to interactions. For example, if you were working for a cosmetics company and wanted to determine the best scents for a new face cream or hand lotion, you would look for the best combination of scents. When mixing two scents (e.g., lavender and Asian pear), it isn't always clear that the combination will be synergistic and result in a better overall scent. It's also possible that two otherwise delightful scents result in a suppression effect and a noxious odor. That's why consumer scientists have to run a series of studies to see which scents produce the best interactions, resulting in the most desirable new scents, and, of course, the highest profits. Without these efforts, we would never get to enjoy scented lotion combinations like coconut, cucumber, and mint, or cypress, lavender, and sage.

Review Questions

1. You are interested in the effect of bystander intervention training on the willingness of employees to speak up and intervene when they witness harassment and/or discrimination in their workplace. You also wonder whether there are gender differences in whether someone is willing to speak up and intervene. Why might you want to analyze this with a factorial ANOVA rather than one-way ANOVAs (or *t*-tests, depending on the number of levels in each factor)?

2. For each, identify the type of interaction.
   a. A nurse at a long-term care facility observes that having plants in a resident's room improves their mood, but that the effect is greater if the resident is also involved in taking care of the plants.
   b. A nature conservation officer observes that interacting with nature increases the amount of money that people donate, but only if the people are not distracted by technology.
   c. A teacher finds that growth mindset lessons are more effective when students are moderately stressed, but not when they are highly stressed.
   d. A clinician finds that both medication and cognitive behavioral therapy are effective at managing ADHD symptoms that patients find distressing. But the effect of the treatments is greatest when they are combined.
   e. A researcher finds that a new intervention is effective at increasing the motivation children have to read in those who do not have a learning disability,

   but it decreases the motivation in those who have a learning disability related to reading.

3. Identify the appropriate statistical test for each research scenario.
   a. You are interested in the effect of screen time on attention in children and whether that varies as a function of age.
   b. A teacher is interested in the effectiveness of a cartoon about numbers and math on number fluency in children. The teacher compares a group of children who regularly watch the cartoon with a group of children who do not regularly watch the cartoon.
   c. A nutritionist is interested in the effects of a new program designed to help parents reduce picky eating behaviors. The number of foods a child is willing to eat is measured before the program starts, at the conclusion of the program, and finally 6 months after the program ends.
   d. A high school chemistry teacher is interested in the effects of gamification on the amount of time students spend studying. The teacher chooses two topics of similar difficulty (and interest) and gamifies one topic but not the other. Then the teacher compares how much students study for each topic.

4. How is the sum of squares total divided up in a 2×2 factorial ANOVA?

5. Let's say we have a research study with 60 participants total, equally divided amongst four groups. Can we assume that the participant scores on the dependent variable are normally distributed?

6. You and your friends are interested in how to learn the material in this course in an effective and efficient manner. You design a study where you vary the study strategy (memorization, retrieval practice, spaced practice, and interleaving), the amount of time spent studying (3 hours, 6 hours, and 9 hours), and the amount of sleep the person has the night before (under 3 hours, 5–6 hours, and 8 or more hours). Then you measure the number of correct responses that are produced on an exam after 4 weeks.
   a. How many factors are there?
   b. How many levels does each variable have?
   c. How many main effects and interactions will be evaluated?
   d. Name the type of ANOVA (e.g., 2 × 2 ANOVA).

7. A doctor is interested in how long it takes a patient to recover from a concussion. They believe that concussion severity (mild versus moderate versus severe) may interact with the level of rest that the patient gets (full rest versus moderate rest versus low rest versus regular activity). They collect data from a total of 72 patients (6 per condition)
   a. What are the degrees of freedom for each main effect and for the interaction?
   b. What are the degrees of freedom within?
   c. What are the critical values for each main effect and for the interaction? Use an alpha of .05.

8. Match the following terms to their definitions: factor; level; cell mean; marginal mean; main effect; interaction

Term	Definition
	A term synonymous with independent variab in the context of a factorial ANOVA
	The groups associated with a given factor in ANOVA
	The mean of all scores for a particular combination of the independent variables' levels
	The mean of all scores in a single row or colum
	How the different levels of one independent variable compare, ignoring any other independent variables
	A unique effect where one independent variable's impact on the dependent variable is different or varies depending on the level of the other independent variables

9. If the interaction and both main effects in a 2 × 3 factorial ANOVA are significant, why do we not pay much attention to the main effects?

10. Based on the following graph, would you expect a main effect of sleep hygiene? A main effect of age? An interaction of sleep and age?

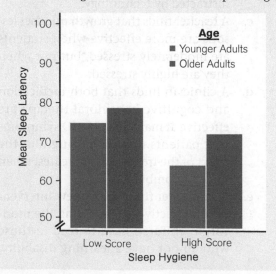

11. Based on the following graph, would you expect a main effect of education? A main effect of group size? An interaction of education and group size?

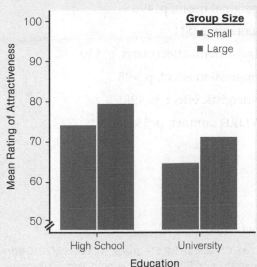

12. A number of fonts have been developed that are intended to improve reading performance in those diagnosed with dyslexia relative to standard fonts. A researcher is interested in a new font that has been developed and wants to assess whether it improves reading performance. They believe that it may also improve reading performance in people not diagnosed with dyslexia, and they wonder whether the improvement is the same in both groups of readers. They recruit eight individuals diagnosed with dyslexia and eight individuals not diagnosed with dyslexia. They randomly assign half of each type of reader to read a passage written in standard font, and the other half to read the same passage written in the newly designed font.

a. What would the populations be?
b. What would the hypotheses be?

c. What are the degrees of freedom within? Degrees of freedom row? Degrees of freedom column? Degrees of freedom for the interaction?
d. Establish the critical value cutoff(s) use an $\alpha = .05$.
e. Determine the sample results.
f. What is the appropriate conclusion?
g. Create an ANOVA source table to display the results.
h. Show cell means, and marginal means in a table.
i. Using this table, along with the hypothesis testing results, what can we determine about the direction of the effects?
j. In order to justify our conclusions in part i, what additional analyses would we need to run, if any?
k. What is the effect size for each main effect and for the interaction? Are they small/medium/large?

	Group 1	Group 2	Group 3	Group 4
	Dyslexia/ New Font	Dyslexia/ Standard Font	No Diagnosis/ New Font	No Diagnosis/ Standard Font
	26	24	41	38
	33	23	38	36
	27	25	37	39
	30	20	36	35
Group Mean	29	23	38	37

Key Concepts

cell mean, p. 498

clustered bar graph, p. 535

crossover effect, p. 519

distributed research network, p. 539

factor, p. 495

factorial analysis of variance (ANOVA), p. 496

interaction, p. 498

main effects, p. 498

marginal mean, p. 498

pilot test, p. 511

simple main effects tests, p. 530

suppression effect, p. 498

synergistic effect, p. 498

WEIRD samples, p. 539

Answers to Your Turn

Your Turn 13.1

1.

	Firmness		
	Strong	**Weak**	
One Hand	10 9 7	2 3 5	**6.00**
	$M_{1.1}$ = **8.67**	$M_{1.2}$ = **3.33**	
Two Hands	7 5 4	1 2 3	**3.67**
	$M_{2.1}$ = **5.33**	$M_{2.2}$ = **2.00**	
	7.00	**2.67**	

(Style — row label on left)

2. (a) 3; (b) 2; (c) 3

3. (a) hybrid; factorial ANOVA; (b) factorial; factorial ANOVA; (c) repeated-measures ANOVA

4. (a) suppression; (b) synergistic

Your Turn 13.2

1. The basic idea is the same (we want to identify variance from our independent variable). The major difference is we now have more than one independent variable, so we need to calculate a sum of squares for each one. We also have the possibility that our independent variables interact or combine with each other, so we also need to calculate a sum of squares for the interaction.

Your Turn 13.3

1. (a) Classical/62 Degrees; Classical/72 Degrees; Smooth Jazz/62 Degrees; Smooth Jazz/72 Degrees; (b)

	Temperature	
	62 Degrees	**72 Degrees**
Classical		
Smooth Jazz		

(Music — row label on left)

2. (a) Population 1: Students who listen to classical in a 62-degree room. Population 2: Students who listen to classical in a 72-degree room. Population 3: Students who listen to smooth jazz in a 62-degree room. Population 4: Students who listen to smooth jazz in a 72-degree room. Sample: The 12 students who sign up to participate.

(b) *Research Hypothesis 1—Main Effect (Music)* (H_1): People who listen to classical music will have different levels of drowsiness compared to those who listen to smooth jazz ($\mu_1 + \mu_2 \neq \mu_3 + \mu_4$). *Null Hypothesis 1:* The population means are equal ($\mu_1 + \mu_2 = \mu_3 + \mu_4$).

Research Hypothesis 2—Main Effect (Temperature) (H_2): People in a room that is 62 degrees will have different levels of drowsiness compared to those in a room that is 72 degrees ($\mu_1 + \mu_3 \neq \mu_2 + \mu_4$). *Null Hypothesis 2:* The population means are equal ($\mu_1 + \mu_3 = \mu_2 + \mu_4$).

Research Hypothesis 3 — Interaction Effect (Music × Temperature) (H_3): When people listen to classical music, temperature's effect on their drowsiness will be different from how temperature effects people who listen to smooth jazz ($\mu_1 - \mu_2 \neq \mu_3 - \mu_4$). *Null Hypothesis 3:* The population means are equal ($\mu_1 - \mu_2 = \mu_3 - \mu_4$).

3. *F* distribution with a shape that ultimately depends on the between-group and within-group degrees of freedom.

4. (a) Significance level (we'll use the standard significance level, $p = .05$), degrees of freedom (between and within) $df_{Music} = 1$, $df_{Temp} = 1$, $df_{Music \times Temp} = 1$, $df_{Within} = 8$; (b) 5.32.

5. (a) Factorial analysis of variance; (b) sums of squares ($SS_{Total} = 47.00$, $SS_{Within} = 4.00$, $SS_{Music} = 21.33$, $SS_{Temp} = 16.33$, $SS_{Music \times Temp} = 5.33$); Mean Squares ($MS_{Music} = 21.33$, $MS_{Temp} = 16.33$, $MS_{Music \times Temp} = 5.33$, $MS_{Within} = .50$); *F*-ratios ($F_{Music} = 42.67$, $F_{Temp} = 32.67$, $F_{Music \times Temp} = 10.67$); c) Nothing. That information should be ignored because it does not relate to the research hypotheses. d)

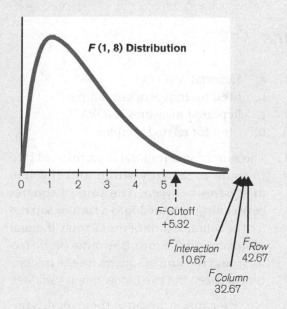

F (1, 8) Distribution

0 1 2 3 4 5

F-Cutoff +5.32

$F_{Interaction}$ 10.67

F_{Column} 32.67

F_{Row} 42.67

6. For each of our between-groups effects (Music, Temperature, Music × Temperature) the *F*-ratios (42.67, 32.67, and 10.67) exceeded the cutoff score of 5.32. Because our sample's results (Step 4) surpassed the critical value (Step 3), we are able to reject each of the null hypotheses that the population means are equal. If we are able to reject the null, the research hypothesis that the population means are different is supported.

7.

Source	SS	df	MS	F
Between				
Row	21.33	1	21.33	42.67
Column	16.33	1	16.33	32.67
Interaction	5.33	1	5.33	10.67
Within	4.00	8	0.50	
Total	47.00	11		

8. (a)

Temperature

	62 Degrees	72 Degrees	
Classical	7 7 6	4 2 3	**4.83**
	$M_{1.1} = 6.67$	$M_{1.2} = 3.00$	
Smooth Jazz	3 3 2	2 1 2	**2.17**
	$M_{2.1} = 2.67$	$M_{2.2} = 1.67$	
	4.67	**2.33**	

(Music)

(b) The music main effect showed that classical music produced more drowsiness than smooth jazz. The temperature main effect showed that a 62-degree room produced more drowsiness than a 72-degree room. The interaction effect showed that when listening to classical music, room temperature had a greater impact on drowsiness than when participants listened to smooth jazz. The combination of classical music and a cool room produced the most drowsiness.

Your Turn 13.4

1. Factorial ANOVAs allow us to test for interactions, whereas one-way between-groups ANOVAs do not. Also, because we are able to look at the effects of multiple independent variables within a single study, we save time and effort.

2. A simple main effect test is a follow-up test to a significant interaction. Simple main effects tests examine how the effect of one independent variable changes across the levels of another independent variable. A main effect, in contrast, tests the effect of an independent variable regardless of the levels of another independent variable.

3. (a) A significant main effect of test timing would reveal that regardless of hypnosis condition, one of the means for test timing is significantly greater than the other. (b) A significant main effect of hypnosis condition would reveal that regardless of test timing, one of the means for hypnosis condition is significantly greater than the other. (c) A significant interaction would reveal that the simple main effect of hypnosis changes across the levels of test timing, or alternatively, that the simple main effect of test timing changes across the levels of hypnosis.

4. (a) Effect size $\eta_p^2 = SS_{Effect}/(SS_{Effect} + SS_{Within}) = 4.05/(4.05 + 77.20) = 4.05/81.25 = 0.05$. (b) Simple main effect of hypnosis within immediate test timing: $SS_{Between} = \Sigma n(M_{Cell} - M_{Row})^2 = 5(14.60 - 14.80)^2 + 5(15.00 - 14.80)^2 = 5(-0.20)^2 + 5(0.20)^2 = 0.20 + 0.20 = 0.40$. $SS_{Within} = 77.20$ (from overall ANOVA). $MS_{Between} = SS_{Between}/df_{Between} = 0.40/1 = 0.40$. $MS_{Within} = 4.83$ (from overall ANOVA). $F = MS_{Between}/MS_{Within} = 0.40/$

$4.83 = 0.083$. Because 0.083 is less than the critical value of 4.49, the simple main effect of hypnosis within immediate test timing is nonsignificant. Simple main effect of hypnosis within delayed test timing: $SS_{Between} = \Sigma n(M_{Cell} - M_{Row})^2 = 5(12.80 - 15.70)^2 + 5(18.60 - 15.70)^2 = 5(-2.90)^2 + 5(2.90)^2 = 42.05 + 42.05 = 84.10$. $SS_{Within} = 77.20$ (from overall ANOVA). $MS_{Between} = SS_{Between}/df_{Between} = 84.10/1 = 84.10$. $MS_{Within} = 4.83$ (from overall ANOVA). $F = MS_{Between}/MS_{Within} = 84.10/4.83 = 17.41$. Because 17.41 is greater than the critical value of 4.49, the simple main effect of hypnosis within immediate test timing is significant. These simple main effects tests reveal that while hypnosis does not improve performance on the memory test when the test is immediate, it does significantly improve performance when the test is delayed.

5. (a) There is a main effect of exercise present. When combined, the two high-exercise conditions have a greater mean than the two low-exercise conditions. (b) There is a main effect of social support present. When combined, the two high social support conditions have a greater mean than the two low social support conditions. (c) There is no interaction effect present. Lines connecting the two low social support bars are parallel to the two high social support bars.

Answers to Review Questions

1. If you analyze the information with a factorial ANOVA, you'll be able to evaluate whether the effectiveness of the training varies as a function of gender—in other words, you'll be able to evaluate both the effects of each independent variable alone as well as whether the variables interact with each other. Another benefit is that the design is more efficient because we can evaluate more than one independent variable at once. This can save us time and resources.

2. a. Synergistic
    b. Suppression
    c. Suppression
    d. Synergistic
    e. Crossover

3. a. Factorial ANOVA
    b. *t*-test for independent samples
    c. Repeated-measures ANOVA
    d. *t*-test for related samples

4. The sum of squares total is partitioned into the sum of squares within and the sum of squares between. The sum of squares between is portioned into a sum of squares for the columns (one of the factors), the sum of squares for the rows (the other of the factors), and the sum of squares for the interaction between the two independent variables.

5. No, we cannot, because the overall sample is large, but each condition has only 15 participants.

6. **a.** There are three factors.
    b. Study strategy has four levels, amount of time spent studying has three levels, and amount of sleep has three levels.
    c. There will be 3 main effects, 3 two-way interactions (study strategy × time; study strategy × sleep; sleep × time), and 1 three-way interaction (study strategy × time × sleep)
    d. 4 × 3 × 3 ANOVA

7. **a.** $df_{Severity} = 2$; $df_{Rest} = 3$; $df_{Interaction} = 6$
    b. $df_{Within} = 60$
    c. Critical value severity = 3.15; critical value rest = 2.76; critical value interaction = 2.25

8.

Term	Definition
Factor	*A term synonymous with independent variable in the context of a factorial ANOVA*
Level	*The groups associated with a given factor in an ANOVA*
Cell mean	*The mean of all scores for a particular combination of the independent variables levels*
Marginal mean	*The mean of all scores in a single row or column*
Main effect	*How the different levels of one independent variable compare, ignoring any other independent variables*
Interaction	*A unique effect where one independent variable's impact on the dependent variable is different or varies depending on the level of the other independent variables*

9. We do not pay much attention to the main effects because the interaction supersedes them in importance. When an interaction is significant, the pattern in a main effect depends on the level of the other independent variable.

10. We would expect a main effect of sleep hygiene—the mean of the low hygiene score is higher than the mean of the high hygiene score. We would expect a main effect of age—the mean of the older adults is higher than the mean of the younger adults. We would expect an interaction—the difference between younger and older adults is smaller when there is low sleep hygiene than the difference between younger and older adults when there is high sleep hygiene.

11. We would expect a main effect of education—the mean of the high school students is higher than the mean of the university students. We would expect a main effect of group size—the mean of the large group size is higher than the mean of the small group size. We would not expect an interaction—the difference between the small and large group sizes for the high school students is approximately the same as the difference between the small and large group sizes for the university students.

12. **a.** Population 1 (μ_1: 1.1): People who are diagnosed with dyslexia and who read the passage in the new font.
    Population 2 (μ_2: 1.2): People who are diagnosed with dyslexia and who read the passage in the standard font.
    Population 3 (μ_3: 2.1): People who are not diagnosed with dyslexia and who read the passage in the new font.
    Population 4 (μ_4: 2.2): People who are not diagnosed with dyslexia and who read the passage in the standard font.

b. Research Hypothesis 1—Main effect (Row/Diagnosis) (H_1): People who are diagnosed with dyslexia and people who are not diagnosed with dyslexia will have different levels of reading performance ($\mu_1 + \mu_2 \neq \mu_3 + \mu_4$).

Null Hypothesis 1: The population means are equal ($\mu_1 + \mu_2 = \mu_3 + \mu_4$). In other words, the populations diagnosed with dyslexia will have the same mean as those not diagnosed with dyslexia.

Research Hypothesis 2—Main effect (Column/Font) (H_2): People who read the new font and people who read the standard font will have different levels of reading performance ($\mu_1 + \mu_3 \neq \mu_2 + \mu_4$)

Null Hypothesis 2: The population means are equal ($\mu_1 + \mu_3 = \mu_2 + \mu_4$). In other words, the populations that read the new font will have the same mean as those reading the standard font.

Research Hypothesis 3—Interaction Effect (Row × Column) (H_3): For people diagnosed with dyslexia, the font's effect on their reading performance will be different from how the font affects people not diagnosed with dyslexia ($\mu_1 - \mu_2 \neq \mu_3 - \mu_4$).

Null Hypothesis 3: The population means are equal ($\mu_1 - \mu_2 = \mu_3 - \mu_4$). In other words, the font's effect on reading performance does not rely on the dyslexia diagnosis.

c. $df_{Within} = 12$, $df_{Row} = 1$, $df_{Column} = 1$, $df_{Interaction} = 1$

d. The critical values are the same (1, 12) = 4.75

e. $SS_{Total} = 671$, $SS_{Within} = 68$, $SS_{Row} = 529$, $SS_{Column} = 49$, $SS_{Interaction} = 25$; $MS_{Within} = 5.67$, $MS_{Row} = 529$, $MS_{Column} = 49$,

$MS_{Interaction} = 25$; $F_{Row} = 93.35$, $F_{Column} = 8.65$, $F_{Interaction} = 4.41$

f. There is a main effect of diagnosis and a main effect of font, but there is no interaction between the variables.

g.

Source	SS	df	MS	F
Between				
Row	529	1	529	93.35
Column	49	1	49	8.65
Interaction	25	1	25	4.41
Within	68	12	5.67	
Total	671	15		

h.

		Font		
		New Font	Standard Font	
Diagnosis	Dyslexia	29	23	26
	No Diagnosis	38	37	37.
		33.5	30	

i. Participants with a dyslexia diagnosis display a lower reading performance than those with no dyslexia diagnosis. Participants reading the new font display a higher reading performance than those reading the standard font. There is no interaction between font and diagnosis.

j. Because the interaction is not significant, and the main effects each have only two levels, then no further analyses are needed. If the interaction had been significant, then we would have had to analyze the simple main effects.

k. Effect size for main effect of diagnosis = 0.89 (large)
Effect size for main effect of font = 0.42 (small)
Effect size for interaction = 0.27 (small)

OPEN STATS LAB

Sharpen your statistics skills with real-life data! Check out OpenStatsLab.com, created by coauthor Kevin McIntyre, to practice running analyses for real published research studies.

Learning Outcomes

After reading this chapter, you should be able to:

● Explain the key question that correlation seeks to answer.

● Identify similarities and differences between *t*-tests and a correlation.

● Identify when it is appropriate to use a correlation.

● Describe the underlying logic for calculating the cross-product of *Z*-scores and correlation coefficient.

● Conduct a *t*-test for correlation.

● Explain what correlation results can and cannot tell us.

Dads. You can spot them a mile away: clunky white athletic shoes, socks pulled up high, jean or cargo shorts, baggy T-shirt (likely tucked in), smartphone clipped to his belt, and sunglasses on their baseball hat. Beneath that slightly disheveled, out-of-style veneer is a superhero, a master of the map, grand grill wizard, and omnipotent ruler of the thermostat. Whether it's teaching us how to change a tire, cook an omelet, or build Ikea furniture; the value of hard work; or how to properly yell at the television during sporting events, our fathers hold a special place in our lives. Sure, mom could just as easily teach us all those things, but there is one area that, at least according to a common stereotype in the United States, seems to be exclusive dad-only territory: jokes.

Dad jokes are short, deliberately unfunny, pun-laden one-liners that are the province and specialty of guys with kids. A joke can become a "dad joke" only once it's apparent. Dads all seem to have jokes about pizza—each one deliciously cheesy: *They don't get a haircut, they get all of them cut. They never play poker in the jungle because there are too many cheetahs.* Dad jokes are infused with so much deliberate corniness that you instinctively recoil, cringe, and roll your eyes. Yet, you simultaneously stifle an involuntary chuckle and try to get him to stop. You: "I'm tired of these jokes." Every dad that hears you say that: "Nice to meet you, Tired."

But really, why do non-dads have a love/hate relationship with these jokes, while dads find them so funny? Whenever dads get asked this type of question, the answer is typically something like, "You'll get it when you're older and wiser. Only a finer intellect can truly appreciate the clever subtlety and nuance in a well-told joke." You can say that again. But it raises an interesting question: Is higher intelligence somehow related to a greater appreciation for dad jokes?

Statistics for Life

Is it possible that this guy actually tells funny jokes?

We know, claiming that being smart relates to thinking dad jokes are funny is such a dad move. Ridiculous? Perhaps, but it doesn't mean dads are necessarily wrong. As a savvy psychology student, you want to check the literature to see just how far-fetched the dad joke–intelligence link may be.

Past research on how people use humor in social interactions suggests that people use humor to signal their intelligence (Howrigan & MacDonald, 2008). It isn't false advertising because other research shows that people who were better at being funny also had higher general and verbal intelligence (Greengross & Miller, 2011). Similarly, other research found that humor ability correlated with fluid reasoning, vocabulary, and broad retrieval ability (Christensen et al., 2018). Interestingly, research also shows that greater emotional intelligence (i.e., being able to effectively recognize and manage emotions) was related to using more adaptive humor that was self-enhancing and sought to build connections, and less aggressive or self-deprecating humor (Gignac et al., 2014). Using humor to make a connection or make themselves look clever sounds like another total dad move.

Okay, that makes it sound like the dads of the world may be onto something. But all of those findings focus on the person telling the jokes. What about the person hearing them? That research linking emotional intelligence and humor also looked at humor appreciation (i.e., whether the listener found things funny or not). But the researchers didn't find a link between emotional intelligence and humor appreciation. However, research on dark humor (jokes that make light of topics like death) finds that people who prefer and better understand dark humor are more intelligent and have more education (Willinger et al., 2017). Although dad jokes are typically anything but dark, it does suggest that certain types of humor may relate more to intelligence than others. To really determine whether smarter people find dad jokes more humorous, we're going to need to do our own study.

Where Do the Data Come From?

It would be a major bonus to show dad some empirical data that shows he's wrong. You decide to try it out first on a couple of friends. It also makes sense to use college-aged participants because you want to convince your dad that people 30 years younger than him don't find him funny.

Duston Todd/Rubberball Productions/Getty Images

To pull this off, you're going to need some dad jokes, so you go right to the source and ask your dad for his "greatest hits." He does not disappoint. Here are his top five:

- *"Which bear is the most condescending? A pan-duh!"*
- *"Do you know Karen? She's a vegan. Never mind, you've probably never heard of herbivore."*
- *"When I went to the zoo, I saw a baguette in a cage. It was bread in captivity."*
- *"I had an interview and they asked if I could perform under pressure. I said, no, but I do a pretty solid Bohemian Rhapsody."*
- *"A century ago, two brothers claimed that it was possible to fly. They were Wright."*

Those are all pretty ridiculous dad jokes. Thanks, dad!

Would anyone find the joke in this Tweet funny? What role might intelligence play?

Now you need to find a measure of intelligence. Rather than relying on book-smart types of tests that focus on verbal ability, you want something more general. One that comes to mind is the Wonderlic test that the National Football League gives to college players entering the pro draft. Skeptical of how good an NFL test could be, you do a quick literature search and find research showing that Wonderlic scores are strongly associated with more standardized measures of cognitive ability, comprehensive knowledge, and overall intellectual function- ing (Matthews & Lassiter, 2007). Okay, sounds legitimate. (Interested in trying the Wonderlic? You can find a quick version here: https:// beatthewonderlic.com/what-is-on-the-wonderlic-test/.)

We put together both measures. One part is the Wonderlic test, which is 50 questions. They'll have 12 minutes to complete it and get one point for each correct answer. This will provide ratio-level data with scores potentially ranging from 0 to 50. The other part has the five jokes and asks people to "Read all five of these dad jokes, and rate how funny you find all of them overall as a group using a 1–10 scale where 1 = Not at All Funny, 5 = Moderately Funny, and 10 = Extremely Funny." This provides us with continuous/interval-scale data. That night you send out a group text to all of your friends and have them come to your apartment. Nine friends show up, and you give each of them both measures. Here is what their data looks like (Figure 14.1).

Participants	Intelligence (X)	Dad Joke Rating (Y)
Cristobal	20	3
Antonia	21	5
Tyron	29	8
Mariann	17	4
Tamisha	33	9
Chandra	24	6
Glenna	19	5
Mignon	44	10
Seymour	27	2

Figure 14.1 Dad Jokes and Intelligence Results

Correlation: What We're Trying to Accomplish

Seeing our data laid out like that should look familiar. If you think back to *t*-tests, especially the *t*-test for dependent means (or paired-samples *t*-test), we also had two scores for each participant. The difference is that back then, both scores were on the exact same measure. Now, each of our friends has two scores, but each is on an entirely different variable.

With two different variables, our key question is how much scores on one relate to scores on the other. Essentially, we want to know if there is a link or connection between our two variables. In our case, we want to answer the question, "Do people who score higher on the Wonderlic find dad jokes funnier?" We can find the answer to this question using **correlation,** which is a statistic that tests the association or relationship between two variables. In other words, if we have more of one variable, how does that relate to how much of the other variable we have?

We can use correlation in a few different design situations:

1. A survey in which the researcher wants to see how scores on two different scales relate to each other (e.g., How does introversion relate to the number of books a person owns?).
2. We can also use correlation to see if a newly created measure is sufficiently similar to an existing measure, or what we call

Want to review the *t*-test for dependent means? SEE CHAPTER 9.

correlation a statistic that tests the association or relationship between two variables.

convergent validity (e.g., Does a new measure of intelligence like the Wonderlic correlate enough with well-established measures of intelligence for us to have confidence in the Wonderlic?).

3. We can also see how consistent a measure is over time, by seeing how much a person's first score correlates with their second score, or what we call **test-retest reliability** (e.g., How much does an IQ test score from elementary school, relate to an IQ test score as an adult?).

In each case, we're interested in the degree of association or strength of relationship between two continuous (noncategorical) variables.

Seeing the Association between Our Variables Before we jump into the math and calculations behind a correlation, let's start a bit more simply. Correlation is about finding associations between variables. One way we can see how two variables relate is by plotting them in a graph called a **scatterplot** (also known as a scatter diagram). On a scatterplot, one variable goes on the x-axis, while the other goes on the y-axis. Each dot represents a single participant's score on both variables. By plotting out the dots for all participants, we start to see a pattern showing how the two variables are linked.

In **Figure 14.2,** boxes (a) and (b) both show a **positive correlation,** which means that high scores on one variable correspond with

convergent validity degree to which a newly created measure is correlated to an existing measure.

test-retest reliability how much a person's first score correlates with their second score on the same test.

scatterplot a depiction of two continuous variables that depicts the relationship between the variables; the X variable is presented on the horizontal axis and the Y variable is presented on the vertical axis; on the graph, each dot represents a single participant's scores on the X and Y variables.

positive correlation a relationship between two variables when high scores on one variable correspond with high scores on the other variable, while low scores on one variable also correspond with low scores on the other.

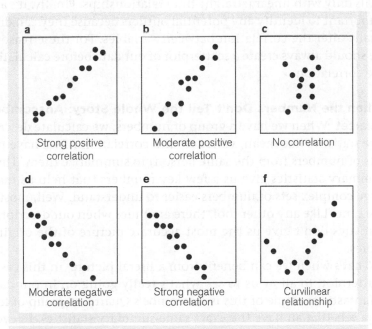

a — Strong positive correlation

b — Moderate positive correlation

c — No correlation

d — Moderate negative correlation

e — Strong negative correlation

f — Curvilinear relationship

Figure 14.2 Dad Jokes and Intelligence

negative correlation a relationship between two variables when high scores on one variable correspond with low scores on the other variable, and vice versa.

no correlation a relationship between two variables when the variables are not related in a meaningful or systematic way.

curvilinear relationship a relationship between two variables when the association between two variables changes over different levels or amounts of the variables.

high scores on the other variable, while low scores on one variable also correspond with low scores on the other. If greater intelligence corresponds with finding dad jokes funnier, this is the pattern we'll see. However, if we're completely wrong and greater intelligence makes people find dad jokes less funny, we'll see a pattern like boxes (d) and (e). They show a **negative correlation,** which means that high scores on one variable correspond with low scores on the other variable, and vice versa. One other thing to notice when interpreting scatterplots for positive and negative correlation is how close the dots are together. When they are more compact, the correlation is stronger—e.g., boxes (a) and (e)—but when the dots are more dispersed, the association between variables is weaker—e.g., boxes (b) and (d).

In terms of our findings, the other way we could be wrong is if our variables are not related in a meaningful or systematic way, or there is **no correlation.** When that happens, the pattern looks like box (c). Our data may also show a **curvilinear relationship,** which happens when the association between two variables changes over different levels or amounts of the variables. In our study, that could happen if people with high intelligence find dad jokes especially funny, those with middle levels of intelligence don't find them very funny at all, but those who have lower intelligence scores also find dad jokes really funny. It's important for us to make sure our data don't depict a curvilinear pattern, because correlation deals only with linear (straight-line) relationships. Finally, it's also important to identify any potential outliers because they can drastically alter the correlation between variables. For these reasons, we should always create a scatterplot of our data before calculating the correlation.

When the Numbers Don't Tell the Whole Story: Anscombe's Quartet When we have a group of numbers, we calculate descriptive statistics like mean, variance, and correlation (if we have two sets of numbers from the same person) to summarize them. These summary statistics give us a few key numbers that help us make large complex sets of numbers easier to understand. Well, most of the time. Like any other tool, there are times when our descriptive statistics don't give us the most accurate picture of the original scores.

That's when we can benefit from a literal picture, in this case a scatterplot, to allow us to see what's really going on in our data. A fantastic example of this is Anscombe's Quartet, a group of four data sets that all have the exact same summary statistics. In every hypothetical data set, the X variable's mean is 9, the Y variable's mean is 7.50. In all four datasets, the variance of X is 11, the variance of Y is 4.12, and the correlation between X and Y is .82. It's easy to assume, then, that all four data sets contain very similar scores. Except they don't. As you can see in **Figure 14.3,** each data set is very different. What we could not see from the summary statistics is abundantly clear when we create the scatterplots: these data are unique. Anscombe's Quartet is another reminder of the importance of plotting our data.

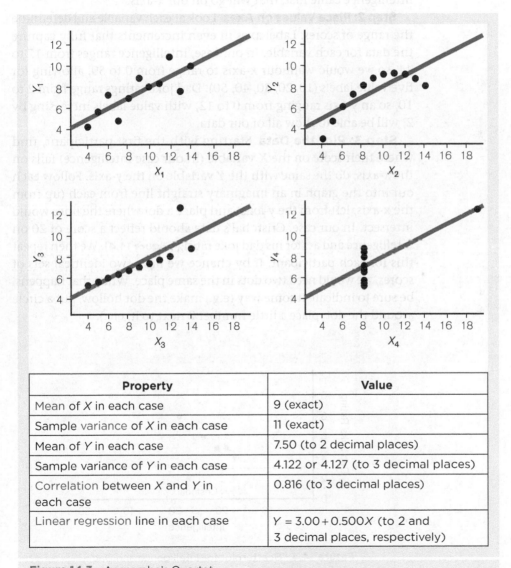

Property	Value
Mean of X in each case	9 (exact)
Sample variance of X in each case	11 (exact)
Mean of Y in each case	7.50 (to 2 decimal places)
Sample variance of Y in each case	4.122 or 4.127 (to 3 decimal places)
Correlation between X and Y in each case	0.816 (to 3 decimal places)
Linear regression line in each case	$Y = 3.00 + 0.500X$ (to 2 and 3 decimal places, respectively)

Figure 14.3 Anscombe's Quartet

Step by Step: Creating a Scatterplot To make our own scatterplot, we can follow these steps:

Step 1: Create and Label Axes We start with a basic graph with an x-axis flat and horizontal on the bottom, and a y-axis standing up vertically, keeping the lengths of each even. We then put one variable on each access. Though the variables can go on either axis, it makes sense to align your axes with how we've worded our research question. In our case, we're wondering "Is higher intelligence somehow related to a greater appreciation for dad jokes?" With that phrasing, since intelligence came first, that will go on our x-axis.

Step 2: Place Values on Axes Look at each variable and determine the range of scores. Label axes in even increments that fully capture the data for each variable. In our case, intelligence ranges from 17 to 44, so we would want our x-axis to range from 0 to 50, allowing for five value labels (10, 20, 30, 40, 50). Dad joke ratings range from 2 to 10, so an y-axis ranging from 0 to 12, with value labels increasing by 2, will be able to show all of our data.

Step 3: Plot the Data Starting with the first participant, find where their score on the X variable (in our case intelligence) falls on the x-axis; do the same with the Y variable on the y-axis. Follow each out into the graph in an imaginary straight line from each (up from the x-axis, left from the y-axis) and place a dot where the lines would intersect. In our case, Cristobal's data should reflect a score of 20 on intelligence and a 3 for his dad joke rating (**Figure 14.4**). We then repeat this for each participant. If by chance we have two identical sets of scores, we would need two dots in the same place. When that happens, be sure to indicate it some way (e.g., make the dot hollow, put a circle around the dot, place a little number 2 next to it, etc.).

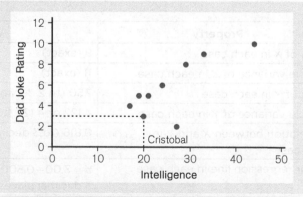

Figure 14.4 Scatterplot for Intelligence and Dad Joke Rating

Your Turn 14.1

1. For each of the following, indicate the appropriate statistic.

a. A researcher wants to see if their new measure of life satisfaction has convergent validity with an existing measure of psychological well-being.

b. A car dealer believes that people are more likely to buy a car after getting a free cup of coffee. To test this, he asks people how motivated they are to buy, then offers them coffee. Once they are done, he again asks them how motivated they are to buy.

c. A movie theater owner wants to see if people who watch action movies buy more popcorn than other people who watch comedies or documentaries.

d. A student working at a tanning salon who works on commission wants to see if the amount of times people tan per month relates to how much they spend on extra services and products.

2. For each of the following scatterplots, identify what type of relationship they show.

a

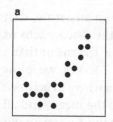

b

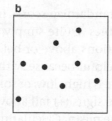

c

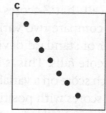

d

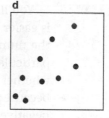

3. a. Create a scatterplot depicting a strong positive correlation between extroversion and enjoying sushi, using at least 10 dots.

b. In a different color, add in 5 additional dots that will weaken the correlation.

4. a. If your X variable's three scores are (2, 5, 8), give three scores on a Y variable (assume a 1–10 scale) that would produce a positive correlation.

b. Now give three scores on a Y variable that would produce a negative correlation.

c. Finally, if your three X-scores were (5, 5, 5), give two different sets of scores for your Y variable, that could result in no correlation.

Correlation: How Does It Work?

Did you notice when we looked at the scatterplots how we were only able to describe positive and negative correlations using words like strong and moderate? If that strikes you as imprecise, you're precisely correct. Not to mention that picking up the distinction between strong and moderate, or moderate and weak correlations based on an array of dots, is fuzzy. To make the exact relationship between our variables more clear, we need a number that clearly expresses how much variable X relates to variable *Y*. That number, the **Pearson *r* product moment correlation coefficient** (or more commonly, just Pearson *r*), is the correlation we calculate when both variables are continuous, measured at the interval or ratio level of measurement.

Getting to Know the Correlation Coefficient Correlation coefficients are actually pretty handy because they pack a lot of information into one number. First, coefficients range only from –1.00 to + 1.00. Any other result is a math error. The larger the number, in either direction, the stronger the association between two variables. A Pearson *r* of +.87 suggests that the two variables are more strongly linked than if *r* was +.23. The same goes for negative correlations: –.72 is stronger than –.13. But correlations of –.72 and +.72 are equally strong because the magnitude of the number is identical. The sign is also informative. If it's positive, that indicates a positive correlation, while negative signs indicate a negative correlation. Correlation coefficients very near 0 indicate no correlation. That's how we interpret the Pearson *r* correlation coefficient; now let's look at where that number comes from.

Correlation Logic: The Return of the *Z* Scores, that is. That's right, we're bringing back one of our old friends. You should know that there are other ways to calculate a correlation, but we're going to focus on using *Z*-scores because it builds directly on what we already learned and more intuitively reveals what the correlation is actually doing behind the scenes.

You'll recall that *Z*-scores standardize scores from any scale, so it is easier to compare two variables. Quite simply, the *Z*-score tells us the number of standard deviations above or below the mean that a particular score falls. This is helpful because with *Z*-scores, we know whether each score on a variable is high, low, or somewhere in between because all scores with positive signs (+) fall above the mean, and all negative scores (–) fall below the mean. Calculating the *Z*-score for our *X* variable (Z_X) and our *Y* variable (Z_Y) helps us see more easily how a score's position on the *X* variable (in our case, intelligence) corresponds to that same person's score on the *Y* variable (dad joke rating). Are both variables high? Both low? One high, one low, or vice versa? Or is one of the scores right near the mean?

In other words, we're interested in the combination of both variables or the *cross-product of Z-scores* ($Z_X Z_Y$), which we get by multiplying a person's *Z*-scores from the *X* and *Y* variables. Now, here's where a little bit of mathematical magic happens. Remember middle school math? What happens when you multiply a positive by a positive? You get a positive. What about multiplying two negatives? That also

Want to review the basics of *Z*-scores? SEE CHAPTER 4.

gives you a positive, because the negatives cancel out. If one number is positive and the other negative, what happens? The result is negative. And if just one number you're multiplying is zero, the result is zero.

It works the exact same way in terms of how the two variables or Z-scores relate to each other. As you can see in **Figure 14.5,** if both are above the mean, their Z-scores are both positive, meaning their cross-product will be positive, indicating a positive correlation. If the X and Y variables are both below the mean, their Z-scores are both negative, meaning their cross-product will be positive because the negatives cancel out. This is also a positive correlation because low numbers in one variable correspond with low numbers in the other. Now if one of the two variables is above the mean and the other is below, there will be one positive Z-score and one negative, resulting in a negative cross-product which indicates a negative correlation. Finally, if one score is near the mean, the Z-score will be near zero, so when that gets multiplied by anything, the result will be low, indicated as no correlation.

Original Scores		Z-Scores		Cross-Product	Correlation
X	**Y**	**Z_X**	**Z_Y**	**$Z_X Z_Y$**	**r**
Above the Mean	Above the Mean	+	+	+	+
Below the Mean	Below the Mean	−	−	+	+
Above the Mean	Below the Mean	+	−	−	−
Below the Mean	Above the Mean	−	+	−	−
Near the Mean	Any	0	Any (+, −, 0)	0	Near 0
Any	Near the Mean	Any (+, −, 0)	0	0	Near 0

Figure 14.5   Cross-Product of Z-score Logic

Multiplying scores on variable X (intelligence) by scores on variable Y (dad joke rating) will give us the cross-product for each pair of scores. However, we want to know about all of the scores together. To determine that, we want to know the average cross-product of Z-scores, so we need to add up all of the cross-products of Z-scores ($\Sigma Z_X Z_Y$). This gives us the total amount of association. However, because this total is also affected by the number of scores in our sample, we divide by the sample size minus 1 ($N-1$). The resulting number is our correlation coefficient (r).

$$r = \frac{\Sigma Z_X Z_Y}{N-1}$$

Your Turn 14.2

1. A study included the following variables: Age, Ethnicity, Income, and a rating of happiness. Which variables could we analyze with a correlation?

2. For each of the following correlation coefficients, identify what type of correlation they show.

a. +.85

b. −.33

c. .02

d. −.99

e. −.04

3. For each pair of X- and Y-scores, complete the chart with + and − signs. Assume the mean for both X and Y is 5.

Original Scores		Z-Scores		Cross-Product	Correlation
X	Y	Z_X	Z_Y	$Z_X Z_Y$	r
9	2				
9	8				
5	10				
3	2				
3	8				
2	5				

Testing Our Data with Correlation: How Does It Work?

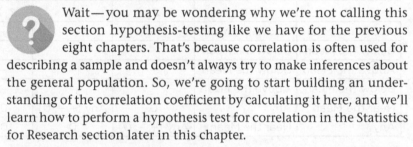

Wait—you may be wondering why we're not calling this section hypothesis-testing like we have for the previous eight chapters. That's because correlation is often used for describing a sample and doesn't always try to make inferences about the general population. So, we're going to start building an understanding of the correlation coefficient by calculating it here, and we'll learn how to perform a hypothesis test for correlation in the Statistics for Research section later in this chapter.

Step by Step: Correlation To make sure we approach our correlation analysis in a systematic way, we're going to follow a series of steps to make sure we do everything we need to answer our research question, "Is higher intelligence somehow related to a greater appreciation for dad jokes?"

Step 1: Plot the Data to Check Linearity We already did this in Figure 14.5. Looking at the pattern in our scatterplot, our data do not appear to be curvilinear. So we can proceed with calculating our Pearson r coefficient.

Step 2: Calculate Z-Scores (Z_x and Z_y) Using what we learned in Chapter 4, we'll convert each of our scores on both variables to Z-scores using the following formula: $Z = (X - M)/SD$. Note that before we can calculate the Z-score, we'll need to determine the mean (M) and sample standard deviation (SD) first. When doing this, make sure to use the X variable's M and SD for the intelligence Z-scores, and the M and SD for the dad joke rating scores when calculating the Z-scores for the Y variable (**Figure 14.6**).

Participants	Intelligence (X)	Deviation Score (X − M)	Squared Deviation Score (X − M)²	Z-Score (Z_X)	Participants	Dad Joke Rating (Y)	Deviation Score (Y − M)	Squared Deviation Score (Y − M)²	Z-Score (Z_Y)	Cross-Product of Z-Scores (Z_X Z_Y)
Cristobal	20	−6.00	36.00	−0.71	Cristobal	3	−2.78	7.72	−1.02	0.72
Antonia	21	−5.00	25.00	−0.59	Antonia	5	−0.78	0.60	−0.29	0.17
Tyron	29	3.00	9.00	0.35	Tyron	8	2.22	4.94	0.81	0.29
Mariann	17	−9.00	81.00	−1.06	Mariann	4	−1.78	3.16	−0.65	0.69
Tamisha	33	7.00	49.00	0.82	Tamisha	9	3.22	10.38	1.18	0.97
Chandra	24	−2.00	4.00	−0.24	Chandra	6	0.22	0.05	0.08	−0.02
Glenna	19	−7.00	49.00	−0.82	Glenna	5	−0.78	0.60	−0.29	0.23
Mignon	44	18.00	324.00	2.12	Mignon	10	4.22	17.83	1.55	3.28
Seymour	27	1.00	1.00	0.12	Seymour	2	−3.78	14.27	−1.38	−0.16
Sum of Scores (ΣX)	234				Sum of Scores (ΣY)	52				
Number of Scores (N)	9				Number of Scores (N)	9			$\Sigma Z_X Z_Y$	6.17
Mean (M_X)	$\Sigma X/N$	26.00			Mean (M_Y)	$\Sigma Y/N$	5.78			
Sum of Squares (SS_x)	$\Sigma(X − M)^2$	578.00			Sum of Squares (SS_y)	$\Sigma(Y − M)^2$	59.56			
Variance (SD^2)	$SS/(N − 1)$	72.25			Variance (SD^2)	$SS/(N − 1)$	7.44			
Standard Deviation (SD_x)	$\sqrt{SD^2}$	8.50			Standard Deviation (SD_y)	$\sqrt{SD^2}$	2.73			
Z-Score (Z_x)	$(X − M)/SD$				Z-Score (Z_y)	$(Y − M)/SD$				
Pearson's r	$\Sigma Z_X Z_Y/N − 1$	0.77								

Figure 14.6 Computations for a Correlation

Step 3: Calculate and Sum Cross-Product of Z-Scores ($Z_X Z_Y$)

For each participant, multiply their Z-score on the X variable/intelligence (Z_X) with their Z-score on the Y variable/intelligence (Z_Y), to create the cross-product. For the first participant Cristobal, his calculation is as follows: $−0.71 \times −1.02 = 0.72$. As you can see, because he was below the mean for both scores, his Z-scores were both negative, resulting in a positive cross-product. Once we've done this for each participant, we add them all up, creating the sum of the cross-products ($\Sigma Z_X Z_Y$); in this case, the result is 6.17.

Step 4: Calculate Pearson r (r)

To determine the average amount of association between the X and Y variables, we'll calculate the average cross-product of Z-scores for each person by dividing the sum ($\Sigma Z_X Z_Y$) by the number of people in the study (N − 1). Doing so gives us the correlation coefficient (r). In our study:

$$r = \frac{\Sigma Z_X Z_Y}{N − 1} = \frac{6.17}{8} = .77$$

Step 6: Decide and Interpret A correlation of .77 indicates a strong positive association between our variables, which indicates that those who scored higher on the Wonderlic rated the dad jokes as funnier, while those who scored lower on the Wonderlic rated the dad jokes as less funny.

 HAND CALCULATION VIDEO TUTORIAL: To learn more, check out the video Performing Pearson Correlation.

Communicating the Result

When communicating our result, we always want to describe the correlation coefficient's direction and strength. Here, there was a strong positive correlation between Wonderlic scores and dad joke ratings. This would seem to support our dad's statement that those with greater intelligence are more likely to find dad jokes funny. It makes sense because the jokes we used require some background knowledge. For example, to make a connection and find humor in the jokes, the listener would need to know about pandas, herbivores, baguettes, the band Queen, and the Wright brothers. Each of those is somewhat trivial and would require some intelligence.

We also have to remember that a strong correlation tells us only about the association between variables. That is, the positive correlation only suggests that those with higher Wonderlic scores tended to find the jokes funnier, and that those with lower Wonderlic scores found the jokes less funny. That correlation does not tell us about any one variable. That is, our results do not tell us whether dad jokes are funny or not. To figure out how funny dad jokes are, we would need to look at the mean rating for dad jokes. On a 10-point scale, the mean rating for dad joke funniness was only a 5.78. That's like getting a 57.8% on a test. Not exactly hilarious. If you're interested in how to present findings using APA Style, please see the next section on Statistics for Research.

Forming a Conclusion

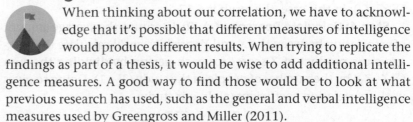 When thinking about our correlation, we have to acknowledge that it's possible that different measures of intelligence would produce different results. When trying to replicate the findings as part of a thesis, it would be wise to add additional intelligence measures. A good way to find those would be to look at what previous research has used, such as the general and verbal intelligence measures used by Greengross and Miller (2011).

We also have to acknowledge that our study only focused on dads delivering jokes. It's possible that telling people they were dad jokes biased the responses. There is research showing that although people assume men are funnier than women, when researchers put that assumption to the test, they found no difference (Hooper et al., 2016). To be gender-neutral, we could just ask people to react to the jokes without knowing it was a "dad" joke.

Your Turn 14.3

Stewie works at a local animal shelter and wants to help adopted animals find the best home possible. After taking a personality course in psychology, Stewie thinks that certain people have personalities that would make them more likely to be "cat people" (that is, prefer cats) while others have personalities that would make them more likely to be "dog people" (that is, prefer dogs). In particular he believes that those with high openness to experience like dogs better, while those with low openness to experience like cats better.

To test this, he asks 12 people who visit the shelter to complete an *openness to experience* item that asks, "I like discovering new ways of doing things that I've never tried before." People rated themselves on a 7-point scale where 1 = Not at All Descriptive of Me and 7 = Extremely Descriptive of Me. Next, they answered the following question, "Would you consider yourself more of a dog person or a cat person?" People rated themselves on a 10-point scale where 1 = Entirely a Dog Person, 5 = Equally a Dog and Cat Person; and 10 = Entirely a Cat Person. Here are the 12 pairs of scores, one from each participant, with *openness to experience* first, followed by dog/cat person rating: (4,5), (2,8), (1,9), (3,10), (4,4), (6,7), (4,9), (7,4), (6,3), (5,2), (5,1), (7,2).

1. Based on what you've read, what type of correlation is Stewie looking for?

2. Calculate the correlation coefficient using the appropriate steps.

Statistics for Research

Digital devices and their screens are all around us. These devices offer access to unprecedented amounts of information, social connection, and entertainment. But is there a downside to having so many screens in our lives? Some researchers suggest that screen time, or the total amount of time that a person spends using electronic devices with screens, may have undesirable physical and psychological effects on people, especially children. For example, research reveals that screen time is associated with less sleep among children (Przybylski, 2019), greater obesity (Stiglic & Viner, 2019), and poor psychological outcomes such as more depression and anxiety (Oswald et al., 2020).

We could also ask an additional research question: Is screen time associated with cognitive development among children? In particular, we may predict that screen time is negatively correlated with attention, meaning that as screen time increases, we expect that children's ability

Is screen time associated with children's attention span?

vinnstock/iStock/Getty Images

to focus their attention for long periods of time decreases. To test this, we will use a correlation analysis.

Here in the Statistics for Research section, we're going to learn about hypothesis testing for correlation, distributions of correlations, assumptions of correlation (including the homoscedasticity assumption), using Spearman correlations for curvilinear relationships, calculating a *t*-score from a correlation, mistakes to avoid when interpreting results, creating a correlation matrix, and understanding spurious correlations.

Where Do the Data Come From?

So, how might we collect data to test our hypothesis that screen time negatively correlates with attention span? Well, measuring screen time should be pretty straightforward. We could ask participants (or their parents) to track their screen time over the course of a day. What about attention span?

One option would be to use the Mackworth Clock Test (Mackworth, 1948), which measures how long participants can pay attention to a clock. During the task, the clock moves in 6-degree increments (the same amount that the second hand moves around the clock). However, sporadically, the clock jumps 12 degrees. Participants need to pay attention to the movement of the clock and indicate any time they see one of these 12-degree jumps by clicking the spacebar on their computer. Now, some versions of the Mackworth Clock Test last 2 hours long (such as one used to train astronauts) and can make participants wait 30 minutes in between jumps. Let's set our version to last as long as it takes for participants to make three mistakes (which we estimate to take about 10 minutes). Presumably, participants with better attention spans will be able to focus on the task better, thereby lasting longer on the task.

Want to try a version of the Mackworth Clock Test? Go to https://www.psytoolkit.org/experiment-library/mackworth.html

Imagine that we collect a sample of 20 first- and second-grade children and (using calculations like we described earlier in the chapter) find a correlation between screen time and attention span of −.47. What does this tell us? Well, it definitely reveals that as screen time increases, attention span decreases, at least in our sample. But does it indicate whether there is an association between screen time and attention span in the population? To answer this question, we need to conduct a hypothesis test for correlation.

Hypothesis Testing for Correlation: What We're Trying to Accomplish

In the first half of this chapter, we learned how to compute the Pearson *r*. We also learned that the correlation coefficient describes both the direction (positive or negative) and the strength of the association between two variables that we observe in our sample. But most of the time, when we conduct research, we want to make conclusions about populations, rather than samples. If we conduct our study and conclude that screen time negatively correlates with attention span, but only for our sample of participants, that would be a very limited conclusion. Instead, we want to know whether there is a correlation among our variables at the population level. To do this, we need to modify an idea that we have encountered many times in this book: the distribution of sample means. Remember that the distribution of sample means is a distribution that we create by taking an infinite number of samples of a fixed sample size and plotting their means in a distribution.

Distributions of sample means are really useful for establishing the population mean's confidence interval, because we know that the sample means' distribution follows the shape of a normal curve. But a distribution of means won't really help us now because we are testing a correlation, not a mean. We can, however, use the same underlying logic that we used when creating a distribution of means to create a **distribution of correlations,** which reflects the correlations between two variables for an infinite number of samples from the population. **Figure 14.7** illustrates what this would look like for three samples taken from the same population. We could imagine taking a sample from the population and measuring the correlation between screen time and attention span. Then, we could draw a second and third sample from the population and recalculate the correlations for each sample. Theoretically, we could then do this again and again until we collected every possible sample from the population. If we took all of the correlations that we observed in our samples and plotted them in a distribution, it would be the distribution of correlations. The only difference between

Want to freshen up on the distribution of means? Look back to CHAPTER 5.

distribution of correlations a distribution comprised of the bivariate correlations for all possible samples of a fixed size.

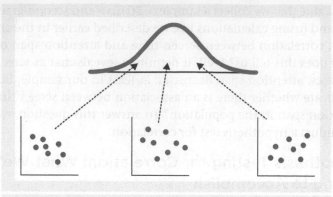

Figure 14.7 Distribution of Correlations

this approach and the distribution of means that we used previously is that we are plotting correlations, rather than means.

Now, the distribution of correlations has some important properties that will help us conduct a hypothesis test for a correlation. Importantly, because the distribution of correlations contains every possible sample from the population, the mean of the sampling distribution of correlations equals the correlation that exists between two variables in the population. Let's think about what this tells us. If the sampling distributions of correlations mean is zero (because the two variables we are interested in are unrelated in the population), then any nonzero correlation we observe in our samples must be due to sampling error. The odds of obtaining a positive correlation or a negative correlation due to sampling error should be equal, resulting in a symmetric distribution of sample correlations. Moreover, we should observe more sample correlations that are close to the correlation in the population, and very few that are far away from the correlation in the population. Thus, the distribution of correlations should take on the shape of a normal curve. In practice, we will use a t-curve (rather than a normal curve) to approximate the distribution of correlations' shape because we don't know the standard error of the population and use our sample to estimate the population variances for our variables.

Once we have this information, we'll be able to estimate the probability of observing a correlation in our sample (the p-value of our correlation), assuming that there is no correlation in the population, which will be our null hypothesis. Several factors affect our hypothesis test's p-value. First, there is the correlation's magnitude: If the correlation in the population is zero, then it should be very surprising for us to observe large correlations in our sample. So, as the observed value of r goes up, our p-value should go down. Second, if the correlation in the population is zero, then it should be very surprising for us to observe nonzero correlations as our sample size gets larger. Bigger samples are better samples typically, so as the value of N goes up, our p-value should go down, given a nonzero correlation in our sample.

Hypothesis Testing for Correlation: How Does It Work?

A hypothesis test is going to weigh the evidence that we have gathered in our sample so that we can make an inference about the population. In this case, if we observe a correlation of $-.47$, with a sample size of 20, do we have enough evidence to believe that there is a correlation between screen time and attention span in the population? Let's find out.

Assumptions of Correlation Analysis Before we can conduct a hypothesis test for correlation, we need to satisfy five assumptions of the test.

1. *The sample is randomly selected from the population and participants' scores are independent.* This assumption states that we used random selection to sample from the population and that the scores of one participant do not affect the scores for any other participant. If we do not use random selection for our sampling method, this can reduce the extent to which we can generalize the results from our sample to the population.

2. *Both the* X *and the* Y *variables are normally distributed, as is the bivariate distribution.* This assumption is not unlike the normality assumption that we have encountered for previous hypothesis tests, but it adds in another requirement. Not only does each variable need to be normally distributed individually, but each variable needs to be normally distributed at each value of the other variable. So, for each score that we observe for screen time, the distribution of scores on attention span should be normally distributed, and vice versa. Although violations of this assumption can affect the value of the correlation coefficient (and p-value for that correlation), its impact is very minimal on our test of significance if we have independent observations (see assumption 1) and our sample size is greater than 15 (Edgell & Noon, 1984; Van den Brink, 1988).

3. *The variance in the* Y *variable is equal across the values of the* X *variable.* This assumption is called the **homoscedasticity assumption** and in many respects is similar to the equality of variances assumption we've seen in other hypothesis tests. Indeed, the Greek roots of the term "homoscedastic" mean "same scatter," which reflects the idea that the variation (scatter) in the Y variable is the same as we move along the values of the

homoscedasticity assumption assumption of correlation and regression analyses that states that the Y variable should exhibit the same amount of variation across the range of scores of the X variable.

X variable. So, the differences in participants' attention span scores (i.e., how much variability they have) should be the same at low, medium, and high levels of screen time. If everyone had the same attention span at low and high screen time, but a wide variety of attention spans at medium screen time, we would violate the homoscedasticity assumption.

Homoscedasticity can be hard to understand, so let's look at an example to help us visualize the issue. **Figure 14.8** presents

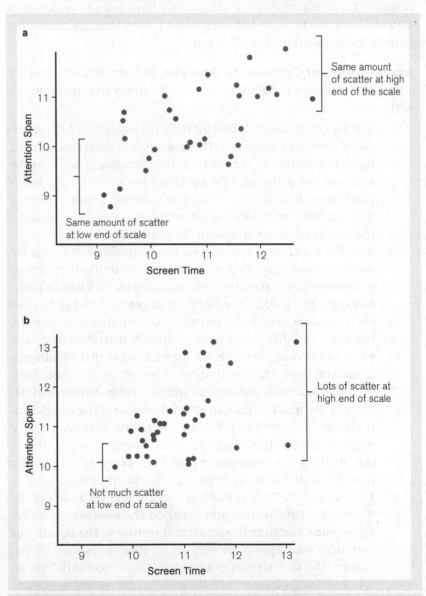

Figure 14.8 Comparing Homoscedastic and Heteroscedastic Scatterplots of Screen Time and Attention Span

two scatterplots, one depicting a homoscedastic association and one that depicts a heteroscedastic association. As we can see in Figure 14.8a, which depicts a homoscedastic association that satisfies the assumption, there is approximately the same amount of variation in attention span when screen time is low as when screen time is high. In contrast, we can see in Figure 14.8b, which depicts a heteroscedastic association that violates the assumption, that there is lower variation in attention span when screen time is low, relative to when screen time is high.

4. *The X, Y association is linear.* This assumption states that the relationship between our variables must be linear. If the association is curvilinear, we will need to use a different type of analysis other than Pearson correlation. For example, we can use the **Spearman correlation** to analyze certain types of curvilinear associations.

5. *We have the correct type of data.* There are different types of correlation based on the type of data (nominal, ordinal, interval, ratio) under consideration. For Pearson *r*, the data for both of our variables should be interval or ratio. There is one exception to this, which is that our *X* variable can be a dichotomous, nominal variable (meaning that it has two and only two groups). In this situation, our measure of correlation is called a point-biserial correlation.

Spearman correlation a type of correlation that analyzes ordinal data and certain curvilinear associations between interval/ratio variables.

Step by Step: Hypothesis Testing Our first step is to specify the populations and hypotheses we are testing.

Step 1: Population and Hypotheses Although we are not directly comparing two (or more) populations such as we have done in previous hypothesis tests, we still need to establish what we are comparing and for whom. In general, we will compare groups of 20 children who will make up our sample, to the population of all children, for the variables screen time and attention.

Population of Interest: A population of first- and second-grade children for whom there is no association between screen time and attention.

Comparison Population: First- and second-grade children like those in our sample for whom there is an association between screen time and attention.

Sample: The 20 children in our sample, each of whom complete a measure of screen time and attention span.

Research Hypothesis: Although we may expect that screen time and attention span are negatively correlated based on previous literature and anecdotal accounts, we should be open to the possibility that they are positively correlated. It's not so outrageous to expect that children who can watch a television screen, tablet, or computer for hours on end will perform better on our measure of attention span. Because either outcome could be possible, our research hypothesis is two-tailed: the correlation in the population is not zero, $\rho \neq 0$ (note that we use the Greek letter ρ or "rho" to refer to the population-level correlation).

Null Hypothesis: The null hypothesis is that the correlation in the population is 0 ($\rho = 0$). In other words, there is no association between screen time and attention span among children.

Step 2: Build Comparison Distribution What would the comparison distribution look like if the null hypothesis is true? Well, the mean would be zero, because the null states that there is no association between our variables, and we know that the distribution of correlations has a mean that is equal to the correlation in the population. If the null is true, we expect to see correlations in our samples that are not zero due to sampling error. Because of this, we need to consider the shape of the distribution of correlations. We said earlier that we will use the t-curve to approximate the shape of the distribution of correlations. In particular, we will use a t-curve with $N - 2$ degrees of freedom. Why $N - 2$? We have $N - 2$ degrees of freedom because degrees of freedom reflect the number of independent observations minus the number of parameters that we are estimating. Here, we are estimating two population parameters (that correspond to the slope and y-intercept of the association, which we'll learn more about in Chapter 15) using our sample's data. So, the degrees of freedom for our comparison distribution is $N - 2 = 20 - 2 = 18$.

Step 3: Establish Critical Value Cutoff Just like any other hypothesis test, we need to figure out the values of t that correspond to our alpha. So, before we can proceed, we need to set our alpha. Let's set it to .05. We are now ready to find the critical values of t. To do so, we will refer to our t-table (**Figure 14.9**). We choose the column that corresponds to our alpha, which we will set to .05, two-tailed. We then scroll down the various rows until we reach the one for 18 degrees of freedom. As we can see, our critical value cutoff is 2.101.

Step 4: Determine Sample Results The next step is to calculate the Pearson correlation coefficient for our sample, and then perform the t-test for correlation. Before we start our calculations, though, we should first make sure that we satisfied the assumptions of the hypothesis test. As we stated earlier, the first assumption states that we randomly selected the sample from the population and that scores between participants are independent. Our study collected a sample of 20 first- and second-grade children but did not use random selection. Thus, this could limit the extent to which our sample results generalize. However, all of the participants' scores were independent. The second assumption is the normality assumption. Recall that this

	One-Tailed Tests Alpha Level		Two-Tailed Tests Alpha Level	
df	0.05	0.01	0.05	0.01
1	6.314	31.821	12.706	63.657
2	2.920	6.965	4.303	9.925
3	2.353	4.541	3.182	5.841
4	2.132	3.747	2.776	4.604
5	2.015	3.365	2.571	4.032
6	1.943	3.143	2.447	3.708
7	1.895	2.998	2.365	3.500
8	1.860	2.897	2.306	3.356
9	1.833	2.822	2.262	3.250
10	1.813	2.764	2.228	3.170
11	1.796	2.718	2.201	3.106
12	1.783	2.681	2.179	3.055
13	1.771	2.651	2.161	3.013
14	1.762	2.625	2.145	2.977
15	1.753	2.603	2.132	2.947
16	1.746	2.584	2.120	2.921
17	1.740	2.567	2.110	2.898
18	1.734	2.553	2.101	2.879
19	1.729	2.540	2.093	2.861
20	1.725	2.528	2.086	2.846
21	1.721	2.518	2.080	2.832
22	1.717	2.509	2.074	2.819
23	1.714	2.500	2.069	2.808
24	1.711	2.492	2.064	2.797
25	1.708	2.485	2.060	2.788
26	1.706	2.479	2.056	2.779
27	1.704	2.473	2.052	2.771
28	1.701	2.467	2.049	2.764
29	1.699	2.462	2.045	2.757
30	1.698	2.458	2.043	2.750
35	1.690	2.438	2.030	2.724
40	1.684	2.424	2.021	2.705

Figure 14.9   *t*-Table Preview

assumption states that not only do each of our variables need to be normally distributed, but so does the bivariate distribution. However, the *t*-test for correlation is robust to violations of normality, so long as our sample size is greater than 15 (Edgell & Noon, 1984; Van den Brink, 1988). Because our sample size is 20, we likely don't need to worry about violations of this assumption. The third assumption is the homoscedasticity assumption. To test this assumption, we can examine the scatterplot of the association. **Figure 14.10** presents the scatterplot for our 20 participants.

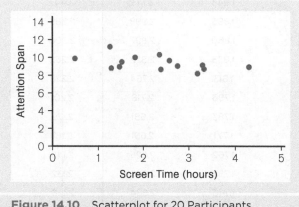

Figure 14.10   Scatterplot for 20 Participants

Our data appear to be homoscedastic, because as we move from low levels of screen time to high levels, the amount of scatter in the data points appears to be equal. Of course, this "eyeball" method may be prone to mistakes, so we'll talk about a more precise method for evaluating homoscedasticity in Chapter 15.

Finally, the fourth assumption of Pearson correlation is that the association between our variables is linear. As we can see in Figure 14.10, the association appears to be linear, rather than curvilinear.

Now that we have satisfied the assumptions, we need to calculate the Pearson correlation coefficient. To do so, we will follow the four steps described in the first half of this chapter.

Correlation Step 1: Plot the data to check linearity. Because we did this when checking our assumptions, we can move on to step 2.

Correlation Step 2: Calculate Z-scores (Z_X and Z_Y). **Figure 14.11** presents all of the relevant calculations. For each score in our data set, we will subtract its relevant mean and then divide by its relevant standard deviation.

Correlation Step 3: Calculate and sum cross-product of Z-scores ($Z_X Z_Y$). Now that each score has been standardized (by converting it to a

Participants	Screen Time (X)	Deviation Score ($X - M$)	Squared Deviation Score ($(X - M)^2$)	Z-Score (Z_x)	Participants	Attention Span (Y)	Deviation Score ($Y - M$)	Squared Deviation Score ($(Y - M)^2$)	Z-Score (Z_y)	Cross-Product of Z-Scores ($Z_x Z_y$)
1	3.18	0.93	0.87	0.93	1	8.06	−1.44	2.06	−1.44	−1.34
2	1.82	−0.43	0.18	−0.43	2	10.51	1.01	1.03	1.02	−0.44
3	0.76	−1.49	2.22	−1.49	3	9.33	−0.17	0.03	−0.17	0.25
4	3.16	0.91	0.83	0.91	4	8.37	−1.13	1.27	−1.13	−1.03
5	1.44	−0.81	0.65	−0.81	5	11.62	2.12	4.51	2.13	−1.72
6	2.68	0.43	0.19	0.43	6	10.79	1.29	1.68	1.30	0.56
7	2.35	0.10	0.01	0.10	7	10.33	0.83	0.70	0.84	0.08
8	0.48	−1.77	3.13	−1.77	8	9.89	0.39	0.16	0.40	−0.70
9	3.19	0.94	0.89	0.94	9	8.19	−1.31	1.70	−1.31	−1.23
10	1.28	−0.97	0.94	−0.97	10	8.8	−0.70	0.48	−0.70	0.67
11	2.57	0.32	0.10	0.32	11	9.66	0.16	0.03	0.16	0.05
12	3.32	1.07	1.15	1.07	12	8.75	−0.75	0.56	−0.75	−0.80
13	1.51	−0.74	0.55	−0.74	13	9.46	−0.04	0.00	−0.04	0.03
14	2.75	0.50	0.25	0.50	14	9.06	−0.44	0.19	−0.44	−0.22
15	4.29	2.04	4.17	2.04	15	8.96	−0.54	0.29	−0.54	−1.09
16	3.3	1.05	1.10	1.05	16	9.14	−0.36	0.13	−0.36	−0.37
17	1.46	−0.79	0.62	−0.79	17	9.04	−0.46	0.21	−0.46	0.36
18	1.25	−1.00	1.00	−1.00	18	11.23	1.73	3.01	1.74	−1.73
19	2.38	0.13	0.02	0.13	19	8.7	−0.80	0.63	−0.80	−0.10
20	1.81	0.44	0.19	0.44	20	10.02	0.52	0.28	0.53	0.23
Sum of Scores (ΣX)	44.98				Sum of Scores (ΣX)	189.91				
Number of Scores (N)	20				Number of Scores (N)	20			$\Sigma Z_x Z_y$	−9.00
Mean (M_x)	$\Sigma X/N$	2.25			Mean (M_x)	$\Sigma X/N$	9.50			
Sum of Squares (SS_x)	$\Sigma(X - M)^2$	19.05			Sum of Squares (SS_x)	$\Sigma(X - M)^2$	18.92			
Variance (SD^2)	$SS/(N - 1)$	1.00			Variance (SD^2)	$SS/(N - 1)$	1.00			
Standard Deviation (SD_x)	$\sqrt{SD^2}$	1.00			Standard Deviation (SD_x)	$\sqrt{SD^2}$	1.00			
Z-Score (Z_x)	$(X - M)/SD$				Z-Score (Z_x)	$(X - M)/SD$				
Pearson's (r)	$\Sigma Z_x Z_y/N - 1$		−0.47		Calculate t-score (t) to find significance	$r/\sqrt{(1 - r^2)/(N - 2)}$				−2.28

Figure 14.11 Computations for a Correlation

Z-score), we calculate the cross-product for each participant, $Z_X Z_Y$, and then sum up the cross-products for the entire sample, $\sum Z_X Z_Y$. As we can see in Figure 14.11, the sum of the cross-products is −9.00.

Correlation Step 4: Calculate Pearson r. The final step is to divide by the sample size. Thus, $r = -9.47/20 = -.47$. The Pearson correlation coefficient is −.47, indicating that as screen time increases, attention span decreases.

We're now ready to calculate the *t*-score for our correlation. To do so, we will convert our Pearson *r* into a *t*-score, using the following formula:

$$t = \frac{r}{\sqrt{\dfrac{1 - r^2}{N - 2}}}$$

$$t = \frac{r}{\sqrt{\dfrac{1 - r^2}{N - 2}}} = \frac{-.47}{\sqrt{\dfrac{1 - (-.47)^2}{20 - 2}}} = \frac{-.47}{\sqrt{\dfrac{.78}{18}}} = \frac{-.47}{.21} = -2.28.$$

Step 5: Decide and Interpret To determine if our *t*-score is significant, we need to compare it to our critical value cutoff, which we found earlier to be +/−2.102. Because we are testing a two-tailed research hypothesis, we will reject the null hypothesis if our *t*-score is smaller than −2.101 or greater than 2.101. In this case, because −2.28 is smaller than −2.101, we can reject the null hypothesis and conclude that there is a negative correlation between screen time and attention span in the population.

Measuring Effect Size As with other hypothesis tests, knowing that the correlation is significant does not reveal whether it represents a large, medium, or small association. Luckily, the correlation coefficient itself can be interpreted directly as indicating the association's magnitude. Thus, we do not need to learn new analyses to convert our correlation coefficient into an effect size measure. We just need to know how to evaluate the correlation that we observe in our study.

To interpret a correlation, we should first look to prior research to see how our observed correlation compares to other correlations. Of course, for some types of research investigations, there may not be a robust literature, making it difficult to use prior work to help interpret the magnitude of a correlation. In these instances, we can rely on conventions. Cohen (1992) suggests that, if we have nothing else to go on, we can consider correlations of .10 to be small, correlations of .30 to be medium, and correlations of .50 to be large.

SPSS Video Tutorial: Correlation

Let's see how we would perform this analysis using SPSS. Watch this SPSS video for this chapter, which demonstrates how to perform correlation using SPSS.

> **SPSS VIDEO TUTORIAL: To learn more, check out the video Correlation.**

Communicating the Result

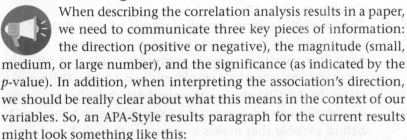

When describing the correlation analysis results in a paper, we need to communicate three key pieces of information: the direction (positive or negative), the magnitude (small, medium, or large number), and the significance (as indicated by the p-value). In addition, when interpreting the association's direction, we should be really clear about what this means in the context of our variables. So, an APA-Style results paragraph for the current results might look something like this:

> A Pearson correlation analysis revealed that there was a medium-large, negative correlation between screen time and attention span ($r = -.47$, $p = .035$), such that increases in screen time were associated with decreases in attention span.

Misinterpreting Our Results As we can see, Pearson correlation is an easy and useful analysis because it tells us the extent to which two variables are associated with one another. Yet, we need to be very careful not to misinterpret our results. For all that a correlation analysis reveals, it's what it doesn't tell us that can get us into trouble. Most importantly, because we do not randomly assign participants to condition in a correlational study, we cannot make conclusions about causality. That is, even if we find a significant, negative correlation between screen time and attention span, we can't conclude that increases in screen time *cause* decreases in attention span. There are at least two reasons for this:

1. *Reverse causality*. We've proceeded working under the assumption that screen time predicts attention span, but what if it's the other way around? Perhaps people with shorter attention spans prefer to use screened devices because they can't concentrate on other types of entertainment (e.g., reading books). So, perhaps

it's the short attention span that leads to increased screen time. The important point is that the correlation coefficient can't tell us, and if we look back to the formula for the Pearson correlation coefficient, we can see why. In the numerator, we multiply the Z-scores for the X variable by the Z-scores for the Y variable. Because $Z_X Z_Y$ leads to the same number as $Z_Y Z_X$, the formula can't distinguish between which is the predictor variable and which is the outcome variable. And as a result, neither can we. So, we need to be especially careful to not assume that a significant correlation means that our X variable causes the changes in the Y variable.

2. *Third variable problem.* Another reason why we can't make causal conclusions based on correlational evidence is that we don't know whether there is another variable that actually drives the correlation that we observe in our study. This issue is called the **third variable problem** and describes the possibility that both our X variable and our Y variable are associated with a third variable that makes it appear as though X and Y are linked to each other. For example, perhaps both screen time and attention span are both correlated with a biological factor, such as the functioning of the prefrontal cortex in the brain that is associated with executive functioning (e.g., planned action; working memory) and self-control. Because we can't measure all possible variables in a given study, there's always a chance that there exists a third variable that is the true cause of the changes in our outcome variable.

In addition to the problem of causality, we can also misinterpret the results of a correlation analysis when we have **restriction of range.** Restriction of range occurs when we are able to measure only a portion of the population and, as a result, we are unable to capture the full range of scores that occurs in the population. For example, it's possible that some people in the population spend so much time in front of a screen that we can't recruit them to participate in our study. As a result of their not being included in our sample, we may find an artificially strong or weak correlation in our sample. **Figure 14.12** illustrates this problem.

The left panel shows the relationship between screen time and attention span for the entire population. The right panel shows the association between screen time and attention span, but leaves out the participants at the extreme low and extreme high end of screen time. If we are unable to measure the full range of scores in the population, the correlation we observe in our sample may be weaker than the correlation that exists in the population.

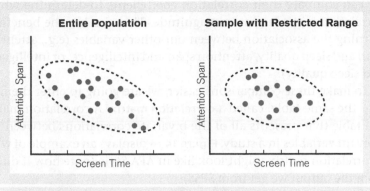

Figure 14.12 Restriction of Range Illustration

A third potential problem that we may encounter when trying to interpret correlation results occurs when the association between our variables isn't linear at all. For example, imagine that we collected a sample of scores to test the association between physiological arousal and attention span. Our variables are definitely associated with each other, but if we calculate the correlation coefficient between them, we would likely find it to be near zero. The reason that the Pearson correlation is near zero, despite these variables being associated with each other, is that the association between arousal and attention span is curvilinear. As we can see in **Figure 14.13,** people at very low levels of arousal (e.g., very sleepy) tend to have poor attention spans, as do people at very high levels of arousal. Yet, because the Pearson correlation tests only for linear associations between variables, it will not be able to pick up on this association.

We can avoid misinterpreting the correlation coefficient for a non-linear association by simply generating a scatterplot for each of the bivariate associations that we are performing. Note that there are methods for describing and testing nonlinear relationships, but they are beyond the scope of our discussion here.

Creating a Correlation Matrix So far in this chapter, we have presented one correlation at a time. In the first half of the chapter, we focused on the correlation between intelligence and how funny people find dad jokes. In the second half of this chapter, we focused on the correlation between screen time and attention span. But one of the advantages of correlation is that we can perform many correlations and easily compare them to each other. For example, we may want to see not only if screen time is associated with attention span, but also screen time's association with other variables such as intelligence and sleep quality. By putting all of these variables into the same study,

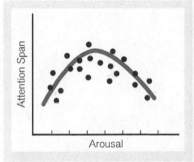

Figure 14.13 Curvilinear Relationship Illustration

> **"**
> **Statistically Speaking**
>
> I feel like my interest in building things with Legos has been curvilinear. I loved it as a kid, lost interest for a while, and now love it again as an adult.
>
> **"**

we can compare their correlation coefficients to determine which correlation is the largest in magnitude. This also has the benefit of learning the association between our other variables (e.g., attention span and sleep quality, attention span and intelligence, or intelligence and sleep quality).

To make these comparisons easier, we are going to enter them all into the same table, called a **correlation matrix.** A correlation matrix is a table that presents all of the bivariate correlations between the relevant variables in a study. **Figure 14.14** displays an example of what a correlation matrix might look like in APA Style (note how it differs from the output we get from SPSS).

correlation matrix a type of table that presents the correlation coefficients for all pairs of variables in a study.

Table 1

Pearson Correlations for Study Variables

Variable	1	2	3	4
1. Attention Span	—			
2. Screen Time	−.47*	—		
3. Intelligence	.27	−.13	—	
4. Sleep Quality	.55**	−.61**	.31	—

Note: *$p < .05$, **$p < .01$.

Figure 14.14 APA-Style Correlation Matrix

As we can see, all of the bivariate correlations appear in the correlation matrix, but only half of the matrix is filled in with numbers. This is because a correlation matrix is symmetric about the diagonal. In other words, because the correlation between attention span and screen time is the same as the correlation between screen time and attention span, we only enter the correlation for each association once. This makes the correlation matrix easier to read. Also, the diagonal of the matrix presents each variable correlated with itself. Because all variables perfectly correlate with themselves (i.e., a correlation of 1.00), this is not interesting information and is usually left out (indicated by the dash).

In terms of interpreting the correlation matrix, we can see that among our predictor variables, sleep quality has the strongest correlation with attention ($r = .55$, $p < .01$), followed by screen time ($r = −.47$, $p < .05$). This would tell us that sleep quality is a slightly better predictor of performance on the Mackworth Clock Test than screen time. We should also note that sleep quality has a positive correlation with attention span, such that higher-quality sleep is associated with better attention span. Finally, intelligence is nonsignificantly correlated with attention span (r = .27, ns), although this may be due to the fact that our sample size was small (N = 20).

Forming a Conclusion

Correlation is a very useful analysis. Not only is it easy to calculate, it is also easy to interpret and can be used in a variety of research contexts. Correlation analyses can tell us important information about the relationship between variables, including the direction of the association, the magnitude, and whether the correlation is likely to exist in the population. Nevertheless, we need to be careful so that we don't misinterpret the results of a correlation. This is especially true when it comes to making causal conclusions based on correlational evidence.

Your Turn 14.4

1. Examine the following scatterplots. Determine whether it is appropriate to use Pearson's correlation coefficient to describe the relationship between X and Y. If not, explain why.

a

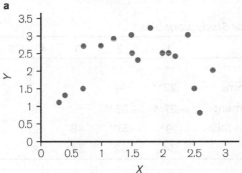

b

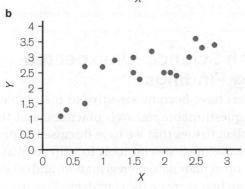

c

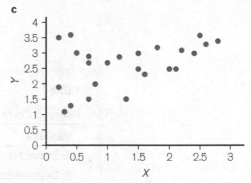

Questions 2–6 relate to the following scenario:

Some people claim that they are good multitaskers, and that when they multitask, they can pay attention to multiple things at the same time, at the same level of quality. You want to test whether this is the case. To test this, you recruit a sample of 122 participants and have them complete a short questionnaire assessing their self-perceived ability to multitask. You then have participants complete three tasks at the same time (drive a car simulator, sing a song, and respond to a text message). You rate their performance on the tasks on a scale from 1 to 10. After performing a correlation analysis, you find positive correlation between self-perceived ability to multitask and actual multitasking performance (r = .11). Is this correlation statistically significant at the alpha = .05 level? Perform the t-test for correlation.

(Continued)

2. Step 1: Population and Hypotheses.

    a. What would the populations and sample be?

    b. What would the hypotheses be?

3. Step 2: Build Comparison Distribution.

    a. What is the distribution of correlations?

    b. How many degrees of freedom does the appropriate distribution have for our current research study?

4. Step 3: Establish Critical Value Cutoff. What are the critical values for your hypothesis test (alpha = .05)?

5. Step 4: Determine Sample Results. What is the value of t?

6. Step 5: Decide and Interpret. What is the appropriate conclusion?

Questions 7–8 relate to the following scenario:

A researcher examines the association between social media use and depression in teens. In the article that describes the results of the study, the researcher writes the following: "Social media use was significantly correlated with risk of depression ($r = .22$, $p = .003$). Thus, we conclude that excessive social media usage may cause teens to be at greater risk of developing depression."

7. Is the researcher justified in making this conclusion? Explain your response.

8. The researcher conducts correlational analyses among several variables that he thinks are associated with depression symptoms, and reports his results in the correlation matrix below.

    a. Which variable has the strongest correlation with depression symptoms?

    b. Interpret the correlation between social media use and academic achievement, noting the direction, magnitude, and significance of the correlation.

Table 1

Pearson Correlations for Study Variables

Variable	1	2	3	4	5
1. Social Media Use	—				
2. Depression Symptoms	.22**	—			
3. Academic Achievement	–.27**	–.38**	—		
4. Emotion Regulation Skills	–.19*	–.51**	.48	—	
5. Target of Bullying	.34	.62	.34	–.06	—

Note: *$p < .05$, **$p < .01$.

Focus on Open Science: Unexpected and Surprising Findings

As researchers have become sensitive to the problems of *p*-hacking, questionable research practices, and the file drawer problem (issues that we have discussed in previous chapters), they have developed several tools to help combat these problems. Open data, open materials, preregistration, and other solutions have helped researchers increase the confidence they have in the findings that are published in the scientific literature.

Kevin Lorenzi/Bloomberg/Getty Images

If you read a report that says apple cider vinegar can cure 57 diseases in a single bound, you would be wise to be skeptical.

But just as important as these approaches have been, proponents of open science also suggest that we change the way we think about scientific findings. In particular, we should focus on the strength and quality of the evidence, rather than on how unexpected or surprising a particular finding is. As an example, imagine that you read an advertisement suggesting that ingesting apple cider vinegar cures acne, allergies, athlete's foot, asthma, and anemia. This would certainly be amazing. It might be true, but our sense of amazement should give us pause and make us a bit skeptical.

Similarly, in psychology, some studies report findings that are surprising and therefore seem interesting. For example, in a study of social priming, researchers asked participants to complete a word task (Bargh et al., 1996). Half of the participants completed the word task using words that referred to elderly stereotypes (e.g., gray, retired), whereas the other half of the participants completed the word task using neutral words. Researchers then measured how long it would take participants to walk down a hallway. The findings revealed that participants primed with the elderly stereotype took longer to walk down the hallway than the control condition, potentially revealing how subtle stereotypes can affect our behaviors. This is a really interesting and surprising finding. And it may be true! But, our feeling of "amazing-ness" should be a signal to us that we should scrutinize the evidence's strength. Are these claims based on large samples? Are they based on randomized, double-blind, clinical trials? Or, are they based on small samples or weaker research designs?

When it comes to surprising research findings and potentially unreliable evidence, one scenario we should be especially sensitive to is when a research study reports a large effect size or large correlation from a small sample size (Simmons, 2020). For example, in the study of elderly stereotypes mentioned earlier, the authors report a significant *t*-test based on a sample size of only 30 participants (Bargh et al., 1996). Yet, when we have small samples, our false positive rate (that is, the number of Type I errors) increases. That's due, in part, because the correlations we observe in small samples can vary widely from the correlations that exist in the population. For example, one simulation (Schönbrodt & Perugini, 2013) demonstrated that small samples ($N < 50$) may not only misestimate the magnitude of association between two variables, but the sign (positive or negative) as well. Based on an analysis of 100,000 samples from a population of 1,000,000 cases, these researchers found that sample correlations stabilize near the true population correlation (ρ) at around 250 observations ($N = 238$ to be precise).

One thing that the open science movement has revealed is that statistical significance, whether it be for a *t*-test, ANOVA, or correlation, does not guarantee that an effect or association is real. We need to scrutinize all results from theoretical, methodological, and statistical perspectives, especially those that seem to be the most interesting because they are surprising or unexpected.

Become a Better Consumer of Statistics

The good news about correlations is that they are fairly simple to do. When we're using statistical software like SPSS, it's even easier to do them in large batches, even on very large data sets. An article from FiveThirtyEight.com entitled *You Can't Trust What You Read About Nutrition* reported on lots of interesting correlations related to food choice, and every single one was statistically significant (Aschwanden, 2016). Here's one: People who have "innie" belly buttons also like cabbage. Weird, but kinda cool, right? Although we like these types of quirky findings, it probably isn't a meaningful association. Rather, it's due to coincidence or some other unknown factor, resulting in what researchers call a **spurious correlation.**

There are lots of reasons why spurious correlations occur. For example, how the researchers measured the variable can influence the outcome, especially if the scales use poor wording or rely too much on a participant's memory. It's also possible to run a lot of correlations that end up being statistically significant, despite the correlation coefficients being small in magnitude. This can happen when the study has a really large sample size. As we know from a previous chapter, statistically significant findings are not necessarily meaningful findings.

The other way to get spurious correlations is to have a lot of variables and run a lot of analyses. The study described in the FiveThirtyEight.com article had over 1,000 variables and ran over 27,000 analyses. Not surprisingly, they found a lot of variables that correlated (**Figure 14.15**). For every one that made theoretical sense

spurious correlation a situation in which two variables are mathematically correlated, but not causally related.

> ❝
> ### Statistically Speaking
> My nephew claims that playing more video games relates to increased scores on the SAT, but to me it sounds like a spurious correlation.
> ❞

EATING OR DRINKING	IS LINKED TO	p-VALUE
Raw tomatoes	Judaism	<0.0001
Egg rolls	Dog ownership	<0.0001
Energy drinks	Smoking	<0.0001
Potato chips	Higher score on SAT math vs. verbal	0.0001
Soda	Weird rash in the past year	0.0002
Shellfish	Right-handedness	0.0002
Lemonade	Belief that "Crash" deserved to win best picture	0.0004
Fried/breaded fish	Democratic Party affiliation	0.0007
Beer	Frequent smoking	0.0013
Coffee	Cat ownership	0.0016
Table salt	Positive relationship with Internet service provider	0.0014
Steak with fat trimmed	Lack of belief in a god	0.0030
Iced tea	Belief that "Crash" didn't deserve to win best picture	0.0043
Bananas	Higher score on SAT verbal vs. math	0.0073
Cabbage	Innie bellybutton	0.0097

Data for this is from fivethirtyeight.com. The web page link is: https://fivethirtyeight.com/features/you-cant-trust-what-you-read-about-nutrition/

Figure 14.15 Spurious Correlations

(e.g., frequency of drinking beer was correlated with frequency of smoking cigarettes), there were others that were hard to believe (e.g., eating potato chips was correlated with higher SAT scores). This is why it is so important to establish a plan before starting analysis. This way, there is no temptation to p-hack by simply running batches of analyses until something works.

Do we really believe that chowing down on potato chips is meaningfully related to higher SAT scores, as one study reported?

Chase Jarvis/Stockbyte/Getty Images

Not only are correlations easy to do, but they're also fairly easy to understand. For this reason, correlational findings are often a favorite for journalists, especially if the study focuses on a flashy topic. The only problem is that scientists often describe findings conservatively and make it clear the variables aren't causing each other. That doesn't always make for exciting headlines, so it is unfortunately all too common for correlational results to take a more causal tone when they appear in nonscientific outlets. When reading about study findings that discuss relationships between variables, it's important to recognize words that suggest correlation and differentiate those from the ones that imply causation (**Figure 14.16**). But be careful—even if an article you read online uses causal language, they may be doing so incorrectly. When in doubt, check their original source.

Words that Imply Correlation	Words that Imply Causation
related	caused
linked to	made
coincide with	led to
tied to	created
connected to	are from
associated with	due to
	blamed for
	attributed to
	because of

Figure 14.16 Words That Imply Correlation and Causation

Interpreting Graphs and Charts from Research Articles

Most studies that conduct correlational analyses report their findings in a correlation matrix because it is possible to report a large number of findings in a reasonably small space. For example, one paper examined the link between screen time, uncontrolled eating, and attention deficit hyperactivity disorder (Ahn et al., 2017). The researchers presented all of the correlations between these variables (and others) in a correlation matrix. Let's take a look at their correlation matrix (**Figure 14.17**) and try to interpret their findings. Before we start, the table note indicates that the authors place a star (*) next to correlations that are significant at the $p < .05$ level, and a cross (†) next to correlations that are significant at the $p < .01$ level.

Table 2
Zero-order correlation matrix for all variables (N = 327)

Variables	1	2	3	4	5	6	7	8	9
1. Gender	1								
2. Age	−0.008								
3. BMI z-score	0.025	−0.048							
4. ADHD symptoms	0.221[†]	0.037	0.280[†]						
5. Uncontrolled eating	0.167[†]	0.148[†]	0.322[†]	0.468[†]					
6. Screen time	0.116*	0.020	0.129*	0.318[†]	0.353[†]				
7. Emotional symptoms	−0.035	−0.028	0.091	0.185[†]	0.101	0.137*			
8. Family SES	0.343[†]	−0.093	0.236[†]	0.202[†]	0.138*	0.162[†]	0.076		
9. Parental smoking	0.041	−0.089	0.055	0.085	0.065	−0.124*	−0.065	0.086	
10. Parental problematic drinking	0.086	0.057	0.091	0.189[†]	0.138*	0.109*	0.181[†]	0.094	0.146[†]

Male gender, presence of parental smoking, and parental problematic drinking were transformed to dummy variable, 1. Family SES: 1 = highest 5 = lowest. *$p < 0.05$, [†]$p < 0.01$. BMI: body mass index, ADHD: attention deficit hyperactivity disorder

Figure 14.17 Example of a Correlation Matrix (Data from Ahn et al., 2017)

As we can see by looking across row six, screen time is positively correlated with BMI ($r = .129$, $p < .05$), attention deficit hyperactivity disorder (ADHD) symptoms ($r = .318$, $p < .01$), and uncontrolled eating ($r = .353$, $p < .01$). To get the other correlations for screen time, we will look down column six, which reveals that screen time is also significantly correlated with emotional symptoms ($r = .137$, $p < .05$), family socioeconomic status ($r = .162$, $p < .01$), parental smoking ($r = −.124$, $p < .05$), and parental problematic drinking ($r = .109$, $p < .05$).

Statistics on the Job

Everyone who works in a school continually looks for ways to make sure the students are happy, healthy, safe, and learning. A school counselor is especially focused on helping students' mental and emotional wellness because of the large impact it can have on academic performance. Within that broad scope, school counselors pay attention to several key variables including school and classroom conduct, number of school absences, and, of course, grades.

Finding correlations is helpful in many facets of work-related activities, such as a school counselor trying to understand what activities might be most effective in boosting a student's academic performance.

SeventyFour/Shutterstock

To help students reach their full potential, a school counselor might be interested in how to help students in each of these areas.

For example, they might have questions about whether the number of one-on-one counseling sessions a student attends relates to the number of times that student acts out in class. Similarly, school counselors might wonder if students who attend more of their programs (e.g., lunch bunch groups, circle of friends, support groups for students with a tough home life) become more engaged and miss less school. School counselors don't just see students outside of class, they also go into the classroom to conduct lessons (e.g., mindfulness, stress reduction, yoga, dealing with bullies, improving study skills). Based on these in-class interactions, the counselor might wonder if students who do well on the lessons also get better grades.

In each of these cases, the school counselor would use correlation to see what experiences (i.e., variables) are associated most strongly with each outcome. By doing so, it can help the counselor spend more time on what seems to improve students' behavior, absenteeism, and grades, and improve the activities that seem less helpful.

Review Questions

1. Which is the appropriate statistical test?
   a. A school counselor wants to know whether attentional regulation is better under low-, medium-, or high-stress conditions.
   b. A human resources department wants to assess whether the active bystander training they have implemented increases a person's intent to intervene when they observe discrimination.
   c. A researcher wants to know whether a person's quality of sleep is related to their emotional regulation.
   d. A clinician wants to know whether the amount of empathy a child has towards animals is related to the amount of empathy they have towards animals as adults.

2. For each of the following correlation coefficients, identify what type of correlation they show.
   a. −0.97
   b. −0.25
   c. +0.07
   d. +0.81

3. One way that a correlation and a *t*-test for dependent means are similar is that they both involve obtaining _____ scores for each participant. One way that they are different is that the with a *t*-test for dependent means, the scores are on _____ variable while for a correlation they are on _____ variables.

4. Look at Table 1 on page 582 that shows the correlation matrix of variables that a researcher believes are associated with depression symptoms.
   a. Which variable has the weakest correlation with emotion regulation skills?
   b. Which pair of variables have the strongest, statistically significant (alpha = .05) correlation overall?
   c. Which variable has the strongest correlation with being the target of bullying, ignoring statistical significance?
   d. Interpret the correlation between social media use and depression symptoms.

5. Look at each of the following graphs and determine whether a Pearson correlation would be appropriate. If it is appropriate, identify if you would expect a positive or a negative correlation value. If it is not appropriate, explain why.
   a.
   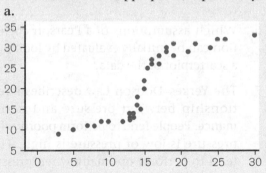
   b.
   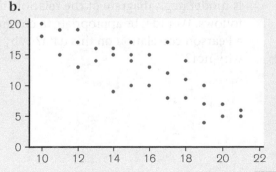

c.

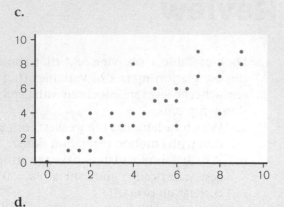

d.

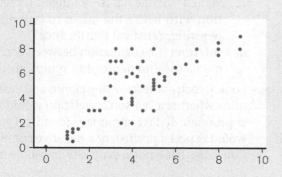

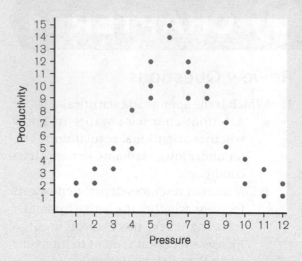

6. Which assumptions of a Pearson correlation can be initially evaluated by looking at a scatterplot of the data?

7. The Yerkes–Dodson Law describes a relationship between pressure and performance. People tend to perform poorly when pressure is low or pressure is high. They tend to perform optimally when pressure is moderate. A diagram of the relationship follows. Would it be appropriate to conduct a Pearson correlation on this data? Why or why not?

8. The city council asks you to assess the value of parks and green spaces on citizens' happiness. You decide to evaluate the amount of greenspace in neighborhoods in your city on a scale from 1 to 15 (where 1 = very low amount of greenspace and 15 = very high amount of greenspace). You go to 10 different neighborhoods and collect a measure of happiness (on a scale from 1 to 10, where 1 = very unhappy and 10 = very happy) from the first adult person you encounter in each neighborhood. Use an alpha = .05.

Neighborhood	Greenspace Rating	Happiness
Citadel	13	10
Strathcona	11	9
Barrhaven	7	6
Highland Creek	14	9
Sherwood	12	7
Fairmount	9	6
Kitsilano	4	7
Lakeview Heights	8	5
Fernwood	3	5
Rockway	6	8

a. What would the population and sample be?
b. What would the hypotheses be?
c. Create a scatterplot of the data.
d. Calculate Pearson *r*.
e. How many degrees of freedom does the comparison distribution have?
f. What are the critical values for the hypothesis test?
g. What is the value of *t*?
h. What is the appropriate conclusion?
i. Is the effect small/medium/large using conventions suggested by Cohen (1992)?

9. Shi and colleagues (2017) reported a correlation between intelligence and creativity was *r* = 0.39 in Chinese children ages 11 and 12 years old. They recruited 568 children for their study. Is this correlation statistically significant at the alpha = .01 level? Perform the *t*-test for correlation.
a. What would the population and sample be?

b. What would the hypotheses be?
c. How many degrees of freedom does the comparison distribution have?
d. What are the critical values for the hypothesis test?
e. What is the value of *t*?
f. What is the appropriate conclusion?
g. Is the effect small/medium/large using conventions suggested by Cohen (1992)?
h. If the researchers had instead recruited 25 children for their study, what would the value of *t* be? What would their conclusion have been?

10. You've heard that the amount of time spent on social media is related to a person's happiness.
a. Define reverse causality and give an example of how it might apply to this correlation.
b. Define the third variable problem and give an example of how it might apply to this correlation.

Key Concepts

Answers to Your Turn

Your Turn 14.1

1. (a) correlation; (b) *t*-test for dependent means; (c) one-way between-groups ANOVA; (d) correlation

2. (a) curvilinear; (b) no correlation; (c) strong negative; (d) moderate positive

3. (a)

(b)

(see plot)

4. (a) 3, 6, 9

(b) 9, 6, 3

(c) 5, 5, 5; or 3, 5, 7 Note because the *X*-scores were all the same, there is no set of *Y* values that could show correlation.

Your Turn 14.2

1. Any two variable combination of age, income, and happiness; note that we can't use a Pearson *r* with ethnicity because that is a categorical variable, and for Pearson *r* we need a continuous variable.

2. (a) strong positive; (b) weak negative; (c) no correlation; (d) strong negative; (e) no correlation

3.

Original Scores		Z-Scores		Cross-Product	Correlation
X	*Y*	Z_X	Z_Y	$Z_X Z_Y$	*r*
9	2	+	−	−	−
9	8	+	+	+	+
5	10	0	+	0	Near 0
3	2	−	−	+	+
3	8	−	+	−	−
2	5	−	0	0	Near 0

Your Turn 14.3

1. Negative correlation

2. Step 1: Plot the data to check linearity.

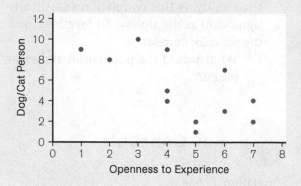

Step 2: Calculate Z-scores (Z_X and Z_Y).

Step 3: Calculate and Sum Cross-product of Z-scores ($Z_X Z_Y$).

Step 4: Calculate Pearson *r* (*r*).

Step 5: Decide and Interpret. A correlation of −.68 indicates a strong negative association between our variables, which indicates that those who scored higher on openness to experience also indicated that they were more of a "dog person," while those who scored lower on openness to experience considered themselves more of a "cat person."

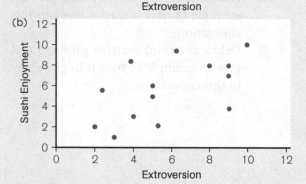

Participants	Openness to Experience (X)	Deviation Score (X − M)	Squared Deviation Score (X − M)²	Z-Score (Z_x)	Participants	Dog/Cat Person (Y)	Deviation Score (Y − M)	Squared Deviation Score (Y − M)²	Z-Score (Z_y)	Cross-Product of Z-Scores (Z_x Z_y)
Melaina	4	−0.50	0.25	−0.27	Melaina	5	−0.33	0.11	−0.11	0.03
Izaak	2	−2.50	6.25	−1.33	Izaak	8	2.67	7.11	0.85	−1.13
Aresnius	1	−3.50	12.25	−1.86	Aresnius	9	3.67	13.44	1.17	−2.17
Fletcher	3	−1.50	2.25	−0.80	Fletcher	10	4.67	21.78	1.48	−1.18
Tao	4	−0.50	0.25	−0.27	Tao	4	−1.33	1.78	−0.42	0.11
Samuel	6	1.50	2.25	0.80	Samuel	7	1.67	2.78	0.53	0.42
Lowell	4	−0.50	0.25	−0.27	Lowell	9	3.67	13.44	1.17	−0.31
Ra'shon	7	2.50	6.25	1.33	Ra'shon	4	−1.33	1.78	−0.42	−0.56
Jen	6	1.50	2.25	0.80	Jen	3	−2.33	5.44	−0.74	−0.59
Furqan	5	0.50	0.25	0.27	Furqan	2	−3.33	11.11	−1.06	−0.28
Elias	5	0.50	0.25	0.27	Elias	1	−4.33	18.78	−1.38	−0.37
Brigitta	7	2.50	6.25	1.33	Brigitta	2	−3.33	11.11	−1.06	−1.41
Sum of Scores (ΣX)	54				Sum of Scores (ΣY)	64				
Number of Scores (N)	12				Number of Scores (N)	12			$\Sigma Z_x Z_y$	−7.43
Mean (M_x)	ΣX/N	4.50			Mean (M_y)	ΣY/N	5.33			
Sum of Squares (SS_x)	Σ(X − M)²	39.00			Sum of Squares (SS_y)	Σ(Y − M)²	108.67			
Variance (SD¹)	SS/(N − 1)	3.55			Variance (SD²)	SS/(N − 1)	9.88			
Standard Deviation (SD_x)	$\sqrt{SD^2}$	1.88			Standard Deviation (SD_y)	$\sqrt{SD^2}$	3.14			
Z-Score (Z_x)	(X − M)/SD				Z-Score (Z_y)	(Y − M)/SD				
Pearson's (r)	$\Sigma Z_x Z_y / N - 1$	−0.68								

Your Turn 14.4

1. (a) No. The association between X and Y appears to be curvilinear. (b) Yes, the association appears to be linear. (c) No. The scatterplot appears to violate the homoscedasticity assumption.

2. (a) Population of Interest: People for whom there is no association between self-perceived ability to multitask and performance while multitasking. Comparison Population: People like those in our sample for whom there is a correlation of $r = .11$. Sample: The 122 participants in our study. (b) Research Hypothesis: There is a correlation between self-perceived ability to multitask and performance while multitasking. Null Hypothesis: There is no correlation between self-perceived ability to multitask and performance while multitasking.

3. (a) The distribution of correlations presents the correlations between two variables for an infinite number of samples from the population. The mean of the distribution of correlations equals the correlation that exists between two variables at the population level. (b) Degrees of freedom are determined by the number of participants minus two: $df = N - 2 = 122 - 2 = 120$.

4. The t-table for 120 degrees of freedom reveals that the critical values are $+/- 1.98$.

5. To convert our Pearson r into a t-score, we use the following formula: $t = r/\sqrt{(1 - r^2)/(N - 2)} = .11/\sqrt{(1 - (.11^2)/(122 - 2)} = .11/\sqrt{(1 - .012)/(120)} = .11/\sqrt{(.99)/(120)} = .11/\sqrt{(.008)} = .11/.089 = 1.23$.

6. We should fail to reject the null hypothesis. We do not have enough evidence to conclude that there is an association between self-reported ability to multitask and performance while multitasking.

7. The researcher is not justified. Although social media use is correlated with depression, the researcher should not claim that social media use *causes* an increase in risk of depression.

8. (a) Emotion regulation skills has the strongest correlation with depression symptoms ($r = -.51$). (b) Social media use has a significant negative correlation with academic achievement ($r = -.27$, $p < .01$), indicating as teens use social media more, they have lower academic achievement.

Answers to Review Questions

1. a. One-way between-groups ANOVA
    b. t-Test for dependent means
    c. Correlation
    d. Correlation

2. a. Strong negative
    b. Weak negative
    c. No correlation
    d. Strong positive

3. Two; the same; different

4. a. Social media use ($r = -.19$)
    b. Emotion regulation skills and depression symptoms ($r = .51$). Note that although being the target of bullying and depression symptoms have a higher correlation value, the correlation is not statistically significant.
    c. Being the target of bullying and depression symptoms.
    d. Social media use has a significant positive correlation with depression symptoms ($r = .22$, $p < .01$) indicating as teens use social media more, they have higher levels of depression symptoms.

5. a. Not appropriate, curvilinear
    b. Appropriate, negative
    c. Appropriate, positive
    d. Not appropriate, heteroscedastic

6. Whether the X and Y variable are normally distributed, linearity, and homoscedasticity.

7. It would not be appropriate to conduct a Pearson correlation on this data because the relationship is curvilinear, and the Pearson correlation is used only with linear relationships.

8. a. Population of interest: a population of adult people living in the city of interest for whom there is no association between greenspace and happiness.
Comparison population: adult people like those in our sample for whom there is an association between greenspace and happiness.
Sample: the 10 people in our sample, who complete a measure of happiness and for whom we can assess the greenspace in their neighborhood.

   b. Research hypothesis: two-tailed; the correlation in the population is not zero, $r \neq 0$.
Null hypothesis: the correlation in the population is zero, $r = 0$.

   c.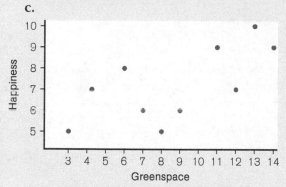

   d. Greenspace: mean = 8.7; $SS = 128.1$; standard deviation = 3.77
Happiness: mean = 7.2; $SS = 27.6$; standard deviation = 1.75
$r = 0.67$

   e. $df = 8$

   f. ± 2.306

   g. $t = 2.55$

   h. Reject the null hypothesis and accept the research hypothesis; conclude that there is a positive correlation between greenspace and happiness.

   i. Large

9. a. Population of interest: a population of children ages 11 and 12 for whom there is no association between intelligence and creativity.
Comparison population: children ages 11 and 12 like those in the sample for whom there is an association between intelligence and creativity.
Sample: the 568 children in the sample, who complete a measure of intelligence and creativity.

   b. Research hypothesis: two-tailed; the correlation in the population is not zero, $r \neq 0$.
Null hypothesis: the correlation in the population is zero, $r = 0$.

   c. $df = 566$

   d. ± 2.617 (note, this value is for $df = 120$, the closest value without going over)

   e. $t = 10.08$

   f. Reject the null hypothesis and accept the research hypothesis; conclude that there is a positive correlation between intelligence and creativity.

   g. Medium

   h. The value of t would be 2.03. They would have failed to reject the null hypothesis; there is no correlation between intelligence and creativity.

10. a. Reverse causality refers to the fact that we cannot distinguish which is the predictor variable and which is the outcome variable. In this case, increases in social media could cause changes in happiness, or increases in happiness could cause changes in social media use.

b. The third variable problem refers to the fact that another variable could be causing changes in both social media use and happiness. Any variable that influences both happiness and social media use could be a third variable, such as age, stress, etc.

 Sharpen your statistics skills with real-life data! Check out OpenStatsLab.com, created by coauthor Kevin McIntyre, to practice running analyses for real published research studies.

15 Regression

Learning Outcomes

After reading this chapter, you should be able to:

- Explain the key questions that regression seeks to answer.

- Identify similarities and differences between correlation and regression.

- Explain when it is appropriate to use a regression.

- Calculate the slope and y-intercept for a linear model.

- Describe the underlying logic for evaluating the predictive power of the regression equation.

- Conduct a hypothesis test for the slope of a regression equation.

- Interpret what regression results can and cannot tell us.

Sports are the ultimate reality show. There are dramatic storylines, complex characters, interesting backstories, thrills and suspense, as well as winners and losers. Sports are captivating because we never know how any one game, tournament, or entire season will turn out. In college sports, we see it during the March Madness college basketball tournament. Every single year, there are major upsets where lowly ranked teams or small schools pull off victories against national powerhouses, and there is the thrill of victory for the ultimate winner. But that excitement starts months before, as teams all around the country work through their seasons to build a win–loss record worthy of making the tournament.

With each new season and new group of players, though, it's difficult to know how well your school's team will do. Wouldn't it be great if there were a way to gain some insight into the basketball team's performance for an upcoming season, even before their first game? If you figure there must be a way to use statistics to predict your team's success in the upcoming season, given the amount of statistics knowledge you have, you're right!

Statistics for Life

What we really need is a way to know what is going to happen, before it does. Though predicting the future seems impossible, we know that meteorologists do this every day when forecasting the weather, and political scientists do this every election when trying to predict the winners. Similarly, if you watch sports broadcasts, they often give the percentage chance that each team has to win. In each case, there must be numbers underlying those predictions, but where do those numbers come from?

As any decent history teacher has told you, it's important to study the past because it gives us insights into the future. That makes sense, but we need to identify which numbers are the best ones to use. That's easier said than done because there are practically an infinite number of factors that influence a game's outcome, like: who the crowd is

How can we know who might make the March Madness tournament this year, before the season even starts?

Bill Wippert//NCAA Photos/Getty Images

pulling for, the referees, how far a particular team had to travel, the coach's experience, and so on. While that's true, the teams' own past performance seems most relevant. Even then, there's lots to choose from (e.g., points scored, points against, rebounds, steals, etc.). Ultimately, every single number we can generate from a game all feed into the one we consider most important: wins.

In particular, we want to see if a team's win total for one season might tell us how many games the team wins the following year. If we know that, then any college basketball fan can look at how well their team did last year to help them know whether they should be excited for the upcoming season and their chances of being in the March Madness tournament.

Where Do the Data Come From?

 Luckily, sports fans and organizations are obsessed with data. The NCAA is no exception and even has a website that provides key numbers for all of college basketball's teams. Within that data we can focus on a team's most recent game, or on entire previous seasons. Based on what we've already learned about statistics, we know that larger sample sizes (i.e., entire seasons vs. the most recent game) will give us a better idea of the team's actual abilities. In other words, the more data, the better. For that reason, we're going to avoid looking at single games, and instead focus on data from full seasons for Division I, which includes many of the elite men's basketball programs in the United States.

Specifically, we'll focus on predicting wins from the 2018–2019 season. Because there are hundreds of teams, to keep the data set manageable, we're going to focus only on the top 16 teams, or

"Sweet 16," from that year's tournament. We know how many games these teams won in 2018–2019, so we want to look back to the 2017–2018 season to see if the team's previous season win total can predict their win total the next year (see **Figure 15.1**). Once we learn how 2017–2018 season wins predicts team wins in 2018–2019, we can then use that association to see how a team's 2018–2019 win total might predict how many games they'll win in a future season. This will help us get an idea of what our team's chances are for getting into the tournament in a given year. Here is what that data look like.

College Basketball Team	2017–2018 Regular Season Wins (X)	2018–2019 Regular Season Wins (Y)
Virginia	31	35
Texas Tech	27	31
Michigan State	30	32
Auburn	26	30
Gonzaga	32	33
Duke	29	32
Kentucky	26	30
Purdue	30	26
Florida St.	23	29
Michigan	32	30
LSU	18	28
Virginia Tech	21	26
North Carolina	26	29
Houston	27	33
Tennessee	26	31
Oregon	23	25

Figure 15.1 College Basketball Season Wins

Prediction: What We're Trying to Accomplish

Data like this will look really familiar because this is exactly what our data looked like for correlation (see Chapter 14). For correlation, we focused on the association or relationship between our two variables. We are still doing that to some degree, but now in *simple linear regression,* we are interested in determining how one variable (X) can predict or forecast the other variable (Y).

In correlation, the association between our two variables was bidirectional. That means that the X variable could influence the Y variable

predictor the *X* variable that we use in regression to forecast, explain, or predict another variable.

criterion the outcome variable being predicted, typically the *Y* variable.

or vice versa. Now, in simple (or univariate) regression, the direction is fixed, which means we focus only on how the *X* variable influences the *Y* variable. For that reason, we typically call the *X* variable the **predictor** because it is the variable that we use in regression to forecast, explain, or predict another variable. Our *Y* variable is the response or outcome, known as the **criterion,** or the variable being predicted. Note that if we manipulate our predictor, we can also call it our independent variable, which would then make the criterion the dependent variable.

We use simple regression in any design where we have two continuous variables and want to determine how knowing scores on one variable can tell us about scores on the other variable. For example, does how many days a week a person goes to the gym predict how many days of work they miss because of illness? Does a client's number of sessions per week predict the number of depressive symptoms they report? Does the number of clicks on an advertisement predict the number of sales? Does the number of wins in one college basketball season predict the number of wins in the following season?

In the case of our research question, though, it may seem a bit magical to take what we learn from previous seasons and apply it to the upcoming season. This is essentially what college admissions offices around the country do. That is, they can look at how successful first-year students from last year were, and see what aspects of their high school experience (e.g., GPA, SAT, extracurricular activities, etc.) predicted their success at college. Based on that information, they have a better idea of the qualities to look for in this year's applicants that will help those students be more successful.

Regression: How Does It Work?

Prediction is all about being able to see into the future. To do that, we need to base those forecasts on something meaningful so that our predictions are as accurate as possible. That process starts by looking at the data we already have for our two variables.

regression line a straight line that serves as a visual representation that best describes how the outcome variable (*Y*) changes relative to changes in the predictor variable (*X*) on a scatterplot.

Seeing the Association Between Our Variables To see how our *X* variable (2017–2018 season wins) predicts our *Y* variable (2018–2019 season wins), we want to see the association between our variables. We can do that by creating a scatterplot, just like we did for correlation. The only difference with using regression to make predictions is that we'll add a trend line, or **regression line,** which is a straight line through our scatterplot (see **Figure 15.2**). That line serves as a visual representation that best describes how the outcome variable (*Y*) changes relative to changes in the predictor variable (*X*).

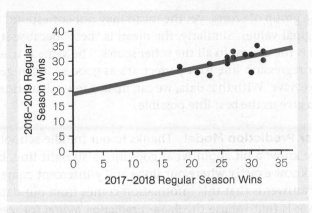

Figure 15.2 Scatterplot with Regression Line

We'll talk more about where this line comes from in a moment, but there are a few features we'd like to point out. First, notice that the line doesn't actually touch or include many of the original data points. Real data won't conform neatly to a straight line, so the regression line is the "line of best fit," or best summary for the pairs of X- and Y-scores, but may not include any of the original pairs.

Second, because the regression line is a straight line, it follows the same principles that you learned back in algebra or geometry. As you may recall, you learned $Y = mx + b$ where m was the line's slope (i.e., how steep or flat the line is) and b was where the line intercepted or crossed the y-axis. Essentially what that equation told you, is that if you take a value for x and multiply it by the slope (m), then add the y-intercept (b), you would learn the value for Y. In terms of regression, the slope roughly corresponds to the correlation between the X and Y variables, while the intercept is what Y's value would be when X equals 0.

What Makes This the Best Line? Earlier we called our regression line the "line of best fit." When it comes to making predictions, we want to make correct forecasts, so what's best is what is most accurate. For that reason, we don't want to just randomly draw any line. Rather, we want to use our data to calculate a line that is the "best" because it is as close as possible to all of the data points. In other words, the best line would have the least amount of deviation from the data. We can determine that by calculating the average distance between our line and each data point, also known as the **standard error of the estimate.**

As long as we base our line on the available data, it will be the "line of best fit," and any other line would be further away from the data points on average. The logic here is very similar to what we discussed in Chapter 3 about means. Recall that the mean is the best score to

standard error of the estimate a calculation of the average distance between our regression line and each data point.

linear prediction model
(also called *regression equation* or *linear prediction rule*) a formula that allows us to make predictions about the criterion or outcome (*Y*) variable based on the predictor (*X*) variable.

represent a group of scores, yet the mean may not correspond to any of the original values. Similarly, the mean is "best" because it is the score that is the closest to all the other scores. The same is true here. While our regression line isn't perfect, it's as good as it can get with the data we have. With that data, we can make a few calculations that are sure to give us the best line possible.

The Linear Prediction Model Thanks to our middle school math classes, we know a bit about what goes into a straight line, but we still don't know exactly where our slope and y-intercept come from. The short answer is that this information comes from our data. The long answer is that we use the **linear prediction model** (or *regression equation*) to create a formula that allows us to make predictions about the criterion or outcome (*Y*) variable based on the predictor (*X*) variable. The regression line is the visual representation of this model. Not coincidentally, you'll notice that the linear prediction model formula, $\hat{Y} = b(X) + a$ (also expressed as: $\hat{Y} = a + b(X)$), looks a lot like the standard formula for a straight line we just discussed.

$$\hat{Y} = b(X) + a$$

One key difference is that *Y* has an extra symbol on top of it to signify that it is a predicted value. We call that symbol a "hat" and refer to $\hat{Y}$ as "*Y*-hat." The slope (what was symbolized as *m* before) in our linear prediction model is the *regression coefficient,* now symbolized as *b*. It is the number that we multiply by *X* (i.e., the score on the predictor variable). As you can see in the statistical formulas shown here, we calculate the regression coefficient (*b*) by dividing our *Y* variable's standard deviation (SD_Y), by our *X* variable's standard deviation (SD_X), then multiplying that by the correlation (*r*) between the *X* and *Y* variables.

$$b = r\,\frac{SD_Y}{SD_X}$$

$$a = M_Y - (b \times M_X)$$

The other piece of the linear prediction model is the y-intercept (previously symbolized as *b* in our straight line formula), which we now call the *regression constant,* symbolized as *a*. It is the number that we add each time we use the formula. We calculate the regression constant (*a*) by multiplying the regression coefficient (*b*) by the mean of our *X* variable (M_X), and subtracting that from the mean of our *Y* variable (M_Y). Overall, in terms of our research question about how a team's previous season's win total predicts the next season's win total, our linear prediction model looks like this: Predicted 2018–2019 Season Wins = b(2017–2018 Season Wins) + a.

Your Turn 15.1

1. For each of the following, indicate the appropriate statistic.

a. A student wants to see if people who wear flip-flops report being happier than another group who wears sneakers.

b. A fellow student decides to see if they can predict how happy a person is based on how many days a week they wear sweatpants.

c. A math professor believes that they can forecast students' semester grades based on the distance a student sits from the front of the class.

d. The Student Government Association on campus wants to see if the price of sporting events relates to attendance.

2. A clinical psychology graduate student is studying whether number of minutes spent dreaming per night one week can reveal a decrease in anxiety symptoms the following week. Identify their criterion and predictor variables.

3. Match up the symbols from the $Y = mx + b$ equation with the symbols for the linear prediction model.

1. b a. $\hat{Y}$
2. Y b. X
3. m c. b
4. X d. a

Testing Our Data with Regression: How Does It Work?

Our goal is to create a linear model that helps us make predictions. At the same time, though, we know that not all of the data points will fall directly on our line of best fit. So, how do you create a regression equation for a line that doesn't exist?

Step by Step: Regression To create our regression equation, we will follow a series of steps to make sure we do everything we need to answer our research question, "Does a college basketball team's number of regular seasons in one year predict their number of wins the next year?" (see **Figure 15.3**).

Step 1: Calculate Pearson (r) Just like we did in Chapter 14, calculate the correlation between the X and Y variables. To refresh, calculate the mean and standard deviation for each variable, calculate Z-scores for all X- and Y-scores, create the cross-product of Z-scores by multiplying Z_X and Z_Y, sum them ($\sum Z_X Z_Y$), and divide by $N - 1$, to calculate the correlation,

$$r = \frac{\sum Z_X Z_Y}{N - 1}$$
$$= \frac{8.91}{15}$$
$$= .594$$

College Basketball Team	2017–2018 Regular Season Wins (X)	Deviation Score ($X - M$)	Squared Deviation Score ($X - M)^2$	Z-Score (Z_x)	College Basketball Team	2018–2019 Regular Season Wins (Y)	Deviation Score ($Y - M$)	Squared Deviation Score ($Y - M)^2$	Z-Score (Z_y)	Cross-Product of Z-Scores ($Z_x Z_y$)
Virginia	31	4.31	18.60	1.08	Virginia	35	5.00	25.00	1.80	1.94
Texas Tech	27	0.31	0.10	0.08	Texas Tech	31	1.00	1.00	0.36	0.03
Michigan State	30	3.31	10.97	0.83	Michigan State	32	2.00	4.00	0.72	0.60
Auburn	26	−0.69	0.47	−0.17	Auburn	30	0.00	0.00	0.00	0.00
Gonzaga	32	5.31	28.22	1.33	Gonzaga	33	3.00	9.00	1.08	1.43
Duke	29	2.31	5.35	0.58	Duke	32	2.00	4.00	0.72	0.42
Kentucky	26	−0.69	0.47	−0.17	Kentucky	30	0.00	0.00	0.00	0.00
Purdue	30	3.31	10.97	0.83	Purdue	26	−4.00	16.00	−1.44	−1.19
Florida St.	23	−3.69	13.60	−0.92	Florida St.	29	−1.00	1.00	−0.36	0.33
Michigan	32	5.31	28.22	1.33	Michigan	30	0.00	0.00	0.00	0.00
LSU	18	−8.69	75.47	−2.17	LSU	28	−2.00	4.00	−0.72	1.56
Virginia Tech	21	−5.69	32.35	−1.42	Virginia Tech	26	−4.00	16.00	−1.44	2.05
North Carolina	26	−0.69	0.47	−0.17	North Carolina	29	−1.00	1.00	−0.36	0.06
Houston	27	0.31	0.10	0.08	Houston	33	3.00	9.00	1.08	0.08
Tennessee	26	−0.69	0.47	−0.17	Tennessee	31	1.00	1.00	0.36	−0.06
Oregon	23	−3.69	13.60	−0.92	Oregon	25	−5.00	25.00	−1.80	1.66
Sum of Scores (ΣX)	427				Sum of Scores (ΣY)	480				
Number of Scores (N)	16				Number of Scores (N)	16			$\Sigma Z_x Z_y$	8.91
Mean (M_x)	$\Sigma X/N$	26.69			Mean (M_y)	$\Sigma Y/N$	30.00			
Sum of Squares (SS_x)	$\Sigma(X - M)^2$	239.44			Sum of Squares (SS_y)	$\Sigma(Y - M)^2$	116.00			
Variance (SD^2)	$SS/(N - 1)$	15.96			Variance (SD^2)	$SS/(N - 1)$	7.73			
Standard Deviation (SD_x)	$\sqrt{SD^2}$	4.00			Standard Deviation (SD_y)	$\sqrt{SD^2}$	2.78			
Z-Score (Z_x)	$(X - M)/SD$				Z-Score (Z_y)	$(Y - M)/SD$				
Pearson's (r)	$\Sigma Z_x Z_y/(N - 1)$	0.594			Slope of the Regression Line / Regression Coefficient (b)	$r (SD_Y/SD_X)$				0.413
Y-intercept / Regression Constant (a)	$M_Y - (b \times M_X)$	18.966								
Enter the Predictor Value (X)				10.00	Predicted Value for Y ($\hat{Y}$)	$b(X) + a$				23.10
Enter the Predictor Value (X)				15.00	Predicted Value for Y ($\hat{Y}$)	$b(X) + a$				25.17
Enter the Predictor Value (X)				20.00	Predicted Value for Y ($\hat{Y}$)	$b(X) + a$				27.23

Figure 15.3 Computations for a Regression

Step 2: Calculate the Regression Coefficient (b) The first piece we need for our linear prediction model is the slope of our regression line, or regression coefficient. The formula for that is $b = r(SD_Y/SD_X)$. We can plug in the numbers as follows:

$$b = 0.594 \left(\frac{2.78}{4.00} \right)$$

$$= 0.594\,(0.695)$$

$$= 0.413.$$

Step 3: Calculate the Regression Constant (a) Now that we have the regression coefficient, we can calculate the y-intercept or regression constant. The formula for that is $a = M_Y - (b \times M_X)$. We can plug in the numbers as follows:

$$a = M_Y - (b \times M_X)$$

$$= 30 - (0.413 \times 26.69)$$

$$= 30 - (11.02)$$

$$= 18.966.$$

Step 4: Complete the Linear Prediction Model We know that the basic formula for our linear regression model is always $\hat{Y} = b(X) + a$. Now that we've calculated the regression coefficient and constant, we can fill those in, which gives us the complete model:

$$\hat{Y} = 0.413(X) + 18.966$$

Or, written out with the variable names:

Predicted 2018–19 Season Wins = 0.413(2017–18 Season Wins) + 18.966

Step 5: Test Out Values of the Predictor Variable (X) With our linear prediction model in place, we can use it in a couple of ways. First, we can test out how our model works for teams that weren't in the Sweet 16. For example, based on our model a team with 10 wins in 2017–2018 would be expected to have won 23.10 games in 2018–2019, a team with 15 wins in 2017–2018 would be expected to have won 25.17 games in 2018–2019, and a team with 20 wins in 2017–2018 would be expected to have won 27.23 games in 2018–2019. Note that for each of the values (10, 20, 40) we used for X, our original data set of 16 teams did not include those values. Yet, we were still able to make a prediction using our model.

We can also use our model another way. Now that we know how 2017–2018 season wins corresponded with 2018–2019 wins, we could apply the same linear prediction model to the 2018–2019 season wins to see how many games our model would predict teams win in the upcoming 2019–2020 season. In **Figure 15.4,** we can see what that looks like for three teams.

Predicting 2019–2020 Regular Season Wins from 2018 to 2019 Regular Season Wins				
Enter the Predictor Value (X): Virginia	35.00	Predicted Value for Y ($\hat{Y}$)	b (X) + a	33.44
Enter the Predictor Value (X): Texas Tech	31.00	Predicted Value for Y ($\hat{Y}$)	b (X) + a	31.78
Enter the Predictor Value (X): Oregon	25.00	Predicted Value for Y ($\hat{Y}$)	b (X) + a	29.30

Figure 15.4   Applying the Linear Prediction Model to the Following Year

Step by Step: Drawing a Regression Line Now that we have our linear prediction model, we can create a regression line by following these steps:

Step 1: Create the Basics of a Scatterplot To do this we can follow the same steps we outlined in Chapter 14. But to refresh, create and label the x- and y-axis, and place values on the axes.

Step 2: Plot the Y-Intercept (*a*) Look at your linear prediction model formula ($\hat{Y} = 0.413(X) + 18.966$, and identify the regression constant (*a*). Place a dot on the y-axis that corresponds to *a*. Note that this is what the predicted value of Y ($\hat{Y}$) would be if the predictor variable (X) was 0.

Step 3: Plot a Value for *X* Select a value for your predictor variable (X) and plot the predicted value of Y ($\hat{Y}$). To make the next step easier, it's best to pick a value in the upper range of values for X. In our example, a value of 40 would work well.

Step 4: Connect the Dots That's it. We need only two points to make a straight line, so we have all that we need. Draw in your line. If you're doing this by hand, a rule or straight edge is a must.

Step 5: Check Yourself . . . Pick an additional one or two values for X, and plot the predicted value of Y ($\hat{Y}$). Any value we select for X should fall on our regression line. If it doesn't, double-check the math and/or the previous steps.

For our study, the resulting line is what you see in Figure 15.2 from earlier.

HAND CALCULATION VIDEO TUTORIAL: To learn more, check out the video Calculating the Regression Equation.

Communicating the Result

We started with a hunch that the number of games a team wins in one season could give us some insight into how many games they might win the following season. Using data from the 2017–2018 and 2018–2019 seasons, we were able to create the following linear prediction model: $\hat{Y} = 0.413(X) + 18.966$. Although we used only data from the 2018–2019 season's Sweet 16 teams, we can use our model to make predictions about other teams. We can also use what we learned about these two seasons and apply it to future seasons (e.g., predicting 2019–2020 wins based on a team's 2018–2019 win total).

Though history can give us a glimpse into what's forthcoming, we also know that the past doesn't always perfectly predict the future. With the men's 2019–2020 college basketball season concluded, it's possible to go back and check how well our model did. Our model is far from perfect, but it's better than if we took random guesses. There's always room for a better model.

Forming a Conclusion

A model is only as good as the data that go into building it. For starters, our model used only data from 16 teams. Not only is that a low number considering all of the teams that play college basketball, but we also focused on the top 16 teams. That may bias our results because those top teams get to play more games. As a result, our model may not generalize well to non-elite programs or those outside of Division I.

Simply because we found that a previous season's win total is a good predictor, it does not mean that it is the best predictor. The NCAA has an abundance of data that we could use to build a model. It is entirely possible that other aspects of a team's performance such as average margin of victory, as well as offensive and defensive numbers like field goal percentage, 3-point shooting, blocked shots, steals, and points allowed per game would be better predictors. We could also look at entirely different types of predictors related to the team's personnel, such as average team height, or average team age, as well as coaching factors such as the number of years coaching, or career wins. In any case, trying out different predictors can get us closer to finding the best predictor. To really leverage the power of more data, we could also look at how using several different predictor variables at once can help our predictions' accuracy.

Statistics for Research

Paul McCartney famously sang "Can't Buy Me Love," a lyric which expresses the idea that people can't buy the things they want the most. But recent evidence suggests that spending money in certain ways may actually increase something that most people desire: happiness. Research reveals, for example, that people report higher levels of happiness when they spend money on other people, compared to when they spend money on themselves (Dunn et al., 2008). Other evidence suggests that people are happier when they buy several small pleasures, rather than a few big ones (Dunn et al., 2011).

Additional research reveals that people report higher levels of happiness when they spend their money on new experiences rather than new possessions (Tambyah & Tan, 2022; Van Boven & Gilovich, 2003), a finding that was replicated with a Chinese sample (Sun et al., 2019). According to this line of research, individuals experience higher levels of happiness for experiential purchases compared to material purchases. But what about among college students? Does spending money on new experiences predict happiness for college students?

Although we might expect college students to have the same types of reactions as other people, we could imagine that there might be differences, too. For example, because they have less stuff than older adults, college students may be happier when they spend money on items that convey social status. In addition, college life is full of new experiences (e.g., new classes, new friends, new romantic relationships, new extracurricular activities, new internships), perhaps to such a degree that the psychological benefits of new experiences are weaker for college students than for other people.

So, to answer this question of whether spending money on new experiences predicts happiness among college students, we will perform a regression analysis. Conducting this analysis will allow us not only to quantify the direction and magnitude of the association between amount spent on new experiences and level of happiness, but also to use the regression model that we generate to make predictions about how much happiness people will have when we know how much they spend on new experiences.

Here in the Statistics for Research section, we're going to learn about prediction error, perfect versus imperfect associations, interpreting scatterplots with a least squares regression line, calculating and interpreting the coefficient of determination (R^2), hypothesis testing with regression, the standardized beta coefficient, and multiple regression.

Does spending money on new experiences make people happy?

Where Do the Data Come From?

To test the association between number of new experiences and happiness, imagine we were to collect a random sample of 30 college students from across the United States. We could ask each student to keep an inventory of all of their expenses during a time when they are likely spending money on new experiences: summer vacation. We could then tally their new experience spending (e.g., a trip to the beach), as opposed to money spent on non-experiences (e.g., a new pair of sunglasses), and the total amount spent on new experiences would be our predictor variable. For our measure of happiness, we could have participants complete the Subjective Happiness Scale (Lyubomirsky & Lepper, 1999), a four-item scale that asks participants to rate the extent to which they consider themselves a happy or unhappy person.

Search for Subjective Happiness Scale to complete an online assessment.

Regression Analysis: What We're Trying to Accomplish

As we learned in the first half of this chapter, regression analysis is all about making predictions. We make these predictions by calculating the equation of the line that best describes the association between our two variables. Calculating the

perfect association a type of linear association where all of the data points fall exactly on the line of best fit; a linear association with zero prediction error.

line's equation is not particularly difficult when there is a **perfect association** between the predictor and criterion variables, as in **Figure 15.5.** When the association is perfect, all of the data points fall exactly in a straight line. By knowing the slope and y-intercept of this regression line, we can perfectly predict a person's score on the criterion variable when we know their score on the predictor variable. In other words, knowing how much a person spent on new experiences allows us to perfectly predict their score on the subjective happiness scale.

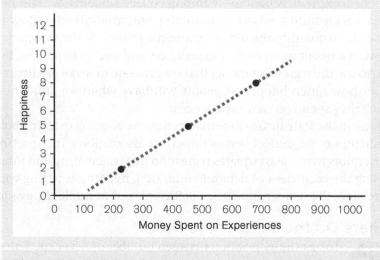

Figure 15.5 Perfect Linear Association Scatterplot

prediction error the difference between the observed values of the criterion variable and the values predicted by the regression equation.

imperfect association a type of linear association where the data points do not fall on the line of best fit.

Another way of saying that our prediction is perfect is to say that there we have zero **prediction error,** which reflects the difference between the observed value and the predicted value of the criterion variable. That is, if we were to calculate the difference between what we actually observed for the criterion variable (Y) versus what our regression model predicted ($\hat{Y}$), the difference would be zero, so we would have zero prediction error.

Of course, associations between psychological variables are rarely perfect. Indeed, most regression analyses are for **imperfect associations,** which describe associations between variables that are linear in nature, but where not all data points fall exactly on a line. For example, in **Figure 15.6,** we can see that some observed values of happiness are higher than what we would predict when using the regression line, some are lower, and some are equal. In an imperfect association, no matter what the slope and the y-intercept of our regression equation

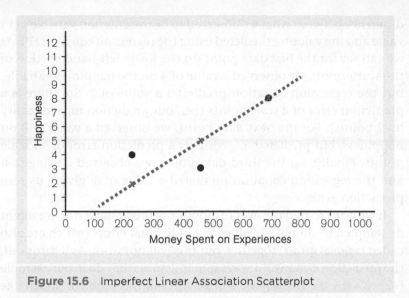

Figure 15.6 Imperfect Linear Association Scatterplot

are, we will always have some amount of prediction error. When the association between two variables is strong, the amount of prediction error goes down. When the association is weak, the amount of prediction error goes up. For this reason, it's helpful to quantify the amount of prediction error that we have when using our regression equation.

To see how this works, take a look at **Figure 15.7**. For each of the data points, we can calculate the prediction error amount by finding the

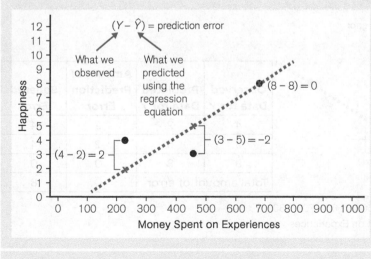

Figure 15.7 Scatterplot with Prediction Errors

difference between what we observed to be the criterion variable's (Y) value and the value we predicted using the regression equation ($\hat{Y}$). As we can see for the first data point (in the lower left-hand portion of the scatterplot), we observed a value of 4 on the happiness variable, but the regression equation predicted a value of 2. So, there is a prediction error of 2 scale points (i.e., our prediction missed reality by 2 points). For the next data point, we observed a value of 3 on happiness, but predicted 5, giving us a prediction error of −2 scale points. Finally, for the third data point, we observed a value of 8 and the regression equation predicted a value of 8, giving us zero prediction error.

If we want to find the overall amount of prediction error, we might be tempted to simply add all of the individual errors (which are also called **residual errors**) together, but this will not work. As it turns out, the prediction errors will always sum to zero, as they do in our example ($-2 + 2 + 0 = 0$). The way we will get around this problem (much like we have done with deviation scores) is to square each of the prediction errors. By squaring them, we will ensure that they no longer sum to zero. Now as we can see in **Figure 15.8,** when we sum the squared errors, they total 8 ($4 + 4 + 0$). This value reflects the total amount of squared error and is called the **sum of squares error.** Its formula is $SS_{Error} = \Sigma(Y - \hat{Y})^2$.

residual error another name for prediction error; the difference between observed and predicted values of the criterion variable.

sum of squares error a statistic that quantifies the total amount of squared prediction error. The line of best fit is the one that minimizes the sum of squares error.

$$SS_{Error} = \Sigma(Y - \hat{Y})^2$$

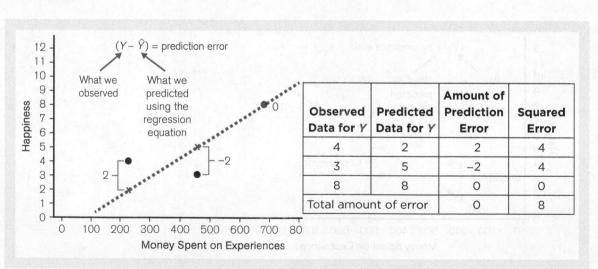

Figure 15.8   Scatterplot with Squared Errors

Observed Data for Y	Predicted Data for Y	Amount of Prediction Error	Squared Error
4	2	2	4
3	5	−2	4
8	8	0	0
Total amount of error		0	8

As it turns out, the line of best fit that we learned to calculate in the first half of this chapter always generates the regression equation that results in the least amount of squared error. For this reason, the line of best fit is also called the **least squares regression line.**

Assessing a Regression Model: The Coefficient of Determination (R^2)

Now, just because the line of best fit has the least amount of squared error, it doesn't actually tell us whether or not the regression line is any good at predicting the criterion variable. The line of best fit simply reveals the values of the slope and y-intercept that result in the least amount of squared error, and unless the squared error is zero, we can't necessarily tell if we have a lot of squared error or a little. So, we need to assess whether or not our regression line is actually useful.

One way to evaluate our regression line is to compare it to a worst case scenario. Let's imagine for a moment that we were trying to predict a person's level of happiness, but we don't know anything about how much they spend on experiences (or anything else about them). What should our prediction for this person's happiness level be in this scenario? Well, without any other information, our best guess would be to predict the outcome or criterion variable's mean. In other words, the safest prediction for everyone is that they would get the mean score on our happiness questionnaire.

Why is this the case? Well, first of all, when we described the mean back in Chapter 3, we said that the mean is the most representative score in a distribution. So, in a worst case situation, when we had to guess a person's score on our criterion variable but didn't know anything about them, our best guess would be use the most representative score in the distribution: the mean (M_Y).

Second, we can see why the mean of Y is our best guess for any particular observation by looking at the regression equation itself: $\hat{Y} = b(X) + a$. If we don't know a person's score on the X variable, the first part of the formula, $b(X)$, becomes irrelevant. Thus, our prediction for Y should be the regression constant (a). We determine the regression constant with the formula $a = M_Y - (b \times M_X)$, and if we don't know the slope (b), this term drops out of the formula, leaving us with $a = M_Y$. In other words, our best guess for Y is the regression constant, which equals Y's mean.

Let's take this insight and apply it to our formula for calculating the sum of squares error. Just like before, we could subtract the observed value of Y from the predicted value, which would be M_Y for all our data points. To see how this works, take a look at **Figure 15.9.** For illustrative purposes, we'll use a sample of three observations with a mean of 5. From these, we can calculate our prediction errors by comparing

least squares regression line another name for the line of best fit. So called because it is the regression line that results in the least amount of squared prediction error.

our observations to the mean. As before, to find the prediction error, we can simply take what we observed (Y) minus our prediction (M_Y). Because these values always sum to zero, we need to square them. As we can see in the figure, if we use the mean to make our predictions, the total amount of prediction error is 15. So, this would be the prediction error amount in the worst case scenario (i.e., using the mean to make all of our predictions).

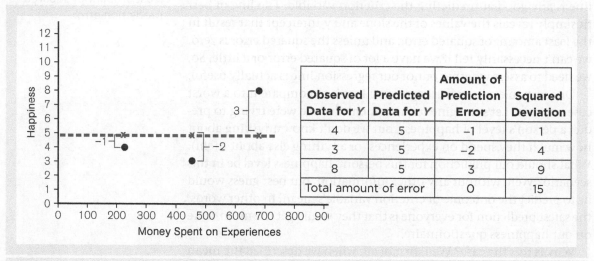

Figure 15.9 Scatterplot with Squared Deviations

Notice, that if we use M_Y to make our predictions, rather than $\hat{Y}$, we calculate our total amount of prediction error with the formula $\Sigma(Y - M_Y)^2$, which is the formula for the sum of squares total (SS_{Total}) that we have encountered numerous times throughout this book. In essence, this reveals that when making predictions for criterion variable scores, we can do no worse than the sum of square total. That is, it represents the maximum possible prediction error for the criterion variable.

Now that we have a benchmark that represents the maximum amount of prediction error possible, we can compare the amount of prediction error we get when using our least squares regression equation to the maximum possible error. Recall that when using our regression equation, our sum of squares error was 8, while the sum of squares total is 15. Thus, we can conclude that our regression equation reduces the amount of prediction error, relative to the total amount of variability. By how much? Well, we can compute this by dividing our sum of squares error by the sum of squares total,

$SS_{Error}/SS_{Total} = \dfrac{\Sigma(Y - \hat{Y})^2}{\Sigma(Y - M_Y)^2} = 8/15 = .53.$ This ratio tells us the proportion of variability in our criterion variable that is unexplained by our regression equation.

Of course, it would be ideal if we calculated the proportion of variability that our regression equation explains, as opposed to the amount that it fails to explain. Luckily, because the variability our regression equation explains plus the amount that it doesn't explain must sum to 1, we can simply take 1 minus the ratio that we just calculated to find the proportion of variability that it explains. In other words, the amount of variability in our criterion variable that our regression equation explains is equal to $1 - (SS_{Error}/SS_{Total}) = 1 - \dfrac{\Sigma(Y - \hat{Y})^2}{\Sigma(Y - M_Y)^2} = 1 - .53 = .47.$ We call this quantity the **coefficient of determination,** or R^2, and it represents the amount of variability in the criterion variable as predicted by the regression equation.

$$R^2 = 1 - \dfrac{\Sigma(Y - \hat{Y})^2}{\Sigma(Y - M_Y)^2}$$

coefficient of determination (R^2) a statistic that quantifies the amount of variability in the criterion variable that is predicted by the regression equation.

Interpreting the Coefficient of Determination (R^2) R^2 is very useful for assessing the regression equation's predictive power. To interpret R^2, we need to know that R^2 ranges from 0 to 1. If R^2 equals 1.00, then the regression equation perfectly predicts scores on the criterion variable. If $R^2 = 0.00$, then the regression equation does no better than guessing the mean of Y for all participants. Also, if we multiply R^2 by 100, it tells us the percentage of variation in the criterion that is predicted by the regression equation. For example, if we found that the R^2 for the association between money spent on new experiences and happiness was .25, we could multiply this by 100 (.25 × 100 = 25%) and conclude that money spent on new experiences predicts 25% of the variation in happiness (with 75% of the variability remaining unexplained). Conversely, if we found that the R^2 for the association between money spent on new experiences and happiness was .65, we could conclude that money spent on experiences predicts 65% of happiness' variation.

Another reason why R^2 is useful for assessing our regression equation's predictive power is that we can easily compare it across different regression equations. For example, let's imagine we wanted to determine which predictor variable did a better job of explaining the variability in happiness: money spent on new experiences, or number of friends on social media. We could calculate the R^2 for each of the two regression equations and compare them directly. For example, if the R^2 for money spent on experiences was .15 and the R^2 for number of friends on social media was .30, we could conclude that number of friends on social media predicted twice as much of the variation in happiness, relative to money spent on new experiences.

One thing we need to be cautious of when interpreting R^2 is that even though it is called the coefficient of determination, it does not tell us about cause and effect. That is, just as with correlation, a regression analysis does not reveal whether two variables are causally related. The R^2 that we observe in a study could be due to the presence of a third variable that relates to both the predictor and the criterion variables. Because of this, we need to choose our words carefully when interpreting our regression results. While it would be appropriate to say that R^2 reveals the amount of variability in the criterion that the predictor variable predicts, we cannot say that R^2 tells us the percentage of the criterion that the predictor variable causes.

Regression Analysis: How Does It Work?

Now that we know about the coefficient of determination, let's see how we calculate it for our complete sample. To start with, we need to calculate the line of best fit first, including the slope and y-intercept. Once we know the line of best fit, we can compare the values of the criterion variable that we observe to what we predict using the regression line ($\hat{Y}$). So, to calculate the line of best fit, we'll follow the steps that we learned in the first half of the chapter (see **Figure 15.10**).

Step by Step: Regression To calculate the slope of our regression equation, we need to know the correlation coefficient. Once we know the correlation coefficient and slope, we can solve for the y-intercept.

Step 1: Calculate Pearson (r) To calculate the correlation coefficient, we convert all of our scores to Z-scores for both the predictor (Z_X) and criterion (Z_Y) variables, multiply these Z-scores together to find the cross-products of Z-scores ($Z_X Z_Y$), add up the cross products, and divide by the sample size minus 1: $r = \dfrac{\Sigma Z_X Z_Y}{N-1} = 0.59$.

Step 2: Calculate the Regression Coefficient (b) To find the slope of our regression equation, we use the formula $b = r(SD_Y / SD_X)$. Thus, the slope for the association between money spent on experiences and happiness is calculated as follows: $b = r(SD_Y / SD_X) = 0.59(1.31/192.91) = 0.004$.

Step 3: Calculate the Regression Constant (a) To find the y-intercept, we use the formula $a = M_Y - (b \times M_X)$. For our current research problem, the regression constant is calculated as follows: $a = M_Y - (b \times M_X) = 3.55 - (0.004 \times 478.82) = 1.64$.

Step 4: Complete the Linear Prediction Model ($\hat{Y} = b(X) + a$)
We're now ready to construct our regression equation: $\hat{Y} = 0.004(X) + 1.64$. This equation tells us our best guess for what the criterion variable should be for any value of the predictor variable. In other words, we can use this equation to predict a person's level of happiness when we know the amount of money they spend on new experiences.

Step by Step: Calculating the Coefficient of Determination (R^2)
Now that we know the equation for the line of best fit, we need to evaluate it. How good of a job does it do in predicting scores on the criterion variable? To answer this question, we need to calculate the coefficient of determination, R^2. Remember that R^2 tells us the amount of variability in the criterion variable that is predicted by the predictor variable. It does this by calculating the ratio of the amount of prediction error relative to the total amount of variability in the criterion variable. So, our first step in calculating R^2 is to use our regression equation to make a prediction for a person's level of happiness, based on the amount of money spent on new experiences.

Step 1: Use the Linear Prediction Model to Find the Predicted Value of Y ($\hat{Y}$) To find our predicted values of Y, we will enter each observed value of the predictor variable into our regression equation: $\hat{Y} = b(X) + a$. Figure 15.10 shows each of these calculations. For example, our first participant spent $710.84 on new experiences. Thus, using our regression equation, we would predict their level of happiness to be $\hat{Y} = b(X) + a = .004(710.84) + 1.64 = 4.47$.

Step 2: Calculate the Amount of Prediction Error Next, we want to compare what our regression equation predicted to the value we actually observed for the criterion variable. The difference between these two scores is our amount of prediction error (also called the residual error), and we can express this idea using the formula $(Y - \hat{Y})$. For example, our first participant had a happiness score of 5.30, but our regression equation predicted a happiness score of 4.47. Thus, our prediction error is $(Y - \hat{Y}) = 5.30 - 4.47 = 0.83$. We repeat this step for all observations in our sample.

Step 3: Calculate the Sum of Squares Error To find our overall amount of prediction error, we need to square each prediction error (so they don't sum to zero) and then add them up. The formula is $SS_{Error} = \Sigma(y - \hat{y})^2 = 32.51$.

Step 4: Calculate the Sum of Squares Total We next need to find the total amount of variability in our criterion variable. In fact, we already made this calculation when we determined the standard deviation. As we can see in Figure 15.10, the formula is $SS_{Total} = \Sigma(Y - M_Y)^2 = 49.67$.

Participant Number	Money Spent on Experiences (X)	Deviation Score (X − M)	Squared Deviation Score (X − M)²	Z-Score (Z_X)	Participant Number	Happiness (Y)	Deviation Score (Y − M)	Squared Deviation Score (Y − M)²	Z-Score (Z_Y)	Cross-Product of Z-Scores (Z_X Z_Y)	Predicted Value of Y (Ŷ)	Prediction Error (Y − Ŷ)	Squared Prediction Errors (Y − Ŷ)²
1	710.84	232.02	53,833.59	1.20	1	5.30	1.75	3.07	1.34	1.61	4.47	0.83	0.69
2	136.06	−342.76	117,483.96	−1.78	2	3.17	−0.38	0.14	−0.29	0.51	2.18	0.99	0.98
3	431.66	−47.16	2,224.00	−0.24	3	2.92	−0.63	0.39	−0.48	0.12	3.36	−0.44	0.19
4	658.39	179.57	32,245.62	0.93	4	6.44	2.89	8.37	2.21	2.06	4.26	2.18	4.74
5	340.09	−138.73	19,245.83	−0.72	5	4.94	1.39	1.94	1.06	−0.77	2.99	1.95	3.79
6	381.48	−97.34	9,474.95	−0.50	6	2.09	−1.46	2.12	−1.11	0.56	3.16	−1.07	1.14
7	307.63	−171.19	29,305.79	−0.89	7	4.88	1.33	1.78	1.02	−0.90	2.86	2.02	4.06
8	388.50	−90.32	8,157.58	−0.47	8	2.31	−1.24	1.53	−0.95	0.44	3.19	−0.88	0.77
9	307.80	−171.02	29,247.61	−0.89	9	1.90	−1.65	2.71	−1.26	1.12	2.87	−0.97	0.93
10	428.54	−50.28	2,528.01	−0.26	10	2.17	−1.38	1.90	−1.05	0.27	3.35	−1.18	1.38
11	886.02	407.20	165,812.38	2.11	11	4.19	0.64	0.41	0.49	1.04	5.17	−0.98	0.96
12	181.60	−297.22	88,339.33	−1.54	12	2.62	−0.93	0.86	−0.71	1.09	2.36	0.26	0.07
13	378.62	−100.20	10,039.91	−0.52	13	2.88	−0.67	0.44	−0.51	0.26	3.15	−0.27	0.07
14	689.38	210.56	44,335.79	1.09	14	4.60	1.05	1.11	0.80	0.88	4.39	0.21	0.05
15	629.26	150.44	22,632.39	0.78	15	4.66	1.11	1.24	0.85	0.66	4.15	0.51	0.26
16	859.84	381.02	145,176.75	1.98	16	5.70	2.15	4.64	1.65	3.25	5.07	0.63	0.40
17	452.89	−25.93	672.33	−0.13	17	2.04	−1.51	2.27	−1.15	0.15	3.44	−1.40	1.97
18	230.73	−248.09	61,548.32	−1.29	18	2.99	−0.56	0.31	−0.43	0.55	2.56	0.43	0.19
19	660.89	182.07	33,149.73	0.94	19	4.99	1.44	2.08	1.10	1.04	4.27	0.72	0.51
20	561.08	82.26	6,766.82	0.43	20	3.40	−0.15	0.02	−0.11	−0.05	3.87	−0.47	0.23
21	579.01	100.19	10,038.17	0.52	21	3.21	−0.34	0.11	−0.26	−0.13	3.95	−0.74	0.54
22	344.38	−134.44	18,073.93	−0.70	22	2.77	−0.78	0.60	−0.59	0.41	3.01	−0.24	0.06
23	362.58	−116.24	13,511.58	−0.60	23	3.34	−0.21	0.04	−0.16	0.10	3.08	0.26	0.07
24	472.38	−6.44	41.47	−0.03	24	2.14	−1.41	1.98	−1.08	0.04	3.52	−1.38	1.91

Figure 15.10 Computations for a Regression

	X	(X − M)	(X − M)²	Z_x		Y	(Y − M)	(Y − M)²	Z_y	$Z_x Z_y$	$\hat{Y}$	(Y − $\hat{Y}$)	(Y − $\hat{Y}$)²
25	539.87	61.05	3,727.18	0.32	25	3.75	0.20	0.04	0.16	0.05	3.79	-0.04	0.00
26	247.33	-231.49	53,587.31	-1.20	26	1.07	-2.48	6.14	-1.89	2.27	2.62	-1.55	2.42
27	483.21	4.39	19.28	0.02	27	4.99	1.44	2.08	1.10	0.03	3.56	1.43	2.03
28	719.31	240.49	57,835.76	1.25	28	4.46	0.91	0.83	0.70	0.87	4.51	-0.05	0.00
29	357.19	-121.63	14,793.69	-0.63	29	3.64	0.09	0.01	0.07	-0.04	3.06	0.58	0.33
30	638.02	159.20	25,344.85	0.83	30	2.85	-0.70	0.49	-0.53	-0.44	4.18	-1.33	1.77

Statistic	Formula	Value (X)	Value (Y)
Sum of Scores (ΣX)		14,364.58	106.41
Number of Scores (N)		30	30
Mean (M_x / M_y)	$\Sigma X / N$; $\Sigma Y / N$	478.82	3.55
Sum of Squares (SS_x / SS_y)	$\Sigma(X - M)^2$; $\Sigma(Y - M)^2$	1,079,193.93	49.67
Variance (SD^2)	$SS/(N - 1)$	37,213.58	1.71
Standard Deviation (SD_x / SD_y)	$\sqrt{SD^2}$	192.91	1.31
Z-Score (Z_x / Z_y)	$(X - M)/SD$; $(Y - M)/SD$		

$\Sigma Z_x Z_y = 17.04$

Statistic	Formula	Value
Pearson's (r)	$\Sigma Z_x Z_y / (N - 1)$	0.59
Slope of the Regression Line / Regression Coefficient (b)	$r\,(SD_y/SD_x)$	0.004
Y-Intercept / Regression Constant (a)	$M_y - (b \times M_x)$	1.64
Coefficient of Determination (R^2)	$1\ N - 1 - (- / \Sigma(Y - M)^2)$	0.35

Sum of Squares Error $\Sigma(Y - \hat{Y})^2 = 32.51$

Step 5: Calculate the Coefficient of Determination (R^2) Now that we know the amount of prediction error and the total amount of variability, we are ready to solve for the R^2. We use the formula:

$$1 - \frac{\Sigma(Y - \hat{Y})^2}{\Sigma(Y - M_Y)^2} = 1 - \left(\frac{32.51}{49.67}\right) = 0.345$$

Step 6: Interpret the Results Perhaps the easiest way to interpret R^2 is to multiply it by 100 and convert it to a percentage: $0.35 \times 100 = 34.50\%$. Thus, the regression equation $\hat{Y} = 0.004(X) + 1.64$ predicts 34.50% of the variability in happiness.

The Relationship Between r and R^2 in a Regression with One Predictor As we've just seen, although each step is easy, calculating R^2 is a multistep, and somewhat time-consuming, process. As it turns out, though, there is a mathematical relationship between the Pearson correlation coefficient (r) and the coefficient of determination that makes calculating R^2 much easier. We can find R^2 by simply squaring the correlation coefficient (r^2). We want to point out that this works only when our regression equation has one predictor variable.

Hypothesis Testing for Regression: How Does It Work?

So far, we have described a way for assessing the predictive power of a regression analysis using the coefficient of determination R^2. But, we don't yet have the ability to evaluate whether the regression equation we found in our sample suggests that there is an association at the population level. In other words, we need to test whether the regression equation that we found in our sample suggests that there is a linear association in the population. We need to conduct a hypothesis test for regression to conclude that our linear model is statistically significant.

Want to review the assumptions of correlation? SEE CHAPTER 14.

Assumptions of the Hypothesis Test for Regression As always, we must satisfy a set of assumptions before we can conduct our hypothesis test. Because regression is an extension of correlation in that we use the Pearson correlation coefficient to solve for our slope and y-intercept, regression and correlation have the same assumptions. So we will summarize the four assumptions below.

1. *The sample is randomly selected from the population and participants' scores are independent.* This assumption states that we selected our sample at random from the population and that scores for any participant do not affect the scores of any other participant.

2. *Both the* X *and the* Y *variables are normally distributed, as is the bivariate distribution.* This assumption states that each variable must be normally distributed, as does the bivariate distribution. Although violating this assumption is problematic, so long as we have satisfied the independent observations part of assumption number 1, violations will have minimal impact on our hypothesis test.

3. *The variance in the* Y *variable is equal across the values of the* X *variable.* This assumption states that the variation (scatter) in the *Y* variable is the same as we move along the values of the *X* variable. As we learned in Chapter 14, this is called the homoscedasticity assumption.

4. *The* X, Y *association is linear.* This assumption states that the relationship between our variables must be linear (i.e., not curvilinear).

Step by Step: Hypothesis Testing Hypothesis testing for regression is essentially the same as it was for correlation. The main difference is that instead of testing the significance of the correlation coefficient, we are testing the significance of the slope. If the slope in the population is zero, it suggests that there is no association between the predictor and criterion variables. If the slope is not zero (either a positive or negative slope), it suggests that there is an association between variables.

Step 1: Population and Hypotheses Our first step is to establish who and what we are testing. So, we will define our populations and hypotheses.

Population of Interest: A population of college students for whom there is no association between money spent on new experiences and happiness.

Comparison Population: College students like those in our sample for whom there is an association between money spent on new experiences and happiness.

Sample: The 30 college students in our sample.

Research Hypothesis: Our research hypothesis is that spending money on new experiences predicts happiness. In other words, the slope of the regression equation at the population level is not zero, $\beta_1 \neq 0$ (note that we use the Greek letter β to symbolize the slope at the population level).

Null Hypothesis: There is no association between spending money on new experiences and happiness; thus, the slope at the population level is zero, $\beta_1 \neq 0$. We will set alpha = .05.

Step 2: Build Comparison Distribution Our next step is to build a comparison distribution. Just like we conceptualized a distribution

distribution of slopes a
distribution that presents
the slopes calculated
from all possible samples
of a certain size from the
population.

of correlations in Chapter 14, here we need to construct a **distribution of slopes,** which represents the distribution that we would create if we collected all possible samples of a certain size from the population and calculated the slope for each. The comparison distribution would be the distribution of slopes if we assume that the null hypothesis is true. If the null hypothesis is true, then the distribution of slope should have a mean of zero, indicating that there is no association between our variables and that any slope that we observe in a sample is due to sampling error. Just as with correlation, we approximate the shape of the comparison distribution with a t-curve with $N - 2$ degrees of freedom. We subtract two degrees of freedom because we are estimating two population parameters: the slope and the y-intercept. For our current study, we had 30 participants, so the appropriate comparison distribution is a t-curve with 28 degrees of freedom ($30 - 2 = 28$).

Step 3: Establish Critical Value Cutoff We need to establish the range of t-scores we would expect to see due to sampling error if the null hypothesis is true. Anything outside of this range would be improbable, and therefore we will reject the null hypothesis. This is exactly what our critical values tell us. If we observe a t-score that falls outside of our critical values, we will reject the null hypothesis and conclude that there is an association between money spent on new experiences and happiness.

To find our critical values, we will refer to the t-table. Because our research hypothesis is two-tailed, and our alpha is .05, we will look at the fourth column of **Figure 15.11.** Similarly, as we established in Step 2, we have 28 degrees of freedom, so we will look to the corresponding row in our t-table. As we can see, our critical value cutoff is +/ − 2.049.

Step 4: Determine Sample Results Before we calculate our t-score, we need to make sure that we satisfied our assumptions. The first assumption is that our sample is randomly selected from the population and that scores are independent between participants. Our sample is a random sample of college students from the United States, so our results may not generalize to college students worldwide. Scores for all participants are independent, so we have satisfied the first assumption. The second assumption states that scores on our variables are normally distributed, as is the bivariate distribution. Because our sample size is sufficiently large, our results are unlikely to be affected by violations of this assumption. The third assumption is the homoscedasticity assumption. As we did in Chapter 14, we can examine the scatterplot of the association to determine whether the amount of scatter is approximately equal along the line of best fit.

	One-Tailed Tests Alpha Level		Two-Tailed Tests Alpha Level	
df	0.05	0.01	0.05	0.01
1	6.314	31.821	12.706	63.657
2	2.920	6.965	4.303	9.925
3	2.353	4.541	3.182	5.841
4	2.132	3.747	2.776	4.604
5	2.015	3.365	2.571	4.032
6	1.943	3.143	2.447	3.708
7	1.895	2.998	2.365	3.500
8	1.860	2.897	2.306	3.356
9	1.833	2.822	2.262	3.250
10	1.813	2.764	2.228	3.170
11	1.796	2.718	2.201	3.106
12	1.783	2.681	2.179	3.055
13	1.771	2.651	2.161	3.013
14	1.762	2.625	2.145	2.977
15	1.753	2.603	2.132	2.947
16	1.746	2.584	2.120	2.921
17	1.740	2.567	2.110	2.898
18	1.734	2.553	2.101	2.879
19	1.729	2.540	2.093	2.861
20	1.725	2.528	2.086	2.846
21	1.721	2.518	2.080	2.832
22	1.717	2.509	2.074	2.819
23	1.714	2.500	2.069	2.808
24	1.711	2.492	2.064	2.797
25	1.708	2.485	2.060	2.788
26	1.706	2.479	2.056	2.779
27	1.704	2.473	2.052	2.771
28	1.701	2.467	2.049	2.764
29	1.699	2.462	2.045	2.757
30	1.698	2.458	2.043	2.750
35	1.690	2.438	2.030	2.724
40	1.684	2.424	2.021	2.705
60	1.671	2.390	2.001	2.661
80	1.664	2.374	1.990	2.639

Figure 15.11 *t*-Table Preview

From the scatterplot (**Figure 15.12**), it appears as though there is an approximately equal amount of scatter all along the length of the line of best fit. Thus, we have satisfied this assumption. Finally, the fourth assumption states that the association between the predictor and criterion variables is linear. Again, we can test this assumption by examining the scatterplot. As we see in Figure 15.12, the association appears to be linear. Thus, we have satisfied this assumption.

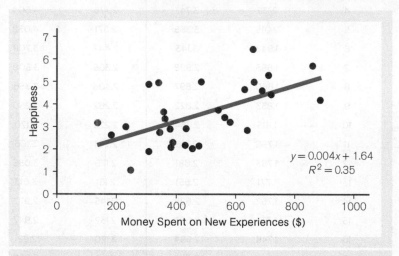

Figure 15.12 Scatterplot of Money Spent on New Experiences and Happiness

Now that we have satisfied the assumptions, we can conduct the *t*-test for the slope. To do this, we need to calculate the *t*-score for the slope of our sample, using the following formula:

$$t = \frac{b}{\frac{\sqrt{\frac{\Sigma(Y - \hat{Y})^2}{N - 2}}}{\sqrt{\Sigma(X - M_X)^2}}}$$

If this looks complicated, don't worry. Each of the components of this formula is something that we have encountered already. In the numerator is the slope, <u>*b*</u>, which we calculated for our sample. In the denominator is the sum of squares error, $\Sigma(Y - \hat{Y})^2$, and the sum of squares total for the predictor variable $\Sigma(X - M_X)^2$, both of which we calculated earlier in Figure 15.12. Beyond this, everything else is straightforward math.

For our current study, $t = \dfrac{.004}{\sqrt{\dfrac{32.51}{\sqrt{\dfrac{30-2}{1079193.93}}}}} = \dfrac{.004}{.001} = 3.84$.

Step 5: Decide and Interpret Is our slope significantly different from zero? To make this determination, we compare our t-score to the critical value, which we found earlier to be $+/- 2.049$. Because 3.84 is greater than 2.049, we can reject the null hypothesis and conclude that there is a statistically significant association between money spent on new experiences and happiness, such that increases in the amount of money spent are associated with increases in happiness.

Interpreting the Magnitude of a Linear Regression Using Standardized Beta Now that we have found a significant regression, we can think about the magnitude of association. One thing that we want to point out is that we cannot use the value of the slope or y-intercept in the regression equation to interpret the magnitude of the association between the predictor and criterion variables. That's because the value of our slope and y-intercepts are unstandardized, such that the values they take on are affected by both the magnitude of the association and the units of measurement. In our example above, money spent on experiences is measured in hundreds of dollars, whereas happiness is measured in points on a 7-point scale. The nature of these units means that we need to move a lot more along the x-axis for each unit change on the y-axis, regardless of the strength of the association.

To fix this issue, we need to calculate the **standardized beta coefficient,** symbolized as β, which specifies the number of standard deviations change in the criterion variable that will occur for each standard deviation change in the predictor variable. To calculate the standardized beta coefficient, we need to multiply the slope by the ratio of the standard deviation of the predictor relative to the standard deviation of the criterion. We can see how this works in the formula:

$$\beta = b \times \left(\dfrac{SD_X}{SD_Y} \right)$$

Note that in linear regressions with one predictor variable, the standardized beta coefficient is equal to the Pearson correlation coefficient (*r*). However, in multiple regression, a type of regression with more than one predictor variable, the standardized beta does not equal the

standardized beta coefficient a statistic used in multiple regression to compare the relative importance of different predictor variables. In regression with one predictor, the standardized beta coefficient equals the correlation coefficient.

correlation coefficient. In both cases, as the standardized beta coefficient approaches −1 or +1, we can conclude that the association is strong.

SPSS Video Tutorial: Regression

 Let's see how we would perform regression analysis using SPSS. Watch the SPSS video on tutorial regression to see how to perform the analyses and interpret the output.

 SPSS VIDEO TUTORIAL: To learn more, check out the video Regression.

Communicating the Result

 When communicating the results of our regression analysis, we need to first consider the importance of the regression equation and the likelihood that other researchers will want to use it to make predictions. Often in **basic research,** which is research conducted for the sake of learning about a phenomenon, researchers hypothesize which variables should be associated with each other (or not) and want to find evidence to support their hypotheses. These researchers don't necessarily intend to use the regression equation to make predictions and, for this reason, don't typically report slope and y-intercept. Instead, they report hypothesis test results for the slope and the R^2, because these are the results that confirm or disconfirm their hypotheses.

In contrast, in **applied research,** which is research conducted to solve a real-world problem, researchers want to generate a linear model so that they can use it. So, these researchers typically focus on reporting the details of the linear model, in addition to the other results.

Because psychological science is most commonly interested in basic research questions, our results paragraph for our current results would look something like this:

> We conducted a regression analysis to examine the association between money spent on new experiences and happiness. The results of the analysis revealed a significant, positive association, $\beta = .59$, $t(28) = 3.84$, $p = .001$, $R^2 = .35$, such that increases in spending on new experiences predicts scores on happiness.

Forming a Conclusion

 Our regression analysis results suggest that increased spending on new experiences predicts college students' happiness levels. Using regression analyses, we found that there is a

basic research research conducted for the sake of learning about a natural phenomenon.

applied research research conducted to solve a real world problem.

significant association between money spent on new experiences and happiness. Specifically, the amount spent on new experiences predicts 34.50% of the variation in happiness.

Despite the useful information that these results provide, we need to keep some important ideas in mind. First of all, it is difficult to make definitive conclusions about the strength of our regression model without the appropriate context. If our model explains 34.50% of the variation in happiness, that seems like a lot. But how does it compare to other predictors? In order to answer this question, we need to compare our results to other findings that exist in the scientific literature.

Second, most psychological outcomes are rarely associated with just one predictor variable. Human psychology is complex and multifaceted, and so we need ways of looking at multiple predictor variables at the same time. This allows us to look at their unique and interactive predictive powers. With this in mind, researchers have developed statistical tools to help us address specific types of research questions. We detail three of these analyses below.

Multiple Regression Multiple regression is a type of analysis that examines whether multiple predictor variables account for the variation in a single criterion variable. For example, we might want to test whether spending money on new experiences predicts variation in happiness above and beyond spending money on possessions. Rather than conducting two separate regression analyses, we could conduct a multiple regression that incorporates both types of spending as predictors simultaneously, while still looking at happiness as our criterion.

When we conduct a multiple regression, we need to evaluate the overall linear model to determine whether our predictor variables combined predict variation in the criterion. But we also need to evaluate the predictor variables individually to see how important each predictor is in the regression model. This is where the standardized beta coefficients that we mentioned earlier come into play. Because they are standardized, we can compare the relative importance of each predictor variable to one another. This allows us to determine, for example, if money spent on new experiences is a stronger predictor of happiness than money spent on possessions.

Mediation Mediation is an extension of multiple regression that looks to see whether a third variable, called the mediator, accounts for the association between a predictor variable and a criterion variable. The goal of this analysis is to examine *why* two variables are associated, by proposing and testing some process or mechanism by which one variable is associated with variation in another. Mediation, therefore, would seek to explain why spending money on new experiences predicts happiness. For example, we might propose that spending money on new

multiple regression a type of analysis that examines whether multiple predictor variables account for the variation in a single criterion variable.

mediation a type of multiple regression that examines whether a third variable explains the association between two variables.

experiences increases individuals' levels of happiness because experiences allow people to develop new skills and hobbies, as well as create meaningful social connections with other people. If this was the case, then we could perform a mediation analysis to determine if developing skills and making social connections is the process or mechanism by which spending money on new experiences is associated with increased happiness.

moderation a type of multiple regression that examines third variables that change the strength or direction of the association between two other variables.

Moderation Moderation is another extension that looks to see whether a third variable, called a moderator, alters the direction or strength of the association between a predictor and criterion variable. The goal of this analysis is to examine *when* or *for whom* there is an association between two variables. Essentially, moderation tests for interactions within a regression context. For example, we might predict that money spent on new experiences predicts happiness, but only for people who are not diagnosed as clinically depressed. The diagnosis of clinical depression serves as a moderator because it reduces the magnitude of the association between money spent on new experiences and happiness to zero.

Moderation is very common in psychology. Often, findings that are present for some people are not present for others. Similarly, findings that are present in some situations are different in other situations. Moderation allows us to test for these changes. Because they sound similar, it's easy to mix up moderation and mediation, but a visual like the one you see in **Figure 15.13** can help make the distinction clearer.

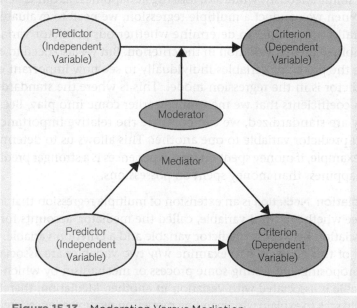

Figure 15.13 Moderation Versus Mediation

Your Turn 15.3

A researcher at a large technology firm wants to study the relationship between money spent on gadgets and happiness. She recruits five participants from a consumer electronics convention and asks them to indicate how much money they spend on gadgets yearly, and has them complete a measure of happiness. Use the data that appear in the table below to answer question 1.

Money Spent on Gadgets ($)	Happiness	Predicted Value of Y Using the Regression Equation ($\hat{Y}$)	Prediction Error $(Y - \hat{Y})$
293.71	3.75		
165.02	4.56		
321.20	6.22		
246.78	6.48		
492.11	5.55		

1. You calculate the regression equation to be $\hat{Y} = .002X + 4.72$. Use the regression equation to solve for the predicted values of Y based on the observed values of X. Then, calculate the amount of prediction error for each observed value of Y.

2. If the sum of squares total for the criterion variable happiness is 5.25, what is the value of the coefficient of determination R^2?

3. What percentage of variation in the criterion variable is predicted by the regression equation?

4. If the sum of squares total for money spent on gadgets is 58,376.39, what is the value of the t-score?

Focus on Open Science: Excluding Data

Our goal as researchers should be to analyze our data in such a way that our results are internally valid (i.e., the independent/predictor variable causes/predicts the changes in the dependent/criterion variable) as well as externally valid (i.e., our results generalize from our sample to the population). To ensure that our results meet these criteria, we sometimes need to exclude observations from our analyses. Most commonly, researchers exclude data when participants fail **attention checks,** which are items embedded in a study to catch participants who aren't paying close attention to the study tasks. For example, in a questionnaire study, researchers may include items that ask participants to respond in a particular way, such as by selecting "slightly disagree" to an item (e.g., "For this item there are several potential responses, but please select 'slightly disagree.'") If the participant responds "strongly agree" (or anything other than "slightly disagree"), it suggests they weren't paying attention to the instructions. It is often best to remove participants who fail attention checks from data analyses because their data are likely of low quality.

attention check an item embedded in a study designed to identify participants who are not paying attention during the study.

It's also common for researchers to remove extreme scores, which we call outliers. We often define outliers as scores that are more than three standard deviations from the distribution's mean. Because outliers are atypical observations, they distort the mean and variability, which can have large impacts on our analyses. For example, in the context of regression, a single outlier can dramatically change the slope and y-intercept of our regression equation.

data plan a document that details all of the ways that researchers will code and analyze their data, including a description of the reasons why participants will be excluded from the final analyses.

While there are perfectly acceptable reasons for excluding data, proponents of open science suggest that researchers create a **data plan,** which is a document that details all of the reasons why the researcher will exclude participants from the final analyses, before they start collecting their data. Data plans are helpful because they force us to determine exclusion criteria prior to having a chance to look at the results. If we wait to make a decision on when to include or exclude data, we may unintentionally base our decision on including/excluding data based on how it impacts the overall results. For example, a research study might exclude outliers, only to discover that the results are no longer statistically significant, at which point the researcher may have second thoughts about removing the outliers.

Overall, without a data plan, researchers have too much flexibility when analyzing their results, which may lead to an increase in false positive findings. Conversely, by having a data plan, and making it public, researchers can demonstrate that they made all data exclusion decisions before beginning the study and that the findings' strength didn't influence those decisions.

Become a Better Consumer of Statistics

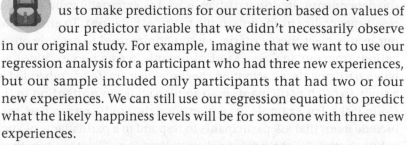

One of the benefits of regression analysis is that it allows us to make predictions for our criterion based on values of our predictor variable that we didn't necessarily observe in our original study. For example, imagine that we want to use our regression analysis for a participant who had three new experiences, but our sample included only participants that had two or four new experiences. We can still use our regression equation to predict what the likely happiness levels will be for someone with three new experiences.

But one thing we need to be cautious about is using our regression model to make predictions that go outside the range of scores that we used to create the regression model. When we use the regression equation to make predictions for values of X that are outside of the range of scores that we used to create the regression equation, we are

Modeling future crop yields accounts for typical rainfall years but would have difficulty projecting for extremes like droughts or floods.

Gerardo Huitrón/iStock/Getty Images

guilty of **extrapolation,** or making predictions that go beyond our data's range. For example, we would be extrapolating from our regression model if we used it to predict the happiness levels of participants who spent $20,000 on new experiences, because the data we used to create our regression model had a range of $136.06 to $886.02 spent on new experiences.

The problem with extrapolation is that regression models assume that variables are linearly associated, but the real association may be nonlinear at extreme values of our predictor variable. For example, let's imagine that we were farmers who wanted to use the amount of rainfall to predict our crop yields. We could construct a linear regression to predict our crop yields, which would be accurate for most typical rainfall levels. But when there are extreme amounts of rainfall, such as during a flood or an extreme drought, all of the crops die and the yield is zero. Our model wouldn't be able to show this, though, because the rainfall levels we used in our model didn't include outlier rainfall levels. So, we need to be somewhat cautious when using regression models to make predictions for extreme values of our predictor variable.

extrapolation an application of a regression equation to make predictions of the criterion variable based on values of predictor that are outside of the range of scores that created the regression equation.

Interpreting Graphs and Charts from Research Articles

A common way for researchers to depict the results of regression analyses is in a scatterplot that includes the line of best fit. By including a scatterplot with their results, not only can researchers show the direction and strength of the linear model, but other scholars can use the regression model to make predictions. For example, in an article looking at the association between income inequality and happiness, researchers (Oishi et al., 2011) presented the scatterplot in **Figure 15.14**.

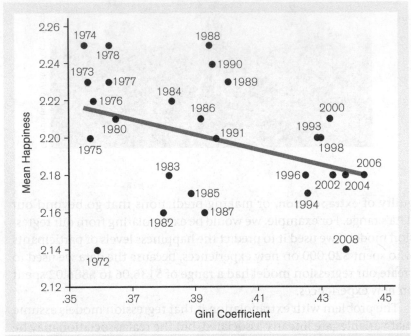

Figure 15.14   Scatterplot (Data from Oishi et al., 2011)

We can clearly see in this scatterplot that income inequality (measured by the Gini coefficient along the x-axis) is negatively associated with happiness (presented along the y-axis), such that in years when there was high income inequality, people reported less happiness. Although the researchers do not give us the exact regression equation, we can use the line of best fit to make predictions for happiness at given levels of inequality. For example, if a given year had an income inequality/Gini coefficient of 0.44, we could predict that people would have a mean happiness score of approximately 2.18.

Statistics on the Job

Of the statistics we cover in this book, regression is likely the one that is most widely used on the job. That's because it is less labor intensive to look for associations between measured variables than to design experiments with manipulated independent variables. Using regression is especially useful in any job where making predictions is useful.

Michael M. Santiago/Getty Images

For example, a strong statistics background is helpful for those in business who want to anticipate market trends, especially those who work with investments and the stock market. For investors, being able to use contributing factors to past stock performance to more accurately anticipate future performance is the key to success (not to mention very large paychecks). Another industry that relies heavily on prediction is insurance. Pricing for insurance policies is rarely one-size-fits-all. Instead, actuaries rely on collecting information about what they are going to insure, and then calculate how much to charge for the policy depending on their predictive models. For this reason, insurance on a sports car costs more than on a minivan, life insurance is cheaper for healthier individuals, and home insurance costs more when the house is further away from the fire department.

Though these are just two examples, it is easy to see how most jobs would benefit from being able to use existing data to make more educated predictions about the future.

Review Questions

1. How are correlations and linear regressions similar? How are they different?

2. If the predictor variable in a regression is manipulated, it can be considered _____. In that situation, the criterion variable could be considered _____.

3. A physician's assistant wants to predict the severity of withdrawal symptoms someone experiences when they attempt to quit smoking based on the average number of cigarettes they smoked the month prior to quitting.
   a. What is the predictor variable?
   b. What is the criterion variable?
   c. What are some potential third variables that could be influencing the results?

4. What are the assumptions of a regression that must be met for it to be appropriate to use?

5. Which is the appropriate statistical test?
   a. A researcher wants to know whether there is a relationship between marital satisfaction and the average duration of fights between partners.
   b. A school administrator wants to predict which children would benefit most from individualized instruction, and wants to use previous grades to make the prediction.
   c. A sales manager wants to know which of four promotions increases sales the most.
   d. A chiropractor wants to know if they can predict how long recovery will take based on the initial reduction of symptoms measured after three weeks of treatment.

6. A professor is interested in determining whether they can predict exam grades based on the number of hours the student studied the content the week before the exam. The professor collects the following data from a random sample of 6 students in class.

Hours Studied (X)	Exam Grade (Y)
10	90
4	55
9	65
11	75
7	80
1	45

   a. Calculate the Pearson r.
   b. Calculate the regression coefficient (b).
   c. Calculate the regression constant (a).
   d. Complete the linear prediction model.
   e. Create a scatterplot of the data and draw the regression line.
   f. Calculate the coefficient of determination (R^2).

7. Your roommate has created a composite depression score that ranges from 1 to 15 and includes factors such as nutrition, amount of time spent in solitary activities, chronic stress, and family history of depression. She believes that she can predict how people will score on more traditional measures of depression based on her composite score. She chooses the Beck Depression Inventory (BDI) and collects data from a random sample of 4 people.

Composite Depression Measure (X)	Beck Depression Inventory (Y)
14	54
6	27
2	24
8	29

   a. Calculate the Pearson r.
   b. Calculate the regression coefficient (b).
   c. Calculate the regression constant (a).
   d. Complete the linear prediction model.
   e. Create a scatterplot of the data and draw the regression line.
   f. Calculate the coefficient of determination (R^2).

8. What is the coefficient of determination? How is it calculated? Can it tell us about cause and effect? Why or why not?

9. Why are there errors in predictions when using a linear regression?

10. Being a member of an honors society (honor society membership) can predict how connected a student feels towards their campus (campus connectedness). But the prediction is only statistically significant if the student is enrolled full time (enrollment status). If they are enrolled part time, then the prediction is not statistically significant. In this example, campus connectedness is a _____ variable, honor society membership is a _____ variable, and enrollment status is a _____ variable.

11. The correlation (r) between offspring survival and group size is 0.20, and the r between offspring survival and food availability is 0.31.
   a. How much variability in offspring survival is predicted by each predictor variable?
   b. How much variability in food availability is predicted by group size?
   c. Which predictor variable does a better job at predicting variability in offspring survival?

12. Explain what is intended by the statement "a model is only as good as the data that go into building it"?

13. Conduct a hypothesis test for the data in Question 6.
   a. What is the population of interest? The comparison population? The sample?
   b. What are the research and null hypotheses?
   c. Build the comparison distribution by calculating the degrees of freedom.
   d. Establish the critical value cutoff (use alpha = .05).
   e. Calculate the t-value.
   f. Decide whether the results are statistically significant and interpret the result.

14. Conduct a hypothesis test for the data in Question 7.

   a. What is the population of interest? The comparison population? The sample?

   b. What are the research and null hypotheses?

   c. Build the comparison distribution by calculating the degrees of freedom.

   d. Establish the critical value cutoff (use alpha = .05).

   e. Calculate the *t*-value.

   f. Decide whether the results are statistically significant and interpret the result.

Key Concepts

applied research, p. 626

attention check, p. 629

basic research, p. 626

coefficient of determination (R^2), p. 615

criterion, p. 600

data plan, p. 630

distribution of slopes, p. 622

extrapolation, p. 631

imperfect association, p. 610

least squares regression line, p. 613

linear prediction model, p. 602

mediation, p. 627

moderation, p. 628

multiple regression, p. 627

perfect association, p. 610

prediction error, p. 610

predictor, p. 600

regression line, p. 600

residual error, p. 612

sum of squares error, p. 612

standard error of the estimate, p. 601

standardized beta coefficient, p. 625

Answers to Your Turn

Your Turn 15.1

1. (a) The *t*-test for independent samples; (b) simple linear regression; (c) simple linear regression; (d) correlation

2. Time spent dreaming is the predictor, while anxiety symptoms are the criterion.

3. 1d; 2a; 3c; 4b

Your Turn 15.2

1. Linear prediction model

2. Step 1: Calculate Pearson (*r*): 0.925

Step 2: Calculate the Regression Coefficient (*b*): 1.821

Step 3: Calculate the Regression Constant (*a*): 1.46

Step 4: Complete the Linear Prediction Model: $\hat{Y} = 1.821(X) + 1.46$

Step 5: Test Out Values of the Predictor Variable (*X*): If someone had zero methods/statistics courses as an incoming student, the predicted performance in the program is 1.46. If someone had four methods/statistics courses, the predicted performance is 8.74.

Graduating PsyD Student	Methods and Statistics GPA (X)	Deviation Score ($X - M$)	Squared Deviation Score ($(X - M)^2$)	Z-Score (Z_x)	Graduating PsyD Student	Program Performance Score (Y)	Deviation Score ($Y - M$)	Squared Deviation Score ($(Y - M)^2$)	Z-Score (Z_y)	Cross-Product of Z-Scores ($Z_x Z_y$)
Jamie	1.00	−0.88	0.77	−1.05	Jamie	4	−0.88	0.77	−0.53	0.56
Foster	3.00	1.13	1.27	1.35	Foster	7	2.13	4.52	1.29	1.74
Traci	1.00	−0.88	0.77	−1.05	Traci	3	−1.88	3.52	−1.14	1.20
Sue	2.00	0.13	0.02	0.15	Sue	6	1.13	1.27	0.69	0.10
Corina	2.00	0.13	0.02	0.15	Corina	5	0.13	0.02	0.08	0.01
Bryce	1.00	−0.88	0.77	−1.05	Bryce	3	−1.88	3.52	−1.14	1.20
Irvin	2.00	0.13	0.02	0.15	Irvin	4	−0.88	0.77	−0.53	−0.08
Rodney	3.00	1.13	1.27	1.35	Rodney	7	2.13	4.52	1.29	1.74
Sum of Scores (ΣX)	15				Sum of Scores (ΣY)	39			$\Sigma Z_x Z_y$	6.48
Number of Scores (N)	8				Number of Scores (N)	8				
Mean (M_x)	$\Sigma X / N$	1.88			Mean (M_y)	$\Sigma Y / N$	4.88			
Sum of Squares (SS_x)	$\Sigma(X - M)^2$	4.88			Sum of Squares (SS_y)	$\Sigma(Y - M)^2$	18.88			
Variance (SD^2)	$SS/(N - 1)$	0.70			Variance (SD^2)	$SS/(N - 1)$	2.70			
Standard Deviation (SD_x)	$\sqrt{SD^2}$	0.83			Standard Deviation (SD_y)	$\sqrt{SD^2}$	1.64			
Z-Score (Z_x)	$(X - M)/SD$				Z-Score (Z_y)	$(Y - M)/SD$				
Pearson's (r)	$\Sigma Z_x Z_y /(N - 1)$		0.925		Slope of the Regression Line / Regression Coefficient (b)		$r(SD_y/SD_x)$			1.821
Y-Intercept / Regression Constant (a)	$M_y - (b \times M_x)$		1.462							
Enter the Predictor Value (X)			0.00		Predicted Value for $Y(\hat{Y})$	$b(X) + a$			1.46	
Enter the Predictor Value (X)			4.00		Predicted Value for $Y(\hat{Y})$	$b(X) + a$			8.74	

3.

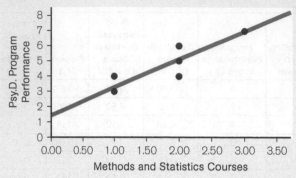

Your Turn 15.3

1.

Money Spent on Gadgets ($)	Happiness	Predicted Value of Y Using the Regression Equation (Y)	Prediction Error ($Y - \hat{Y}$)
293.71	3.75	5.31	−1.56
165.02	4.56	5.05	−0.49
321.20	6.22	5.36	0.86
246.78	6.48	5.21	1.27
492.11	5.55	5.70	−0.15

2. To solve this problem we first need to calculate the sum of squares error. We square each of the prediction errors that we found in the previous problem and add them together: $SS_{Error} = (-1.56^2) + (-.49^2) + (.86^2) + (1.27^2) + (-.15^2) = 2.43 + .24 + .74 + 1.60 + .02 = 5.03$. To solve for R^2, we use the formula $R^2 = 1 - (SS_{Error}/SS_{Total}) = 1 - (5.03/5.25) = .042$.

3. To solve, we multiple R^2 by 100 to convert it into a percentage: $.042 \times 100 = 4.2\%$.

4. To solve for t, we use the formula $t = b/\left(\sqrt{(\Sigma(Y - \hat{Y})^2/(N - 2)}/\sqrt{(\Sigma(X - M_X)^2}\right) = .002/\sqrt{(5.03/3)}./\sqrt{(58376.39)} = .002/(1.29/241.61) = .002/.005 = 0.4$.

Answers to Review Questions

1. They are similar in that they look for a relationship or connection between 2 variables. They differ in that regression seeks to predict the value of one variable based on knowledge of the other (i.e., there is directionality in the relationship). The assumptions of both statistical tests are the same. Finally, in a regression, one variable (the predictor) is sometimes manipulated.

2. An independent variable; a dependent variable.

3. a. Average number of cigarettes smoked the month prior to quitting.
   b. Severity of withdrawal symptoms.
   c. Answers will vary, potential answers might be whether the person has tried quitting smoking before, how many years the person has smoked, and the age of the person.

4. The sample must be randomly selected. The observations must be independent. Both variables (X and Y) need to be normally distributed, as well as the bivariate distribution. Homoscedasticity is necessary. Finally, there needs to be a linear association between the variables.

5.
a. Correlation
b. Regression
c. ANOVA
d. Regression

6.
a. 0.828
b. 3.581
c. 43.266
d. $\hat{Y} = 3.581(X) + 43.266$
e.

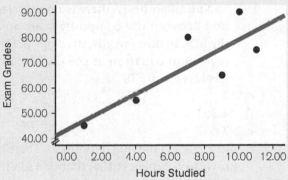

f. 0.686 (68.6%)

7.
a. 0.931
b. 2.573
c. 14.200
d. $\hat{Y} = 2.573(X) + 14.200$

e.

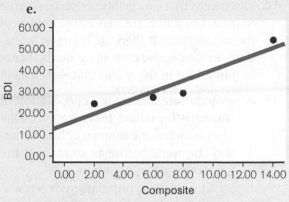

f. 0.867 (86.7%)

8. It is a measure of how good the regression is at predicting the criterion variable. It is the proportion of variability in our criterion variable that is predicted by our regression equation.

To calculate it, you can use the formula:

$$R^2 = 1 - \frac{\Sigma(Y - \hat{Y})^2}{\Sigma(Y - M_Y)^2}.$$

It cannot tell us about cause and effect; a third variable could be present that relates to both the predictor and criterion variables.

9. A linear regression only uses one variable to predict another, and associations between variables in psychology are rarely perfect.

10. Criterion; predictor; moderator

11.
a. 4.00% of variability in offspring survival is predicted by group size; 9.61% of variability in offspring survival is predicted by food availability.
b. This is not able to be determined based on the information given.
c. Food availability does a better job at predicting offspring survival.

12. This means that the quality of the data we use to build the model influences the quality of the model itself. If there are biases or limitations on the data we used, there are also biases or limitations in the model that was created.

13. **a.** Population of interest: a population of students for whom there is no association between the number of hours studied the week before an exam and the grade earned on the exam.

    Comparison population: a population of students like those in our sample for whom there is an association between the number of hours studied the week before an exam and the grade earned on the exam.

    Sample: the 6 students in our sample.

    b. Research hypothesis: the number of hours spent studying content the week before an exam predicts the grade earned on the exam. In other words, the slope of the regression equation at the population level is not zero, $b \neq 0$.

    Null hypothesis: there is no association between the number of hours spent studying content the week before an exam and the grade earned on the exam. In other words, the slope of the regression equation at the population level is zero, $b = 0$.

    c. 4

    d. 2.776

    e. 2.956

    f. Reject the null hypothesis and accept the research hypothesis. There is a significant association between the number of hours spent studying content the week before an exam and the grade earned on the exam.

14. **a.** Population of interest: a population of people for whom there is no association between the composite measure of depression created by your roommate and the BDI.

    Comparison population: a population of people like those in our sample for whom there is an association between the composite measure of depression created by your roommate and the BDI.

    Sample: the 4 people in our sample.

    b. Research hypothesis: the composite score predicts the BDI score a person will obtain. In other words, the slope of the regression equation at the population level is not zero, $b \neq 0$.

    Null hypothesis: there is no association between the composite score and the BDI. In other words, the slope of the regression equation at the population level is zero, $b = 0$.

    c. 2

    d. 4.303

    e. 3.607

    f. Fail to reject the null hypothesis. There is no reason to believe that there is a significant association between the composite score and the BDI.

Sharpen your statistics skills with real-life data! Check out OpenStatsLab.com, created by coauthor Kevin McIntyre, to practice running analyses for real published research studies.

16 Chi-Square Tests

Learning Outcomes

After reading this chapter, you should be able to:

- Explain the key questions that chi-square tests seek to answer.

- Identify similarities and differences between parametric and nonparametric tests.

- Describe when it is appropriate to use a chi-square goodness of fit test and chi-square test of independence.

- Conduct hypothesis tests using the chi-square goodness of fit test and chi-square test of independence.

- Describe the underlying chi-square logic that compares expected results to observed results in terms of how well the model "fits" the data.

- Interpret what chi-square results can and cannot tell us.

"Have you ever noticed?" It's a classic question for many of life's curious observations. For example, comedian Jerry Seinfeld once pointed out, "Ever notice when you blow in a dog's face he gets mad at you? But when you take him in a car he sticks his head out the window."

If you're looking for a great way to start a conversation, asking "Have you ever noticed?" will surely get things going. Have you ever noticed how people who post how awesome their relationship is always seem to break up soon after? Have you ever noticed how you never see baby pigeons or squirrels around? Or ever noticed as soon as you learn a new word you never heard of before you start hearing it all the time?

Insights often come from observation. For anyone interested in delving into human behavior, people-watching is where it all starts. While your school's dining hall or cafeteria may not be the best place for fine dining, it is a wonderful people-watching spot. From your favorite table, you and your friends notice how people walking together tend to match their strides or how people reflexively fix their hair and adjust their appearance right before they enter the crowded part of the dining hall. You also observe how everyone seems to be on their phone, but it seems women are more likely to have white smartphones.

Statistics for Life

Lunch table observations can generate interesting insights. However, we can't automatically accept our observations as completely accurate statements of fact. That is, just because it seems like women own more white smartphones, it may not actually be true.

Importantly, we know about confirmation bias, or that once we form a conclusion, we tend to seek out and notice information that agrees with us (Nickerson, 1998). Though confirmation bias can be intentional, it also happens without our awareness and can shape our

Are women more likely to have a white smartphone?

beliefs about groups of people based on their race, sexual orientation, or gender. Despite large-scale studies with thousands of participants failing to find meaningful male–female differences, those beliefs persist (Zell et al., 2015). Yet, people think they see differences all the time. This is why we need to test our observation more thoroughly.

Where Do the Data Come From?

 So far we've done some very limited observations on campus. It's possible that this white phone phenomenon is unique to our school, or applies only to college students. To see if women's proclivity toward white phones is a real pattern, we should observe it in another setting with a different group of people to see if it generalizes. In other words, we want to see if the pattern we observe on campus replicates elsewhere.

We decide to set up in a local mall that is busy during the day. To make sure we avoid any potential bias in who we notice, we set up rules for our observation. We will pick the busiest entrance and only make note of women's phone color as they leave since that is when many people will naturally have their phone out. We decide ahead of time that we'll code the first 100 women we see who have their phone out. After spending a few hours loitering at the mall entrance near the food court, here is what that data look like (see **Figure 16.1**). Note that because we collected data about so many people, the ". . ." indicates that we also had data from participants 7–95 that we aren't showing.

Participant	Phone Color
1.00	White
2.00	White
3.00	White
4.00	Black
5.00	Black
6.00	White
. . .	. . .
96.00	Black
97.00	White
98.00	White
99.00	Black
100.00	White

Figure 16.1 Women's Phone Color at the Mall

Chi-Square: What We're Trying to Accomplish

We have data from 100 different participants, and categorical information (i.e., white vs. black) about their phone color. Looking at that data, it does not appear that we could do much to analyze it. Based on what we've learned so far, the most we could do with this is create a frequency table.

One key difference is that we did speculate about the phone color frequencies we would find. When we have one nominal variable from a single population and want to see how the reality of what we observe compares to our preconceived expectations, we use the **chi-square goodness of fit test (χ^2).** What if we have two variables? Well, we'll talk about another type of chi-square test to analyze two nominal variables in the Statistics for Research section of this chapter. For now, we'll focus on just a single nominal variable.

We have actually had a fair amount of experience with statistics focusing on a single variable. The Z-test, single sample t-test, and t-test for dependent means, all analyze data from one source. The key difference is that those previous tests all analyzed data for variables that used either interval or ratio measurement scales. Here, with the chi-square goodness of fit test, our variable is categorical and uses a nominal measurement scale. That is, we only have frequencies of those groups (i.e., how many phones are either black or white), instead of the degree to which a phone is a color.

When we think of "fit" in terms of the chi-square goodness of fit test, we need to be careful. Here, "fit" does not involve any prediction, but instead has to do with how well our sample matches the population. If it matches well, and there is a good "fit," in terms of hypothesis testing, we fail to reject the null hypothesis. In other words, our sample is no different from the population. However, if we have a poor "fit" between our sample and the population, it indicates that our sample is significantly different from the population, allowing us to reject the null during hypothesis testing.

Chi-square is also different from t-tests because it is a type of **nonparametric test,** which is any test that does not rely on assumptions about the population, typically when we have nominal- or ordinal-scale data. For example, we would not assume the underlying distribution for smartphone color is normal. This is common when we have categorical data because there is no expectation that categories will generally fall around a mean (in fact, it is hard to know what a mean of a categorical variable would even tell us). Contrast this with previous parametric tests like the t-test for independent samples or analysis of variance that have continuous (interval or ratio scale) variables as the outcome. In those cases we assume that most scores will be near the outcome's mean, with increasingly fewer scores as we move away from the mean (i.e., a normal distribution).

We can use chi-square goodness of fit in two different design situations:

1. Data from an observation, survey, and so on, where the researcher wants to see if outcomes on a categorical variable

chi-square goodness of fit test (χ^2) statistical test we use when we have a nominal or categorical variable from a single population and want to see how the reality of what we observe compares to our preconceived expectations.

Want to review the single sample t-test, and t-test for dependent means? SEE CHAPTER 9.

nonparametric test any test that does not rely on assumptions about the population, typically when we have nominal or ordinal scale data.

differ from what we might expect by chance in the population (e.g., are women more likely to have white smartphones than black smartphones?).

2. Reported data where we want to see if statements or claims about outcome frequencies are valid (e.g., a graduate program claims that 60% of master's students in a counseling program get their first choice for internship placement, 30% get their second choice, and 10% get their third choice, and we want to see if that actually happens in this year's cohort).

In each case, we're interested in how the data we actually observe matches up with what we thought would happen for a categorical (nominal-scale) outcome.

Chi-Square Goodness of Fit: How Does It Work?

In life, we all have expectations. Seeing how that compares to reality can often be illuminating. Among YouTubers, there is a popular format where vloggers show some idealized version of how a life experience may transpire. Next, they reveal how things actually turned out. The contrast is often startling and amusing. This is essentially what we're doing with chi-square analyses. Ahead of time we establish the expected frequency for an outcome, then compare that to the frequency we actually observe (see **Figure 16.2**). By comparing expected and observed frequencies, we learn whether what we saw happen is truly different from what we anticipated happening.

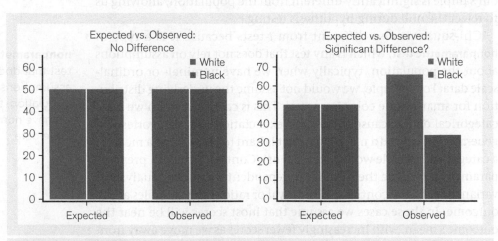

Figure 16.2 Expected Versus Observed Outcomes

But, what should we expect? When in doubt, we should anticipate that there is nothing special happening—in other words, the null hypothesis. For frequencies, that would be that any impact on our variable is random. That is, there should be no clear pattern or difference in the frequencies. If we observe 100 women at the mall, 50 should have a white phone and 50 a black phone. Similarly, if we were flipping a coin, we would expect it to turn up half heads and half tails, and with dice rolls we would expect each of the six numbers to occur at the same frequency.

Mathematically, we'll determine the expected frequency (E) by dividing the sample size (N) by the number of categories of our nominal variable ($N_{Categories}$, which is sometimes symbolized k).

$$E = \frac{N}{N_{Categories}}$$

So, as we mentioned a moment ago, if we have a sample of 100 women, and are observing two categories of color (black and white), the expected frequency for each color would be equal to $\frac{100}{2}$ or 50. If, instead, we were looking at the frequency of three colors of phone (black, white, and gray), the expected frequency for each color would be equal to $\frac{100}{3}$ or 33.33.

The chi-square goodness of fit examines whether what we expected matches what we actually observed. If we find a discrepancy between what we thought was going to happen and what actually happens, we can't automatically conclude that there was a difference. To do that, we need to use our chi-square statistic to determine if what we're observing is likely to have happened by chance, or if what we observed was unlikely to have occurred by chance and suggests a pattern.

Finding the Fit The basis of the chi-square goodness of fit is the comparison of expected outcomes to observed outcomes. First, we need to remember that we aren't interested in each individual person (e.g., what color phone the 10th woman we observed had). Instead, we are focusing on the overall frequencies of the outcome from the entire group (e.g., how many women had white phones vs. black phones). Then we turn to our chi-square goodness of fit formula to find the difference between observed frequency (O) and the expected frequency (E). Once we have the difference score ($O - E$), we square it. We need to square these values because otherwise they would add up to zero. This should feel familiar because it fairly parallels what we do when calculating squared deviations.

The final step is to divide our squared expected-observed difference scores by the expected frequency of that category: $(O - E)^2/E$.

We do that in order to put the distance between our expectation and observation in the proper context. That is, if we find a difference between the expected and observed frequency of 1, that would be small if our expected frequency for that category was 50. However, if our expected frequency for the category was only 2, a difference of 1 is more substantial. Now that our squared differences between observed and expected are weighted, we sum up the results, $\Sigma(O - E)^2/E$, giving us our chi-square goodness of fit statistic.

$$\chi^2 = \Sigma \frac{(O - E)^2}{E}$$

Your Turn 16.1

1. For each of the following, indicate the appropriate statistic.

a. A researcher knows that the average TikTok user stays on the app for an average of 89 minutes per day. She wants to see if clients who follow a meditation program stay on less than the average.

b. A researcher wants to see if babies prefer looking at someone in person or on a video screen.

c. The president of your school wants to see if alumni are more likely to donate to the school before or after they receive a free university window cling in the mail.

d. The English Department wants to test the belief that reading more classic works (e.g., Shakespeare) is associated with average annual income.

e. A baseball card company promised that 10% of the cards in every pack will feature a rookie/first-year player.

2. Fritz is in charge of testing the ball machines at lottery headquarters. The machine he needs to check has 10 balls, numbered 1–10, that blow around in a chamber, until someone presses a button and a single ball gets selected. For the lottery to be valid, the results should be random. Say Fritz tests the machine 100 times.

a. What should be the results if the outcomes truly are random?

b. What might the results look like if the 3 ball was weighted differently and more likely to get selected?

Hypothesis Testing with Chi-Square Goodness of Fit: How Does It Work?

Even though the chi-square is a nonparametric test, the good news is that the hypothesis test's steps for nonparametric analyses are all the same as what we did before.

Step by Step: Chi-Square Goodness of Fit Hopefully by now, these steps feel very familiar.

Step 1: Population and Hypotheses The way we think about populations with the chi-square goodness of fit, we have a population that matches our expectations and one that does not. Of the two populations, the one that matches expectations would indicate that nothing special is happening. That would be the comparison population (or the situation when our null hypothesis is true). Our population of interest is the case where we think there is something unique taking place. In other words:

Population of Interest: Women with smartphones similar to those we observe at the mall.

Comparison Population: Women from the general population who are just as likely to have a white smartphone as a black smartphone.

Sample: The 100 women we observe at our local mall's exit.

Next, we need to make a prediction about what we think will happen. Generally speaking, our research hypothesis is always the same in chi-square: our two populations are different. Similarly, the null hypothesis is always that our two populations are the same.

Research Hypothesis (H_1): The women who we observe at the mall will have a different frequency of white versus black smartphones compared to women in the general population who are just as likely to have a white smartphone as a black smartphone.

Null Hypothesis (H_0): The women who we observe at the mall will be just as likely to have a white smartphone as a black smartphone, similar to women in the general population.

Step 2: Build Comparison Distribution Similar to how we handled comparison distributions for *t*-tests and analysis of variance, chi-square has a different comparison distribution for each degree of freedom (see **Figure 16.3**).

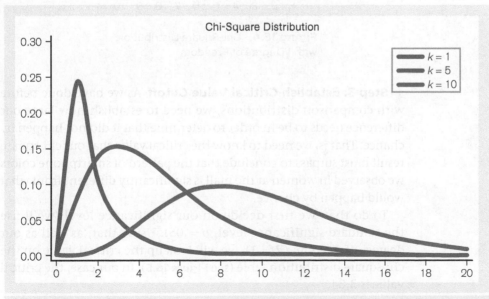

Figure 16.3 Comparison of Several Chi-Square Distributions

The one wrinkle here is that our degrees of freedom are not based on the number of participants. Instead, we focus on the number of different categories (sometimes symbolized as k) ($df = N_{Categories} - 1$). In our study, we have two categories (white phones and black phones), so our degrees of freedom are:

$$df = N_{Categories} - 1 = 2 - 1 = 1.$$

We might also notice another difference between the chi-square distribution and the normal curve and t-curves: the chi-square is a positively skewed distribution. A big reason for this is that we square the differences between the observed and expected frequencies, so chi-square can never produce a negative number. This means that the chi-square distribution must start at zero and go only in the positive direction.

Now that we know the degrees of freedom, we can find the correct shape (see **Figure 16.4**).

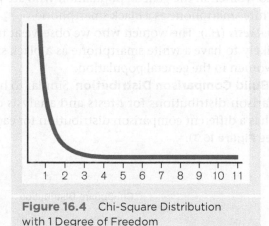

1 2 3 4 5 6 7 8 9 10 11

Figure 16.4   Chi-Square Distribution with 1 Degree of Freedom

Step 3: Establish Critical Value Cutoff As we have done before with comparison distributions, we need to establish how large our difference needs to be in order to determine that it did not happen by chance. That is, we need to know the critical value that our chi-square result must surpass to conclude that the pattern of smartphone colors we observed in women at the mall is significantly different from what would happen by chance.

To do that, we first decide on our significance level (we'll use the standard significance level, $p = .05$). Using that, as well as our degrees of freedom ($df = 1$), we will look up the critical value on the chi-square distribution table (see **Figure 16.5**). In our case, the critical value is 3.84.

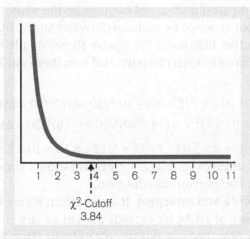

	Significance (Alpha) Level		
df	.10	.05	.01
1	2.706 →	3.841	6.635
2	4.605	5.992	9.211
3	6.252	7.815	11.345
4	7.780	9.488	13.277
5	9.237	11.071	15.087
6	10.645	12.592	16.812
7	12.017	14.067	18.475
8	13.362	15.507	20.090
9	14.684	16.919	21.666
10	15.987	18.307	23.209

Figure 16.5 Chi-Square Distribution Table Preview

Thus, the chi-square we calculate must be greater than 3.84. Our last step is indicating the critical value on our comparison distribution, which you can see in **Figure 16.6**.

χ^2-Cutoff
3.84

Figure 16.6 Chi-Square Distribution with Critical Value Cutoff

Step 4: Determine Sample Results First, we have to look at our data from all 100 observations and get a count of how many white and black phones we saw (i.e., the observed frequency). We'll save you a step here and count them for you: there were 66 white smartphones and 34 black smartphones. Those numbers are different from the 50/50 split we expected based on chance, but is it different enough to be significant? For that, we need to calculate the chi-square goodness of fit (see **Figure 16.7**).

Category	Observed (*O*)	Expected (*E*)	Difference Score (*O* − *E*)	Squared Difference Score (*O* − *E*)^2	Squared Difference Weighted by Expected Frequency (*O* − *E*)^2/*E*
White	66	50	16.00	256.00	5.12
Black	34	50	−16.00	256.00	5.12
Number of Categories (*N_{Categories}*)	2			Sum (Σ)	10.24
Degrees of Freedom (*df*)	(*N_{Categories}* − 1)	1			
Chi-Square (χ^2)	Σ[(*O* − *E*)^2/*E*]	10.24			

Figure 16.7 Computations for Chi-Square Goodness of Fit

Here, we compare our observed frequencies (66 white and 34 black phones) with our expected frequencies (50 white and 50 black phones), by calculating the difference. We square those, divide them by the expected frequency in each category, and sum them up. That gives us the following:

White Phones = $(O - E)^2/E = (66 - 50)^2/50 = (16)^2/50 = 256/50 = 5.12$
Black Phones = $(O - E)^2/E = (34 - 50)^2/50 = (-16)^2/50 = 256/50 = 5.12$

Now we add those up, $\Sigma(O - E)^2/E = 5.12 + 5.12 = 10.24$, which is our chi-square goodness of fit test (χ^2). Next, we should show where our χ^2 falls on the comparison distribution.

Step 5: Decide and Interpret It is clear from **Figure 16.8** that our sample's χ^2 score of 10.24 far exceeds the chi-square cutoff score of 3.84. Decision time. Because our sample's results (Step 4) exceed the critical value (Step 3), we are able to reject the null hypothesis (H_0) that the two populations are the same. If we are able to reject the null, we can also say that we are able to support the research hypothesis (H_1) that the women who we observe at the mall will have a different frequency of white versus black smartphones compared to women in the general population.

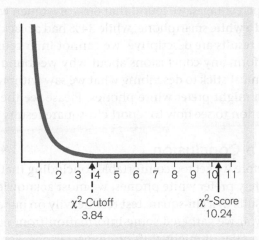

Figure 16.8 Sample Results on the Comparison Distribution

For a demonstration of the hand calculations involved in chi-square goodness of fit, watch this video.

 HAND CALCULATION VIDEO TUTORIAL: To learn more, check out the video Performing Chi-Square Goodness-of-Fit.

SPSS Video Tutorial: Chi-Square Goodness of Fit

Let's see how we would perform the chi-square goodness of fit analysis using SPSS by watching this video.

 SPSS VIDEO TUTORIAL: To learn more, check out the video Chi-Square Goodness-of-Fit.

Communicating the Result

Based on an offhand observation at the dining hall, we thought that women were more likely to own a white smartphone than a black smartphone. To test that out, we decided to test our hunch in another group, so we headed out to the mall to make observations of women's phones. Based on those observations and a subsequent chi-square goodness of fit test, women do appear to be more likely to own a white phone than a black phone.

When communicating results from frequencies, it is better to give percentages than the frequency count. In our case, since we had 100 participants, the numbers are the same, but we would still want to convey the percentages: we found that 66% of women we observed at the mall had a white smartphone, while 34% had a black smartphone. Because our results are descriptive, we cannot infer cause and effect, nor can we form any conclusions about why we found this pattern. Instead, we must stick to describing what we saw without speculating why women might prefer white phones. Please see the Statistics for Research section to see how to report chi-square results in APA Style.

Forming a Conclusion

 Before we get too comfortable concluding that women definitely prefer white phones, we must acknowledge that our results in a chi-square test rely heavily on our expectations. In our study, if we gathered some information from manufacturers about phone sales, it might shift our expectations. For example, we might now expect that 60% of women would have a white phone and 40% a black phone (see **Figure 16.9**). When we use those new expectations, our results would no longer be significant.

Category	Observed (O)	Expected (E)	Difference Score (O − E)	Squared Difference Score (O − E)²	Squared Difference Weighted by Expected Frequency (O − E)²/E
White	66	60	6.00	36.00	0.60
Black	34	40	−6.00	36.00	0.90
Number of Categories ($N_{Categories}$)	2			Sum (Σ)	1.50
Degrees of Freedom (df)	($N_{Categories}$ − 1)	1			
Chi-Square (χ^2)	Σ[(O − E)²/E]	1.50			

Figure 16.9 Computations for Chi-Square Goodness of Fit — Alternate Expectations

For this reason, when establishing expectations in a study, whenever possible we need to carefully justify them based on previous results, or theoretical considerations. Also, because our observations focused only on women, we cannot simply conclude that if women prefer white, men must prefer black. In fact, men may also prefer white smartphones. Therefore we should try to extend our findings by conducting 100 additional observations at the mall, this time focusing on men's phones to see if they are more likely to have a black phone.

Your Turn 16.2

You are an employee at the LaLa Lime store, and your manager asks for your thoughts on the upcoming order of new leggings. She has to pick how many pairs of each color to get for the store and thinks it is best to order the same number of each of the season's new colors (Morning Mist-Gray, Periwinkle, Smokey Blush-Pink, and Camouflage). You disagree and think some colors will be more popular than others (especially Morning Mist and Camouflage). Your manager ignores your ideas (typical) and orders the same number of each color. Convinced that you know what you're talking about, and hoping to elevate your role and pay, you want to show your manager that you were correct about customers' color preference. Use the steps of hypothesis testing to see if you were right based on what color leggings the first 200 customers purchase.

1. Step 1: Population and Hypotheses.

   a. What would the populations be?

   b. What would the hypotheses be?

2. Step 2: Build a Comparison Distribution.

   a. What does the comparison population look like? What shape is it?

   b. How many degrees of freedom does our study have?

3. Step 3: Establish Critical Value Cutoff. What is the critical value cutoff score?

4. Step 4: Determine Sample Results. Based on the first 200 customers, you see that they have purchased 81 Morning Mist-Gray, 44 Periwinkle, 11 Smokey Blush-Pink, and 64 Camouflage.

   a. What are the expected frequencies for each color?

   b. Calculate a chi-square goodness of fit.

   c. Show the result on the comparison distribution, including the critical value.

5. Step 5: Decide and Interpret. What is the appropriate conclusion?

Statistics for Research

For better or worse, most romantic relationships eventually end. According to the Centers for Disease Control (CDC) 630,505 people in the United States got divorced in 2020 (CDC, 2020) and countless others in nonmarital relationships decided to call it quits. Given the prevalence of relationship dissolution and the impact that breakups have on people, it's not surprising that lots of research has examined the variables that predict what contributes to relationships ending (see Le et al., 2010, for a meta-analysis).

There are several common strategies for breaking up with a romantic partner. These include the open confrontation strategy, where a partner directly communicates their desire to end the relationship; the de-escalation strategy, where a partner gradually ends the relationship by being less responsive to their partner over time; the mediated communication strategy, where a partner uses impersonal forms of communication, such as text messages or email, to end the relationship; and the ghosting strategy, where a partner cuts off all forms of personal and impersonal communication, acting as though the ex-partner doesn't exist (e.g., Collins & Gillath, 2012; Koessler et al., 2019).

Does breakup strategy influence whether a couple remains friends after breaking up?

faidzzainal/E+/Getty Images

But what happens next can be surprising. After breaking up, many former romantic partners decide to stay friends. Whether it be because they have children together, because they want to keep their ex-partner as a source of emotional support, or because they have a lot of positive memories of good times with their former partner, research shows that approximately 59% of people have a friend who was previously a romantic partner (Griffith et al., 2017). Note, however, that this is for all of our friends and not the likelihood any single romantic relationship will end and shift to friendship.

One variable that could affect whether people stay friends after breakup is the strategy they used to end the relationship. Perhaps if people use a more personal and positive approach, such as the open confrontation strategy or the mediated communication strategy, people may be more likely to remain friends afterwards. In contrast, former partners may be less likely to remain friends when using the de-escalation or ghosting strategies.

Let's imagine that we wanted to determine whether breakup strategy is associated with whether or not a romantic couple decides to stay friends after breaking up. When we want to look at the association between variables, we have performed a correlation or regression analysis. But, that was when our variables were all interval- or ratio-level variables. Now, both of our variables (breakup strategy and friendship status) are nominal variables, so we can't use correlation or regression because they require interval- or ratio-level data. As we learned in the first half of the chapter, an approach for analyzing nominal variables is the chi-square goodness of fit test, but we use that test when we have only one nominal variable.

Here in the Statistics for Research section, we have two nominal variables (see **Figure 16.10**). So, we need to learn a new form of chi-square test called the **chi-square test of independence,** which examines whether two nominal variables are associated with each other (or are independent from one another). Not only are we going to learn about

chi-square test of independence a type of statistical analysis we use to determine whether two nominal variables are associated (or independent).

	Chi-Square Goodness of Fit Test	Chi-Square Test of Independence
Sample Type	Single Sample from Population	Single Dependent Sample
Key Question	Is the sample different from the population?	Is there an association between variables?
Type of Data	Single nominal variable	Two nominal variables
Key Comparison	Observed sample variable to theoretical population	Two observed variables from the sample to each other
Degrees of Freedom	$df = N_{Categories} - 1$ or $df = k - 1$	$df = (N_{Rows} - 1) \times (N_{Columns} - 1)$

Figure 16.10 Chi-Square Test Comparison

this new chi-square test, but we'll also discuss contingency tables, and hypothesis testing with the chi-square test of independence.

Where Do the Data Come From?

To determine whether breakup strategy is associated with whether or not people remain friends, imagine we recruited 130 people who had recently experienced a breakup. We could ask them to report which of the four breakup strategies the initiator (i.e., the partner who ended the relationship) used. We could also have participants indicate whether they are still friends with their former partner (yes or no). Simple and straightforward.

Once we have collected our data, we should summarize it in a **contingency table** (also called a *crosstabulation table*), which is a table where the categories of one variable comprise the rows of the table, and the categories of the other variable comprise the columns. The cells of the table present the observed frequencies for each combination of rows and columns. For example, we could present our data in a contingency table like in **Figure 16.11**.

contingency table (also called a *crosstabulation table*) a table used to depict the data in a chi-square test of independence. The rows of the table represent the categories of one nominal variable and the columns represent the categories of a second nominal variable.

	Friendship Status		
Breakup Strategy	**Not Friends**	**Stay Friends**	**Total**
Open Confrontation	17	27	44
De-escalation	11	7	18
Mediated Communication	31	20	51
Ghosting	14	3	17
Total	73	57	130

Figure 16.11 Contingency Table for Breakup Strategy and Friendship Status

As we can see, when a partner used an open confrontation strategy during the breakup, 17 respondents did not stay friends with their former partner, but 27 did. Similarly, when a partner used de-escalation, 11 participants did not remain friends with their partner, but 7 did. In addition to presenting the observed frequencies, our contingency table also presents the row and column totals (also called marginal totals). Thus, out of the 130 observations, 44 used open confrontation, 18 used de-escalation, 51 used mediated communication, and 17 used ghosting. Similarly, 73 respondents did not remain friends with their ex, while 57 did.

Presenting our data in a contingency table not only helps us keep our data organized, but it will help us perform our calculations. Indeed, we will need to use both the observed frequencies and the row and column totals when we calculate the chi-square test score. In addition, these contingency tables help us describe our overall design. Just as we did with factorial ANOVA in Chapter 13, we will name our design according to the number of categories for each of our variables.

In this case, our first variable is breakup strategy, and it has four levels. Our second variable is friendship status, and it has two levels. Thus, our design, and contingency table, is a four-by-two (4×2) chi-square test of independence. If we decided to include a fifth breakup strategy in our study, we would have a 5×2 design. If we decided to add a third variable, marital status, with two levels (married vs. not married), we would have a $4 \times 2 \times 2$ (four types of breakup strategies, 2 levels of marital status, and 2 levels of friendship status). A useful aspect of this naming convention for our research designs is that if we multiply the number of levels per variable together, the product is the total number of cells in our contingency table ($4 \times 2 = 8$ cells).

Chi-Square Test of Independence: What We're Trying to Accomplish

 Now that we have our data organized, we need to determine whether there is an association between breakup strategy and friendship status. In essence, we want to see whether the frequency of observations across the levels of one of our variables is contingent upon the levels of the other variable. In other words, does the tendency to remain friends following breakup depend upon which breakup strategy was used?

How are we going to test this? We can take the same general approach that we used to solve for the chi-square goodness of fit. In particular, we will assess the extent to which our observed data fit or match what we would expect if there were no association between our variables. If the difference between what we observe and what we expect is small, it suggests that the variables are independent.

For example, if breakup strategy is independent from (i.e., unrelated to) friendship status, then our observed frequencies should match our expected frequencies. In that case, our observed data will not differ from the pattern we should expect if there is no association between our variables. However, if breakup strategy is associated with friendship status, the observed data should not match what we would expect if there is no association. In other words, we should see a large difference between our observed data and our expected data.

Chi-Square Test of Independence: How Does It Work?

So, we want to compare what we observed to what we expect if the two variables are independent. But, what should we expect? We might just take a simple approach and take our sample size divided by the total number of cells in our contingency table and make all of our expected frequencies equal. This approach would work, but only if each of the row totals were equal and each of the column totals were equal. In other words, if people used each of the breakup strategies equally often, and people were just as likely to remain friends as not.

Unfortunately, research is typically more complicated than that. First of all, breakup strategies likely do not occur with equal frequencies. Do we really think that ghosting (a relatively new and uncommon breakup strategy) should occur at the same rate as open confrontation or de-escalation? It seems unlikely. Second, do we really expect half of all breakups to end in friendships? As much as that might be a nice sentiment, it too seems unlikely. Instead, it's probably the case that more former partners choose to not remain friends after breaking up than stay friends. So how are we going to generate expected frequencies if we don't think that each of the categories will occur with equal frequencies?

The answer is to consider how likely the various categories are separately and then combine their likelihoods together. To do this, we start by converting our observed frequencies for each row and column into a relative frequency.

Relative frequency tells us how common a particular response is out of total number of responses. So, how likely is each strategy in the context of all breakup strategies? Well, open confrontation occurred 44 times out of the 130 total breakups, which equates to a relative frequency of .3384 (44/130 = .3384). We can multiply this by 100 to think about it as a percentage (.3384 × 100 = 33.84%). Thus, in our sample, participants report that their breakups occurred via open

Need a refresher on relative frequency? SEE CHAPTER 2.

confrontation 33.84% of the time. We can take the same approach to compute the relative frequency for

de-escalation (18/130 = .1384 or 13.84%),

mediated communication (51/130 = .3923 or 39.23%), and

ghosting (17/130 = .1307 or 13.07%).

After solving for the relative frequencies of the breakup strategies, we need to do the same for whether or not people stay friends. In our sample, the relative frequency for

staying friends (57/130 = .4384 or 43.84%),

not staying friends (73/130 = .5615 or 56.15%).

Figure 16.12 presents all of the relative frequencies for each of the rows and columns in our contingency table.

Breakup Strategy	Friendship Status			Relative Frequency
	Not Friends	Stay Friends	Total	
Open Confrontation	17	27	44	.3384
De-escalation	11	7	18	.1384
Mediated Communication	31	20	51	.3923
Ghosting	14	3	17	.1307
Total	73	57	130	
Relative Frequency	.5615	.4384		

Figure 16.12 Contingency Table for Breakup Strategy and Friendship Status with Relative Frequencies

Now that we know the relative frequencies for breakup strategies and friendship status separately, we need to look at them together. Essentially, we need to know the joint probability for each particular breakup strategy when paired with each level of friendship status. To get that, we first need the joint probability—which, you will recall from Chapter 5, was the probability of two events occurring at the same time—and we calculate it by multiplying the probabilities of each separate event together. So, if we want to know the probability of a particular observation using the open confrontation strategy and staying friends, we would multiply the probability of using open confrontation (.3384) by the probability of staying friends (.4384) to get an overall probability of .1483 (.3384 × .4384 = .1483). Thus, we should expect 14.83% of our sample to use an open confrontation strategy and stay friends.

There's just one final thing to do to determine our expected frequencies. To convert this joint probability to an expected frequency, we need to multiply it by our total sample size. This will tell us the number of participants that we should expect to see in a particular cell. Thus, the formula for the expected frequency of a particular cell is as follows: $(rf_{Row} \times rf_{Column}) \times N$, where rf_{Row} is the relative frequency of the row to which the cell belongs, rf_{Column} is the relative frequency of the column to which the cell belongs, and N is the total sample size.

$$E = (rf_{Row} \times rf_{Column}) \times N$$

So, to calculate the expected frequency for the open confrontation/ stay friends cell, we would multiply the joint probability .1483 by our total sample size of 130, which comes out to be 19.29 (.1483 × 130 = 19.29). Thus, if there is no association between breakup strategy and friendship status, we should expect to see 19.29 observations in the open confrontation/stay friends cell of our contingency table. **Figure 16.13** presents all of the observed frequencies and calculations of the expected frequencies.

Breakup Strategy	Friendship Status		Total	Relative Frequency
	Not Friends	**Stay Friends**		
Open Confrontation	17 (.3384 × .5615) × 130 = 24.70	27 (.3384 × .4384) × 130 = 19.29	44	.3384
De-escalation	11 (.1384 × .5615) × 130 = 10.10	7 (.1384 × .4384) × 130 = 7.89	18	.1384
Mediated Communication	31 (.3923 × .5615) × 130 = 28.64	20 (.3923 × .4384) × 130 = 22.36	51	.3923
Ghosting	14 (.1307 × .5615) × 130 = 9.54	3 (.1307 × .4384) × 130 = 7.45	17	.1307
Total	73	57	130	
Relative Frequency	.5615	.4384		

Figure 16.13 Contingency Table for Breakup Strategy and Friendship Status with Observed and Expected Frequencies

Finding the Fit Just like with the chi-square goodness of fit test, now that we know our expected frequencies, we want to determine whether our observed data fit these expected frequencies or do not fit. Recall that the expected frequencies tell us what we should observe if there is no association between our variables. Thus, if our observed data do not match the expected frequencies, it tells us that our variables are associated.

To find the fit, we will use the exact same formula as we did for the chi-square goodness of fit test. We will find the difference between the observed and expected frequencies $(O - E)$ for each cell in our contingency table, square this quantity $(O - E)^2$, and divide by the expected frequency: $(O - E)^2/E$. We will do this for each cell in the table and then add the results together, $\Sigma(O - E)^2/E$.

$$\chi^2 = \Sigma \frac{(O - E)^2}{E}$$

Hypothesis Testing with Chi-Square Test of Independence: How Does It Work?

Is breakup strategy associated with whether people stay friends after breakup? To determine this, we will need to conduct a hypothesis test. As with the other tests that we have learned, finding that two variables are associated for a sample is interesting, but we really want to know whether the evidence in our sample is strong enough to make conclusions about the population. To make these conclusions, we need to perform a hypothesis test.

Assumptions of Chi-Square For both the chi-square goodness of fit test and chi-square test of independence, we must satisfy several assumptions in order for our tests to work properly.

1. *We have measured each variable at the nominal level.* Both versions of the chi-square test examine nominal-level variables.
2. *Scores are independent from one another.* No participant's responses should influence any other responses. For this reason, chi-square must be between-participants.
3. *The expected frequencies for all cells are 1 or greater.* If any of the expected frequencies are less than 1, our ability to estimate the p-value of our test statistic will be in doubt. In general, we should aim for expected frequencies that are at least 5. Essentially, this assumption states that there is a minimum number of participants that our study should have, based on the number of categories of our variable(s). If we calculate our expected frequencies and find that we have any that are less than 1, or some that are less than 5, we should collect more data or collapse/combine our variables so that they have fewer levels.

For example, if we had expected frequencies that were too small for our breakup study, we might consider combining the mediated communication and ghosting strategies, because both of these strategies involve technology in some way. Doing so would increase the size of the expected frequencies.

Step by Step: Chi-Square Test of Independence Before we can perform our hypothesis test, we want to specify exactly what we are testing.

Step 1: Population and Hypotheses In chi-square, we will compare people like those in our sample that are similar to the general population that would exist if the null hypothesis is true.

Population of Interest: People who have recently experienced a breakup.

Comparison Population: People in the population for whom there is no association between breakup strategy and friendship status.

Sample: The 130 participants who have recently experienced a breakup.

So, to test our hypothesis, we will compare the people in our sample to what the population would look like if there was no association. Next, we need to establish our research and null hypotheses. These take the same format for all chi-square test of independence analyses. Under the null hypothesis, we will state that there is no association between our variables. In other words, the observed frequencies will match the expected frequencies. Our research hypothesis will therefore state that there is an association between our variables, and that the observed frequencies will not match the expected frequencies. Because we are able only to evaluate whether or not there is an association between our variables, all chi-square test of independence analyses are two-tailed. In other words, we do not need to specify exactly how the observed and expected frequencies will not match.

Research Hypothesis (H_1): There will be an association between breakup strategy and friendship status, such that some breakup strategies will be associated with an increased likelihood of remaining friends following breakup, whereas others will be associated with a decreased likelihood of remaining friends.

Null Hypothesis (H_0): Breakup strategy and friendship status are independent. There is no association between them.

Step 2: Build Comparison Distribution As we learned in the first half of this chapter, the chi-square distribution changes shape based on the degrees of freedom. We also learned that the degrees of freedom come from our variables' number of categories, rather than on the sample size.

With a bit of logic, this makes sense. For most tests, we are comparing means, and the individual scores determine what the means are. If we change any of the scores within a variable, we change the mean. So, if we know that there are three scores in a distribution, 1, 2, and x (an unknown score), and we know the overall mean is 2, we can determine that the missing score must be 3. So, here we would have $N-1$ degrees of freedom.

But that's not how the chi-square tests work. Here, we compare the number of scores in variables' different categories. So, if we know that there were 200 observations overall, and these observations fall into two categories, one of which has 150 observations and the other is unknown, we can deduce that the other category must have 50 observations. If there are three categories, one of which has 150 observations, we can't say for sure how many observations fall into either of the remaining categories. This is why we base the degrees of freedom for chi-square on the number of categories, rather than on the sample size.

For the chi-square test of independence, we have two variables, each with a certain number of categories. To solve for the overall number of degrees of freedom, we multiply the number of rows minus one by the number of columns minus one, like so: $df = (N_{Rows}-1) \times (N_{Columns}-1)$. For our study of breakup strategies and friendship status, we have four rows (each representing the various breakup strategies) and two columns (representing whether or not people stay friends). Thus, our degrees of freedom are: $df = (N_{Rows}-1) \times (N_{Columns}-1) = (4-1) \times (2-1) = 3$.

Step 3: Establish Critical Value Cutoff Figure 16.14 presents the critical values for different chi-square curves. We have established

	Significance (Alpha) Level		
df	.10	.05	.01
1	2.706	3.841	6.635
2	4.605	5.992	9.211
3	6.252	7.815	11.345
4	7.780	9.488	13.277
5	9.237	11.071	15.087
6	10.645	12.592	16.812
7	12.017	14.067	18.475
8	13.362	15.507	20.090
9	14.684	16.919	21.666
10	15.987	18.307	23.209

Figure 16.14 Chi-Square Distribution Table Preview

that the relevant comparison distribution is a chi-square curve with three degrees of freedom. We can establish the critical value cutoff by scrolling down the rows until we reach the row for three degrees of freedom and scroll across the columns until we reach the column for an alpha of .05. As we can see, our critical value is 7.81. This represents the chi-square value that corresponds to a probability of .05, so we know that if our chi-square score is equal to or greater than 7.81, the probability of our observed data is less than our alpha, and we should therefore reject the null hypothesis.

Step 4: Determine Sample Results To start, we need to make sure that we have satisfied the assumptions of the chi-square test. The first assumption states that the variables in our analysis must be measured at the nominal level. Both breakup strategy and friendship status are nominal, so we satisfy this assumption. The second assumption states that the observations are independent, and they are. Our study is between-participants and the participants did not interact with each other. The final assumption states that our expected frequencies must be greater than 1 (and ideally greater than 5). Looking back at Figure 16.14, we can see that all of the expected frequencies are greater than 5 (the smallest being 7.45), so we have satisfied this assumption.

Given that we satisfied the assumptions, we are ready to calculate the chi-square score. For each of the cells in our contingency table, we will calculate the amount of mismatch between the observed and expected frequencies, using the formula $(O-E)^2/E$. We'll then sum up all of these values.

Based on our calculations provided in **Figure 16.15,** our chi-square test of independence test score (χ^2) is 10.85.

Step 5: Decide and Interpret Because our test score of 10.85 is greater than our critical value of 7.81, we can reject the null hypothesis and conclude that there is an association between breakup strategy and friendship status.

Now that we know there is an association, we want to figure out why. So, we'll compare the observed and expected frequencies. Given that there are eight possible comparisons to make (one for each of the eight cells in our contingency table), we should start by looking for the largest difference between observed and expected frequencies. Doing so will help us understand the nature of the association more easily.

Here, we can see that the largest difference between what we observed and what we expected (if there was no association) is for the open confrontation and friendship status cells, with a

Cell	Observed (O)	Expected (E)	Difference Score (O − E)	Squared Difference Score (O − E)²	Squared Difference Weighted by Expected Frequency (O − E)²/E
Open Confrontation/ Not Friends	17.00	24.70	−7.70	59.29	2.40
Open Confrontation/ Stay Friends	27.00	19.29	7.71	59.44	3.08
De-escalation/Not Friends	11.00	10.10	0.90	0.81	0.08
De-escalation/Stay Friends	7.00	7.89	−0.89	0.79	0.10
Mediated Communication/ Not Friends	31.00	28.64	2.36	5.57	0.19
Mediated Communication/ Stay Friends	20.00	22.36	−2.36	5.57	0.25
Ghosting/Not Friends	14.00	9.54	4.46	19.89	2.09
Ghosting/Stay Friends	3.00	7.45	−4.45	19.80	2.66
Number of Rows (N_{Rows})	4.00			Sum (Σ)	10.85
Number of Columns ($N_{Columns}$)	2.00				
Degrees of Freedom (df)	$(N_{Rows}-1)(N_{Columns}-1)$		3.00		
Chi-Square (χ^2)	$\Sigma[(O-E)^2/E]$		10.85		

Figure 16.15 Computations for Chi-Square Test of Independence

difference between the observed and expected frequencies of 7.7. We can see that when a partner used open confrontation to break up, more couples remained friends afterwards (and by extension, fewer were not friends) than we would expect if there were no association.

The next-largest difference was for ghosting, where more couples did not stay friends after breakup than we would expect, with a difference between the observed and expected frequencies of 4.5. The third-largest difference was for mediated communication, where couples were slightly less likely to remain friends than we would expect, with a difference between observed and expected frequencies of 2.4. Finally, there is not much of a difference between the observed and expected frequencies for de-escalation, suggesting that this breakup strategy is not associated with a change in likelihood of staying friends.

Ready to see a demonstration of the hand calculations involved in the chi-square test of independence? Watch this video.

HAND CALCULATION VIDEO TUTORIAL: To learn more, check out the video Performing the Chi-Square Test of Independence.

SPSS Video Tutorial: Chi-Square Test of Independence

Let's see how we would perform the chi-square test of independence analysis using SPSS by watching this video.

SPSS VIDEO TUTORIAL: To learn more, check out the video Chi-Square Test of Independence.

Communicating the Result

After interpreting our output, we want to write up our results. Because the chi-square test of independence is more uncommon than other tests that we have learned, it's a good idea to explain why this is the appropriate test. We then want to describe the test results and our interpretation of them. Thus, our results paragraph might look something like this:

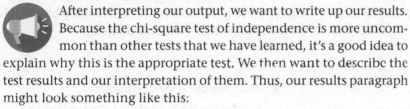

Because breakup strategy and friendship status were both measured at the nominal level, we performed a 4 (breakup strategy: open confrontation, de-escalation, mediated communication, ghosting) × 2 (friendship status: not friends, stay friends) chi-square test of independence to determine if breakup strategy was associated with friendship status. The results of this test were significant, $\chi^2(3) = 10.85$, $p = .013$. The pattern of results suggest that open confrontation resulted in greater likelihood to remain friends, while ghosting resulted in less likelihood of remaining friends. Mediated communication and de-escalation results were similar to what we would expect if there was no association.

Forming a Conclusion

When we have nominal-level variables, we are limited in the types of analyses that we can perform. With the chi-square test of independence, we are able to examine whether two nominal variables are associated (or independent). This approach allowed us to test the association between the strategy used to end a relationship and the likelihood that the couple remained friends after dissolution.

In many ways, the chi-square test of independence is similar to a correlation analysis, and forming a conclusion is no different. Just as we can't make cause-and-effect conclusions when interpreting correlational results, we generally shouldn't do that for chi-square results, either. In particular, it could be that people who were on more friendly terms to begin with at the time of their breakup were more amenable to open confrontation, while people who had a particular hostility toward their ex-partner were more likely to use ghosting. In other words, the chi-square test of independence doesn't tell us which of our variables is the cause and which is the effect. Similarly, there could be third variables that contribute to the association.

That said, there is a situation in which it might be possible to make a cause-and-effect interpretation for the results of a chi-square test of independence. If the experimenters manipulated one of the variables and randomly assigned participants to a condition, it could be possible to make causal conclusions (which we didn't do here).

Your Turn 16.3

A developmental psychologist is interested in determining whether children's attachment styles are associated with their parent's parenting styles. To test this, he categorizes children into one of four attachment styles (secure, anxious-ambivalent, anxious-avoidant, and disorganized) based on a behavioral assessment. He then categorizes each child's primary caregiver into one of three parenting styles (authoritative, authoritarian, and permissive) based on a battery of questionnaires.

1. Based on the description provided, what type of analysis should the researcher conduct? Why?

2. Construct a generic contingency table for the current study. How many rows are present? How many columns?

For the next several problems, use the steps of hypothesis testing to determine whether there is an association between attachment style and parenting style.

3. Step 1: Population and Hypotheses.

a. What are the populations involved in this study?

b. What is the research hypothesis? What is the null hypothesis?

4. Step 2: Build a Comparison Distribution. Determine the number of degrees of freedom. Based on this, what is the appropriate comparison distribution?

5. Step 3: Establish Critical Value Cutoff. What is the critical value cutoff score, using alpha = .05.

6. Step 4: Determine Sample Results. The researcher collects data on 315 children and presents the observed frequencies in the contingency table:

Attachment Style	Parenting Style		
	Authoritative	Authoritarian	Permissive
Secure	68	16	33
Anxious-Ambivalent	28	45	9
Anxious-Avoidance	12	18	20
Disorganized	16	29	21

(Continued)

a. Calculate the row and column totals.

b. Calculate the relative frequencies for each row and column.

c. Calculate the expected frequencies for each cell.

d. Determine whether all of the expected frequencies are greater than 1.

e. Calculate the chi-square test of independence.

7. Step 5: Decide and Interpret.

a. Make a decision regarding the null hypothesis.

b. Interpret the results.

Focus on Open Science: Combatting Science Fraud

Throughout this textbook, we have discussed the reasons for the move toward open science. We noted that there was a replication crisis in psychology where a high percentage of findings were not replicated in subsequent studies. We also discussed various issues that call into question the legitimacy of the scientific process, including HARKing (i.e., hypothesizing after results known), the file drawer problem, and p-hacking. Along the way, we've discussed potential solutions to these problems, such as preregistration of hypotheses and posting research materials and data online.

Of course, one thing we want to recognize is that no matter what procedures we put in place to encourage transparency and promote high-quality research practices, there will always be people who try to cut corners and engage in shoddy science. There will also be people who engage in outright fraudulent behavior, including the creation of fake data and the manipulation of real data to show a desired result. These types of **data fraud** will likely continue to exist (hopefully in smaller and smaller numbers) no matter what safeguards are put in place to help prevent them.

> ## Statistically Speaking
>
> My friend from high school is trying to sell supplements. They claim to have done research showing it works, but I'm pretty sure they made it up and are engaging in data fraud.

data fraud deliberate creation of false data, or manipulation of otherwise genuine data, to ensure a particular outcome of a data analytic test occurs.

There will always be fraudulent actors in science, as there is in every profession, but we can take concrete steps to minimize the frequency of fraud and its effects.

Illia Uriadnikov/Alamy Stock Photo

To combat these forms of science fraud, we need to develop the ability to distinguish among high-quality and low-quality (and possibly fraudulent) findings. To that end, we should have more confidence in findings that have the following five characteristics:

1. *Data plan and hypotheses are preregistered.*
2. *Materials and data are available for analysis by others.*
3. *Results are based on large samples.*
4. *Not only are results statistically significant, but effect sizes suggest the effect is important.*
5. *Findings replicate across time and across different researchers.*

Conversely, we should have less confidence in findings that have these five characteristics:

1. *Findings from a single study are surprising and counterintuitive.*
2. *Findings are based on small samples.*
3. *Hypotheses are not preregistered.*
4. *The researchers have conflicts of interest.*
5. *The results just barely reach statistical significance.*

Become a Better Consumer of Statistics

As consumers of statistics, we need to consider what information we know and what information we don't know. Throughout this chapter, we have learned that in order to analyze a nominal variable, we need to know both the observed frequencies for a variable and the expected frequencies. We can't simply compare the observed frequencies to each other, as they tell us only part of the relevant information. Yet, often in everyday life, people try to interpret observed frequencies alone.

To understand this further, let's imagine that we are reading a research article about a psychological intervention for couples who are having problems with their relationships and considering breaking up. Fifty couples went through the therapy program, and the researchers tracked the number of couples that stayed together versus the number who broke up (see **Figure 16.16**). The researchers report the following data:

	Relationship Status	
	Break Up	Stay Together
Therapy Program	15	35

Figure 16.16 Therapy Program Contingency Table

We might be tempted on the basis of this information to conclude that the therapy program helps couples stay together, because 20 more couples stayed together ($N = 35$) than broke up ($N = 15$). But do we really have enough information to make this conclusion? No. We are seeing only one side of the story. To properly evaluate the effectiveness, we also need to have a sense of what to expect if people didn't go through the therapy program.

What we need is a comparison group. Let's imagine that we collected data from couples ($N = 360$) that did not go through the therapy program (see **Figure 16.17**), and we observed the following results:

	Relationship Status	
	Break Up	**Stay Together**
Therapy Program	15	35
No Therapy	150	210

Figure 16.17 Therapy Program Contingency Table

Is the therapy program effective? Hopefully, it is obvious that we can't compare the observed frequencies to each other (e.g., 35 vs. 210). Doing so would fail to take into account the fact that there were many more couples who did not undergo therapy than there were who did. The only way to evaluate whether the therapy program is effective is to compare the observed frequencies to the expected frequencies. Because the expected frequencies take into account the likelihood of being in each condition, they provide a fair comparison for us to evaluate whether the observed frequencies are higher or lower than we would expect if there were no effect.

The take-home message is that sometimes the evidence in front of us is not enough to make a conclusion. We need to consider the missing information, the information we would need to make a fair comparison.

Interpreting Graphs and Charts from Research Articles

When presenting the results of chi-square analyses, it's not uncommon for researchers to include the contingency table that presents the observed frequencies for each of the combination of variables. Let's take a look at an example from a research article that examined how people react to learning that their partners' have faults (Murray & Holmes, 1999). The authors proposed that there are three reactions that people might make: they might see the fault as an isolated characteristic and not make links to other aspects of the partner (e.g., my partner is messy); they might see the fault as linked to other faults (e.g., my partner is messy because they are not a systematic person); or they might see a fault as linked to a virtue (e.g., my partner is messy, but it's because they are so creative). The researchers looked to see whether these interpretations of their partners' faults were associated with various outcomes, such as their level of well-being (measured as either high or low). The researchers predicted that people who are able to link faults to virtues should be most likely to display high levels of well-being.

To test this prediction, the authors conducted a chi-square test of independence, because the authors measured both the interpretation of the fault and well-being at the nominal level. They presented their results in the contingency table in **Figure 16.18**.

Table 5						
Nature of Attributes Linked to the Partner's Greatest Fault as a Function of Well-Being, Positive Illusions, and Stability						
	Well-being composite		**Illusions composite**		**Stability**	
Nature of link	**Low**	**High**	**Low**	**High**	**No**	**Yes**
No link made	17	19	22	14	13	23
Fault linked to fault	22	22	24	20	15	29
Fault linked to virtue	15	41	16	40	20	36
$\chi^2(2, N = 136)$	6.70*		11.46**		0.04	
*p < .05, **p < .01.						

Figure 16.18 Contingency Table (Data from Murray & Holmes, 1999)

As we can see in the table, the results for the association between interpretation of the partners' fault (called Nature of link) has three categories (No link made, Fault linked to fault, and Fault linked to virtue) and Well-being composite has two levels (Low, High). For this analysis, we can see that the chi-square test score (based on 2 degrees of freedom and a total sample size of 136) was significant, $\chi^2 = 6.70$, $p < .05$. The contingency table presents only the observed frequencies, not the expected frequencies, which makes the results a bit harder to interpret. But, using this information plus the information that the authors provide in the results section of the paper, we can see that people who tended to link their partners' faults to virtues were more likely to be high in well-being than would be expected if there were no association.

Statistics on the Job

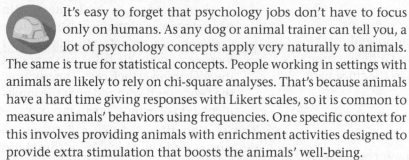

It's easy to forget that psychology jobs don't have to focus only on humans. As any dog or animal trainer can tell you, a lot of psychology concepts apply very naturally to animals. The same is true for statistical concepts. People working in settings with animals are likely to rely on chi-square analyses. That's because animals have a hard time giving responses with Likert scales, so it is common to measure animals' behaviors using frequencies. One specific context for this involves providing animals with enrichment activities designed to provide extra stimulation that boosts the animals' well-being.

To help boost animals' well-being, caretakers often incorporate enrichment activities to provide animals with extra stimulation. These are often things like toys (e.g., a ball that elephants can kick around), new challenges (e.g., placing food in feeders that require animals to solve a puzzle), or activities (e.g., a new sliding board in the dog kennel) that are incorporated into the animals' living space. To see what they like best, you can set up two different types of enrichment and observe the animals over time to see which they choose. In this case, if there is no preference, we'd expect the animals to select the two enrichment options equally. However, if we observe them choosing one more frequently, we can be sure to provide animals with more of that enrichment type. Anyone who works at a pet store, at a zoo, in animal research, or as an animal trainer should have a vested interest in their animals, and learning what types of enrichment are best is a great step toward doing that.

Andrew Linscott/Alamy Stock Photo

You may not expect the person caring for the animals at your local zoo to be using statistics, but chances are they do.

Review Questions

1. How is the key question addressed by the chi-square goodness of fit test different from the key question addressed by the chi-square test of independence?

2. In your own words, explain what a chi-square test does.

3. What are the two key differences between parametric and nonparametric tests?

4. Identify the general category of statistic (parametric or nonparametric) that you would want to use in the following situations, and then identify the specific statistic that you would use (e.g., *t*-test, ANOVA, chi-square test of independence).

   a. A student at a local high school believes that people are more likely to wear school colors (versus non-school colors) to sporting events.

   b. A waitress is wondering whether the method of payment (cash versus card) influences the amount of tip a person leaves after a meal.

   c. An academic dean wants to know whether the frequency of academic integrity violations (e.g., cheating, plagiarism) is higher in required courses (versus electives) and whether it is also influenced by the difficulty of the course (low, moderate, high).

   d. A clinician believes that the incidence of other learning disorders (e.g., dyslexia) is higher in individuals diagnosed with Attention-Deficit/Hyperactivity Disorder (ADHD) than in those not diagnosed with ADHD.

   e. A volunteer at a youth club is interested in which type of reinforcement (verbal praise versus physical rewards) result in a greater increase of desirable behaviors amongst the adolescents at their club. They measure the behaviors before and after the implementation of reinforcement protocols.

5. The section titled *Statistics for Research* describes a study in which friendship status and breakup strategy are the variables of interest. Could both individuals from a relationship be included in the study? Why or why not?

6. Why are the degrees of freedom in a chi-square test calculated based on the number of categories in the variable(s) rather than based on sample size?

7. Why are all chi-square tests of independence two-tailed?

8. Someone in the United States needs a blood transfusion every 2 seconds. There are 4 main types of blood (A, B, AB, and O). Since more people can receive blood from an O type donor, donation campaigns target people with that blood type more than other blood types. If the campaigns are successful, the proportion of donors with O type blood should be different from the proportion of people in the general population with O type blood. In the general population of the United States, 42% of people have A type blood, 10% have B type blood, 4% have AB type blood, and 44% have O type blood. You obtain data from your local blood donation clinic on the last 1,000 donors and find the following:

Blood Type	Frequency
A	380
B	100
AB	30
O	490

a. What type of analysis is appropriate?
b. What are the populations involved in the study?
c. What are the hypotheses?
d. Determine the number of degrees of freedom.
e. Establish the critical value cutoff.
f. Determine the sample results.
   i. Calculate the expected frequencies for each blood type.
   ii. Determine whether all of the expected frequencies are greater than 1.
   iii. Calculate the chi-square.
g. Make a decision regarding the null hypothesis.
h. Interpret the results.

9. In the section titled *Become a Better Consumer of Statistics*, a study is described that evaluates the association between relationship status (break up, stay together) and the efficacy of a psychological intervention for couples who are having problems with their relationships and are considering breaking up (therapy protocol: therapy program, no therapy).
a. What type of analysis is appropriate?
b. What are the populations involved in the study?
c. What are the hypotheses?

d. Determine the number of degrees of freedom.
e. Establish the critical value cutoff.
f. Determine the sample results.
   i. Calculate the row and column totals.
   ii. Calculate the relative frequencies for each row and column.
   iii. Calculate the expected frequencies for each cell.
   iv. Determine whether all of the expected frequencies are greater than 1.
   v. Calculate the chi-square.
g. Make a decision regarding the null hypothesis.
h. Interpret the results.

10. Why do we need to square the difference scores when calculating a chi-square analysis? How is this similar to the process of calculating a standard deviation?

11. The larger the difference between the observed and expected frequencies, the _____ likely we are to reject the _____ hypothesis and find support for the _____ hypothesis.

12. How do the concepts of reverse causality and the third variable problem (introduced in Chapter 14) apply to a chi-square test of independence?

 ## Key Concepts

chi-square goodness of fit test (χ^2), p. 643

chi-square test of independence, p. 654

contingency table, p. 655

data fraud, p. 667

nonparametric test, p. 643

Answers to Your Turn

Your Turn 16.1

1. (a) single sample *t*-test; (b) chi-square goodness of fit; (c) *t*-test for dependent samples; (d) correlation; (e) chi-square goodness of fit

2. (a) Each number (1–10) comes up exactly 10 times. (b) The 3 ball would get selected 19 times and all the other balls would get selected 9 times. The exact numbers here don't matter, but the answer should reflect the 3 ball coming up many more times than the others (which should be relatively evenly selected).

Your Turn 16.2

1. (a) Population of Interest: Customers similar to those who shopped in our LaLa Lime store. Comparison Population: Customers from the general population who are equally as likely to buy any of the 4 color options. Sample: The first 200 women who purchase the spring season's leggings in our store. (b) Research Hypothesis: The customers who buy leggings in our store will buy more of some legging colors than others compared to customers in the general population who are just as likely to buy each color. Null Hypothesis: The customers who buy leggings are equally likely to buy all four colors of leggings, similar to women in the general population.

2. (a) It is a chi-square distribution with a shape ultimately determined by the degrees of freedom. (b) Our degrees of freedom are: $df = N_{Categories} - 1 = 4 - 1 = 3$.

3. For a chi-square distribution with 3 degrees of freedom and using the standard significance level ($p = .05$), the critical value is 7.81 (which we get from the chi-square distribution table).

4. (a) 50 for each; (b) See table below.

4. (c)

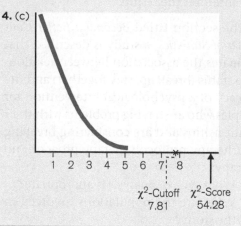

χ^2-Cutoff
7.81

χ^2-Score
54.28

Category	Observed (O)	Expected (E)	Difference Score (O − E)	Squared Difference Score (O − E)²	Squared Difference Weighted by Expected Frequency (O − E)²/E
Morning Mist-Gray	81	50	31.00	961.00	19.22
Periwinkle	44	50	−6.00	36.00	0.72
Smokey Blush-Pink	11	50	−39.00	1521.00	30.42
Camouflage	64	50	14.00	196.00	3.92
Number of Categories ($N_{Categories}$)	4			**Sum (Σ)**	54.28
Degrees of Freedom (*df*)	($N_{Categories} - 1$)		3		
Chi-Square (χ^2)	$\Sigma[(O - E)^2/E]$		54.28		

5. Our sample's χ^2 score of 54.28 far exceeds the chi-square cutoff score of 7.81. We are able to reject the null hypothesis (H_0) that the two populations are the same. We are also able to support the research hypothesis (H_1) that the customers who bought leggings at our store will have a different frequency of purchasing the four colors of leggings compared to women in the general population who are equally likely to buy each color.

Your Turn 16.3

1. The researcher should conduct a chi-square test of independence because he is testing whether two nominal variables are associated with one another.

2.

Attachment Style	Parenting Style		
	Authoritative	**Authoritarian**	**Permissive**
Secure			
Anxious-Ambivalent			
Anxious-Avoidance			
Disorganized			

3. (a) Population of Interest: children similar to those in the study. Comparison population: children for whom attachment style is independent from the primary caregiver's parenting style. (b) Research Hypothesis: Attachment style will be associated with parenting style. Null Hypothesis: Attachment style will be independent from parenting style.

4. $df = (N_{Rows} - 1) \times (N_{Columns} - 1) = (4 - 1) \times (3 - 1) = 6$. The appropriate comparison distribution is a chi-square distribution with six degrees of freedom.

5. The critical value is 12.59.

6. (a) See table below.

Attachment Style	Parenting Style			Row Total
	Authoritative	**Authoritarian**	**Permissive**	
Secure	68	16	33	117
Anxious-Ambivalent	28	45	9	82
Anxious-Avoidance	12	18	20	50
Disorganized	16	29	21	66
Column Total	124	108	83	315

(b)

Attachment Style	Parenting Style			Row Total	Relative Frequency
	Authoritative	**Authoritarian**	**Permissive**		
Secure	68	16	33	117	.37
Anxious-Ambivalent	28	45	9	82	.26
Anxious-Avoidance	12	18	20	50	.16
Disorganized	16	29	21	66	.21
Column Total	124	108	83	315	
Relative Frequency	.39	.34	.26		

(c-e)

Cell	Observed (O)	Expected (E)	Difference Score (O − E)	Squared Difference Score (O − E)²	Squared Difference Weighted by Expected Frequency (O − E)²/E
Secure/Authoritative	68	46.06	21.94	481.49	10.45
Secure/Authoritarian	16	40.11	−24.11	581.50	14.50
Secure/Permissive	33	30.83	2.17	4.72	0.15
Anxious-Ambivalent/Authoritative	28	32.28	−4.28	18.31	0.57
Anxious-Ambivalent/Authoritarian	45	28.11	16.89	285.13	10.14
Anxious-Ambivalent/Permissive	9	21.61	−12.61	158.92	7.36
Anxious-Avoidant/Authoritative	12	19.68	−7.68	59.02	3.00
Anxious-Avoidant/Authoritarian	18	17.14	0.86	0.73	0.04
Anxious-Avoidant/Permissive	20	13.17	6.83	46.59	3.54
Disorganized/Authoritative	16	25.98	−9.98	99.62	3.83
Disorganized/Authoritarian	29	22.63	6.37	40.60	1.79
Disorganized/Permissive	21	17.39	3.61	13.03	0.75
Number of Rows (N_{Rows})	4.00			**Sum (Σ)**	56.12
Number of Columns ($N_{Columns}$)	3.00				
Degrees of Freedom (df)	$(N_{Rows} - 1)(N_{Columns} - 1)$		6.00		
Chi-Square (χ^2)	$\Sigma[(O - E)^2/E]$		56.12		

7. (a) A chi-square test of independence score (χ^2) is 56.12, which is greater than the critical value of 12.59, thus we reject the null hypothesis. (b) Looking at the differences between the observed and expected frequencies, the results reveal that securely attached children were more likely to have authoritative parents and less likely to have authoritarian parents than would be expected if there were no association between attachment style and parenting style. Also, there was a greater frequency of anxious-ambivalent children having authoritarian parents than was expected.

Answers to Review Questions

1. The key question of the chi-square goodness of fit test is whether the observed frequencies in a sample are different from the expected frequencies in a population on a single variable. The key question of a chi-square test of independence is whether there is an association between two (or more) variables.

2. We need a chi-square analysis to statistically evaluate whether the difference between the observed and expected frequencies are greater than what would be expected by chance.

3. Nonparametric tests are used with nominal measurement scale variables, while parametric tests are used with interval or ratio measurement scale variables.

   Nonparametric tests do not make assumptions about the population (e.g., that the underlying distribution is normal) while parametric tests do make assumptions about the population.

4. a. Nonparametric, chi-square goodness of fit test
   b. Parametric, *t*-test for independent samples
   c. Nonparametric, chi-square test of independence
   d. Nonparametric, chi-square test of independence
   e. Parametric, *t*-test for related samples

5. No they could not both be included in the study because the scores within a couple would not be independent of each other.

6. This is because we compare the number of observations in different categories rather than the mean of individual scores. In the case of a chi-square, if we know the frequency of the observations in all but one category and we know the overall number of observations, then we can calculate the number of scores in the remaining category.

7. They are all two-tailed because we can only evaluate whether there is an association between the variables. We cannot specify how the observed and expected frequencies will not match.

8. a. Chi-square goodness of fit
   b. Population of Interest: blood donors similar to those who donated after the most recent donation campaign at our local blood donation center.

      Comparison Population: blood donors from the general population in the United States who match the frequency of blood types in the general population.

      Sample: the most recent 1,000 blood donors who donated blood at our local blood donation center.
   c. Research Hypothesis: Donors will have some blood types more frequently compared to people in the general population.

      Null Hypothesis: Donors will have the same distribution of blood types as the general population.
   d. 3
   e. 7.81
   f. i. A type blood: expected frequency = 420

      B type blood: expected frequency = 100

      AB type blood: expected frequency = 40

      O type blood: expected frequency = 440
      ii. All expected frequencies are greater than 1
      iii. 11.99
   g. Reject the null hypothesis that the blood donors are the same as the general population. Support the research hypothesis that the blood donors will have a different distribution of blood types than the general population.
   h. The largest difference between expected and observed frequencies is that there are more O type donors than expected. The next largest difference is that there are fewer A type donors than expected.

9. **a.** Chi-square test of independence
   b. Population of Interest: couples similar to those in the study.

   Comparison Population: couples for whom relationship status is independent of therapy protocol.

   Sample: the 410 participants who were considering breaking up.
   c. Research Hypothesis: Relationship status will be associated with therapy protocol.

   Null Hypothesis: Relationship status will be independent of therapy protocol.
   d. 1
   e. 3.84
   f. **i.** Therapy protocol: therapy program = row total = 50

   Therapy protocol: no therapy = row total = 360

   Relationship status: stay together = column total = 245

   Relationship status: break up = column total = 165
   ii. Therapy protocol: therapy program = relative frequency = 0.1220

   Therapy protocol: no therapy = relative frequency = 0.8780

   Relationship status: stay together = relative frequency = 0.5976

   Relationship status: break up relative frequency = – 0.4024
   iii. Therapy program/stay together = expected frequency = 29.88

   Therapy program/break up = expected frequency = 20.12

   No therapy/stay together = expected frequency = 215.12

   No therapy/break up = expected frequency = 144.88
   iv. All expected frequencies are greater than 1
   v. 2.48
   g. Fail to reject the null hypothesis (2.48 < 3.84)
   h. Couples who participate in the therapy protocol are not more likely to stay together than those who do not participate in the therapy protocol.

10. The scores need to be squared; otherwise, they will sum to 0. When calculating a standard deviation, we need to square the deviation scores before calculating the sum of squares.

11. More; null; research

12. In most chi-square tests we cannot make cause-and-effect conclusions because the test does not tell us which variable is the cause and which is the effect. However, if a researcher manipulates one of the variables and the researcher uses random assignment, then causal conclusions could be possible. In terms of the third variable problem, like a correlation, there could be variables not measured in the study that influence the association.

 OPEN STATS LAB

Sharpen your statistics skills with real-life data! Check out OpenStatsLab.com, created by coauthor Kevin McIntyre, to practice running analyses for real published research studies.

A

Mathematics Refresher

Learning Outcomes

After reading this Appendix, you should be able to:

● Perform basic mathematical operations.

● Recognize common mathematical symbols and notations.

● Solve equations using the proper order of operations.

● Reorganize equations to solve for unknown quantities.

A s we mentioned in Chapter 1, the math involved in a statistics course is more straightforward than many students think it is. At the same time, we don't want to discount the feelings you might be experiencing as you start on your statistical journey. It may also have been a while since you were enrolled in a math class, so a refresher of some of the concepts may be helpful. Regardless of your current comfort level, reviewing this material is likely to be beneficial. If you find it basic, then consider it a boost to your confidence. If you find it difficult, then consider it a well-timed lesson that will help set you up for success in the course.

We include a *Statistics Readiness Quiz* to help you evaluate your current familiarity with the material. This quiz is broken down into sections to help you understand which concepts you may need to review. Each question evaluates slightly different things, so for the most accurate results, don't skip any questions. After the quiz, we provide a general review of the material, worked examples, and a second quiz. Review the content that you struggled with, or that you want further information about. Then take the second quiz and see how you do after reviewing the material. If you continue to struggle, reach out to your instructor(s) or a tutor for some additional help.

Remember, your ability to use math and understanding of statistical concepts are not finished products! This course is all part of the process to increase your capacity to work with numbers in ways that will help you in research, at work, and in your life. Always keep in mind, you are taking this course to learn the material; you are not expected to know it already. So, let's get started.

Math Skills Readiness Quiz

The best way to evaluate if you are ready to perform the math in this textbook is to take a quick quiz that requires you to use various math skills. Try to solve each of the problems listed below. Note that the problem sets get a bit trickier as you move on. You might want to have a calculator handy.

A.1

1. $-5^2 =$ _____
2. $-2 - (-7) =$ _____
3. $-10 \times -8 =$ _____
4. $16 \div -4 =$ _____
5. $\sqrt{81} =$ _____

A.2

6. $1 + (7 - 18)(2) =$ _____
7. $8 - 2^2 \div 4 =$ _____
8. $-24 \div 6 + 3 \times 10 =$ _____
9. For the set of scores $X = 14, 5, 9$
   $\Sigma(X - 10) + 100 =$ _____
10. For the set of scores $X = 3, 15, 21, 9$
    $\Sigma(3 - X)^2 \div 8 =$ _____

A.3

11. Solve for X.
    $(X - 23)^2 - 1 = 24$
    $X =$ _____
12. Solve for X.
    $32/(7 + X) = 4$
    $X =$ _____
13. Solve for X.
    $Y = mX + b$
    $X =$ _____
14. Solve for X.
    $p = \sqrt{\dfrac{D^2}{X}}$
    $X =$ _____
15. Solve for X.
    $\sqrt{X - 211} = 256$
    $X =$ _____

To see how you did, compare your responses to the answers that are listed at the end of this appendix. For any problems that you solved incorrectly, try to figure out what went wrong.

Were there symbols that you weren't familiar with and didn't know how to use? Was it an order of operations mistake? If so, the next two sections of this mathematics refresher will help. The first focuses on mathematical symbols and notations. The second focuses on order of operations.

A.1 Mathematical Symbols and Notations

The basic mathematical symbols that are used in this book are listed in the table below. Many are likely familiar to you, but a quick review of them may be helpful, especially if you haven't used them recently. For example, students sometimes have difficulty working with negative numbers and with exponents, so we include some worked examples below.

Another tip: make sure to familiarize yourself with the calculator(s) you will use when taking a test. You want to avoid surprises on the exams you take in your statistics course. We've had students confused on an exam because the output of their calculator doesn't match the answers listed on their exam. You don't want to find yourself in a situation, for example, where your calculator produces a fraction when you need a decimal (or vice versa).

Symbol	Meaning	Example
+	Addition	$7 + 3 = 10$
−	Subtraction	$7 - 3 = 4$
×, ( )	Multiplication	$7 \times 3 = 21, 7(3) = 21$
÷, /	Division	$7 \div 3 = 3.5, 7/3 = 3.5$
>	Greater than	$7 > 3$
<	Less than	$3 < 7$
≥	Greater than or equal to	$7 \geq 3, 7 \geq 7$
≤	Less than or equal to	$3 \leq 7, 3 \leq 3$
≠	Not equal to or not the same as	$7 \neq 3$
Σ	Sum a set of numbers	$x = 1, 3, 5$ $\Sigma x = 1 + 3 + 5 = 9$

Worked Examples

Let's take a look at several examples of each of the types of symbols listed in the table above. We're going to focus on situations that are often more difficult for students, or where there are relevant patterns that we should know.

Addition and Subtraction Addition and subtraction are among the basic mathematical operations that you learned a long time ago. Still, we're starting at the beginning. Let's focus on adding and subtracting negative numbers, because this can be tricky.

1. Adding negative numbers: the result is the same as subtracting a positive number.

    $7 + (-3) = 4$

    $7 - 3 = 4$

2. Subtracting negative numbers: the result is the same as adding a positive number.

    $7 - (-3) = 10$

    $7 + 3 = 10$

Multiplication and Division Multiplication and division are also basic mathematical operations. Let's focus on some patterns that we might observe when multiplying and dividing negative numbers.

3. Multiplying two negative numbers: the result is positive.

    $-7 \times -3 = 21$

    $-7(-3) = 21$

4. Multiplying one negative number and one positive number: the result is negative.

    $-7 \times 3 = -21$

    $-7(3) = -21$

5. Dividing one negative number by one positive number (or dividing one positive number by one negative number): the result is negative.

    $-7 \div 2 = -3.5$

    $-7/2 = -3.5$

6. Dividing a negative number by a negative number: the result is positive.

    $-7 \div -2 = 3.5$

    $-7/-2 = 3.5$

Exponents Exponents are used to indicate that a number (the base) should be multiplied by itself. The value of the exponent indicates how many times that number should be multiplied. A common error we see among our students is in example number 9 below (a negative base raised to an even exponent).

$$7^3 \leftarrow \text{exponent}$$
$$\uparrow$$
$$\text{Base}$$

7. Base is positive and exponent is even: the result is positive.

    $7^2 = 7 \times 7 = 49$

8. Base is positive and exponent is odd: the result is positive.

    $7^3 = 7 \times 7 \times 7 = 343$

9. Base is negative and exponent is even: the result is positive.

    $-7^2 = -7 \times -7 = 49$

10. Base is negative and exponent is odd: the result is negative.

    $-7^3 = -7 \times -7 \times -7 = -343$

Keep in mind that square roots are exponents.

$$\sqrt{X} = X^{0.5}$$

Summation Notation One mathematical symbol that you may not have encountered in previous courses, or that you may not have a lot of experience with, is summation (or sigma) notation. This notation is represented by the symbol Σ, which is the Greek uppercase letter S, called sigma. The Σ symbol indicates to us that we are to sum the values indicated.

For example, if you see the formula

$$\Sigma X$$

you are to sum all the values of X in a given data set.

As with other mathematical operations, it can be combined in sequence with other operations. (See section A.2, "Order of Operations," for details on when the summation notation should be computed when it appears in a formula.)

11. A dataset composed of the following numbers: 3, 7, 1, 8, 12

$$\Sigma X = 3 + 7 + 1 + 8 + 12 = 31$$

A.2 Order of Operations

Equations often include more than one mathematical operation. In those instances, it is important to perform the operations in a specific order. When operations are performed in different orders, you will likely get the wrong answer to an equation. The following is the order in which mathematical operations should be performed. Here, we can think back to the acronym PEMDAS that you may have learned back in middle school—but with the added order of Summation added in.

1. **P**arentheses: complete calculations within parentheses first, following the order of operations sequence if there is more than one operation contained within a set of parentheses.

2. **E**xponents (this includes square roots): complete any exponents (in this textbook that will primarily consist of squaring).

3. **M**ultiplication and/or **D**ivision: progressing from left to right, complete all multiplication and division in the order in which they are encountered.

4. **S**ummation using the Σ notation: recall that this notation means add up all of the values.

5. **A**ddition and/or **S**ubtraction: progressing from left to right, complete all addition and subtraction in the order in which they are encountered. Remember that summation (indicated by Σ) is equivalent to addition.

Worked Examples

In the examples below, the numbers highlighted in red identify the operations that we perform at each step.

12.

$(7 + 3)^2 + 5 \times 6$	Parentheses
$(10)^2 + 5 \times 6$	Exponents
$100 + 5 \times 6$	Multiplication
$100 + 30$	Addition
130	Answer

13.

$6 \div 3 \times 2 + 5^2$	Exponents
$6 \div 3 \times 2 + 25$	Division
$2 \times 2 + 25$	Multiplication
$4 + 25$	Addition
29	Answer

14.

$2 \times 3^2 + 7$	Exponents
$2 \times 9 + 7$	Multiplication
$18 + 7$	Addition
25	Answer

15. For the set of scores $X = 7, 3, 11$

$$\Sigma(X + 1)^2$$

$(7 + 1)^2 + (3 + 1)^2 + (11 + 1)^2$	Parentheses
$8^2 + 4^2 + 12^2$	Exponents
$64 + 16 + 144$	Summation
224	Answer

Order of Operations for Two Equations Used in this Textbook

16. Standard deviation (population)

$SD = \sqrt{\left(\dfrac{\Sigma(X - M)^2}{N}\right)}$	Parentheses (calculate deviation scores)
$SD = \sqrt{\left(\dfrac{\Sigma(\textit{deviation score})^2}{N}\right)}$	Exponent (square each deviation score)
$SD = \sqrt{\left(\dfrac{\Sigma(\textit{squared deviation score})}{N}\right)}$	Summation (sum the squared deviation scores)

$SD = \sqrt{\left(\dfrac{SS}{N}\right)}$	Division (divide the sum of the squared deviation scores by the sample size)
$SD = \sqrt{Variance}$	Exponent (square root the variance)
SD	Answer

17. Chi-Square Goodness of Fit

$\chi^2 = \Sigma\left(\dfrac{(O - E)^2}{E}\right)$	Parentheses (subtract the expected frequency from each observed frequency)
$\chi^2 = \Sigma\left(\dfrac{difference\ score^2}{E}\right)$	Exponents (square each difference score)
$\chi^2 = \Sigma\left(\dfrac{squared\ difference\ score}{E}\right)$	Division (divide the squared difference scores by the expected frequencies)
$\chi^2 = \Sigma(results)$	Summation (sum the results)
χ^2	Answer

A.3 Solving Equations

There are going to be situations where you will need to rearrange an equation so that a value (or variable) is isolated. This is also known as solving an equation. To remove an operation from one side of an equation, perform the opposite operation to *both* sides of the equation.

Worked Examples

Single Unknown Variable

18.

$X + 3 = 7$	
$X + 3 - 3 = 7 - 3$	Subtract 3 from each side to isolate X
$X = 4$	

19.

$X - 7 = 3$	
$X - 7 + 7 = 3 + 7$	Add 7 to each side to isolate X
$X = 10$	

20.

$X * 7 = 70$	
$(X * 7) \div 7 = 70 \div 7$	Divide each side by 7 to isolate X
$X = 10$	

21.

$X \div 3 = 5$	
$(X \div 3) \times 3 = 5 \times 3$	Multiply each side by 3 to isolate X
$X = 15$	

22.

$(X + 3) \div 10 = 7$	
$(X + 3) \div 10 \times 10 = 7 \times 10$	Work backward through the order of operations (see section A.2)
$(X + 3) - 3 = 70 - 3$	
$X = 67$	

More Than One Unknown Variable You will encounter many equations in this book where there is more than one variable in the equation. The equation may already be solved for the variable you are trying to find. Other times, you may need to rearrange the equation to isolate a different variable. The good news is that just like you can add or subtract a number from each side of an equation, you can add or subtract a variable from each side of the equation.

$z = \dfrac{X - M}{SD}$	
$z \times SD = \dfrac{X - M}{SD} \times SD$	Multiply each side by SD
$z \times SD + M = X - M + M$	Add M to each side to isolate X
$X = z \times SD + M$	

*Note: SD refers to standard deviation (see Chapter 3).

Realizing that these are all the same formula can make the course feel less overwhelming.

$$z = \frac{X - M}{SD} \quad X = z(SD) + M \quad M = X - z(SD)$$

$$SD = \frac{X - M}{z}$$

Knowing the parallels in the formulas is also helpful because you may sometimes feel like you don't have the correct formula to solve a question, when what you really need to do is rearrange a formula you already have. For example, say you have this formula (from Chapter 3):

$$M = \frac{\Sigma X}{n}$$

If you want to calculate n, you have the formula you need if you rearrange the one above.

$M = \dfrac{\Sigma X}{n}$	
$M \times n = \dfrac{\Sigma X}{n} \times n$	Multiply each side by n
$Mn \div M = \Sigma X \div M$	Divide each side by M
$n = \dfrac{\Sigma X}{M}$	

Math Skills Re-Evaluation Quiz

Now let's take a second quiz to see how much this has helped refresh your memory about these basic mathematical concepts. Again, you may not get all of them correct, which is fine! Remember, learning statistics is a process, and we are at the very beginning of this process. There will be challenges along the way, as there is when we try to learn anything. Everyone learns at different paces, but we assure you that by the end, we will all end up in the same place—together!

A.1

1. $\sqrt{121} =$
2. $6 + 3 =$
3. $5 - (-1) =$
4. $-10 \div 5 =$
5. $-3^2 =$

A.2

6. $6^2 \div (3 + 1) =$
7. $-1 + 4 \times 3 =$
8. $16 + 8 \div 2 + 2 =$
9. For the set of scores $X = 4, 6, 3$
   $\Sigma(X^2) - 4 =$
10. For the set of scores $X = 12, 5, 10, 2$
    $\Sigma(X - 4)^2$

A.3

11. Solve for X.
    $(X + 3)^2 = 36$
12. Solve for X.
    $45 \div X + 10 = 5$
13. Solve for X.
    $s = \dfrac{(X - M)^2}{N}$
14. Solve for X.
    $\sqrt{X + 2} = 12$
15. Solve for k.
    $b = (k - 4) \div X$

Answers to Math Skills Readiness Quiz

A.1

1. 25
2. 5
3. 80
4. −4
5. 9

A.2

6. −21
7. 7
8. 26
9. 98
10. 63

A.3

11. 28
12. 1
13. $X = (Y - b) \div m$
14. $X = D^2/p^2$
15. 65,747

Answers to Math Skills Readiness Re-Evaluation Quiz

A.1

1. 11
2. 9
3. 6
4. −2
5. 9

A.2

6. 9
7. 11
8. 22
9. 57
10. 105

A.3

11. 3
12. −9
13. $X = M + \sqrt{N \times s}$
14. 142
15. $k = b \times X + 4$

Where Does Data Come From? A Primer on Research Methods and Design

Learning Outcomes

After reading this Appendix, you should be able to:

- Explain in general terms how researchers collect data.

- Explain how researchers use conceptual and operational definitions.

- Differentiate nonexperimental and experimental designs.

- Differentiate between between-groups and within-groups designs.

- Identify several data collection techniques.

- Identify the proper statistical analysis based on a study description.

peer review a process in which fellow experts from the field examine the study to make sure the quality is sufficiently high to warrant publication.

A statistics textbook can easily leave the impression that data miraculously appear, ready to analyze, and with a clear indication of which statistical analysis we should perform. Though we hope that our approach in *Statistics for Research and Life* doesn't create this impression, we want to provide a quick background on research methods and design, or, in other words, what happens before we get the numbers. Ultimately, statistics are a tool that provides answers to our research questions. Knowing the questions and a bit about the methods involved in generating the numbers we're using provides useful context. Rather than dealing with a bunch of anonymous and seemingly random numbers, learning their origin story helps bring the numbers to life.

Research Starts with a Question

Sometimes getting started feels like the hardest part. But in research, the opposite is often true. Every research study begins when a scientist has a question about how something works. That question could arise from personal experience (e.g., "Because books are prominent in our house, will our kids like to read more, or less?"), observing others (e.g., "Do left-handed people post better pictures on Instagram?"), or something they read in a scientific journal (e.g., "A study claims that people look longer at their romantic partner's faces than strangers' faces. Is this a way for anxious people to feel reassured?").

Regardless of our question's origin, the next step is to consult the literature to learn what previous studies already may know about the topic. We do this to sharpen our ideas and make sure we are not accidentally doing a study that's already been done (as we discuss in Chapter 8, when we purposefully re-do a previous study, we call that replication). When doing a literature search, we focus on studies that have undergone a **peer-review** process in which fellow experts from the field examine the study to make sure the quality is sufficiently high to warrant publication. Essentially, peer review is a quality control device. The best way to find these articles is through databases like PsychARTICLES or PsycINFO. Researchers read these articles, take notes, and refine their ideas to build on what other researchers have already learned. Once a researcher has sufficient background understanding of a topic, they formulate their hypotheses.

From Questions to Answers

When creating a study, researchers don't start with a predetermined idea of which approach they'll take. Rather, they look carefully at their research questions and hypotheses, then craft the best design to answer their questions and test the hypotheses.

Identify Key Variables

conceptual definition
what a variable focuses on within the study.

operational definition
a description of a construct in terms of concrete, observable, and measurable characteristics.

To design a study, we need to identify our variables, or aspects that we expect to vary, have different values, or change. Once we know our variables, we need to move from a **conceptual definition,** or what a variable focuses on within the study, to an **operational definition,** or how the researcher will implement or use that variable within the study. For example, from the question "Because books are prominent in our house, will our kids like to read more, or less?" we would need to clarify what "books are prominent in our house" means. It could focus on how visible books are, how much we talk about them in the house, or simply how many books we have. Once the researcher settles on the conceptual definition of the number of books as the best way to answer the question, they next need to decide how to count. Though it seems straightforward, there are ambiguous aspects (e.g., how do magazines, newspapers, e-books, audiobooks, children's books, cookbooks, etc., count?). It's important because the operational definition impacts how others interpret the results. When operationally defining variables, researchers also need to decide how much information they need, or their scale of measurement (i.e., nominal, ordinal, interval, and ratio).

Identify the General Design

correlational (or non-experimental) design
a design where researchers are curious about what happens or describing what some behavior or trait looks like. They do not manipulate any variables, and are therefore unable to establish cause-and-effect relationships.

Researchers must also decide what type of question they're asking or what they want to learn, because that will determine the general research design. When researchers are curious about what happens or describing what some behavior or trait looks like, they use a **correlational (or nonexperimental) design.** These designs look at associations between predictor (explanatory) and response (criterion) variables, and they can show what happens to a variable when another increases or decreases but is unable to pinpoint why.

However, if a researcher wants to understand what causes a change in a variable, they use an **experimental design,** by manipulating or purposefully changing the independent variable to determine the effects on the outcome or dependent variable. Within experimental designs, researchers typically compare groups, or levels of the independent variable. When doing so, one group generally gets the treatment, while other groups receive something very similar but lacking the key ingredient. When each study participant receives every level of the independent variable, we consider it a **within-groups design.** However, when different groups of participants receive different levels of the independent variable, we consider it a **between-groups design.**

Conduct the Study

When starting a study, researchers need to decide who would be best to include in their study and where to get those participants. Once the sampling strategy is in place, the researcher needs to know how they are going to carry out the study. If participants will simply complete a series of questions, those steps are relatively straightforward. However, in an experiment, there is often a **research protocol** that maps out the specific steps the researcher should follow during the study. In any study, the first step before collecting any information from participants is to obtain informed consent where participants learn about the study, including any potential risks and a reminder that they are free to quit at any time. After giving consent, participants will complete the study, then receive a debriefing where the researcher fully explains the study's purpose and answers any questions.

Data Collection Techniques

There are a lot of ways for researchers to gather information from their sample. They can use observation to watch and record how people behave and what they say. Archival methods allow researchers to gather information from previously existing sources. Self-report directly asks the participant to indicate their thoughts and feelings through an interview or a survey questionnaire presented on paper, via the web, or through an app. Researchers can also capture physiological data by measuring heart rate, skin conductance, or brain waves/activity, or by analyzing saliva samples.

Identifying the Proper Analysis

Every statistics program that can be run on a computer is dumb. That is, it will do pretty much whatever analysis the researcher tells it to do. For that reason, one of the most essential skills to master

experimental design a design where researchers manipulate or purposefully change the independent variable to determine the effects on the outcome or dependent variable.

within-groups design when each study participant receives every level of the independent variable.

between-groups design when different groups of participants receive different levels of the independent variable.

research protocol the specific steps the researcher should follow during the study.

is knowing the right analysis to run based on the design and measurement level of our data. Luckily, the steps are very similar to the decisions a researcher makes when designing their study. But if you didn't happen to be the researcher, picking the right statistics is a bit like a forensic case where we have to unpack what the researcher did based on the clues left behind in the study description. Much like a researcher doesn't pick their design, but instead allows the question to determine the design, we don't pick which statistic to run. Instead, we use the elements of the design and the variables to inform our decision.

Know What to Ignore

Research studies collect a lot of data, and we won't need to use every variable in every analysis. Rather, we should focus only on the variables that directly address the one research question or hypothesis we are analyzing at the time. Different hypotheses are going to require different variables. Knowing what to leave out is a big part of the variable. There will be a lot of information that isn't necessary. When in doubt, review the research question/hypothesis.

Is It an Experiment? You can start to determine if a study uses an experimental or nonexperimental design by looking at the research question or hypothesis. Experiments focus on figuring out cause and effect — that is, answering why something happened. But because other techniques can seek to answer questions about cause and effect that aren't experiments per se, we need to dig a bit deeper into what makes a study an experiment. Really, there are two key characteristics of experiments. The first is that the researcher manipulates the independent variable. This means that the researcher treats one group of participants differently from the other. For example, we might test whether ibuprofen (a drug used to relieve pain) helps reduce the feeling of social pain that occurs after a person is excluded from a group. In this case, we could give some of the participants ibuprofen and others a placebo. Because we, the researchers, are manipulating the independent variable (the presence or absence of ibuprofen), we have satisfied the first key characteristic of an experiment. The second key characteristic is that researchers must randomly assign participants to the conditions of the study. This means that we need to sort participants into our different treatment groups on a random basis. For example, we might use a random number generator to figure out whether a particular participant is assigned to the ibuprofen condition or the placebo condition.

If you've met the criteria for an experiment, you next need to identify the level of measurement (or measurement scale) of the independent variable and dependent variable. The independent variable(s) will always be nominal, because this variable reflects the group to which the participant was assigned (e.g., experimental condition or control condition). The dependent variable is typically an interval or ratio variable, but could be nominal or ordinal as well. Next, you need to count how many independent variables there are, and how many levels each one has. Finally, you need to determine if participants receive every level of the independent variable (a within-groups design), or if different groups of participants receive different levels of the independent variable (a between-groups design).

Using this information, look at **Table B.1** to identify the research design and the statistic that goes with it. Careful—just because one hypothesis from a study requires a certain analysis, it does not guarantee that every hypothesis from that study uses the exact same analysis. For example, a multigroup study comparing three different types of therapy's ability to decrease depressive symptoms may require a one-way ANOVA for the main hypothesis. However, if a researcher wanted to see if there was a difference between men and women on depressive symptoms, that would require a t-test for independent samples. That is, we can treat categorical (nominal) variables as quasi-independent variables when we cannot easily manipulate the variable in question. You have to let your data tell you which analysis is best.

What if It's NOT an Experiment?

In a nonexperimental study, the researcher hasn't manipulated anything and therefore can't randomly assign participants to condition. Most often, these are correlational designs that involve the researcher observing participants, using existing data, or giving people a survey. In these studies, it's even more important to focus on the variables that each hypothesis uses. As before, we'll want to identify key variables and determine their level of measurement (i.e., nominal, ordinal, interval, ratio).

If we're dealing exclusively with nominal variables, we will use a chi-square analysis. If there is only one nominal variable, we'll need a chi-square goodness of fit; however, if there are two or more nominal variables, we'll need a chi-square test of independence.

If we have all interval or ratio variables and want to see the association between two of them, we'll use a Pearson's correlation.

Table B.1 Matching Research Design Elements to the Proper Statistic

Design Elements	Example	Statistic	Textbook Chapter
1 variable of any type (that you want to summarize or describe)	What is the average relationship length of Tinder relationships? Do they vary a lot, or are they mostly the same length?	Descriptives (frequencies; central tendency; variability)	Chapter 3
Two-Group (Comparing Your Sample to the Population): 1 continuous (interval/ratio) variable	Was my sample's score on life satisfaction significantly greater than the scale's midpoint?	Single sample t-test (one-sample t-test)	Chapter 9
Two-Group/Pre-Post Design: 1 nominal IV (2 levels; Within-Groups); 1 DV (interval/ratio)	Optimism before and after a mindfulness exercise.	t-test for dependent means (paired samples t-test)	Chapter 9
Two-Group/Simple Experiment: 1 nominal IV (2 levels; Between-Groups); 1 DV (interval/ratio)	Effectiveness of cognitive-behavioral therapy vs. psychoanalysis on anxiety.	t-test for independent means (independent samples t-test)	Chapter 10
Multi-Group Design: 1 nominal IV (3+ levels; Between-Groups); 1 DV (interval/ratio)	Studying alone, studying in a group, or no studying's impact on psychology test scores.	One-way between-groups analysis of variance (ANOVA)	Chapter 11
Multi-Group Design/Repeated Measures: 1 nominal IV (3+ levels; Within-Groups); 1 DV (interval/ratio)	Verbal aggression measured each week following either a week of playing sports video games, first-person shooter games, puzzle games, or no games.	Repeated-measures analysis of variance (ANOVA)	Chapter 12
Factorial Design: 2+ nominal IV (2+ levels each; Between-Groups); 1 DV (interval/ratio)	Test the effect of a story (personal vs. general) and type of appeal (emotional vs. factual) on willingness to donate to a GoFundMe page.	Factorial analysis of variance (ANOVA)	Chapter 13
Mixed Design: 1 nominal IV (2+ levels; Between-Groups); 1 nominal IV (2+ levels; Within-Groups); 1 DV (interval/ratio)	Test if there is a change in mood before/after listening to music and if it varies by listening format (headphones vs. speakers).	Factorial mixed-design analysis of variance (ANOVA)	Chapter 13
2 continuous (interval/ratio) variables	Determine the association between happiness and income.	Correlation (Bivariate)/ Pearson's r	Chapter 14
2+ continuous (interval/ratio) variables involving a prediction	Determine the best predictor of empathy from several possibilities (emotional intelligence; verbal intelligence; introversion).	Regression (linear)	Chapter 15
1 nominal/categorical variable	Does the number of men who enroll in a yoga class differ from what we expected?	Chi-square goodness of fit	Chapter 16
2 nominal/categorical variables	Does the number of men and women differ by the type of exercise class at the gym (spin class, kickboxing, boot camp)?	Chi-square test of independence	Chapter 16

If there are two or more interval or ratio variables, and we're interested in a prediction among them, we'll use a regression.

If we have one or more nominal variables and want to see how they relate to an interval or ratio outcome, our analysis will be similar to what we did for an experiment. If we have one nominal variable with two levels, we would perform a *t*-test. If we have one nominal variable with three or more levels, we would use an ANOVA. If we had two (or more) nominal variables, we would use a factorial ANOVA.

Finally, if we're looking at a single variable and want to describe or summarize it (e.g., to describe our sample in the participants section of the Method), regardless of the variable's scale of measurement, we would use descriptive statistics (i.e., frequencies, central tendency, variability).

Communicate the Findings

For science to exist, grow, and improve, we must communicate our findings. Doing so not only helps others scientists conduct their research, but it also benefits nonscientists because their lives can improve based upon the findings.

APA Style Research Report

The most common way we communicate findings in psychology is through an APA-Style research report. To make it easy to navigate, APA reports follow a predictable format. They start with a title page, which includes the paper's title and author information. On page 2, there is an abstract, which is a short summary of the report's most important information. Next, the report includes an introduction, which gives the reader a foundational understanding of the key variables and previous research, as well as the present study's research question(s) or hypothesis(es).

The next major section, the method, provides information about the participants that were in the study, the material or measures, the study design, and the procedure, or what the researcher did to conduct the study. After describing how they did the study, the researchers will describe what they found in the results section. Here you will find key information related to the descriptive or inferential analyses, the numerical results, and a very brief explanation of the results, along with references to any tables or figures.

The next section in an APA-Style research report is the discussion, where the researcher provides a summary of the overall findings, interpretations of the findings and their implication, the study's limitations and strengths, suggestions for future directions, and a conclusion. The remaining sections include (in order): references, footnotes, tables, and figures. See **Table B.2** for summary.

Table B.2 APA-Style Report: Main Sections

Title Page	Gives the paper's title, author names, and affiliations. Also includes any Author Notes.
Abstract	Gives a short (150–200 words) summary of the key points from the report, along with a list of key words related to the research.
Introduction	Gives the reader context for understanding the key variables from the present study, including defining key terms, describing relevant theories, and summarizing previous research on the topic. It also provides information about the research questions or hypotheses.
Method	Gives information that fellow researchers would need to replicate the research. This includes information on who the participants were, the materials the researcher used, the design, and the procedure for data collection.
Results	Gives information about which statistical analyses the researcher used to test each hypothesis, and results from any descriptive and inferential statistics, along with a quick narrative summary of what the numerical results indicate. This section also includes references to any tables or figures that help make the results clearer.
Discussion	Gives an overall summary of the findings, interprets them in the context of past research, points out the study's strengths and weaknesses, includes future research suggestions, and provides a conclusion.
References	Gives information regarding the sources cited in the paper so that readers can locate the original study and read more on the topic.

Statistical Tables

Table C-1

Standard Normal Cumulative Probability Table

Cumulative probabilities for negative z-values are shown in the following table:

z	0.00	0.01	0.02	0.03	0.04	0.05	0.06	0.07	0.08	0.09
−3.4	.0003	.0003	.0003	.0003	.0003	.0003	.0003	.0003	.0003	.0002
−3.3	.0005	.0005	.0005	.0004	.0004	.0004	.0004	.0004	.0004	.0003
−3.2	.0007	.0007	.0006	.0006	.0006	.0006	.0006	.0005	.0005	.0005
−3.1	.0010	.0009	.0009	.0009	.0008	.0008	.0008	.0008	.0007	.0007
−3.0	.0013	.0013	.0013	.0012	.0012	.0011	.0011	.0011	.0010	.0010
−2.9	.0019	.0018	.0018	.0017	.0016	.0016	.0015	.0015	.0014	.0014
−2.8	.0026	.0025	.0024	.0023	.0023	.0022	.0021	.0021	.0020	.0019
−2.7	.0035	.0034	.0033	.0032	.0031	.0030	.0029	.0028	.0027	.0026
−2.6	.0047	.0045	.0044	.0043	.0041	.0040	.0039	.0038	.0037	.0036
−2.5	.0062	.0060	.0059	.0057	.0055	.0054	.0052	.0051	.0049	.0048
−2.4	.0082	.0080	.0078	.0075	.0073	.0071	.0069	.0068	.0066	.0064
−2.3	.0107	.0104	.0102	.0099	.0096	.0094	.0091	.0089	.0087	.0084
−2.2	.0139	.0136	.0132	.0129	.0125	.0122	.0119	.0116	.0113	.0110
−2.1	.0179	.0174	.0170	.0166	.0162	.0158	.0154	.0150	.0146	.0143
−2.0	.0228	.0222	.0217	.0212	.0207	.0202	.0197	.0192	.0188	.0183
−1.9	.0287	.0281	.0274	.0268	.0262	.0256	.0250	.0244	.0239	.0233
−1.8	.0359	.0351	.0344	.0336	.0329	.0322	.0314	.0307	.0301	.0294
−1.7	.0446	.0436	.0427	.0418	.0409	.0401	.0392	.0384	.0375	.0367
−1.6	.0548	.0537	.0526	.0516	.0505	.0495	.0485	.0475	.0465	.0455
−1.5	.0668	.0655	.0643	.0630	.0618	.0606	.0594	.0582	.0571	.0559

Table C-1 continued

z	0.00	0.01	0.02	0.03	0.04	0.05	0.06	0.07	0.08	0.09
−1.4	.0808	.0793	.0778	.0764	.0749	.0735	.0721	.0708	.0694	.0681
−1.3	.0968	.0951	.0934	.0918	.0901	.0885	.0869	.0853	.0838	.0823
−1.2	.1151	.1131	.1112	.1093	.1075	.1056	.1038	.1020	.1003	.0985
−1.1	.1357	.1335	.1314	.1292	.1271	.1251	.1230	.1210	.1190	.1170
−1.0	.1587	.1562	.1539	.1515	.1492	.1469	.1446	.1423	.1401	.1379
−0.9	.1841	.1814	.1788	.1762	.1736	.1711	.1685	.1660	.1635	.1611
−0.8	.2119	.2090	.2061	.2033	.2005	.1977	.1949	.1922	.1894	.1867
−0.7	.2420	.2389	.2358	.2327	.2296	.2266	.2236	.2206	.2177	.2148
−0.6	.2743	.2709	.2676	.2643	.2611	.2578	.2546	.2514	.2483	.2451
−0.5	.3085	.3050	.3015	.2981	.2946	.2912	.2877	.2843	.2810	.2776
−0.4	.3446	.3409	.3372	.3336	.3300	.3264	.3228	.3192	.3156	.3121
−0.3	.3821	.3783	.3745	.3707	.3669	.3632	.3594	.3557	.3520	.3483
−0.2	.4207	.4168	.4129	.4090	.4052	.4013	.3974	.3936	.3897	.3859
−0.1	.4602	.4562	.4522	.4483	.4443	.4404	.4364	.4325	.4286	.4247
0.0	.5000	.4960	.4920	.4880	.4840	.4801	.4761	.4721	.4681	.4641

Cumulative probabilities for positive *z*-values are shown in the following table:

z	0.00	0.01	0.02	0.03	0.04	0.05	0.06	0.07	0.08	0.09
0.0	.5000	.5040	.5080	.5120	.5160	.5199	.5239	.5279	.5319	.5359
0.1	.5398	.5438	.5478	.5517	.5557	.5596	.5636	.5675	.5714	.5753
0.2	.5793	.5832	.5871	.5910	.5948	.5987	.6026	.6064	.6103	.6141
0.3	.6179	.6217	.6255	.6293	.6331	.6368	.6406	.6443	.6480	.6517
0.4	.6554	.6591	.6628	.6664	.6700	.6736	.6772	.6808	.6844	.6879
0.5	.6915	.6950	.6985	.7019	.7054	.7088	.7123	.7157	.7190	.7224
0.6	.7257	.7291	.7324	.7357	.7389	.7422	.7454	.7486	.7517	.7549
0.7	.7580	.7611	.7642	.7673	.7704	.7734	.7764	.7794	.7823	.7852
0.8	.7881	.7910	.7939	.7967	.7995	.8023	.8051	.8078	.8106	.8133
0.9	.8159	.8186	.8212	.8238	.8264	.8289	.8315	.8340	.8365	.8389
1.0	.8413	.8438	.8461	.8485	.8508	.8531	.8554	.8577	.8599	.8621
1.1	.8643	.8665	.8686	.8708	.8729	.8749	.8770	.8790	.8810	.8830
1.2	.8849	.8869	.8888	.8907	.8925	.8944	.8962	.8980	.8997	.9015
1.3	.9032	.9049	.9066	.9082	.9099	.9115	.9131	.9147	.9162	.9177
1.4	.9192	.9207	.9222	.9236	.9251	.9265	.9279	.9292	.9306	.9319

z	0.00	0.01	0.02	0.03	0.04	0.05	0.06	0.07	0.08	0.09
1.5	.9332	.9345	.9357	.9370	.9382	.9394	.9406	.9418	.9429	.9441
1.6	.9452	.9463	.9474	.9484	.9495	.9505	.9515	.9525	.9535	.9545
1.7	.9554	.9564	.9573	.9582	.9591	.9599	.9608	.9616	.9625	.9633
1.8	.9641	.9649	.9656	.9664	.9671	.9678	.9686	.9693	.9699	.9706
1.9	.9713	.9719	.9726	.9732	.9738	.9744	.9750	.9756	.9761	.9767
2.0	.9772	.9778	.9783	.9788	.9793	.9798	.9803	.9808	.9812	.9817
2.1	.9821	.9826	.9830	.9834	.9838	.9842	.9846	.9850	.9854	.9857
2.2	.9861	.9864	.9868	.9871	.9875	.9878	.9881	.9884	.9887	.9890
2.3	.9893	.9896	.9898	.9901	.9904	.9906	.9909	.9911	.9913	.9916
2.4	.9918	.9920	.9922	.9925	.9927	.9929	.9931	.9932	.9934	.9936
2.5	.9938	.9940	.9941	.9943	.9945	.9946	.9948	.9949	.9951	.9952
2.6	.9953	.9955	.9956	.9957	.9959	.9960	.9961	.9962	.9963	.9964
2.7	.9965	.9966	.9967	.9968	.9969	.9970	.9971	.9972	.9973	.9974
2.8	.9974	.9975	.9976	.9977	.9977	.9978	.9979	.9979	.9980	.9981
2.9	.9981	.9982	.9982	.9983	.9984	.9984	.9985	.9985	.9986	.9986
3.0	.9987	.9987	.9987	.9988	.9988	.9989	.9989	.9989	.9990	.9990
3.1	.9990	.9991	.9991	.9991	.9992	.9992	.9992	.9992	.9993	.9993
3.2	.9993	.9993	.9994	.9994	.9994	.9994	.9994	.9995	.9995	.9995
3.3	.9995	.9995	.9995	.9996	.9996	.9996	.9996	.9996	.9996	.9997
3.4	.9997	.9997	.9997	.9997	.9997	.9997	.9997	.9997	.9997	.9998

Table C-2

The *t* Distributions

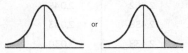

	One-Tailed Tests Alpha Level		Two-Tailed Tests Alpha Level	
df	0.05	0.01	0.05	0.01
1	6.314	31.821	12.706	63.657
2	2.920	6.965	4.303	9.925
3	2.353	4.541	3.182	5.841
4	2.132	3.747	2.776	4.604
5	2.015	3.365	2.571	4.032
6	1.943	3.143	2.447	3.708

Table C-2 continued

df	One-Tailed Tests Alpha Level		Two-Tailed Tests Alpha Level	
	0.05	0.01	0.05	0.01
7	1.895	2.998	2.365	3.500
8	1.860	2.897	2.306	3.356
9	1.833	2.822	2.262	3.250
10	1.813	2.764	2.228	3.170
11	1.796	2.718	2.201	3.106
12	1.783	2.681	2.179	3.055
13	1.771	2.651	2.161	3.013
14	1.762	2.625	2.145	2.977
15	1.753	2.603	2.132	2.947
16	1.746	2.584	2.120	2.921
17	1.740	2.567	2.110	2.898
18	1.734	2.553	2.101	2.879
19	1.729	2.540	2.093	2.861
20	1.725	2.528	2.086	2.846
21	1.721	2.518	2.080	2.832
22	1.717	2.509	2.074	2.819
23	1.714	2.500	2.069	2.808
24	1.711	2.492	2.064	2.797
25	1.708	2.485	2.060	2.788
26	1.706	2.479	2.056	2.779
27	1.704	2.473	2.052	2.771
28	1.701	2.467	2.049	2.764
29	1.699	2.462	2.045	2.757
30	1.698	2.458	2.043	2.750
35	1.690	2.438	2.030	2.724
40	1.684	2.424	2.021	2.705
60	1.671	2.390	2.001	2.661
80	1.664	2.374	1.990	2.639
100	1.660	2.364	1.984	2.626
120	1.658	2.358	1.980	2.617
∞	1.645	2.327	1.960	2.576

Table C-3

The *F* Distributions

Within-Groups *df*	Significance (Alpha) Level	Between-Groups Degrees of Freedom					
		1	2	3	4	5	6
1	0.01	4052	5000	5404	5625	5764	5859
	0.05	162	200	216	225	230	234
2	0.01	98.50	99.00	99.17	99.25	99.30	99.33
	0.05	18.51	19.00	19.17	19.25	19.30	19.33
3	0.01	34.12	30.82	29.46	28.71	28.24	27.91
	0.05	10.13	9.55	9.28	9.12	9.01	8.94
4	0.01	21.20	18.00	16.70	15.98	15.52	15.21
	0.05	7.71	6.95	6.59	6.39	6.26	6.16
5	0.01	16.26	13.27	12.06	11.39	10.97	10.67
	0.05	6.61	5.79	5.41	5.19	5.05	4.95
6	0.01	13.75	10.93	9.78	9.15	8.75	8.47
	0.05	5.99	5.14	4.76	4.53	4.39	4.28
7	0.01	12.25	9.55	8.45	7.85	7.46	7.19
	0.05	5.59	4.74	4.35	4.12	3.97	3.87
8	0.01	11.26	8.65	7.59	7.01	6.63	6.37
	0.05	5.32	4.46	4.07	3.84	3.69	3.58
9	0.01	10.56	8.02	6.99	6.42	6.06	5.80
	0.05	5.12	4.26	3.86	3.63	3.48	3.37
10	0.01	10.05	7.56	6.55	6.00	5.64	5.39
	0.05	4.97	4.10	3.71	3.48	3.33	3.22
11	0.01	9.65	7.21	6.22	5.67	5.32	5.07
	0.05	4.85	3.98	3.59	3.36	3.20	3.10
12	0.01	9.33	6.93	5.95	5.41	5.07	4.82
	0.05	4.75	3.89	3.49	3.26	3.11	3.00
13	0.01	9.07	6.70	5.74	5.21	4.86	4.62
	0.05	4.67	3.81	3.41	3.18	3.03	2.92
14	0.01	8.86	6.52	5.56	5.04	4.70	4.46
	0.05	4.60	3.74	3.34	3.11	2.96	2.85
15	0.01	8.68	6.36	5.42	4.89	4.56	4.32
	0.05	4.54	3.68	3.29	3.06	2.90	2.79

Table C-3 continued

Within-Groups *df*	Significance (Alpha) Level	Between-Groups Degrees of Freedom					
		1	2	3	4	5	6
16	0.01	8.53	6.23	5.29	4.77	4.44	4.20
	0.05	4.49	3.63	3.24	3.01	2.85	2.74
17	0.01	8.40	6.11	5.19	4.67	4.34	4.10
	0.05	4.45	3.59	3.20	2.97	2.81	2.70
18	0.01	8.29	6.01	5.09	4.58	4.25	4.02
	0.05	4.41	3.56	3.16	2.93	2.77	2.66
19	0.01	8.19	5.93	5.01	4.50	4.17	3.94
	0.05	4.38	3.52	3.13	2.90	2.74	2.63
20	0.01	8.10	5.85	4.94	4.43	4.10	3.87
	0.05	4.35	3.49	3.10	2.87	2.71	2.60
21	0.01	8.02	5.78	4.88	4.37	4.04	3.81
	0.05	4.33	3.47	3.07	2.84	2.69	2.57
22	0.01	7.95	5.72	4.82	4.31	3.99	3.76
	0.05	4.30	3.44	3.05	2.82	2.66	2.55
23	0.01	7.88	5.66	4.77	4.26	3.94	3.71
	0.05	4.28	3.42	3.03	2.80	2.64	2.53
24	0.01	7.82	5.61	4.72	4.22	3.90	3.67
	0.05	4.26	3.40	3.01	2.78	2.62	2.51
25	0.01	7.77	5.57	4.68	4.18	3.86	3.63
	0.05	4.24	3.39	2.99	2.76	2.60	2.49
26	0.01	7.72	5.53	4.64	4.14	3.82	3.59
	0.05	4.23	3.37	2.98	2.74	2.59	2.48
27	0.01	7.68	5.49	4.60	4.11	3.79	3.56
	0.05	4.21	3.36	2.96	2.73	2.57	2.46
28	0.01	7.64	5.45	4.57	4.08	3.75	3.53
	0.05	4.20	3.34	2.95	2.72	2.56	2.45
29	0.01	7.60	5.42	4.54	4.05	3.73	3.50
	0.05	4.18	3.33	2.94	2.70	2.55	2.43
30	0.01	7.56	5.39	4.51	4.02	3.70	3.47
	0.05	4.17	3.32	2.92	2.69	2.53	2.42
35	0.01	7.42	5.27	4.40	3.91	3.59	3.37
	0.05	4.12	3.27	2.88	2.64	2.49	2.37
40	0.01	7.32	5.18	4.31	3.83	3.51	3.29
	0.05	4.09	3.23	2.84	2.61	2.45	2.34

Within- Groups df	Significance (Alpha) Level	Between-Groups Degrees of Freedom					
		1	2	3	4	5	6
45	0.01	7.23	5.11	4.25	3.77	3.46	3.23
	0.05	4.06	3.21	2.81	2.58	2.42	2.31
50	0.01	7.17	5.06	4.20	3.72	3.41	3.19
	0.05	4.04	3.18	2.79	2.56	2.40	2.29
55	0.01	7.12	5.01	4.16	3.68	3.37	3.15
	0.05	4.02	3.17	2.77	2.54	2.38	2.27
60	0.01	7.08	4.98	4.13	3.65	3.34	3.12
	0.05	4.00	3.15	2.76	2.53	2.37	2.26
65	0.01	7.04	4.95	4.10	3.62	3.31	3.09
	0.05	3.99	3.14	2.75	2.51	2.36	2.24
70	0.01	7.01	4.92	4.08	3.60	3.29	3.07
	0.05	3.98	3.13	2.74	2.50	2.35	2.23
75	0.01	6.99	4.90	4.06	3.58	3.27	3.05
	0.05	3.97	3.12	2.73	2.49	2.34	2.22
80	0.01	6.96	4.88	4.04	3.56	3.26	3.04
	0.05	3.96	3.11	2.72	2.49	2.33	2.22
85	0.01	6.94	4.86	4.02	3.55	3.24	3.02
	0.05	3.95	3.10	2.71	2.48	2.32	2.21
90	0.01	6.93	4.85	4.01	3.54	3.23	3.01
	0.05	3.95	3.10	2.71	2.47	2.32	2.20
95	0.01	6.91	4.84	4.00	3.52	3.22	3.00
	0.05	3.94	3.09	2.70	2.47	2.31	2.20
100	0.01	6.90	4.82	3.98	3.51	3.21	2.99
	0.05	3.94	3.09	2.70	2.46	2.31	2.19
200	0.01	6.76	4.71	3.88	3.41	3.11	2.89
	0.05	3.89	3.04	2.65	2.42	2.26	2.14
1000	0.01	6.66	4.63	3.80	3.34	3.04	2.82
	0.05	3.85	3.00	2.61	2.38	2.22	2.11
∞	0.01	6.64	4.61	3.78	3.32	3.02	2.80
	0.05	3.84	3.00	2.61	2.37	2.22	2.10

Table C-4

The Chi-Square Distributions

df	Significance (Alpha) Level		
	0.10	0.05	0.01
1	2.706	3.841	6.635
2	4.605	5.992	9.211
3	6.252	7.815	11.345
4	7.780	9.488	13.277
5	9.237	11.071	15.087
6	10.645	12.592	16.812
7	12.017	14.067	18.475
8	13.362	15.507	20.090
9	14.684	16.919	21.666
10	15.987	18.307	23.209

Table C-5

The q Statistic (Tukey *HSD* Test)

Within-Groups df	Significance (Alpha) Level	k = Number of Treatments (Levels)										
		2	3	4	5	6	7	8	9	10	11	12
4	0.05	3.93	5.04	5.76	6.29	6.71	7.05	7.35	7.60	7.83	8.03	8.21
	0.01	6.51	8.12	9.17	9.96	10.58	11.10	11.54	11.92	12.26	12.57	12.84
5	0.05	3.64	4.60	5.22	5.67	6.03	6.33	6.58	6.80	6.99	7.17	7.32
	0.01	5.70	6.98	7.80	8.42	8.91	9.32	9.67	9.97	10.24	10.48	10.70
6	0.05	3.46	4.34	4.90	5.30	5.63	5.90	6.12	6.32	6.49	6.65	6.79
	0.01	5.24	6.33	7.03	7.56	7.97	8.32	8.61	8.87	9.10	9.30	9.48
7	0.05	3.34	4.16	4.68	5.06	5.36	5.61	5.82	6.00	6.16	6.30	6.43
	0.01	4.95	5.92	6.54	7.01	7.37	7.68	7.94	8.17	8.37	8.55	8.71
8	0.05	3.26	4.04	4.53	4.89	5.17	5.40	5.60	5.77	5.92	6.05	6.18
	0.01	4.75	5.64	6.20	6.62	6.96	7.24	7.47	7.68	7.86	8.03	8.18
9	0.05	3.20	3.95	4.41	4.76	5.02	5.24	5.43	5.59	5.74	5.87	5.98
	0.01	4.60	5.43	5.96	6.35	6.66	6.91	7.13	7.33	7.49	7.65	7.78

Within-Groups df	Significance (Alpha) Level	k = Number of Treatments (Levels)										
		2	3	4	5	6	7	8	9	10	11	12
10	0.05	3.15	3.88	4.33	4.65	4.91	5.12	5.30	5.46	5.60	5.72	5.83
	0.01	4.48	5.27	5.77	6.14	6.43	6.67	6.87	7.05	7.21	7.36	7.49
11	0.05	3.11	3.82	4.26	4.57	4.82	5.03	5.20	5.35	5.49	5.61	5.71
	0.01	4.39	5.15	5.62	5.97	6.25	6.48	6.67	6.84	6.99	7.13	7.25
12	0.05	3.08	3.77	4.20	4.51	4.75	4.95	5.12	5.27	5.39	5.51	5.61
	0.01	4.32	5.05	5.50	5.84	6.10	6.32	6.51	6.67	6.81	6.94	7.06
13	0.05	3.06	3.73	4.15	4.45	4.69	4.88	5.05	5.19	5.32	5.43	5.53
	0.01	4.26	4.96	5.40	5.73	5.98	6.19	6.37	6.53	6.67	6.79	6.90
14	0.05	3.03	3.70	4.11	4.41	4.64	4.83	4.99	5.13	5.25	5.36	5.46
	0.01	4.21	4.89	5.32	5.63	5.88	6.08	6.26	6.41	6.54	6.66	6.77
15	0.05	3.01	3.67	4.08	4.37	4.59	4.78	4.94	5.08	5.20	5.31	5.40
	0.01	4.17	4.84	5.25	5.56	5.80	5.99	6.16	6.31	6.44	6.55	6.66
16	0.05	3.00	3.65	4.05	4.33	4.56	4.74	4.90	5.03	5.15	5.26	5.35
	0.01	4.13	4.79	5.19	5.49	5.72	5.92	6.08	6.22	6.35	6.46	6.56
17	0.05	2.98	3.63	4.02	4.30	4.52	4.70	4.86	4.99	5.11	5.21	5.31
	0.01	4.10	4.74	5.14	5.43	5.66	5.85	6.01	6.15	6.27	6.38	6.48
18	0.05	2.97	3.61	4.00	4.28	4.49	4.67	4.82	4.96	5.07	5.17	5.27
	0.01	4.07	4.70	5.09	5.38	5.60	5.79	5.94	6.08	6.20	6.31	6.41
19	0.05	2.96	3.59	3.98	4.25	4.47	4.65	4.79	4.92	5.04	5.14	5.23
	0.01	4.05	4.67	5.05	5.33	5.55	5.73	5.89	6.02	6.14	6.25	6.34
20	0.05	2.95	3.58	3.96	4.23	4.45	4.62	4.77	4.90	5.01	5.11	5.20
	0.01	4.02	4.64	5.02	5.29	5.51	5.69	5.84	5.97	6.09	6.19	6.28
24	0.05	2.92	3.53	3.90	4.17	4.37	4.54	4.68	4.81	4.92	5.01	5.10
	0.01	3.96	4.55	4.91	5.17	5.37	5.54	5.69	5.81	5.92	6.02	6.11
30	0.05	2.89	3.49	3.85	4.10	4.30	4.46	4.60	4.72	4.82	4.92	5.00
	0.01	3.89	4.45	4.80	5.05	5.24	5.40	5.54	5.65	5.76	5.85	5.93
40	0.05	2.86	3.44	3.79	4.04	4.23	4.39	4.52	4.63	4.73	4.82	4.90
	0.01	3.82	4.37	4.70	4.93	5.11	5.26	5.39	5.50	5.60	5.69	5.76
60	0.05	2.83	3.40	3.74	3.98	4.16	4.31	4.44	4.55	4.65	4.73	4.81
	0.01	3.76	4.28	4.59	4.82	4.99	5.13	5.25	5.36	5.45	5.53	5.60
120	0.05	2.80	3.36	3.68	3.92	4.10	4.24	4.36	4.47	4.56	4.64	4.71
	0.01	3.70	4.20	4.50	4.71	4.87	5.01	5.12	5.21	5.30	5.37	5.44
∞	0.05	2.77	3.31	3.63	3.86	4.03	4.17	4.28	4.39	4.47	4.55	4.62
	0.01	3.64	4.12	4.40	4.60	4.76	4.88	4.99	5.08	5.16	5.23	5.29

Glossary

A

68–95–99 approximation in any normal distribution, there are similar percentages of cases between standard deviations (roughly 68% within 1 *SD* of the mean, 95% within 2 *SD* of the mean, and 99% within 3 *SD*).

A/B Testing a method used in business where two versions of a product or message are used simultaneously until hypothesis testing reveals one version to be superior to the other.

actuarial science the field of science devoted to understanding risk in everyday life through the use of probabilities.

additive probability the probability that any one of several events occurs as the result of a trial

algorithm a strategy that relies on carefully following a clearly planned and logical sequence of rules.

alpha (α) level (also called the *significance level*) establishes the value of *p* that, when observed, determines when the null hypothesis should be rejected.

analysis plan a document that describes how data will be collected, processed, and analyzed.

applied research research conducted to solve a real world problem.

assumptions of a hypothesis test the preconditions that must be satisfied for the results of a hypothesis test to be valid.

attention check an item embedded in a study designed to identify participants who are not paying attention during the study.

B

bar graph a chart for displaying frequencies of nominal data.

basic research research conducted for the sake of learning about a natural phenomenon.

between-groups design when different groups of participants receive different levels of the independent variable.

bimodal distribution a distribution that has two "peaks," indicating the two most frequently occurring scores.

Bonferroni correction a type of post hoc test that divides the experimentwise alpha by the number of hypothesis tests to determine the testwise alpha.

C

ceiling effect a negatively skewed distribution that occurs when most participants respond at the extreme high end of the measurement scale.

cell mean the mean of all scores for a particular combination of the independent variables' levels.

Central Limit Theorem a statistical concept describing the shape of a distribution of sample means. As the sample size increases, the distribution of sample means more closely resembles a normal distribution, even if the original population is not normally distributed.

central tendency value that summarizes all of the other obtained measurements or values for a particular variable.

chi-square goodness of fit test (χ^2) statistical test we use when we have a nominal or categorical variable from a single population and want to see how the reality of what we observe compares to our preconceived expectations.

chi-square test of independence a type of statistical analysis we use to determine whether two nominal variables are associated (or independent).

clustered bar graph a bar graph used to depict the results of a factorial ANOVA.

coefficient of determination (R^2) a statistic that quantifies the amount of variability in the criterion variable that is predicted by the regression equation.

Cohen's d a measure of effect size used for comparing two means.

comparison distribution a distribution we use to compare a sample to that depicting the population's characteristics if the null hypothesis is true.

computational reproducibility describes the extent to which different researchers are able to reach the same statistical conclusions when analyzing the same data set.

conceptual definition what a variable focuses on within the study.

confidence interval a range of scores that likely includes the population's true mean.

confirmatory research research that is intended to test a particular hypothesis, using a specific methodology and analysis.

conflict of interest occurs when a researcher is motivated to find a particular outcome for a study.

confounds variables that vary along with the independent variable that can cause changes in the dependent variable.

CONSORT diagram a figure included in research articles that documents the flow of participants in a study from recruitment to data analysis.

construct a variable that is not directly observable but describes a collection of traits, behaviors, or cognitions related to the same idea or concept.

contingency table (also called a *crosstabulation table*) a table used to depict the data in a chi-square test of independence. The rows of the table represent the categories of one nominal variable and the columns represent the categories of a second nominal variable.

continuous variable a variable whose value is obtained by measuring and, as a result, can include fractions or decimals; often interval or ratio scale data.

convenience sample a sampling strategy in which a researcher selects participants based on the ease at which they are recruited into the study.

conventional levels of significance the typical alpha levels that researchers use in hypothesis testing (5% and 1%, or $\alpha = .05$ and $\alpha = .01$).

convergent validity degree to which a newly created measure is correlated to an existing measure.

correlation a statistic that tests the association or relationship between two variables.

correlational (or non-experimental) design a design where researchers are curious about what happens or describing what some behavior or trait looks like. They do not manipulate any variables, and are therefore unable to establish cause-and-effect relationships.

correlation matrix a type of table that presents the correlation coefficients for all pairs of variables in a study.

criterion the outcome variable being predicted, typically the Y variable.

critical region the part of the comparison distribution where a score must fall in order to reject the null hypothesis.

critical value the cutoff point on the comparison distribution at which we are able to reject the null hypothesis.

crossover effect a type of interaction that occurs when the effect of one independent variable produces the opposite effect across the levels of the other independent variable.

curvilinear relationship a relationship between two variables when the association between two variables changes over different levels or amounts of the variables.

D

data fraud deliberate creation of false data, or manipulation of otherwise genuine data, to ensure a particular outcome of a data analytic test occurs.

data plan a document that details all of the ways that researchers will code and analyze their data, including a description of the reasons why participants will be excluded from the final analyses.

degrees of freedom the number of independent observations in a sample that are free to vary.

degrees of freedom total (df_{Total}) the sample size minus 1, or the sum of the between and within degrees of freedom.

dependent variable the variable in a study that changes in response to the independent variable; the outcome or effect.

descriptive statistics a branch of statistics used to summarize the basic characteristics of a sample dataset.

deviation score a calculation of how far each score is from the mean by subtracting the mean (M) from each score (X), or ($X - M$).

difference score the difference between the pretest and posttest measurements.

directional hypothesis a type of research hypothesis that specifies whether the sample mean will be less than or greater than the population mean.

discrete variable a variable whose value is obtained by counting and, as a result, can only take the form of a whole, positive integer; often nominal and ordinal scale data.

distributed research network a team of scholars working across the globe on the same research project.

distribution of correlations a distribution comprised of the bivariate correlations for all possible samples of a fixed size.

distribution of sample means a distribution that depicts the means of all possible samples drawn from a population.

distribution of slopes a distribution that presents the slopes calculated from all possible samples of a certain size from the population.

E

effect size a measure of the strength of an association between two variables; or the practical,

rather than statistical, importance of a research finding.

equality of variances assumption (also called the *homogeneity of variances assumption*) an assumption that two population variances are equal. Used in the *t*-test for independent samples to justify the pooling of samples' variances to estimate the population's variance.

error fluctuations in scores caused by how we measure a variable (i.e., measurement error), experimenter expectations and biases (i.e., experimenter error), or participants' expectations and biases (i.e., participant error).

error bars lines added to the bars in a bar graph that express the amount of variability in a variable. Error bars may represent the standard deviation, standard error, confidence interval, or any other measure of variability.

error variance variations in scores due to extraneous variables, measurement error, or random error (e.g., luck or chance factors).

eta squared (or η^2) measure of effect size used in one-way ANOVA. Helps researchers determine the practical or meaningfulness of a significant result and is measured by dividing sum of squares between ($SS_{Between}$) by the sum of squares total (SS_{Total}).

ethics a set of moral guidelines that shape behavior and inform decisions.

experimental design a design where researchers manipulate or purposefully change the independent variable to determine the effects on the outcome or dependent variable.

experiment a type of research study that compares at least two groups of participants that are equivalent in every way, except on the independent variable. The goal of an experiment is to show that changes in the independent variable cause changes to the dependent variable.

experimentwise error rate the overall Type I error rate for an experiment when conducting multiple hypothesis tests.

exploratory research research that is not intended to test a particular hypothesis, but rather to learn more about a psychological phenomenon.

extrapolation an application of a regression equation to make predictions of the criterion variable based on values of predictor that are outside of the range of scores that created the regression equation.

F

face validity extent to which, on the surface, something appears to effectively accomplish its goal.

factor a term synonymous with independent variable in the context of factorial ANOVA.

factorial analysis of variance (ANOVA) (also known as *factorial ANOVA* when there are two factors) a statistic that lets us determine if two or more categorical or nominal independent variables influence a continuous (interval or ratio) dependent variable.

false-positive findings results that support a hypothesis, even though the hypothesis is incorrect.

F **distribution** a distribution of all possible *F*-ratios, the shape of which shows that for most comparisons the *F*-ratio will be very close to one, with large *F*-ratios being increasingly rare.

file drawer problem problem arising when scholars do not attempt to publish nonsignificant findings.

floor effect a positively skewed distribution that occurs when most participants respond at the extreme low end of the measurement scale.

F-**ratio** score representing how the between-groups estimate of population variance compares to the within-groups estimate of population variance ($F = S^2_{Between}/S^2_{Within}$).

frequency distribution any graphical representation of data frequencies.

frequency polygon a graph of frequencies that uses a continuous line to visualize the shape of a frequency distribution.

frequency table an ordered list of each specific possible value, along with a tally of how often or how many times each data point occurred.

G

gambler's fallacy the mistaken belief that random sequences will match their expected probabilities over the short term.

generalizability the ability to make accurate conclusions about those who were not in the study.

grand mean (*GM*) a mean calculated from a group of other means.

grouped frequency table an ordered list of groupings of values, along with a tally of how often values in each interval occurred.

H

HARKing describes the questionable research practice where researchers make their predictions only after analyzing their data.

heuristic a strategy that relies on mental shortcuts, or quick solutions that are often practical but imperfect.

histogram a visual representation of data for a single variable that uses bars to chart values on the x-axis and shows frequencies on the y-axis.

homoscedasticity assumption assumption of correlation and regression analyses that states that the *Y* variable should exhibit the same amount of variation across the range of scores of the *X* variable.

hypothesis testing a sequence of steps that help us to determine whether the evidence (a sample's results) support the hypothesis for the population.

I

imperfect association a type of linear association where the data points do not fall on the line of best fit.

independent events two events are independent when the occurrence of one event does not impact the probability of the other.

independent groups design (also called a *between-subjects design*) a type of study where different groups of participants experience the different levels of the independent variable.

independent variable the variable in an experiment that is manipulated to determine if it causes a change in the dependent variable; the cause.

inferential statistics a branch of statistics used to make conclusions about a population based on the data from a sample.

infographic a visual technique for conveying data that relies on images, figures, and tables presented in an appealing way.

interaction a unique effect where one independent variable's impact on the dependent variable is different or varies depending on the level of the other independent variable.

interval the range of scores used to create a grouped frequency table or histogram.

interval scale a level of measurement in which scores reflect the actual amount of a variable and differences of one unit reflect the same amount across the number line; zero, however, does not reflect an absence of the variable.

J

joint probability describes the probability that two or more events occur simultaneously, or successively.

K

kurtosis a measure of the "tailedness" of a distribution; kurtosis is high when a distribution has many extreme scores, and kurtosis is low when there are few or no extreme scores.

L

law of large numbers in random sequences, observed probabilities match expected frequencies only over a large number of trials.

least squares regression line another name for the line of best fit. So called because it is the regression line that results in the least amount of squared prediction error.

leptokurtic distribution a distribution that has more scores in the tails than a normal curve.

level a condition of a factor.

level of measurement (or *scale of measurement*) the types and characteristics of the information that numbers convey.

Levene's Test for Equality of Variances a statistical analysis used to test the equality of variances assumption.

linear prediction model (also called *regression equation* or *linear prediction rule*) a formula that allows us to make predictions about the criterion or outcome (Y) variable based on the predictor (X) variable.

line graph a type of graph where means are connected by lines. Used to depict the results of repeated-measures analyses.

M

main effects how different levels of one independent variable compare, ignoring any other independent variables.

Mann-Whitney U a statistical test that compares two independent samples for a dependent variable that is ordinal.

marginal mean the mean of all scores in a single row or column.

matched-samples design study methodology in which two different participants are matched on the basis of a shared characteristic, which results in their being treated as dependent means.

Mauchly's Test of Sphericity a hypothesis test used to assess the sphericity assumption of repeated-measures ANOVA.

mean sometimes called the arithmetic mean, a measure of central tendency that indicates the average of the numbers (sum of all numbers divided by the number of cases).

mean square between (MS_B) the mean amount of squared deviation between the groups.

mean square within (MS_W) the mean of the squared variation within groups.

median a measure of central tendency that indicates the place in a series of numbers that represents the midpoint location where half of the actual scores are above and half of the actual scores fall below.

mediation a type of multiple regression that examines whether a third variable explains the association between two variables.

mesokurtic distribution a distribution that is similar in kurtosis to a normal curve.

meta-analysis a type of research study that combines results from all relevant research.

mode a measure of central tendency indicating the number that occurs most often.

moderation a type of multiple regression that examines third variables that change the strength or direction of the association between two other variables.

multimodal distribution a distribution that has more than two modes.

multiple regression a type of analysis that examines whether multiple predictor variables account for the variation in a single criterion variable.

N

negative correlation a relationship between two variables when high scores on one variable correspond with low scores on the other variable, and vice versa.

negative skew values on the right side of a distribution are more frequent than values on the left.

no correlation a relationship between two variables when the variables are not related in a meaningful or systematic way.

nominal scale a level of measurement in which scores reflect not an amount of a variable but, rather, membership within a group or category.

nondirectional hypothesis a type of research hypothesis that predicts that the sample mean will be different from the population mean, but does not state the direction of the difference.

nonparametric test any test that does not rely on assumptions about the population, typically when we have nominal or ordinal scale data.

normal curve the theoretical symmetrical distribution shape when there is a large number of observations that are continuous scores. The curve depicts the probability or likelihood of observations occurring. Also known as the normal distribution, Gaussian distribution, or bell curve.

null hypothesis (H_0) a declaration that counters the research hypothesis by stating there is no effect or difference, and that the populations are the same.

nullification fallacy describes the mistaken assumption that nonsignificant findings are caused only by the absence of an effect of the independent variable.

O

one-sample Z-test a type of hypothesis test used to compare a single sample mean to a population mean.

one-tailed a comparison distribution that has a single critical region within only one of the distribution's tails.

one-way analysis of variance (or ANOVA) a hypothesis test that lets us determine if three or more samples are from different populations when we have continuous (interval or ratio) data.

open materials a principle of open science in which researchers make all study materials needed to reproduce the findings publicly available, typically on the Internet.

open science a series of key practices, including preregistration, sharing study methods, and sharing datasets, designed to encourage greater collaboration and transparency in the research process.

operational definition the specific way a researcher describes a construct in terms of concrete, observable, and measurable characteristics.

ordinal scale a level of measurement in which scores can be rank ordered.

outlier an extreme score; more technically, a score that occurs at least three standard deviations away from the mean.

P

partial eta squared (η_p^2) an effect size measure. In repeated-measures ANOVA, it indicates the amount of variation in the dependent variable attributable to the differences between condition means, after removing the participant variance.

participant effect changes in the participants' scores that are due to participants' expectations or beliefs about the purpose of an experiment, rather than the independent variable.

Pearson *r* product moment correlation coefficient (or more commonly just *Pearson* r) the correlation we calculate when both variables are continuous.

peer review a process in which fellow experts from the field examine the study to make sure the quality is sufficiently high to warrant publication.

percentile rank reflects the percentage of scores that occur below a particular value on the normal curve.

perfect association a type of linear association where all of the data points fall exactly on the line of best fit; a linear association with zero prediction error.

***p*-hacking** the questionable research practice whereby researchers manipulate their data until they find significant results.

pie chart a circle that represents 100% of responses and is divided to represent categories as percentages.

pilot test a trial run that allows us to refine the study prior to running a full-scale study.

platykurtic distribution a distribution that has fewer scores in its tails than a normal curve.

population every single person, animal, or object that has relevant data about a research question.

positive correlation a relationship between two variables when high scores on one variable correspond with high scores on the other variable, while low scores on one variable also correspond with low scores on the other.

positive skew values on the left side of a distribution are more frequent than values on the right.

post hoc tests statistical analyses performed after rejecting the null hypothesis of an ANOVA and used to identify specific differences between pairs of groups.

posttest a measurement taken after the introduction of the independent variable.

power analysis an analysis conducted prior to the start of a study that has the goal of determining the sample size needed to achieve a specified level of power.

power the likelihood that a research study can correctly reject the null hypothesis.

prediction error the difference between the observed values of the criterion variable and the values predicted by the regression equation.

predictor the *X* variable that we use in regression to forecast, explain, or predict another variable.

preregistration openly and clearly stating a study's purpose and hypotheses before collecting any data.

preregistration of hypotheses a procedure to increase research transparency where researchers post their predictions in a public forum, such that they can later prove that they made these predictions before analyzing their data.

pretest a measurement taken prior to the introduction of the independent variable.

probability how likely an event, case, or outcome is to occur, relative to all potential outcomes.

probability distribution a probability distribution is a listing of all possible outcomes of an experiment and their associated probabilities.

publication bias tendency for scholarly journals to publish only papers that report statistically significant findings.

***p*-value** probability of obtaining sample data (e.g., sample mean) if the null hypothesis is true.

***p*-value approach** approach to hypothesis testing that calculates the exact probability of the test statistic and compares that to alpha.

Q

questionable research practice (QRP) analytical techniques that are acceptable under certain conditions but that can be exploited to produce a specific result or confirm a particular hypothesis.

R

random sampling (also called *random selection*) a sampling strategy by which every single person in the entire population has the same chance of being included in the sample.

range a measure of variability that indicates how far apart the top score is from the bottom score.

ratio scale a level of measurement in which scores reflect the amount of a variable present, and a zero score indicates the absence of the variable; ratio variables have the property that one can calculate meaningful ratios.

raw data numerical information that has not been processed, changed, or analyzed in any way.

registered report type of scholarly article that is accepted for publication prior to collection of data, based on the importance of the hypothesis it is testing and the procedures used to test the hypothesis.

regression line a straight line that serves as a visual representation that best describes how the outcome variable (Y) changes relative to changes in the predictor variable (X) on a scatterplot.

relative frequency the number of times that a particular score occurs in a data set, relative to the total number of observations.

repeated-measures analysis of variance (also known as *one-way within-groups ANOVA*) a statistic that lets us determine if three or more scores from the same sample are significantly different when we have continuous (interval or ratio) data and when we don't know the variance.

repeated-measures design (also called *within-subjects design*) study methodology in which each participant is measured twice on the dependent variable: prior to the introduction of the independent variable (called the *pretest*), and after the introduction of the independent variable (called the *posttest*).

replication (also called *reproducibility*) the notion in science that all findings should survive repeated testing before they are accepted.

replication crisis a crisis that exists in psychology and other sciences as a result of the failure to replicate findings that were previously accepted.

representative sample a smaller subset that shares the same characteristics of the larger overall population.

research hypothesis (H_1) states how we believe the populations will compare to each other or how the populations will differ.

research protocol the specific steps the researcher should follow during the study.

residual error another name for prediction error; the difference between observed and predicted values of the criterion variable.

residual score the absolute value of a deviation score ($X - M$).

restriction of range situation that occurs when researchers are only able to sample a part of the full range of scores that occurs in the population for a variable. Impacts the value of the correlation coefficient that we observe in a sample.

S

sample subset of people selected from the population using some defined procedure.

sampling error the difference between a sample statistic and the population, caused by analyzing a subset of the population.

sampling technique how participants were recruited into the study.

sampling with replacement a sampling technique in which individuals included in a sample are replaced in the population such that they could be sampled again.

scatterplot a depiction of two continuous variables that depicts the relationship between the variables; the X variable is presented on the horizontal axis and the Y variable is presented on the vertical axis; on the graph, each dot represents a single participant's scores on the X and Y variables.

score a participant's individual result on a variable.

significance fallacy describes the mistaken assumption that statistically significant findings are meaningful or useful in a practical context.

simple main effects tests hypothesis tests that help us understand why an interaction is significant. Simple main effects tests examine how the effect of one independent variable changes across the levels of the other independent variable.

single sample *t*-test (also called *one-sample* t-*test*) a statistic that lets us determine if a single sample is different from a population when we have continuous (interval or ratio) data and when we don't know the variance.

skewness the degree to which a distribution is not symmetrical; distributions can be positively or negatively skewed.

Spearman correlation a type of correlation that analyzes ordinal data and certain curvilinear associations between interval/ratio variables.

sphericity assumption assumption of repeated-measures ANOVA that states that all pairs of difference scores should have equal variances.

spurious correlation a situation in which two variables are mathematically correlated, but not causally related.

standard deviation (*SD*) a measure of variability that indicates how far scores are dispersed from the mean using the same units as the original scale. It is the square root of the variance, or $\sqrt{SD^2}$. They are the most widely used statistic for describing variability.

standard error (*SE*) name given to the standard deviation of a sampling distribution.

standard error of the estimate a calculation of the average distance between our regression line and each data point.

standardized beta coefficient a statistic used in multiple regression to compare the relative importance of different predictor variables. In regression with one predictor, the standardized beta coefficient equals the correlation coefficient.

standard normal distribution a normal curve with a mean of 0 and a standard deviation of 1.

statistically significant results that are highly unlikely to have happened if in reality the null hypothesis is true.

statistics the science of identifying, gathering, organizing, summarizing, analyzing, and interpreting numerical information to draw conclusions about the world.

Studentized Range statistic (*q_k*) a statistic that controls for our experimentwise error by taking into account the sample size and number of conditions we are comparing.

sum of squares between (*SS_Between*) the sum of squared deviation scores, which measures the total between-groups variation.

sum of squares error a statistic that quantifies the total amount of squared prediction error. The line of best fit is the one that minimizes the sum of squares error.

sum of squares (*SS*) the sum of the squared deviation scores, or $\Sigma(X - M)^2$.

sum of squares total (*SS_Total*) the difference between each score and the grand mean.

sum of squares within (*SS_Within*) the sum of squared deviation scores, which measures the total within-groups variation.

suppression effect when the combination of independent variables produces an effect less than its parts.

symmetrical distribution a type of distribution where the pattern of scores to the left of the middle is approximately identical to the pattern of scores to the right of the median; the median, mean, and mode occur at the same point.

synergistic effect when the combination of independent variables produces an effect greater than its parts.

syntax file the file generated by statistical software programs that records the set of data analyses that a researcher performs, rather than the results of those analyses.

T

test-retest reliability how much a person's first score correlates with their second score on the same test.

test statistic the computed statistic used to evaluate the null hypothesis.

testwise error rate the probability of making a Type I error for any particular hypothesis test.

third variable problem problematic situation where the correlation between two variables is due to a third variable that is correlated with each variable separately. This problem affects our ability to make causal conclusions when interpreting correlational results.

***t*-test for dependent means** (also called *paired samples* t-*test*) a type of hypothesis test used to compare two sets of non-independent scores. Typically used to compare scores measured from the same participants, such as in a repeated measures design.

***t*-test for two independent samples** (also called *independent samples* t-*test*) a statistical test that lets us determine if two samples are from different populations when we have a continuous (interval or ratio) dependent variable and when we don't know the population variance.

Tukey's Honestly Significant Difference (HSD) a post hoc test that seeks to identify the smallest difference (called the HSD) between any pair of means that would be significant at a specific level of alpha.

two-tailed a comparison distribution that has two critical regions, one in both of the distribution's tails.

Type I error rejecting the null hypothesis when you should not (i.e., saying there is an effect when there is not).

Type II error failing to reject the null when you should (i.e., missing an effect that was there).

U

uniform distribution a distribution in which all of the values occur with approximately the same frequency.

unimodal distribution a distribution that has one "peak," representing the most frequently occurring value.

V

values any possible outcomes for a variable.

variability how spread out the scores are in a distribution.

variable anything that can change.

variance (SD^2) a measure of variability that generally lets us know how far, on average, numbers in the distribution are spread out from the mean, $\sum(X - M)^2/N$, or SS/N.

volunteer bias a problem encountered when recruiting participants for a study where the people who volunteer to participate in a study are systematically different than the people do not volunteer. As a result, a sample may not be representative of the population.

W

weighted average a way of calculating the mean in which some ratings are multiplied in order to give them more importance.

WEIRD samples acronym that describes samples from Western, Educated, Industrialized, Rich, and Democratic cultures.

within-groups design when each study participant receives every level of the independent variable.

Z

***Z*-score** a transformation that takes an individual raw score and coverts it into a standardized format where the mean is 0 and standard deviation is 1.

References

Ahn, J. S., Min, S., & Kim, M. H. (2017). The role of uncontrolled eating and screen time in the link of attention deficit hyperactivity disorder with weight in late childhood. *Psychiatry Investigation, 14*, 808–816.

Akinola, M., & Mendes, W. B. (2008). The dark side of creativity: Biological vulnerability and negative emotions lead to greater artistic creativity. *Personality and Social Psychology Bulletin, 34*(12), 1677–1686.

Allan, G. M., & Arroll, B. (2014). Prevention and treatment of the common cold: Making sense of the evidence. *Canadian Medical Association Journal, 186*(3), 190–199. https://doi.org/10.1503/cmaj.121442

American Psychological Association (APA). (2018). *School psychology.* http://www.apa.org/ed/graduate/specialize/school.aspx

American Psychological Association (APA). (2020). *Stress in America 2020: A national mental health crisis.* Stress in America Survey. https://www.apa.org/news/press/releases/stress/2020/sia-mental-health-crisis.pdf

Appleby, D. C. (2015). *An online career-exploration resource for psychology majors.* Society for the Teaching of Psychology's Office of Teaching Resources. http://www.teachpsych.org/Resources/Documents/otrp/resources/appleby15students.docx

Aschwanden, C. (2016, January 6). *You can't trust what you read about nutrition.* FiveThirtyEight.com. https://fivethirtyeight.com/features/you-cant-trust-what-you-read-about-nutrition/

Asendorpf, J. B., Conner, M., De Fruyt, F., De Houwer, J., Denissen, J. J., Fiedler, K., Fiedler, S., Funder, D. C., Kliegl, R., Nosek, B. A., Perugini, M., Roberts, B. W., Schmitt, M., van Aken, M. A. G., Weber, H., & Wicherts, J. M. (2013). Recommendations for increasing replicability in psychology. *European Journal of Personality, 27*, 108–119. https://doi.org/10.1002/per.1919

Bakker, M., van Dijk, A., & Wicherts, J. M. (2012). The rules of the game called psychological science. *Perspectives on Psychological Science, 7*, 543–554.

Bandelow, B., Reitt, M., Röver, C., Michaelis, S., Görlich, Y., & Wedekind, D. (2015). Efficacy of treatments for anxiety disorders: A meta-analysis. *International Clinical Psychopharmacology, 30*, 183–192.

Bargh, J. A., Chen, M., & Burrows, L. (1996). Automaticity of social behavior: Direct effects of trait construct and stereotype activation on action. *Journal of Personality and Social Psychology, 71*(2), 230–244.

Baumeister, R. F., Bratslavsky, E., Muraven, M., & Tice, D. (1998). Ego depletion: Is the active self a limited resource? *Journal of Personality and Social Psychology, 74*, 1252–1265.

Benjamin, D. J., Berger, J. O., Johannesson, M., Nosek, B. A., Wagenmakers, E. J., Berk, R., Bollen, K. A., Brembs, B., Brown, L., Camerer, C., Cesarini, D., Chambers, C. D., Clyde, M., Cook, T. D., De Boeck, P., Dienes, Z., Dreber, A., Easwaran, K., Efferson, C., . . . Johnson, V. E. (2018). Redefine statistical significance. *Nature Human Behaviour, 2*, 6–10. https://doi.org/10.1038/s41562-017-0189-z

Berger, J., & Barasch, A. (2015). Posting posed, choosing candid: Photo posters mispredict audience preferences. *Advances in Consumer Research, 43*, 52–53.

Birdee, G. S., Legedza, A. T., Saper, R. B., Bertisch, S. M., Eisenberg, D. M., & Phillips, R. S. (2008). Characteristics of yoga users: Results of a national survey. *Journal of General Internal Medicine, 23*, 1653–1658.

Blackwell, L. S., Trzesniewski, K. H., & Dweck, C. S. (2007). Implicit theories of intelligence predict achievement across an adolescent transition: A longitudinal study and an intervention. *Child Development, 78*(1), 246–263. https://www.jstor.org/stable/4139223

Boaler, J. (2013). Ability and mathematics: The mind-set revolution that is reshaping education. *Forum, 55*, 143–152.

Bureau of Labor Statistics, U.S. Department of Labor. (2022, April 18). *Occupational Outlook Handbook: Mathematicians and Statisticians.* https://www.bls.gov/ooh/math/mathematicians-and-statisticians.htm

Byrne, M. (2014). *Instagram statistics.* OpticalCortex.com. https://opticalcortex.com/instagram-statistics/

Centers for Disease Control and Prevention (CDC). (2018). *Use of yoga and meditation becoming more popular in U.S.* https://www.cdc.gov/nchs/pressroom/nchs_press_releases/2018/201811_Yoga_Meditation.htm

Centers for Disease Control and Prevention (CDC). (2020). *National marriage and divorce rate trends for 2000–2020.* https://www.cdc.gov/nchs/fastats/marriage-divorce.htm

Chambers, C. (2019). What's next for registered reports? *Nature, 573*, 187–189.

Chan, B. L., Witt, R., Charrow, A. P., Magee, A., Howard, R., Pasquina, P. F., Heilman, K. M., & Tsao, J. W. (2007). Mirror therapy for phantom limb pain. *New England Journal of Medicine, 357*(21), 2206–2207. https://doi.org/10.1056/NEJMc071927

Christensen, A. P., Silvia, P. J., Nusbaum, E. C., & Beaty, R. E. (2018). Clever people: Intelligence and humor production ability. *Psychology of Aesthetics, Creativity, and the Arts, 12*(2), 136–143.

Cohen, J. (1988). *Statistical power analysis for the behavioral sciences.* Lawrence Erlbaum Associates.

Cohen, J. (1992). Statistical power analysis. *Current Directions in Psychological Science, 1*(3), 98–101. https://doi.org/10.1111/1467-8721.ep10768783

Cohen, S., Kamarck, T., & Mermelstein, R. (1983). A global measure of perceived stress. *Journal of Health and Social Behavior, 24*, 385–396.

Collins, T. J., & Gillath, O. (2012). Attachment, breakup strategies, and associated outcomes: The effects of security enhancement on the selection of breakup strategies. *Journal of Research in Personality, 46*(2), 210–222. https://doi.org/10.1016/j.jrp.2012.01.008

Corsi, P. M. (1972). Human memory and the medial temporal region of the brain. *Dissertation Abstracts International, 34*(02), 891B (University Microfilms No. AAI05-77717).

Cowan, N. (2010). The magical mystery four: How is working memory capacity limited, and why? *Current Directions in Psychological Science, 19*, 51–57.

Cumming, G. (2014). The new statistics: Why and how. *Psychological Science, 25*(1), 7–29. https://doi.org/10.1177/0956797613504966

Cumming, G., Fidler, F., & Vaux, D. L. (2007). Error bars in experimental biology. *The Journal of Cell Biology, 177*, 7–11. https://doi.org/10.1083/jcb.200611141

Dar-Nimrod, I., Hansen, I. G., Proulx, T., Lehman, D. R., Chapman, B. P., & Duberstein, P. R. (2012). Coolness: An empirical investigation. *Journal of Individual Differences, 33*(3), 175–185. https://doi.org/10.1027/1614-0001/a000088

Deater-Deckard, K., Mullineaux, P. Y., Beekman, C., Petrill, S. A., Schatschneider, C., & Thompson, L. A. (2009). Conduct problems, IQ, and household chaos: A longitudinal multi-informant study. *Journal of Child Psychology and Psychiatry, and Allied Disciplines, 50*(10), 1301–1308. https://doi.org/10.1111/j.1469-7610.2009.02108.x

de Vries, A. M., Schulz, T., Westerhuis, R., Navis, G. J., Niesing, J., Ranchor, A. V., & Schroevers, M. J. (2017). Goal disturbance changes pre/post-renal transplantation are related to changes in distress. *British Journal of Health Psychology, 22*, 524–541. https://doi.org/10.1111/bjhp.12243

Dowdy, A., Hantula, D. A., Travers, J. C., & Tincani, M. (2021). Meta-analytic methods to detect publication bias in behavior science research. *Perspectives on Behavior Science, 45*(1), 37–52. https://doi.org/10.1007/s40614-021-00303-0

Draganski, B., Gaser, C., Busch, V., Schuierer, G., Bodgahn, U., & May, A. (2004). Changes in grey matter induced by training. *Nature, 427*, 311–312.

Draganski, B., Gaser, C., Kempermann, G., Kuhn, H. G., Winkler, J., Büchel, C., & May, A. (2006). Temporal and spatial dynamics of brain structure changes during extensive learning. *The Journal of Neuroscience, 26*(23), 6314–6317. https://doi.org/10.1523/JNEUROSCI.4628-05.2006

Dunn, E. W., Aknin, L., & Norton, M. I. (2008). Spending money on others promotes happiness. *Science, 319*, 1687–1688. https://doi.org/10.1126/science.1150952

Dunn, E. W., Gilbert, D. T., & Wilson, T. D. (2011). If money doesn't make you happy, then you probably aren't spending it right. *Journal of Consumer Psychology, 21*(2), 115–125. https://doi.org/10.1016/j.jcps.2011.02.002

Edgell, S. E., & Noon, S. M. (1984). Effect of violation of normality on the *t* test of the correlation coefficient. *Psychological Bulletin, 95*(3), 576–583.

Farrell Pagulayan, K., Busch, R. M., Medina, K. L., Bartok, J. A., & Krikorian, R. (2006). Developmental normative data for the Corsi block-tapping task. *Journal of Clinical and Experimental Neuropsychology, 28*, 1043–1052.

Finley, A. (2021). *How college contributes to workforce success: Employer views on what matters most.* Association of American Colleges and Universities. https://dgmg81phhvh63.cloudfront.net/content/user-photos/Research/PDFs/AACUEmployerReport2021.pdf

Fismer, K. L., & Pilkington, K. (2012). Lavender and sleep: A systematic review of the evidence. *European Journal of Integrative Medicine, 4*, e436–e447.

Forbes.com. (2020, April). *The world's highest-paid celebrities.* https://www.forbes.com/celebrities/list/#tab:overall

Franzen, S., van den Berg, E., Goudsmit, M., Jurgens, C. K., van de Wiel, L., Kalkisim, Y., Uysal-Bozkir, Ö., Ayhan, Y., Nielsen, T. R., & Papma, J. M. (2020). A systematic review of neuropsychological tests for the assessment of dementia in non-western, low-educated or illiterate populations. *Journal of the International Neuropsychological Society, 26*(3), 331–351. https://doi.org/10.1017/S1355617719000894

Fredrickson, B. L. (2001). The role of positive emotions in positive psychology: The broaden-and-build theory of positive emotions. *American Psychologist, 56*(3), 218–226. https://doi.org/10.1037/0003-066X.56.3.218

Gale, A., & Lewis, M. B. (2019). When the camera does lie: Selfies are dishonest indicators of dominance. *Psychology of Popular Media, 9*(4), 447–455. https://doi.org/10.1037/ppm0000260

Gathercole, S. E., Dunning, D. L., Holmes, J., & Norris, D. (2019). Working memory training involves learning new skills. *Journal of Memory and Language, 105*, 19–42. https://doi.org/10.1016/j.jml.2018.10.003

Gazzaley, A., Cooney, J. W., Rissman, J., & D'Esposito, M. (2005). Top-down suppression deficit underlies working memory impairment in normal aging. *Nature Neuroscience, 8*(10), 1298–1300. https://doi.org/10.1038/nn1543

Gerber, P., Schlaffke, L., Heba, S., Greenlee, M. W., Schultz, T., & Schmidt-Wilcke, T. (2014). Juggling revisited—A voxel-based morphometry study with expert jugglers. *NeuroImage, 95*, 320–325. https://doi.org/10.1016/j.neuroimage.2014.04.023

Gewin, V. (2016). Data sharing: An open mind on open data. *Nature, 529*(7584), 117–119.

Gignac, G. E., Karatamoglou, A., Wee, S., & Palacios, G. (2014). Emotional intelligence as a unique predictor of individual differences in humour styles and humour appreciation. *Personality and Individual Differences, 56*, 34–39.

Gollwitzer, P. M. (1999). Implementation intentions: Strong effects of simple plans. *American Psychologist, 54*, 493–503.

Goodstein, D. (1994). Pariah science: Whatever happened to cold fusion? *The American Scholar, 63*, 527–541.

Gordon, W. (2020, December 1). Social media can be toxic. Here's how to make sure your feeds aren't. *Popular Science.* https://www.popsci.com/story/diy/avoid-social-media-toxicity-guide/

Greengross, G., & Miller, G. (2011). Humor ability reveals intelligence, predicts mating success, and is higher in males. *Intelligence, 39*(4), 188–192.

Griffith, R. L., Gillath, O., Zhao, X., & Martinez, R. (2017). Staying friends with ex-romantic partners: Predictors, reasons, and outcomes. *Personal Relationships, 24*(3), 550–584. https://doi.org/10.1111/pere.12197

Gruber, C., Keil, T., Kulig, M., Roll, S., Wahn, U., Wahn, V., & MAS-90 Study Group. (2008). History of respiratory infections in the first 12 yr among children from a birth cohort. *Pediatric Allergy and Immunology, 19*(6), 505–512. https://doi.org/10.1111/j.1399-3038.2007.00688.x

Guilford, J. P., Merrifield, P. R., & Wilson, R. C. (1958). *Unusual uses test*. Sheridan Psychological Services.

Hao, N., Yuan, H., Cheng, R., Wang, Q., & Runco, M. A. (2015). Interaction effect of response medium and working memory capacity on creative idea generation. *Frontiers in Psychology, 6*, 1582.

Hardy, J. L., Nelson, R. A., Thomason, M. E., Sternberg, D. A., Katovich, K., Farzin, F., & Scanlon, M. (2015). Enhancing cognitive abilities with comprehensive training: A large, online, randomized, active-controlled trial. *PLoS ONE, 10*(9), e0134467.

Harp, N. R., Freeman, J. B., & Neta, M. (2022). Mindfulness-based stress reduction triggers a long-term shift toward more positive appraisals of emotional ambiguity. *Journal of Experimental Psychology: General, 151*(9), 2160–2172. https://doi.org/10.1037/xge0001173

Hart Research Associates. (2015). *Falling short? College learning and career success*. Association of American Colleges & Universities. https://www.aacu.org/sites/default/files/files/LEAP/2015employerstudentsurvey.pdf

Henrich, J., Heine, S. J., & Norenzayan, A. (2010). The weirdest people in the world? *Behavioral and Brain Sciences, 33*(2–3), 61–83.

Hirst, W., Phelps, E. A., Meksin, R., Vaidya, C. J., Johnson, M. K., Mitchell, K. J., Buckner, R. L., Budson, A. E., Gabrieli, J. D. E., Lustig, C., Mather, M., Ochsner, K. N., Schacter, D., Simons, J. S., Lyle, K. B., Cuc, A. F., & Olsson, A. (2015). A ten-year follow-up of a study of memory for the attack of September 11, 2001: Flashbulb memories and memories for flashbulb events. *Journal of Experimental Psychology: General, 144*, 604. https://doi.org/10.1037/xge0000055

Hooper, J., Sharpe, D., & Roberts, S. G. B. (2016). Are men funnier than women, or do we just think they are? *Translational Issues in Psychological Science, 2*(1), 54–62.

Howarth, A., Smith, J. G., Perkins-Porras, L., & Ussher, M. (2019). Effects of brief mindfulness-based interventions on health-related outcomes: A systematic review. *Mindfulness, 10*, 1957–1968. https://doi.org/10.1007/s12671-019-01163-1

Howrigan, D. P., & MacDonald, K. B. (2008). Humor as a mental fitness indicator. *Evolutionary Psychology, 6*(4), 625–666.

Isen, A. M., Daubman, K. A., & Nowicki, G. P. (1987). Positive affect facilitates creative problem solving. *Journal of Personality and Social Psychology, 52*(6), 1122–1131.

Ito, Y., Browne, C. A., & Yamamoto, K. (2022). The impacts of mindfulness-based stress reduction (MBSR) on mindfulness and well-being for regular and novice meditators. *Mindfulness, 13*(6), 1458–1468. https://doi.org/10.1007/s12671-022-01888-6

John, L. K., Loewenstein, G., & Prelec, D. (2012). Measuring the prevalence of questionable research practices with incentives for truth telling. *Psychological Science, 23*(5), 524–532. https://doi.org/10.1177/0956797611430953

John, O. P., Donahue, E. M., & Kentle, R. L. (1991). *The Big Five Inventory—Versions 4a and 54*. University of California, Berkeley, Institute of Personality and Social Research.

Kaminske, A. N. (2020, January 9). How to choose the right way to study for you: Advice for students. *The Learning Scientists*. https://www.learningscientists.org/blog/2020/1/9-1

Kaminski, J., Call, J., & Fischer, J. (2004). Word learning in a domestic dog: Evidence for "fast mapping." *Science, 304*, 1682–1683.

Kensinger, E. A., & Corkin, S. (2003). Memory enhancement for emotional words: are emotional words more vividly remembered than neutral words? *Memory & Cognition, 31*(8), 1169–1180. https://doi.org/10.3758/bf03195800

Kirschbaum, C., Pirke, K. M., & Hellhammer, D. H. (1993). The "Trier Social Stress Test"—A tool for investigating psychobiological stress responses in a laboratory setting. *Neuropsychobiology, 28*(1–2), 76–81.

Klein, R. A., Vianello, M., Hasselman, F., Adams, B. G., Adams, R. B., Jr., Alper, S., Aveyard, M., Axt, J. R., Babalola, M. T., Bahník, Š., Batra, R., Berkics, M., Bernstein, M. J., Berry, D. R., Bialobrzeska, O., Binan, E. D., Bocian, K., Brandt, M. J., Busching, R., . . . Nosek, B. A. (2018). Many Labs 2: Investigating variation in replicability across samples and settings. *Advances in Methods and Practices in Psychological Science, 1*(4), 443–490. https://doi.org/10.1177/2515245918810225

Koessler, R. B., Kohut, T., & Campbell, L. (2019). When your boo becomes a ghost: The association between breakup strategy and breakup role in experiences of relationship dissolution. *Collabra: Psychology, 5*(1), 29, 1–18. https://doi.org/10.1525/collabra.230

Kühberger, A., Fritz, A., Lermer, E., & Scherndl, T. (2015). The significance fallacy in inferential statistics. *BMC Research Notes, 8*, 84.

Landrigan, J. F., Bell, T., Crowe, M., Clay, O. J., & Mirman, D. (2020). Lifting cognition: A meta-analysis of effects of resistance exercise on cognition. *Psychological Research, 84*, 1167–1183. https://doi.org/10.1007/s00426-019-01145-x

Le, B., Dove, N. L., Agnew, C. R., Korn, M. S., & Mutso, A. A. (2010). Predicting nonmarital romantic relationship dissolution: A meta-analytic synthesis. *Personal Relationships, 17*(3), 377–390. https://doi.org/10.1111/j.1475-6811.2010.01285.x

LeBel, E. P., Campbell, L., & Loving, T. J. (2017). Benefits of open and high-powered research outweigh costs. *Journal of Personality and Social Psychology, 113*, 230–243. https://doi.org/10.1037/pspi0000049

Lee, K., Sidhu, D. M., & Pexman, P. M. (2021). Teaching sarcasm: Evaluating metapragmatic training for typically developing children. *Canadian Journal of Experimental Psychology/Revue canadienne de psychologie expérimentale, 75*(2), 139–145. https://doi.org/10.1037/cep0000228

Lee, M. S., Choi, J., Posadzki, P., & Ernst, E. (2012). Aromatherapy for health care: An overview of systematic reviews. *Maturitas, 71*, 257–260. https://doi.org/10.1016/j.maturitas.2011.12.018

Leon, A. C., Davis, L. L., & Kraemer, H. C. (2011). The role and interpretation of pilot studies in clinical research. *Journal of Psychiatric Research, 45*(5), 626–629.

Lilienfeld, S. O. (2007). Psychological treatments that cause harm. *Perspectives on Psychological Science, 2*, 53–70.

Limakatso, K., Bedwell, G. J., Madden, V. J., & Parker, R. (2020). The prevalence and risk factors for phantom limb pain in people with amputations: A systematic review and meta-analysis. *PLoS ONE, 15*(10), 1–21. https://doi.org/10.1371/journal.pone.0240431

Lister, M. (2022, July). Thirty-one mind-boggling Instagram stats & facts for 2022. *The WordStream Blog*. https://www.wordstream.com/blog/ws/2017/04/20/instagram-statistics

Liu, Y., Zhu, J., & He, J. (2022). Can selfies trigger social anxiety? A study on the relationship between social media selfie behavior and social anxiety in Chinese youth group. *Frontiers Psychology, 13*, 1016538. https://doi.org/10.3389/fpsyg.2022.1016538

López-Muñoz, F., & Alamo, C. (2009). Monoaminergic neurotransmission: The history of the discovery of antidepressants from 1950s until today. *Current Pharmaceutical Design, 15*, 1563–1586.

Lyubomirsky, S., & Lepper, H. S. (1999). A measure of subjective happiness: Preliminary reliability and construct validation. *Social Indicators Research, 46*(2), 137–155. https://doi.org/10.1023/A:1006824100041

Mackworth, N. H. (1948). The breakdown of vigilance during prolonged visual search. *Quarterly Journal of Experimental Psychology, 1*, 6–21.

Manning-Schaffel, V. (2018, February). *The world's 20 most popular bucket list activities*. LiveStrong.com. https://www.livestrong.com/slideshow/1012668-worlds-20-popular-bucket-list-activities/

Maras, D., Flament, M. F., Murray, M., Buchholz, A., Henderson, K. A., Obeid, N., & Goldfield, G. S. (2015). Screen time is associated with depression and anxiety in Canadian youth. *Preventive Medicine, 73*, 133–138.

Mårtensson, J., Eriksson, J., Bodammer, N. C., Lindgren, M., Johansson, M., Nyberg, L., & Lövdén, M. (2012). Growth of language-related brain areas after foreign language learning. *NeuroImage*, *63*, 240–244.

Matthews, T. D., & Lassiter, K. S. (2007). What does the Wonderlic Personnel Test measure? *Psychological Reports*, *100*(3, pt. 1), 707–712.

Maxwell, S. E. (2004). The persistence of underpowered studies in psychological research: Causes, consequences, and remedies. *Psychological Methods*, *9*, 147–163.

Messer, W. S., Griggs, R. A., & Jackson, S. L. (1999). A national survey of undergraduate psychology degree options and major requirements. *Teaching of Psychology*, *26*(3), 164–171. https://doi.org/10.1207/S15328023TOP260301

Miller, C. C. (2018, January 18). The U.S. fertility rate is down, yet more women are mothers. *The New York Times*. https://www.nytimes.com/2018/01/18/upshot/the-us-fertility-rate-is-down-yet-more-women-are-mothers.html

Miller, G. A. (1956). The magical number seven, plus or minus two: Some limits on our capacity for processing information. *Psychological Review*, *63*, 81–97.

Miyazaki, A., Okuyama, T., Mori, H., Sato, K., Kumamoto, K., & Hiyama, A. (2022). Effects of two short-term aerobic exercises on cognitive function in healthy older adults during COVID-19 confinement in Japan: A pilot randomized controlled trial. *International Journal of Environmental Research and Public Health*, *19*(10), 6202. https://doi.org/10.3390/ijerph19106202

Moyer, C. A., Rounds, J., & Hannum, J. W. (2004). A meta-analysis of massage therapy research. *Psychological Bulletin*, *130*(1), 3–18.

Murray, S. L., & Holmes, J. G. (1999). The (mental) ties that bind: Cognitive structures that predict relationship resilience. *Journal of Personality and Social Psychology*, *77*(6), 1228–1244. https://doi.org/10.1037/0022-3514.77.6.1228

Nickerson, R. S. (1998). Confirmation bias: A ubiquitous phenomenon in many guises. *Review of General Psychology*, *2*(2), 175–220. https://doi.org/10.1037/1089-2680.2.2.175

Nosek, B. A., Ebersole, C. R., DeHaven, A. C., & Mellor, D. T. (2018). The preregistration revolution. *Proceedings of the National Academy of Sciences*, *115*, 2600–2606.

Nouchi, R., Taki, Y., Takeuchi, H., Hashizume, H., Nozawa, T., Kambara, T., Sekiguchi, A., Miyauchi, C. M., Kotozaki, Y., Nouchi, H., & Kawashima, R. (2013). Brain-training game boosts executive functions, working memory and processing speed in the young adults: A randomized controlled trial. *PLoS ONE*, *8*, e55518. https://doi.org/10.1371/journal.pone.0055518

Office of Research Integrity, U.S. Department of Health and Human Services. (2017, September 25). *A brief overview on conflict of interests*. https://ori.hhs.gov/conflicts-interest-and-commitment

Oishi, S., Kesebir, S., & Diener, E. (2011). Income inequality and happiness. *Psychological Science*, *22*(9), 1095–1100. https://doi.org/10.1177/0956797611417262

Open Science Collaboration. (2015). Estimating the reproducibility of psychological science. *Science*, *349*, aac4716.

Oswald, T. K., Rumbold, A. R., Kedzior, S. G. E., & Moore, V. M. (2020). Psychological impacts of "screen time" and "green time" for children and adolescents: A systematic scoping review. *PLoS One*, *15*(9), e0237725. https://doi.org/10.1371/journal.pone.0237725

Parsons, C. A., Alden, L. E., & Biesanz, J. C. (2021). Influencing emotion: Social anxiety and comparisons on Instagram. *Emotion*, *21*(7), 1427.

Patterson, A. (2015). The daily word counts of 39 famous authors. *WritersWrite.co.za*. https://writerswrite.co.za/the-daily-word-counts-of-39-famous-authors-1/

Pautasso, M. (2010). Worsening file-drawer problem in the abstracts of natural, medical and social science databases. *Scientometrics*, *85*(1), 193–202.

Pilley, J. W., & Reid, A. K. (2011). Border collie comprehends object names as verbal referents. *Behavioural Processes*, *86*, 184–195.

Popper, K. (1959). *The logic of scientific discovery*. Hutchison.

Przybylski, A. K. (2019). Digital screen time and pediatric sleep: Evidence from a preregistered cohort study. *The Journal of Pediatrics, 205*, 218–223.

Puah, S., Khalid, M., Looi, C., & Khor, E. (2021). Investigating working adults' intentions to participate in microlearning using the decomposed theory of planned behaviour. *British Journal of Educational Technology, 53*, 367–390. https://doi.org/10.1111/bjet.13170

Rogers, T., & Milkman, K. L. (2016). Reminders through association. *Psychological Science, 27*, 973–986.

Rosenthal, R. (1979). The file drawer problem and tolerance for null results. *Psychological Bulletin, 86*(3), 638–641. https://doi.org/10.1037/0033-2909.86.3.638

Sakaluk, J. K. (2016). Exploring small, confirming big: An alternative system to the new statistics for advancing cumulative and replicable psychological research. *Journal of Experimental Social Psychology, 66*, 47–54.

Schneider, P., Scherg, M., Dosch, H. G., Specht, H. J., Gutschalk, A., & Rupp, A. (2002). Morphology of Heschl's gyrus reflects enhanced activation in the auditory cortex of musicians. *Nature Neuroscience, 5*, 688.

Schönbrodt, F. D., & Perugini, M. (2013). At what sample size do correlations stabilize? *Journal of Research in Personality, 47*(5), 609–612.

Schroeder, B. (2021, June 11). The data analytics profession and employment is exploding—three trends that matter. *Forbes*. https://www.forbes.com/sites/bernhardschroeder/2021/06/11/the-data-analytics-profession-and-employment-is-exploding-three-trends-that-matter/

Sedgewick, J. R., Flath, M. E., & Elias, L. J. (2017). Presenting your best self(ie): The influence of gender on vertical orientation of selfies on Tinder. *Frontiers in Psychology, 8*.

Settanni, M., & Marengo, D. (2015). Sharing feelings online: Studying emotional well-being via automated text analysis of Facebook posts. *Frontiers in Psychology, 6*, 1–7.

Shi, B., Wang, L., Yang, J., Zhang, M., & Xu, L. (2017). Relationship between divergent thinking and intelligence: An empirical study of the threshold hypothesis with Chinese children. *Frontiers in Psychology, 8*, 254. https://doi.org/10.3389/fpsyg.2017.00254

Simmons, J. P. (2020, February 28). What do true findings look like? In E. J. Masicampo & N. Toosi (Chairs), *What do we know and what should we be teaching others about our field?* [Symposium]. Society for Personality and Social Psychology Annual Conference, New Orleans, LA, United States.

Simmons, J. P., Nelson, L. D., & Simonsohn, U. (2017, November 6). *How to properly preregister a study* [Web log post]. http://datacolada.org/64

Simons, D. J., Boot, W. R., Charness, N., Gathercole, S. E., Chabris, C. F., Hambrick, D. Z., & Stine-Morrow, E. A. L. (2016). Do "brain-training" programs work? *Psychological Science in the Public Interest, 17*(3), 103–186.

Sizemore, O. J., & Lewandowski, G. W., Jr. (2009). Learning might not equal liking: Research methods course changes knowledge but not attitudes. *Teaching of Psychology, 36*(2), 90–95. https://doi.org/10.1080/00986280902739727

Smid, C. R., Karbach, J., & Steinbeis, N. (2020). Toward a science of effective cognitive training. *Current Directions in Psychological Science, 29*(6), 531–537. https://doi.org/10.1177/0963721420951599

Snyder, C. R., Sympson, S. C., Ybasco, F. C., Borders, T. F., Babyak, M. A., & Higgins, R. L. (1996). Development and validation of the State Hope Scale. *Journal of Personality and Social Psychology, 70*(2), 321–335. https://doi.org/10.1037//0022-3514.70.2.321

Spreen, O., & Strauss, E. (1991). *A compendium of neuropsychological tests: Administration, norms, and commentary*. Oxford University Press.

Spurk, D., Keller, A. C., & Hirschi, A. (2016). Do bad guys get ahead or fall behind? Relationships of the dark triad of personality with objective and subjective career success. *Social Psychological and Personality Science, 7*, 113–121.

Srivastava, S, John, O. P., Gosling, S. D., & Potter, J. (2003). Development of personality in early and middle adulthood: Set like plaster or persistent change? *Journal of Personality and Social Psychology, 84*, 1041–1053.

Statista.com. (2015, March). *Average number of Instagram followers of teenage users in the United States as of March 2015.* https://www.statista.com/statistics/419326/us-teen-instagram-followers-number/

Statista.com. (2022). *Number of monthly active Instagram users from January 2013 to December 2021 (in millions).* https://www.statista.com/statistics/253577/number-of-monthly-active-instagram-users/

Steele, C. J., & Zatorre, R. J. (2018). Practice makes plasticity. *Nature Neuroscience, 21*(12), 1645–1646. https://doi.org/10.1038/s41593-018-0280-4

Stiglic, N., & Viner, R. M. (2019). Effects of screentime on the health and well-being of children and adolescents: A systematic review of reviews. *BMJ Open, 9,* e023191. https://doi.org/10.1136/bmjopen-2018-023191

Stowell, J. R., & Nelson, J. M. (2007). Benefits of electronic audience response systems on student participation, learning, and emotion. *Teaching of Psychology, 34,* 253–258.

Stuart, J., & Kurek, A. (2019). Looking hot in selfies: Narcissistic beginnings, aggressive outcomes? *International Journal of Behavioral Development, 43*(6), 500–506.

Sun, Y., Wang, R., Xu, Y., & Jiang, J. (2019). Will recalling a purchase increase your well-being? The sequential mediating roles of postpurchase sharing and relatedness need satisfaction. *Asian Journal of Social Psychology, 22*(4), 391–400. https://doi.org/10.1111/ajsp.12382

Takeda, A., Watanuki, E., & Koyama, S. (2017). Effects of inhalation aromatherapy on symptoms of sleep disturbance in the elderly with dementia. *Evidence-Based Complementary and Alternative Medicine, 2017.* https://doi.org/10.1155/2017/1902807

Talarico, J. M., & Rubin, D. C. (2003). Confidence, not consistency, characterizes flashbulb memories. *Psychological Science, 14,* 455–461.

Tambyah, S. K., & Tan, S. J. (2022). Consuming for happiness. In L. R. Kahle, T. M. Lowrey, & J. Huber, *APA handbook of consumer psychology* (pp. 637–646). American Psychological Association. https://doi.org/10.1037/0000262-028

Templer, D. I., Salter, C. A., Dickey, S., Baldwin, R., & Veleber, D. M. (1981). The construction of a pet attitude scale. *The Psychological Record, 31,* 343–348. https://doi.org/10.1007/BF03394747

Thompson, M., Vodicka, T. A., Blair, P. S., Buckley, D. I., Henghan, C., Hay, A. D., & TARGET Programme Team. (2013). Duration of symptoms of respiratory tract infections in children: Systematic review. *British Medical Journal, 347.* https://doi.org/10.1136/bmj.f7027

Tiggemann, M., Anderberg, I., & Brown, Z. (2020). Uploading your best self: Selfie editing and body dissatisfaction. *Body Image, 33,* 175–182. https://doi.org/10.1016/j.bodyim.2020.03.002

Tukey, J. W. (1980). We need both exploratory and confirmatory. *The American Statistician, 34,* 23–25.

Twenge, J. M., Sherman, R. A., & Wells, B. E. (2017). Sexual inactivity during young adulthood is more common among U.S. millennials and iGen: Age, period, and cohort effects on having no sexual partners after age 18. *Archives of Sexual Behavior, 46*(2), 433–440. https://doi.org/10.1007/s10508-016-0798-z

Van Boven, L., & Gilovich, T. (2003). To do or to have? That is the question. *Journal of Personality and Social Psychology, 85*(6), 1193–1202. https://doi.org/10.1037/0022-3514.85.6.1193

Van Dam, N. T., van Vugt, M. K., Vago, D. R., Schmalzl, L., Saron, C. D., Olendzki, A., Meissner, T., Lazar, S. W., Kerr, C. E., Gorchov, J., Fox, K. C. R., Field, B. A., Britton, W. B., Brefczynski-Lewis, J. A., & Meyer, D. E. (2018). Mind the hype: A critical evaluation and prescriptive agenda for research on mindfulness and meditation. *Perspectives on Psychological Science, 13,* 36–61. https://doi.org/10.1177/1745691617709589

Van den Brink, W. P. (1988). The robustness of the *t* test of the correlation coefficient and the need for simulation studies. *British Journal of Mathematical and Statistical Psychology, 41*(2), 251–256.

Van Gorp, W. G., Satz, P., Kiersch, M. E., & Henry, R. (1986). Normative data on the Boston Naming Test for a group of normal older adults. *Journal of Clinical and Experimental Neuropsychology, 8,* 702–705.

Veldhuis, J., Alleva, J. M., Bij de Vaate, A. J. D. (Nadia), Keijer, M., & Konijn, E. A. (2018). Me, my selfie, and I:

The relations between selfie behaviors, body image, self-objectification, and self-esteem in young women. *Psychology of Popular Media*, *9*(1), 3–13. https://doi.org/10.1037/ppm0000206

Wagenmakers, E. J., Wetzels, R., Borsboom, D., van der Maas, H. L., & Kievit, R. A. (2012). An agenda for purely confirmatory research. *Perspectives on Psychological Science*, *7*, 632–638.

Werch, C. E., & Owen, D. M. (2002). Iatrogenic effects of alcohol and drug prevention programs. *Journal of Studies on Alcohol*, *63*, 581–590.

Westfall, P. H. (2014). Kurtosis as peakedness, 1905–2014. R.I.P. *The American Statistician*, *68*, 191–195. https://doi.org/10.1080/00031305.2014.917055

Willinger, U., Hergovich, A., Schmoeger, M., Deckert, M., Stoettner, S., Bunda, I., Witting, A., Seidler, M., Moser, R., Kacena, S., Jaeckle, D., Loader, B., Mueller, C., & Auff, E. (2017). Cognitive and emotional demands of black humour processing: The role of intelligence, aggressiveness and mood. *Cognitive Processing*, *18*(2), 159–167.

Woods, S. L., & Rockman, P. (2021). *Mindfulness-based stress reduction: Protocol, practice, and teaching skills*. New Harbinger Publications.

Wright, D. B., & McDaid, A. T. (1996). Comparing system and estimator variables using data from real line-ups. *Applied Cognitive Psychology*, *10*, 75–84. https://doi.org/10.1002/(SICI)1099-0720(199602)10:1%3C75::AID-ACP364%3E3.0.CO;2-E

Zajonc, R. B. (1968). Attitudinal effects of mere exposure. *Journal of Personality and Social Psychology*, *9*, 1–27.

Zell, E., Krizan, Z., & Teeter, S. R. (2015). Evaluating gender similarities and differences using metasynthesis. *American Psychologist*, *70*(1), 10–20. https://doi.org/10.1037/a0038208

Zhang, K., Liu, Y., Liu, J., Liu, R., & Cao, C. (2021). Detecting structural and functional neuroplasticity in elite ice-skating athletes. *Human Movement Science*, *78*, 102795. https://doi.org/10.1016/j.humov.2021.102795

Name Index

Subject Index

definition, 64
different from mean, 95
how it works, 64–65
when to use, 80–81
mediation, 627–628
memory, 8
score, 8–9
mesokurtic distribution, 42
meta-analysis, 273
mindfulness meditation, research on, 361–377
conclusion, forming, 377
data sources, 362–363
hypothesis testing with t-test for two independent samples, 363–375
results, communicating, 375–376
t-test for two independent samples, 363
mode, 63–64
calculating, 63–64
communicating results, 75–76
definition, 63
how it works, 63–64
when to use, 79–80
moderation, 628
multimodal distribution, 35
multiple regression, 627
multiplication, A-3

N
negative correlation, 556
negative emotions on Twitter, research on
conclusion, forming, 93
data sources, 77–78
measures of central tendency, 78–85
measures of variability, 85–92
results, communicating, 93
negative skew, 36, 37
New Year's resolutions, research on, 308–326
conclusion, forming, 325–326
data sources, 309–310
hypothesis testing with t-test for dependent means, 311–324

results, communicating, 325
t-test for dependent means, 310–311
no correlation, 556
NOIR, 11
nominal scale, 11
nondirectional hypothesis, 227–228
definition of, 227
two-tailed test, 228
nonexperimental study, B-5–B-7
nonparametric test, 643
normal curve, 42, 110–113. *See also* normal distribution
bell curve, 111
characteristics of, 111
definition of, 110
purpose of, 122–123
ratio of scores in peak versus tails, 123–124
use in research, 120–123
normal distribution. *See also* normal curve
comparing using z-scores, 133–134
finding percentile rank for any score in, 125–130
finding raw score that corresponds to percentile rank in, 131–133
null hypothesis (H_0), 182
nullification fallacy, 273
number line
plotting individual scores on, 108–110
numbers, what they tell, 16–17

O
one-sample t-test. *See* single sample t-test
one-sample Z-test, 233–234
one-tailed hypothesis testing, 226–227
vs. two-tailed hypothesis testing, 228–229, 243–244
one-way analysis of variance (ANOVA), 392–437

between-groups estimate, 397–400
conclusion, forming, 409, 433
definition of, 392
hypothesis testing with, 403–409
partitioning the variance, 395
results, communicating, 409, 431–432
uses of, 392–394
within-groups estimate, 395–397
one-way within-groups ANOVA. *See* repeated-measures analysis of variance (RM ANOVA)
open data, 49–50
open materials, 97–98
open science
combatting science fraud, 667–668
computational reproducibility, 169–170
conflict of interest, 433–434
definition of, 15
distributed research networks, 539
and ethics in statistics, 14–15
effect size, power, and replication, 284
excluding data, 629–630
exploratory versus confirmatory research, 378–379
file drawer problem, 482–483
one-versus two-tailed tests, 243–244
open data, 49–50
open materials, 97–98
outliers and questionable research practices, 137–138
p-hacking, 327–328
preregistration, 205–206
unexpected and surprising findings, 582–585
operational definition, 8, 106, B-2
order of mathematical operations, A-4–A-5
ordinal scale, 11
outlier, 43, 134–135

P

paired-samples *t*-test. *See t*-test for dependent means
partial eta squared, 478
participant effect, 324
Pearson *r* product moment correlation coefficient, 560
peer-review, B-1–B-2
PEMDAS, 3, A-4
percentile rank, 125–130
   for any score in a normal distribution, 125–130
   definition, 125
   finding the raw score that corresponds to, in a normal distribution, 131–133
perfect association, 609–610
p-hacking, 327–328
pie chart, 52
   proportions, exaggerating, 52
pilot test, 280, 511
platykurtic distribution, 42
population, 7, 145
   purpose of, 147
positive and negative emotions' effect on creativity, research on, 512–534
   conclusion, forming, 537–538
   data sources, 513–514
   factorial analysis of variance (ANOVA), 514–520
   hypothesis testing with factorial analysis of variance (ANOVA), 520–534
   results, communicating, 534–536
positive correlation, 555–556
positive skew, 36, 37
post hoc tests, 425–426, 474–477
posttest, 309
power, 269
   determining hypothesis test's sensitivity, 277–281
   forming conclusions, 282–283
power analysis, 279–281
prediction, 597–600

prediction error, 610
predictor, 600
preregistration, 15
   of hypotheses, 205–206
pretest, 309
probability, 154–157
   calculating, 155–157
   definition of, 155
   and distribution of sample means, 162–168
   forming conclusions, 157
   and sampling, how they connect, 159–160
   thinking probabilistically, 156–157
probability distribution, 162
Project DARE, 243
PsychARTICLES, B-2
PsycINFO, B-2
publication bias, 482
Publication Manual of the American Psychological Association, 47
p-value, 197
p-value approach, 190, 197

Q

q statistic (Tukey *HSD* test), C-8–C-9
questionable research practice (QRP), 137

R

random sampling, 148
random selection, 148
range, 86
   calculating, 68–69
   definition, 68
   how it works, 68–69
   when to use, 86
ratio scale, 12
raw data, 31
registered report, 483
regression, 597–633
   assumptions of hypothesis test for, 620–621
   coefficient, 605
   conclusion, forming, 607–608, 626–628

constant, 605
   how it works, 600–603
   hypothesis testing for, 620–626
   results, communicating, 607, 626
   testing data with, 603–607
regression analysis, 616–620
regression equation. *See* linear prediction model
regression line, 600
relative frequency, 28
repeated-measures analysis of variance (RM ANOVA), 448–486
   assumptions of, 466
   vs. between-groups ANOVA, 451
   conclusion, forming, 462, 481–482
   definition of, 450
   hypothesis testing with, 454–461
   partitioning the variance, 452–454
   purpose of, 450–454, 464–465
   results, communicating, 461, 480–481
   uses of, 450–451
repeated-measures design, 309
replication, 284
replication crisis, 284
representative sample, 147
research design elements, matching to the proper statistic, B-6
researchers, need for statistics, 7–9
research hypothesis (*H*₁), 182
research methods and design, B-1–B-8
   data, analyzing, B-3–B-7
   data collection techniques, B-3
   experiment, B-4–B-5
   findings, communicating, B-7–B-8
   general research design, B-2–B-3
   key variables, identifying, B-2
   nonexperimental study, B-5–B-7
   questions, B-1–B-2
   study, conducting, B-3
research protocol, B-3
residual error, 612
residual score, 422
restriction of range, 578, 579